C000062085

The Political Economy of Economic Growth in 1960–2000

The period from 1960 to 2000 was one of remarkable growth and transformation in the world economy. Why did most of Sub-Saharan Africa fail to develop over this period? Why did a few small African economies succeed spectacularly? *The Political Economy of Economic Growth in Africa, 1960–2000* is by far the most ambitious and comprehensive assessment of Africa's post-independence economic performance to date. Volume 1 examines the impact of resource wealth and geographical remoteness on Africa's growth and develops a new dataset of governance regimes covering all of Sub-Saharan Africa. Separate chapters analyze the dominant patterns of governance observed over the period and their impact on growth, the ideological formation of the political elite, the roots of political violence and reform, and the lessons of the 1960–2000 period for contemporary growth strategy. Volume 2 contains the twenty-six detailed country studies on which these analyses are based. These volumes are an invaluable resource for researchers and policy-makers concerned with the economic development of Africa.

BENNO J. NDULU is Governor of the Central Bank of Tanzania.

STEPHEN A. O'CONNELL is Eugene M. Lang Research Professor of Economics at Swarthmore College.

ROBERT H. BATES is Eaton Professor of the Science of Government at Harvard University.

PAUL COLLIER is a Professor of Economics at the University of Oxford.

CHUKWUMA C. SOLUDO is Governor of the Central Bank of Nigeria.

The Political Economy of Economic Growth in Africa, 1960–2000

Volume 1

Edited by

BENNO J. NDULU

STEPHEN A. O'CONNELL

ROBERT H. BATES

PAUL COLLIER

CHUKWUMA C. SOLUDO

CAMBRIDGE
UNIVERSITY PRESS

CAMBRIDGE UNIVERSITY PRESS
Cambridge, New York, Melbourne, Madrid, Cape Town, Singapore, São Paulo, Delhi

Cambridge University Press
The Edinburgh Building, Cambridge CB2 8RU, UK

Published in the United States of America by Cambridge University Press, New York

www.cambridge.org
Information on this title: www.cambridge.org/9780521127752

© African Economic Research Consortium 2008

This publication is in copyright. Subject to statutory exception
and to the provisions of relevant collective licensing agreements,
no reproduction of any part may take place without
the written permission of Cambridge University Press.

First published 2008
First paperback Edition 2009

Printed in the United Kingdom at the University Press, Cambridge

A catalogue record for this publication is available from the British Library

ISBN 978-0-521-87848-7 hardback
ISBN 978-0-521-12775-2 paperback

Cambridge University Press has no responsibility for the persistence or accuracy of URLs
for external or third-party internet websites referred to in this publication, and does not
guarantee that any content on such websites is, or will remain, accurate or appropriate.
Information regarding prices, travel timetables and other factual infromation given in
this work are correct at the time of first printing but Cambridge University Press does
not guarantee the accuracy of such information thereafter.

Contents

Figures

Tables

Contributors

Jean-Paul Azam is a Professor of Economics at the University of Toulouse and at the Institut Universitaire de France. He is the Director of Atelier de Recherche Quantitative Appliquée au Développement Economique (ARQADE) and a Research Fellow at Institut d'Economie Industrielle (IDEI), both in Toulouse, and a Fellow of the European Development Network and the Institute for the Study of Labor (IZA, in Bonn). Dr. Azam has extensive field experience in Africa and Asia and has served as a consultant to the World Bank and EU. His research spans a wide variety of topics, including migration, ethnic discrimination, wage determination, pro-poor growth, and the determinants of civil war and terrorism. His recent book *Trade, Exchange Rate and Growth in Sub-Saharan Africa* (Cambridge University Press, 2007) emphasizes the role of domestic institutions (formal or informal) in determining the impacts of economic policy on poverty and growth.

Robert H. Bates is Eaton Professor of the Science of Government at Harvard University, where he is a member of the faculty of the Department of Government and of the Department of African and Afro-American Studies. He is also a member of the Political Instability Task Force of the United States Government and serves as a Resource Person for the African Economic Research Consortium (AERC). Among recent honors, Professor Bates was a Carnegie Scholar in 2001–2 and a Moore Distinguished Scholar in 2003–4. Co-author or co-editor of thirteen books on the political economy of development, his most recent is *Prosperity and Violence* (W. W. Norton, 2001). Professor Bates has conducted research in many countries in Africa and in Colombia and Brazil.

Paul Collier is a Professor of Economics at Oxford University where he is the founding Director of the Centre for Study of African Economies (CSAE). He is a Professor Associate of CERDI (Université d'Auvergne) and of the Sorbonne. From April 1998 to April 2003, he was Director of the Development Research group at the World Bank; more recently he served as senior advisor to Tony Blair's Commission on Africa. He works on a wide range of topics in the economics of African development, including trade and macroeconomic policy, the causes and consequences of civil war, the effects of aid, and the problems of democracy in low-income and natural-resource-rich societies.

Augustin Kwasi Fosu is Deputy Director of the World Institute for Development Economics Research (WIDER) at the United Nations University in Helsinki. Until recently, he was at the UN Economic Commission for Africa, Addis Ababa, where he served as Director of the Economic and Social Policy Division and as Senior Policy Advisor and Chief Economist. From May 1998 to January 2004, Dr. Fosu was Director of Research of the AERC. Until August 2002, he was Professor of Economics at Oakland University (USA), where he served on the faculty for over twenty years. Dr. Fosu is a past president of the National Economic Association (1997) and the African Finance and Economics Association (1998 and 1999), both based in the USA. He is coeditor of the *Journal of African Economies* and has published extensively in economic growth and development and in labor economics.

Jan Willem Gunning is Professor of Development Economics at the Free University of Amsterdam and Director of the Amsterdam Institute for International Development. Previously he was Professor of Economics and Director of the CSAE at the University of Oxford. Gunning has published widely on trade shocks, firm and household behavior, and macroeconomic management in Africa. He is a former staff member of the World Bank and conducted (with Kwesi Botchwey, Paul Collier, and Koichi Hamada) the first-ever external evaluation of the IMF. He served for ten years as an AERC Resource Person and holds an honorary doctorate from the Université d'Auvergne where he is a Professor Associate of CERDI.

Anke Hoeffler is a research officer at the CSAE, University of Oxford. She specializes in macroeconomic research, and in particular the analysis of civil war in developing countries. She has published a range of papers on the causes of war, the determinants and impact of military expenditure, the dynamics of post-conflict economies, the effect of aid, and the problems of democracy in low-income and natural-resource-rich societies. Her most recent publication is the co-authored chapter on civil war in the *Handbook of Defence Economics* (with Paul Collier).

Benno J. Ndulu is Governor of the Central Bank of Tanzania. He was previously at the World Bank, as an Advisor to the Vice President in the Africa region after supervising Bank-wide Research Support in the office of the Chief Economist and Senior Vice President. Dr. Ndulu is best known for his involvement in setting up and developing one of the most effective research and training networks in Africa, the AERC. He served first as its Research Director and later as its Executive Director. Dr. Ndulu received an honorary doctorate from the Institute of Social Studies (The Hague), in recognition of his contributions to capacity-building and research on Africa and his intellectual contributions to the democratic change in South Africa. He has published widely on growth, adjustment, governance, and trade, and has been involved in policy advisory roles world-wide.

Stephen A. O'Connell is Eugene M. Lang Research Professor of Economics at Swarthmore College. He has been a visiting researcher at the Universities of Nairobi, Dar es Salaam, and Oxford, and a consultant to the IMF, the World Bank, and the Tanzanian government. He serves as a Resource Person for the AERC, where he is also a member of the Programme Committee. Professor O'Connell co-edited *Parallel Exchange Rates in Developing Countries* (Macmillan, 1997, with Miguel Kiguel and J. Saul Lizondo) and has published widely on macroeconomic management, governance, foreign aid, and growth in Sub-Saharan Africa.

Chukwuma C. Soludo is Governor of the Central Bank of Nigeria. He previously served as the Economic Advisor to President Obasanjo and was the Founding Director of the African Institute for Applied Economics, Enugu, Nigeria. Professor Soludo has been appointed a member of the Chief Economist Advisory Council of the World Bank and the International Advisory Group of the UK Department for International Development (DFID). Before joining government he was Professor of Economics at the University of Nigeria, Nsukka. Among other publications, he is the author (with Thandika Mkandawire) of *Our Continent, Our Future: African Perspectives on Structural Adjustment* (Africa World Press, NJ, 1999) and a co-author of *Can Africa Claim the 21st Century?* (World Bank, 2000). Professor Soludo's research spans a wide set of topics in African development, with a focus on macroeconomic management, monetary and financial policies, and international trade.

Foreword

Throughout many of the first decades following independence, Africa's economies failed to grow; indeed in 2000 *per capita* incomes in several countries were lower than they had been in 1960. In this two-volume study, the African Economic Research Consortium (AERC) probes the nature and the roots of Africa's economic performance in the first decades of independence. We seek to describe Africa's growth experience in the latter decades of the twentieth century, to account for it, and to extract lessons to guide future policy-making in the continent.

The timing of this two-volume assessment could not be more propitious. Debates over growth strategy have renewed as the region emerges from decades of economic decline and policy reform. Growth itself reignited in the mid-1990s, supported by policy reforms and also by rising commodity prices, a revival of aid flows, and the resolution of costly civil conflicts. What constitutes a pro-growth policy environment? What constrains the achievement of that environment? These questions were central to this examination of Africa's immediate past. The answers to them should feature in debates over how best to secure its economic future.

We all recognize that the forces out of our control – the vagaries of commodity prices and climatic conditions, the rigors of fierce competition in fast-changing global markets, and the uncertainties of donor priorities and commitments – place limits on what we can attain. Even at the domestic level, important factors constrain our choices. The political reforms of the 1990s widened the scope for popular restraints on government, for example; but they also increased the level of uncertainty regarding the direction of future policy choices. And in a number of countries, the pursuit of growth awaits the end of armed conflict. Despite such limitations, however, policy-makers can identify country-specific opportunities for growth and build upon them, drawing lessons from a country's own history and from experiences elsewhere in Africa and the developing world. In these volumes, the scholars of the AERC seek to make the historical and comparative record available to those whose choices will affect our economic future.

The core of the "Explaining African Economic Growth" project appears in volume 2, which contains eighteen detailed country studies (plus an additional eight on the CD-ROM that accompanies the volume) conducted by African research teams. These case studies use a common methodology that identifies key turning points in the governance environment and grounds each country's experience in the global evidence on growth. In volume 1, the project's steering committee draws on the country evidence to analyze the determinants of growth. With its two-fold emphasis on geography and governance – or, more broadly, on growth opportunities and choices – the synthesis provides a platform for the analysis of country-specific and region-wide growth strategies in contemporary Africa. Taken together, these two volumes constitute the most ambitious and comprehensive study of the African growth experience to date.

This study would not have been possible without the continuing support of AERC Core funders. We are very grateful to them for their unflinching support of the abiding goals of the AERC, namely, strengthening the African capacity to conduct rigorous, independent, and policy-relevant research which is grounded in local realities and, hence, provides support for evidence-based policy-making in Africa, especially in the context of a dynamic and evolving environment. This mission rests on two basic premises. First, that development is more likely to occur where there is sustained sound management of the economy. Second, that such management is more likely to happen where there is an active, well-informed cadre of locally based professionals to conduct policy-relevant research.

The AERC is building that cadre of professionals through a program that has two primary components, one devoted to policy-relevant research and the other to graduate training in economics. The research component, in turn, comprises thematic research, as the bedrock of capacity-building, and collaborative research, which is designed to engage senior African researchers with their colleagues from outside the continent in conducting research into topical and policy-relevant issues pertinent to enhancing economic development in Africa. This study is a sterling example of the AERC's collaborative research program. It received specific financial support from the Swedish International Development Co-operation Agency (Sida), the Swiss Agency for Development Cooperation (SDC), the Norwegian Agency for Development Cooperation (NORAD), the UK's Department for International Development (DFID), the United States Agency for International Development (USAID), and the World Bank (IBRD) through the Global Development Network, and for this support we are very grateful.

We are also grateful to a variety of research organizations for their contributions over the course of the study. In this regard, we thank the Weatherhead Center for International Affairs at Harvard University, for supporting the launching conference in 1999 and the culminating conference in March 2005; Stanford University's Institute for Advanced Study in the Behavioral and Social Sciences, for hosting a week-long meeting in August 2003 during which the basic structure of the synthesis was developed; the Ford Foundation, for supporting the Stanford meeting through the Institute for International Education; Dr. Pauline Boerma, for hosting an editors' conference in

Goelo, France, in August 2004; and the Rockefeller Foundation, for sponsoring an editors' meeting at the Bellagio Study Center in October 2005.

We owe a debt of gratitude to Robert Bates, Paul Collier, Benno Ndulu, and Ademola Oyejide, who designed the project; and to the project's Steering Committee, which was intimately involved at all stages of the research. Members of the Steering Committee included Olusanya Ajakaiye (the current Director of Research) and Augustin Fosu (his predecessor), Jean-Paul Azam, Robert Bates, Paul Collier, Shantayanan Devarajan, Jan Willem Gunning, Dominique Njinkeu (former AERC Deputy Director of Research), Benno Ndulu, Stephen O'Connell, and Chukwuma Soludo. We are grateful also to Robert Bates and Macartan Humphreys for conducting a key training session on political economy analysis.

The project was co-ordinated by Benno Ndulu, Stephen O'Connell, and Chukwuma Soludo, whose intellectual guidance and high standards of excellence are evident throughout these pages. Particular thanks go to Steve, who managed the revision of draft chapters and their preparation for publication.

Dr. Joseph Karugia, Ms. Angelina Musera, Ms. Pamellah Lidaywa and, indeed, the entire staff of the AERC Secretariat deserve special thanks for providing superb technical and administrative support. We also thank Swarthmore College students Elizabeth Upshur, Matthew Meltzer, Dann Naseemullah, Isaac Sorkin, Daniel Hammer, Sikandra Christian, Bree Bang-Jensen, and Jennifer Peck for excellent research and editorial assistance, and our copy-editor, Barbara Docherty, for her great patience and expertise. We thank the scholars and policymakers – too many to enumerate here – who provided comments on work-in-progress; we trust that they will find, in these volumes, an ample return on their efforts. Finally, we are very grateful to Chris Harrison, our commissioning editor at Cambridge, for his guidance and support throughout the publication phase of this study.

Olusanya Ajakaiye
Director of Research, AERC

William Lyakurwa
Executive Director, AERC

Acronyms

AERC	African Economic Research Consortium
AGOA	Africa Growth and Opportunity Act (USA)
ANC	African National Congress (South Africa)
APC	All People's Congress (Sierra Leone)
APRM	African Peer Review Mechanism
AU	African Union
BDP	Botswana Democratic Party
CAR	Central African Republic
CFA	Communauté Financière d'Afrique
CFAF	CFA franc
CNR	Conseil National de la Révolution (Republic of the Congo)
CPI	consumer price index
CPIA	Country Policy and Institutional Assessment (World Bank)
CPP	Convention People's Party (Ghana)
DRC	Democratic Republic of Congo
ECA	Economic Commission for Africa
EITI	Extractive Industries Transparency Initiative
EPI	elite political instability
EPLF	Eritrean People's Liberation Front
EPZ	Export-Processing Zone
ERP	Economic Recovery Program
FDI	foreign direct investment
FORD	Forum for the Restoration of Democracy (Kenya)
FP	Front Populaire (Burkina Faso)
FRELIMO	Mozambican Liberation Front
FSP	financial stabilization program
G7	Canada, France, Germany, Italy, Japan, United Kingdom, United States
GDP	gross domestic product
GEP	*Global Economic Prospects* (World Bank)
GNI	gross national income
HDIs	human development indicators
IBRD	International Bank for Reconstruction and Development
ICOR	incremental capital–output ratio
ICRG	*International Country Risk Guide*

ICRISAT	International Crops Research Institute for the Semi-Arid Tropics (India)
IDA	International Development Association (World Bank)
ILO	International Labour Organization
IMF	International Monetary Fund
KANU	Kenya African National Union
LDC	less-developed country
MFA	Multi-Fiber Agreement
MIGA	Multinational Investment Guarantee Agency
MPLA	Popular Movement for the Liberation of Angola
NAM	Non-aligned Movement
NEPAD	New Partnership for African Development
NGB	Nigerian Grains Board
NTRCB	Nigerian Tuber and Root Crops Board
OAU	Organization of African Unity
ODA	official development assistance
OECD	Organization for Economic Co-operation and Development
OFNACER	Cereal Office (Burkina Faso)
OPAT	Office des Produits Agricoles du Togo
OPEC	Organization of Petroleum-Exporting Countries
PPP	purchasing power parity
PRIO	Peace Research Institute, Oslo
PRS	Political Risk Services
PWT	Penn World Tables
RENAMO	Mozambican National Resistance
RMA	Rand Monetary Area
RPF	Rwandan Patriotic Front
RUF	Revolutionary United Front (Sierra Leone)
SACU	Southern African Customs Union
SAP	structural adjustment program
SLPMB	Sierra Leone Produce Marketing Board
SLPP	Sierra Leone People's Party
SSA	Sub-Saharan Africa
TEXCO	National Textile Corporation (Tanzania)
TFP	total factor productivity
TLAIA	Tanzanian Leather Associated Industries
TPLF	Tigray People's Liberation Front (Ethiopia)
UNIP	United National Independence Party (Zambia)
UPC	United People's Congress (Uganda)
WDI	World Development Indicator (World Bank)
WDR	*World Development Report* (World Bank)
WEO	*World Economic Outlook* (IMF)

PART 1

Overview

1 | Policy plus: African growth performance, 1960–2000

Benno J. Ndulu and Stephen A. O'Connell

World Bank and Swarthmore College. This chapter was written with financial support to O'Connell from the NSF (Grant SES-0213754) and a Swarthmore College Lang Faculty Fellowship. Views expressed here are those of the authors, not necessarily those of the World Bank Group or affiliated organizations. We are grateful to Robert Bates, Jean-Claude Berthélemy, Paul Collier, Susan Collins, Anke Hoeffler, Cathy Pattillo, James Robinson, Lemma Senbet, Jeffrey Williamson, participants at the March 2005 Harvard Weatherhead Center Workshop, and Growth Project researchers for their suggestions on work-in-progress, and to Lopa Chakraborty for research assistance. Steering committee members Olusanya Ajakaiye, Jean-Paul Azam, Robert Bates, Paul Collier, Shanta Devarajan, Jan Willem Gunning, Augustin Fosu, Dominique Njinkeu, and Chukwuma Soludo provided many useful discussions. Any errors and omissions remain our own.

Table 1.1 *Regional growth comparisons, 1960–2000 (cross-country averages within regions).*

Region	N	Initial values (1960 or earliest year before 1965, or as indicated)				End-to-end annual growth rates (earliest year before 1965 to latest year between 1995 and 2000)					Ending values (latest year between 1995 and 2000)			
						Real GDP		Real GDP *per capita*						
		Real GDP *per capita* (1996 PPP$)	Gross primary enrollment rate (1970)	Adult illiteracy rate (1970)	Life expectancy at birth	Total	Population	Total	Workers *per capita*	Real GDP per worker	Real GDP *per capita* (1996 PPP$)	Gross primary enrollment rate	Adult illiteracy rate	Life expectancy at birth
SSA	35	1,278.1 (15.0)	53.8 (52.8)	55.8	41.1 (58.5)	3.20	2.63	0.56	−0.15	0.72	2,047.5 (8.4)	90.1 (86.4)	41.2	47.8 (61.1)
OTHER DEVELOPG	43	2,591.5 (30.5)	90.5 (88.9)	26.5	53.2 (75.8)	4.28	2.16	2.12	0.23	1.90	6,409.1 (26.2)	107.4 (103.0)	17.9	69.7 (89.1)
LAC	22	3,338.4 (39.2)	99.1 (97.3)	17.4	56.4 (80.3)	3.52	2.08	1.44	0.42	1.03	6,268 (25.6)	113 (108.3)	11.1	70.8 (90.5)
SASIA	5	934.4 (11.0)	58.6 (57.6)	55.5	45.3 (64.5)	4.34	2.23	2.10	−0.32	2.42	2,186.3 (8.9)	100.1 (96.0)	45.2	63.8 (81.6)
EAP	9	1,833.1 (21.5)	94 (92.3)	20.4	50.6 (72.1)	5.48	2.07	3.41	0.16	3.29	8,691 (35.5)	101.3 (97.1)	11.4	69.6 (89.0)
MENAT	7	2,402.5 (28.2)	81.9 (80.5)	42.3	51.7 (73.6)	5.09	2.48	2.61	0.13	2.48	6,934.7 (28.3)	103 (98.8)	27.8	70.6 (90.3)
INDUST	22	8,507.6	101.8	–	70.2	3.45	0.71	2.74	0.34	2.41	24,489.2	104.3	–	78.2
Total	100	3,433.3	80.4	38.1	52.7	3.72	2.00	1.71	0.12	1.60	8,860.2	100.6	27.1	63.9
SSA v. SASIA		(136.8)	(91.8)	(100.5)	(90.7)	–	–	–	–	–	(93.7)	(90.0)	(91.2)	(74.9)
SSA v. OtherDev		(49.3)	(59.4)	(210.6)	(77.3)	–	–	–	–	–	(31.9)	(83.9)	(230.2)	(68.6)

Notes: Except in the final two rows, the numbers in parentheses give the relevant developing-country mean as a percentage of the industrial-country mean. The final two rows show the SSA mean as a percentage of the SASIA mean and the mean for all non-SSA developing countries.
Source: Penn World Tables (PWT)6.1 and World Development Indicators. Regions: SSA=Sub-Saharan Africa; OTHER DEVELOPG=Other Developing (LAC=Latin America and Caribbean, SASIA=South Asia, EAP=East Asia and Pacific, MENAT=Middle East, North Africa and Turkey); INDUST=Industrial countries.

1 Overview

A collaborative effort of the African Economic Research Consortium (AERC), Harvard University, and Oxford University, the Growth Project was designed to produce the first comprehensive assessment by African research economists of the growth experience of Sub-Saharan Africa (SSA) in the post-independence period.[1] At the core of the project is a tight integration of country-level research with global econometric evidence on economic growth. In this chapter we provide the building blocks of this approach and a perspective on the lessons it produced. The themes introduced here are developed in detail throughout this volume and in the accompanying volume 2 of country studies. In the course of our analysis we provide a road map to the remaining chapters of this synthesis volume.

1.1 Economic growth in Africa, 1960–2000

Africa's growth record appears in table 1.1, which focuses on the period from 1960 to 2000 and applies to all developing countries with continuous data. The post-1960 period corresponds closely to the era of political sovereignty in SSA (table 1.2).[2] It is also by far the most intensively studied period in the global growth econometrics literature, reflecting the availability of comparable cross-country data on the contemporary nation-states of the developing world.

Simple cross-country averages suggest, at best, a story of modest progress. Human development indicators (HDIs) showed a decided improvement over the forty-year period, and real GDP *per capita* rose by 60 percent.

But, on a deeper look, the record is profoundly unsettling. Non-African growth consistently outpaced African growth after 1960, with the result that Sub-Saharan real incomes fell by over 35 percent relative to incomes in other developing regions, and by nearly half relative to industrial countries. Human development gaps widened rather than narrowed over time, and Africa's cumulative progress was insufficient, by 2000, to reach the levels of human development the rest of the developing world had already attained in 1960.

More troubling still is the picture of absolute deprivation that emerges from a continent-wide perspective. As emphasized in chapter 2,

---

[1] The structure of the Growth Project reflects the sustained collaboration of a steering committee composed of Olusanya Ajakaiye, Jean-Paul Azam, Robert Bates, Augustin Fosu, Benno Ndulu, Dominique Njinkeu, Paul Collier, Shanta Devarajan, Jan Willem Gunning, Stephen O'Connell, and Chukwuma Soludo.

[2] See table 1.2 for a comparison of SSA's march to political independence with that of other regions.

Table 1.2 *Dates of political independence, developing countries.*

Region	*n*	Proportion of countries politically independent				
		10%	*25%*	*50%*	*75%*	*All*
SSA	46	1957	1960	1961	1966	1993
Other developing	66	1830	1830	1946	1961	1981
of which:						
LAC	27	1818	1825	1840	1962	1981
ASIA	20	1816	1933	1948	1956	1975
MENAT	19	1816	1932	1948	1962	1971
Total	112	1822	1907	1960	1964	1993

Source: Gleditsch database. LAC = Latin America and Caribbean, ASIA = Asia, MENAT = Middle East, North Africa, and Turkey.

cross-country averages obscure the impact on African *populations* of slow growth in the continent's largest countries. Average real income *per capita* for the region as a whole barely increased between 1960 and 2000. Household survey data, moreover, suggest a sharp increase in income inequality over much of the period. In the context of slow overall growth, this meant an increase in income poverty. At the turn of the millennium, nearly half of the SSA population fell below an income poverty line of $1.50 (PPP-adjusted) per day, up from 35 percent in 1970. Using the same poverty line, the global incidence of poverty fell from 20 percent to 7 percent over the same period (Sala-i-Martin 2006).

While our central task is to explain persistent and widespread economic stagnation, the trends in table 1.1 conceal a wide diversity of experience at the country level. In figure 1.1 we line up the countries of SSA from left to right, in descending order of the long-run average growth rate of real GDP *per capita*.[3] Dots indicate country-specific long-run averages, and for each country we use upper- and lower-case three-letter labels to indicate the extremes of medium-term growth experience, measuring these as the fastest and slowest ten-year moving averages of growth over the course of the sample.[4] Figure 1.1 provides a snapshot of the level and variability of long-run growth in the individual countries of SSA between 1960 and 2000.

[3] Upper-case horizontal labels identify Growth Project countries. Figure 1.1 excludes Liberia, the slowest-growing African country over the whole period. Liberia's measured real GDP *per capita* contracted at an average rate of 25.7 percent between 1986 and 1995, a rate large enough to throw off the scaling for the whole diagram. Our empirical work excludes Liberia, for which very little data are available.

[4] The idea for this diagram comes from Ben Jones and Ben Olken, who presented a similar diagram at an NBER conference in April 2006.

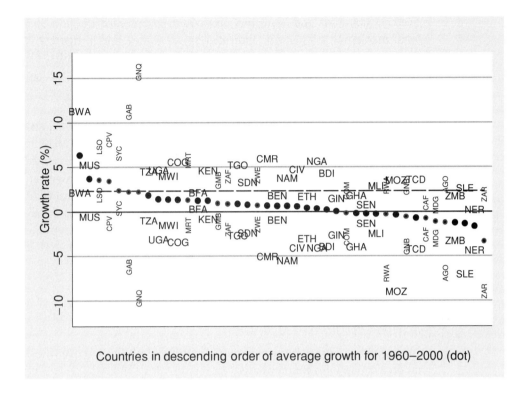

Countries in descending order of average growth for 1960–2000 (dot)

Figure 1.1 Country-level growth performance in SSA, 1960–2000.
Notes: The figure ranks the countries of SSA from left to right, in descending order of
the long-run average growth rate of real GDP *per capita*. Heavy dots indicate the
country-specific long-run averages, and the dashed horizontal line shows the global
median (2.3 percent). For each country, three-letter labels indicate the upper and lower
extremes of medium-term growth experience, measuring these as the fastest and
slowest ten-year moving averages of growth over the course of the sample. Thus for
example: Botswana (the left-most country) has the highest long-run growth, at above
6 percent per annum; its fastest ten-year moving average was above 11 percent and its
slowest was just below the global mean. Horizontal (vertical) labels and larger (smaller)
dots indicate case study (non-case study) countries. We exclude Somalia for lack of data
and Liberia for scaling purposes (a moving average of its logarithmic growth rate from
1985 to 1995 is −25.7): Liberia's long-run growth is −3.5, slightly below that of the
Democratic Republic of Congo (DRC) at −3.3. Annual growth rates are log differences
of real GDP *per capita* in local currency units from the World Bank, supplemented in a
few cases of unavailable World Bank data by log differences of real GDP *per capita* in
constant international dollars from the Penn World Tables (PWT) 6.1. For Tanzania,
we use the PWT6.1 series, but treat 1988 as a missing observation because the series
shows an erroneous massive downward adjustment in that year. The resulting long-run
average, with this observation excluded, is close to the average calculated using PWT5.6.

Led by Botswana and Mauritius, five countries exceeded the non-SSA global median of 2.3 percent (indicated by the dotted line in figure 1.1, p. 7) over the full period. But many more grew at this rate, or faster, for extended periods. Nearly three-quarters out-performed the global median on a decadal-average basis, and some did so for considerably longer periods, including Côte d'Ivoire until the late 1970s, Ghana since the early 1980s, and Uganda since the late 1980s. More than one in four countries in SSA experienced at least one extended episode of extremely rapid growth after 1960, as indicated by a decadal moving average exceeding 5 percent. Not surprisingly, these within-SSA growth differentials mattered for human development: an increase of one standard deviation in the long-run growth rate of real GDP *per capita* was associated with an increase of nearly half a standard deviation in an index of cumulative human development constructed from the measures in table 1.1.[5] The diversity in figure 1.1 suggests that models of development success exist not just outside Africa but within the continent itself.

1.2   Scope and structure of the Project

Two research questions motivated the Growth Project.[6] For SSA as a whole and on a country-by-country basis,

- What were the key growth opportunities and constraints after 1960?
- What explains success or failure in seizing the opportunities?

We approached these questions by combining global evidence on the determinants of growth with country-based work on the microeconomic behavior of firms and households, the organization of markets, and the political economy of policy and institutions. In a two-stage approach, research teams first used cross-country regression models to place their country's growth in comparative perspective and identify its major proximate

---

[5] Our index of human development is

$$0.5*[(100 - illit) + primenr] + 0.5*lifxnorm,$$

where *illit* is the adult illiteracy rate (percent), *primenr* is the gross primary enrollment ratio (percent), and *lifxnorm* is a normalized life expectancy measure, which we calculate as the percentage ratio of years of life expectancy to average life expectancy (over the whole 1970–2000 period) in industrial countries. Using cross-sectional data on thirty-five SSA countries, we regressed the average annual change in this index between 1970 and 2000 on the average logarithmic growth rate of real GDP *per capita*, controlling for the initial 1970 level of human development. The coefficient on growth is 0.1037, with a robust *t*-statistic of 2.14 (significant at the 5 percent level) and an implied beta coefficient of 0.41 ($R^2 = 0.35$).

[6] Portions of this sub-section and the next draw from O'Connell (2004) and Fosu and O'Connell (2006).

determinants over time. The bulk of the research then took place at the country level, where the task was to marshal evidence on why the determinants evolved as they did. Episodes that were poorly captured by the first stage motivated a search for country-specific mechanisms omitted from the cross-country models. The two stages of analysis disciplined and informed each other, producing unified and comparable accounts of individual-country experience.

With twenty-six country studies covering over 75 percent of regional population, the Growth Project is by far the most comprehensive country-based assessment of Africa's growth experience to date.[7] Table 1.3 shows the country cases along with their GDP and population shares in SSA and the ratios of their GDPs *per capita* to the regional average (all in 1960). The sample intentionally over-weights countries with large populations, reflecting their greater importance for region-wide performance and implicitly shifting the unit of analysis from African nation-states to the experiences of African people. At the other extreme the sample includes Botswana and Mauritius, both tiny in terms of population; these countries loom large as examples of sustained growth success, not just within Africa but on a global basis. Collapsed states like the Democratic Republic of Congo (DRC) and Somalia, where data limitations are severe, are under-represented to some degree although, as we shall see, state breakdown represents a plausible characterization of over 10 percent of the country-years in our sample. The most important omission among our case studies is South Africa, a country representing nearly 8 percent of population and 30 percent of regional GDP in 1960. We are fortunately able to draw on a rich existing literature here, so that the South African case contributes materially throughout this volume.

Figure 1.2 depicts the episodal analysis the country teams were asked to adopt in organizing the central themes of their case study. Each country's growth experience was to be divided into a small set of episodes corresponding to major changes in the incentive structure facing private economic activity, particularly with respect to government interventions in markets. Within each episode, researchers focused on two questions:

- First, how did policies and shocks combine to produce the observed growth outcomes? Researchers developed microeconomic evidence linking policies and shocks to the resource allocation decisions of households and firms, and particularly to the scale and *ex ante* efficiency of investment

---

[7] A number of country teams had access to excellent recent country studies from the *EAGER* project and/or the *Emerging Africa* project (Berthélemy and Soderling (2001, 2002)), both of which provide sustained treatments of country-level growth experience that are deeply informed by the cross-country literature.

Table 1.3 *Countries in the Growth Project.*

Country	Average growth in real GDP per capita (1961–2000)	Percentage share in total SSA: Population (1960)	Percentage share in total SSA: GDP (1960)	Ratio of GDP per capita to SSA average (1960)	Authors of country study (chapter in vol. 2 in parentheses)
Coastal (CO) opportunity group					
Benin	0.63	1.03	0.82	0.74	Antonin S. Dossou, Jean-Yves Sinzogan, and Sylviane Mensah (22)
Côte d'Ivoire	0.57	1.73	2.06	1.10	Marcel Kouadio Benie (23)
Ghana	−0.21	3.11	1.91	0.57	Ernest Aryeetey and Augustin K. Fosu (9)
Kenya	1.23	3.82	2.20	0.53	Francis F. Mwega and Njuguna S. Ndung'u (10)
Mauritius	3.70	0.30	0.69	2.11	Shyam Nath and Yeti Nisha Madhoo (11)
Mozambique	−0.38	3.42	3.96	1.07	Clara Ana de Sousa and José Sulemane (14)
Senegal	−0.24	1.46	1.98	1.25	Mansour Ndiaye (12)
Tanzania	1.83	4.68	1.32	0.26	Nkunde Mwase and Benno Ndulu (13)
Togo	0.86	0.70	0.46	0.61	Tchabouré Aimé Gogué and Kodjo Evlo (14)
CO group	**0.89**[a]	**20.24**[b]	**15.39**[b]	**0.92**[a]	
Landlocked (LL) opportunity group					
Burkina Faso	1.25	2.12	1.20	0.52	Kimseyinga Savadogo, Siaka Coulibaly, and Coleen A. McCracken (20)
Burundi	0.20	1.35	0.51	0.35	Janvier D. Nkurunziza and Floribert Ngaruko (2)
Chad	−0.72	1.40	1.22	0.80	Jean-Paul Azam and Nadjiounoum Djimtoïngar (3)
Ethiopia[c]	0.41	10.44	4.05	0.36	Alemayehu Geda (4)
Malawi	1.36	1.62	0.50	0.29	Chinyamata Chipeta and Mjedo Mkandawire (5)
Mali	−0.27	1.99	1.46	0.68	Massa Coulibaly and Amadou Diarra (21)
Niger	−1.65	1.46	1.74	1.11	Ousmane Samba Mamadou and Mahaman Sani Yakoubou (6)
Sudan[c]	0.75	5.22	3.89	0.69	Ali Abdel Gadir Ali and Ibrahim A. Elbadawi (7)
Uganda	1.40	3.01	1.24	0.38	Louis A. Kasekende and Michael Atingi-Ego (8)
LL group	**0.31**[a]	**28.61**[b]	**15.83**[b]	**0.58**[a]	
Resource-rich (RR) opportunity group					
Botswana	6.33	0.22	0.16	0.67	Gervase S. Maipose and Thapelo C. Matsheka (15)
Cameroon	0.66	2.43	3.03	1.16	Georges Kobou, Dominique Njinkeu, and Bruno Powo Fosso (16)
Congo, Rep.	1.33	0.45	0.15	0.31	Célestin Tsassa and Benjamin Yamb (25)
Guinea	0.02	1.44	2.92	1.88	Sékou F. Doumbouya and Fodé Camara (17)
Namibia	0.62	0.28	0.69	2.24	Tekaligne Godana and John E. Odada (26)
Nigeria	0.32	18.71	14.30	0.71	Milton A. Iyoha and Dickson E. Oriakhi (18)
Sierra Leone	−1.36	1.03	0.82	0.74	Victor A. B. Davies (19)
Zambia	−1.25	1.44	1.24	0.80	Inyambo Mwanawina and James Mulungushi (27)
RR group	**0.83**[a]	**26.00**[b]	**23.31**[b]	**1.06**[a]	
Total	**0.67**[a]	**74.85**[b]	**54.53**[b]	**0.84**[b]	

Note: [a]Average for category; [b]Total for category. The comparisons are *vis-à-vis* all forty-two countries in SSA for which we have data on population and real GDP at international prices. The RR group contains all countries classified in chapter 2 as resource-rich for more than half of the 1960–2000 period; [c]Ethiopia and Sudan are included in the LL group for analytical purposes; see chapter 2 and the appendix to chapter 7 on Sudan by Ali and Elbadawi in volume 2.

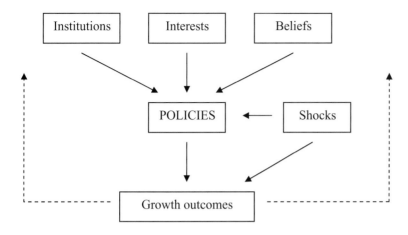

Figure 1.2 Episodal growth analysis.

in human and physical capital. Where growth appeared to be dominated by factors poorly proxied in cross-country growth regressions, these factors were identified and evidence brought to bear on their importance.

• Second, why were these policies chosen? Researchers developed evidence on the beliefs of the political elite, the interests to which they responded, and the institutions through which political competition was mediated.

1.3   A taxonomic approach to synthesis

The structure of this volume reflects a two-way taxonomy developed by the project editors in the course of reviewing draft versions of the country studies. To proxy for growth *opportunities*, we re-grouped the country studies – previously organized by sub-region – by aspects of location and resource endowment that have powerfully differentiated growth experience on a global basis. As discussed in detail in chapter 2, the high-opportunity *coastal, resource-scarce* group includes countries such as Tanzania or Senegal; the low-opportunity *landlocked, resource-scarce* group includes countries such as Burkina Faso and Burundi; the *resource-rich* group includes economies such as Botswana or Nigeria.[8]

---

[8] In chapter 2, Collier and O'Connell use time-varying criterion to identify resource-rich countries. Thus Nigeria (for example) becomes resource-rich in 1971 when its exploitation of oil resources passes a set of quantitative thresholds; for 1960–70, Nigeria is classified as coastal and resource-scarce. The resource-rich group in table 1.3 is composed of countries classified by Collier and O'Connell as resource-rich for more than half of the 1960–2000 period.

After an intensive review of the draft country studies, the editorial team identified four broad anti-growth syndromes that emerged repeatedly in the country evidence. Three directly reflect the choices of incumbent state actors – in turn, control or *regulatory* regimes that severely distort productive activity and reward rent-seeking, regimes of *ethno-regional redistribution* that compromise efficiency in order to generate resource transfers to subnational political interests, and regimes of *intertemporal redistribution* that aggressively transfer resources from the future to the present. The fourth, *state breakdown*, refers to situations of civil war or intense political instability in which a government fails to provide security or to project a coherent influence in a substantial portion of the country. We asked country teams to corroborate our proposed classification of episodes and syndromes for their country, a process that led in some cases to substantial modifications. The editorial team then extended this judgmental classification to all other African countries, based on a consultation of the relevant literature. These syndromes do not exhaust the ways in which African governments have actively shaped the growth environment, and in a substantial portion of episodes countries avoided all four syndromes, a category we call *syndrome-free*. Nor do the patterns revealed in our two-way taxonomy constitute a complete account of growth outcomes; this requires controlling for exogenous shocks and initial conditions, and for a wide range of detailed and often country-specific opportunities and choices. But the analysis of opportunities, episodes, and syndromes constitutes the heart of our contribution to understanding African growth experience.

1.4   A guide to this volume

Parts 1–4 of this volume, respectively, provide an overview of Africa's growth experience, an analysis of the anti-growth syndromes and their impacts, an explanation of observed policy patterns in terms of political and economic geography, and an application of the syndrome taxonomy to issues of contemporary growth strategy.

The chapters of part 1 (chapters 1–3) provide an integrated review of Africa's post-independence growth experience, adopting in turn an econometric, analytical, and descriptive perspective on the evidence. Our task in the present chapter is to provide the context for subsequent contributions, in the form of a self-contained review of the stylized facts and the growth econometrics literature. In chapter 2, Paul Collier and Stephen O'Connell develop the taxonomy of opportunities and choices and present a full classification of anti-growth syndromes for forty-six countries of SSA between 1960 and 2000. They apply the taxonomy to cross-country growth differentials and show that Africa's growth opportunities – weighed down by physical remoteness and natural resource wealth – and its policy choices – undermined by narrow political interests and weak institutions – provide a powerful account of the region's overall growth shortfall. Coastal and resource-scarce economies, which prospered globally after 1980, did particularly poorly in SSA; their failure, Collier and O'Connell argue, worsened the growth environment for their landlocked neighbors. Anti-growth syndromes have a large impact on growth across all opportunity groups, and where syndrome-free status was sustained over time, moderate growth was also sustained. Rapid growth was virtually never sustained in the absence of syndrome-free status. Moreover, these impacts are robust to the possible endogeneity of policy. In chapter 3, Augustin Fosu draws extensive illustrations of each of the syndromes from the twenty-six country studies of the project. Fosu also initiates the analysis of adoption and abandonment of syndromes, themes taken up further in parts 2 and 3. Among the key influences, Fosu highlights the importance of initial conditions (including group-identity rivalries, global development paradigms, the backgrounds of initial leaders, and the quality of initial institutions), natural-resource endowments, supply shocks, domestic institutions (especially the military), and economically driven political expediency.

The chapters of part 2 (chapters 4–8) provide sustained explorations of each of the four main anti-growth syndromes. In chapter 4, Robert Bates assesses the economic tactics and domestic politics of African "control" regimes, drawing on the country evidence to reassess his celebrated treatment of these regimes during their heyday (Bates 1981). In chapter 5, Paul Collier and Jan Willem Gunning explore the economic trajectory and political-economy logic of intertemporally unsustainable regimes. These include the public spending booms that have sometimes accompanied reversible commodity price shocks, but also the more acute phenomenon of "looting" by narrow political elites. In chapter 6, Jean-Paul Azam reinterprets the use of redistributive policy instruments in the context of political polarization. When *ex ante* ethno-regional polarization is high, some form of redistribution may be a necessary component of nation-building. Accomplishing this credibly and efficiently constitutes a challenge of critical and continuing relevance for many African countries. In chapter 7, Robert Bates turns to violence and state failure, endogenizing the security of property and the quality of the investment environment as functions of the government's tax base, its discount rate, and its access to natural-resource rents.

Jan Willem Gunning closes out part 2 in chapter 8 by studying the impact of risk on growth, a theme of relevance in both the presence of anti-growth syndromes and the absence of policy-related risks. He shows that when farms and households must rely on risky assets as stores of value, their attempts to self-insure against future consumption volatility may well involve a reduced rate of overall wealth accumulation. Microeconomic evidence suggests that this negative effect of risk on growth can be large. The relevant risks may be exogenous, but policy-induced risks – such as inflation-induced risks to currency and bank liabilities, tax-rate risks to investment in export crops, or property risks associated with inadequate security – may also contribute to the persistence of poverty by undermining microeconomic incentives for capital accumulation.

Part 3 (chapters 9–11) pushes further into the task of explanation. What historical, structural, and institutional features of African economies explain the adoption and abandonment of anti-growth syndromes? Benno Ndulu begins in chapter 9, by examining the role of outside influences in the evolution of development paradigms in SSA. In chapter 10, Robert Bates turns to the role of domestic political institutions, focusing particularly on how the nature of political succession affects the incidence and durability of pro-market economic reforms. In chapter 11, Paul Collier and Robert Bates (with Anke Hoeffler and Stephen O'Connell) develop a theory of political evolution under conditions of sub-national regional polarization. They use it to endogenize the policy choices of political elites as functions of economic structure and the degree of ethno-regional polarization. They show empirically that the incidence of anti-growth syndromes reflects the nature of the party system, the size and composition of the selectorate, and the level of knowledge possessed by political leaders.

Chapter 12, by Paul Collier, Jan Willem Gunning, Stephen O'Connell, and Benno Ndulu, concludes the volume in part 4 by putting the synthesis taxonomy to work. If growth depends on opportunities and choices (chapter 2), then country-level growth strategies must be opportunity-specific. In terms of our own opportunity categories, resource-rich countries must spend public resources well; landlocked and resource-scarce countries must upgrade infrastructure and exploit regional markets; coastal and resource-scarce countries must focus on creating competitive platforms for serving global markets. If there is a single central lesson from the Growth Project, however, it is that recognizing opportunities is only half the battle. The other half is building the political and economic institutions for seizing these opportunities on a sustainable basis. Chapter 12 takes a first cut at this two-fold analysis by exploring not only the nature of growth opportunities but also the political foundations for seizing them.

The remainder of the present chapter provides a foundation for what follows and a summary assessment of lessons learned. In sections 2 and 3, we lay out the main stylized facts of African growth and interpret these observations from the viewpoint of the growth econometrics literature. Section 4 then previews the main conclusions of the synthesis, including the argument that avoiding anti-growth syndromes is both a necessary condition for sustained rapid growth and a sufficient condition for the avoidance of

short-run collapses. In section 5, we take a forward-looking stance, returning to the growth literature and the country evidence to explore the scope
for opportunity-specific growth strategies in the period ahead.

2   Five features of African growth

We begin by setting out five key features of the African growth record.[9]

2.1   Divergence

The most widely noted feature of African growth after 1960 is the divergence
of African incomes from incomes in other developing regions (table 1.1).[10]
Divergence is not solely an African phenomenon (consider Haiti, for example, or North Korea), and there are dramatic exceptions within the region,
as we saw above. But the African growth "tragedy" – the term comes from
Easterly and Levine (1997) and Artadi and Sala-i-Martin (2003) – is a staple
of the cross-country growth literature, and one that easily matches its distant
counterpart, the East Asian "miracle," in its cumulative impact on thinking
about economic growth.

Table 1.4 places the contemporary record in a longer-term perspective,
using region-wide GDP and population estimates constructed by Angus

---

[9] The global econometric literature relevant to understanding Africa's growth experience is
immense. Recent Africa-focused surveys include Collier and Gunning (1999) and our
own framework paper for the Growth Project (O'Connell and Ndulu 2001), which cover
the literature through the late 1990s. Much has been added since then, and we provide a
compressed update in section 3 below. The cross-country literature on economic growth
now has its own journal (the *Journal of Economic Growth*, since 1995), a PhD-level text by
Barro and Sala-i-Martin (1995), undergraduate-level texts by Jones (1998) and Van den
Berg (2001), a two volume handbook from North-Holland (Aghion and Durlauf 2005),
and another handbook forthcoming from Edward Elgar. As many have observed, most of
the important ideas in the modern growth literature have precursors dating from the
1950s or earlier. The emergence in the late 1980s of global datasets with wide
developing-country coverage provided key impetus for the contemporary literature, as
did the successes of "new growth theorists" in formally breaking out of the neoclassical
tradition of diminishing returns to capital and exogenous technological progress. Easterly
(2001) provides a masterful introduction to the interaction between the modern growth
literature and post-Second World War development experience. Hayami (2001) provides
a complementary account with deep roots in the development economics literature and
the history of economic thought.

[10] In the cross-country growth literature, *convergence* refers to a situation in which
cross-country differences in real income *per capita* shrink over time and *divergence* to the
opposite phenomenon. See Barro and Sala-i-Martin (1995) for a thorough discussion and
Pritchett (1997) for a demonstration of the long-run divergence between the now-rich
and now-poor countries of the world.

Table 1.4 *Long-run growth rates of regional population, GDP, and GDP per capita.*

	SSA	Total	LAC	ASIA	MENAT
			Other developing regions		
			of which:		
Population					
1820–70	0.3	0.2	1.3	0.1	0.5
1870–1913	0.9	0.6	1.6	0.6	0.3
1913–50	1.6	1.0	2.0	0.9	1.3
1950–2001	2.6	2.0	2.3	1.9	2.7
Peak year[a]	1983	1971	1960	1971	1981
Peak rate[a]	3.00	2.52	2.87	2.52	3.34
Real GDP (PPP-adjusted 1990 dollars)					
1820–70	0.6	0.1	1.2	0.0	1.0
1870–1913	1.1	1.3	3.5	1.1	1.6
1913–50	2.7	1.5	3.4	0.9	2.5
1950–2001	3.3	5.0	4.0	5.4	4.9
Real GDP per capita (PPP-adjusted 1990 dollars)					
1820–70	0.2	−0.1	0.0	−0.1	0.5
1870–1913	0.2	0.7	1.8	0.5	1.2
1913–50	1.1	0.5	1.4	−0.1	1.1
1950–2001	0.7	3.0	1.7	3.4	2.2
No. of countries	53	90	27	42	21

Note: [a]Peak year and peak rate correspond to the earliest year after which all subsequent population growth rates are lower.
Source: Maddison (2001). The table pertains to region-wide totals. SSA comprises Maddison's *Africa* excluding North Africa. LAC comprises Maddison's *Latin America* and includes the Caribbean. ASIA is Maddison's *East Asia*. MENAT (Middle East, North Africa, and Turkey) corresponds to Maddison's *West Asia* plus North Africa. Libya could not be separated out and is therefore included here in SSA rather than in MENAT.

Maddison (Maddison 2001). Data limitations are severe before 1960, and particularly so for SSA where the GDP aggregate is based on scaled-up estimates for Ghana and South Africa. With this caveat in mind we stress three observations. The first is that protracted slow growth, with divergence from similar or higher-income cohorts, is not an outlier by historical standards. The stagnation of African incomes between 1950 and 2001 matches that of the entire non-African periphery during the last great phase of globalization, between 1870 and 1913. Second, however, if we focus on the period since the Industrial Revolution, Africa's divergence appears to be concentrated after 1950. Having weathered the disintegration of the world economy between 1913 and 1950, perhaps even with modestly greater success than the non-African periphery, African populations missed out on the unprecedented economic transformation that took place in the rest of the developing world after 1950. The comparison with Asia, which looms large here by virtue of its large population, is striking: *per capita* growth in Asia advanced by almost 4 percentage points relative to SSA, between the 1913–50 and 1950–2001 periods.

Third, comparing tables 1.1 and 1.4, the data suggest a sharper divergence between African and non-African *populations* than between African and non-African *countries*. We saw a hint of this in figure 1.1, where the collective population (in 1990) of the five Sub-Saharan countries that exceeded the global median growth rate over the full period was fewer than 5 million people. This is in sharp contrast with global experience since 1960, which tends to display divergence across countries but convergence across people. As emphasized by Sala-i-Martin (2006), divergence across countries is largely driven by slow growth within the numerous African sub-sample, while divergence across people is driven by the strong growth performance of populous non-African countries such as China, India, and Indonesia. Figure 1.3 follows Collier and O'Connell (chapter 2) in comparing unweighted and population-weighted regional time series for African and non-African developing countries. Large population has been positively correlated with growth among non-African developing countries, particularly after 1980. This effect is largely absent in SSA, however, where the population-weighted data suggest, if anything, lagging performance by the larger countries. Within SSA, not a single country among the thirteen with populations exceeding 10 million in 1990 grew faster than 2 percent over the 1960–2000 period.

As a final dimension of divergence, we focus on the time pattern of Africa's growth shortfall. Africa's unweighted average growth rate shows a decidedly U-shaped pattern in figure 1.3: highest in the 1960s, then falling steadily through the early 1990s before rebounding strongly for most of the decade. The shortfall relative to other regions shows a muted version of this U-shaped pattern, complicated by a transitory narrowing during the early-to-mid-1980s as commercial borrowers in other regions weathered the international debt crisis. But the population-weighted comparison again suggests a dramatic U-shape: Africa's relative performance deteriorates sharply in the 1970s, before beginning a fitful recovery that gathers final steam only after 1994. Both in absolute terms and by comparison with other regions, therefore, Africa's shortfall is sharpest during the twenty-year period from roughly 1974 to 1994.

Table 1.5 *Regional growth-accounting decompositions (annual growth rates except where noted).*

| | | | | | | | | Contributions of: | | |
Region	N	Real GDP	Population	Real GDP per capita	Workers per capita	Real GDP per worker	K per worker	Educ. per worker	Resid.
SSA	**18**	**3.25**	**2.70**	**0.54**	**−0.07**	**0.61**	**0.36**	**0.25**	**0.00**
Other developing:									
LAC	21	3.49	2.17	1.32	0.39	0.92	0.41	0.34	0.18
SASIA	4	4.45	2.23	2.22	−0.32	2. 4	1.11	0.32	1.11
EAP	7	6.21	2.04	4.17	0.22	3.95	2.11	0.49	1.35
MENAT	9	4.84	2.19	2.65	0.13	2.52	1.19	0.44	0.90
Total	**59**	**4.01**	**2.32**	**1.68**	**0.14**	**1.54**	**0.76**	**0.34**	**0.43**
SSA minus Other developing		−1.10	0.55	−1.64	−0.31	−1.33	−0.57	−0.13	−0.63

Source: PWT6.1; initial capital stock and educational contribution from Susan Collins. For definition of regions see table 1.1.

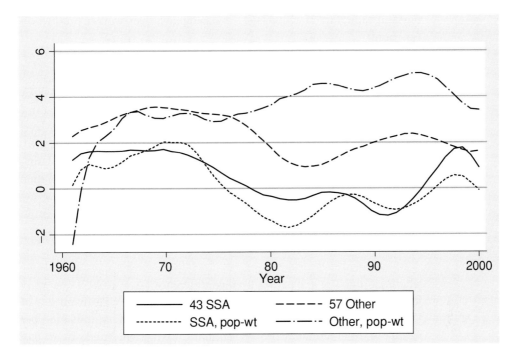

Figure 1.3 Smoothed average growth in real GDP *per capita*, 1960–2000 (countries with a full set of growth observations)
Notes: We smoothed the data using a kernel-weighted polynomial smoother of degree 1 (with an Epanechnikov kernel). Alternative approaches yield similar results.

2.2   Slow accumulation and productivity growth

Early development theorists viewed low national investment as the essential constraint on development (e.g. Lewis 1954). To what degree can Africa's growth performance be traced to a shortfall of capital accumulation? Table 1.5 employs an economy-wide growth-accounting framework to decompose the growth in real GDP per worker into the contributions of physical and human capital accumulation per worker and a productivity growth residual. The sample is considerably smaller than in previous tables and figures, mainly reflecting the limited availability of survey data on education per worker. The underlying production function is Cobb–Douglas in physical capital and effective labor, where the latter is measured as human capital per worker multiplied by the population of working age.[11] Exploiting the assumption of constant returns to scale, we can divide output and

---

[11] Human capital per worker is calculated by applying a fixed percentage wage premium of 7 percent to each additional year of schooling, as described in Collins and Bosworth (1996). As described in n. 12, we have recalculated the Collins–Bosworth growth accounts using

physical capital by effective labor and obtain the per-worker production function[12]

$$ypw_{it} = A_{it} \cdot kpw_{it}^{\alpha} hpw_{it}^{1-\alpha}, \tag{1}$$

where ypw_{it}, kpw_{it} and hpw_{it} are real GDP per worker, physical capital per worker, and human capital per worker, respectively, in country i in year t. Capital stocks are measured at the beginning of period t, and A_{it} is the level of total factor productivity (TFP). Following Collins and Bosworth (1996), we set the share of physical capital in national income to $\alpha = 0.35$. Using the difference in logs as an approximation to the growth rate, we can then obtain the implied growth of TFP over any k-year period from the exact decomposition

$$\Delta_k \ln ypw_{it} = 0.35 \Delta_k \ln kpw_{i,t} + 0.65 \Delta_k \ln hpw_{i,t} + \Delta_k \log A_{it}, \tag{2}$$

where Δ_k denotes a k-period average difference ($\Delta_k x_t \equiv k^{-1}(x_t - x_{t-k})$ for any variable x_t). The second and third terms on the right-hand side of (2) give the contributions of physical and human capital accumulation per worker to the growth of real GDP *per capita*; on the right-hand side, *ex post* TFP growth is calculated as a residual.

Table 1.5 shows regional averages of country-by-country calculations using (2), for the full period 1960–2000. In the bottom row we compare the eighteen countries in SSA for which data are available with forty-one other developing countries. Measured capital accumulation accounts for about half of the long-run differential in growth rates of real GDP per worker; the other half, by definition, reflects the stagnation of African productivity. The striking fact is that on a country-by-country basis between 1960 and

PPP-adjusted data, but without changing the contribution of human-capital accumulation. We thank Susan Collins for access to an updated version of the Collins and Bosworth (1996) dataset.

[12] Collins and Bosworth (1996) perform the same calculation using GDP and capital stock series measured in constant local currency. They assume a Cobb–Douglas production function with effective labor input given by hL, where h is a measure of education per worker and L is the labor force. Capital's share is 0.35. The capital stock is estimated from starting values in 1960 using the perpetual inventory method with a depreciation rate of 5 percent. To apply the decomposition to PPP-adjusted real GDP series, we first converted the initial capital stock to PPP dollars by assuming the same ratio between PPP-adjusted and constant-local-currency initial capital stocks as between PPP-adjusted and constant-local-currency investment rates (this is required to reflect the very different relative price of investment in PPP-adjusted data versus national accounts: investment tends to be much more expensive at international than domestic prices in low-income countries). We then recalculated the capital stock series using investment at constant international prices.

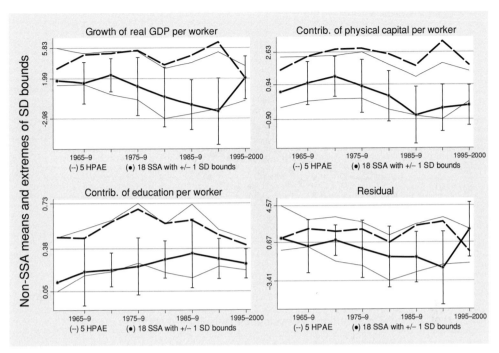

Figure 1.4 Growth accounting over time, fifty-nine developing countries, 1965–2000.
Notes: For each indicator, the heavy line shows the SSA mean calculated at
non-overlapping five-year intervals (dotted heavy lines show the high-performing
Asian economies). Vertical bars show bounds of plus and minus one "within-SSA,
within period" standard deviation around these means. Thin lines show +/− 1
standard deviation bounds around the half-decadal means for all other developing
countries. The *y*-axis scale shows the long-run non-SSA mean and, for purposes of
scaling, the range of the non-SSA +/− 1 standard deviation bounds.

2000, cumulative productivity growth in SSA was as likely to be negative as
positive.[13]

We noted above the U-shaped time pattern of Africa's average growth
shortfall. This pattern reappears in the growth-accounting sub-sample. As
indicated by the heavy lines in figure 1.4, the bulk of Africa's shortfall occurs
between the mid-1970s and the mid-1990s. The early portion of this pattern is associated with a steady decline in physical capital accumulation per
worker, in both absolute terms and relative to other developing regions.
Africa's recovery in the second half of the 1990s, by contrast, is entirely

---

[13] Using a similar methodology, Hall and Jones (1999) estimated the *level* of TFP in the late
1980s, for a global sample of countries. They showed that the differences in PPP-adjusted
incomes in table 1.2 are mainly driven by differences in the apparent productivity of
measured inputs, rather than by differences in their availability per worker.

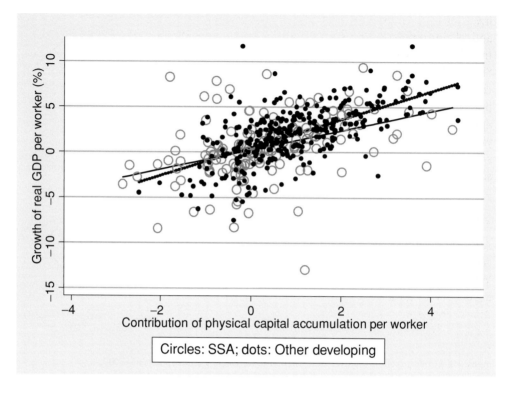

Figure 1.5 Capital accumulation and growth.
Notes: Observations are non-overlapping half-decadal averages between 1960–4 and 1995–2000 (144 observations from SSA, 328 from non-SSA developing countries). The slope coefficients from a pooled regression with separate slopes and intercepts are 1.55 ($t = 14.11$) for non-SSA and 1.07 ($t = 5.47$) for SSA. An *F*-test rejects equality of slope coefficients ($p = 0.033$).

accounted for by rapid increases in the productivity residual, an observation emphasized by Berthélemy and Soderling (2001).

As indicated in figure 1.5, the empirical link between physical capital accumulation and growth was weaker in SSA than it was in other developing regions between 1960 and 2000.[14] This suggests a low *ex ante* yield on investment in SSA, a phenomenon widely observed in the growth literature and consistent with evidence of substantial capital flight from the region (Collier, Hoeffler, and Pattillo 2004). The dominant interpretation stresses failures in governance, citing the predominance of inefficient public sector

[14] In figure 1.5, the estimated slope coefficient on physical capital's contribution to growth in real GDP per worker is 45 percent higher for non-SSA countries than in the SSA sample. The difference in slopes is highly statistically significant (an *F*-test for equality of coefficients yields $p = 0.03$).

investment (Artadi and Sala-i-Martin 2003), the prevalence of tax avoidance and self-insurance by firms and households (Collier and Pattillo 2000), and the diversion of resources into rent-seeking and corruption (Vishny and Shleifer 1993). Our country studies provide powerful evidence for these channels, and in subsequent chapters the editors explore their roots in political conflict. A more speculative but potentially complementary view appeals to increasing returns and threshold effects, arguing that investment yields would have been sharply higher if investment rates had been well above historical averages (Sachs *et al.* 2004). We return to this possibility in section 5.

2.3   *Limited structural transformation*

African economies were overwhelmingly rural in 1960, with agriculture accounting for some 40 percent of GDP and 85 percent of the labor force. While the rural share of the population fell steadily over the next forty years, in 2000 it was still, at 63 percent, slightly above the 1960 average for non-SSA developing countries. In the context of very rapid population growth, this modest shift meant that rural population density increased substantially, reversing Africa's initial advantage in arable land *per capita* relative to other developing regions. It also meant that urban populations, given their small initial size, grew spectacularly.

A contraction of the agricultural share of the labor force is one of the most durable features of the structural transformation that takes place in the course of development. In a closed-economy context, this transfer can be sustained only if labor productivity in agriculture increases rapidly enough to feed a growing urban population. In an open economy food can be imported, but agricultural productivity remains a key determinant of overall living standards and an essential source of foreign exchange for imported capital goods. Consistent with Africa's slow overall growth, there is little evidence that the modest observed shift out of agriculture was driven by advances in rural labor productivity. Agricultural value added per worker rose at a trend rate of 0.5 percent per year in SSA, less than a third of the prevailing rate within other developing regions. Cereal yields did only slightly better, rising at 0.74 percent per year as compared with 2.4 percent outside of SSA. Relative food prices show little evidence of a systemic food crisis, but the answer may lie in rising food imports: the ratio of net imports of food to GDP rose by 1.4 percentage points a decade in SSA, eight times faster than outside of SSA.

The massive growth rate of urban populations in Africa – exceeding 6 percent per annum through about 1980 – was initially associated with a marked increase in the shares of industry and especially services (including the public sector) in GDP. This process came to a halt during the 1980s,

Table 1.6 *Regional comparisons of volatility.*

		Regional averages of country-level standard deviations				Correlation between current and lagged growth	
		Annual data		Non-overlapping five-year averages			
Region	N	Growth of real GDP *per capita*	Prediction error	Growth of real GDP *per capita*	Prediction error	Five-year periods	Decades
SSA	38	7.31	6.91	3.36	2.56	0.07	0.30
MENAT	8	5.92	5.51	2.71	1.94	0.03	−0.10
Other developing	37	4.30	4.04	2.31	2.01	0.39	0.42
INDUST	22	2.69	2.43	1.69	1.30	0.31	0.41
Total	105	5.18	4.85	2.59	2.06	0.25	0.41
SSA intercept[a]		2.147***	2.081***	0.912***	0.399	–	–
Robust standard error		0.600	0.583	0.285	0.277	–	–

Note: [a]Coefficient on an SSA dummy variable in a cross-sectional regression of country-level standard deviations on the log of PPP-adjusted *per capita* real GDP ($N = 105$; $R^2 = 0.424$ and 0.421 using annual data and 0.238 and 0.154 using five-year averages).
*** = significant at the 1% level.

Source: PWT6.1. Prediction errors are calculated from country-by-country annual or half-decadal AR(2) processes for the growth rate of real GDP *per capita*. For definition of regions see table 1.1.

however, and was partly reversed during the 1990s as the GDP share of agriculture actually rose, at the expense of the industrial share (the share of services remaining constant).

Export diversification is a second area in which the structural transformation of African economies has been limited (Gersovitz and Paxson 1990; Berthélemy and Soderling 2001, 2002). Exports have tended to remain concentrated in a narrow band of primary commodities, and in many cases have become more concentrated over time via the exploitation of mineral resources. In chapter 2, Collier and O'Connell use global data on primary commodity exports and rents from energy, mineral, and forest resources to identify resource-rich economies. Comparing SSA with other developing regions outside of the Middle East and North Africa, they find that a stark difference already existed in 1960, with 12.5 percent of the SSA sample and only 7 percent of the non-SSA sample classified as resource-rich. Over time, however, this difference expanded: another 16.7 percent of the African sample acquired resource-rich status by 2000, compared to only 10.5 percent of the non-African sample. While this suggests a hardening of the continent's existing primary commodity specialization, Collier and O'Connell also find in chapter 2 that among coastal and resource-scarce countries, significant export diversification has taken place among countries that have maintained the trade-promoting policy reforms undertaken by the early 1990s.

2.4 Lingering volatility

Table 1.6 examines the intertemporal variation of growth rates within countries, both on a year-to-year basis and over longer periods. Annual growth in SSA has been highly volatile, and this is true both of growth itself and of the unpredictable component of growth, proxied here by the prediction error from a country-by-country AR(2) process. Five-year averages smooth out this volatility considerably – consistent with the presence of transitory shocks to growth (including classical measurement error) – but medium-term volatility remains distinctly higher in SSA than elsewhere.

Since volatility tends to decrease with income on a global basis, we check at the bottom of table 1.6 whether African volatility remains high after conditioning on the region's low income. The answer is "yes" for the annual data: the standard deviation is roughly 2 percentage points higher for African countries than would be predicted on the basis of income alone. But the volatility of African growth looks less distinctive when we move to five-year periods: the SSA effect becomes small and statistically insignificant. Africa's medium-term volatility is therefore not unusual once we control for low income. What is unusual, as we emphasized above, is the persistence of low income and the concomitant lack of structural diversification, during a period of global growth. These have implied a continued exposure to substantial medium-term volatility.

Within countries, period-to-period correlations between five- and ten-year non-overlapping averages provide a further indication of the episodal character of African growth. Such correlations are virtually zero across five-year periods but rise to 0.30 across decades, consistent with protracted but ultimately temporary periods of boom and bust.

2.5   Diversity

As a final broad feature of growth experience in Africa we return to the cross-country diversity noted in figure 1.1. The variation in long-run growth within SSA dwarfs the difference between average growth in SSA and average growth in any other region. This is true not just for overall growth outcomes, but also for each of the growth-accounting components that appear in table 1.5 (recall figure 1.4 in which we showed the half-decadal contributions of physical capital, human capital, and productivity growth, with standard-deviation bounds to indicate the wide range of outcomes in SSA). These observations underscore the perils of regional generalization as well as the urgency of understanding the sources of differential growth success within Africa.

3   The view from growth econometrics

What are the *determinants* of the growth record we have just outlined? Cross-country regressions provide a natural approach to this question, and in the Growth Project we used the growth econometrics literature to structure the country studies and to develop our synthesis of the case material. The literature identifies *resource endowments* and *governance* as the critical determinants of growth performance in SSA. Some of the most fundamental issues of growth strategy lie at the intersection of these two areas, a premise that underscores the significance of case study analysis and motivates our taxonomy by opportunities and choices. We begin, however, with a brief digression on the interpretation of regression evidence and its use in country analysis.

3.1   Regression models of growth

Like growth accounting, the typical growth equation starts from an aggregate production function. In the augmented Solow model of Mankiw, Romer, and Weil (1992), for example, the aggregate production function takes the form

$$Y_{it} = K_{it}^{\alpha} H_{it}^{\beta} (A_{it} \cdot L_{it})^{1-\alpha-\beta},$$

where K, H, and L are aggregate physical capital, human capital, and raw labor, α and β are the shares of physical and human capital in national income, and A is the level of productivity (assumed to be embodied in raw labor; the implied measure of total factor productivity is $A^{1-\alpha-\beta}$). With $\alpha + \beta < 1$, the production function is subject to decreasing returns to scale in physical and human capital per effective worker, implying that output per effective worker, $\tilde{y} \equiv Y/AL$, approaches a unique steady-state value. Convergence is monotonic, at a speed that is proportional to the distance from the steady state. The average growth of output per *actual* worker, $y = Y/L$, over any k-year period is therefore given by

$$\Delta_k \ln y_{it} = -\gamma \ln y_{i,t-k} + \gamma \ln \tilde{y}_i^* + \Delta_k \ln A_{it} - \gamma \ln A_{i,t-k}, \quad (3)$$

where Δ_k is defined as above (see (2)) and $\gamma > 0$ is the speed of convergence to the steady-state path.[15]

Equation (3) is the basis for regression models of the form

$$\Delta_k \ln y_{it} = -\gamma \ln y_{i,t-k} + \phi' x_{it} + \lambda' z_i + \varepsilon_{it}, \quad (4)$$

where ε_{it} is a country-period disturbance. The presence of initial income is a hallmark of the neoclassical or "conditional convergence" paradigm, in which diminishing returns to all forms of reproducible capital (including human) ultimately limit the contribution of capital accumulation to growth. In this paradigm, countries that are poorer *relative to their country-specific steady states* grow faster. The vectors x_{it} and z_i enter the equation as time-varying and time-invariant determinants of the three other variables in (3): steady-state income per effective worker, the rate of productivity growth, and the initial level of productivity.

Applications of the conditional convergence paradigm range from the parsimonious augmented Solow model, in which productivity is exogenous and steady-state output y^* is a function of a few behavioral parameters,[16] to the looser tradition initiated by Barro (1991), in which the x and z variables include a wide array of theoretically plausible determinants of either

---

[15] *Conditional* convergence refers to convergence towards a country-specific steady state. It is to be distinguished from *absolute* convergence, which refers to a tendency for poor countries to grow faster than rich ones (as if all countries were converging to the same steady-state path), see Barro and Sala-i-Martin (1995). Our earlier discussion of divergence refers to absolute convergence.

[16] See Hoeffler (2002) for an application to Africa. The key behavioral parameters are the national investment rate and the population growth rate.

factor accumulation or productivity (e.g. policy variables, institutional quality, political instability, geographical location). A version of (4) can also be
derived directly from the production function, by differentiating it to obtain
an equation like (2) and then modeling factor accumulation and productivity growth as functions of other variables (Temple 1999). In such cases
conditional convergence is not necessarily implied, and initial income is
therefore excluded; the x and z variables operate directly on long-run growth
rates, via either factor accumulation or productivity growth. Applications
within the endogenous growth tradition typically take this form.[17]

3.2   Interpreting regression evidence

Cross-country regressions rely on two types of pooling to extract information on the growth process. The first is implied by the level of analysis: any
study of country-wide growth outcomes ends up aggregating the information, constraints, and choices of diverse agents interacting in complex ways
over time. The second is more explicit and takes place across countries: in
the absence of controlled experiments, each country's experience is used as
a counterfactual for the experience of other countries.

If observations for different countries and time periods are governed by
the same joint distribution of variables, regression models estimated using
ordinary least squares (OLS) provide a good approximation to the expected
value of growth conditional on observed determinants (Wooldridge 2003).
As such, these models (i) have very strong descriptive content; (ii) provide a
reliable basis for conditional predictions within any sample drawn from the
joint distribution that produce the data at hand; and (iii), very importantly
for our purposes, can exert a powerful discipline on any causal account of
growth.[18] In our framework paper for the Growth Project, we used least-
squares "conditional models" to help country authors place their country's
experience in global perspective and to identify leading themes to be explored
at the disaggregated levels of sectors, markets, and agents. We provide an
updated version of this analysis in sub-section 3.4.2.

Economists remain sharply divided, however, over whether growth
regressions can be given a causal interpretation (Temple 1999; Brock and
Durlauf 2001). At issue here is the nature of the regression counterfactual. If
the determinants of growth were assigned to countries on an experimental
basis, OLS regressions would pick up the *ceteris paribus* impact on growth of

---

[17] In models with constant or increasing returns to reproducible capital per worker (e.g.
Lucas 1988), conditional convergence is not implied.

[18] Any causal account implies a particular joint distribution of growth and its determinants,
and therefore a particular form for the conditional expectation of growth. OLS
regressions are therefore capable of ruling out certain causal claims about growth, even if
the determinants are not econometrically predetermined.

each determinant, given a sufficiently large set of observations. But history is not a controlled experiment. The typical growth regression is therefore likely to be subject to some degree of endogeneity bias, whether from true simultaneity – investment determines growth, but growth also determines investment – or from the omission of key determinants that are correlated with the included variables. OLS regressions retain their status as conditional expectations in the face of these realities, but something is unavoidably lost: if the determinants of growth are not statistically predetermined, then each country's experience no longer represents a clear counterfactual – an indication of well-defined opportunities seized or missed – against which to assess the experience of other countries in the sample.[19]

Growth regressions can be pushed beyond description and conditional prediction by isolating predetermined variation in the determinants of growth. There are a variety of ways of doing this, each with some cost in terms of description and prediction, and in box 1.1 we briefly review the main approaches. The bottom line, however, is that no single econometric approach can do justice to the growth evidence. In our framework paper (O'Connell and Ndulu 2001), therefore, we used the full set of approaches – conditional models, reduced-form models, fixed-effects estimation, and instrumental variables – to identify the key determinants of African growth on a country-by-country basis. We follow the same approach below in summarizing the literature, generally relying on the reader to consult the methodologies adopted in the original papers.

Two observations will become clearer as we proceed. First, the cross-country literature provides an indispensable resource for country-level growth analysis. Country studies face a massive degrees-of-freedom problem: with only four decadal (eight half-decadal) observations on long-run growth, there is too little information to run an empirical horse race among alternative hypotheses about what drove observed growth outcomes. By identifying systematic features of the growth process and documenting their relative importance on a global basis, growth regressions can direct country-level work into its most productive areas (Collier and Gunning 1999).[20] Second, however, detailed country research remains indispensable.

---

[19] Observing a large and positive coefficient on the investment rate, for example, one can always say that Sierra Leone's predicted growth rate would have been 3 percentage points higher if Sierra Leone's investment rate had equaled Singapore's. It does not follow that low investment determined low growth in Sierra Leone, or that a policy package that raised Sierra Leone's investment rate to that of Singapore could be expected to close the growth gap between the two countries.

[20] Cross-country regressions also face a degrees-of-freedom problem, given the large number of potential determinants and the non-experimental, one-time nature of the data. For systematic approaches to identifying "robust" determinants, see Levine and Renelt (1993) and Sala-i-Martin, Doppelhofer, and Miller (2004).

Box 1.1 The endogeneity problem in growth econometrics

OLS regressions uncover a causal relationship only if the determinants under consideration are uncorrelated with the residual. If they are not, then OLS coefficients contain an endogeneity bias that cannot be eliminated even with an arbitrarily large data sample. In the growth context, the two most troubling sources of endogeneity are simultaneity and omitted variables.

The most common approach to endogeneity bias is to purge the regression of endogenous determinants by modeling these variables, at least implicitly, as functions of predetermined variables. The investment rate may be eliminated, for example, in favor of demographic variables that affect investment via national saving and are more plausibly predetermined over the five- or ten-year span of country-period observations. In the limit, this approach produces an econometric reduced form, in which all explanatory variables are predetermined and causality flows unambiguously from the explanatory variables to growth. A drawback of this approach is that it places an increasing distance between the included determinants and growth outcomes, in the process often suppressing the structural relationships of most interest to the investigator.

If endogeneity arises from the omission of unobserved but time-invariant attributes of countries or regions (e.g. cultural attributes that affect both growth and the included determinants), a second approach is to eliminate all cross-country or cross-region variation from the data. This can be done by estimating the regression model using deviations from country or region averages (the "fixed-effects" estimator). The cost here is that many of the most important growth determinants vary more strongly across countries than within countries; a substantial amount of information is therefore lost.

A final approach relies on uncovering sources of quasi-experimental variation in the potentially endogenous determinants. "Instrumental" variables are predetermined variables that affect the determinants of interest but are not otherwise correlated with growth. If such variables can be identified, their variation can be used to induce predetermined variation in the otherwise endogenous determinants. While this approach represents the state of the art in growth econometrics, its success depends very strongly on the quality of the instruments. In general, when the instruments only weakly predict the endogenous determinants, small-sample bias is known to be severe; when they strongly predict these determinants, it is less likely that they are predetermined. Controversy therefore abounds here, and particularly so in the growth context where good instruments are difficult to find.

See Wooldridge (2003) for a thorough treatment of these issues and Angrist and Krueger (2001) for details on instrumental variables and related approaches.

The scope for regression-based counterfactual analysis is narrower than is often acknowledged, and even the best growth regression falls short, by construction, of addressing a set of research questions that are of central importance at the country level (O'Connell 2004):

- With respect to opportunities and constraints: what evidence is available to corroborate the importance of particular growth determinants in particular countries, and to identify the channels through which these variables operated?
- Why did the growth determinants evolve as they did, particularly when subject to policy choice?
- What features of country experience might account for why growth was more rapid, or less rapid, than predicted?

Cross-country econometrics and case analysis therefore have powerfully complementary roles to play in the analysis of growth.

3.3 A shifting platform: geography and human resources

The growth econometrics literature took off in the late 1980s as large sets of comparable cross-country data became available from the World Bank and the UN's Income Comparison project. Early contributions (e.g. Barro 1991) noted that a dummy variable for SSA typically accounted for between 1 and 2 percentage points of growth, suggesting that a substantial portion of Africa's overall shortfall was unaccounted for by included determinants. An Africa-focused sub-literature has subsequently labored to uncover the forces proxied by the Africa dummy variable, largely by introducing novel growth determinants that matter for growth on a global basis and that tend to cluster, within SSA, in the upper or lower portions of the global distribution.[21] A number of cross-country studies have focused explicitly on explaining within-Africa growth differentials, either by restricting attention to Africa-only samples or by allowing parameters to vary across regional sub-samples; notable among these are Ghura and Hadjimichael (1996) on sources of African growth, Block (2001) on differences between African and non-African growth dynamics, Fosu (1992, 2002) on political instability, and Berthélemy and Soderling (2001) on episodes of rapid growth.

The current state of the literature can be summarized under the headings of resource endowments and governance. We begin with resource endowments, first considering demographics and human development, two areas not strongly emphasized in the individual country studies, and then turning to geography, which constitutes one of the two dimensions of our synthesis.

---

[21] This is not the only strategy; Hoeffler (2002) finds that the Africa dummy disappears when the Arellano–Bond GMM technique (Arellano and Bond 1991) is applied to instruments for investment and initial income in the augmented Solow model.

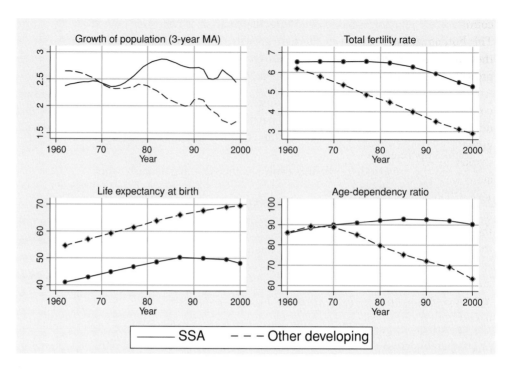

Figure 1.6 Demographic pressures, SSA versus Other developing regions, 1960–2000.
Source: World Bank, World Development Indicators 2005. The figures show simple
averages of country observations, for all countries with continuously available
observations.

3.3.1   Demography

Both theory and evidence suggest that a population explosion is responsible
for some portion of Africa's economic divergence after 1960. In figure 1.6,
African fertility rates, age dependency ratios, and population growth rates
were similar to those of other regions in the 1960s. The demographic picture diverged sharply over the next forty years, however, as public health
improvements reduced infant mortality rates and raised life expectancies
throughout the developing world. Outside Africa fertility rates fell rapidly
enough that population growth declined. Within Africa fertility behavior
barely changed, and as a result population growth accelerated. Starting in
the early 1970s (and through the remainder of the century), African populations grew more rapidly than non-African populations had *ever* grown
on a sustained basis.

Growth theory stresses two channels of the adverse impact of population growth on real incomes. The first arises from diminishing returns, as
land and physical capital are spread over more workers. This effect can be

counteracted by higher investment rates per worker or faster increases in TFP but, as we have seen, there was no systematic tendency for either of these to occur. The second arises from the impact of increased population growth on the ratio of dependents to working-age population. In figure 1.6, Africa's dependency ratio rises steadily, exceeding historical developing-country norms by 1970 and remaining above them through the remainder of the century. Rising dependency ratios have a mechanical impact on growth, by diluting the contribution of any given real GDP growth per worker to real GDP growth *per capita*: table 1.1 indicates that this effect alone is worth nearly 0.4 percent of *per capita* growth per year over the full 1960–2000 period, comparing SSA with other developing regions.[22] Bloom and Sachs (1998) emphasize additional adverse impacts operating through the discouraging effect of high dependency ratios on national saving and the quality of human capital formation.

The fertility rate began to decline in Africa in the mid-1980s, suggesting entry into the final phase of the demographic transition, during which family sizes begin to shrink as parents invest more intensively in a smaller number of children. Maddison's data place the turning point for regional population growth at 1983 (table 1.4). As stressed by Artadi and Sala-i-Martin (2003) and Lucas (2003), any acceleration in this development will bode well for Africa's future growth.

3.3.2 Human development

In global growth regressions, the initial health and – less robustly – education status of the population are often strong predictors of subsequent growth. In table 1.1 we showed that, over the entire 1960–2000 period, the gap between African life expectancies and literacy rates and those in other developing regions did not widen as rapidly as did the gap in incomes. Figure 1.7 provides an alternative perspective on the same phenomenon. We plot the estimated coefficients $\hat{\gamma}_t, \hat{\gamma}_{t+1}, \ldots, \hat{\gamma}_{2000}$, along with their 2-standard-deviation bounds, from OLS regressions of the form

$$d_{it} = \alpha + \beta \ln y_{it} + \sum_{j=t}^{2000} \gamma_j (SSA_i \cdot year_t),$$

where d is the life expectancy rate at birth, or the adult illiteracy rate, for country i in year t, and y (as before) is PPP-adjusted real income *per capita*. The estimated coefficients provide a measure of year-by-year gaps in average human development between countries in SSA and other developing regions, controlling for the gap readily attributable to differences in real

[22] Bloom and Williamson (1998) emphasize the "demographic dividend" that accrued to East Asian countries over this period as a result of a falling ratio of dependents to workers.

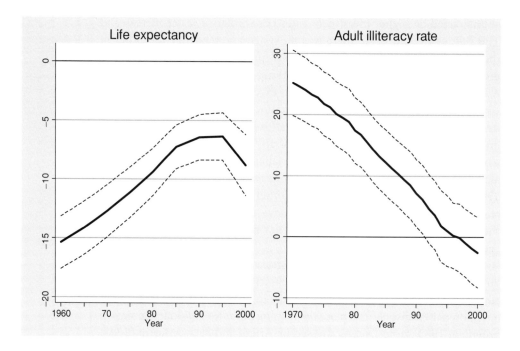

Figure 1.7 Life expectancy and adult illiteracy, SSA/year interactions and 2SD bounds, 1960–2000
Note: Dotted lines show $+/-$ 2 standard errors around the estimated coefficients.

GDP *per capita*. At the time of political independence for much of SSA, life expectancy rates were fifteen years below those of countries with similar incomes globally, and adult illiteracy rates were 25 percentage points higher. By the early 1990s, African illiteracy rates were statistically indistinguishable from those of similar-income countries. Life expectancy rates had also converged steadily to global income-adjusted norms for much of the period but, in contrast with literacy rates, they show a marked slowdown starting in the mid-1980s and a striking reversal with the onset of HIV/AIDS in the 1990s.

While figure 1.7 documents a reasonably rapid convergence of African human development measures to income-adjusted global norms, the adjustment for income is crucial. We have already seen that, on average, African incomes stagnated over the period, diverging sharply from incomes in other regions. Figure 1.7 simply confirms that human development measures did better: they continued to advance at a slow pace, in the face of very limited improvements in overall living standards.[23]

[23] Easterly (1999) argues that in global samples, HDIs display a broad tendency to improve that is not tightly tied to differences in national growth performance.

The growth impact of education has been the subject of a celebrated conundrum in growth econometrics. Microeconomic evidence suggests that the private returns to education are substantial, and growth theory routinely imputes a social return to human capital investment that is at least as great as the private return. But growth researchers have had an extraordinarily difficult time finding statistically significant and economically plausible impacts of educational variables in global growth regressions (Pritchett 2001). In our own framework paper (O'Connell and Ndulu 2001), measures of educational attainment and enrollment performed very poorly in conditional OLS regressions incorporating demographic measures and life expectancy rates, and their limited availability dramatically reduced the size of the African sub-sample.

More recent research has begun to reconcile the microeconomic and growth evidence via better measurement of educational attainment and greater care in the treatment of collinearity and endogeneity. Using an improved dataset on educational attainment, Cohen and Soto (2001) and Soto (2002) uncover statistically significant impacts of human capital investment on growth that are in the range of 7 to 10 percent.[24] Others have found significant impacts once thresholds are passed; Barro (1999), for example, finds that school attainment at the secondary and higher levels for males aged twenty-five and over has a positive effect on the subsequent rate of economic growth. The estimated impact for this category is such that an additional year of schooling raises the growth rate impact by 0.7 percent per year, a very large effect indeed for slow growers. This impact is mediated predominantly via improved capabilities to absorb technological advances.

Barro's results are consistent with those of Borensztein, De Gregorio, and Lee (1998), who find that the productivity advantages latent in foreign direct investment (FDI) are subject to human-capital threshold effects. These authors find that the growth contribution of FDI exceeds that of domestic investment only when the host country's average secondary-school attainment exceeds 0.52 years (for the male population of working age). This level is far above that of the majority of African countries. Consistent with these results, the vast bulk of FDI into Africa flows into the mineral and energy sectors. Within Africa, Lumbila (2005) finds a similar threshold effect using secondary enrollment rather than attainment rates: returns to FDI are significantly higher in countries with secondary enrollment rates exceeding 25 percent.

---

[24] There is some evidence that human-capital accumulation induces accumulation of additional physical capital. Taking this indirect effect into account, these authors estimate the total long-run impact of an additional average year of education on income *per capita* at between 12 and 16 percent.

3.3.3   Geography

Cross-country evidence has played a central role in the revival of geographically based explanations of African growth. The dominant strands in this literature focus on the disadvantages of location in the ecological tropics, the physical isolation of African populations, and the costs of resource-based comparative advantage. A final line of argument, overlapping with the others but raising a separate set of issues, emphasizes vulnerability to external shocks.

Location

Bloom and Sachs (1998) and Masters and McMillan (2001) show that, in global samples, malaria prevalence and location in the ecological tropics are associated with systematically slower growth. While a high disease burden (to humans, animals, or both) would be expected to undermine productivity in agriculture and the quality of labor input more generally, these are *level* effects on real income; the channels through which a hostile natural environment affects the rate of factor accumulation or the growth rate of productivity are less obvious. In the case of human capital, factor accumulation effects may come from the impact of poor health on the returns to education. Evidence from northern Kenya, for example, suggests that treatment for intestinal worms has a major impact on school attendance (Miguel and Kremer 2004). A second, indirect impact on both human and physical capital accumulation per worker may come via population growth, if high levels of fertility reflect a demand for surviving children as old-age security.[25] The regression evidence implicates productivity growth as a key channel as well, since these regressions typically hold national saving or investment rates (and sometimes measures of human capital accumulation) constant.

Isolation

The original geography of economic growth comes from Adam Smith, who in his *Wealth of Nations* placed the extent of the market at the heart of both accumulation and productivity growth. African populations are in fact unusually isolated, both from each other and from global populations. Frankel and Romer (1999) use a gravity model to calculate the distance of countries from potentially important trading partners, and then use this distance variable as an instrument for actual international trade.[26] They

---

[25] As proxied by life expectancies, health standards have generally been rising over most of the period. This mechanism can explain the persistence of high fertility behavior only if anticipated morbidity lags actual morbidity.

[26] See section 3.2 and box 1.1. The idea here is that distance is more plausibly predetermined with respect to economic growth than trade is, so that variation in distance induces

find that distance strongly undermines growth, via its impact on international trade. Africa is by far the most remote continent by this measure and, as we confirmed in our framework paper, trade is an even stronger predictor of growth for African countries than it is for non-African countries (O'Connell and Ndulu 2001). Bloom and Sachs (1998), Gallup, Sachs with Mellinger (1999), and Limão and Venables (2002) examine economic isolation more broadly and show that political landlockedness, remoteness of populations from ports or ocean-navigable rivers, large over-land transport distances, and poor transport infrastructure all reduce growth in global samples. African populations face unusually high costs in each of these areas.

Endowments

The *natural resource curse* refers to a broad empirical consensus – illustrated by the travails of many oil-exporting countries, including Nigeria, starting in the 1970s – that natural-resource exporters grow more slowly, other things equal, than exporters of manufactures and services (Sachs and Warner 1997, 2001). While the inability of African countries to break out of narrow commodity specialization has been widely noted (Gersovitz and Paxson 1990), the sources of this pattern remain contentious. Wood and Berge (1997) appeal to geography, arguing that Africa's low ratio of skilled labor to natural resources generates a deep comparative advantage in primary exports. Collier (1997) focuses on governance, arguing that natural-resource exports dominate because they are unusually robust to institutional failures in the public sector. In chapter 2, Collier and O'Connell document a divergence in African trade patterns starting in the 1990s: the emergence of new oil exporters has sharpened the primary commodity specialization of the continent, but among coastal and resource-scarce countries those that have maintained strong policy environments have experienced significant diversification into manufacturing and services.

The literature identifies two main channels through which natural-resource wealth may undermine long-run growth. Both involve failures of governance, a topic we treat more directly in section 3.4. The first is through a market failure associated with other sectors that produce traded goods. If agriculture, manufacturing or traded services (e.g. tourism) generate learning-by-doing effects or other positive externalities, then the tendency for these sectors to shrink as natural-resource exports are exploited undermines aggregate growth (Rajan and Subramanian 2005). This is the "Dutch disease"; it implies a policy error because an optimal subsidy to traded goods can internalize the externality and convert commodity wealth into a source of net gains (Adam and O'Connell 2004).

quasi-experimental variation in trade, making it possible to isolate the causal component of the observed positive correlation between trade and growth.

Other channels for the natural-resource curse implicate governance even more directly, by characterizing resource rents as a source of institutional failure in the public sector. An important strand of this literature focuses on short-run commodity booms rather than long-run resource endowments, and here the cross-country evidence is, at first glance, puzzling: terms of trade improvements play a notoriously modest role in explaining growth cross-country regressions. But this is consistent with an extensive case study literature that emphasizes the diversity of country-level policy responses.[27] Nigeria and Indonesia, for example, received similar oil windfalls in the 1970s but undertook dramatically different policy responses and experienced divergent growth outcomes (Bevan, Collier, and Gunning 1999). The management of natural resource rents features critically in many of the country studies of the Growth Project, particularly within the "resource-rich" category where these rents were typically the dominant source of government revenues. Chapters 6, 7, and 8 draw on the case study evidence to explore the impact of these rents on fiscal sustainability, violence, and political accountability.

Vulnerability

A final line of argument, included here with some violence to the "geography" category, emphasizes the vulnerability of non-diversified economies to external shocks (Guillaumont, Guillaumont-Jeanneney, and Brun 1999). Cross-country evidence confirms that countries with more volatile growth rates – recall table 1.6 – grow more slowly on average (Ramey and Ramey 1995; Gunning, chapter 8 in this volume). While a substantial portion of observed volatility is driven by economic policy (Gavin and Hausmann 1998), external shocks contribute both directly and via the policy responses they provoke. In table 1.7 we show cross-country regressions of growth volatility on the standard deviations of rainfall shocks (weighted by the share of agriculture in total employment), terms of trade shocks (weighted by the share of exports in GDP), and partner-country growth rates (weighted by bilateral trade shares). Each of these variables provides some leverage over cross-country differences in volatility. Low-income economies face larger income risks in these arenas, as suggested by the declining size and significance of the lagged income variable when these regressors are incorporated.

We noted earlier that growth rates in African countries are unusually volatile on an inter-annual basis, even after controlling for income. This effect appears to be mediated by our measures of externally induced volatility, because an SSA dummy variable falls considerably in size and loses

---

[27] It should also be recalled that terms of trade shocks are first-order shocks to national income, not to GDP. Impacts on growth would occur via factor accumulation or productivity growth.

Table 1.7 *External shocks and the volatility of growth.*
Dependent variable: standard deviation of growth in real GDP per capita.

Variable	(1)	(2)	(3)	(4)
ln($yinit$)	−1.089	−0.647	−0.552	−0.337
	(0.225)***	(0.340)*	(0.356)	(0.447)
sd[xsh*dln(tot)]	–	–	0.424	0.392
	–	–	(0.069)***	(0.075)***
sd[ash*dln($rain$)]	–	–	0.139	0.118
	–	–	(0.082)*	(0.080)
sd[dln(ytp)]	–	–	1.685	1.794
	–	–	(0.757)**	(0.754)**
SSA	–	1.483	–	0.858
	–	(0.661)**	–	(0.591)
Constant	13.361	9.428	4.780	2.812
	(1.794)***	(2.850)***	(3.902)	(4.767)
Observations	110	110	110	110
R-squared	0.14	0.20	0.42	0.44
F-stat	23.443	19.624	24.333	20.204
Prob>F	0.0000	0.0000	0.0000	0.0000

Robust standard errors in parentheses (*significant at 10%; **5%; ***1%).
Notes: Observations are countries. The notation "dln" refers to the change in the log from year to year, and "sd" refers to a country-level standard deviation calculated over the 1960–2000 period. *yinit* is initial (= 1960) real GDP *per capita* at international prices; *xsh* is the average ratio of merchandise exports to GDP over the full period, and *tot* is the barter terms of trade (price index of merchandise exports divided by price index of merchandise imports); *ash* is the average ratio of agricultural value added to GDP at current prices over the full period; *rain* is area-weighted average annual rainfall in millimeters, based on gridded climatology data; *ytp* is the trade-weighted average growth rate of real GDP *per capita* among trading partners; and SSA is a dummy variable for SSA.

significance when these variables are included (compare regressions (2) and (4) in table 1.7). In separate regressions (not shown) we find that Africa's exposures to rainfall volatility and partner-growth volatility are not in fact unusually high, given the region's low income. The exposure of African countries to terms of trade volatility, by contrast, is over 50 percent higher than that of other developing countries after controlling for income. The estimated difference exposure is statistically significant and is consistent with the region's unusually strong dependence on a few primary exports.

With rudimentary domestic financial markets and pro-cyclical (if any) access to foreign capital markets, credit markets provide very limited scope for the management of shocks to income in SSA. At the macroeconomic level, international reserves provide scope for offsetting temporary shocks to net foreign exchange receipts, but until the 1990s few countries out-side of Botswana maintained prudent levels of reserves. Foreign aid is in principle a natural source of countercyclical finance, and the level of aid is large in SSA,[28] but the evidence suggests that aid has been a net source of volatility in foreign exchange receipts, not of insurance (Bulir and Hamman 2003).

With risks to income persisting at the microeconomic level, households and firms are likely to turn to self-insurance mechanisms in an effort to reduce their *ex ante* exposure to shocks. Such mechanisms may operate in such disparate domains as fertility behavior, the choice of crops or seed varieties, the speed of adoption of new technologies, the scale of commer-cial enterprises, and the size of business inventories. The hallmark of self-insurance is to sacrifice expected yield for greater safety, thereby reducing the average yield on investments in physical and human capital. An increase in income uncertainty may therefore reduce the expected growth rate of income even if the volume of investment – as suggested by theories of pre-cautionary saving – rises.[29] In chapter 8 Gunning takes this argument a step further by arguing that rural households in SSA typically lack access to a safe asset. This undermines the precautionary saving motive to such a degree that increases in uninsured income risk now sharply reduce long-run asset accumulation by rural households.

It is difficult, however, to econometrically disentangle the effects of *ex ante* uncertainty and *ex post* shocks. This is particularly true in aggregate data, where uncertainty changes only slowly over time as a function of observed shocks. This is an active and as yet inconclusive area of research. In the com-modity price arena, Blattman, Hwang, and Williamson (2007) use panel data to distinguish trend from volatility in the terms of trade before the First World War. They find that among countries in the periphery of the industrial world, *ex ante* volatility undermined growth, in part by discour-aging direct foreign investment. Dehn (2000), however, finds that in a panel of contemporary developing countries, measures of *ex ante* volatility have very little impact on growth, relative to the impacts of actual shocks (par-ticularly adverse ones). Research on rainfall shocks is beginning to proceed in the same spirit; O'Connell and Ndulu (2001) and Miguel, Satyanatah, and Sergenti (2004) confirm the importance of rainfall shocks for growth in Africa-only samples, but as yet little is known about the relative macroe-conomic importance of shocks and *ex ante* exposure.

---

[28] The median ratio of net official development assistance to GNP was 13.4 percent for SSA during the 1990s, as compared with a global median of 4.5 percent for all aid recipients (O'Connell and Soludo 2001).

[29] Note also that an increase in income uncertainty may reduce *domestic* investment even if overall saving rises, if it stimulates a shift into foreign assets.

3.4   Governance and growth

It is tempting to read the evidence on resource endowments and growth, and particularly on the salience of geographical variables, as uncovering essentially permanent sources of slow growth in Africa. But there is nothing in what we have reviewed that would sharply distinguish North from South Korea in 1960, Botswana from Zambia at independence, China before and after 1980, or Uganda before and after 1986. These contributions map out *diagnosis* rather than *destiny*. They reveal systematic tendencies, but unexplained variance remains very high. Moreover, where geographical constraints are important, their salience is ultimately endogenous to human action.[30]

This brings us to governance, a central preoccupation of the literature on African economic growth since the early 1980s. The study of governance is the study of how states deploy the coercive power that distinguishes them from markets or communities (Hayami 2001). Even at this high level of abstraction, two distinct but complementary questions can be distinguished. First, like any collective good, national growth will be under-provided by markets and communities in the absence of institutional structures to compel collective action (Olson 1965). But what are the appropriate spheres of such action? A minimalist tradition dating from Adam Smith and reinforced by the new institutional economics of North (1981, 1991) places the security of individual rights to property and income at the center. In 1755 Smith reduced the core functions of government to "peace, easy taxes, and a tolerable administration of justice," famously arguing that these were sufficient for rapid growth.[31] North and his contemporaries are closer to viewing these functions as *necessary* rather than sufficient, and contemporary minimalists invariably place some categories of public infrastructure investment (e.g. in ports, agricultural research, and primary education) among the necessary conditions (Lal 2000; Easterly 2001). But as emphasized by Bates in chapter 4 and Ndulu in chapter 9, African governments initially embraced a very different view of the appropriate division of labor between markets and states.

Second, regardless of how state power is acquired, it is ultimately exercised by private individuals. What prevents the use of coercive power for private or community ends, rather than national ones? A rational-choice tradition

---

[30] Jeffrey Sachs is by far the single most influential contributor to the geography-and-growth literature (see the references in the text), and at the same time the most urgent champion of a big push to overcome these constraints (e.g. Sachs *et al.* 2004).

[31] "Little else is requisite to carry a state to the highest degree of opulence from the lowest barbarism, but peace, easy taxes, and a tolerable administration of justice; all the rest being brought about by the natural order of things." The date 1755 comes from Jay (1996), who cites Smith's 1795 *Essays on Philosophical Subjects.*

dating at least from the *Federalist Papers*[32] views the problem of institutional design in government as one of aligning the incentives of government officials with the general interest in economic progress. A misalignment of incentives, from this perspective, leaves policy prey to the parochial interests of incumbent political elites and may convert the public sector into an arena for costly distributional struggle. Chapters 6, 7, 10, and 11 study this problem in the African context, drawing extensively on evidence from the country studies in volume 2.

In contrast to slowly moving geographical variables, the governance environment has been in flux in many of the countries of SSA over the period since 1960. We emphasize two key dimensions before turning briefly to the treatment of governance in growth econometrics.

First, the novelty of sovereignty itself is often overlooked. It came later and much more rapidly to SSA than to other developing regions, with nearly three-quarters of the region securing independence between 1956 and 1966 (table 1.2).[33] Anti-colonialist movements had begun to acquire weight within the European colonial empires during the 1930s and 1940s, but in Africa the end of colonialism was more powerfully driven more by the realignment of global power in the Second World War than by the mobilization of national collective action against colonialism (Oliver and Atmore 1994). In retrospect, the transfer of sovereignty *per se* had unclear implications for growth. In their own interests, the colonial powers had developed a physical and institutional infrastructure for the efficient exploitation of resource-based exports, mainly in agriculture but also, particularly in Southern Africa, in minerals. The transfer of sovereignty would therefore allow a fundamental redirection of development strategy – "Seek ye first the political kingdom," said Ghana's Kwame Nkrumah, "and all the rest shall be added unto ye." But it would also transfer the "rents to sovereignty"[34] and the responsibility for core functions – peace, policy, property rights, and infrastructure – to such local political elites as would acquire the instruments of state power. Growth could falter if these functions were subordinated to other agendas or undermined by the collapse of state authority.

A second and more widely remarked phenomenon is the evolving nature of executive power in independent Africa. The politically plural constitutions adopted at independence gave way during the 1960s and 1970s to one-party

---

[32] Writing under the pen name "Publius," Alexander Hamilton, John Jay, and James Madison published *The Federalist* as a series of eighty-five newspaper essays in 1787 and 1788, in an effort to rally the citizens of New York behind adoption of the proposed US Constitution. See http://thomas.loc.gov/home/histdox/fedpapers.html for the full text.

[33] Only three countries – Ethiopia (ancient), Liberia (1947), and South Africa (1910) – existed as independent states in 1955, and in South Africa, black majority rule would not come until 1994.

[34] This term is due to Nkurunziza and Ngaruko, who use it to powerful effect in their country study of Burundi in volume 2.

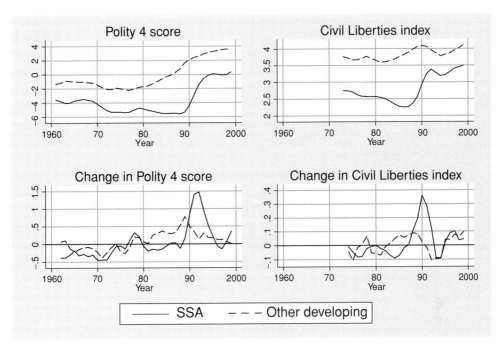

Figure 1.8 Democracy/autocracy and civil liberties, 1960–2000.
Note: The figure applies to all countries with continuous coverage.

states and military dictatorships through much of the region (Collier 1982; Bratton and van de Walle 1997). Meanwhile currency boards, customs unions, and other colonial-era "agencies of restraint" were replaced by national institutions that were rapidly subordinated to executive authority (Collier 1991).[35] Using the Polity 4 democracy/autocracy scale, figure 1.8 documents the repudiation by African political elites of institutional constraints on their power in the first decade or so after independence – and then the restoration of these constraints, after a lag of two decades, in the process of democratization that swept the continent between 1988 and 1994.[36]

---

[35] The CFA countries retained their colonial-era monetary integration with France, but transferred its governance into African hands in the mid-1970s (O'Connell 1997). Masson and Pattillo (2005) provide a thorough institutional history of monetary policy in independent Africa.

[36] The Polity 4 measure of political regimes varies between −10 for high autocracy and +10 for high democracy, with 0 representing a regime that is neutral between the two extremes. Higher values correspond to deeper and more effective political constraints on executive tenure and autonomy. The data represent the judgments of a panel of experts and emphasize the *de facto* situation when this departs from the impression given by formal institutions (e.g. a democratically elected leader actively violating constitutional constraints gets a low score). Figure 1.8 also shows the Freedom House civil liberties index, which is similarly constructed and after reversing the scale runs from 1 (worst) to 7 (best).

As with the transfer of sovereignty, the consolidation of executive authority *per se* had unclear implications for economic growth. On a global basis, the average growth performance of authoritarian governments after 1960 was little different from that of democracies, and in East and Southeast Asia, authoritarian rule often delivered very high growth (Alesina and Perotti 1994). The opposite proved true in Africa, however. The continent's long detour into authoritarian rule corresponds roughly to the U-shaped evolution of its growth performance. Its highest performers – Botswana and Mauritius – are among its few consistently democratic regimes (Ndulu and O'Connell 1999; Bratton and van de Walle 1997). Chapters 10 and 11 provide a theory of political institutions that grounds this correlation in Africa's economic and political geography.

With this background, we turn to the treatment of governance in growth econometrics, focusing on the core functions discussed above. We then turn to political polarization as a potentially deep determinant of the quality of governance.

3.4.1 Peace

Civil wars represent the most dramatic failure of a state to command a monopoly of coercion over its own territory. Their incidence trended upwards within the developing world through most of the period, but Africa's experience diverged sharply from that of other developing regions in the early 1990s. Figure 1.9 dates the relative deterioration in Africa's security situation to the democratization period of 1988–94 and suggests a lingering effect of this deterioration through the 1990s. In the global data, civil war costs over 2 percentage points of growth on an annual basis, while increasing the risk of subsequent conflict (Collier and Hoeffler 2002, 2004). Low incomes and primary commodity exports substantially increase the risk of civil war and imply a relatively high underlying exposure in SSA.

In chapter 7, Bates expands the analysis of state failure to include situations in which political leaders turn the instruments of state power to predatory purposes and private groups arm themselves in order to defend and pursue their own interests. A failure of political order, in this analysis, undermines economic growth even before the situation degenerates (if it does) into civil war. Leaders impose confiscatory taxes and stop securing private property; private groups devote productive resources to a zero-sum deterrence game. Mirroring the civil war literature, Bates finds that the prevalence of political conflict is a decreasing function of *per capita* income and an increasing function of natural-resource rents. He also finds that private military groups emerge more frequently in the presence of competitive political systems than under military dictatorships or one-party states, consistent with the shorter expected tenure of leaders under contested elections. The latter result suggests that the rapid re-introduction of multi-party elections between

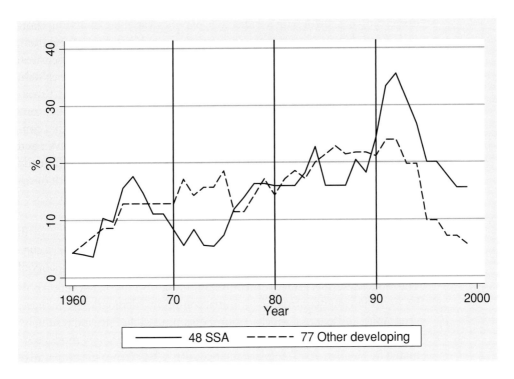

Figure 1.9 Proportion of countries in civil war, 1960–2000.
Source: Civil war dummy variable constructed by N. Sambanis. Data end in 1999.

1988 and 1994 may have contributed, in the short run, to an increase in political violence and a deterioration in the growth environment.

3.4.2　Policy

Functioning states affect the economic environment for growth by intervening in markets, producing or distributing goods and services, providing social overhead capital, and defining and/or enforcing property rights. The first two categories comprise what is conventionally treated as "economic policy" in the growth econometrics literature.[37]

Policy failures are at the heart of a critique of African governance that began with Bates (1981) and the World Bank's "Berg Report" (World Bank 1981)[38] and gathered force in the early 1980s with the emergence of structural adjustment lending throughout Africa and Latin America. In our framework paper for the Growth Project, we documented the strong

---

[37] We treat the final two categories (in reverse order) in sub-sections 3.4.3 and 3.4.4.
[38] So called after its head author, Elliot Berg.

association of growth with a wide range of policy variables, including inflation, fiscal deficits, government consumption, the black market premium, and exchange rate over-valuation, as well as with a variety of policy-sensitive variables including the size of the financial sector (O'Connell and Ndulu 2001). Controlling for initial conditions and exogenous shocks, policy measures were strongly correlated with growth, both in unrestricted global samples (using five-year non-overlapping averages) and in regressions that controlled for unobserved country heterogeneity by including country fixed effects.[39] We found little evidence that policy variables operated differently in SSA than elsewhere, with the exception of trade openness, which had a stronger impact on predicted growth within SSA than outside.

Regression-based growth decompositions

Table 1.8 shows a set of regressions based on the pooled conditional specification we developed in our framework paper (O' Connell and Ndulu 2001). The model describes growth outcomes conditional on alternative sets of policy variables, after controlling for initial conditions, demographic changes, geography, and external shocks. Country teams used the "fits and residuals" from this model (and from a version of the augmented Solow model estimated by Hoeffler 2002) to place their country's experience in comparative perspective.

Column (1) shows the original pooled conditional model, updated to 2004. The model is robust to the extension of the sample. All coefficients retain their magnitudes and expected signs, and the income effect of the terms of trade is nearly significant at the 10 percent level while all other variables are significant at better than 5 percent with the exception of landlocked status, which has a very similar point estimate to its original one. An SSA dummy variable is both economically and statistically insignificant when added to the specification (coefficient -0.21, $p = 0.75$).

In columns (2)–(4) we replace the Barro–Lee (1994) "unproductive government consumption" variable – which measures government consumption at international prices, net of spending on education and defense – with the overall government consumption ratio, which is much more widely available, particularly after the mid-1980s. We also include measures of real exchange rate misalignment and monetary depth, two variables often implicated in discussions of the sectoral bias of policy in Africa.

---

[39] In the latter case, correlations derive only from within-country variation in policy and growth. Any (spurious) growth effects that are driven by cross-country correlations between policy performance and unobserved country attributes are eliminated, because the regression implicitly uses only the deviations of all variables from country-specific means. See box 1.1.

Table 1.8 *Pooled conditional regressions.*
Dependent variable: growth of real GDP per capita

Variable	(1)	(2)	(3)	(4)
Initial real GDP	−1.363	−1.259	−1.115	−0.740
per capita	(0.000)***	(0.000)***	(0.000)***	(0.015)**
Initial years of life	0.065	0.085	0.064	0.049
expectancy	(0.045)**	(0.001)***	(0.011)**	(0.078)*
Age dependency ratio	−0.044	−0.043	−0.046	−0.042
	(0.001)***	(0.000)***	(0.000)***	(0.003)***
Growth of potential LF	0.655	0.965	0.924	1.009
participation	(0.008)***	(0.001)***	(0.004)***	(0.006)***
Landlocked	−0.469	0.010	0.179	0.662
	(0.256)	(0.979)	(0.686)	(0.202)
Trading-partner growth	0.551	0.378	0.304	0.416
	(0.001)***	(0.030)**	(0.094)*	(0.059)*
Income effect of TOT	0.032	0.036	0.043	0.049
improvements	(0.154)	(0.012)**	(0.005)***	(0.004)***
Political instability	−0.292	−0.240	−0.257	−0.212
	(0.000)***	(0.001)***	(0.001)***	(0.009)***
Inflation rate (<500)	−0.010	−0.016	−0.016	−0.015
	(0.015)**	(0.011)**	(0.010)**	(0.011)**
Black market premium	−0.014	−0.013	−0.012	−0.014
(<500)	(0.023)**	(0.002)***	(0.020)**	(0.003)***
Over-valuation index	–	–	−0.007	−0.009
	–	–	(0.017)**	(0.016)**
Unproductive govt	−0.099	–	–	–
consump./GDP	(0.001)***	–	–	–
Total govt consump./GDP	–	−0.031	−0.024	−0.024
	–	(0.022)**	(0.114)	(0.172)
log of M2/GDP ratio	–	–	–	0.173
	–	–	–	(0.020)**

(*cont.*)

Table 1.8 *(cont.)*

Variable	(1)	(2)	(3)	(4)
Constant	11.575	9.014	9.908	6.601
	(0.000)***	(0.000)***	(0.000)***	(0.029)**
Observations	495	676	592	415
R-squared	0.356	0.339	0.357	0.357
F-stat	12.441	13.214	14.012	20.268
Prob>F	0.0000	0.0000	0.0000	0.0000

Robust *p*-values are in parentheses (*significant at 10%; ** significant at 5%; *** significant at 1%).

Notes: Observations are half-decadal averages or initial half-decadal values (as indicated) from 1960–4 to 2000–4. The sample is unbalanced (not all countries have a full set of observations). The regressions contain a full set of half-decadal dummy variables whose coefficients are not reported here.

Definition of variables: Initial real GDP per capita is at international prices. The *age dependency ratio* is the ratio of population below fifteen or over sixty-five to total population. *Growth of potential LF (labor force) participation* is the growth rate of the ratio of population of working age to overall population. *Trading-partner growth* is the trade-weighted average growth of real GDP *per capita* among trading partners. The *income effect of TOT improvements* is the average income effect of the change in the terms of trade using the final year of the previous half-decade as base: higher values represent more favorable terms of trade movements. *Political instability* is the number of strikes, revolutions, or assassinations. The *inflation rate* is calculated as $100^* \ln(1 + \pi)$, where π is the CPI inflation rate. The *black market premium* is the percentage excess of the annual average black market exchange rate over the annual average official exchange rate. For both π and the black market premium, we omit half-decadal observations where these take values above 500 percent. The *over-valuation index* extends the index constructed for 1976–85 by Dollar (1992): we constructed the bilateral real exchange rate against the US dollar as $e_{it} = CPI_{it}/(E_{it} \cdot CPI_{USA,t})$, where E_{it} is country *i*'s average nominal official exchange rate in year t (locals per US dollar), and then re-based this series to equal Dollar's over-valuation index on average for 1976–85. Values greater than 100 denote over-valuation. *Unproductive government consumption* is defined as government consumption at international prices excluding spending on defense and education; this variable was introduced by Barro and Lee (1994) and we have extended it past 1984 using IMF data on government spending categories. Both government consumption variables use data at international prices. For data sources and further details on construction of the variables, see O'Connell and Ndulu (2001); all variables are as described there, with the exception of the inflation variable (in O'Connell and Ndulu 2001, we used π itself rather than the log transformation which we have adopted here).

Over-valued exchange rates impose an anti-export bias while also indicating macroeconomic unsustainability; monetary depth reflects the influence of financial repression on intermediation by the banking sector.

Consistent with our earlier discussion, demographic variables – which vary mainly across countries rather than over time – play a very powerful role in differentiating Africa's predicted growth from that of other regions. Across all four regressions, differences in the demographic variables consistently predict two-thirds of the observed difference between average growth in SSA and in other developing regions (table 1.9). The landlockedness variable, by contrast, is puzzling at first: its coefficient is unstable and fails to reach statistical significance. The declining premium on coastal location in regressions (2)–(4) is driven in part by the inclusion of a much broader post-1985 sample: as Collier and O'Connell show in chapter 2, African coastal economies very strongly under-performed their global counterparts after 1980. Within the set of included variables, however, landlockedness consistently exerts a strong indirect effect on predicted growth, via the initial conditions and demographic variables.[40]

The policy coefficients in table 1.9 are estimated reasonably precisely and display reasonable stability across forty years of dramatic change in the global policy environment. To verify the latter, we constructed regression-weighted policy aggregates by summing up the policy variables in regressions (1)–(4), multiplied by their estimated coefficients. By construction, these aggregates have a coefficient of one when entered in place of the individual policy variables. We interacted these variables with the period-by-period dummy variables in order to allow policy impacts to vary over time, and then tested for equality of these coefficients across periods. We were not able to reject equality at conventional significance levels, except in regression (2) where an F-test produces a p-value of 0.073 and the point estimates suggest (figure 1.10) a modest increase in policy coefficients late in the period.

But does policy *matter* in the sense of substantially affecting predicted growth, holding other determinants constant? If we look at regional growth differentials, the answer is "yes," though with varying strength across specifications. Regression (1) implies a very strong impact: holding other determinants constant, well over half $(0.66/1.18 = 0.56)$ of Africa's total growth shortfall relative to other developing regions $(1.09 + 0.09 = 1.18)$ is

---

[40] For example: in regressions (2)–(4), if we sum up the regression-weighted contributions of initial conditions and demographic variables and regress this variable on landlocked status, we get a coefficient that is positive and large and has a p-value below 1 percent. The sum of this coefficient and the coefficient on landlockedness, as a measure of the net (direct plus indirect) impact of landlockedness on predicted growth, is 0.68, 0.35, and 0.17, respectively, in the three regressions.

Table 1.9 *Regression-based growth decompositions.*

Deviations from sample mean	Regression (1)			Regression (2)			Regression (3)			Regression (4)		
	SSA	Other	Indust.	SSA	Other	Indust.	SSA	Other	Indust.	SSA	Other	Indust.
Growth	−1.09	0.09	0.60	−1.14	0.24	0.92	−1.20	0.12	0.98	−1.09	0.46	1.22
Contribution of:												
Initial conditions	0.49	0.33	−0.81	0.08	0.27	−0.58	0.25	0.22	−0.63	−0.02	0.06	−0.51
Demography	−0.91	−0.14	0.82	−0.84	0.09	0.84	−0.92	0.02	0.87	−0.70	0.29	0.85
Landlocked status	−0.12	0.04	0.02	0.00	0.00	0.00	0.04	−0.02	−0.01	0.14	−0.06	−0.11
Shocks	−0.01	−0.02	0.03	−0.02	−0.02	0.05	−0.03	−0.02	0.07	−0.04	0.00	0.17
Political instability	0.11	−0.09	0.06	0.07	−0.08	0.06	0.08	−0.09	0.07	0.08	−0.06	0.15
Policy	−0.71	−0.05	0.56	−0.20	−0.14	0.49	−0.29	−0.08	0.43	−0.32	0.11	0.66
Period fixed effects	0.11	−0.01	−0.05	−0.07	−0.01	0.1	−0.22	0.00	0.21	−0.12	0.04	0.25
Residual	−0.06	0.03	−0.01	−0.17	0.13	−0.04	−0.11	0.08	−0.02	−0.11	0.08	−0.24

Note. Where the contributions do not add exactly to the growth deviation, this is due to rounding.
Source. Regressions in table 1.8. Contributions are average regional deviations from the sample mean, multiplied by the relevant regression coefficients. *Initial conditions* include initial income and life expectancy; *Demography* includes age dependency ratio and the growth in the potential LF participation rate; *Shocks* include the income effect of the TOT and the partner-country growth rate; *Policy* includes the inflation rate and all variables listed below it in table 1.8.

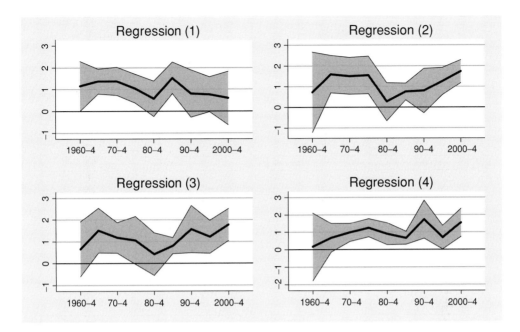

Figure 1.10 Policy coefficients, by half-decade, 1960–2004.
Note: Shaded region shows $+/- 2$ standard errors around the estimated coefficients.

predicted on the basis of differences in the policy variables.[41] The impact is more modest in specifications that replace the Barro–Lee government spending variable and draw more heavily from the period after 1985, but it remains considerable in specifications (3) and (4) at 16 and 28 percent, respectively.

Policy variables over time

Given the overall importance of policy in these regressions, does the time profile of policy variables display the U-shape we have seen in the growth

[41] In table 1.9 we use the regressions in columns (2) and (3) to decompose the deviation of period t growth from the sample mean ($g_{it} - \bar{g}$, into the sum of a country-period residual and the regression-weighted sum of country-period deviations in the growth determinants. Using a hat ($^\wedge$) to denote an OLS estimate, the table reports a version of

$$g_{it} - \bar{g} = -\hat{\gamma}(\ln y_{i,t-k} - \overline{\ln y}) + \sum_j \hat{\phi}^j \left(x_{it}^j - \bar{x}\right) + \sum_l \hat{\lambda}^l \left(z_i^l - \bar{z}\right) + \hat{\varepsilon}_{it}$$

with the variables re-grouped by analytical category (see table 1.8) and the country-period observations aggregated over time. Since the average OLS residual is zero by construction, the decomposition is exact. The orthogonality of fit and residual also affords a clean attribution of the relative contributions of observed and unobserved determinants of growth to the overall conditional mean. The latter property does not hold for individual determinants, however, because they are mutually correlated.

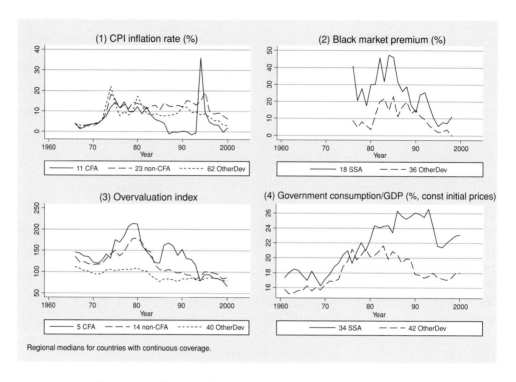

Figure 1.11 Policy variables over time, 1960–2000.

outcomes? Figure 1.11 tracks the policy variables one by one, in each case using the largest sample with continuously available data (a sample considerably larger than the regression sample). The broad answer is "yes": policy variables tend to deteriorate in the 1970s and 1980s before improving, both absolutely and relative to other developing regions, starting in the mid-1980s.

Panel (3) reflects what is probably the single most dramatic macroeconomic policy development of the post-independence period: the emergence of strongly over-valued exchange rates throughout SSA in the 1970s, and their gradual resolution through real depreciation starting in the early 1980s. A sharp distinction is apparent here between the countries of the CFA zone, comprising a pair of monetary unions with currencies pegged to the French franc, and countries outside the zone operating independent monetary policies.[42] Outside of the CFA zone, real depreciation got underway by the mid-1980s, driven by nominal depreciation and the loosening of

---

[42] Not all non-CFA countries operate independent monetary policies; the South African rand circulates in Lesotho, Namibia, and Swaziland, who together with South Africa form the Rand Monetary Area (RMA). Monetary policy in the RMA is set by the Reserve Bank of South Africa. Botswana left the RMA in the mid-1970s.

exchange controls that in many cases had been extended to the current account during the turbulent 1970s. Panel (2) shows the associated reductions in the black market premium outside of the CFA zone: the process of exchange rate unification was interrupted only briefly by the period of political instability in the early 1990s. By the mid-1990s virtually all of SSA had formally abjured exchange controls on the current account by adopting "Article VIII" status in the IMF.[43]

In contrast with the countries operating independent monetary policies, exchange controls were effectively absent in the CFA countries by virtue of a convertibility guarantee extended by the French government. While balance of payments pressures were in many cases similar to those faced outside the CFA zone – particularly in the net-oil-importing West African monetary union, which included Côte d'Ivoire, one of SSA's few commercial borrowers – exchange rate adjustment was delayed within the CFA zone until 1994. In the meantime over-valuation persisted, and the adjustment to balance of payments pressure took place via monetary and fiscal contraction. The resulting divergent trends in inflation are apparent in panel (1); adjustment was deflationary in the CFA zone during the 1980s and early 1990s. The inflation spike in CFA countries in 1994 was driven by a 50 percent devaluation of the CFA franc, widely viewed as long overdue.

Government consumption ratios (panel (4)) show a sharp divergence for SSA as a whole starting in the late 1970s, with Africa's ratios continuing to climb as the debt crisis enforced fiscal austerity in other regions. A delayed and rapid adjustment took place in the early 1990s, coinciding roughly with a decline of similar magnitude in foreign aid following the collapse of the Soviet Union (O'Connell and Soludo 2001).

Assessing the policy environment

As we emphasized in our framework paper (O'Connell and Ndulu 2001), the "contributions" in table 1.9 reflect sample correlations rather than clean policy counterfactuals. In large part this reflects the inherent difficulty of measuring the aspects of policy that matter for growth and are plausibly predetermined. The challenges here are well known:

- *Reverse causality*: policy variables often reflect policy outcomes rather than policy settings. An increase in the black market premium or the fiscal deficit, for example, may be driven by a collapse in export performance, inducing a correlation with growth even if neither the exchange control regime nor the structure of fiscal policy have changed.

---

[43] When an IMF country accepts Article VIII status, it agrees not to employ multiple currency practices or to impose payments' restrictions on current account transactions, without IMF approval. In effect, it adopts full convertibility of its currency, at a single exchange rate, for current account purposes. For details, consult the IMF's Articles of Agreement at www.imf.org/external/pubs/ft/aa/index.htm.

- *Dimensionality*: the range of potentially important policy instruments is wide enough that the same policy orientation – e.g. export promotion or state-led industrialization – may be expressed in a wide variety of intercorrelated policy settings, some of which are unobserved and no single one of which has a robust impact on growth in any limited sample of data.
- *Expectations*: the same policy intervention, expected to be sustained in one country and reversed in another, may have extremely different impacts on resource allocation.[44]

These problems make case study analysis indispensable. For cross-country empirical work, however, policy *rules* are more likely to be predetermined with respect to growth than are policy outcomes; *groups* of policy variables are more likely to be robust to the detailed institutional differences among countries; and *judgmental assessments* can be used to distinguish deep from superficial policy commitments. Sachs and Warner (1995) exploited these points in their analysis of openness and growth, classifying a country as "closed" over the 1965–90 period if it satisfied any one of a set of measures of inward-looking distortions, ranging from deep policy commitments (social-ist government) to particular institutional structures (export marketing monopolies) to standard policy variables (a persistently high black market premium or effective tariff rate). In the policy taxonomy developed in chapter 2, the Growth Project editors apply a similar but more qualitative logic to a set of policy syndromes that were observed repeatedly in the case study evidence. By contrast with the Sachs–Warner variable, which covers only eighteen African countries and is virtually time-invariant (only two of the eighteen are classified as open for more than three of the twenty-six years), our syndrome classification covers forty-seven African countries and captures major shifts in the governance environment *within* the 1960–2000 period.

In chapter 2, Collier and O'Connell use an instrumental variables approach to handle the potential endogeneity from growth outcomes to policy syndromes. They find that policy impacts are, if anything, stronger once endogeneity is taken into account. This may reflect a tendency of growth-reducing policy regimes to persist as long as other, unobserved variables keep growth from collapsing.

3.4.3   The institutional environment

The mid-1990s witnessed an explosion of interest within the growth econometrics literature in what institutional economists call the "rules of the game," the basic institutional environment within which economic activity

---

[44] Oyejide, Elbadawi, and Collier (1999) emphasize the reversibility of African trade reforms as a major cause of their failure.

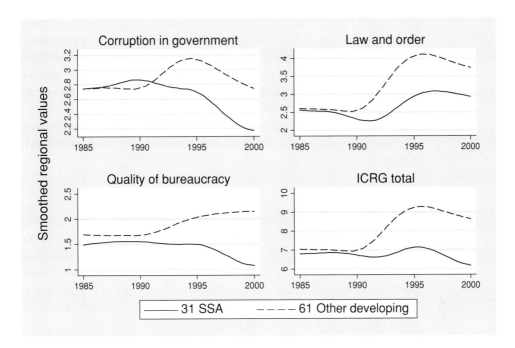

Figure 1.12 ICRG institutional performance measures, countries with full set of observations, 1985–2000.

Note: ICRG total is the sum of the other three measures.

is organized (Williamson 1998). A burgeoning literature documents the correlation of public sector corruption (Mauro 1995), the rule of law (Knack and Keefer 1995), and the quality of the government bureaucracy with investment and growth, and particularly with the *level* of real GDP *per capita*. Like the indexes of political institutions we examined earlier, measures of the institutional environment typically reflect expert judgments about actual practice, rather than compilations of formal rules. They therefore reflect the interplay between formal rules – legal and regulatory structures, formal administrative practices – and the informal norms and expectations that guide the conduct of public officials. None of the most widely used institutional variables are available before the mid-1980s and, like geographical variables, measures of institutional performance tend to change only slowly over time. Their role in growth regressions has generally been limited to explaining cross-sectional rather than intertemporal variation in growth.

In contrast to measures of policy and political institutions, measures of the institutional environment show little broad tendency to improve in SSA during the 1990s. Figure 1.12 tracks annual averages of monthly *ICRG* indexes of government corruption, the rule of law, and the quality of the government bureaucracy from 1984 (the earliest year) to 2000;[45] if anything, these variables suggest a deterioration in SSA during the 1990s, in both absolute terms and relative to other developing regions. This is consistent with the persistence of clientilist norms in the face of economic and political reforms (van de Walle 2001) and perhaps with the impact of political liberalization on public awareness of malfeasance by public officials. Bates' chapter 10 suggests a more powerful adverse link between political liberalization and institutional performance, based on the shortening horizons of political leaders.

3.4.4   Infrastructure

A final core function of growth-promoting government is the provision of social overhead capital – public investments in transport and communications infrastructure, agricultural productivity, and primary education and health. The evidence we reviewed earlier (section 3.3) provides both direct and indirect support for the importance of such infrastructure. A great deal remains to be understood, however, about the role of such investment in Africa's growth performance. We return to this issue in section 5.

3.4.5   Polarization

Why might governments fail to provide an enabling environment for private investment and economic growth? In chapter 9, Ndulu documents the influence of global development paradigms and external patrons, through at least the early 1980s, in creating an environment favorable to heavy state intervention. But the efficacy of such intervention and the extent of policy distortions varied across countries, and the average quality of policy in SSA, as we have seen, fell short of that in other regions. To *explain* this variation – our regressions *conditioned* on it – our country studies in volume 2 repeatedly appeal to the predominance of sectional over national interests, both as a source of policy failures and as a source of violent conflict and state breakdown. In doing so they develop themes rooted both in the African political economy literature and in recent growth econometrics.

In an influential early contribution, Bates (1981) focused on policy towards export agriculture and argued on the basis of case evidence that the punitive taxation of agriculture had less to do with development strategy or political ideology than with the systematic advantages of urban-based interest groups in exerting pressure on political elites (see also Ake 1996;

---

[45] The *International Country Risk Guide* (*ICRG*) is produced by the PRS Group and contains judgmental indexes of a variety of measures of country risk. The indexes of corruption, law and order, and bureaucracy quality run from 0 (worst) to 6 (best).

McMillan 2001; and chapter 4 in this volume). At the heart of this argument
is a conflict of interest that leads narrowly based political elites to prefer local or regional collective goods to national ones (Olson 1965). While
Bates focused on the rural–urban divide, the insight is a general one: Adam
and O'Connell (1999) show that in the absence of effective institutional
restraints, the policy choices of a government captured by *any* sufficiently
narrow group will tend to trade off growth for inefficient redistribution,
with greater distortions and slower growth the more narrow the favored
group and the higher the discount rate of political elites.

While experience varies, the political geography that emerges from our
country studies is more often defined on ethno-regional lines than by economic sector or urban–rural location. The salience of ethno-regional interests may have deep roots in the region's physical geography and colonial
history. Collier (2002) notes that the predominance of subsistence risks and
low population density in SSA favored the historical emergence of strong and
localized identities based on kinship. From early on, however, the colonial
powers re-posed issues of economic and political management on a larger
spatial scale, encouraging the re-organization of collective action around
the more fluid and socially determined categories of tribe and ethnicity. By
late in the colonial period, these "imagined identities" had acquired a powerful salience, often underpinned by a common language and/or religion.
When issues of political self-determination came to the fore, ethno-regional
political parties were the dominant basis for political competition in many
countries.

While "nation-building" was a staple of the early post-independence
political science literature (e.g. Carter 1962, 1963, 1966), Easterly and Levine
(1997) were the first in the growth econometrics literature systematically
to explore the implications of internal political polarization for growth.
They noted that the degree of ethno-linguistic fractionalization – measured by the probability that two randomly chosen individuals from the
same country spoke a different first language – was much higher in most
African countries than it was in non-African countries. They interpreted
this (time-invariant) variable as a measure of latent political conflicts and
showed that it predicted growth-reducing policy distortions in global samples. Rodrik (1999), in a similar vein, found that external shocks undermined growth by more where ethno-linguistic fractionalization was high
than where it was low.

Measures of ethnic fractionalization are both economically and statistically insignificant when added to the conditional regression models
in table 1.9, suggesting that effects on predicted growth, if any, must be
indirect. In table 1.10 we investigate this by running a set of auxiliary regressions relating the contributions of included determinants to the measure

Table 1.10 *Ethnic fractionalization and growth.*

Dependent variable	Regression from table 1.8			
	(1)	(2)	(3)	(4)
Main regression				
Growth in real	−0.522	−0.236	−0.198	0.252
GDP *per capita*	(0.500)	(0.736)	(0.795)	(0.782)
Auxiliary regressions				
Initial conditions	−0.432*	−1.276***	−1.012***	−1.180***
and demography	(0.071)	(0.000)	(0.000)	(0.000)
Political instability	−0.048	0.012	0.007	0.070
	(0.594)	(0.846)	(0.919)	(0.374)
Policy	−1.146***	−0.652***	−0.528***	−0.539*
	(0.000)	(0.000)	(0.001)	(0.052)

Robust *p*-values are in parentheses (*=significant at the 10% level; **=5%; ***=1%).
Notes: The entries show estimated coefficients on the Fearon (2003) cultural fractionalization variable. In the main regression, this variable is simply added to the list
already present in table 1.8. In the auxiliary regressions, the dependent variables are the
regression-weighted values of groups of determinants that appear in the relevant main
regression. Thus for initial conditions and demography and column (2), the dependent
variable is the sum of initial real GDP *per capita*, the initial life expectancy at birth, the
age dependency ratio, and the growth of the potential LF participation rate, all weighted
by their regression coefficients from column (2) of table 1.8.

of ethnic fractionalization developed by Fearon (2003).[46] Fractionalization
has a statistically significant indirect impact not only via policy but also
via the initial conditions and demographic variables. The total indirect
impact is substantial: an increase in fractionalization equal to the difference
between Africa's average (0.77) and that of other developing regions (0.43)
reduces predicted growth by between 0.5 and 0.6 of a percentage point of
annual growth.

The literature subsequent to Easterly and Levine (1997) has begun to
develop a more nuanced picture of the impact of ethnic diversity on growth,
by incorporating civil wars, differentiating dominance from fractionalization, and studying the mediating effect of political institutions.

Collier and Hoeffler (2004) focus on civil war. In global data, the risk
of civil war is maximized when the single largest ethno-linguistic group

---

[46] Fearon's fractionalization measure refers to "culture" rather than ethnicity *per se*; it
measures the probability that two people drawn at random belong to the same culture.
Results are very similar using the Easterly and Levine (1997) measure of ethno-linguistic
fractionalization. The cross-country correlation between the two measures is 0.77.

comprises between 45 and 90 percent of the population. Situations of ethnic dominance, in which a single large group constitutes a permanent majority of the population (e.g. Rwanda or Burundi) and ethnic polarization, in which two or three large groups coexist (e.g. Nigeria) are distinctly more prone to state breakdown than situations of either homogeneity (e.g. Botswana) or acute fractionalization (e.g. Tanzania). These non-linearities may help explain the absence of a linear effect of fractionalization on political instability in table 1.10. Within SSA, Collier and Hoeffler (2004) find that the level of fractionalization is sufficiently high in most countries to generate a net protective effect, actually reducing the risk of civil war relative to global norms (low incomes and commodity export specialization, as we emphasized earlier, have the opposite effect). They explain this result by appealing to the difficulties of identity-based recruitment by rebel groups in ethnically diverse societies.

Rodrik (1999) and Collier (2000) study the intermediating effect of political institutions. Both find that fractionalization has its most deleterious effects on growth in the absence of democratic institutions, a combination characteristic of much of SSA between the mid-1970s and the early 1990s. Bates and his co-authors take up this theme in chapter 12, providing an empirically grounded analysis of policy choice under alternative political regimes. The central empirical result – that exposure to anti-growth syndromes is greatest when autocratic regimes are combined with ethnic diversity – runs directly counter to the pronouncements of dictators both in Africa and elsewhere, who routinely justify a monopoly on power by appealing to the social costs of pluralism.

In chapter 6, Azam brings policy and conflict together by studying the role of regional redistribution in buying off potential conflict. He argues that, in a situation of historically determined regional polarization, the counterfactual to a policy of regional redistribution may be civil war. Economic reforms, in this view, should be geared towards making redistribution transparent, enforceable, and efficient, but should seek to limit its overall scope only where political stability can be secured by other means.

Azam's analysis points to a potentially deep conundrum in ethnically divided societies: a policy of "buying off" threats to security may enhance growth in the short run but reduce it in the long run by validating ethno-regional claims as a basis for national politics and policy. Nationally funded public education has immediate appeal from this perspective – it creates a transfer to lower-income regions while potentially serving also as a solvent of narrowly defined social capital over time.[47]

---

[47] Miguel (2004) argues that President Nyerere in Tanzania used curricular initiatives and other instruments (notably the enforcement of Swahili as a national language) to break down ethnic cleavages, with the result that by the 1990s the impact of ethnic

3.5   From growth econometrics to case analysis

The growth econometrics literature locates the stylized facts of African growth in a combination of geography and governance. These categories appear in our synthesis taxonomy as the "opportunities" and "choices" that influence growth outcomes across episodes. Growth opportunities, from this perspective, are latent in a country's physical geography and resource endowment at a point in time, and perhaps in its internal political geography; choices influence the degree to which these opportunities are seized (or not) over the medium run, and modified (or not) over the long run.

The intersection between geography and governance, operating over a much longer historical horizon, is at the heart of recent growth research. In a study of long-run growth in the Americas, for example, Engerman and Sokoloff (1997) argue that landed elites tended to emerge during the colonial period in areas favorable to the development of plantation-based agriculture. These elites subsequently captured political institutions and prevented a redistribution of either political power or economic wealth. Where local conditions favored smallholder agriculture, more inclusive political institutions, with greater openness to innovation and growth, were able to take hold and flourish over time. In a parallel vein Acemoglu, Johnson, and Robinson (2001) argue that differences in contemporary institutional performance reflect experimental variation induced by the response of European colonial regimes to local geography. In this view, the colonial powers introduced predatory and extractive institutions where local health conditions produced high mortality among European soldiers and missionaries, as in most of SSA, and growth-oriented institutions where conditions favored permanent settlement, as in North America. These institutions were then reproduced over time, remaining resistant to fundamental reshaping even with the departure of the colonial regimes.

These contributions take the search for experimental variation deeper, in the hope of unraveling cause from correlation in the cross-country data. In the process, however, much of what we seek to understand – Africa's post-independence growth performance, both across countries and over time – threatens to recede as unexplained variation around a set of slow-moving and predetermined characteristics. The task of country-level research is to get inside this variation. Guided by the cross-country evidence and the episodal structure laid out in figure 1.1, our country studies in volume 2 sought to establish how governments perceived the constraints and opportunities facing them, how they shaped the incentive environment facing households

fractionalization on local public goods provision was significantly lower in a set of Tanzanian villages near Lake Victoria than it was in a similarly situated set of Kenyan villages across the border.

and firms, and how these agents responded to the incentive environment while also seeking to influence it.

4   Opportunities and choices: learning from the country evidence

Throughout this volume we emphasize four often interrelated factors that play a powerful role in the global growth evidence and that emerge repeatedly in our country studies:

- Resource endowments that invite a narrow commodity specialization and provide large and volatile rents to political incumbents.
- Policy-driven distortions in the composition of investment and the allocation of labor and capital across sectors or firms.
- Diversion of productive resources into rent-seeking and other forms of distributional struggle, including civil war.
- Remoteness from middle-to-high-income world markets, implying high costs of trade and technology transfer.

The salience of the first three factors varies not just across countries but also within countries, in many cases shaping the periodization chosen by the country author and serving as a central theme in the overall story line. The fourth factor is closer to being time-invariant, and its importance therefore emerges mainly at the synthesis stage.

Resource endowments and geographical location form the basis of our division of countries by growth opportunities, and we return to this theme in section 5. Here we focus briefly on policy distortions and distributional struggle, which are at the heart of our analysis of policy syndromes.

Chapter 2 provides the full syndrome classification developed by the editorial team, in the form of a time line indicating the periods during which a clear anti-growth bias can be detected in each country's governance environment. Collier and O'Connell discuss the analytical basis for each of the syndromes and the judgmental criteria employed by the editorial team in identifying its occurrence. In table 1.11 we show the incidence of syndromes over time by opportunity category. Regulatory regimes form the largest category by far, and occur most frequently in resource-scarce countries. Their prevalence among *coastal* resource-scarce countries – where they might be expected to be maximally damaging to growth – is greater than that of any other syndrome–category combination. Syndrome-free cases come second: in a challenge to the highly pejorative thrust of the African political economy literature, we find that African governments steered clear of our anti-growth syndromes fully one-third of the time. Only Botswana, The

Table 1.11 *Frequency of syndromes, by opportunity category.*

	Coastal	Landlocked	Resource-rich	Total
Distribution of post-independence country-years				
%	45.4	30.3	24.3	100
Frequency of syndromes (% of country-years)[a]				
Regulatory	48.8	46.2	35.1	44.7
Redistributive	24.2	35.4	30.0	29.0
Intertemporal	10.5	8.1	18.2	11.6
State breakdown	10.3	18.5	13.3	13.5
Syndrome-free	31.7	26.9	45.5	33.6

Notes: The table uses all observations for forty-eight African countries, from the earlier of 1960 and the year of independence to 2000. For the population-weighted incidence of syndromes see chapter 2, table 2.7.

[a] Column sums exceed 100% because countries can exhibit multiple syndromes.

Gambia, Lesotho, Malawi, and Swaziland, however, achieved syndrome-free status over the full period since independence. Inefficient ethno-regional redistribution comes next, accounting for nearly 30 percent of country-years. The coastal and resource-scarce economies did best here, though the differences by opportunity category are small. Intertemporal failures and state breakdown come next, each occurring in fewer than 15 percent of country-years. The combined exposure to redistributive and intertemporal regimes – in effect, to redistributive failure, whether across existing interests or over time – is greatest among the resource-rich countries.

Figure 1.13 tracks the occurrence of syndromes over time (see also chapter 3). Regulatory regimes show a distinct inverted-U-shaped pattern: already prevalent in 1960, they increase sharply during the 1970s and reach a peak in the early 1980s. They decline slowly throughout the 1980s and then sharply between the late 1980s and early 1990s. Redistributive regimes show a similar but more muted pattern, with the result that syndrome-free status declines steadily, from over 60 percent of countries in 1960 to below 20 percent by the mid-1970s. The restoration of syndrome-free status comes gradually during the 1980s and then increases sharply in the early 1990s before stabilizing at just under half of the sample. Most aspects of the governance environment therefore display the same broad U-shaped pattern we noted in Africa's overall growth shortfall. While causation may run in both directions, Collier and O'Connell argue in chapter 2, on the basis of instrumental variables estimation, that the causal link from governance to growth is, if anything, somewhat stronger than the raw correlation.

State breakdown is the only syndrome that shows a monotonic trend over time. The incidence of breakdown rises gradually through much of

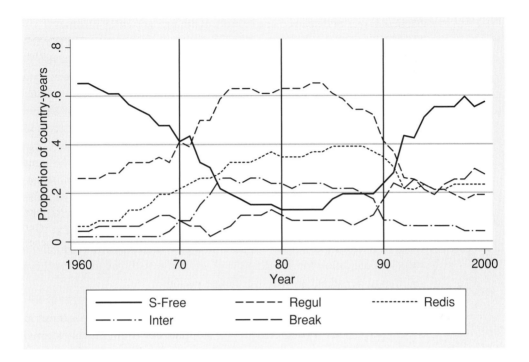

Figure 1.13 The policy environment over time, forty-six countries of SSA, independence to 2000, 1960–2000.
Key: *S-Free* = Syndrome-free; *Regul* = Excessive regulatory controls; *Redis* = Inefficient redistribution; *Inter* = Unsustainable intertemporal redistribution; *Break* = State breakdown.
Source: Judgmental classification by the editorial committee based on the country studies in volume 2 and the broader literature. The syndromes are analyzed in detail in chapter 2 of this volume. The sample includes Eritrea (a 47th country) starting in 1994.

the period before increasing sharply starting in the late 1980s. By 2000, state breakdown characterizes more than a quarter of the countries in SSA. The governance environment therefore shows a sharp divergence across countries during the 1990s, as regulatory and redistributive regimes are replaced by a combination of syndrome-free status and state breakdown.

Fosu explores the sources of these developments in chapter 3, which are then analyzed in detail in chapters 4–7 on the individual syndromes. In chapter 9, Ndulu assesses the influence of the global intellectual environment on the development strategies embraced by African leaders. The implications of the syndromes for growth are investigated empirically by Collier and O'Connell in chapter 2.

Using an early version of the synthesis classification, Fosu and O'Connell (2006) aggregated the four anti-growth syndromes into a single dichotomous variable indicating whether a country was syndrome-free in a particular year or displayed one or more of the anti-growth syndromes. They identified a *growth collapse* as a year in which a three-year centered moving average of growth was negative, and a period of *sustained growth* as a year in which a five-year centered moving average exceeded 3.5 percent (roughly a point above the long-run developing-country median). In chapter 4, Bates reproduces this calculation using the final syndrome classification, with very similar results.[48] The probability of sustained growth is below 20 percent in the presence of one or more syndromes; it is 44 percent for syndrome-free countries, and the difference is highly statistically significant. At the same time, the probability of a growth collapse is below 20 percent for syndrome-free countries and nearly 50 percent for countries displaying one or more syndromes. As stressed by Fosu and O'Connell (2006) and underscored by the empirical analysis in chapter 2, syndrome-free status emerges as (virtually) a necessary condition for sustained growth in SSA and (virtually) a sufficient condition for avoiding the short-run growth collapses that have so often undermined growth over longer periods.

Our own compressed representation of the country evidence goes as follows. State breakdown disproportionately affected landlocked countries in SSA; but wherever it occurred, growth stopped. For countries that steered clear of breakdown, avoiding the regulatory, redistributive, and intertemporal syndromes constituted a second critical step. Where these syndromes emerged, growth again stopped, with high probability. If a single dominant lesson emerges, it is that in the opening decades of political independence, African governments systematically under-prioritized the core functions of securing peace, husbanding national assets, and creating a minimally supportive environment for trade and private investment. Governments that succeeded in performing these functions avoided growth collapses and created a platform for moderate to rapid growth. The spread in outcomes among syndrome-free countries was wide, however, reflecting the diversity of *ex ante* opportunities and perhaps, at the deepest level, the differential success of countries at identifying and removing binding constraints.

Subsequent chapters explore the reasons for the continent's long detour into growth syndromes and the growth prospects uncovered by the economic and political reforms that swept the continent beginning in the mid-1980s. Strong political leadership is a feature of all sustained high performers in our sample – notably Mauritius among coastal, resource-scarce economies, Malawi among landlocked, resource-scarce economies, and Botswana among resource-rich economies. Institutional legacies feature importantly in some cases (Botswana, Mauritius), but in many others the

---

[48] The editorial committee reviewed the full syndrome classification in October 2005, in a process that produced a number of data revisions.

institutional performance of the public sector has displayed little internal inertia, depending instead on the political dispensation of powerful leaders (Malawi, Uganda since the mid-1980s). In the latter cases, high performance has not often outlasted political succession. Ethno-regional polarization poses a continuing challenge to effective governance in many of our cases (Azam, chapter 6 and Bates, chapter 7) and in concert with low education levels complicates the short-run relationship between democratization and the growth environment (Ndulu, chapter 9).

Do growth-promoting governments "merely" perform core functions, or do they intervene at an ambitious scale to remove binding constraints on growth? The dichotomy is misleading, because the manifest difficulty of committing to core functions suggests that governments that steered clear of syndromes achieved this as a matter of ambitious and purposive strategy. Two features appear common across our cases of sustained growth success: first, the degree of market intervention was kept in proportion to government capability – remaining a good bit lower, for example, in Botswana and post-conflict Uganda than in Mauritius. Second, successful governments articulated growth strategies that committed government to adequate provision of core functions and accommodated private sector accumulation as a central component of development. Where such a commitment emerged from policy reform – as in most cases – the duration over which policy remained syndrome-free played a key role in establishing credibility.

5 Conclusions

In closing, we emphasize three lessons that emerge from our review of the global econometric evidence and our interpretation of Growth Project findings. The first relates to the critical role of core functions in any growth strategy. Put simply, while remaining syndrome-free is a deeply non-trivial task, it is the single most important choice for closing the growth gap between Africa and other regions. The second moves from errors of omission to errors of commission related to the under-provision of critical public goods. While African countries face unusually severe natural and locational disadvantages, these are not destiny: they can be offset by appropriate investments and policy choices. The domain of these choices is partly national but also partly regional. The third relates to the shifting human-resource platform for growth. We return to educational thresholds and demographic change, two arenas in which time is beginning to turn in Africa's favor, potentially opening new growth opportunities in the period ahead.

Let us now elaborate these points.

5.1   Avoiding syndromes

We showed in sub-section 3.4.2 that averaging across forty years of African growth experience and controlling for differences in the composition of opportunities, the impact of poor policy accounts for something between a quarter and half of the difference in predicted growth between African and non-African developing countries. Comparing SSA with East Asia, Easterly and Levine (1997), Elbadawi, Ndulu, and Ndung'u (1997), and O'Connell and Ndulu (2001) found similar impacts: differences in policy variables generate between 1 and 3 percentage points of predicted growth differential.

Governments affect the environment for growth in ways that are poorly proxied by conventional policy variables. Building directly on the country evidence in volume 2, we have constructed a detailed new assessment of governance patterns covering all of SSA since 1960. The empirical leverage of anti-growth syndromes for growth is large. In chapter 2, Collier and O'Connell use a counterfactual analysis to estimate the contribution of syndromes to the growth differential with other regions; they find that syndromes robbed African countries of roughly 2 percentage points of growth out of the (population-weighted) 3.5 percentage point overall differential. In dramatic contrast to many of the leading variables in the growth econometrics literature, our syndrome classification plays as powerful a role in differentiating growth outcomes *within* Africa and over time as it does on the cross-regional dimension: in a regression analysis controlling for shocks and opportunity categories, syndrome-free status is worth roughly 2 percentage points of annual growth (chapter 2). The impact is, if anything, greater after controlling for the potential endogeneity of syndromes. Over the period of study, syndrome-free status emerges as a necessary condition for sustained growth and a sufficient condition for avoiding short-term growth collapse.

Throughout this study, Growth Project researchers have sought to *explain* observed patterns of governance in terms of the incentives confronting political elites. These incentives are shaped not only by existing patterns of political polarization but also by the institutions that govern political succession and the exercise of power. As emphasized in chapter 12, successful growth strategies will have to combine two inputs: an opportunity-specific diagnosis of high-return activities for the public sector, and a set of parallel investments in political institutions capable of credibly underpinning these choices.

5.2   Overcoming locational disadvantages

Collier and O'Connell (chapter 2) find that over a quarter of Africa's long-run growth shortfall can be attributed to the unusually small proportion of its population residing in "high-opportunity" coastal and resource-scarce countries. By the 1990s, 35 percent of the region's population resided in landlocked and resource-scarce countries, as against 1 percent for other developing regions; another 30 percent resided in resource-rich countries, as against 11 percent for other regions.

Geographical endowments condition not only the nature of growth opportunities but also the incentives of policy-makers and the costs of error. Thus landlocked countries did poorest in terms of overall syndrome exposure and were particularly prone to state breakdown; resource-rich countries, and particularly those with polarized political geography, were particularly exposed to intertemporal errors and inefficient redistribution. The incidence of debilitating regulatory controls was highest among the coastal and resource-scarce group, perhaps a surprising result given the potentially high returns to more market-oriented policies; what is less surprising, given the differential sensitivity of growth to allocative distortions in this group (chapter 12), is that these countries under-performed their global counterparts by more than did the other opportunity groups.

We have emphasized that maintaining syndrome-free status is necessary but not sufficient for achieving truly rapid growth on a sustained basis. The growth econometrics literature suggests a potentially important role for public investments aimed at reducing the unusually high cost of development in African countries. Among these Ndulu (2004) emphasizes the disease burden associated with tropical location and the high transport costs associated with low population density, remote location, and multiplicity of national borders. These are two major areas in which the provision of national and regional public goods may play a critical role in unlocking long-run growth.

We have emphasized the high variance of outcomes among the resource-rich countries, but the variance within *each* of our opportunity groups is larger than the differences between groups. Geography is not destiny. Botswana is both landlocked and natural-resource-dependent, but it was the fastest-growing economy in Africa between 1960 and 2000 and among the fastest globally. Botswana exemplifies strong economic management; it prospered through the successful management of natural-resource wealth, in turn the result of strong state capacity rooted in a combination of highly participatory indigenous institutions and strong leadership (see chapter 3 and the country study by Nath and Madhoo in volume 2). Botswana has also benefited, however – as have landlocked Lesotho, Swaziland and, to a much lesser degree, Malawi – from its integration with the South African economy. The latter has not only underpinned stability and restraint in important aspects of economic policy, but has also meant access to high-quality infrastructure. Improvements in regional transport infrastructure, and in supporting frameworks of cross-border cooperation, may have a high return in other areas of SSA.

5.3   Building human resources

One of our stylized facts is that SSA has done a bit better on HDIs than it has done on real GDP growth. If initial conditions matter, this suggests that SSA has a more solid starting point for growth now than in the 1960s. For at least two additional reasons, we believe that the contribution of human resources to Africa's growth is likely to be considerably larger in the region's second forty years of independence than it was in the first.

The first relates to thresholds in educational attainment. We have cited the evidence of FDI complementarities that may begin to be activated as African countries approach threshold levels of secondary attainment. Other writers have appealed to more general threshold effects of education in the growth process (e.g. Azariadis and Drazen 1990; Berthélemy 2006). If these are present, the steady advance of educational attainment in Africa has brought the region closer to supporting the rapid expansion of new and more education-intensive activities in the manufacturing and service sectors. Large stocks of human and financial flight capital exist outside many African countries and should be in the vanguard of any such development. Their role as catalyst is undoubtedly contingent on the maintenance of economic and political reforms as well as on improved institutional performance of the public sector.

Second, Africa's demographic evolution posed a set of distinctively difficult challenges during the 1960–2000 period. Demographic patterns are slow-moving and largely predetermined. They hardly feature in the country studies and are not often integrated into discussions of growth strategy. Yet the combination of persistently high fertility with falling mortality produced historically unprecedented rates of population growth in the period after independence. The resulting high and rising dependency ratios diluted labor input *per capita* and may have undermined growth indirectly by reducing the quantity and/or quality of human capital investment and diverting public resources from critical areas of infrastructure development. In the pooled conditional regressions of sub-section 3.4.1, we found that holding other determinants constant, demographic variables predicted between 0.75 and 1 percentage point of average growth differential between SSA and other developing regions – roughly two-thirds of the observed differential.

Late in the period and mainly as a result of the HIV/AIDS epidemic, SSA became the only developing region in the whole post-1960 sample to experience a sustained reverse trend in life expectancy.

Fertility has begun to decline in many African countries, driven by a combination of improved labor market opportunities for women, greater knowledge and availability of contraceptives, public health improvements that enhance the return to investment in children, and changing behavioral norms. Population growth will continue to be rapid even with falling fertility rates, posing continued challenges for capital deepening and in sharpening the local competition for resources. But we have also stressed the long-run costs of low population density. Increasing population densities represent an opportunity for institutional developments and agglomeration effects that are favorable to long-run growth. Meanwhile falling dependency ratios will produce at least a modest growth dividend in much of the region in the decades ahead.

5.4   Final thoughts

Our aim in this chapter has been to provide a self-contained review of the stylized facts of African growth and the insights offered by the growth econometrics literature. These ingredients shaped the country studies in volume 2 and provided the basic dimensions of the synthesis taxonomy. If we have whetted the reader's appetite for the contributions that follow, then we shall have succeeded. As for the past, our privilege has been to see it whole, through the eyes of Growth Project researchers intimately familiar with their countries' economic histories and personally invested in what comes ahead. May the next forty years belong to Africa, and to them.

References

Acemoglu, Daron, Simon Johnson, and James Robinson (2001), "The Colonial Origins of Comparative Development: An Empirical Investigation," *American Economic Review* 91, December: 1369–1401

Adam, Christopher S. and Stephen A. O'Connell (1999), "Aid, Taxation, and Development in Sub-Saharan Africa," *Economics and Politics* 11(3), November: 225–54

 (2004), "Aid versus Trade Revisited: Donor and Recipient Policies in the Presence of Learning-by-Doing," *Economic Journal* 114(492), January: 150–73

Aghion, Philippe and Steven Durlauf, eds. (2005), *Handbook of Economic Growth, Volumes 1A and 1B.* Handbooks in Economics 22. Amsterdam and San Diego, CA: Elsevier, North Holland

Ake, Claude (1996), *Democracy and Development in Africa.* Washington, DC: The Brookings Institution

Alesina, Alberto and Roberto Perotti (1994), "The Political Economy of Growth: A Critical Survey of the Recent Literature," *World Bank Economic Review* 8(3), September: 351–71

Angrist, Joshua and Alan Krueger (2001), "Instrumental Variables and the Search for Identification: From Supply and Demand to Natural Experiments," *Journal of Economic Perspectives* 15(4), Fall: 69–85

Arellano, M.D. and S.D. Bond (1991), "Some Tests of Specification for Panel Data," *Review of Economic Studies* 58: 277–94

Artadi, Elsa V. and Xavier Sala-i-Martin (2003), "The Economic Tragedy of the XXth Century: Growth in Africa," National Bureau of Economic Research Working Paper 9865, July

Azariadis, Costas and Allan Drazen (1990), "Threshold Externalities in Economic Development," *Quarterly Journal of Economics* 105(2), May: 501–26

Barro, Robert J. (1991), "Economic Growth in a Cross-Section of Countries," *Quarterly Journal of Economics* 106(2), May: 407–43

  (1999), "Human Capital and Growth in Cross-Country Regressions," *Swedish Economic Policy Review* 6(2), Autumn: 237–77

Barro, R. and Jong-Wha Lee (1994), "Sources of Economic Growth," *Carnegie–Rochester Conference Series on Public Policy* 40

Barro, Robert J. and Xavier Sala-i-Martin (1995), *Economic Growth.* New York: McGraw-Hill

Bates, Robert H. (1981), *Markets and States in Tropical Africa: The Political Basis of Agricultural Policies.* Berkeley, CA: University of California Press

Berthélemy, Jean-Claude (2006), "Convergence and Development Traps: How Did Emerging Economies Escape the Underdevelopment Trap?," in François Bourguignon and Boris Pleskovic, eds., *Growth and Integration: Annual World Bank Conference on Development Economics 2006.* Washington, DC: The World Bank: 127–51

Berthélemy, Jean-Claude and Ludvig Soderling (2001), "The Role of Capital Accumulation, Adjustment and Structural Change for Economic Take-Off: Empirical Evidence from African Growth Episodes," *World Development* 29(2): 323–43

  (2002), "Will There Be New Emerging-Market Economies in Africa by the Year 2020?," IMF Working Paper WP/02/131, August

Bevan, David L., Paul Collier, and Jan Willem Gunning (1999), *Nigeria and Indonesia.* New York: Oxford University Press for the World Bank

Blattman, Christopher, Jason Hwang, and Jeffrey G. Williamson (2007), "Winners and Losers in the Commodity Lottery: The Impact of the Terms of Trade Growth and Volatility in the Periphery, 1870–1939," *Journal of Development Economics* 82(1), January: 156–79

Block, Steven A. (2001), "Does Africa Grow Differently?," *Journal of Development Economics* 65: 443–67

Bloom, David and Jeffrey D. Sachs (1998), "Geography, Demography, and Economic Growth in Africa," *Brookings Papers on Economic Activity* 2: 207–73

Bloom, David and Jeffrey G. Williamson (1998), "Demographic Transitions and Economic Miracles in Emerging Asia," *World Bank Economic Review* 12(3), September: 419–55

Borensztein, Eduardo, José De Gregorio, and Jong-Wha Lee (1998), "How Does Foreign Direct Investment Affect Economic Growth?," *Journal of International Economics* 45(1), June: 115–35

Bratton, Michael and Nicolas van de Walle (1997), *Democratic Experiments in Africa.* Cambridge: Cambridge University Press

Brock, William A. and Steven Durlauf (2001), "Growth Empirics and Reality," *World Bank Economic Review* 15(2): 229–72

Bulir, A. and A. J. Hamann (2003), "Aid Volatility: An Empirical Assessment," *IMF Staff Papers* 50(1): 64–89

Carter, Gwendolen M., ed. (1962), *African One-Party States*. Ithaca, NY: Cornell University Press

(1963), *Five African States: Responses to Diversity*. Ithaca, NY: Cornell University Press

(1966), *National Unity and Regionalism in Eight African States*. Ithaca, NY: Cornell University Press

Cohen, Daniel and Marcelo Soto (2001), "Growth and Human Capital: Good Data, Good Results," CEPR Discussion Papers 3025/2001. London: Centre for Economic Policy Research

Collier, Paul (1991), "Africa's External Relations, 1960–1990," *African Affairs* 90(3): 339–56

(1997), "Globalization: Implications for Africa," in Zubair Iqbal and Mohsin S. Khan, eds., *Trade Reform and Regional Integration in Africa*. Washington, DC: International Monetary Fund: 147–81

(2000), "Ethnicity, Politics and Economic Performance," *Economics and Politics* 12(3), November: 225–45

(2002), "Implications of Ethnic Diversity," *Economic Policy* 32, April: 129–66

Collier, Paul and Jan Willem Gunning (1999), "Explaining African Economic Growth," *Journal of Economic Literature* 37, March: 64–111

Collier, Paul and Anke Hoeffler (2002), "On the Incidence of Civil War in Africa," *Journal of Conflict Resolution* 46(1), February: 13–28

(2004), "Greed and Grievance in Civil War," *Oxford Economic Papers* 56(4), October: 563–95

Collier, Paul, Anke Hoeffler, and Catherine Pattillo (2004), "Capital Flight and the Brain Drain as Portfolio Decisions," *Journal of African Economies* 13 (Supplement 2): 15–54

Collier, Paul and Catherine Pattillo (2000), *Investment and Risk in Africa*. London: Macmillan

Collier, Ruth Berins (1982), *Regimes in Tropical Africa: Changing Forms of Supremacy, 1945–75*. Berkeley, CA: University of California Press

Collins, Susan and Barry P. Bosworth (1996), "Economic Growth in East Asia: Accumulation versus Assimilation," *Brookings Papers on Economic Activity* 2: 135–203

Dehn, Jan (2000), "Commodity Price Uncertainty and Shocks: Implications for Economic Growth," Centre for the Study of African Economies Working Paper WPS/2000–10, May

Dollar, David (1992), "Outwar oriented Developing Economies Really Do Grow More Rapidly. Evidence from 95 LDCs, 1976–1985," *Economic Development and Cultural Change* 40(3), April: 523–44

Easterly, William (1999), "Life During Growth," *Journal of Economic Growth* 4(3), September: 239–75

(2001), *The Elusive Quest for Growth: Economists' Adventures and Misadventures in the Tropics*. Cambridge, MA: MIT Press

Easterly, William and Ross Levine (1997), "Africa's Growth Tragedy: Policies and Ethnic Divisions," *Quarterly Journal of Economics* 112: 1203–50

Elbadawi, Ibrahim A., Benno J. Ndulu, and Njuguna S. Ndung'u (1997), "Dealing with the Debt Burden of the Highly Indebted Poor African Countries," in Zubair Iqbal and Ravi Kanbur, eds., *External Finance for Low Income Countries*. Washington, DC: International Monetary Fund

Engerman, Stanley L. and Kenneth L. Sokoloff (1997), "Factor Endowments, Institutions, and Differential Paths of Growth Among New World Economies," in Stephen Haber, ed., *How Latin America Fell Behind*. Stanford, CA: Stanford University Press

Fearon, James (2003), "Ethnic and Cultural Diversity by Country," *Journal of Economic Growth* 8(2), June: 195–222

Fosu, Augustin K. (1992), "Political Instability and Economic Growth: Evidence from Sub-Saharan Africa," *Economic Development and Cultural Change* 40(4): 829–41

(2002), "Political Instability and Economic Growth: Implications of Coup Events in Sub-Saharan Africa," *American Journal of Economics and Sociology* 61(1): 329–48

Fosu, Augustin K. and Stephen A. O'Connell (2006), "Explaining African Economic Growth: The Role of Anti-growth Syndromes," in François Bourguignon and Boris Pleskovic, eds., *Annual World Bank Conference on Development Economics 2006: Growth and Integration*. Washington, DC: The World Bank

Frankel, Jeffrey A. and David Romer (1999), "Does Trade Cause Growth?," *American Economic Review* 89(3), June: 379–99

Gallup, John Luke, Jeffrey D. Sachs with Andrew Mellinger (1999), "Geography and Economic Development," in Boris Pleskovic and Joseph E. Stiglitz, eds., *Annual World Bank Conference on Development Economics 1998*. Washington, DC: The World Bank

Gavin, Michael and Ricardo Hausmann (1998), "Macroeconomic Volatility and Economic Development," in Silvio Borner and Martin Paldam, eds., *The Political Dimension of Economic Growth: Proceedings of the IEA Conference held in San Jose, Costa Rica*. IEA Conference Volume 119. New York: St. Martin's Press: 97–116

Gersovitz, Mark and Christina Paxson (1990), *The Economies of Africa and the Prices of Their Exports*. Princeton Studies in International Finance 68. Princeton, NJ: Princeton University, Department of Economics, International Finance Section

Ghura, Dhaneshwar and Michael T. Hadjimichael (1996), "Growth in Sub-Saharan Africa," *IMF Staff Papers* 43, September: 605–34

Guillaumont, Patrick, Sylviane Guillaumont-Jeanneney, and Jean-François Brun (1999), "How Instability Lowers African Growth," *Journal of African Economies* 8(1), 87–107

Hall, Robert J. and Robert Jones (1999), "Why Do Some Countries Produce So Much More Output Than Others?," *Quarterly Journal of Economics* 114(1): 83–116

Hayami, Yujiro (2001), *Development Economics: From the Poverty to the Wealth of Nations*, 2nd edn. Oxford: Oxford University Press

Hoeffler, Anke (2002), "The Augmented Solow Model and the African Growth Debate," *Oxford Bulletin of Economics and Statistics* 64(2), May: 135–58

Jay, Antony (1996), *The Oxford Book of Political Quotations.* New York: Oxford University Press

Jones, Charles I. (1998), *Introduction to Economic Growth.* New York: W. W. Norton

Knack, Stephen and Philip Keefer (1995), "Institutions and Economic Performance: Cross-Country Tests Using Alternative Institutional Measures," *Economics and Politics* 7, November: 207–27

Lal, Deepak (2000), *The Poverty of "Development Economics."* Cambridge, MA: MIT Press

Levine, Ross and David Renelt (1993), "A Sensitivity Analysis of Cross-Country Growth Regressions," *American Economic Review* 82(4), September: 942–63

Lewis, W. Arthur (1954), "Economic Development with Unlimited Supplies of Labor," *The Manchester School of Economic and Social Studies* 22, May: 139–92

Limão, Nuno and Anthony J. Venables (2002), "Transport Costs, Infrastructure and Growth," *World Bank Economic Review* 15(3): 451–79

Lucas, Robert E. (1988), "On the Mechanics of Economic Development," *Journal of Monetary Economics* 22(1), July: 3–42

    (2003), "The Industrial Revolution: Past and Future," in Federal Reserve Bank of Minneapolis, *Annual Report: The Region.* Minneapolis, MN: Federal Reserve Bank of Minneapolis, http://minneapolisfed.org/pubs/region/04-05/essay.cfm

Lumbila, Kevin N. (2005), *Risk, FDI and Economic Growth: A Dynamic Panel Analysis of the Determinants of FDI and its Growth Impact in Africa.* PhD dissertation, American University

Maddison, Angus (2001), *The World Economy: Historical Statistics.* Paris: Organization for Economic Co-operation and Development

Mankiw, N. Gregory, David Romer, and David N. Weil (1992), "A Contribution to the Empirics of Economic Growth," *Quarterly Journal of Economics* 107(2), May: 407–37

Masson, Paul R. and Catherine Pattillo (2005), *The Monetary Geography of Africa.* Washington, DC: The Brookings Institution

Masters, William and Margaret S. McMillan (2001), "Climate, Scale and Economic Growth," *Journal of Economic Growth* 6(3): September

Mauro, Paolo (1995), "Corruption and Growth," *Quarterly Journal of Economics* 110: 681–712

McMillan, Margaret (2001), "Why Kill the Golden Goose? A Political Economy Model of Export Taxation," *Review of Economics and Statistics* 83(1), February: 170–84

Miguel, Edward (2004), "Tribe or Nation? Nation-Building and Public Goods in Kenya versus Tanzania," *World Politics* 56, April: 327–62

Miguel, Edward and Michael Kremer (2004), "Worms: Identifying Impacts on Education and Health in the Presence of Treatment Externalities," *Econometrica* 72(1), January: 159–217

Miguel, Edward, Shanker Satyanatah, and Ernest Sergenti (2004), "Economic Shocks and Civil Conflict: An Instrumental Variables Approach," *Journal of Political Economy* 112(4): 725–53

Ndulu, Benno J. (2004), "Infrastructure, Regional Integration and Growth in Sub-Saharan Africa: Dealing with the Disadvantages of Geographical and Sovereign Fragmentation," Paper presented at the AERC Plenary Session, Nairobi, December 4

Ndulu, Benno J. and Stephen A. O'Connell (1999), "Governance and Growth in Sub-Saharan Africa," *Journal of Economic Perspectives* 13(3), Summer: 41–66

North, Douglass (1981), *Structure and Change in Economic History*. New York: W. W. Norton

     (1991), "Institutions," *Journal of Economic Perspectives* 5: 97–112

O'Connell, Stephen A. (1997), "Macroeconomic Harmonization, Trade Reform and Regional Trade in Sub-Saharan Africa," in A. Oyejide, I. Elbadawi, and Paul Collier, eds., *Regional Integration and Trade Liberalization in SubSaharan Africa, Volume I: Framework, Issues and Methodological Perspectives*. London: Macmillan: 89–158

     (2004), "Explaining African Economic Growth: Emerging Lessons from the Growth Project," Paper presented at the AERC Plenary Session, Nairobi, May 26

O'Connell, Stephen A. and Benno J. Ndulu (2001), "Explaining African Economic Growth: A Focus on Sources of Growth," AERC Growth Project, Nairobi, April; downloadable: www.aercafrica.org

O'Connell, Stephen A. and Charles C. Soludo (2001), "Aid Intensity in Africa," *World Development* 29(9), September: 1527–52

Oliver, Roland and Anthony Atmore (1994), *Africa Since 1800*. Cambridge: Cambridge University Press

Olson, Mancur, Jr. (1965), *The Logic of Collective Action: Public Goods and the Theory of Groups*. Cambridge, MA: Harvard University Press

Oyejide, T. Ademola, Ibrahim Elbadawi, and Paul Collier, eds. (1999), *Regional Integration and Trade Liberalization in Africa*. New York: St. Martin's Press

Pritchett, Lant (1997), "Divergence, Big Time," *Journal of Economic Perspectives* 11(3), Summer: 3–17

     (2001), "Where Has All the Education Gone?," *World Bank Economic Review* 15(3): 367–91

Rajan, Raghuram and Arvind Subramanian (2005), "What Undermines Aid's Impact on Growth?," IMF Working Papers 05/126. Washington, DC: International Monetary Fund

Ramey, G. and V. A. Ramey (1995), "Cross-Country Evidence on the Link Between Volatility and Growth," *American Economic Review* 85(5), December: 1138–51

Rodrik, Dani (1999), "Where Did All the Growth Go? External Shocks and Growth Collapses," *Journal of Economic Growth* 4(4), December: 384–412

Sachs, Jeffrey D., John W. McArthur, Guido Schmidt-Traub, Margaret Kruk, Chandrika Bahadur, Michael Faye, and Gordon McCord (2004), "Ending Africa's Poverty Trap," *Brookings Papers on Economic Activity* 1: 117–241

Sachs, Jeffrey D. and Andrew Warner (1995), "Economic Reform and the Process of Global Integration," *Brookings Papers on Economic Activity* 1: 1–95

     (1997), "Sources of Slow Growth in African Economies," *Journal of African Economies* 6(3): 335–76

(2001), "The Curse of Natural Resources," *European Economic Review* 45(4–6): 827–38

Sala-i-Martin, Xavier (2006), "The World Distribution of Income: Falling Poverty and . . . Convergence, Period," *Quarterly Journal of Economics*, 121(2), May: 351–97

Sala-i-Martin, Xavier, Gernot Doppelhofer, and Ronald I. Miller (2004), "Determinants of Long-Term Growth: A Bayesian Averaging of Classical Estimates (BACE) Approach," *American Economic Review* 94(4), September: 813–35

Soto, Marcelo (2002), "Rediscovering Education in Growth Regressions," OECD Development Centre Technical Paper 202. Paris: Organization for Economic Co-operation and Development

Temple, Jonathan (1999), "The New Growth Evidence," *Journal of Economic Literature* 37(1), March: 112–56

van de Walle, N. (2001), *African Economies and the Politics of Permanent Crisis.* Cambridge: Cambridge University Press

Van den Berg, Hendrik (2001), *Economic Growth and Development.* Boston: McGraw-Hill Irwin

Vishny, R. and A. Shleifer (1993), "Corruption," *Quarterly Journal of Economics* 108(3): 599–617

Williamson, Oliver (1998), "Transaction Cost Economics: How it Works, Where it is Headed," *De Economist* 146(1): 23–58

World Bank (1981), *Accelerated Development in Sub-Saharan Africa: An Agenda for Action.* Washington, DC: The World Bank

Wood, Adrian and Kersti Berge (1997), "Exporting Manufactures: Human Resources, Natural Resources, and Trade Policy," *Journal of Development Studies* 34(1), October: 35–59

Wooldridge, Jeffrey M. (2003), *Introductory Econometrics: A Modern Approach.* Mason, OH: Thompson South-Western

2 | Opportunities and choices

Paul Collier and Stephen A. O'Connell

1 Introduction

Growth depends upon the interaction of opportunities and choices. A country, or an entire region, may fail to grow either because there are no opportunities, or because choices are made that preclude opportunities being taken. The stark phenomenon we are trying to understand is that

Oxford University and Centre for Study of African Economies; and Swarthmore College and Centre for Study of African Economies. We thank Befekadu Degefe, Catherine Pattillo, Lemma Senbet, Nicholas van de Walle, James Robinson, Jeffrey Williamson, Growth Project editors and researchers, and seminar participants at the AERC, Harvard, Oxford, the IMF, and the World Bank for helpful comments.

for forty years Africa stagnated while other developing regions grew. This chapter attempts to explain this alarming phenomenon in terms of the distinctive opportunities open to the region and the distinctive choices which were made.

Before explanation comes description. The comparison of regional growth rates must surely seem a straightforward matter. In fact, especially for Africa, it is sensitive to apparently arcane choices. To date, in our view scholars have invariably got these choices wrong and so we must begin with a brief discussion of these issues.

The basic unit for reporting GDP and its growth is the nation: regional figures on GDP are built up from these observations at the level of the nation. The most widely cited regional growth rates come from the *World Economic Outlook (WEO)* of the IMF and the *Global Economic Prospects (GEP)* of the World Bank. In both cases, the regional figures are half-way houses on the road to estimates of the growth of global GDP. Necessarily, in such an approach, the growth rates of regional and global GDP are simply arrived at from the total level of GDP and its comparison with the previous year. This is equivalent to averaging the annual growth rates of each country *weighted by the GDP of each country*. Around half of the GDP of SSA is generated by South Africa, so that this approach gives a huge weight to the growth performance of South Africa. While the approach is appropriate if the question concerns total African GDP, it can be highly misleading as a description of the growth experienced by the typical African.

The alternative common approach to reporting Africa's growth rate is the easy procedure of taking the simple average of the underlying national growth rates. However, just as Africa's forty-eight countries differ by GDP, with South Africa being the whale, so they differ by population, with Nigeria being the whale. The simple average is driven by a group of minnows that between them have both negligible population and negligible GDP. For some purposes, the experience of each country is indeed equally important – each country constitutes a "natural experiment" in how opportunities and choices combine to determine growth, and so generates equivalently valuable information *for analysis*. But as a *description* of the region's experience, a simple average of country growth rates is clearly indefensible.

Our own approach is to weight the underlying national growth rates by the share of each country's population. While this will give us the wrong answer to the question of how Africa's GDP grew in aggregate, it will give a more accurate picture of the growth experienced by the typical African. For example, it assigns Nigeria its true importance as the home of one in five Africans. If the growth process fails in Nigeria that is indeed more important *for Africans* than if it fails in South Africa – though it is less important *for global GDP*. For the *WEO* and the *GEP* it is global GDP that is important;

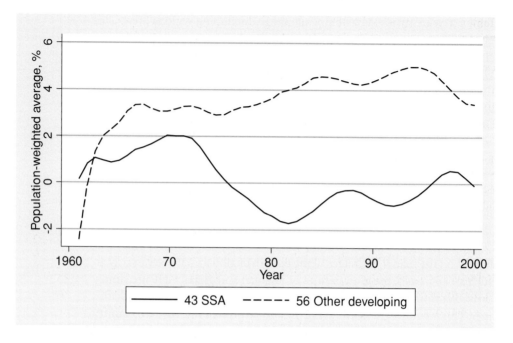

Figure 2.1 Smoothed growth rates of real GDP *per capita*, countries with full set of observations, 1960–2000
Notes: We applied a kernel-weighted local polynomial smoother to the data, using the Epanechnikov kernel and polynomial order 1. Alternative smoothing approaches produce similar results.

for our purposes it is the experience of Africans. We then compare *per capita* growth rates, decade-by-decade, for two groups: forty-three African countries and fifty-six non-African developing countries. To our knowledge, such population-weighted growth rates have not previously been calculated.

The results are shown for the forty years 1960–99 in figure 2.1, and by decade in table 2.1. Over the entire period the average annual growth rate for Africa was a mere 0.13 percentage points. Taking into account the likely range of measurement inaccuracies, such a negligible growth rate is effectively zero. In other words, over the forty-year period considered in this volume, the region stagnated. This absence of growth was distinctive to the region. For the rest of the developing world the *per capita* growth rate was higher than at any previous period in history, at 3.63 percentage points.

Thus, stagnation was divergence. Yet, more seriously, the degree of divergence was accelerating. Whereas in the 1960s the difference in growth rates was only around 1 percentage point, since 1980 it has been around 5 percentage points. This widening difference was due both to growth acceleration in the rest of the developing world and to growth deceleration – to the extent of being negative – in Africa.

Table 2.1 *Population-weighted growth, by decade.*

Decade	43 SSA	56 Other developing	Difference
1960s	1.04	2.29	1.25
1970s	0.86	3.23	2.37
1980s	−0.79	4.32	5.11
1990–2000	−0.46	4.46	4.92
Total	0.13	3.63	3.50

Note: The sample consists of all developing countries with full availability. See note to table 2.2.

We now turn from description to analysis: why did Africa stagnate? In section 2 we develop a simple classification of opportunities. We use this to build an estimate of the extent to which the differences between Africa's opportunities and those of other regions account for the observed difference in growth outcomes. In section 3 we turn to policy choices. Building up from our twenty-six country case studies in volume 2, we develop a typology of *policy error*: episodes when some major choice was clearly mistaken. We use this classification for all forty-eight African countries. In section 4 we bring the two analyses together in an attempt to explain the divergence in growth rates as being due to the interaction of choices and opportunities.

2   Africa's opportunities

Opportunities for economic growth differ between countries. In this section we first develop a simple classification of opportunities. We then apply it to developing countries globally, bringing out the differences between Africa and the other developing regions.

2.1   A basic classification of opportunities

Two features of an economy that the literature suggests might influence its potential for growth are *endowments* and *location*. These form the basis for our classification.

2.1.1   Endowments

All developing countries share, to a degree, the characteristic of labor abundance relative to developed countries, but they differ massively as to "land" abundance. Africa is a land-abundant region in the literal sense that it has a large land area per inhabitant compared with all other developing regions. However, there are obviously enormous differences in the value of land depending upon characteristics such as rainfall and the natural resources that potentially can be discovered. In measuring the endowment of "land" we therefore have a choice as to whether to use simply the area of land per inhabitant, or to introduce an economic concept based on the value of the resources contained in that land. The former approach has been adopted by Adrian Wood (2003), who argues that Africa is basically similar to Latin America, both being land-abundant in contrast to Asia. However, introducing a measure of economic value to this land has considerable advantages – without it, the average inhabitant of Niger, with a large acreage of landlocked, resource-free desert, will be characterized as much better endowed than the average inhabitant of Equatorial Guinea, living on a small island surrounded by oil. This is the approach taken here – we define "land" abundance in terms of the value of the "rents" contained in the exports of primary commodities as a share of GDP. The rents reflect the excess of world prices over production costs, commodity-by-commodity. This approach has the disadvantage, as compared with land area, of being endogenous to the choices that a society makes. For example, in Chad the absolute value of the rents was endogenous because the investment needed for oil exporting was delayed due to internal conflict. More obviously, the share of rents in GDP depends upon the choices that influence the growth of non-"land" GDP. The precise share of natural-resource rents in GDP is thus clearly endogenous. To reduce this problem we classify according to a threshold: if an economy generates more than 10 percent of GDP from primary commodity rents it is deemed to be a "natural-resource" economy. Because prices of commodities fluctuate, potentially some economies flip backwards and forwards across this threshold year-to-year. Since our basic analysis is going to rest on political economy, with processes that do not switch on and off with such high frequency, we impose a somewhat greater degree of stability on the data.[1]

---

[1] Construction of the resource-rich variable: we classify a country as resource-rich starting in the first year the country satisfies the following three conditions:

- current rents from energy, minerals, and forests exceed 5 percent of gross national income (GNI)
- a forward moving average of these rents exceeds 10 percent of GNI
- the share of primary commodities in exports exceeds 20 percent for at least a five-year period following this initial year.

These criteria are meant to identify countries in which natural-resource wealth is large enough to play a central role in economic management and in the interface of the country with global markets. Judgmental adjustments are required to "back-cast" this classification to the first part of the sample, because the resource rent data are available only since 1970. We therefore back-dated the initial year to 1960 if the three criteria held in 1970 *and* the share of primary commodities in exports was already above 20 percent in 1965. If the three criteria held in 1970 and the share of primary commodities was above 20 percent in 1970

2.1.2   Location

Especially in the period since 1960, international trade has become increasingly important to the global economy. A potential impediment to participating in this trade is for a country to be landlocked. Sachs and his colleagues (Sachs *et al.* 2004) have pioneered research into this phenomenon which they have shown to be globally significant. Being landlocked is itself a very crude measure of the problem. For example, Switzerland is landlocked but this does not constitute an impediment, since its neighboring coastal countries – Germany, Italy, and France – are not so much in the way of reaching its market, but themselves *constitute* its market. Hence, it might be more appropriate to nuance physical geography with an economic concept of distance to market. Initially, however, we take a simple geographic definition. Sachs has argued that even countries with a coastline can be effectively landlocked if their populations live a long way inland – for example, due to disease vectors. However, the great difference between a landlocked country and a coastal country whose population lives inland is that the latter has the potential for migration without legal impediment. Sachs has also emphasized the importance of other aspects of location, notably the incidence of disease, and Masters and McMillan (2001) have extended the concern to diseases of crops, showing the effect of the incidence of frost. Such refinements might indeed turn out to be critical. However, for the present we investigate how far a very simple classification can take us.

2.1.3   Endowments and location in growth regressions

The disaggregation according to endowment and location potentially generates four mutually exhaustive categories: (1) landlocked, resource-rich; (2) landlocked, resource-scarce; (3) coastal, resource-rich; (4) coastal, resource-scarce. However, there are both theoretical and empirical grounds for conflating the two resource-rich categories ((1) and (3)). From the perspective of theory, the rents on most natural resources are sufficiently high for the additional transport costs incurred by being landlocked not to be a binding constraint upon their exportation. Whereas the "Dutch disease" effect of natural-resource exports would tend to preclude diversification into manufactured exports even if the country was coastal. Hence, whether coastal or landlocked, a resource-rich country might be expected to have rather similar opportunities. This is borne out by the growth regression reported in table 2.2. Here, all developing countries are classified into the mutually

but below 20 percent in 1965, we linearly interpolated the primary commodity share between 1965 and 1970 and back-dated the initial "resource-rich" year to the first year the interpolated share exceeded 20 percent. Additional judgmental adjustments were made for Equatorial Guinea (1996), Sierra Leone (1960), and Algeria (1960) based on country information.

Table 2.2 *Geography and growth, disaggregating into four groups.*
Dependent variable: growth in real GDP per capita.

Variable	Estimated coefficient and standard error
GCoastal	1.542***
	0.275
GCoastal*RR	−0.592*
	0.329
GLandlocked*RR	1.397**
	0.594

$N = 3{,}959$, Adjusted $R^2 = 0.027$, RMSE $= 6.405$, $F = 4.066$ (prob$>F = 0.000$)

$^*p < 0.1;\ ^{**}p < 0.05;\ ^{***}p < 0.01.$

Notes: Estimation is by OLS for the full-availability developing-country sample (ninety-nine developing countries with at least thirty-nine of forty annual observations available). A full set of year effects is included. The labels "GCoastal" and "GLandlocked" refer to geographically based, time-invariant coastal or landlocked status (with the exception of Ethiopia which changes in 1994, and DRC and Sudan, which we classify judgmentally as landlocked based on access to the coast). Here RR = resource-rich is a cross-cutting category defined as indicated in n. 1.

exclusive groups of coastal or landlocked, with the landlocked category as the default. All countries are then further divided into the mutually exclusive categories of resource-rich or resource-scarce.

Globally, being coastal augments growth relative to being landlocked by over 1.5 percentage points. However, the interactions with resource abundance are profoundly different for coastal and landlocked economies. Resource abundance significantly reduces growth in coastal economies, whereas it significantly increases growth in landlocked economies. Hence, as theory predicts, resource abundance wipes out the growth opportunity otherwise inherent in a coastal location, replacing it with a lesser opportunity which is equally available whether the country is coastal or landlocked. In our subsequent analysis we therefore collapse the disaggregation into three groups: (5) resource-rich (whether coastal or landlocked); (6) coastal, resource-scarce; and (7) landlocked, resource-scarce.

We first investigate whether the distinctions between resource-rich, coastal, non-resource-rich, and landlocked, non-resource-rich, are significant in a regression of growth over the relevant period 1960–2000, for developing countries as a whole (table 2.3).

Regression (1) finds that the distinctions are indeed significant. The coastal, resource-scarce countries tended to grow markedly more rapidly than the resource-rich countries, which in turn grew much more rapidly

Table 2.3 *Geography and growth, resource-rich; coastal, resource-scarce; landlocked, resource-scarce.*
Dependent variable: growth in real GDP per capita.

Variable	Estimated coefficients and standard errors		
	(1)	(2)	(3)
Coastal	1.542***	0.673**	1.191***
	0.275	0.298	0.409
Resource-rich	1.003***	0.319	0.715
	0.378	0.402	0.492
Coastal*SSA	–	–	−1.778***
			0.253
Landlocked*SSA	–	–	−1.082**
			0.481
Resource-rich*SSA	–	–	−1.458**
			0.586
SSA	–	−1.630***	–
		0.230	
N	3,959	3,959	3,959
Adjusted R^2	0.028	0.041	0.040
RMSE	6.404	6.361	6.362
F	4.772	5.253	5.413
Prob$>F$	0.000	0.000	0.000

*$p < 0.1$; **$p < 0.05$; ***$p < 0.01$.
Note: Estimation is by OLS for the full-availability developing-country sample (see note to table 2.2). All regressions include a full set of year effects.

than the landlocked, resource-scarce countries. Since our focus will be on Africa, we next investigate whether, controlling for these global differences, African countries had significantly distinctive growth. We first introduce a dummy variable for Africa: it is significantly negative (2). We then inter-act the dummy with each of the three geographic categories (3). All the interaction terms are significant and negative: within each category African countries under-performed the global average. However, beyond this there is a clear pattern. The under-performance was most severe for Africa's coastal, resource-scarce economies, and least severe for Africa's landlocked, resource-scarce economies.

The contrasting distributions of the populations of Africa and other developing regions are shown in table 2.4 (appendix table 2.A1, p. 126, provides the information for each country). The classification of countries changes from time to time, according to the value of the rents from primary

Table 2.4 *Population distribution, by opportunity category.*

Group and decade	Coastal	Landlocked	Resource-rich
43 SSA countries			
1960s	67	29	4
1970s	47	29	23
1980s	42	29	29
1990–2000	35	35	30
Total	47	31	22
56 Other developing countries			
1960s	96	1	3
1970s	90	1	10
1980s	88	1	11
1990–2000	88	1	11
Total	91	1	9

Note: The sample is all developing countries with full availability.

commodity exports. Both Africa and other developing regions have had resource discoveries that have increased the proportion of the population living in resource-rich countries, but this has been much more pronounced for Africa.

By the 1990s only 35 percent of Africa's population was living in coastal, resource-scarce economies as opposed to 88 percent in the rest of the developing world. Resource-rich economies accounted for 30 percent, as opposed to only 11 percent elsewhere. However, the most striking difference is in the proportion of the population living in landlocked, resource-scarce economies. Outside Africa, this category was negligible – a mere 1 percent; within Africa, it was 35 percent. Because of these differences in opportunities, any systematic global differences in growth rates *between the opportunity groups* will give rise to differences between African and non-African growth rates.

2.2   Differential growth performance and its decomposition

We now compare the growth performance of the African region against that of the rest of the developing world, using this three-way disaggregation. To introduce an initial sense of how performance evolved, we break the information down by decade (table 2.5).

Table 2.5 *Growth differential, by opportunity category and decade.*

Decade	Overall 43 SSA	Overall 56 Other	Coastal 43 SSA	Coastal 56 Other	Landlocked 43 SSA	Landlocked 56 Other	Resource-rich 43 SSA	Resource-rich 56 Other
1960s	1.04	2.29	1.36	2.25	0.16	0.74	2.08	3.85
1970s	0.86	3.23	1.32	3.18	−0.31	1.26	1.42	3.89
1980s	−0.79	4.32	−0.85	4.68	0.14	1.56	−1.67	1.50
1990–2000	−0.46	4.46	0.27	4.74	−1.30	1.91	−0.42	2.47
Total	0.13	3.63	0.50	3.79	−0.36	1.40	0.29	2.89
	Difference		Difference		Difference		Difference	
1960s	1.25		0.89		0.58		1.77	
1970s	2.37		1.86		1.57		2.47	
1980s	5.11		5.53		1.42		3.17	
1990–2000	4.91		4.47		3.21		2.89	
Total	3.50		3.29		1.76		2.60	

Note: The sample includes all developing countries with full availability. Growth rates are population-weighted; the overall differential corresponds to that in table 2.1. Population weights differ for the two regions, so it is possible (in the bottom half of the table) for the opportunity-specific differences in this table to each be below the overall differential.

We start with the performance of the non-African developing countries. There were indeed large differences in growth rates between the three opportunity categories. The most successful of the three groups were the coastal, resource-scarce economies. Their average *per capita* growth over the forty years was 3.78 percent. Such rapid growth is without historical precedent and is cumulatively transforming. After forty years of such growth – about the typical period of a working life – *per capita* incomes have increased by a factor of 4.6.[2] The resource-rich economies were less successful, despite their apparently more favorable opportunities. Their growth rates were 1 percentage point lower than the coastal, resource-scarce economies. Nevertheless, growth was sufficient to be transforming over a single working lifetime. After forty years of such growth incomes have risen by a factor of 3.2. The least successful were the landlocked, resource-scarce economies. The lack of both the basic opportunities identified in our classification evidently mattered. Indeed, it mattered a lot:

[2] Throughout the chapter we use log differentials in growth calculations. The cumulative changes reported here are therefore given by $y_{t+40}/y_t = \exp(40 \cdot g)$, where g is the relevant average growth rate from table 2.5.

growth was barely half that even of the resource-rich economies. For these economies growth was insufficient to be truly transforming over a working lifetime, but there was still progress: over forty years incomes rose only 0.75 percent.

In Africa, as in the rest of the world, the worst-performing group was the one with least opportunities – the landlocked, resource-scarce group. In Africa this group was in gradual absolute decline. Cumulatively over the forty years, for the quarter of Africa's people living with these limited opportunities, *per capita* incomes fell by nearly 15 percent. Whereas in absolute terms Africa's landlocked, resource-scarce countries performed worst, in relative terms their performance was nevertheless much better than the other African opportunity groups. The African resource-rich group diverged from the rest of the opportunity group, at 2.60 percentage points per year. However, much the widest gap was that for the coastal, resource-scarce economies. In Africa the group barely grew, and the growth gap with other regions was 3.29 percentage points. That Africa's coastal, resource-scarce economies missed out on the transformation experienced elsewhere is the most important single factor in Africa's overall growth shortfall. Not only was this divergence substantial, it was widening. In other regions the growth of the coastal, resource-scarce regions was accelerating. By contrast, in Africa it was decelerating. As a result the growth gap tended to widen drastically over the decades: -0.89; -1.86; -5.53; -4.47.

Bringing together tables 2.4 and 2.5, it is evident that African opportunities were heavily skewed towards the categories that in the rest of the world were least successful. The share of Africa's population living in the slowest-growing category – landlocked, resource-scarce – was thirty-five times that of the other developing regions, and it also had treble the share living in the other slow-growing category – resource-rich. To what extent did this difference in opportunities account for the slower overall growth of Africa with which we started?

In table 2.6 we decompose the difference in the overall growth rate between Africa and the rest of the developing world into that part due to the difference in their opportunity structures, and the differences in the opportunity-specific growth rates. Column (1) repeats the overall growth differential shown in table 2.1. Column (2) shows that part due to differences in opportunity structure. This is arrived at by calculating the growth rate that Africa would have had were each of its opportunity groups to have had the growth rate of that opportunity group in other developing regions. That is, we combine non-African opportunity-specific growth rates with the African structure of opportunities. The effect of differences in opportunities is far from negligible – overall it accounts for a slower growth rate for Africa of 0.96 percentage points. Yet this is only 27 percent of the growth gap to be

Table 2.6 *Decomposition of growth differential, by opportunity composition and opportunity-specific growth.*

Decade	Difference (1)	Contribution of:	
		Opportunity composition (2)	Opportunity-specific growth (3)
1960s	1.25	0.42	0.83
1970s	2.36	0.43	1.94
1980s	5.11	1.48	3.63
1990–2000	4.92	1.41	3.51
Total	3.50	0.96	2.54

Note: The formula is

$$g_O - g_S = \sum_{c=1}^{3} (\omega_{Oc} - \omega_{Sc}) \cdot g_{Oc} + \omega_{Sc} \cdot (g_{Oc} - g_{Sc}),$$

where g_O and g_S are population-weighted growth in the "56 Other" and "43 SSA" regions and ω_{jc} is the share of category c in population of region j. The regional population-weighted growth rates are from table 2.1.

explained. Evidently, the main explanation for Africa's slow growth must look beyond this distinction between opportunities.

The crux of Africa's growth divergence is well illustrated in figure 2.2, which shows the evolution of the three opportunity groups for Africa and other developing regions. We calculate these growth paths by setting real incomes equal to the relevant opportunity-specific regional averages in 1960, and then applying opportunity-specific regional growth rates for subsequent years. Outside of Africa, the rapid growth of the coastal, resource-scarce economies, especially post-1980, took them by the end of our period comfortably into the middle-income range. Similarly, the resource-rich economies were able to grow out of poverty. The relatively few landlocked, resource-scarce economies still posed a development challenge, although even here if the trend continued by 2020 they would have reached the lower-middle-income level. In Africa, all three categories stay resolutely in the low-income category. On these trends, quite soon the low-income world would become synonymous with Africa.

2.3 Key questions

Africa's growth under-performance, on the above analysis, is proximately explained first and foremost by the failure of its coastal, resource-scarce economies to replicate the growth pattern of other such economies as of

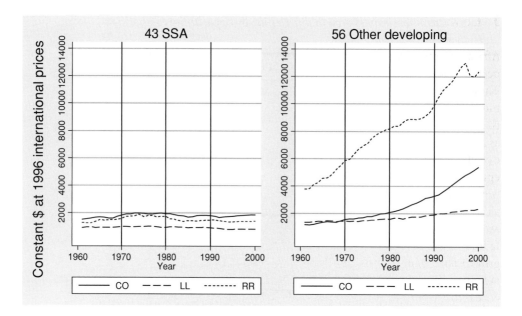

Figure 2.2 Simulated real GDP *per capita*, 1960–2000.
Note: The simulated paths show how GDP per capita would have evolved in each region and opportunity group if initial real incomes per capita had subsequently grown at observed region- and group-specific population-weighted annual growth rates. Note that the country composition of the group averages changes as the group composition evolves.
Source: PWT6.1, World Bank, and authors' calculations.

around 1980. Additionally, it is relatively dependent upon natural-resource economies which globally under-performed, and which in Africa performed markedly worse than the global average, though the pattern is very uneven both over time and between countries. Finally, Africa is the region with the largest share of landlocked, resource-scarce economies which themselves somewhat under-performed relative to the already dismal global pattern.

These three proximate explanations generate three further questions:

- Why, as of around 1980, did coastal Africa not participate in the global pattern?
- Why did most of Africa's resource-rich economies fall short of the global average, and fall so far short of the successful pattern established by Botswana?
- Under what counterfactual would performance for Africa's landlocked, resource-scarce economies have been significantly better?

It is now time to turn from opportunities to choices.

3   Choices

Africa is diverse. Although for the region taken as a whole over the forty-year period that we consider there was stagnation, stagnation is not the norm. The average conceals enormous variation between countries, and also enormous variation over time. In this study our focus or units of observation are country-episodes, periods within a country that can broadly be considered as a unity for the purpose of understanding the growth experience. Since the overall growth experience is so dismal, our main concern is to understand episodes during which the growth process failed. However, our characterization of episodes is not defined by the growth outcomes, but rather by various dysfunctional political-economy configurations which we refer to as "syndromes." The core of our study is to understand the overall growth failure in terms of four distinct syndromes, each of which accounts for growth failures in particular countries at particular times. The syndromes are not exhaustive of African experience. We do not attempt to force experience into the syndromes. Rather, in reviewing the accounts provided by our twenty-six case studies it became apparent that although no single overarching account of Africa's growth failure could be sustained, neither was each country's experience entirely unique. Our identification of four groups of syndromes came out of this review of our case study histories: some patterns became evident.

Having identified the syndromes to which African countries appear to have been prone, we then carefully reviewed each country's forty-year history with the country authors, to establish whether and when its experience is well described by one or other of these syndromes. Some countries never experience any of the syndromes; others are characterized by more than one syndrome at the same time. Where a country-episode was characterized by multiple syndromes it became a matter of judgment whether one of them was of over-riding importance, or whether to understand the growth outcome multiple syndromes needed to be taken into account. Hence, some episodes feature in two or more chapters in our syndrome-specific analysis of part 2 of this volume. In a final step, we reviewed the economic histories of twenty-two additional African countries in order to extend the syndrome classification to all of SSA.

The syndromes are not intended to be exhaustive of the ways in which growth can fail. Rather, they represent salient episodes of purposive failure attributable to human agency within the society – whether by leaders, governments, or groups outside government such as rebel movements. A country may avoid these syndromes yet fail to grow – for example, because it is unlucky in being hit by shocks, or because it is very badly endowed. We shall of course be considering such explanations of growth failure, and indeed sometimes they are central to understanding growth outcomes, but they are not included in our syndromes. Similarly, because our syndromes are defined by the choices of key actors rather than by growth outcomes, in principle a country-episode might be characterized by one of our syndromes and yet experience sustainable growth. However, where this happens, unless there is some manifest lucky event, our characterization of the behavior pattern as a syndrome must be called into question. A behavior pattern within which several countries achieved sustainable growth could not reasonably be regarded as a syndrome.

We now discuss the syndromes. They fall into four major groupings of behavior: regulatory, distributive, intertemporal, and state breakdown, and we consider them in turn. Appendix table 2.A2 (p. 132) provides the full classification for the forty-eight countries.

3.1 Regulatory syndromes

Most African countries became independent at a time when socialist and communist strategies of economic development were fashionable. In chapters 3 and 9, Fosu and Ndulu discuss discuss in detail the nature of such influences on African policy choices – in effect, why some of the syndromes were particularly common in Africa. Here we simply recognize that as a matter of fact many African countries adopted socialist or communist strategies of development. Our concern here is purely with the consequences of these choices for growth. The core of socialist and communist economic strategies was the regulation of economic activity, the ownership of productive enterprises by the state, and an industrialization strategy modeled, at least loosely, on that of the USSR and pursued behind high trade barriers financed through the taxation of exports. Additionally, at the level of political institutions, socialism and communism at least in Africa were used to justify one-party states. While this was common to both socialist and communist strategies, there were substantial differences in the extent to which regulation and state ownership were applied. While there is a continuum of the intensity of these economic regimes the differences along the continuum are sufficiently pronounced for it to be useful to distinguish between what we term "hard controls" – in effect something close to the full communist vision – and "soft controls," where some parts of the economy would be regulated and some nationalized, but in which the ambition or efficacy of the policies was much more moderate. For example, in a "hard-control" regime such as Congo Brazzaville, or Tanzania 1973–85, the banks and other "commanding heights" of the economy would be nationalized, and virtually all private economic activity subject to regulations which substantially changed behavior through price controls and investment licensing. In a "soft-control" regime such as Zambia 1963–91, substantial parts of the economy – such as the banks – remained private, and price controls, although significant, were less pervasive. Just as there is an element of judgment as to where along a continuum it is best to distinguish between hard- and soft-control regimes, so it is a matter of judgment where soft-control regimes stop and other types of economic strategies start. In the 1960s planning was so fashionable that virtually all states had five-year plans. Similarly, virtually all states controlled some prices, or at least passed legislation which notionally set controlled prices. For example, Malawi had some price and interest rate controls, along with major state and quasi-state enterprises. By the standards of the 1990s these policy stances look quite interventionist. Yet we judge them to be markedly less interventionist than the strategies pursued in states such as Zambia and so do not include them in our category of "soft controls." Even the softest of the "soft-control" states involves regulation and state ownership outside the range found in the European social-market economies. To summarize, we have two types of regulatory syndrome – hard- and soft-control regimes. Each of these was quite common in Africa. If we take as our measure of exposure to syndromes the number of years in which any country in our sample experienced them, we find that between them the two variants of the regulatory syndrome accounted for around 35 percent of African economic history during 1960–2000. The soft-control regime was about twice as common as the hard-control regime.

3.2 Redistributive syndromes

We now turn to the second type of syndrome, which concerns policies towards the redistribution of income between ethno-regional groups. Around 44 percent of African economic history during our period is characterized by this syndrome. All governments intervene in order to redistribute income between households, most commonly from richer to poorer. This is not our concern. Rather, we regard as potentially damaging for growth those situations in which the basic units of redistribution are ethno-regional. However, not all such redistributions are dysfunctional. Growth can potentially be damaged by both errors of commission and errors of omission.

We begin with errors of commission: the power of the state is used to redistribute substantial amounts of income from one ethno-regional group to another, and this has side-effects which reduce growth. For example, public revenues might be used to benefit a particular group rather than to provide public goods. This can adversely affect growth because some of the public goods that are neglected are capital goods. Another channel by which growth is adversely affected is if high costs are inflicted upon the economy in order to raise the revenues that are needed to finance redistribution. A third channel is if large-scale redistribution between ethnic groups so inflates the returns to power that substantial resources are devoted to the struggle to gain power – the concept known as "rent-seeking."

Conversely, errors of omission occur if the state fails to redistribute between ethno-regional groups in a situation in which such redistribution would be growth-enhancing. One such situation is if one ethnic group is so much poorer than the other that the ordering is almost lexicographic: virtually all members of one ethnic group are poorer than those in the other. In such a situation there are reasonable grounds for expecting redistribution between ethnic groups to raise growth – for example, because households in the poorer group are credit constrained. Another situation in which inter-ethnic redistribution can raise growth is if it pre-empts a strategy of violence on the part of the poorer ethnic group. In the absence of a voluntary transfer, the rational strategy for a poor-but-strong group may be to use violence to enforce a transfer. Pre-emptive redistribution can then be cost-effective even for the victim group because it avoids the costs of violence.

The first type of ethno-regional redistribution has been common in Africa during our period. An example of such an episode would be Kenya under President Moi. During this long episode an alliance of minor, and relatively poor, regions held power and used it to redistribute from the rich and previously favored region of Central Province and Nairobi. An example of how growth was sacrificed was the telecommunications strategy. The post office was used to create employment for the Kalenjin, the ethnic group at the core of President Moi's constituency, and to ensure the profitability of the post office it was cross-subsidized from telecommunications in a merged enterprise. In turn, to maintain the public telecommunications business profitable, competition in telecommunications was circumscribed, resulting in a service that was both bad and high-cost. Since globally good telecommunications was becoming regarded as an essential feature of an environment conducive for growth, this ethnic transfer program thus inflicted high costs on the economy.

At the extreme end of ethno-regional redistribution, we find "looting." By this, we mean a situation in which assets, whether private or public, are stripped outside the context of the rule of law and due process. Often this is done by a leader and his small entourage who run the government for their personal financial advantage. In such a polity power will necessarily become highly concentrated because the leader cannot expect his objective to be widely shared. The power amassed by the head of state then becomes used to generate opportunities for personal wealth. Even were the dictator confident that his family would remain in power in perpetuity, such a concentration of power would be likely to affect growth adversely. However, personal rule is unlikely to be sustainable beyond one generation and since the dictator and his family are likely to recognize this, the intertemporal aspects of the looting syndrome are similar to those of elite end-games to be discussed below. Long-term growth of the economy is of little value to the dictator because he does not expect to benefit from such growth. Indeed, to the extent that growth would strengthen the position of actors other than the dictator and his entourage, it might weaken his hold on power. Further, because power is concentrated and the objective for which that power is used is so malign, other private actors can have little confidence that their legitimate interests will be respected. Few African leaders have been entirely altruistic or indeed entirely honest, and there is a continuum of personal corruption which at some point shades into the looting syndrome. However, we have reserved this classification for cases in which the personal aggrandizing behavior of the head of state was sufficiently dramatic to become a major explanation of macroeconomic performance. For example, we consider both Idi Amin in Uganda and General Abacha in Nigeria not just as clear cases of centralized personal power used for corrupt purposes, but that the economic history of these countries during their periods of rule cannot be understood without reference to this behavior.

Looting is not synonymous with dictatorship. Most dictators are not looters, and some democracies not only permit but actually induce looting. In Africa the most serious single episode of looting was indeed under the auspices of democracy, namely the Shagari regime in Nigeria, 1979–83. Nigeria accounts for a fifth of Africa's population and this period was the peak of the oil boom, potentially providing the country with massive finance for productive investment. This opportunity, probably the most important in Africa for our entire forty-year period, was missed due to looting during democracy.

Whereas most of Africa's redistribution syndromes have been errors of commission, there have been some cases of errors of omission. The clearest case of a failure to redistribute between ethnic groups being directly dysfunctional for growth was South Africa under apartheid. A reasonable case can be made that redistribution would have enhanced the productivity of the poor ethnic group by more than it would have reduced the productivity of the richer group. Judgments as to failures to make pre-emptive redistributions are more difficult. An example is Chad prior to 1990. In Chad northerners tend to have a comparative advantage in military power and southerners in productive economic activity. Hence, unless the south redistributes to the north on a voluntary basis the north is liable to attempt to enforce redistribution through violent conflict. Post-1990 Chad established a sometimes fragile peace, partly due to such redistribution. Prior to 1990 the failure to adopt voluntary redistribution may have contributed to continuing conflict.

3.3 Intertemporal syndromes

We now turn to the third type of syndrome in which the key errors were intertemporal. Obviously, since our story concerns growth – or, rather, the failure of growth – in one sense all the syndromes involved intertemporal errors. However, a useful distinction can be drawn between errors which had often inadvertent adverse consequences for growth – as in the control regimes – and errors which directly involved an under-valuation of the future. We estimate that intertemporal syndromes account for around 18 percent of African economic history. We distinguish between two types of intertemporal syndrome: anticipated redistributions, and unsustainable spending.

Anticipated redistribution occurs when an elite group anticipates a loss of power. For some reason it comes to believe that it will be unable to defend its level of income and, more particularly, its ownership of assets. The group therefore sees itself as in an "end-game" in which its critical objectives are to amass wealth as rapidly as possible and to shift existing wealth abroad. The group may come to believe that its period in power is limited for various reasons, but the most likely is that the elite is an ethnic minority faced by mounting popular pressure for political reform. Typically, the minority will have been in a position of entrenched power. For the period when it was confident of power it may have run a redistributive syndrome, or it may have managed the economy for the objective of economic growth – with income concentrated in the hands of the elite, growth delivers the elite disproportionate benefits. However, once the elite begins to doubt its ability to sustain itself in power the objective of growth become less attractive. The clearest example in Africa of such a switch in elite expectations occurs outside our sample – in Angola, following the Portuguese revolution of 1974. Suddenly, the Angolan elite was confronted with a radically changed political situation in which it was evident that Portugal would not sustain the elite in power. This produced a dramatic economic exodus in which assets were shipped out of the country. Within our sample such end-games have been relatively rare, but important. The most substantial one is probably South Africa after 1980. During the late 1970s political events in Southern Africa transformed prospects for continued Afrikaner rule in South Africa. By the early 1980s the South African economy – largely controlled by white interests – had switched from a configuration of high investment and rapid growth to one of low investment and stagnation. We attribute this at least in part to an emerging fear on the part of the white elite that the returns on further investment would be subject to high taxation or other forms of redistribution. This state of affairs continued until the handover of power, and to an extent has continued even under African National Congress (ANC) rule. A similar characterization applies, we think, to Burundi, where the Tutsi elite came to doubt its ability to hang on to power given that it formed such a small minority of the population. In the event, the elite did manage to hang on to power for a long time, but in heavily contested circumstances, so that the retention of elite power continued to look precarious.

The other intertemporal syndrome we term "unsustainable spending." The related concept of "unsustainable growth" is normally used in the context of environmental degradation – for example, growth achieved by destroying forests. Although destroying forests is an unsustainable *activity*, it does not necessarily imply unsustainable *growth*. If the profits from deforestation are well invested, the economy can simply move to some other activity at a sustainably higher path of income. The unsustainable spending syndrome occurs when a country fails to transform temporary income into permanent income. A period of unsustainable growth ensues: good times are followed by a period of reversion. While the burst of unsustainable growth is a missed opportunity, a pernicious variant is where the good times sow the seeds of subsequent destruction: the future is worse than if the temporary boom had never occurred. Environmental destruction indeed sometimes takes this form. However, there are two other routes to impoverishment that are particularly pertinent for our subsequent analysis: debt accumulation and irreversible expenditures. In the former the country amplifies temporarily favorable circumstances by borrowing internationally, but does not transform the borrowed resources into productive assets. In the latter, the country uses temporary income to lock into a pattern of expenditures which cannot easily be reversed, so that as income reverts to its former level damage is incurred by reducing expenditures which are more valuable than those into which the country has become locked.

Africa has a high natural-resource endowment *per capita*. Natural resources most obviously tempt a country into environmental unsustainability: depletion of the resource without adequate replacement with other assets. The depletion of Zambian copper is an example: the issue is not that the copper should have been left in the ground – the resource depletion itself was clearly appropriate – but that other assets should have been accumulated. However, natural resources also lure a country into unsustainability by other routes. The price shocks common to natural resources may induce periods of high income in which debt is accumulated and irreversible expenditure commitments are made. Nigeria during the oil boom of 1974–86 is the classic example of a temporary boom being geared up by debt accumulation. The oil boom was approximately doubled by debt accumulation. By the mid-1980s the country hit its borrowing constraint, coincident with a collapse in the oil price, so that real expenditure roughly halved over a very short period. Côte d'Ivoire during the 1970s was another example of unsustainable spending, in which public expenditure rose at an astonishingly fast pace, creating commitments, notably a government payroll, that could not be reduced during the following decade. A variant of unsustainable spending occurs where an unsustainable strategy is chosen in the context of a control regime. For example, in Congo Brazzaville the oil boom was used to expand manufacturing industry behind heavy import protection. Statistically, this produced a phase of rapid growth, followed by a post-boom phase of equally rapid collapse, so that the economy appeared to have grown and then contracted. However, because the control regime heavily distorted domestic prices from opportunity costs, some of this growth was illusory. In effect, an unproductive activity was induced which was misleadingly recorded in the national accounts as productive. Hence, the growth might have been illusory rather than merely unsustainable.

The various forms of unsustainable spending are particularly pernicious because of their potential for confusion. Growth – often rapid growth – is coincident with the policy error, followed some years later by rapid decline. It is easy to mis-diagnose the decline as being due to errors made during the decline, and to see the growth phase as a success. A classic instance of such mis-diagnosis is the popular critique of the "structural adjustment program" (SAP) in Nigeria in the late 1980s. Because living standards were in radical decline during this period, the policies adopted were blamed, despite the astonishing achievement that the growth of output was actually faster during this period than during the oil boom itself.

3.4   State breakdown

The final syndrome is where the state is unable to maintain internal security. Again there is a continuum here from an inability to control crime through to large-scale sustained rebellion. During our period, Africa was increasingly affected by violent rebellion, although in our sample it accounts for only around 14 percent of African experience. Nevertheless, the impact upon growth has been considerable. During civil war economies go into steep decline. For example, by the end of its period of conflict *per capita* incomes in Sierra Leone had fallen to only one-third of their pre-conflict level. Further, many of these costs prove persistent – military spending remains high in post-conflict periods, and the social disruption, notably worsened health states, can last for a generation. Finally, many of the costs of a civil war spill over to neighbors. This can occur due to rivalries in military spending, to demand spillovers, migration, and the disruption of transport routes. For example, the civil war in Mozambique approximately doubled the costs of international transport for Malawi, and the civil war in the DRC prevented the Central African Republic (CAR) from using its normal river route to the sea.

3.5   Syndromes and opportunities

The population-weighted distribution of syndromes across the opportunities is shown in table 2.7. Each person-year is an observation. For the coastal countries the most common syndrome was regulatory. Unsurprisingly, for

Table 2.7 *Frequency of syndromes, by opportunity category.*

	Coastal	Landlocked	Resource-rich	Total
Distribution of person-years				
%	44.4	30.9	24.7	100
Frequency of syndromes (% of person-years)[a]				
Regulatory	37.8	37.0	25.8	35.2
Redistributive	28.4	46.2	79.8	44.0
Intertemporal	15.1	4.8	46.7	18.2
State breakdown	9.3	25.6	8.5	14.1
Syndrome-free	33.8	20.5	9.3	24.9

Notes: The table uses annual observations for forty-seven African countries, from the later of 1960 and the year of independence to 2000. Frequencies are population-weighted and therefore refer to person-years rather than country-years.
[a] Column sums exceed 100% because a country can exhibit multiple syndromes in a given year.

the resource-rich the most common were redistributive and intertemporal: there was a lot for the state to redistribute, and both the volatility of income and the scope for borrowing provided scope for intertemporal error. Perhaps as a result of these greater opportunities, the resource-rich countries were overall much more prone to the syndromes. The landlocked were differentially prone to state breakdown, and differentially free of the intertemporal syndrome.

A more formal test of whether the opportunity groups differed in their proneness to each syndrome is set out in table 2.8, which reports probit regressions with the landlocked category as the default and with yearly dummy variables included to control for unobserved effects common to all countries.[3] The landlocked, resource-scarce countries are significantly less likely to be syndrome-free than their coastal counterparts. This is consistent with a long-standing hypothesis of Jeffrey Sachs that landlocked countries have worse policies because the returns to good policies are lower (Gallup and Sachs 1997). They are also significantly more likely to suffer state breakdown than either of the other groups and less likely to suffer intertemporal syndromes, perhaps because the societies are too poor to accumulate either assets or debts. As between the resource-rich and the coastal, resource-scarce groups, the former are significantly more prone to the redistributive

---

[3] These probit regressions are population-weighted, so the results refer (for example) to coastal and resource-scarce populations rather than coastal and resource-scarce countries. All of the comparisons discussed in this paragraph hold true for unweighted probits as well, however, in terms of both sign and statistical significance.

Table 2.8 *Incidence of syndromes, by opportunity group.*

	Dependent variable				
Opportunity group	Syndrome-free	Regulatory	Redistributive	Intertemporal	State breakdown
Coastal	0.516***	0.016	−0.541***	0.591***	−0.712***
Resource-rich	−0.201	−0.698***	0.804***	1.679***	−0.699***
N	1,894	1,894	1,894	1,894	1,894
Pseudo-R^2	0.258	0.179	0.154	0.346	0.105
chi^2	325.595	213.428	149.981	325.350	121.017
prob>chi^2	0.000	0.000	0.000	0.000	0.000
Marginal impact of category on probability of syndrome:					
Coastal	0.141***	0.006	−0.206***	0.082***	−0.130***
Resource-rich	−0.052	−0.224***	0.312***	0.406***	−0.099***
Significance test for equality of coastal and resource-rich coefficients:					
prob>chi^2	0.000	0.000	0.000	0.000	0.929
Reject CO = RR?	Yes	Yes	Yes	Yes	No

$^*p < 0.1; ^{**}p < 0.05; ^{***}p < 0.01.$

Note: The dependent variable is a dummy variable for the occurrence of the syndrome. Coefficients are from population-weighted probit regressions with year effects. Landlocked is the omitted category.

and intertemporal syndromes, and less prone to the regulatory. The greater proneness of the coastal, resource-scarce group to the regulatory syndrome may reflect the greater relative importance of trade and the private sector in the economy: regulation is both feasible and lucrative.

Table 2.9 summarizes how the prevalence of the syndromes in aggregate evolved decade-by-decade. During the 1990s the incidence of the syndromes declined sharply, but on average during the decade around 60 percent of Africans were still living in syndrome conditions.

Table 2.10 shows the evolution by opportunity group, taking into account the distribution of Africa's population. Although on average over the forty years the coastal, resource-scarce economies were least prone to syndromes, this differed markedly over time. During the 1980s, when in the rest of the world the coastal, resource-scarce countries started to take off, only 4 percent of the coastal, resource-scarce economies, and hence less than 2 percent of Africa's population, was living in those which were syndrome-free. Between the 1980s and the 1990s there were two dramatic changes. The coastal countries largely broke free of the regulatory syndrome, and the resource-rich countries largely broke free of the intertemporal syndrome.

Table 2.9 *Distribution of not-syndrome-free population, by opportunity category and decade.*

	Share of 48-country SSA population exhibiting at least one syndrome			
		Location of population		
Decade	Overall	Coastal	Landlocked	Resource-rich
1960s	0.52	0.28	0.23	0.01
1970s	0.89	0.41	0.26	0.22
1980s	0.94	0.40	0.26	0.27
1990–2000	0.61	0.17	0.20	0.24
Total	0.74	0.31	0.24	0.19

Note: The table classifies all country-years for forty-eight SSA countries, 1960–2000.

Table 2.10 *Distribution of population, by opportunity, syndrome, and decade.*

Category and decade	Share of category in SSA population	Share of population in opportunity category affected by:[a]				
		Syndrome-free	Regulatory	Redistributive	Intertemporal	State breakdown
Coastal						
1960s	0.68	0.57	0.19	0.24	0.01	0.11
1970s	0.49	0.13	0.59	0.25	0.23	0.07
1980s	0.43	0.04	0.72	0.32	0.23	0.07
1990–2000	0.36	0.56	0.19	0.18	0.08	0.07
Total	0.49	0.33	0.42	0.25	0.13	0.08
Llocked						
1960s	0.29	0.20	0.37	0.33	0.00	0.33
1970s	0.29	0.08	0.57	0.59	0.09	0.11
1980s	0.28	0.07	0.57	0.52	0.09	0.20
1990–2000	0.35	0.40	0.13	0.35	0.04	0.32
Total	0.30	0.19	0.41	0.45	0.05	0.24
Resrich						
1960s	0.04	0.84	0.08	0.00	0.00	0.08
1970s	0.23	0.07	0.24	0.77	0.76	0.04
1980s	0.29	0.04	0.46	0.78	0.70	0.07
1990–2000	0.29	0.18	0.08	0.76	0.07	0.11
Total	0.21	0.28	0.21	0.59	0.38	0.07

Notes: The table covers all country-year observations between 1960 and 2000 for forty-eight countries in SSA.

[a] The sum across all five columns can exceed 1 because a given country-year may exhibit more than one syndrome.

4 Consequences of the syndromes for growth

4.1 Possible effects of the syndromes on opportunities

Between them, these syndromes occupy around three-quarters of African experience. Potentially, this could imply that one-quarter of the countries in Africa completely avoided the syndromes and three-quarters were permanently stuck in them. In practice, few countries were permanently in these syndromes but even fewer escaped them altogether. In our sample, only Malawi, Botswana, and Mauritius escaped all the syndromes for a sustained substantial period – more than two decades. All other countries at best had relatively brief episodes free from them. While growth was often reasonable during these syndrome-free episodes, they were too brief to raise incomes substantially.

The effect of the syndromes, or their absence, has to be evaluated against some counterfactual which reflects opportunities forgone.

The natural-resource economies, of which Africa has a considerable number, are the most dependent upon governance. Natural resources generate large rents which accrue to government, and so the extent to which the rents are harnessed to growth depends critically upon government decisions. The sensitivity of performance to governance is well illustrated by the contrast between Botswana and Sierra Leone. At the beginning of our period the two economies had approximately equal *per capita* incomes, and both were endowed with diamonds. By the end of our period the difference in *per capita* incomes was approximately ten to one, with Botswana having sustained one of the fastest growth rates in the world and Sierra Leone one of the fastest rates of decline. Recall that Botswana is one of the very few countries which we judge to have avoided all of the syndromes, and this appears to have made a spectacular difference. It serves as an interesting counterfactual to the dismal growth performance of all the other natural-resource economies that fell victim to one or other of the syndromes. Not all the syndromes are likely to have been equally damaging to natural-resource economies. For such economies the key government decisions are intertemporal – the rents extracted must be turned into productive investment either by the state itself or by the private sector. The costs of the redistributive syndrome are also likely to be large, not because redistribution is costly to finance – tax distortions are not needed to accomplish it – but because so much of the economy is at stake in securing an efficient pattern of investment and avoiding distributional struggle. By contrast soft controls *per se* may not be particularly damaging for resource-rich countries: the state is necessarily going to be large, and in the absence of the intertemporal or redistributive syndromes the distortions associated with soft controls may remain relatively minor.

The coastal economies without natural resources had the opportunity to follow the development path common in East Asia, by which countries integrated into the world economy through labor-intensive manufactured exports. Such exports are transactions-intensive with very low margins of profitability, and so performance is sensitive to economic policies. Success requires reasonable economic infrastructure and relative prices that come reasonably close to reflecting social opportunity cost. The opportunity for penetrating global markets deteriorated during our period because by the 1990s China (in manufactures) and India (in services) were so successful that there was considerably less room for other entrants to the market. Unfortunately, no mainland African coastal economy had policies conducive to manufactured exports for a sustained period prior to 1990. During the 1970s Côte d'Ivoire began to break into European markets for manufactures, but this was killed off by the end of the decade due to growing exchange rate over-valuation. The only African economy which succeeded in global manufactures was Mauritius – like Botswana a country we judge to have avoided all of the syndromes for an extended period. Mauritius is now by far the richest country in Africa in terms of *per capita* income, and so this again gives some insight into the opportunity cost of the syndromes in other coastal economies without natural resources. Unlike the natural-resource economies, for manufactured exports the key decisions are not intertemporal but rather concern the costs of doing business. Hence, for this group of economies we would expect that the control regimes – both hard and soft – would be particularly damaging, as would a prioritization of redistribution over efficiency.

The landlocked economies without natural resources had dramatically worse opportunities for growth. Being landlocked they were precluded from significant entry into the global market for manufactures and without high-value natural resources they were left dependent upon agriculture. Globally, there is no example of such a country experiencing rapid growth during this period. One African country in this category we judge to have avoided all the syndromes for the entire forty-year period is Malawi. Yet its growth performance was modest. Uganda, another landlocked economy, performed well in the 1990s but to a substantial extent this was a recovery from previous collapse. Just as there is little upside potential for such economies, they may be relatively resilient to policy errors and predation. Peasant farmers have the option of retreating into subsistence and so defending their incomes. Hence, this group of economies may have lost least, both in absolute terms and relative to the counterfactual of potential growth, from their experience of the syndromes. State breakdown is probably an exception; civil wars increase the risk of subsequent conflict, and where growth opportunities are already limited the likelihood of a continuing conflict/low-income trap is greater.

An Africa that had been free from the syndromes would thus, in our view, have looked very different, not just in terms of overall growth but in terms of the relative performance of countries. We would have expected to see the natural-resource economies performing equivalently to Botswana – in effect reaching lower-middle income status. We would have expected the coastal, resource-scarce economies to have done better – during our period, those countries that succeeded in breaking into manufactured export markets experienced spectacular growth. There seems no natural obstacle to countries such as Côte d'Ivoire, Ghana, Kenya, Madagascar, Mozambique, and Tanzania having similar growth experiences to Mauritius and Thailand. Such growth would have produced massive inequalities in income between African countries, with the landlocked economies without natural resources experiencing severe relative decline. This, in turn, would presumably have fueled substantial migration from the landlocked economies to the coast. This was indeed the pattern early in our period, before African growth decelerated. Malawi had a massive outflow of workers to South Africa, and Burkina Faso had a massive outflow to Côte d'Ivoire. In effect, Africa would have seen population movements similar to the migration to the coast that has occurred as a result of geographically skewed growth in China. Africa's relatively uniform lack of growth is thus, in our view, not the product of a uniform phenomenon, but rather the interaction of distinct syndromes with differential effects in different countries according to their opportunities.

4.2   How important were the syndromes?

Just as we have investigated the contribution of differences in opportunities to accounting for the difference between African growth rates and those of other developing countries, so we can potentially do the same for the syndromes. In table 2.11 we make an extreme "working assumption" that we subsequently investigate, namely that other developing regions did not suffer from the syndromes. This assumption is not realistic, but it enables us to calculate an extreme bound as to how important the syndromes might have been. If the opportunity-specific growth rates differ little between syndrome and syndrome-free periods, then as a matter of logic the syndromes cannot account for Africa's slow growth. Table 2.11 is constructed by taking as a counterfactual that without the syndromes each African opportunity group would have grown during a decade at the rate of the syndrome-free countries in the group in that decade. Column (1) takes from table 2.6 the growth difference to be explained once we have controlled for Africa's distinctive opportunities. Column (2) shows the difference accounted for by the gap between the syndrome-free growth rate in each opportunity group in Africa,

Table 2.11 *Contribution of syndromes to the growth differential.*

		Of which:	
Decade	Contribution of opportunity-specific growth to overall growth differential[a] (1)	Differential between African syndrome-free growth and growth in other regions (2)	Within-Africa syndrome effect (3)
1960s	0.83	−0.33	1.16
1970s	1.94	−0.12	2.06
1980s	3.63	1.16	2.46
1990–2000	3.51	1.63	1.88
Total	2.54	0.63	1.91

Note: Supposing the syndromes are unique to SSA, African population-weighted growth in category c is then

$$g_{Ac} = \omega_{Acf} g_{Acf} + \omega_{Acn} g_{Acn} = g_{Acf} - \omega_{Acn}(g_{Acf} - g_{Acn}),$$

where ω_{Ack} is the population share for $k =$ free or not-free. Then SSA can fall short either through unfortunate composition or because of syndromes. Substituting for g_{Ac} in the earlier equation, we can decompose growth as

$$g_O - g_A = \sum_{c=1}^{3}(\omega_{Oc} - \omega_{Ac}) \cdot g_{Oc} + \omega_{Ac} \cdot (g_{Oc} - g_{Acf}) + \omega_{Ac}\omega_{Acn} \cdot (g_{Acf} - g_{Acn}).$$

[a] This column is the same as column (3) of table 2.6.

and that in other developing regions. Column (3) shows the contribution of the syndromes.

Taking the forty years as a whole, the syndrome effect is by far the most important of the three explanatory factors. It accounts for around half (52 percent) of the overall growth differential. Taken together with the 27 percent accounted for by differences in opportunity structures, the residual accounted for by the difference between Africa's syndrome-free growth rate and that of other regions is only 0.72 percentage points. So, conditional upon the extreme assumption that the syndromes were unique to Africa they provide a lot of explanatory power. Decade-by-decade, the story is a little more complicated. The syndromes become less important, both absolutely and relatively, in the 1990s.

Table 2.11 is based on differences between Africa and other developing regions. A different approach is to analyze growth within Africa through regression analysis and estimate the effect of the syndromes. The effect of the syndromes in aggregate is shown in table 2.12.

Table 2.12 *Robust regressions, controlling for shocks.*
Dependent variable: growth in real GDP per capita

	Country fixed effects not included				Country fixed effects included	
A. *Syndrome-free status not instrumented*						
Variable	(1)	(2)	(3)	(4)	(5)	(6)
Syndrome-free	2.076***	2.040***	1.890***	2.071***	2.162***	2.147***
	0.241	0.332	0.249	0.318	0.303	0.366
Partner growth	0.296***	–	0.299***	–	0.298***	–
	0.096	–	0.094	–	0.101	–
Dry year	−0.463*	−0.174	−0.309	−0.224	−0.265	−0.252
	0.264	0.259	0.250	0.306	0.333	0.328
Coastal	–	–	0.476	0.008	–	–
	–	–	0.364	0.306	–	–
Resrich	–	–	0.050	−0.254	–	–
	–	–	0.415	0.357	–	–
N	1,492	1,770	1,492	1,770	1,492	1,770
Pseudo-R^2	0.028	0.049	0.029	0.050	0.066	0.092
B. *Syndrome-free status instrumented*						
Variable	(7)	(8)	(9)	(10)	(11)	(12)
Syndrome-free	3.182***	5.100***	3.209***	5.196***	2.150**	3.765
	0.882	1.231	0.877	1.076	0.882	1.355***
Partner growth	0.335***	–	0.234**	–	0.358**	–
	0.106	–	0.112	–	0.166	–
Dry year	−0.750**	−0.308	−0.784**	−0.431	−0.653	−0.283
	0.339	0.319	0.340	0.357	0.441	0.463
Coastal	–	–	0.164	−0.236	–	–
	–	–	0.471	0.344	–	–
Resrich	–	–	−0.067	−0.087	–	–
	–	–	0.578	0.487	–	–
N	1,183	1,313	1,183	1,313	917	965
Pseudo-R^2	0.016	0.050	0.018	0.053	0.045	0.090
Pseudo-R^2 from stage 1 probit	0.13	0.16	0.17	0.19	0.34	0.47

Notes: Reported coefficients are from Least Absolute Deviation (LAD) regressions. Bootstrapped standard errors appear below the coefficient estimates (*$p < 0.1$; **$p < 0.05$; ***$p < 0.01$). In panel B we obtain instrumental variables estimates by running a stage 1 probit equation for syndrome-free status on all exogenous variables and all three instruments (rule by fear*ethnic fractionalization, socialist government, and a 1961–89 "Cold War" dummy), and then estimating a LAD regression in stage 2 with syndrome-free replaced by the predicted probability from stage 1. To obtain consistent standard errors in panel B, we bootstrap the full two-stage process, except in column (12) where there were insufficient observations to do so. (Thus in column (12) we report the bootstrapped standard errors from the stage 2 regression. These were very close to the "fully bootstrapped" standard errors in the cases of columns (7)–(11).) All regressions that exclude partner growth include a full set of annual dummy variables (period fixed effects). The *dry year* variable is a dummy variable equaling 1 when rainfall is more than one country-specific standard deviation below its country-specific long-run mean.

The regressions control for rainfall shocks and opportunity categories. The syndromes in aggregate are always highly significant. Depending on which of the six specifications is chosen, the syndromes are found to have lowered the growth rate by between 1.9 and 2.2 percentage points, which is compatible with the inference of table 2.11 that the syndromes on average reduced growth by around 1.9 percentage points.

The results of table 2.12, panel A are potentially exposed to the critique that the syndromes are endogenous to economic performance. This could arise both because as researchers we may have inadvertently tended to categorize as syndromes those periods in which growth was low, or because periods of economic decline make a society more prone to various of the syndromes. We have tried to guard against the former, but the latter is undoubtedly a potential problem: for example, other research has established that periods of economic decline make African societies more prone to civil war (Miguel, Satyanath, and Sergenti 2004). We first test for endogeneity. This is not straightforward, since the regressions in table 2.12 are quantile regressions and so not directly amenable to endogeneity tests. To perform such tests we therefore take a standard least-squares approach. Using a Hausman test we cannot reject that syndrome-free status is exogenous. However, because we have some *a priori* reason to be concerned about endogeneity, we adopt the approach of using instruments for the syndromes. Our instruments are taken from chapter 11, where we indeed attempt to endogenize the syndromes. There we find that the syndromes collectively are made much more likely by the conjunction of ethnic fractionalization with an extreme form of dictatorship which we term "rule by fear." While this is more fully discussed in chapter 11, here we note that it is the combination of these features, rather than their direct effects, that produces the syndromes. Ethnic fractionalization is evidently likely to be exogenous to the syndromes. While the political system itself might be endogenous, there is less reason to be concerned that the political system will be endogenous only in the context of ethnic fractionalization, so that the combination is a reasonable instrument for the syndromes. Our second instrument is the end of the Cold War, which is clearly exogenous to any developments in African politics. Our third instrument is a dummy variable for whether the head of state was avowedly "socialist." As discussed by Ndulu in chapter 9, African heads of state tended to get their ideas from prevailing international intellectual fashions rather than from the experience of their own societies. To a considerable extent, whether leaders had "socialist" ideas did not derive from the recent economic performance of their own societies. Table 2.12, panel B reports the results of using these three variables as instruments for the syndromes. The results are qualitatively unchanged: the syndromes are growth-reducing. Quantitatively, the effect of being syndrome-free is now even larger, with the effect on the growth rate ranging between 2 and

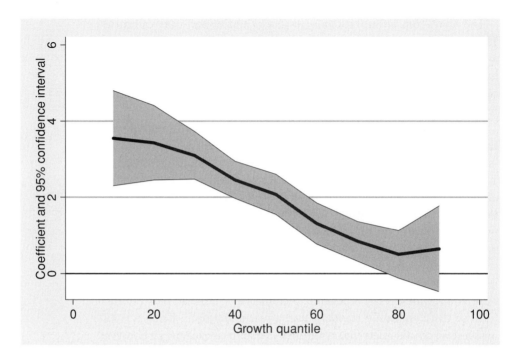

Figure 2.3 Estimated growth impact of avoiding syndromes.
Note: Estimated specification appears in column (1) of table 2.12, panel A.

5 percentage points. Each of these variables is thus a reasonable instrument for the syndromes, although the first and third can potentially be
questioned. Even when each of the three variables is used in turn as the sole
instrument the results remain significant: being syndrome-free substantially
augments growth.[4]

Given that the adverse effect of the syndromes appears to be robust we
next investigate in what contexts they were particularly damaging to the
growth process. For this we use quantile regressions, the results of which
are reported in figure 2.3, together with the bounds showing the 95 percent confidence interval. Coefficients are estimated for each decile, the fifth
decile corresponding precisely to the results reported in table 2.12, panel A.
The quantile regression shows that the syndromes have different effects at
different deciles of "fortune." For those countries with the very best fortune,
avoidance of syndromes makes only a modest difference. For those with the
worst fortune it makes an enormous difference. This implies that avoidance of the syndromes is a *sufficient condition* for avoiding growth collapses:

[4] For reasons of space we do not report these results, but they are available upon request.

Table 2.13 *Robust regressions, controlling for shocks, all syndromes.*
Dependent variable: growth in real GDP per capita.

Variable	Country fixed effects not included				Country fixed effects included	
	(1)	(2)	(3)	(4)	(5)	(6)
Regulatory	−0.972***	−0.900**	−0.944***	−0.902***	−1.626***	−1.627***
	0.327	0.377	0.227	0.349	0.347	0.448
Redistributive	−0.983***	−0.783*	−0.952**	−0.774**	−0.723	0.028
	0.262	0.403	0.415	0.354	0.735	0.474
Intertemporal	−0.450	−0.851	−0.597	−0.862	−0.048	−0.871
	0.604	0.708	0.531	0.532	0.837	0.575
Breakdown	−1.767***	−1.973***	−1.788**	−1.963***	−1.872*	−1.986***
	0.650	0.443	0.696	0.424	0.989	0.643
Partner growth	0.303***	–	0.309***	–	0.332***	–
	0.106		0.098		0.123	
Rainfall anomaly	−0.425*	−0.295	−0.379	−0.276	−0.466	−0.396
	0.231	0.231	0.366	0.200	0.314	0.325
Coastal	–	–	0.383	−0.033	–	–
			0.378	0.392		
Resrich	–	–	0.230	−0.036	–	–
			0.400	0.352		
N	1,492	1,770	1,492	1,770	1,492	1,770
Pseudo-R^2	0.025	0.047	0.026	0.047	0.062	0.091

Notes: See table 2.12.

if a country is syndrome-free even extreme ill fortune is not ruinous for the growth process. Being syndrome-free is not a necessary condition for rapid growth of real GDP: if the country is sufficiently fortunate it can grow rapidly on a temporary basis, almost regardless of its choices. Thus, Equatorial Guinea has discovered so much oil that its GDP is growing despite continued predation by a narrow political elite; in Sudan, oil-based growth is temporarily robust to state breakdown. But poor choices sharply deteriorate the lower tail of growth outcomes, reducing the probability that an episode of rapid growth will be sustained over the medium to long term. Figure 2.3 implies that being syndrome-free is a necessary condition for *sustaining* rapid growth across periods of good and bad fortune.

Hence, the intra-African evidence is consistent with that from the comparison of Africa with other regions, although the latter is currently predicated on the extreme assumption that the syndromes were unique to Africa.

In table 2.13 we deepen the analysis by investigating differences between the syndromes, using the same approach as in table 2.12. This reveals a large difference between the damage done by state breakdown and the other three

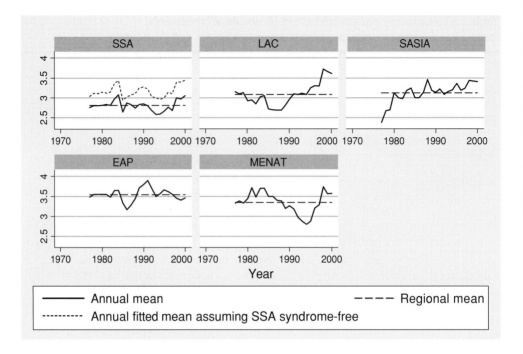

Figure 2.4 CPIA, by region, 1977–2000.
Note: ECA economies excluded to preserve scaling.

syndromes, although all four are adverse. Depending on which of the six specifications is adopted, state breakdown reduces growth by between 1.8 and 2 percentage points. This is consistent with the global estimate of the effects of civil war of 2.2 percentage points off the growth rate (Collier 1999). The other three syndromes each generate costs of around 1 percentage point off the growth rate.

So far, the only basis for the classification of syndromes has been our own subjective assessment, drawing on the accounts of the case studies. There are two ways of validating these classifications – objective evidence on policies and the subjective judgments of other informed observers. In chapter 3 we follow the former route, assessing the extent to which our judgments correspond to objective information. Here we follow the alternative route and investigate whether our assessments correspond to other subjective judgments. The source we use for this is the annual rating system of World Bank economists, the "Country Policy and Institutional Assessment" (CPIA). The advantage of this rating system is that it is undertaken globally to a common standard and the series goes back to 1977. Hence, it is possible to compare Africa with other developing regions. Figure 2.4 shows the CPIA by region. The dashed line shows the average CPIA score over the period. The bold line shows the evolution of the CPIA year-by-year. Evidently, the policy and

Table 2.14 *Syndromes and the CPIA, annual panel regressions.* Dependent variable: CPIA score.

Variable	OLS	FE
Constant	3.442***	3.251***
	0.078	0.081
Soft	−0.149***	−0.333***
	0.051	0.068
Hard	−0.556***	−0.694***
	0.068	0.08
Redistributive	−0.595***	−0.182***
	0.055	0.070
Intertemporal	0.119*	0.085
	0.066	0.074
Breakdown	−0.721***	−0.419***
	0.076	0.063
N	1,007	1,007
Adjusted R^2	0.290	0.113
RMSE	0.688	0.513
F	17.948	7.213
Prob>F	0.000	0.000

Note: All regressions include year effects. The FE regression also includes country effects. The panel is unbalanced because we use all available observations. The omitted category is syndrome-free.

institutional environment has on average been judged to be worse in Africa than those of other developing regions.

We first investigate whether within Africa our classification of some periods as syndromes corresponds to markedly worse CPIA ratings: that is, within Africa, does our judgment correspond to those of other informed observers. In table 2.14 we report annual panel regressions of the CPIA score on each syndrome. We control for year and for country fixed effects. Table 2.14 shows that each of the syndromes other than the intertemporal is significant in explaining the CPIA score. The intertemporal syndrome is, indeed, marginally significant *with the wrong sign*. Recall that the main intertemporal syndrome is unsustainable spending. We have already noted how pernicious this is from the perspective of whether the society correctly judges policy: during the upswing of this syndrome growth is rapid. While our disagreement with the CPIA may indicate that our judgment of these episodes is unduly adverse, it may instead indicate that during these misleading upswings the judgment of World Bank staff was systematically too favorable. From table 2.14 we can conclude that with the notable exception of these episodes of unsustainable spending, our intra-African distinctions are largely shared by other observers.

Recall that our initial working assumption above has been that other regions did not experience policy and institutional dysfunction as severely as Africa: although countries elsewhere obviously made policy errors, the syndromes were unique to Africa. This working assumption is obviously inaccurate: other regions had countries with some deeply dysfunctional policies and institutions. We are now in a position to determine the extent to which our assumption is inaccurate. We begin in table 2.15, which shows the average CPIA score for other regions, that for the years in Africa that were syndrome-free, and that for those that were subject to one or other of the syndromes. The CPIA is a 1–5 scoring system, with low scores indicating worse policies and weaker institutions. In practice, the range of the scores is very largely confined to 2–4, with 2 indicating extremely bad circumstances, and 4 relatively good circumstances.

Table 2.15 suggests that our working assumption is not as inaccurate as might have been supposed. Taking the means of the CPIA scores, there is no significant difference between the entire non-African group and the group of African syndrome-free country-years. By contrast, there is a large and significant difference between the African syndrome years on the one hand and both syndrome-free Africa and other regions, on the other. This is true both for the entire period for which we have data, 1977–2000, and for each sub-period individually, with the sole exception of 1985–92 when Africa's syndrome-free economies are rated above the economies of other regions, significant at 5 percent. Strikingly, for our final period 1993–2000, the CPIA scores for syndrome-free Africa (3.30) and for other developing regions (3.34) are virtually identical. This does not imply that the syndromes were unique to Africa: obviously they were not. However, it does suggest that the greater prevalence and intensity in Africa of the policy problems that these syndromes describe may approximate to the extent to which Africa's policy environment was distinctive.

In figures 2.4 and 2.5 we use the above results to infer the contribution, year-by-year, of the syndromes to the difference between Africa's CPIA score and that for other developing regions. In figure 2.4, the dotted line shows what the CPIA would have been for Africa in the absence of the syndromes, based on the regression of the first column of table 2.14. Derived from this, figure 2.5 shows the estimated shortfall in the CPIA for Africa, year-by-year, attributable to the syndromes.

Table 2.14 and figure 2.5 are merely statements about averages. By definition, none of the African syndrome-free years was subject to syndromes, whereas undoubtedly some of the non-African countries experienced syndromes. This is indicated by the larger standard deviations for the non-African group. While table 2.15 suggests that on average the difference

Table 2.15 *Overall CPIA score, by opportunity group, region, and syndrome status.*

Region or period	Sample statistics			Tests for difference in means (row mean − column mean)		chi² test for differences in variances (*p*-value)
	Mean	Std dev.	Freq.			
By opportunity group						
All non-industrial countries						
CO	3.129	0.798	1,449	CO	LL	
LL	2.860	0.769	479	LL −0.270***	−	
RR	2.956	0.905	620	RR −0.173***	0.096	
Total	3.036	0.827	2,548			0.000
SSA only						
CO	2.860	0.744	439	CO	LL	
LL	2.701	0.791	309	LL −0.159**	−	
RR	2.731	0.921	282	RR −0.129	0.03	
Total	2.777	0.812	1,030			0.000
By region and syndrome status						
All years 1977–2000						
SSA sfr	3.311	0.614	313	SSA sfr	SSA nfr	
SSA nfr	2.542	0.784	694	SSA nfr −0.770***	−	
Other	3.213	0.790	1,518	Other −0.099	0.670***	
Total	3.041	0.828	2,525			0.000
1977–84						
SSA sfr	3.363	0.615	43	SSA sfr	SSA nfr	
SSA nfr	2.715	0.729	260	SSA nfr −0.647***	−	
Other	3.264	0.833	424	Other −0.099	0.548***	
Total	3.073	0.829	727			0.007
1985–92						
SSA sfr	3.318	0.813	77	SSA sfr	SSA nfr	
SSA nfr	2.516	0.843	262	SSA nfr −0.802***	−	
Other	3.009	0.881	492	Other −0.309**	0.493***	
Total	2.882	0.902	831			0.541
1993–2000						
SSA sfr	3.297	0.518	193	SSA sfr	SSA nfr	
SSA nfr	2.320	0.709	172	SSA nfr −0.977***	−	
Other	3.343	0.634	602	Other 0.046	1.023***	
Total	3.152	0.737	967			0.000

*$p < 0.1$; **$p < 0.05$; ***$p < 0.01$.

Notes: SSA sfr and SSA nfr refer to syndrome-free, and not-syndrome-free, respectively. Other refers to all non-SSA observations. The test for differences in means is Bonferroni's test. The test for differences in variances is Bartlett's test.

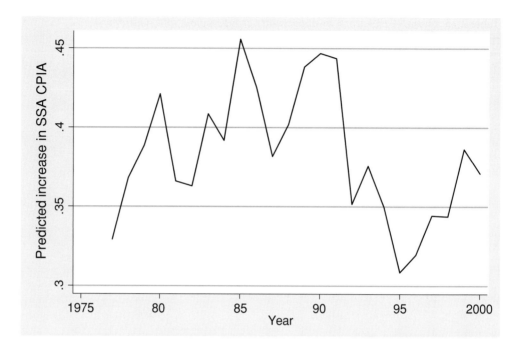

Figure 2.5 Effect on CPIA of avoiding syndromes, 1977–2000
Note: Based on regression in column (1) of table 2.14.

between Africa and other low-income developing regions is *equivalent* to other regions not having experienced syndromes, evidently other regions did experience syndromes. We now infer how the incidence of syndromes evolved in Africa relative to other regions. We do this by using the observed relationship between the CPIA and syndromes in Africa to predict the incidence in other regions, through probit analysis. The results by decade are shown in table 2.16.

Due to well-known limitations of probit models, the overall incidence is of less interest than the trend. What is striking is that the predicted incidence of syndromes in other developing regions more than halves between the late 1970s and the 1990s. By contrast, the predicted incidence of syndromes in Africa falls much less sharply, by around a third. Other regions most surely suffered from syndromes, but they appear to have escaped from them much more rapidly.

4.3 Syndromes and the foreclosing of opportunities

We have suggested that different countries of Africa have faced different opportunities: that successful growth strategies during the period we analyze

Table 2.16 *Predicted incidence of syndromes over time, by region.*

Period and region	Row proportion		Column proportion
1977–2000	*Not free*	*Free*	Total
Other	55.27	44.73	57.22
SSA	69.43	30.57	42.78
Total	61.33	38.67	100
1977–1979	*Not free*	*Free*	Total
Other	81.51	18.49	51.05
SSA	85.00	15.00	48.95
Total	83.22	16.78	100
1980–89	*Not free*	*Free*	Total
Other	82.65	17.35	55.32
SSA	84.26	15.74	44.68
Total	83.37	16.63	100
1990–2000	*Not free*	*Free*	Total
Other	30.25	69.75	60.08
SSA	52.00	48.00	39.92
Total	38.94	61.06	100

Notes: Predictions are from a probit regression of syndrome-free status on the CPIA score, for all SSA country-years with available CPIA values 1977–2000. The estimated coefficient on *cpia* is 1.025, with a standard error of 0.079 (significant at the 1% level). This implies that a one-unit increase in CPIA increases the probability of syndrome-free status by 31.5 percent. The probit equation includes a full set of year effects. The pseudo-R^2 is 0.3102 and the Wald chi^2 for overall fit is 256.80, with prob>chi^2 of 0.000.

would inevitably have differed across the region. The coastal, resource-scarce economies had the chance to follow the labor-intensive manufacturing route; the resource-rich economies needed to have effective public spending; while the landlocked, resource-scarce economies were dependent upon successful growth strategies in their neighbors. We now develop these hypotheses and subject them to some testing.

4.3.1   Coastal, resource-scarce economies

We start with the coastal, resource-scarce economies. Recall that this is indeed the biggest single factor in Africa's growth divergence with other regions. Further, the gap in performance between Africa and other regions in this opportunity category only really opens up from the 1980s and then rapidly becomes dramatically wide. This is at least consistent with the timing

Table 2.17 *Coastal, resource-scarce economies compared.*

	Developing countries				Low-income developing countries[a]			
	All		Excluding China and India		All		Excluding China and India	
Decade	(1)		(2)		(3)		(4)	
Number of countries								
	Other	*SSA*	*Other*	*SSA*	*Other*	*SSA*	*Other*	*SSA*
1960s	46.7	24.0	44.7	24.0	11.0	17.0	9.0	17.0
1970s	41.0	21.1	39.0	21.1	10.0	14.8	8.0	14.8
1980s	39.0	17.9	37.0	17.9	10.0	12.9	8.0	12.9
1990–2000	39.0	16.9	37.0	16.9	10.0	12.4	8.0	12.4
Total	41.2	19.8	39.2	19.8	10.2	14.1	8.2	14.1
Population-weighted growth differential (Other minus SSA)								
1960s	0.89		1.34		1.05		1.22	
1970s	1.86		1.87		1.72		0.52	
1980s	5.53		2.61		6.39		3.89	
1990–2000	4.46		1.75		4.98		1.96	
Total	3.28		1.90		3.63		1.92	

Notes: [a] Low-income economies are those whose average PPP-adjusted real GDP *per capita* between 1973 and 1977 was below $2,450 at 1996 international prices.

of Asia's breakthrough into labor-intensive manufactured and service exports. The first issue we investigate is whether the population-weighted divergence of Africa and other developing regions in this opportunity category is entirely driven by China and India. Of course, even if this is the case, the divergence is a real phenomenon. Nevertheless, it is important to establish whether the exceptional phenomenon is the take-off of these two populous countries relative to all other low-income coastal, resource-scarce countries, or whether the exceptional phenomenon is the divergence of Africa. Table 2.17 compares the performance of African and other coastal, resource-scarce economies, with various exclusions from the non-Africa group. The key part is column (4) of table 2.17, which compares Africa with other economies that were low-income in the mid-1970s but which excludes China and India. The growth differential is indeed lower than when China and India are included, but it is still substantial, and it is still much higher post-1980 than pre-1980. Pre-1980 the differential is only around 1.3 percentage points, whereas post-1980 it is around 3.0 percentage points. There is thus some basis for concluding that Africa's coastal, resource-scarce economies did indeed diverge massively from somewhat similar economies elsewhere after 1980.

Perhaps the most striking feature of economic development during our period is that, beginning in around 1980, developing countries have succeeded in breaking into the global market in manufactures, a change which became explosive. Between 1980 and 2000 the share of manufactures in developing countries' exports rose from 25 percent to 80 percent. Such explosive growth is consistent with the industrial agglomeration models of Krugman and Venables (Krugman and Venables 1995, 1996), with an initial agglomeration advantage for the rich countries being breached as the wage differential widened to a critical threshold. In these models, once industry begins to relocate, the initial agglomeration advantage declines and so growth in the "South" – or, at least, in that part of it where industry initially chooses to locate – explosively catches up the North. The role of the syndromes in closing off the opportunity to break into manufactured exports at the crucial time before Asia established economies of agglomeration is thus a contending explanation for why coastal Africa did not participate in this process. During the decade of the 1980s the coastal, resource-scarce economies of Africa were virtually all in the grip of one or other of the syndromes. Going through the countries in the coastal, resource-scarce category, Côte d'Ivoire and Senegal were handicapped by the combination of minimum wage laws and the franc zone, which prevented them inflating away from uncompetitive real wages. Mozambique and Ethiopia were war-torn. Sudan, as well as being periodically war-torn is, as Sachs would argue, scarcely a coastal economy, since the overwhelming bulk of its population and its cities are landlocked.[5] South Africa was entering a period of anticipated redistribution and consequent high uncertainty. The remaining economies in the category were Ghana, Kenya, Mauritius, Tanzania, and Togo. Of these, Ghana emerged from syndromes during the late 1980s and it is an important question to what extent by the end of our period it had succeeded in diversifying its exports. Tanzania emerged from syndromes a little later than Ghana and so the same question applies. Kenya was in the grip of regional redistribution for the entire post-1980 period, as was Togo, where this was compounded by the legacy of a mismanaged commodity boom. Only Mauritius was syndrome-free for the entire post-1980 period. It did indeed succeed in breaking into manufactured and service exports and became a middle-income economy.

[5] The same consideration applies to Ethiopia. Eritrea's independence in 1993, which left Ethiopia fully landlocked, was the culmination of thirty years of civil war between the coastal regions and the rest of Ethiopia. As noted earlier, we classify both Sudan and Ethiopia as landlocked in our empirical work.

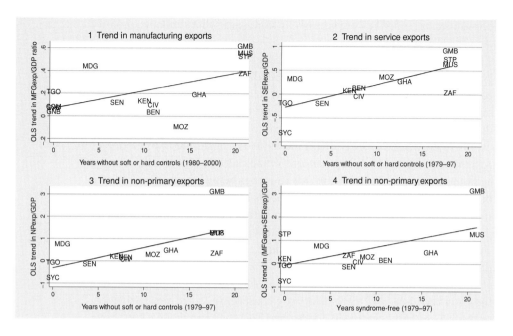

Figure 2.6 Syndromes and export diversification, coastal SSA, 1979–2000
Note: See table 2.18.

We next investigate whether there is a statistical relationship between the extent to which Africa's coastal, resource-scarce economies expanded their manufactured and service exports and the extent to which they avoided the syndromes. Specifically, we consider whether the number of years that an economy was free from syndromes post-1979 is significant in explaining the trend in the share of manufactured and service exports in GDP. When we aggregate all the syndromes many of the countries are concentrated around zero years syndrome-free. To remedy this loss of variation we also consider only the regulatory syndrome which is both the most common one for the coastal economies and also probably the most destructive for export opportunities. We consider manufacturing and service exports both separately and together. Figure 2.6 graphs the relationship and table 2.18 reports the regression results. The persistence of the regulatory syndrome in the coastal, resource-scarce economies is indeed significant in reducing the growth of manufacturing exports, service exports, and their combination. Despite the lack of variation, the persistence of the totality of syndromes is also significant except for manufactured exports. Not only are the results statistically significant, they are large. Because our dependent variable is the trend in exports, an implication is that the effect of removing the syndromes

Table 2.18 *African coastal economies, syndrome status and export diversification, 1980–2000.*

Variable	Dependent variable: estimated linear trend, 1980–2000, in:					
	Manufactured exports/GDP		Commercial service exports/GDP		Non-primary exports/GDP	
Constant	0.147*	0.025	−0.091	−0.275	−0.067	−0.312
	0.069	0.068	0.215	0.193	0.33	0.299
Years syndrome-free	0.012	–	0.034*	–	0.078*	–
	0.007		0.016		0.04	
Years control-free	–	0.015***	–	0.048**	–	0.091**
		0.005		0.016		0.037
N	15	15	13	13	13	13
Adjusted R^2	0.046	0.236	0.237	0.508	0.276	0.379
RMSE	0.216	0.193	0.396	0.318	0.814	0.754
F	1.666	6.822	4.831	8.114	3.429	5.96

*$p < 0.1$; **$p < 0.05$; ***$p < 0.01$.

Note: Estimation is by OLS. Robust standard errors are below the coefficient estimates.

is gradual and cumulative. By the end of two decades, the difference between a country such as Mauritius, which was free of the syndrome for the entire period, and a country such as Togo which maintained the syndrome for twenty-one of the twenty-four years covered in table 2.18, is predicted to be $20 \ years * (21 \cdot 0.078) = 32.8$ percent of GDP (for manufacturing $+$ service exports). However, an out-of-sample extrapolation would imply that this is a widening difference: Mauritius is on an export growth path, whereas Togo is not.

4.3.2 Resource-rich economies

Turning to the second of our questions, recall that in the 1960s there were virtually no resource-rich economies in Africa. However, post-1970, when such economies started to become more common, only a small minority have been syndrome-free. Indeed, even during the 1990s of the 30 percent of Africa's population living in resource-rich economies, all but 4 percent were living with one or other of the syndromes. The most frequent syndromes in the resource-rich economies were redistributive and intertemporal. Indeed, the two syndromes often coexisted: for example, the government would borrow internationally in order to magnify its transfers to its favored group.

Although almost all of Africa's resource-rich economies failed to harness their potential for growth, Botswana stands out as an extraordinary exception analogous to Mauritius among the coastal economies. Botswana maintained standards of governance that enabled it to use its resource wealth to attain middle-income status, growing exceptionally fast even by global standards. Evidently, globally resource wealth posed problems for governance, but with the exception of Botswana the other African resource-rich countries did significantly worse than the global average. Why might this have happened?

Resource wealth poses in its starkest form the choice between public goods and transfers. A result already well established in the literature is that when small, clearly defined groups hold power they have an incentive to prioritize transfers over the public good of growth (Adam and O'Connell 1999). Ethnicity is obviously the most potent such social cleavage. Hence theory would predict that ethnic diversity makes autocracy particularly damaging: the power base for the autocracy being a single ethnic group, there is a strong incentive for redistribution over growth. This prediction is consistent with the global econometric evidence. Although there is usually no clear relationship between democracy and growth, once ethnic diversity is introduced as an interaction with democracy, there is a clear and substantial effect: democracy promotes growth in the context of ethnic diversity (Collier 2000; Alesina and La Ferrara 2004). Further, globally, resource rents significantly increase the probability of autocracy (Collier and Hoeffler 2005).

African societies are distinctively different from those of other regions in two respects that are pertinent for these global relationships. First, as is well known, they are characterized by atypically high ethnic diversity. Secondly, during our period, they have been atypically prone to autocracy. The implication of these characteristics and the above global relationships is that we would indeed expect Africa's resource-rich economies to have differentially worse performance than other regions. On this explanation, Africa's resource-rich countries under-performed those of other regions because they were more likely to be characterized by the toxic combination of ethnic diversity and autocracy. This is borne out in table 2.19, which measures the political regime and ethnic diversity by opportunity group and decade for both Africa and for other regions. We present the results both unweighted and with population weights: the former are more pertinent as a description of the typical country, and the latter for growth outcomes. Our key interest is the conjunction of high ethnic diversity with low democracy. Using standard scoring systems we first consider the average of this ratio over the entire forty years. The result is striking: among the six categories generated by the three opportunity groups and the distinction between Africa and other regions, Africa's resource-rich countries come top. On the unweighted data the difference is dramatic: for Africa's resource-rich countries the ratio is more than double that of other regions, though for the weighted data the difference is narrower. Turning to the decade-by-decade data, we see that the 1960s are

Table 2.19 *Democracy and ethnic fractionalization, by opportunity category and decade.*

Variable, region, and decade	Unweighted			Population-weighted		
	CO	LL	RR	CO	LL	RR
Polity 4 democracy score						
SSA 1960s	2.11	1.35	1.57	2.84	1.77	2.55
1970s	1.53	0.68	0.98	1.39	0.77	0.91
1980s	1.47	0.60	0.88	1.44	1.22	2.35
1990–2000	3.23	1.97	2.16	3.44	1.65	1.10
Total	*2.07*	*1.15*	*1.41*	*2.26*	*1.36*	*1.54*
Other 1960s	3.22	0.10	2.50	3.36	0.08	1.16
1970s	2.88	0.00	1.99	3.18	0.00	0.72
1980s	3.68	0.42	2.76	3.37	1.36	1.13
1990–2000	5.71	4.02	3.69	4.43	5.64	2.24
Total	*3.89*	*1.20*	*2.85*	*3.60*	*1.76*	*1.38*
Ethnic fractionalization index[a]						
SSA 1960s	68.06	57.00	68.80	77.43	64.69	74.57
1970s	67.12	57.45	68.40	73.73	64.85	84.06
1980s	64.62	57.50	71.20	72.31	64.85	84.38
1990–2000	64.39	58.08	71.20	72.96	65.81	84.38
Total	*66.21*	*57.52*	*70.20*	*74.54*	*65.12*	*83.88*
Other 1960s	32.64	50.67	37.29	62.18	61.49	46.17
1970s	31.74	46.33	40.59	61.40	59.57	59.89
1980s	29.58	42.00	45.15	61.55	59.57	59.31
1990–2000	29.58	42.00	45.15	61.55	59.57	59.31
Total	*30.93*	*45.79*	*42.85*	*61.68*	*60.14*	*58.09*
Ratio: ethnic fractionalization/(1 + democracy score)						
SSA 1960s	50.67	51.44	46.54	49.29	51.54	35.15
1970s	51.78	51.48	59.48	58.91	58.77	74.70
1980s	45.56	49.00	63.62	55.83	50.43	61.78
1990–2000	33.83	40.81	43.75	38.62	46.04	64.55
Total	*46.20*	*47.83*	*54.19*	*51.37*	*51.13*	*65.22*
Other 1960s	16.12	46.13	23.93	18.81	58.40	44.45
1970s	17.92	46.33	28.72	14.70	59.57	57.33
1980s	13.92	20.48	27.44	13.88	25.20	52.82
1990–2000	7.04	6.61	19.72	8.39	9.45	43.07
Total	*13.68*	*31.78*	*24.74*	*13.95*	*38.86*	*50.01*

Notes: The table uses all countries with at least thirty years of data on the democracy index between 1960 and 2000.

[a]The fractionalization index applies to the early 1960s and is time-invariant. Averages change over time as the country composition varies by opportunity category.

anomalous. During 1970–2000 Africa's resource-rich countries were consistently far more characterized by the cocktail of high ethnic diversity and low democracy than both the other African opportunity groups and the resource-rich countries of other regions. Finally, looking to the underlying ethnic diversity and democracy scores, we see that this was generally driven both by higher diversity and by lower democracy. By the 1990s, although globally the resource-rich countries were lagging behind in terms of democratization, outside Africa such countries were substantially more democratic than their African counterparts.

As we argue in chapter 5 on intertemporal syndromes, there may be a further catch: democracy is prone to malfunction in the context of resource wealth. Empirically, the global relationship between resource wealth, democracy, and growth is adverse: when resource rents are substantial democracy significantly reduces growth (Collier and Hoeffler 2005). One explanation for this result is that resource rents tend to subvert democracy by providing the finance that makes patronage politics the dominating electoral strategy. Collier and Hoeffler (2005) show that empirically the problem of democracy in the context of resource rents comes only from electoral competition; checks and balances, the other feature of democracy, are differentially beneficial to growth in the context of resource rents. Presumably, sufficient checks and balances make patronage politics infeasible even in the context of resource wealth. Hence, it is not democracy *per se*, but rather the type of democracy that matters: resource-rich societies need a form of democracy characterized by checks and balances rather than by intense electoral competition. This happens to describe Botswana. Electoral competition is rather limited: despite continuous democracy there has never been a change of government. Yet, perhaps because democracy has been continuous, the non-electoral checks and balances that work through due process have never been undermined. Nigeria under Shagari, although also a democracy, was clearly at the other end of the spectrum: a brief period of electoral competition in a context in which due process had already collapsed under previous military regimes. The Shagari regime presided over the single most important missed opportunity for growth that resource-rich Africa has had during our period.

4.3.3   Landlocked, resource-scarce economies

Finally, we turn to the landlocked, resource-scarce economies. Our hypothesis here is that globally the performance of such economies should be dependent upon whether more fortunately endowed neighbors are growing. This is because the most obvious growth strategy for such a country is to service the markets of its neighbors. In table 2.20 we test this hypothesis both for other regions and for Africa in a growth regression. To check robustness we use three approaches, OLS, IV, and LAD (the LAD

Table 2.20 *Neighbor effects on growth: 1.*
Dependent variable: growth of real GDP per capita.

Variable	OLS regressions			IV regressions[a]		
	(1)	(2)	(3)	(4)	(5)	(6)
Landlocked (LL)	−1.003***	−1.003***	−1.633***	−1.118***	−1.136***	−1.942**
	0.291	0.291	0.526	0.298	0.299	0.794
Resource-rich (RR)	−0.819***	−0.821***	−0.746**	−0.649**	−0.643**	−0.533
	0.306	0.306	0.341	0.318	0.319	0.423
Island	1.852***	1.852***	1.777***	2.378***	2.413***	2.252***
	0.253	0.253	0.267	0.309	0.311	0.341
Neighbor growth	0.428***	0.428***	0.392***	0.719***	0.742***	0.659***
	0.046	0.046	0.06	0.11	0.113	0.14
CO*SSA	−0.967***	−0.957***	−1.027***	−0.382	−0.4	−0.549
	0.299	0.304	0.319	0.362	0.425	0.453
LL*SSA	0.002	−0.017	0.546	0.68	0.727	1.381*
	0.426	0.427	0.571	0.505	0.514	0.822
RR*SSA	0.361	0.317	0.178	0.69	0.985	0.728
	0.57	0.57	0.573	0.597	0.645	0.654
Island*SSA	−0.765	−0.774	−0.699	−1.394**	−1.373*	−1.218*
	0.638	0.641	0.646	0.664	0.703	0.714
Neighbor growth*LL	–	–	0.318**	–	–	0.418
	–	–	0.157	–	–	0.309
Neighbor growth*RR	–	–	−0.083	–	–	−0.135
	–	–	0.09	–	–	0.211
Nbr growth*CO*SSA	–	−0.313***	−0.278***	–	−0.529*	−0.463
	–	0.085	0.093	–	0.312	0.317
Nbr growth*LL*SSA	–	−0.181**	−0.462***	–	−0.579	−0.925*
	–	0.091	0.165	–	0.434	0.51
Nbr growth*RR*SSA	–	−0.391***	−0.270**	–	−0.097	0.117
	–	0.128	0.137	–	0.282	0.313
Nbr growth*SSA	−0.304***	–	–	−0.584***	–	–
	0.072	–	–	0.119	–	–
Dry year	−0.302	−0.304	−0.322	−0.305	−0.236	−0.268
	0.212	0.212	0.211	0.216	0.233	0.233
N	5620	5620	5620	5399	5399	5399
Adjusted R^2	0.097	0.098	0.101	0.084	0.07	0.078
RMSE	6.263	6.262	6.249	6.338	6.389	6.361
F	9.800	9.494	9.234	9.22	8.849	8.731

*$p < 0.1$; **$p < 0.05$; ***$p < 0.01$.
Notes: All regressions include a full set of year effects.
[a] Instruments for variables involving neighbor growth are the first and second lags of
all such variables.

regressions are in appendix table 2.A3). Globally, the growth of neighbors matters, which is unsurprising. Further, globally the landlocked, resource-scarce economies indeed are more dependent than other economies on the growth of their neighbors: from the OLS results, whereas the typical growth spillover of an additional 1 percentage point on the growth rate of neighbors is 0.4 percentage points, for the landlocked, resource-scarce it is 0.7 percentage points. However, all African economies depart from this global pattern: neighborhood growth spillovers are much weaker, and indeed for Africa's landlocked, resource-scarce countries there are no significant neighborhood growth spillovers.

The most likely explanation for this striking result is that Africa's internal barriers to trade are much higher than those of other regions. This is consistent with evidence on both the actual practice of trade policies and the very high level of transport costs. The differential lack of a growth spillover effect for Africa's landlocked economies, contrasted with the differentially large effect for such economies elsewhere, suggests that such barriers may be atypically high even by African standards. This is plausible: being landlocked not only raises costs of transport to global markets but also raises them to other African markets.

Paradoxically, to date this isolation of Africa's landlocked, resource-scarce economies from their neighborhoods has not mattered very much for their growth. Although as a group these countries have grown more slowly than their more fortunately endowed neighbors, the gap has been much narrower than that in other regions. The lack of integration of Africa's landlocked economies matters more for the future when its more fortunate countries indeed succeed in harnessing their opportunities. Then, in an ideal world, the landlocked, resource-scarce would be carried along by the growth of their neighbors, as in other regions. In Africa, on past levels of integration, even when the countries with better opportunities succeed in harnessing them, there is going to be no such spillover effect. The most credible growth prospect for the poorest countries of Africa is currently closed off by the region's internal barriers.

5   A preliminary conclusion

Misunderstanding the past makes it harder to change the future. What have we learned from this chapter that might be helpful for the shaping of African development strategies?

5.1   Understanding the past

Changing Africa's future from the trends of 1960–2000 is evidently of global concern: the region was stagnant during a period of unprecedented global growth. It is currently fashionable to come up with single explanations for this massive failure of the growth process: the region is irretrievably aid-dependent (Lal 1999); it has uniquely unfavorable geography (Gallup and Sachs 1997; Sachs *et al.* 2004); it has inherited dysfunctional institutions (Acemoglu, Johnson, and Robinson 2001). We have argued that such explanations ignore important variation: geographic opportunities differed across Africa, and choices also differed. While introducing variation we have been parsimonious: Africa's forty-eight countries and forty years of behavior – 1,920 observations – have been collapsed into three opportunity groups and a choice between being syndrome-free and four syndromes.

Our foremost objective has, of course, been to provide an account of the past failure of the growth process. The annual growth shortfall to be explained is 3.5 percentage points. Of this, we attribute around 1 percentage point to Africa's inherently inferior growth opportunities: its population is heavily skewed away from the fast-growth opportunity of being resource-scarce and coastal. We attribute nearly 2 percentage points to the damage done by one or other of the four policy syndromes: regulatory, intertemporal, redistributive, and state breakdown. The shortfall in Africa's policies and institutions relative to other regions was closely equivalent to the effect of these syndromes.

Our account of the failure of the growth process is thus in essence as follows. Globally, there have been two autonomous paths to middle-income status. Resource-rich economies can succeed, but since such economies will necessarily have a large state, the critical governance issue is how the state spends money. Coastal, resource-scarce economies can also succeed, but since their success depends upon keeping costs at globally competitive levels, the critical governance issue is that the state should not be predatory upon the export sector. The landlocked, resource-scarce economies lack an autonomous path to middle-income status, unless their more fortunate neighbors harness their growth opportunities. Conditional upon this, such economies succeed by integrating within their region, servicing their fast-growing neighbors.

In Africa, the relative balance of autonomous growth opportunities was distinctive because the two paths were equally important whereas globally the labor-intensive exports path was far more important. Africa's socio-political structure was unusually ill suited to this importance of resource wealth. Globally, the cocktail of resource-wealth, ethnic diversity, and autocracy has usually been toxic for growth. This manifested itself as a high incidence of the redistributive and intertemporal syndromes in these economies. The resource-scarce coastal economies were disproportionately prone to the regulatory syndrome. During the critical decade of the 1980s, when these countries could potentially have matched Asia in breaking in to new global markets, only Mauritius was syndrome-free. Since the 1980s it has become much harder to follow this growth path because of the agglomeration economies now built up by China and India. Nevertheless, those African coastal economies that have escaped from syndromes have started to succeed in new export markets. Africa's landlocked, resource-scarce economies have faced a triple bind. Their more fortunate neighbors had usually foreclosed their growth opportunities through one or other of the syndromes. Over and above this, the landlocked countries faced transport and policy barriers to regional integration that made it difficult to latch onto neighboring success in the rare cases where it occurred. Perhaps the prevailing stagnation reduced the political incentive for integration. Finally, the landlocked economies were disproportionately prone to the syndromes. Again, this might have been because, lacking a viable growth strategy, there was less incentive to avoid them.

Because of the radically greater importance of countries with resource wealth and countries that lacked such wealth and were landlocked, Africa's needed priorities were distinctive. The region needed to make the "big state" work effectively, and it needed regional integration. Whether external policy pressure has had much effect is beyond our scope, but we note that these two issues have not been its priorities. External priorities towards the state have been to reduce its size, and towards trade they have been external liberalization. These priorities were probably appropriate predominantly for the minority of economies that were coastal and resource-scarce.

5.2   Facing the future

We close by speculating about Africa's future growth. Clearly, on our thesis, the syndromes have been the proximate impediments to African growth. Hence, the first priority is to avoid them. This may be extremely difficult because some of them may develop a trap-like persistence. Options for avoidance are discussed in the chapters devoted to each specific syndrome. Here our main concern is the implications of an environment beyond the syndromes. The key issue is whether, by avoiding the syndromes, Africa can replicate the success of other regions. Again we start from the two autonomous growth strategies.

Were the resource-rich countries to avoid the syndromes there seems no reason why they could not grow. Botswana is the practical demonstration of this possibility. However, it may be extremely difficult for the rest of resource-rich Africa to follow this path. We have argued that in the African context autocracies are likely to handle resource wealth very badly, but that democracies face equivalent problems from patronage politics unless they are able to construct effective checks and balances through due process. Such checks and balances are not an automatic concomitant of electoral competition, and democratic patronage politics has no incentive to construct them. Worse, the corruption that is at the center of the problems of these societies may be highly persistent (Tirole 1996). Thus, the legacy of the syndromes might be the trap of corruption.

Were the coastal, resource-scarce economies now to escape the syndromes it is much more of an open question whether they would match the growth of other regions. During the 1990s even those economies that avoided the syndromes grew markedly less rapidly than other regions. There are three broad explanations for this shortfall. One is simply that there are inevitable lags between reform and private investment. On our evidence, after a decade of being syndrome-free such economies can expect to be raising their share of manufactured and service exports in GDP at around 0.2 percentage points a year, and after two decades at around 0.4 percentage points a year: *success is accelerating*. A second explanation is more disturbing: coastal Africa has missed the boat. Whereas in the 1980s Africa could have broken into global markets, now that Asia is established Africa has no comparative advantage in labor costs to offset its disadvantage in the lack of agglomeration. If this is right, coastal Africa must look elsewhere for growth, perhaps by emulating Latin America in adding value to its resource-based exports. On the third explanation the avoidance of syndromes is necessary but insufficient for success in new exports. Success requires some positive actions by the state, such as the provision of infrastructure or education. In our view there is currently insufficient evidence decisively to reject any of these three explanations with radically different implications.

On the basis of our analysis of the past, the landlocked, resource-scarce economies have little prospect of a growth path to middle-income status until their more fortunate neighbors succeed. Even then, they are dependent upon infrastructure and trade policies that integrate their economies with their neighbors, and this evidently requires the cooperation of their neighbors. This may be overly pessimistic. The growth opportunities for landlocked, resource-scarce economies may be transformed through two new opportunities. First, there is a whole new class of service exports that are not significantly handicapped by being landlocked. Secondly, many landlocked countries have untapped natural-resource wealth and can transform themselves into resource-rich economies.

Thus, while the analysis of the past offers some guidance, it leaves major uncertainties. A safety-first strategy would evidently allow for these. Given the uncertainty attaching to autonomous processes of governance reform in the resource-rich countries, and the importance of such reform for the landlocked, resource-scarce economies, the latter have good reason to attempt to reinforce internal processes of reform with neighborhood pressure through the African Union. Given the uncertainty attaching to the prospect of coastal economies breaking into export markets, governments would be wise to adopt a maximal strategy: taking positive actions beyond avoiding the syndromes. Given the uncertainty of other options, the landlocked, resource-scarce economies would be wise to encourage resource prospecting, and to invest in the facilities necessary for the new service exports.

Achieving growth in Africa is thus unlikely to be an easy matter for its societies. For different reasons, Botswana and Mauritius are deceptive models for growth. Africa's resource-rich economies will find it extremely difficult to construct the checks and balances that have enabled Botswana to grow. Africa's coastal economies will find the global market much more difficult to penetrate than did Mauritius which broke in before low-income Asia was established and additionally benefited from substantial protection from Asian competition. The third of Africa's population that is in landlocked, resource-scarce economies with consequently reduced opportunities has no parallel in other regions. However, actions at the country, regional, and international level would each be improved by recognizing the distinctiveness of the opportunities and problems that Africa faces.

Appendix

Table 2.A1 *Global sample for growth of real GDP per capita.*

Country	In39	In35	Population, 1990 (million)	Average growth, 1960–2000 or available years	First year resource-rich
SSA: Coastal					
Benin	1	1	4.71	0.63	.
Cape Verde	1	1	0.34	3.43	.
Comoros	1	1	0.43	−0.18	.
Côte d'Ivoire	1	1	11.80	0.57	.
Gambia, The	1	1	0.93	0.92	.
Ghana	1	1	15.14	−0.21	.
Guinea-Bissau	1	1	0.95	−0.58	.
Kenya	1	1	23.35	1.23	.
Madagascar	1	1	11.63	−1.11	.
Mauritius	1	1	1.06	3.70	.
Mozambique	1	1	14.15	−0.38	.
Senegal	1	1	7.33	−0.24	.
Seychelles	1	1	0.07	2.35	.
South Africa	1	1	35.20	0.88	.
Tanzania	1	1	25.47	1.83	.
Togo	1	1	3.45	0.86	.
Djibouti	0	0	0.47	−4.80	.
Eritrea	0	0	3.14	2.48	.
São Tomé and Principe	0	0	0.12	−1.06	.
Somalia	0	0	7.16	.	.

Table 2.A1 (cont.)

Country	In39	In35	Population, 1990 (million)	Average growth, 1960–2000 or available years	First year resource-rich
SSA: Landlocked					
Burkina Faso	1	1	8.88	1.25	.
Burundi	1	1	5.46	0.20	.
CAR	1	1	2.94	−0.75	.
Chad	1	1	5.75	−0.72	.
DRC	1	1	37.00	−3.35	.
Ethiopia[a]	1	1	51.18	0.41	.
Lesotho	1	1	1.68	3.57	.
Malawi	1	1	8.51	1.36	.
Mali	1	1	8.46	−0.27	.
Niger	1	1	7.71	−1.65	.
Rwanda	1	1	6.94	−0.33	.
Sudan[a]	1	1	24.82	0.75	.
Uganda	1	1	16.33	1.40	.
Zimbabwe	1	1	10.24	0.71	.
SSA: Resource-rich					
Angola	1	1	9.57	−1.23	1974
Botswana	1	1	1.28	6.33	1970
Cameroon	1	1	11.61	0.66	1979
Congo, Rep.	1	1	2.23	1.33	1974
Equatorial Guinea	1	1	0.35	2.21	1996
Gabon	1	1	0.94	2.21	1960
Guinea	1	1	5.76	0.02	1974
Liberia	1	1	2.43	−3.49	1960
Mauritania	1	1	1.99	1.30	1960
Namibia	1	1	1.38	0.62	1979
Nigeria	1	1	96.20	0.32	1971
Sierra Leone	1	1	4.00	−1.36	1960
Zambia	1	1	7.78	−1.25	1960
Swaziland	0	0	0.77	2.03	1960
LAC: Coastal					
Argentina	1	1	32.53	0.95	.
Bahamas, The	1	1	0.26	1.33	.
Barbados	1	1	0.26	2.67	.
Belize	1	1	0.19	2.91	.
Brazil	1	1	147.96	2.44	.
Colombia	1	1	34.97	1.82	.
Costa Rica	1	1	3.05	1.76	.
Dominican Republic	1	1	7.06	2.75	.

(cont.)

Table 2.A1 *(cont.)*

Country	In39	In35	Population, 1990 (million)	Average growth, 1960–2000 or available years	First year resource-rich
El Salvador	1	1	5.11	0.74	.
Guatemala	1	1	8.75	1.30	.
Haiti	1	1	6.47	−0.99	.
Honduras	1	1	4.87	0.82	.
Jamaica	1	1	2.39	0.54	.
Mexico	1	1	83.23	2.11	.
Nicaragua	1	1	3.82	−0.87	.
Panama	1	1	2.40	2.02	.
Peru	1	1	21.57	0.56	.
Puerto Rico	1	1	3.54	3.62	.
St Vincent & Grenadines	1	1	0.11	4.79	.
Uruguay	1	1	3.11	1.14	.
Antigua and Barbuda	0	0	0.06	4.40	.
Bermuda	0	0	.	.	.
Cuba	0	0	10.63	−2.45	.
Dominica	0	0	0.07	3.17	.
Grenada	0	0	0.09	4.00	.
St. Kitts and Nevis	0	0	0.04	5.08	.
St. Lucia	0	0	0.13	3.22	.
LAC: Landlocked					
Paraguay	1	1	4.15	1.62	.
LAC: Resource-rich					
Bolivia	1	1	6.57	0.35	1970
Chile	1	1	13.10	2.48	1970
Ecuador	1	1	10.26	1.52	1974
SASIA: Coastal					
Guyana	1	1	0.73	0.81	1960
Trinidad and Tobago	1	1	1.22	2.59	1960
Venezuela, RB	1	1	19.50	−0.30	1960
Suriname	0	0	0.40	0.60	1960
Bangladesh	1	1	110.03	1.36	.
India	1	1	849.52	2.30	.
Pakistan	1	1	107.98	2.62	.
Sri Lanka	1	1	16.27	2.88	.
SASIA: Landlocked					
Nepal	1	1	18.14	1.38	.
Bhutan	0	0	0.60	4.16	.

Table 2.A1 (cont.)

Country	In39	In35	Population, 1990 (million)	Average growth, 1960–2000 or available years	First year resource-rich
SASIA: Resource-rich					
<no cases>					
EAP: Coastal					
China	1	1	1135.19	5.42	.
Fiji	1	1	0.74	1.66	.
Hong Kong, China	1	1	5.70	5.26	.
Korea, Rep.	1	1	42.87	5.75	.
Philippines	1	1	61.04	1.16	.
Singapore	1	1	3.05	5.92	.
Taiwan, China	1	1	20.23	6.37	.
Thailand	1	1	55.60	4.51	.
Cambodia	0	0	9.15	2.33	.
Macao, China	0	0	0.37	2.18	.
Vietnam	0	0	66.20	4.33	.
EAP: Landlocked					
Lao PDR	0	0	4.13	2.88	.
Mongolia	0	0	2.11	0.52	.
EAP: Resource-rich					
Indonesia	1	1	178.23	3.51	1970
Malaysia	1	1	18.20	3.98	1976
Papua New Guinea	1	1	3.98	1.30	1972
MENAT: Coastal					
Cyprus	1	1	0.68	4.40	.
Egypt, Arab Rep.	1	1	52.44	3.05	.
Israel	1	1	4.66	2.94	.
Jordan	1	1	3.17	1.15	.
Malta	1	1	0.36	5.42	.
Morocco	1	1	24.04	1.69	.
Turkey	1	1	56.15	2.29	.
Lebanon	0	0	3.63	1.34	.
MENAT: Landlocked					
<no cases>					
MENAT: Resource-rich					
Algeria	1	1	25.02	0.86	1960
Iran, Islamic Rep.	1	1	54.40	1.50	1960
Oman	1	1	1.63	5.35	1967
Saudi Arabia	1	1	15.80	1.46	1960
Syrian Arab Republic	1	1	12.12	2.28	1974

(cont.)

Table 2.A1 *(cont.)*

Country	In39	In35	Population, 1990 (million)	Average growth, 1960–2000 or available years	First year resource-rich
Tunisia	1	1	8.15	3.02	1974
Kuwait	0	1	2.13	−3.70	1960
Bahrain	0	0	0.50	0.14	1960
Iraq	0	0	18.08	.	1960
Qatar	0	0	0.49	.	1960
United Arab Emirates (UAE)	0	0	1.84	−3.90	1973
Yemen, Rep.	0	0	11.88	1.51	1990
EEFSU: Coastal					
Romania	1	1	23.21	1.94	.
Georgia	0	1	5.46	−0.80	.
Latvia	0	1	2.67	1.82	.
Russian Federation	0	1	148.29	1.54	.
Bulgaria	0	0	8.72	0.73	.
Croatia	0	0	4.77	−0.55	.
Estonia	0	0	1.57	0.49	.
Lithuania	0	0	3.70	−3.28	.
Poland	0	0	38.12	2.65	.
Slovenia	0	0	2.00	1.88	.
Ukraine	0	0	51.89	−6.17	.
Yugoslavia, Fed. Rep.	0	0	10.53	.	.
EEFSU: Landlocked					
Hungary	1	1	10.36	3.17	.
Armenia	0	0	3.55	−4.58	.
Belarus	0	0	10.19	−1.02	.
Czech Rep.	0	0	10.36	0.21	.
Kyrgyz Rep.	0	0	4.42	−2.53	.
Macedonia, FYR	0	0	1.90	−0.78	.
Moldova	0	0	4.36	−4.22	.
Slovak Rep.	0	0	5.28	0.58	.
Tajikistan	0	0	5.30	−7.92	.
EEFSU: Resource-rich					
Albania	0	0	3.28	0.37	1984
Azerbaijan	0	0	7.16	−4.41	1992
Kazakhstan	0	0	16.35	−3.06	1990
Turkmenistan	0	0	3.67	−4.97	1993
Uzbekistan	0	0	20.51	−1.16	1991
INDUST: Coastal					
Australia	1	1	17.07	2.13	.
Belgium	1	1	9.97	2.75	.

Table 2.A1 *(cont.)*

Country	In39	In35	Population, 1990 (million)	Average growth, 1960–2000 or available years	First year resource-rich
Canada	1	1	27.79	2.31	.
Cyprus	1	1	0.68	4.40	.
Denmark	1	1	5.14	2.15	.
Finland	1	1	4.99	2.97	.
France	1	1	56.74	2.61	.
Greece	1	1	10.16	3.11	.
Iceland	1	1	0.25	2.83	.
Ireland	1	1	3.51	4.10	.
Italy	1	1	56.72	2.88	.
Japan	1	1	123.54	4.18	.
Netherlands	1	1	14.95	2.41	.
New Zealand	1	1	3.44	1.28	.
Norway	1	1	4.24	3.04	.
Portugal	1	1	9.90	3.90	.
Spain	1	1	38.84	3.34	.
Sweden	1	1	8.56	2.17	.
United Kingdom	1	1	57.56	2.12	.
United States	1	1	249.44	2.21	.
Germany	0	0	79.43	1.99	.
INDUST: Landlocked					
Austria	1	1	7.73	2.85	.
Luxembourg	1	1	0.38	3.20	.
Switzerland	1	1	6.71	1.44	.

INDUST: Resource-rich

<no cases>

Notes:

[a] Ethiopia became landlocked in 1994 with the independence of Eritrea. Sudan is classified as landlocked for reasons discussed in the text. See also the appendix to Ali and Elbadawi's chapter 7 on Sudan in volume 2. Growth rates are calculated for available years. *In39* means at least 39 of 40 annual growth observations 1961–2000 available. *In35* means at least 35 of 40 annual growth observations 1961–2000 available. Most of our empirical work excludes the industrial countries and also excludes any country without at least 39 observations.

Table 2.A2 *Syndrome classification (downloadable).*

Country (**bold** = case study)/ chapter in vol. 2 (in parentheses)	Regulatory syndromes		Redistributive syndromes		Intertemporal syndromes		State breakdown	Syndrome-free
	Soft controls	Hard controls	Regional	Looting	Unsustainable spending	Anticipated redistribution		
Angola	1991–2005	1975–90	1975–2005	1990–2005	1994–2005	1972–5	1975–2002	1960–71
Benin (22)	1960–74, 2004–5	1975–89	–	–	–	–	–	1990–2003
Botswana (15)	–	–	–	–	–	–	–	1960–2005
Burkina Faso (20)	1960–82	1983–90	–	–	–	–	–	1991–2005
Burundi (2)	1972–88	–	1972–88	1972–88	1972–88	–	1960–72, 1988–2005	–
Cameroon (16)	1960–77	–	–	–	1978–93	–	–	1994–2005
Cape Verde	1975–91	–	–	–	–	1974–5	–	1960–73, 1992–2005
CAR	1965–2005	–	–	1965–79	–	–	1996–2003	1960–4
Chad (3)	1960–2005	–	1960–90	–	–	–	1979–84	–
Comoros	1979–2005	1976–8	1979–2005	1979–89	–	–	1976–8, 1990–2005	1960–75
DRC	–	–	1965–73	1973–97	–	–	1960–5, 1996–2005	–
Congo (25)	1963–8	1969–91	1969–91	–	1982–91	–	1993, 1997, 2002	1960–2, 1994–6, 1998–2001, 2003–5
Côte d'Ivoire (23)	1980–9	–	–	1970–90	–	–	–	1960–9, 1991–2000
Djibouti	–	–	1977–2005	–	–	–	1991–2000	1960–76
Equatorial Guinea	–	–	–	1968–2005	–	–	1968–79	1960–7
Eritrea	–	1999–2005	–	–	–	–	1999–2000	1993–8
Ethiopia (4)	–	1974–91	–	–	–	–	–	1960–73, 1992–2005
Gabon	1960–97	–	–	–	–	–	–	1998–2005
Gambia, The	–	–	–	–	–	–	–	1960–2005

Country								
Ghana (9)	1972–8, 1984	1960–8, 1979–83	1960–8	–	–	–	–	1969–71, 1985–2005
Guinea (17)	1960–3, 1978–84	1964–77	–	–	1973–84	–	–	1985–2005
Guinea-Bissau	1974–2005	–	–	–	–	1960–73	1998–2005	–
Kenya (10)	1972–90	–	1978–2002, 2003–5	–	–	–	–	1960–71
Lesotho	–	–	–	–	–	–	–	1960–2005
Liberia	–	–	1980–90	1997–2003	–	–	1980–97, 2000–3	1960–79, 2004–5
Madagascar	1972–5, 1986–96	1976–85	–	–	–	1972–7	2002	1960–71, 1997–2001, 2003–5
Malawi (5)	–	–	–	–	–	–	–	1960–2005
Mali (21)	–	1960–8	–	1968–91	–	–	–	1992–2005
Mauritania	1974–85	–	–	–	–	–	–	1960–73, 1986–2005
Mauritius (11)	1960–70	–	–	–	–	–	–	1971–2005
Mozambique (24)	1960–76	1977–86	–	1974–6	–	1969–74	1974–91	1992–2005
Namibia (26)	–	–	–	–	–	1975–89	1990–9	1960–74, 1990–2005
Niger (6)	1960–89	–	–	–	1974–89	–	1966–70	1999–2005
Nigeria (18)	–	1983–6	1967–2003	1973–87, 1993–8	1970–87	–	–	1960–5, 2004–5
Rwanda	–	–	1973–94	–	–	–	1993–4	1960–72, 1995–2005
São Tomé and Príncipe	NA	NA	NA	NA	NA	NA	NA	NA

(cont.)

Table 2.A2 (cont.)

Country (bold = case study)/ chapter in vol. 2 (in parentheses)	Regulatory syndromes		Redistributive syndromes		Intertemporal syndromes		State break-down	Syndrome-free
	Soft controls	Hard controls	Regional	Looting	Unsustainable spending	Anticipated redistribution		
Senegal (12)	1960–93	–	–	–	1974–8	–	–	1994–2005
Seychelles	1993–2005	1972–92	–	–	–	–	–	1960–71
Sierra Leone (19)	–	1970–89	1970–2000	1970–2000	–	–	1967–9, 1990–2000	1960–6, 2001–5
Somalia	–	1969–75	–	1975–91	–	–	1991–2005	1960–8
South Africa	1960–91	–	1960–91	–	–	1977–93	–	1994–2005
Sudan (7)	1970–89	–	–	–	–	–	1962–72, 1985–2005	1960–1
Swaziland	–	–	–	–	–	–	–	1960–2005
Tanzania (13)	1986–94	1970–85	–	–	–	–	–	1960–9, 1995–2005
Togo (14)	1974–2005	–	1975–2000	1994–2005	1974–89	1994–2000	1991–3	1960–73
Uganda (8)	1960–7, 1971–91	1968–70	1966–70	1971–9	–	–	1979–86	1992–2005
Zambia (27)	1968–91	–	–	–	1973–89	–	–	1960–7, 1992–2005
Zimbabwe	1965–99	1900–2005	–	1998–2005	–	1976–80, 1991–7	1976–80	1960–4

Source: Judgmental classification by project editors and country authors.

Notes: NA denotes inadequate basis for classification. These data can be downloaded as an excel spreadsheet or STATA data set from www.swarthmore.edu/SocSci/soconnel/aercgrth.html.

Table 2.A3 *Neighbor effects on growth: 2.*

	LAD regressions		
Variable	(7)	(8)	(9)
Landlocked (LL)	−0.535***	−0.491**	−1.182***
	0.201	0.204	0.286
Resource-rich (RR)	−0.597***	−0.601**	−0.716***
	0.217	0.256	0.195
Island	1.465***	1.481***	1.350***
	0.089	0.231	0.174
Neighbor growth	0.319***	0.321***	0.280***
	0.036	0.042	0.032
CO*SSA	−1.143***	−1.136***	−1.219***
	0.218	0.295	0.231
LL*SSA	−0.950***	−1.012**	−0.388
	0.332	0.423	0.362
RR*SSA	−0.204	−0.201	−0.179
	0.289	0.219	0.283
Island*SSA	−1.122***	−1.084**	−0.964*
	0.41	0.479	0.54
Neighbor growth*LL	–	–	0.201***
			0.077
Neighbor growth*RR	–	–	0.04
			0.083
Nbr growth*CO*SSA	–	−0.213***	−0.181**
		0.075	0.072
Nbr growth*LL*SSA	–	0.032	−0.123
		0.073	0.092
Nbr growth*RR*SSA	–	−0.282***	−0.279***
		0.079	0.099
Neighbor growth*SSA	−0.186***	–	–
	0.067		
Dry year	−0.09	−0.05	−0.099
	0.134	0.148	0.101
N	5,620	5,620	5,620
Pseudo-R^2	0.0626	0.0639	0.0647

*$p < 0.1$; **$p < 0.05$; ***$p < 0.01$.
Notes: Bootstrapped standard errors. All regressions include a full set of year effects.

References

Acemoglu, Daron, Simon Johnson, and James Robinson (2001), "The Colonial Origins of Comparative Development: An Empirical Investigation," *American Economic Review* 91(5) December: 1369–1401

Adam, Christopher and Stephen O'Connell (1999), "Aid, Taxation and Development in Sub-Saharan Africa," *Economics and Politics* 11(3), November: 225–54

Alesina, Alberto and Eliana La Ferrara (2004), "Ethnic Diversity and Economic Performance," NBER Working Paper 10313

Collier, Paul (1999), "On the Economic Consequences of Civil War," *Oxford Economic Papers* 51(1): 168–83

Collier, Paul and Anke Hoeffler (2000), "Ethnicity, Politics and Economic Performance," *Economics and Politics* 12(3), November: 225–45

  (2005), "Democracy and Resource Rents," CSAE, Department of Economics, Oxford University

Gallup, J. and Jeffrey Sachs (1997), "Geography and Economic Growth," in B. Pleskovic and J. Stiglitz, eds., *Proceedings of the World Bank Conference on Development Economics*. Washington, DC: The World Bank

Krugman, Paul and Anthony J. Venables (1995), "Globalization and the Inequality of Nations," *Quarterly Journal of Economics* 110(4), November: 857–80

  (1996), "Integration, Specialization, and Adjustment," *European Economic Review* 40(3–5), April: 959–67

Lal, Deepak (1999), "Foreign Aid: An Idea Whose Time Has Gone," in Deepak Lal, *Unfinished Business: India in the World Economy*. Oxford: Oxford University Press

Masters, William and Margaret McMillan (2001), "Climate and Scale in Economic Growth," *Journal of Economic Growth* 6(3), September

Miguel, E., S. Satyanath, and E. Sergenti (2004), "Economic Shocks and Civil Conflict: An Instrumental Variables Approach," *Journal of Political Economy*, 112(4): 725–53

Sachs, Jeffrey *et al.* (2004), "Africa's Poverty Trap," *Brookings Papers on Economic Activity* 1: 117–240

Tirole, Jean (1996), "A Theory of Collective Reputations (with Applications to the Persistence of Corruption and to Firm Quality)," *Review of Economic Studies* 63(1), January: 1–22

Wood, Adrian (2003), "Could Africa be like America?," in Boris Pleskovic and Nicholas Stern, eds., *Annual World Bank Conference on Development Economics, 2003*. New York: Oxford University Press

3 | Anti-growth syndromes in Africa: a synthesis of the case studies

Augustin Kwasi Fosu

1 Introduction: the anti-growth syndromes

As part of the Collaborative Research project conducted by the African Economic Research Consortium (AERC) on "Explaining African Economic Growth Performance" (the "Growth Project"), a number of anti-growth syndromes were identified by the project's editorial committee based on previously commissioned project case studies and other evidence.[1] These

Director, Economic and Social Policy Division, UN Economic Commission for Africa, Addis Ababa, Ethiopia, and RDRC Research Fellow, University of California, Berkeley, CA, USA. Neither institution is responsible for the views expressed here. An earlier version of the chapter was presented at the AERC/Harvard workshop, Harvard University, Cambridge, MA, USA, March 18–19, 2005. The author is particularly grateful to Stephen O'Connell for helpful suggestions.

[1] The first stage of this exercise was undertaken by Jean-Paul Azam, Robert Bates, Paul Collier, Augustin Fosu, Jan Willem Gunning, Benno Ndulu, and Stephen O'Connell in August 2003, based on draft versions of the country studies in volume 2. The classification was assessed by country authors at a November 2003 conference and refined in response to their comments. In August 2004 the editorial committee undertook a similar judgmental exercise to extend the sample to most of Africa: see chapter 2 for the full classification.

Table 3.1 *Anti-growth syndromes: relative frequencies of occurrence from independence to year 2000, forty-six [twenty-six] SSA countries (percent).*

	State controls	Adverse redistribution	Intertemporal	State breakdown	Syndrome-free
Unweighted	33.8 [37.1]	21.9 [18.2]	8.8 [11.5]	10.2 [8.8]	25.4 [24.4]
Population-weighted	26.3	31.6	13.1	10.2	18.9

Notes: The first row comprises the set of non-weighted relative frequencies, with figures for the twenty-six-country case study sample (see table 3.2) in square brackets. The forty-six-country sample also includes Eritrea (as a forty-seventh country) for 1994–2000. The second row is weighted by the respective 1980 country populations.

Source: The syndrome data are reported in full in chapter 2. The format of the above table follows Fosu and O'Connell (2005), table 3.3. Figures differ because of revisions in the syndrome data, but more importantly because the current figures are conditioned on the sample space. Here each syndrome observed in a country-year, rather than each country-year itself, is treated as an observation (as is each syndrome-free country-year). The frequencies therefore sum by construction to 100 percent.

classifications for practically all of SSA, involving forty-six countries, as well as for the sample of twenty-six country cases, over the period between country official independence from colonial rule and the year 2000, are presented in table 3.1. These are: State controls (SC), Adverse redistribution (AR), Intertemporally unsustainable spending (IUS), and State breakdown (SB); also presented is the complementary Syndrome-free (SF) category.[2]

As the non-weighted row of table 3.1 indicates, the classification with the largest relative frequency is SC (34 percent), followed by SF (25 percent), then AR (22 percent), SB (10 percent), and IUS (9 percent). Considering the population-weighted frequencies (table 3.1), however, the ranking changes somewhat. The AR category is now first (32 percent), followed closely by SC (26 percent), then by SF (19 percent), IUS (13 percent), and SB (10 percent). Thus, larger countries tend to be relatively skewed toward AR and IUS, while SF is less prevalent in larger states and SB is invariant to country size.

The estimates for the twenty-six case countries,[3] also reported in table 3.1, somewhat over-estimate the incidence of SC and IUS, and slightly under-estimate that of AR and SB, relative to the forty-six-country (non-weighted) sample. These differences are small, however, so that with respect to the overall syndrome classification, the case study sample closely resembles the region as a whole.

Figure 3.1 depicts the evolution of these categories over time for the forty-six countries. The picture that emerges is that during the initial stages of

[2] In chapter 2 and elsewhere in the volume the SC, AR, and IUS syndromes are referred to as the regulatory, redistributive, and intertemporal syndromes, respectively.

[3] See table 3.2 for the list of the case countries. In this chapter we include South Africa among the case study aggregates based on a periodization by the project editors.

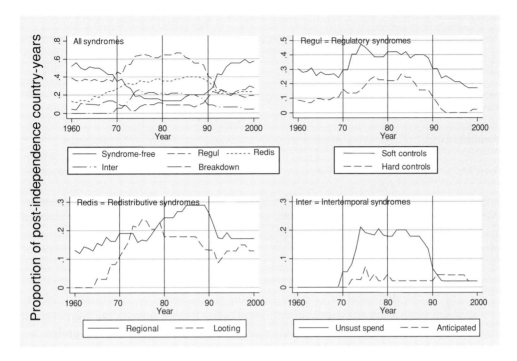

Figure 3.1 Policy syndromes in forty-six SSA countries, 1960–2000
Notes: Based on judgmental classification by the editorial committee based on country studies and broader literature (adapted from Fosu and O'Connell (2006), figure 4). *Key*: *S-free* = Syndrome-free; *Regul* = State control syndromes (*Soft Controls* or *Hard Controls*); *Redis* = Adverse redistribution syndromes (*Regional* or *Looting*); *Inter* = Intertemporal syndromes (*Unsustainable Spending* or *Anticipated Redistribution*); Breakdown = State failure. The vertical axis is the proportion of year-countries.

independence in the 1960s, the dominant category was SF, followed closely by SC. The other categories were rather minimal. However, SF steadily declined in prevalence and bottomed out in the early 1980s, began to rise steadily as of the mid-1980s, and leveled off beginning in the mid-1990s. In contrast, the incidence of SC was relatively steady until about 1970 when it overtook SF, rising steadily and remaining high until the mid-1980s when it began to decline, becoming less prevalent than SF in the early 1990s. Meanwhile, IUS and AR rose from the time of independence, and leveled off as of the mid-1970s. Most remarkably, however, the frequency of SB rose substantially in the 1990s. As figure 3.1 further shows, the incidence of SB increased during the immediate post-independence period, dipped in the early 1970s, picked up slightly as of the mid-1970s, and leveled off thereafter prior to the rise beginning in the late 1980s.

The central hypothesis of the Growth Project is that the quality of economic policy has a powerful effect on whether countries seize the growth opportunities implied by global technologies and markets and by their own

Table 3.2 *Country cases in the Growth Project, by sub-region and opportunity group.*

	Coastal and resource-poor	Landlocked and resource-poor	Resource-rich
Eastern and Central Africa	Kenya	Burundi, Chad, Ethiopia,[a] Niger, Sudan,[a] Uganda	Cameroon, Congo
Southern Africa	Mauritius, Mozambique, Tanzania	Malawi	Botswana, Namibia, Zambia
West Africa	Benin, Côte d'Ivoire, Ghana, Senegal, Togo	Burkina Faso, Mali	Guinea, Nigeria, Sierra Leone

Note: [a]Ethiopia (literally landlocked after 1993) and Sudan are classified as landlocked for analytical purposes. The opportunity groups are defined in chapter 2.

initial conditions. But precisely how does policy succeed or fail, and why are successful or unsuccessful policies chosen? The syndrome classification aggregates multi-dimensional policy into broad patterns that occurred repeatedly in the case study evidence and that both theory and global evidence identify as discouraging to growth. The evidence that the syndromes reduce growth is strong: Fosu and O'Connell (2006) find, for example, that avoiding the syndromes is simultaneously a necessary condition for attaining sustainable growth in SSA and a nearly-sufficient condition for preventing growth collapse (see also chapter 2). Indeed, being syndrome-free may add as much as 2 percentage points per year to *per capita* growth (chapter 2). In the current chapter, we take the next step. Based on evidence from twenty-six country cases (listed in table 3.2), we attempt to analyze the above syndromes, as well as the syndrome-free category, in terms of their genesis and expiry. Why did these syndromes occur to begin with, and why were they ended? We shall first provide several illustrative examples for each of the syndromes,[4] and then synthesize the case study evidence over a number of attributes.

2   Illustrative examples of the syndromes

2.1   *State controls*

There are two types of state controls, depending on the degree to which economic activities were controlled: "soft" and "hard." Under both, the state

---

[4] These illustrations are derived from the AERC Growth Project case studies listed respectively in the reference list and included in volume 2.

intervened via altering market incentives, usually involving the distortion of market prices: internally such as direct or indirect price controls of basic commodities of transportation, foodstuffs, finance, etc.; and externally via fixing the price of foreign exchange, along with the use of quantity controls as a rationing mechanism, such as import and export licensing. In many instances, marketing boards were set up to administer prices, and other state enterprises engaged in production and distribution. Under soft controls, the degree of pervasiveness was considerably mild. In contrast, hard controls would be relatively severe, with harsh enforcement of comparatively binding constraints, normally involving a radical Marxist *modus operandi* that seriously restricted private operation and individual choice, to the point where much of resource allocation was subject to government control. Most African countries engaged in either or both forms of controls in their respective histories. Illustrative examples follow.

2.1.1   Burkina Faso: 1960–1982 (soft control); 1983–1990 (hard control)

Following independence in 1960, Burkina Faso pursued "state interventionism, in the absence of a dynamic private sector" (Savadogo, Coulibaly, and McCracken 2007: 7). There was relatively little intervention in the market for cereals (sorghum, millet, and maize) in the first decade after independence. After the drought of the mid-1970s, however, the Cereal Office (OFNACER), originally set up to handle food aid, became a bilateral monopolist on cereal trade and restricted private trade. The key factor contributing to the 1960–82 period being soft rather than hard control is the relatively political conservative leadership (President Maurice Yaméogo, 1960–6; General Sangoulé Lamizana, 1966–80; and Colonel Saye Zerbo, 1980–2), which provided a considerable, but uneven, latitude for private sector activity.

The 1960–82 period was one of considerable political instability, however, as reflected by the coups of 1966, 1980, and 1982. The first two were apparently in response to the dissatisfaction with economic conditions as *per capita* GDP growth averaged less than 1 percent annually.[5] The era of soft control ended when a more radical officer corps led by the charismatic Thomas Sankara overthrew the government via a coup in August 1983, and imposed a more severe form of "state capitalism." The government's role became much more pervasive, and remained so until the end of the decade. For example, a draconian rental law required landlords to transfer a whole year of rent to the government; for 1984 rent was declared free. The 1983–90 hard-control period was punctuated by a bloody coup in October 1987,

---

[5] Savadogo, Coulibaly, and McCracken (2007) emphasize that the first coup was actually a popular uprising rather than conventional *coup d'état*. Labor unions were instrumental in organizing the uprising, and the excesses of the first President, Mr. Yaméogo (1960–6), played an important catalytic role.

when Sankara was killed as part of a power play among the radicals and was replaced by Blaise Compaoré. The ensuing severe financial imbalances and economic difficulties, however, forced the Compaoré government to seek salvation from the Bretton Woods institutions, with the election of Compaore under a new constitution in 1991 (Savadogo, Coulibaly, and McCracken 2007).

2.1.2   Cameroon: 1960–1977 (soft control)

Cameroon obtained its independence from France in 1960. Ahmadou Ahidjo, its first president, pursued soft-control policies amid early attempts at industrialization based on import substitution. The adoption of a soft-control regime emanated in great part from Ahidjo's relatively politically conservative background. However, more market-friendly laissez-faire policies were precluded by the need for the government to engage in peace-building at the early stages of independence due to the ethnically based insurrection during the pre-independence years. This period of soft controls ended with the production and exportation of oil in 1978 when the availability of huge revenue windfalls led to intertemporally unsustainable government spending (Kobou, Njinkeu, and Powo Fosso 2007).

2.1.3   Chad: 1960–2000 (soft control)

As cotton has historically been the primary export product capable of generating foreign exchange, it has attracted some form of government control in the form of taxes and the involvement of a parastatal company. The control then provided a mechanism for the provision of foreign exchange revenues to the government. The entire period may, however, be characterized as soft, rather than hard, control as much of the political system has never been particularly radicalized (Azam and Djimtoïngar 2007).

2.1.4   Ghana: 1960–1966, 1972–1983 (hard control)

At the time of independence in 1957, the clear choice was between Mr. J. B. Danquah, a politically conservative politician from the majority Akan ethnic group who favored a go-slow market-friendly federal approach, and Mr. Kwame Nkrumah, from the minority Nzimma ethnic group, who preferred a socialistic modality with a strong role for government. Nkrumah won the election based in part on the appeal of the promises of faster economic progress through the government's active role in the economy and partly out of fear of possible Akan domination.

Transforming the country to a one-party state by 1960, as the Republic of Ghana, Nkrumah assumed a strong role as President from his initial position as Prime Minister at the time of independence. The government embarked on a radical path of industrialization, with the state playing the leading role. The socialistic ideology of collective ownership, later dubbed "Nkrumahism," rather than capitalistic individual owner-ship, reigned supreme. Thus, nearly all large-scale business operations were owned by the state. In the process, private enterprises, especially those of medium-to-large size, were squeezed out, through political intimidation or via financial starvation. Huge spending on nationally unproductive projects, given Nkrumah's rather large vision of total liberation of the African conti-nent from colonialism and imperialism, led the country rapidly toward fiscal difficulties. By 1966, Ghana's net international reserves were in a deficit of US$391 million, down from a surplus of US$269 million at the time of inde-pendence. Corresponding economic difficulties included an increase in the inflation rate from 1 percent in 1957 to 22.7 percent in 1966, and a fall in *per capita* GDP from $500 in 1960 to about $470 by 1966 (1987 real US dollars). Thus, when the military overthrew Nkrumah's government in a coup in February 1966, there was much celebration in the streets to welcome the change.

The 1972–83 period of hard controls began when General Ignatius Acheampong overthrew the economically liberal government of Prime Min-ister Kofi Busia in a coup in 1972, using as the primary pretext a recent gov-ernment devaluation of the domestic currency. This period was one of "mud-dling through" (Aryeetey and Fosu 2007), with a series of five governments, primarily military, coming to power through coups and counter-coups, except for a very brief period of a civilian government of Hilla Limann, 1979–81. Governments responded to economic difficulties by imposing further constraints, particularly price and import controls, which became necessary in the face of macroeconomic imbalances associated with the severely over-valued local currency, the cedi. Cognizant of the high likelihood of coup incidence when such devaluations occurred, governments were unwilling to run the risk of devaluing the cedi (Fosu 1992). Except for the explicitly ideological tinge of the Rawlings regime, however, which came to power in a coup in December 1981 (following a brief coup by Rawlings in 1979), these governments were not particularly radical, but viewed the control policies as the way out. The Acheampong military government (1972–9) had, for example, engaged in non-radical schemes such as "Operation Feed Yourself," and flirted with a "Uni-government" that would include both the military and civilians. Nonetheless, much resource allocation was done through strict controls.

Severe fiscal difficulties were apparent in the early 1980s. By 1983, inci-dentally a year of very severe drought, central government revenues had shrunk to only 5 percent as a proportion of GDP, compared with a rate of 20 percent in 1970; inflation had accelerated from 18 percent in 1974 to 116 percent in 1981, even though prices were supposed to be controlled; domestic investment had fallen to less than 4 percent, from its value of

14 percent in 1974; and the current account balance was US$175 million in deficit, with the country experiencing major arrears and no loans or grants to finance these deficits or arrears. Thus, the radical-leaning Rawlings government appeared to have little choice but to succumb to the IMF/World Bank-sponsored Economic Recovery Program (ERP),[6] which was ushered in during April 1983, followed by the Structural Adjustment Program (SAP) in 1986. The 1984–2000 period is characterized as syndrome-free (see below) (Aryeetey and Fosu 2007).

2.1.5   Sierra Leone: 1975–1989 (hard control)

Sierra Leone gained independence in 1961. The ascendancy of the All People's Congress (APC) to power in 1968, following a period of acute elite political instability that saw three successful coups in one year, eventually spelled the end of conservative politics and market-friendly policies. It took some time for the new government to consolidate power; hence, the hard-control regime that emerged did not occur until several years later, aided by the negative oil supply shocks of the 1970s. These shocks propelled the implementation of wide-scale price and foreign-exchange rate controls and financial repression. Meanwhile, the government borrowed heavily to finance grandiose public projects, such as the 1980 summit of the Organization of African Unity (OAU) held in Freetown, which consumed more than 60 percent of the 1980 government revenues. Export crops – palm kernel, cocoa, and coffee – were also subjected to both explicit and, perhaps more significantly, implicit taxation by the monopsonistic Sierra Leone Produce Marketing Board (SLPMB). Meanwhile, import subsidies and price controls became a source of economic rents for redistribution to political allies, including Northern interests. Severe macroeconomic imbalances surfaced. By 1981–5, the exchange rate over-valuation index had reached 229, from its level of 190 in 1961–5. The economic situation deteriorated steadily, reaching crisis proportions in the mid-to-late 1980s. By 1987, the poverty rate had reached 80 percent, inflation rates topped 180 percent, and tax revenues dwindled to less than 10 percent of GDP, about one-half of their value in the early 1980s. The government sought relief from the IMF and World Bank in the form of an SAP late in 1989, but economic reforms were interrupted by the civil war that began in 1991 (Davies 2007).

2.1.6   Tanzania: 1970–1985 (hard control); 1986–1994 (soft controls)

The genesis of the imposition of strict controls was the strong belief by Julius Nyerere, the first President of Tanzania, that the socialistic model

---

[6] One might argue that Rawlings had also learned his economic lessons by 1983, when it became clear that the political intimidation of suppliers of products accused of hoarding, including bulldozing of the Makola Market, would not solve the economic difficulties.

was the best strategy for Tanzania's rapid development, as apparent in the Arusha Declaration of 1967. This ideology of African Socialism incorporated strong government intervention. The strategy culminated in the establishment of the "Ujamaa" villages of farmers, modeled after Mao Tse Tung's Chinese communes.[7] The individual form of decision-making was, therefore, transformed to a collective one. Meanwhile, to achieve equity, government revenues were used to heavily subsidize production in remote areas, directly through production input subsidies, and indirectly via the system of "pan-territorial prices," introduced in the early 1970s to equalize prices across regions. Stringent price controls, particularly on food, were put in place beginning in the early 1970s, especially in response to increasing inflation from oil-supply and drought shocks. Import controls were imposed as foreign reserves declined sharply because of the government policy to provide universal access to social services. By 1985, the exchange rate premium had reached its peak of 200 percent. Shortages of consumer goods became chronic, while parallel underground economic activities emerged and intensified as controls became more stringent.

As long as government could muster the resources to finance the controls, the resulting economic difficulties could be tolerated. Such resources emanated from the coffee boom of the 1970s and continued inflows of external aid, which went into financing government investment. However, the end of the coffee boom in 1978 and the oil price shock of 1979, as well as the costly war against Uganda's Idi Amin in 1979, led to severe fiscal difficulties and to additional tightening of controls, resulting in further economic stresses. Rapidly dwindling revenues compelled the government to employ deficit spending, which exacerbated the inflation problem, resulting in additional economic difficulties. As the fiscal problems mounted and became very severe, the government, still unconvinced of the deleteriousness of its ideologically based policies, was forced to tepidly accept World Bank-administered reforms and to soften controls beginning in 1985, though it was not until 1995 that Tanzania was transformed to a market-based economy.

Thus, the period of soft controls began in 1986, marked by "government withdrawal from direct involvement in production, processing and marketing activities retaining only its role in setting policies" (Mwase and Ndulu 2007: 15). Major price controls, including foreign exchange, were also dismantled. However, the institutional and legal remnants of the hard control regime remained. For example, government parastatals such as state-owned

---

[7] This resulted in a major increase of the population residing in Ujamaa villages from only 5 percent at the beginning of the program to as much as 60 percent at the end of 1975 (Mwase and Ndulu 2007).

banks continued to serve as a source of rents for political operators. The 1986–94 period could thus be viewed as a transition from hard controls to a market-based economy, a transition that required substantial political machinations, as discussed below (Mwase and Ndulu 2007).

2.2   Adverse redistribution

Redistribution could be favorable to growth in cases where it reduced polarization.[8] However, its effect might be perverse if it increased polarization, especially in cases where government officials used redistribution as a mechanism to reward their cronies or regional constituencies that were often ethnically defined. This latter form, adverse redistribution, could be vertical as well. Many SSA governments engaged in adverse redistribution as a mechanism for shoring up their respective power bases, usually based on ethnicity. Several examples follow.

2.2.1   Burundi: 1975–1987

As a strategy of "rents to sovereignty" (Nkurunziza and Ngaruko 2007), the Tutsi-dominated government created a large number of public corporations that distributed rents to members of the Tutsi political elite, mostly Bururi-Tutsis, who formed the political base for the ruling group. Meanwhile, to maintain political control the army-led Tutsis perpetrated severe political repression against the majority Hutus, following a massacre of the Tutsi minority by Hutus in 1972. This strategy then constituted an ethnically based form of vertical redistribution, which presumably ended only about 1989, following external and internal pressure, when Major Pierre Buyoya replaced Colonel Jean-Baptiste Bagaza via a coup in 1987. The redistributive policy, coupled with political repression by the minority Tutsis, was likely rationalized on the basis of perceived Tutsi fear of domination by the majority Hutus in a general democratic political contestation. Thus, in the

---

[8] Jean-Paul Azam has, for instance, argued that the failure of some governments to provide sufficient redistribution to less well-off segments of their population has encouraged such segments to take up arms and resulted in civil wars (Azam 1995, 2001, and chapter 6). An important example is Côte d'Ivoire, where the government of President Félix Houphouët-Boigny was able to "buy" peace by sharing the Southern wealth of cocoa revenues, for example, with the North through subsidization. The failure to continue that policy after the Houphouët-Boigny era is believed to have contributed to the ensuing civil war between the North and South (Azam 2005). Similarly, the government of Kwame Nkrumah in Ghana provided a similar policy favoring the North, a policy that appears to have survived to the present and may have contributed to national peace enjoyed by the country since independence. Another important case is Mauritius where the ability of the government, through appropriate multi-party political coalition, to redistribute income toward greater equity avoided conflict that could have derailed the growth process (Nath and Madhoo 2007).

short run at least, such a redistributive strategy to maintain the political base of the Tutsi-dominated government appears to be a politically optimal strategy. This state of affairs, however, led to a subsequent period of state breakdown, as discussed below (Nkurunziza and Ngaruko 2007).

2.2.2   Sierra Leone: 1969–1990

The redistributive behavior of the government during this period was based on inter-ethnic rivalry between the North-based Temne and South-eastern Mende groups, each of which commanded roughly 30 percent of the population. The former group dominated the APC political party, which assumed political power in 1968. To consolidate its political base, the new government engaged in regional redistribution from the Mende in favor of their politically allied Temne. The redistribution, however, disenfranchised the Mende and increased inter-ethnic polarization, which is believed to have contributed to the subsequent civil war that broke out in 1991 (Davies 2007).

2.2.3   Togo: 1976–1990

There was substantial regional redistribution in favor of the Kabyes, President Gnassingbe Eyadema's ethnic group of the Kara region in the North, mainly through the ballooned and monopolized public sector, financed initially from revenue windfalls from phosphate and the coffee boom of the late 1970s. Even in response to the SAP begun in the mid-1980s when retrenching of the public sector was in effect, the Kabyes are believed to have retained the lion's share of desirable employment. While such a strategy likely shored up President Eyadema's political base, it fanned inter-ethnic polarization, which may have subsequently contributed to acute political instability in the early 1990s, with major demonstrations and strikes (Gogué and Evlo 2007).

2.3   Intertemporally unsustainable spending

Intertemporally unsustainable spending has most frequently been associated with temporary revenue windfalls from increases in the prices of export commodities, such as bauxite, coffee, oil, and phosphate. Thus, this syndrome occurred usually in resource-rich countries. The revenue boom would lead the government to undertake certain projects. Additional resources were often necessary, however, for reaching spending targets, thus calling for supplemental borrowing, which was further encouraged in the 1970s by cheap "petro-dollars." The government would eventually run into fiscal difficulties when the commodity price boom ended, resulting in a curtailment of public spending. The upshot was that many projects remained uncompleted. Given the lumpiness of investment, moreover, projects' values of marginal product were seldom realized. The subsequent period, therefore, often experienced substantially reduced economic growth, as the previous period's growth had been fueled in part by pure spending not matched by real output increases. Several case examples follow.

2.3.1   Burundi: 1975–1985

Following the coffee boom of the 1970s, the government undertook a massive program of public investment, which increased from a mere 5.6 percent of total investment in 1971 to 42.8 percent in 1980. Much of this went toward the creation of a large number of public corporations, which were used to redistribute economic rents to the political elite, mostly Bururi Tutsis. Between 1977 and 1982, for example, some 100 state enterprises "were created and put in the hands of cronies" (Nkurunziza and Ngaruko 2007: 34). As many of these corporations were mismanaged, however, large infusions of government subsidies were required to keep them afloat. This required substantial borrowings to finance the widening fiscal deficits in the 1970s, leading to onerous and unsustainable debt servicing requirements in the early-to-mid-1980s. The resulting macroeconomic imbalances propelled the government to adopt an IMF/World Bank SAP in 1986 (Nkurunziza and Ngaruko, 2007).

2.3.2   Cameroon: 1982–1993

Oil was produced and exported, beginning in 1978. The revenues were removed from the normal budget process and placed in a special account managed directly by President Paul Biya, who had replaced President Ahmadou Ahidjo in 1982 upon the latter's voluntary retirement. However, a failed coup attempt in 1984, presumably orchestrated by Ahidjo, led Biya to solidify his grip on power. This strategy entailed major spending, thanks in part to the oil revenues under his direct control, in an increasing effort to build an ethnically based political alliance. The introduction of multi-party competitive politics in 1990 further fueled political rivalry and intensified spending intended to win electoral authority. The end of the oil-financed boom, coupled with the inability to allow the CFA franc to adjust downward, resulted in a post-1985 growth collapse, which ended only following the devaluation of the currency in 1994 (Kobou, Njinkeu, and Powo Fosso 2007).

2.3.3   Nigeria: 1974–1986

The major positive oil supply shocks in the third quarter of 1973 and in 1979 endowed Nigeria with huge revenues. In the wake of the oil boom, "export revenues skyrocketed, producing major increases in foreign exchange reserves, imports, and domestic incomes" (Iyoha and Oriakhi 2007: 3). By the early 1980s, petroleum production accounted for 20–25 percent of GDP, 90 percent of foreign exchange earnings, and 70 percent of budgetary revenues. This commodity boom led to a spending boom, a substantial portion of which was channeled into the building and expansion of much-needed infrastructure, such as roads, airports, schools, universities, and hospitals. There were, however, some adverse impacts of the commodity boom that became a harbinger of the precarious future. These included notably the "Dutch Disease," where the non-oil tradable sector (agriculture) declined in response to appreciation of the domestic currency, the naira, despite the huge amount of government resources heaped upon agriculture. By 1975, Nigeria had become a net importer of food for the first time.

Government programs and parastatals also proliferated in the 1970s, many in agriculture: Integrated Agriculture Development Projects, the Nigerian Grains Board (NGB), Nigerian Tuber and Root Crops Board (NTRCB), Operation Feed the Nation, Green Revolution Programme, etc. Indeed, the setup of the NGB and NTRCB in 1976 signaled the advent of government intervention in the marketing and distribution of staple food – that is, in addition to the already existing boards on cash crops, such as the Cocoa Marketing Board. There was also major spending on import substitution activities, with the result that manufacturing production, heavily subsidized with the revenue windfall, grew substantially from a GDP share of 5.6 percent in 1962–3 to 8.7 percent by 1986. That the spending boom generated unsustainably high growth can be demonstrated by the fact that between 1970 and 1977, *per capita* income grew at an astronomically high annual rate of 12 percent.

The oil boom ended in 1982, however. In response to a more than 50 percent depreciation in the world price of oil by early 1986, Nigeria's petroleum export earnings tumbled from nearly US$25 billion in 1980 to US$6.4 billion in 1986. Such a drastic loss of foreign earnings spawned a host of economic problems, including on the external side, "unsustainable balance-of-payments deficits, a rapidly escalating debt stock, and a crushing debt-service burden"[9] (Iyoha and Oriakhi 2007: 3). "Internally, the economic problems included unsustainable fiscal deficits, rising unemployment, and galloping inflation" (Iyoha and Oriakhi 2007: 3).

---

[9] Nigeria's external debt stock was only US$1 billion in the late 1970s, or 8 percent of income in 1977. Following the oil collapse, however, the country became one of the most heavily indebted countries in SSA, with total external debt peaking at over US$33 billion in 1990. Accordingly, Nigeria's debt servicing requirements became astronomically high, cresting at approximately 40 percent of exports in 1986, about twice the SSA average. The debt servicing became apparently so crushing that the government unilaterally decided not to honor some of its scheduled payments (indeed, the Nigerian government decided in 1993 to limit its actual debt service payments to no more than 30 percent of net oil revenues), thus reducing the actual debt service ratio to 22 percent and 14 percent in 1990 and 1996, respectively. Consequently, the country accumulated substantial external debt arrears, most of these owed to the Paris Club.

Much of the debt accumulation arose from the need to sustain certain politically driven spending commitments within an environment of ethnic polarization. For example, competition for economic rents may have contributed to the high frequency of government changes within the 1974–86 period, most originating from military coups: the civilian presidential government of Alhaji Shehu Shagari (1979–83), and military regimes headed by General Murtala Mohammed (1975–6), General Olusegun Obasanjo (1976–9), and General Muhammad Buhari (1983–5). The frequent changes in administration, especially involving military coups, did not auger well for economic growth, as observed for SSA countries generally (Fosu 1992, 2002); nor did the fragmentation of the military elites along ethnic lines. Except for Obasanjo, all of the above leaders came from the North, while the oil revenues derived from the South, with the implied redistribution of the oil revenues northward. For example, General Buhari, a northerner, created an additional seven states, set up the machinery to move the capital from Lagos in the South to the more central location of Abuja, and completed an expensive fertilizer plant in Kaduna in the North. President Alhaji Shagari also drastically reduced the share of oil royalties provided to the South, from 30 percent to 2 percent.

By 1985, investment, most of it public,[10] had collapsed to 9 percent of GDP from its peak of 31.5 percent in 1976. Fiscal deficits had also ballooned from 5.3 percent of GDP in 1983 to 10.4 percent by 1986, while the external debt had skyrocketed from US$1 billion in the 1970s to US$26 billion by 1986. Meanwhile, the reserve–import ratio tumbled from nearly 40.0 months in 1983 to only 5.4 months in 1986. These severe fiscal difficulties led the Nigerian government to seek the assistance of the Bretton Woods institutions, and to adopt a SAP in July 1986 (Iyoha and Oriakhi 2007).

2.3.4 Togo: 1974–1989

Despite the negative oil-supply shock of 1973, the phosphate boom of 1974 and 1975 (a five-fold price increase) and the substantial coffee price rise in 1977 produced a windfall in public revenues. Correspondingly, government spending rose substantially, with public investment skyrocketing from 13.4 percent in 1973 to 47 percent by the late 1970s, matched by more than a doubling of the workforce in the formal industrial sector, mostly public, between 1973 and 1979. By the late 1970s, however, Togo had already begun to experience fiscal difficulties, thanks to the bust in the coffee and phosphates markets coupled with high government expenditures, which forced the country to seek major increases in external borrowings, resulting in a

---

[10] The public share of total investment was nearly 80 percent in 1976 – that is, 24.4 percent public investment/GDP ratio versus 31.5 percent total investment ratio.

gargantuan rise in its external debt, from 15.1 percent of GDP in 1970 to 116.4 percent in 1978. This period of unsustainable spending compelled the government to seek an IMF-administered financial stabilization program (FSP) negotiated in 1979 as well as a series of SAPs beginning in 1982. Public investment then shrank from nearly 50 percent of GDP in the late 1970s to 20 percent by 1989, while an employment freeze reduced the civil service by 13 percent between 1985 and 1988. Although the syndrome of unsustainable spending was virtually over by 1990, the emergence of civil strife in 1990 and the restoration of repressive military dictatorship in 1991 ensured that the subsequent period was not syndrome-free (Gogué and Evlo 2007).

2.4   State breakdown

State breakdown (often denoted "state failure" in the political economy literature) is said to occur when conditions are such that law and order breaks down and the government is unable to carry out its basic functions. This situation usually results from civil war. It may also occur when there is acute elite political instability such as very high frequency of coups d'état. A few examples follow.

2.4.1   Burundi: 1988–2000

Following the long history of redistribution in favor of the minority Tutsis, who controlled both the government and the military, and harsh political repression of the majority Hutus, the background was prepared for severe political instability, with a civil war in 1988. A year before, Pierre Buyoya, a Bururi Tutsi, had seized power in a military coup. In 1993, Buyoya lost in the country's first presidential election to a Hutu, Melchior Ndadaye. The latter was, however, assassinated in the same year in a Tutsi raid on the presidential palace. This incident ignited the second civil war, which ended only in 2003. Thus, the whole of 1988–2003 could be characterized as one of state breakdown, though the period of political instability continued beyond 1993 when there was a high frequency of government changes (Nkurunziza and Ngaruko 2007).

2.4.2   Chad: 1979–1984, 1985–1993

Chad gained independence in 1960 as a highly polarized country, with the relatively educated and cotton-producing South controlling the political and administrative apparatus of government, headed by François Tombalbaye until his deposition and death in a 1975 coup. During this period, the government failed to share southern wealth sufficiently with the North, leading initially to a rebellion in the North and to an all-out civil war in 1979 that lasted until 1984. Following the 1975 coup, General Félix Malloum, another Southerner, attempted to bridge the political divide with the North by appointing Hissène Habré, a former rebellion leader from the North, as Prime Minister. Unfortunately, Habré's actions, viewed by his supporters as an aggressive anti-corruption drive but by others as intimidation of the South, alienated the Southern elites and led to the civil war.

Even though the civil war formally ended in 1984, the North severely repressed the South politically, leading to post-war acute political instability, which was attenuated only after Idriss Déby took over the government in 1990. But even then there was a 1993 massacre in the South under his watch. Hence, this acute form of political instability, which could reasonably be judged as state breakdown, was not over before the 1993 massacre, following which Déby wittingly established a regional power-sharing government, with General Kamougue, who formerly led the resistance in the South, as President of the national assembly. The devaluation of the CFA franc in 1994 also helped stabilize the economic environment, especially for cotton production (Azam and Djimtoïngar 2004).

2.4.3   Sierra Leone: 1967–1968, 1991–2000

The 1967–8 period was one of severe elite political instability that saw three successful coups within a short period of one year. This followed the closely fought election of March 1967, which was won by the APC opposition party. A 1967 coup, however, prevented the APC from taking office. It took a third coup in 1968 for the APC to be able to assume office. The genesis of this acute form of elite political instability could be traced in part to concerns about the radical leanings of the APC as opposed to the political conservatism that had characterized the political history of Sierra Leone. Perhaps more importantly, however, it could also be viewed in the context of the deep-seated rivalry between the northern Temne that supported the APC and the southern Mende that backed the incumbency. Nonetheless, the severe nature of the impasse meant that government became dysfunctional.

To shore up its political base, especially in such a highly polarized environment, the APC engaged in ethnic-based regional redistribution in favor of the Temne in the North, further disenfranchising the southern Mende. The APC, moreover, alienated many others through its autocratic rule that prevented any smooth transfer of power, compelling a rebel movement of the Revolutionary United Front (RUF) to take up arms against the government in 1991, thus starting a civil war which raged on for over a decade, fueled by the easy availability of alluvial diamonds. It was not until January 2002 that the war officially ended following a defeat of the RUF via external intervention (Davies 2007).

2.5   Syndrome-free

By default, syndrome-free status tends to identify politically stable regimes with reasonably market-friendly policies. In the immediate post-independence era, syndrome-free status was typically associated with politically conservative governments. To some extent, the incidence of syndrome-free, precipitated by political conservatism, could be viewed as a political accident. Indeed, the data show that among the forty-six SSA countries, roughly the same number opted for syndrome-free policies as those adopting syndrome policies (see figure 3.1). A syndrome-free regime could also occur, at least briefly, when a military coup replaced an authoritarian government with a disastrous economic record. More recent syndrome-free cases in Africa, however, appear to have emanated from major fiscal difficulties that compelled countries to adopt reforms in exchange for financial assistance from the Bretton Woods institutions. Several case examples follow.

2.5.1   Botswana: 1960–2000

Botswana is the shining example of a syndrome-free country in Africa. The genesis of this positive phenomenon is the democratic multi-party political arrangement based on the conservative Tswana traditional political culture, which also served to protect the interest of minority groups. The state-led development, unlike the case of most other African countries, was based on strategic facilitation of the private sector rather than state suppression. Furthermore, unlike the historically authoritative governments of China and East Asia that have nonetheless experienced strong growth, the government of Botswana has been democratic from the onset.

Why did Botswana succeed in establishing such a market-friendly democratic government when so many countries failed or never even attempted it? One possible answer is the decision by the time of independence in 1966 to base the government on the pre-colonial traditional conservative Tswana culture of widespread political participation, thus creating "an indigenous developmental state" (Maundeni 2001). Botswana has also had a relatively small (less than 2 million even today), largely homogenous population. Consequently, the country did not suffer as much pre-independence polarization as did many other African countries with much more inter-ethnic rivalry. In addition, the interests of the members of government, mostly cattle raisers, coincided with the pursuit of market-friendly policies that favored the rural sector. Botswana, therefore, avoided the characteristically rural-unfriendly urban-biased policies, such as over-taxing the rural sector via the use of state marketing boards (Bates 1981 and chapter 4) or over-valuation of the exchange rate (Fosu 2003).

Botswana also enjoyed an advantage with its natural endowment of diamonds, the main pillar of the economy. Unlike the case of the alluvial diamonds of Sierra Leone, for example, Botswana's diamond deposits required deep-earth mining. Thus the marginal cost of extraction without appropriate state sanctioning was relatively high, attenuating the use of diamonds as a financing tool for insurgency. Another geographical benefit is Botswana's proximity to South Africa. Being a member of both the Southern African Customs Union (SACU) and the RMA helped maintain exchange rate and monetary stability. The country was, moreover, the beneficiary of generous donor support based on its status as a democratic state on the doorstep of apartheid South Africa. Unlike most other SSA countries, however, Botswana did not become dependent on external aid, thanks in no small part to its good governance which helped ensure proper management of the aid (Maipose and Matsheka 2007).

2.5.2 Burkina Faso: 1991–2000

The Burkina Faso economy was relatively market-driven during 1991–2000, with a new constitution adopted in June 1991 that ushered in political liberalization followed by a devaluation of the CFAF in the franc zone in 1994. The genesis of this outcome was the set of fiscal difficulties faced by the military regime in the late 1980s. Captain Blaise Compaoré of the Front Populaire (FP) came to power in October 1987 through a coup. The FP "first attempted to continue the revolutionary mood" (Savadogo, Coulibaly, and McCracken 2007: 56), but faced major fiscal/economic difficulties and was compelled to seek assistance through an SAP of the IMF/World Bank (Savadogo, Coulibaly, and McCracken 2007).

2.5.3 Ghana: 1968–1972, 1984–2000

Following the overthrow of the Kwame Nkrumah regime via a military coup in February 1966, the military began a process of liberalizing the economy, including a devaluation of the cedi. The civilian government of Prime Minister Kofi Busia later accelerated this liberalization process upon assumption of office in 1969. The market-friendly era ended, however, when General Ignatius Acheampong staged another military coup in 1972, subsequent to a major devaluation of the Ghanaian currency by the Busia government.

The next syndrome-free phase, starting in 1984, was arrived at following the very harsh economic and fiscal conditions described earlier (section 2.1.4). These conditions compelled the socialistic radical-leaning government of Jerry Rawlings to accept the bitter IMF/World Bank medicine of an ERP starting in April 1983 (though 1984 marked the beginning of effective liberalization). Under the ERP, the economy was deregulated and liberalized, followed by the SAP that began in 1986. After years of muddling through, with the economy on its knees, and with little revenue to turn the situation around and no hope for external financial support, the radicals had to bow to reason and accept the reforms. In addition, it was clear that after years of coups and counter-coups, and with nothing to show for the record, another coup would not necessarily be the solution[11] (Aryeetey and Fosu 2007).

2.5.4   Sierra Leone: 1961–1966

The politically conservative leadership of the Protectorate-based Sierra Leone People's Party (SLPP), comprising chiefs and others from the hinterland, facilitated a market-friendly set of policies. The SLPP also maintained political stability by forging an alliance with the relatively educated Freetown-based Creoles. The stability ended, and with it the syndrome-free phase, when the closely fought election of March 1967 resulted in a successful coup that prevented the winner, the APC, from taking office. The APC was finally able to assume office in 1968 only as a result of a third successful coup following the election. The more socialistic APC began to put in place relatively market-distorting and adverse redistributive measures of state controls (Davies 2007).

2.5.5   Tanzania: 1961–1967, 1995–2000

The period immediately following independence in 1961 represented essentially a continuation of market-friendly policies of the colonial era. Capital formation and income growth were strong during this initial period, with *per capita* income advancing at an average rate of 4.1 percent annually during the 1961–7 period. However, there was impatience within the government of Julius Nyerere that the speed of industrialization was too slow and, perhaps more importantly, that the lot of the rural population required special attention. The government believed, furthermore, that socialism as a mode of development constituted the best mechanism to achieve the twin goal of development with equity, propelled by rapid industrialization and substantial redistribution to the majority rural population. This belief was crystallized into the 1967 Arusha Declaration, which provided the turning point for economic policies, as discussed above.

Severe economic and fiscal difficulties emanating from radical socialistic policies of state controls in the 1970s and early 1980s compelled the government to accept a World Bank-administered market-based reform program in 1986. It was not until 1995, though, that Tanzania could be considered as transformed to a market-friendly economy. The path toward this syndrome-free period was not smooth, however. The role played by external aid in this whole process is particularly interesting in the Tanzanian

---

[11] Though Fosu (2002) shows that a successful coup could actually raise growth when an economy is that dismal with very low investment, there was no guarantee that a coup attempt would necessarily succeed; instead, an abortive coup would likely only exacerbate the economic plight (Fosu 2002).

case. The country had remained a darling of aid donors for years in spite of (or because of) its socialistic mode of development, cushioning the adverse impact of the concomitant policies and thus postponing Tanzania's need to undertake reforms. Similarly, it was the substantial scale-down of aid in the early 1980s, precipitated in part by the world-wide paradigm change away from the socialistic mode of development, which further deepened the fiscal crisis and forced the government to change direction. Yet, it was also the substantial increase in aid following Tanzania's adoption of reforms that cushioned the accompanying socio-economic hardships, thus rendering the reform program more socially palatable.[12] Furthermore, when the program appeared to be off-track in the early 1990s, another round of substantial withdrawal of aid seems to have helped put it back on track.

Despite the formal adoption of reforms in 1986, political commitment to market-based policies was still lacking, a situation that was further exacerbated by the advent of competitive multi-party politics. Ideological debates raged between the "nationalistic liberalizers," who favored limited and guided liberalization, and those preferring faster and more extensive liberalization, the "free marketers." Helping to turn the tide toward the latter school of thought was the conditional aid policy exercised by donors in favor of rewarding commitment to reform while punishing policy reversals.[13] Meanwhile, the set-up of the "Helleiner process" in 1994, intended to smooth out relations with donors and augment aid effectiveness, helped to increase external aid to Tanzania. To boost national ownership and support for the reform program, the government also conducted nation-wide consultative and awareness campaigns to underscore the potential benefits of reforms. Beginning in 1995, Tanzania was transformed to a market-based economy, supported by multi-party democracy (Mwase and Ndulu 2007).

2.5.6   Togo: 1960–1973

Market-friendly policies were generally in place, despite the successful coups of 1963 and 1967 and the assassination of the politically conservative and economically liberal President Sylvanus Olympio during the former coup. The genesis of this policy regime is traceable to the background of Olympio as a former executive of an international trading company, as well as to the influence of the business community that constituted his support base. The

---

[12] For example, foreign assistance excluding technical assistance surged from 4.2 percent in 1985 to 17.4 percent of GDP in 1990 when President Ali Hassan Mwinyi was re-elected. The re-election mitigated the effects of competitive politics, paving the way for a return to the adjustment program.

[13] Commitment to reforms weakened again due in part to the apparent lame-duck nature of Mwinyi's presidency, leading once more to "an erosion of donor confidence resulting in wide scale exodus of donor aid" (Mwase and Ndulu 2007: 52).

syndrome-free period ended following the phosphate and coffee booms of the mid-1970s when revenue windfalls became available and the government engaged in intertemporally unsustainable spending, as discussed above (Gogué and Evlo 2007).

3   A synthesis

The explanations of why syndrome or syndrome-free regimes were begun or ended, based on the review of the case studies, may be synthesized along the following attributes: initial conditions; supply shocks (negative and positive); opportunity; the role of institutions, especially that of the military; and economically driven political expediency.

3.1   Initial conditions

Initial conditions at the time of independence from colonial rule played a very salient role in the adoption of policies by African governments. Such conditions may be classified into: reigning international paradigms; experience of the initial leaders; degree of group-identity rivalry, defined to include ethnic, linguistic, and religious forms of rivalry; initial institutions; and the role of government in fulfilling society's time preference for development.

3.1.1   Reigning international paradigms

The nature of policies pursued since independence depended considerably on the extent to which the initial leaders were influenced by the competing dual international development paradigms at the time: generally, capitalism versus socialism.[14] The adoption of socialistic policies usually meant a more extensive involvement of government in the economy, which entailed the adoption of non-market policies of state controls, in turn providing the basis for the redistribution intended to reduce income inequality. Many early African leaders found the socialistic direction particularly attractive. This attraction may help explain why, among the forty-six SSA countries, the frequency of controls was only slightly lower than that of syndrome-free status in 1960 but overtook syndrome-free status by the late 1960s; it was not until the early 1990s that syndrome-free status again began to dominate controls (figure 3.1). Indeed, for the twenty-six case countries, the relative frequency of controls was highest among all the syndromes and syndrome-free status in 1960, but otherwise followed a similar pattern as that for the forty-six countries (see figure 3.2).

---

[14] See Ndulu (chapter 9) for a discussion of the influence of international paradigms on African leaders' policy choice.

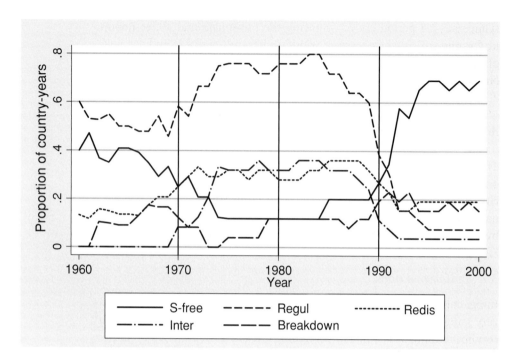

Figure 3.2 Policy syndromes in twenty-six case-study countries, post-independence years
Notes: See notes and key to figure 3.1. The sample appears in table 3.2.

The attraction of the early African leadership to socialism could be explained by several factors. First, a number of the leaders were strong believers in the need for a relatively equitable growth, and viewed capitalism as a mechanism for a few individuals to become richer at the expense of the masses. Second, the private sector was very much non-existent in many of these countries; thus the state was viewed as the primary agent for economic growth and development. Third, the government's role was envisaged as preserving the state, which normally comprised different and adversarial ethnic groups; that objective was seen as requiring a strong central authority with the power for resource redistribution to be targeted at attenuating centrifugal forces.

3.1.2   Experience of the initial leaders

The experience of the initial leaders seems to have mattered in the choice of policies. Those leaders who were politically conservative tended to favor market-friendly policies – e.g. Jomo Kenyatta of Kenya (Mwega and Ndulu 2007), Félix Houphouët-Boigny of Côte d'Ivoire (Kouadio Benie 2007), Sir Seretse Khama of Botswana (Maipose and Matsheka 2007), Sylvanus Olympio of Togo (Gogué and Evlo 2007), and Hastings Banda of Malawi

(Chipeta and Mkandawire 2007). In contrast, the politically liberal/radical leadership preferred a larger role for the government – e.g. Kwame Nkrumah of Ghana (Aryeetey and Fosu 2007), Julius Nyerere of Tanzania (Mwase and Ndulu 2007), Kenneth Kaunda of Zambia (Mwanawina and Mulungushi 2007), Modibo Keïta of Mali (Coulibaly and Diarra 2007), and Sékou Touré of Guinea (Doumbouya and Camara 2007). The sphere of influence on the leadership emanated considerably from the international arena based on the competing socialist and capitalist paradigms (chapter 9), as well as from the professional or traditional backgrounds of the leadership. In Togo, for example, the adoption of market-oriented policies is believed to have resulted from the background of Togo's first President, Sylvanus Olympio, as a former executive of an international trading company, buttressed by the business community as his support base (Gogué and Evlo 2007). Similarly, in Botswana, the rural origins of the leadership provided guidance toward rural-friendly measures, thus avoiding urban-biased policies (Maipose and Matsheka 2007). And, in Côte d'Ivoire (Kouadio Benie 2007), Kenya (Mwega and Ndung'u 2007), and Malawi (Chipeta and Mkandawire 2007), the agricultural backgrounds of the early leaders help explain their relatively supportive policies toward agriculture.

3.1.3 Group-identity rivalry

The need to preserve the non-cohesive embryonic nation following independence was the preoccupation of the vast majority of African leaders. Such preoccupation would dominate most of the policies pursued. In Ghana, for example, where there was considerable rivalry within the Akan, dominated by the Asante, as well as between the Akan and the other ethnic groups, the Nkrumah leadership believed that a strong central government was required to tame the centrifugal ethnic tendencies in order to preserve the nation-state (Aryeetey and Fosu 2007). In contrast, a federal system of government was chosen in Nigeria in order to accommodate the heterogeneous ethnic groups (Iyoha and Oriakhi 2007). Unfortunately, such a federal system may have enhanced the state-failure episode of the Biafran war of separation during the latter 1960s (Garba and Garba 2005).

Socialist policies may have succeeded, initially at least, in suppressing the tendencies toward state failure in the form of open warfare in many parts of Africa (Fosu 2005). Instead, elite political instability in the form of coups reigned in many African countries (Fosu 2005). Botswana succeeded in adopting market-friendly policies at the time of independence leading to its syndrome-free status throughout, in part because of the non-rivalrous nature of the relatively small homogenous population.[15] While the Tswana

---

[15] It is important to underscore the fact that Botswana's majority-Tswana leadership was also able to accommodate the rights of the minority group, thus paving the way for harmony under its multi-party democracy (Maipose and Matsheka 2007).

majority was able to undertake measures to safeguard the rights of their competing ethnic minority, it is also true that the minority was no threat to the Tswana. It is interesting to note that though Botswana has been able to maintain a multi-party democracy, there has been one dominant party since independence, namely, the Botswana Democratic Party (BDP) (Maipose and Matsheka 2007), suggesting that the lack of significant competition from the small parties likely helped tolerate their existence.

Indeed, group-identity rivalry has contributed considerably to various forms of anti-growth syndromes, as observed above, including adverse redistribution and even state failure. Economic rents generated from controls, for instance, would often be redistributed on the basis of ethnicity and, thus, represented "rents to sovereignty" (Nkurunziza and Ngaruko 2007) or, alternatively, "rents to political survival." Furthermore, multi-party competition seems to have further exacerbated this form of redistribution in some African countries – e.g. Cameroon in the 1980s under Paul Biya (Kobou, Njinkeu and Powo Fosso 2007) and Sierra Leone in the 1970s and 1980s under the APC (Davies 2007). In a number of African countries, moreover, the "North–South" divides, usually ethnic and religion-based, have served as centrifugal forces against state formation, resulting in state failures – e.g. Nigeria (Iyoha and Oriakhi 2007), Chad (Azam and Djimtoïngar 2007), Sudan (Ali and Elbadawi 2007), and Côte d'Ivoire (Kouadio Benie 2007).

3.1.4   Initial institutions

At the time of independence in African countries, there was often the colonial administration, on the one hand, and the rival chieftaincies, on the other. The colonial institution was usually rejected especially by the socialistic-leaning leadership, which also tended not to embrace the use of the traditional institutions as a base for governance either. Instead, colonial institutions were *selectively* adopted where they seemed to serve the interest of the leadership. For example, a number of former English and French colonies chose to maintain the no-limit terms of office for the head of state but not the concomitant checks and balances, as many opted for practically unlimited powers of the President. Meanwhile, the military was, at least initially, strengthened to protect the executive, usually from potential internal forces. As the strength of the military grew, however, it became the only real institution strong enough to change the entrenched leadership of the executive, with implications for elite political instability and possible state failure. Indeed, many of these heads of state later resorted to weakening the power of the military and empowering their own coteries of guards.[16]

---

[16] In Ghana, for example, a special force of Presidential Guards, who enjoyed better treatment than the military and police, protected President Nkrumah.

3.1.5 The role of government and time preference

In a number of cases where the leadership at the time of independence was politically conservative with market-friendly policies, the governments did not last long.[17] There was much political agitation for the government to lead the charge toward improving the lot of the people, especially given the paltry infrastructure and the rather slow pace at which the relatively undeveloped private sector was able to deliver the expected development outcomes for the population at large. Sooner or later, therefore, such governments were supplanted by more politically radical leaders, which preached the need for governments to quickly improve the conditions of the masses through more active intervention. These relatively interventionist, but initially popular, governments also tended to resort to autocratic measures, including the use of controls for redistribution (regional or vertical), in order to solidify their political position. Resorting to controls is consistent with such a strategy for two reasons: (1) government control of resources through marketing boards was intended to generate monopoly/monopsony rents for redistribution (Bates 1981 and chapter 4); and (2) price and foreign exchange controls were used as rationing mechanisms for shortages, but also served as ways to reward the elite constituency through implicit subsidies, as in the case of over-valuation of foreign currency, while at the same time providing economic-rent opportunities for the political coalition (Fosu 2003). Thus, it was unsurprising that the frequency of syndrome-free regimes decreased steadily through the 1970s, while the incidence of syndromes, particularly controls and intertemporally unsustainable spending, rose into the 1970s (see figures 3.1 and 3.2).

3.2 Supply shocks

3.2.1 Negative supply shocks

Negative supply shocks would usually be transformed to price increases in a non-regulated market, but to shortages in the case of price-controlled markets. Such supply shocks were typically the OPEC-orchestrated petroleum-supply reductions of particularly 1973 and 1979, as well as droughts

---

[17] There were several notable exceptions. For example, Ahmadou Ahidjo of Cameroon voluntarily retired in 1982 (Kobou and Njinkeu 2007), and Félix Houphouët-Boigny of Côte d'Ivoire (Kouadio Benie 2007), and Hastings Banda of Malawi (Chipeta and Mkandawire 2007) continued in power till retirement. Most importantly, Botswana was able to continue with its multi-party democracy without military intervention. One reason behind this feat might be that there was little ethnic rivalry to be taken advantage of by coalitions of a fractionalized military, as was the case in many other African countries. Another, perhaps more significant, rationale is that the military was not an important institution in Botswana (Maipose and Matsheka 2007).

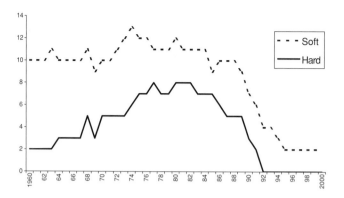

Figure 3.3 Evolution (frequencies) of control type, twenty-seven SSA case studies, 1960–2000
Notes: See notes and key to figure 3.1. The sample includes South Africa (hence twenty-seven cases rather than twenty-six).

occurring in many of the case countries. Since the large majority of African countries have traditionally been net consumers of petroleum, the events of the 1970s resulted in negative supply shocks. These shocks led directly to both stagnation and inflation in these economies, and indirectly via the resulting recessions in the rest of the world, which in turn engendered decreases in the demand for Africa's exports. Both effects should result in at least "implicit" domestic price increases and an over-valuation of the domestic currency, as most African countries operated fixed exchange rates in the 1970s. In addition, these negative supply shocks led to substantial deterioration in the terms of trade of many of the countries as of the mid-1970s-to-early 1980s.

As price pressures built up, there was the temptation by governments to regulate even further. Countries operating relatively free markets felt politically compelled to adopt controls, while those with controls tended to tighten them up. Thus there was the tendency for greater prevalence of controls generally in SSA in the 1970s, as observed in figure 3.1 for the forty-six African SSA countries. For the case study countries as well, as figure 3.2 indicates, the frequency of controls increased substantially in the 1970s and remained high until about the mid-1980s when several of the countries began IMF/World Bank-administered reform programs. Furthermore, as figure 3.3 shows, the relative frequency of hard to soft controls increased, starting in the mid-1970s. Both types of controls began to fall considerably as of the mid-1980s, however, and by the early 1990s there was no trace of hard controls. Meanwhile, even the prevalence of soft controls had reached its historical nadir by the early 1990s.

3.2.2   Positive supply shocks

Positive supply shocks provided countries with revenue windfalls. Many of these countries spent such windfalls as if they were sustainable over time. Either the revenues were used to meet short-term political objectives, thus providing (unsustainable) short-run benefits to the relevant political constituency, or were allocated based on policy errors resulting from myopia. In the first case, the spending was usually in the form of redistribution to the leaders' cronies or geographical constituencies. In the second, grandiose national projects with longer-term gestation periods were undertaken, with the erroneous expectations that the revenues would continue. As revenues subsequently dwindled, however, governments were forced to borrow in order to complete the projects, resulting in increased onerous debts and eventual fiscal difficulties. Furthermore, many of these projects were abandoned or curtailed from their original respective optimal sizes, thus resulting in sub-optimal cost–return outcomes.

3.3   Opportunity

The opportunity set available to countries played an important role in the prevalence of syndromes.[18] The intertemporally unsustainable syndrome would normally require the existence of a boom–bust episode associated with a natural resource: such as phosphate in Togo, 1974–89 (Gogué and Evlo 2007); oil in Cameroon, 1982–93 (Kobou, Njinkeu, and Powo Fosso 2007); phosphates and groundnuts in Senegal, 1974–9 (Ndiaye 2007); bauxite in Guinea, 1973–84 (Doumbouya and Camara 2007); coffee in Burundi, 1975–85 (Nkurunziza and Ngaruko 2007); uranium in Niger, 1974–85 (Samba Mamadou and Yakoubou 2007); and oil in Nigeria, 1974–86 (Iyoha and Oriakhi 2007). In some situations, such revenues led to outright looting, as in the case of oil in Nigeria during 1974–86 by several governments and during 1993–8 by Sani Abacha (Iyoha and Oriakhi 2007), and coffee in Uganda at the time of Idi Amin, 1971–8 (Kasekende and Atingi-Ego 2007). Similarly, the revenue-generating natural resources would provide the basis for redistribution, especially regionally. They could also fuel war and hence state breakdown (Collier and Hoeffler 1998), as the case of diamonds in Sierra Leone (Davies 2007), as well as oil in Angola (Roque 2005) and in Nigeria (Garba and Garba 2005; Iyoha and Oriakhi 2007). The lesson here is that a more transparent and judicious management of revenues from natural resources of the Chadian type, for example, is required.[19]

---

[18] See chapter 2 for a detailed discussion of the relationship between opportunity and syndromes.

[19] Under pressure from the World Bank, Chad set up a watchdog agency, the Revenue Oversight Committee, intended to scrutinize the use of oil revenues (The Economist 2003).

3.4 The role of institutions/political system

3.4.1 The military

The military has played a strong role in most of Africa since independence. Unfortunately, indigenous institutions were often supplanted by embryonic modern institutions, while the executive superseded the other forms of government, such as parliament and the judiciary, and entrenched itself in power. The military, then, became the only real competitor of the executive. Indeed, the rampancy of coups d'état across the African continent following independence could be traced in great part to the lack of a smooth and transparent process for leadership change.[20] Thus, by default, the military was transformed as the only real agent for political change in many of the countries, especially in autocratic countries.

Yet, the double-edged-sword role of the military became apparent, as it also overthrew embryonic democratic governments with syndrome-free policies that it considered to be politically unpalatable. Examples include, in Ghana, the 1972 overthrow of the government of Prime Minister Busia by General Acheampong (Aryeetey and Fosu 2007), and, in Togo, the assassination of Sylvanus Olympio and overthrow of his government by the military in the early 1960s (Gogué and Evlo 2007). The military was also used as an agent for settling scores and grievances associated with ethnic and other rivalries. Hence, in a positive sense, it represented a form of pressure valve, such that an all-out civil war was averted. The recourse to open rebellion (extreme form of state failure) became more likely where the use of coups was no longer a viable option for meeting such objectives (Fosu 2005).[21] Yet, the incidence of coups was in of itself a reflection of the underlying problems of institutional weakness (Fosu 2005).

3.4.2 Political system

The nature of institutions had a particularly salient role to play in fomenting or averting anti-growth syndromes. For example, the Fabian socialism adopted in many African countries contributed to the regulatory syndrome, as well as to adverse redistribution. Moreover, the rigid nature of such

---

[20] "The post-independence era in SSA has been marked by rampant events of coups d'état, with over 60 'successful' coups that resulted in government overthrows, 70 abortive coups and 125 officially reported coup plots" (Fosu 2003: 69)

[21] The RUF of Sierra Leone, for example, seems to have taken up arms against the APC when it became apparent that the military could not be used to loosen the APC's grip on power (Davies 2007). Similarly, the Hutu armed rebellion of Burundi appears to have been motivated by the feeling that there was no recourse through the military, which was controlled by the minority Tutsis (Nkurunziza and Ngaruko 2007). The genesis of the Liberian civil war can be traced in great part to the inability of the Samuel Doe antagonists to overthrow him via the regular military (Davies 2005).

Table 3.3 *Relative frequencies of syndrome-free and state breakdown, for forty-six [twenty-six] SSA countries, by sub-period.*

	Syndrome-free	State breakdown
1960–9	0.49 [0.38]	0.10 [0.10]
1970–9	0.23 [0.17]	0.08 [0.06]
1980–9	0.16 [0.16]	0.09 [0.12]
1990–5	0.41 [0.51]	0.22 [0.19]
1996–2000	0.57 [0.68]	0.26 [0.17]

Notes: Frequencies for the twenty-six-country case study sample appear in brackets.

governments led to elite political instability in the form of *coups d'état* – successful, abortive, or plots. Ironically, as observed above, such political instability might have actually helped to avert complete state breakdown in the form of armed insurrections (Fosu 2005). According to figures 3.1 and 3.2, the frequency of state failure was minimal until the latter part of the 1980s. In contrast, as the political space was liberalized in the late 1980s in many African countries, and the frequency of syndrome-free statuses surged, so did the incidence of state failure (figures 3.1 and 3.2). Indeed, as table 3.3 shows, the relative frequency of syndrome-free status jumped from 16 percent in the 1980s to nearly 50 percent in the 1990s for the forty-six SSA countries, while state breakdown more than doubled from 9 percent in the 1980s to 24 percent in the 1990s. A similar evolution holds for the twenty-six case countries as well, though the increase in the relative frequency of state breakdown between the 1980s and 1990s was less dramatic. The ability of governments to engage in virtuous redistribution, whether under dictatorship or multi-party politics, could also help obviate state breakdown and potentially achieve the syndrome-free regime.[22]

3.5 Economically driven political expediency

The upsurge in syndrome-free cases as of the late 1980s could be traced to the necessity for African governments to escape from dire fiscal straits in which

---

[22] For example, President Félix Houphouët-Boigny, a virtual dictator, is credited with uniting the northern and southern people of Côte d'Ivoire for many years by virtuously redistributing resources toward the relatively resource-poor North. However, the advent of multi-party competitive politics seems to have eroded this special arrangement and may have contributed significantly to the state breakdown that has essentially split the country into the northern and southern constituents (Azam 2005). Similarly in the case of Mauritius, successive democratic governments were able to buy peace by redistributing resources in favor of the majority native population (Nath and Madhoo 2007).

they had found themselves, usually following episodes of controls or unsustainable spending, and thus for accepting the IMF/World Bank liberalization reforms – e.g. Benin, 1990 (Dossou and Sinzogan, with Mensah 2007); Burkina Faso, 1991 (Savadogo, Coulibaly, and McCracken 2007); Republic of Congo, 1991 (Tsassa and Yamb 2007); Ethiopia, 1989 (Alemayehu 2003); Ghana, 1983 (Aryeetey and Fosu 2007); Guinea, 1985 (Doumbouya and Camara 2007); Mozambique, 1987 (de Sousa and Sulemane 2007); Niger, 1990 (Samba Mamadou and Yakoubou 2007); Sierra Leone, 1991 (Davies 2007); and Togo, 1980 (Gogué and Evlo 2007).[23] While the eclipse of ideological dualism – capitalist versus socialist – in the international arena and the emergence of a globally dominant paradigm of market-friendly policies played an important part in the transition, the thawing of the Cold War at the time also contributed to the exigencies faced by many socialistic African countries that could no longer count on the USSR for assistance. In addition, the substantial erosion of terms of trade in the late 1970s and early 1980s meant that many African countries faced major fiscal difficulties and had reluctantly to accept market-friendly policies accompanying IMF/World Bank bailouts.

4 Conclusion

Avoiding syndromes is a near-sufficient condition for preventing growth collapse and is also necessary for sustainable growth (Fosu and O'Connell, 2006). The absence of syndromes could increase *per capita* GDP growth by as much as 2.0 percentage points (Fosu and O'Connell 2006). This potential gain is huge for a sub-continent where overall *per capita* growth during the last four decades has averaged roughly 0.5 percent annually (Fosu 2001a). Thus, an appropriate growth-maximizing strategy would entail the minimization of the prevalence of syndromes. It is, therefore, heartening to observe a substantial increase in the frequency of syndrome-free status as of the late 1980s in Africa.

This recent rise in the frequency of syndrome-free status may be traced to two major developments: (1) the convergence of the international paradigm toward market-friendly policies as the best strategy for producing economic growth and development, and (2) the realization by African countries that external support requires adherence to these policies. The first development is particularly salient, as it has attenuated the uncertainty in policy-making. African leaders committed to growth and development in their

---

[23] For CFA economies, the period of reforms could not really materialize until the regional depreciation of the CFAF in 1994.

respective countries can now concentrate on mechanisms required to foster a syndrome-free environment.

The case studies have taught us that at the time of independence in many African countries, strong central governments were perceived as the optimal mechanism for nation-building. Controls from the central authority and redistribution were among the strategies employed. In many instances, these efforts appear to have actually succeeded in preventing state breakdown in terms of open rebellion. Unfortunately, however, the strategies adopted then also resulted in the various anti-growth syndromes of controls, adverse redistribution and intertemporally unsustainable spending. Without the appropriate checks and balances, the executive was free to carry out policies unencumbered, a process that seems to have spawned many of the syndromes. Meanwhile, the military became the only real credible agent for changing governments through *coups d'état*. This situation resulted in elite political instability (EPI), which has been deleterious to growth in Africa (Fosu 1992, 2001b). In its severe form, furthermore, EPI could constitute state failure, a phenomenon that tends to be the most growth-inhibiting syndrome (Fosu and O'Connell 2006, table 8).

What is now apparent is that if syndrome-free status is to be achieved and sustained, the appropriate institutions are required to provide the checks and balances that would prevent unencumbered action on the part of the executive, and to keep the military at bay. While dictatorships need not be anti-growth (Clague *et al.* 1996), the history of the continent has revealed that growth and dictatorships are unlikely to coexist. Thus, current efforts such as the New Partnership for African Development (NEPAD) and the African Peer Review Mechanism (APRM) to improve good governance would seem to constitute steps in the right direction. Meanwhile, it is imperative that the potential downside risks, including redistributive politics associated with multi-party democracy (Bratton and van de Walle 1997) and state breakdown,[24] be minimized.

Achieving a syndrome-free state would require compromises. Given the inherent group-identity nature of many African countries, such compromises would entail not only political power-sharing across groups, but also group-identity-based economic redistribution, *de jure* or *de facto*. In particular, it may be worthwhile to revisit the group-identity political representation framework proposed by Claude Ake (1996), despite the potentially unwieldy problem of its implementation (Fosu 1998). As Azam (1995, 2001), for instance, argues, proper regional redistribution could indeed "buy" peace.

---

[24] The case studies show a considerable rise in the frequency of state failure since the late 1980s when many African countries embarked on competitive democratic politics. It must be stressed, though, that such incidence is dwarfed by the frequency of syndrome-free status during the same period (see figures 3.1 and 3.2).

Above all, the establishment of appropriate institutions is the *sine qua non* for fostering the capable state necessary for undertaking optimal economic decisions, including the intertemporal allocation of resources. Building such institutional capacities requires time, local effort, and ownership; however, the role of the international community is just as salient, through policy coherence and augmentation of development capacity.

References

Ake, Claude (1996), *Democracy and Development in Africa*. Washington, DC: Brookings Institution

Alemayehu, Geda (2003), "The Political Economy of Growth in Ethiopia," *AERC Growth Project*, Nairobi

Ali, Ali Abdel Gadir and Ibrahim A. Elbadawi (2007), "Explaining Sudan's Economic Growth Performance," chapter 7 in Benno J. Ndulu, Stephen A. O'Connell, Jean-Paul Azam, Robert H. Bates, Augustin Kwasi Fosu, Jan Willem Gunning, and Dominique Njinkeu, eds., *The Political Economy of Economic Growth in Africa, 1960–2000*, vol. 2. Cambridge: Cambridge University Press

Aryeetey, Ernest and Augustin K. Fosu (2007), "Economic Growth in Ghana, 1960–2000," chapter 9 in Benno J. Ndulu, Stephen A. O'Connell, Jean-Paul Azam, Robert H. Bates, Augustin Kwasi Fosu, Jan Willem Gunning, and Dominique Njinkeu, eds., *The Political Economy of Economic Growth in Africa, 1960–2000*, vol. 2. Cambridge: Cambridge University Press

Azam, Jean-Paul (1995), "How to Pay for the Peace? A Theoretical Framework with Reference to African Countries," *Public Choice* 83: 173–84

   (2001). "The Redistributive State and Conflicts in Africa," *Journal of Peace Research* 38(4): 429–44

   (2005), "Political Geography and Redistribution," Paper presented at the AERC/Weatherhead Center Workshop on Explaining African Economic Growth, Harvard University, Cambridge, MA, March 18–19

Azam, Jean-Paul and Nadjiounoum Djimtoïngar (2007), "Cotton, War, and Growth in Chad, 1996–2000," chapter 3 in Benno J. Ndulu, Stephen A. O'Connell, Jean-Paul Azam, Robert H. Bates, Augustin Kwasi Fosu, Jan Willem Gunning, and Dominique Njinkeu, eds., *The Political Economy of Economic Growth in Africa, 1960–2000*, vol. 2. Cambridge: Cambridge University Press

Bates, Robert H. (1981), *Markets and States in Tropical Africa*. Berkeley, CA: University of California Press

Bratton, Michael and Nicolas van de Walle (1997), *Democratic Experiments in Africa*. Cambridge: Cambridge University Press

Chipeta, Chinyamata and Mjedo Mkandawire (2007), "Man-made Opportunities and Growth in Malawi," chapter 5 in Benno J. Ndulu, Stephen A. O'Connell, Jean-Paul Azam, Robert H. Bates, Augustin Kwasi Fosu, Jan Willem Gunning, and Dominique Njinkeu, eds., *The Political Economy of Economic Growth in Africa, 1960–2000*, vol. 2. Cambridge: Cambridge University Press

Clague, C., P. Keefer, S. Knack, and M. Olsen (1996), "Property and Contract Rights in Autocracies and Democracies," *Journal of Economic Growth* 1: 243–76

Collier, Paul and Anke Hoeffler (1998), "On Economic Causes of Civil War," *Oxford Economic Papers* 50(4): 563–75

Coulibaly, Massa and Amadou Diarra(2005). "Liberia and Sierra Leone: Interwoven Civil Wars," in Augustin K. Fosu and Paul Collier, eds., *Post-conflict Economies in Africa.* New York: Palgrave Macmillan: 77–90

(2007), "Mali: du 'tout Etat' à la croissance invisible," chapter 21 in Benno J. Ndulu, Stephen A. O'Connell, Jean-Paul Azam, Robert H. Bates, Augustin Kwasi Fosu, Jan Willem Gunning, and Dominique Njinkeu, eds., *The Political Economy of Economic Growth in Africa, 1960–2000*, vol. 2. Cambridge: Cambridge University Press

Davies, Victor A. B. (2007), "Sierra Leone's Economic Growth Performance, 1961–2000," chapter 19 in Benno J. Ndulu, Stephen A. O'Connell, Jean-Paul Azam, Robert H. Bates, Augustin Kwasi Fosu, Jan Willem Gunning, and Dominique Njinkeu, eds., *The Political Economy of Economic Growth in Africa, 1960–2000*, vol. 2. Cambridge: Cambridge University Press

de Sousa, Clara Ana and José Sulemane (2007), "Mozambique's Growth Performance, 1960–1996," chapter 24 in Benno J. Ndulu, Stephen A. O'Connell, Jean-Paul Azam, Robert H. Bates, Augustin Kwasi Fosu, Jan Willem Gunning, and Dominique Njinkeu, eds., *The Political Economy of Economic Growth in Africa, 1960–2000*, vol. 2. Cambridge: Cambridge University Press

Dossou, Antonin S. and Jean-Yves Sinzogan, with Sylviane Mensah (2007), "Economic Growth in Benin: Lost Opportunities," chapter 22 in Benno J. Ndulu, Stephen A. O'Connell, Jean-Paul Azam, Robert H. Bates, Augustin Kwasi Fosu, Jan Willem Gunning, and Dominique Njinkeu, eds., *The Political Economy of Economic Growth in Africa, 1960–2000*, vol. 2. Cambridge: Cambridge University Press

Doumbouya, Sékou and Fodé Camara (2007), "Explaining Economic Growth in Africa: The Case of Guinea," chapter 17 in Benno J. Ndulu, Stephen A. O'Connell, Jean-Paul Azam, Robert H. Bates, Augustin Kwasi Fosu, Jan Willem Gunning, and Dominique Njinkeu, eds., *The Political Economy of Economic Growth in Africa, 1960–2000*, vol. 2. Cambridge: Cambridge University Press

Economist, The (2003), "Can Oil Ever Help the Poor?," December 6: 37–8

Fosu, A. K. (1992), "Political Instability and Economic Growth: Evidence from Sub-Saharan Africa," *Economic Development and Cultural Change* 40(4): 829–41

(1998), "Review of Claude Ake, Democracy and Development in Africa," *Journal of Development Studies* 34(4): 171–2

(2001a), "The Global Setting and African Economic Growth," *Journal of African Economies* 10(3): 282–310

(2001b), "Political Instability and Economic Growth in Developing Economies: Some Specification Empirics," *Economics Letters* 70: 289–94

(2002), "Political Instability and Economic Growth: Implications of Coup Events in Sub-Saharan Africa," *American Journal of Economics and Sociology* 61(1): 329–48

(2003), "Political Instability and Export Performance in Sub-Saharan Africa," *Journal of Development Studies* 39(4): 68–82

(2005), "Post-conflict Economies in Africa: Synthesis and Lessons," in Augustin K. Fosu and Paul Collier, eds., *Post-conflict Economies in Africa*. New York: Palgrave Macmillan: 231–40

Fosu, Augustin K. and Stephen A. O'Connell (2006), "Explaining African Economic Growth: The Role of Anti-growth Syndromes," in François Bourguignon and Boris Pleskovic, eds., *Annual World Bank Conference on Development Economics 2006: Growth and Integration*. Washington, DC: The World Bank

Garba, A. G. and P. K. Garba (2005), "The Nigerian Civil War: Causes and the Aftermath," in Augustin K. Fosu and Paul Collier, eds., *Post-conflict Economies in Africa*. New York: Palgrave Macmillan: 91–108

Godana, Tekaligne and John E. Odada (2007), "A Case Study of Namibia," chapter 26 in Benno J. Ndulu, Stephen A. O'Connell, Jean-Paul Azam, Robert H. Bates, Augustin Kwasi Fosu, Jan Willem Gunning, and Dominique Njinkeu, eds., *The Political Economy of Economic Growth in Africa, 1960–2000*, vol. 2. Cambridge: Cambridge University Press

Gogué, Tchabouré A. and Kodjo Evlo (2007), "Togo: Lost Opportunities for Growth," chapter 14 in Benno J. Ndulu, Stephen A. O'Connell, Jean-Paul Azam, Robert H. Bates, Augustin Kwasi Fosu, Jan Willem Gunning, and Dominique Njinkeu, eds., *The Political Economy of Economic Growth in Africa, 1960–2000*, vol. 2. Cambridge: Cambridge University Press

Iyoha, Milton A. and Dickson E. Oriakhi (2007), "Explaining African Economic Growth Performance: The Case of Nigeria," chapter 18 in Benno J. Ndulu, Stephen A. O'Connell, Jean-Paul Azam, Robert H. Bates, Augustin Kwasi Fosu, Jan Willem Gunning, and Dominique Njinkeu, eds., *The Political Economy of Economic Growth in Africa, 1960–2000*, vol. 2. Cambridge: Cambridge University Press

Kasekende, Louis A. and Michael Atingi-Ego (2007), "Restarting and Sustaining Growth in a Post-conflict Economy: The Case of Uganda," chapter 8 in Benno J. Ndulu, Stephen A. O'Connell, Jean-Paul Azam, Robert H. Bates, Augustin Kwasi Fosu, Jan Willem Gunning, and Dominique Njinkeu, eds., *The Political Economy of Economic Growth in Africa, 1960–2000*, vol. 2. Cambridge: Cambridge University Press

Kobou, Georges, Dominique Njinkeu and Bruno Powo Fosso (2007), "The Political Economy of Cameroon's Post-independence Growth Experience," chapter 16 in Benno J. Ndulu, Stephen A. O'Connell, Jean-Paul Azam, Robert H. Bates, Augustin Kwasi Fosu, Jan Willem Gunning, and Dominique Njinkeu, eds., *The Political Economy of Economic Growth in Africa, 1960–2000*, vol. 2. Cambridge: Cambridge University Press

Kouadio Benie, Marcel (2007), "Explication de la croissance en Côte d'Ivoire," chapter 23 in Benno J. Ndulu, Stephen A. O'Connell, Jean-Paul Azam, Robert H. Bates, Augustin Kwasi Fosu, Jan Willem Gunning, and Dominique Njinkeu, eds., *The Political Economy of Economic Growth in Africa, 1960–2000*, vol. 2. Cambridge: Cambridge University Press

Maipose, Gervase S. and Thapelo C. Matsheka (2007), "The Indigenous Developmental State and Growth in Botswana," chapter 15 in Benno J. Ndulu, Stephen A. O'Connell, Jean-Paul Azam, Robert H. Bates, Augustin Kwasi Fosu, Jan

Willem Gunning, and Dominique Njinkeu, eds., *The Political Economy of Economic Growth in Africa, 1960–2000*, vol. 2. Cambridge: Cambridge University Press

Maundeni, Z. (2001), "State Culture and Development in Botswana and Zimbabwe," *Journal of Modern African Studies* 40(1): 105–32

Mwanawina, Inyambo and James Mulungushi (2007), "Zambia," chapter 27 in Benno J. Ndulu, Stephen A. O'Connell, Jean-Paul Azam, Robert H. Bates, Augustin Kwasi Fosu, Jan Willem Gunning, and Dominique Njinkeu, eds., *The Political Economy of Economic Growth in Africa, 1960–2000*, vol. 2. Cambridge: Cambridge University Press

Mwase, Nkunde and Benno Ndulu (2007). "Tanzania: Explaining Four Decades of Episodic Growth," chapter 13 in Benno J. Ndulu, Stephen A. O'Connell, Jean-Paul Azam, Robert H. Bates, Augustin Kwasi Fosu, Jan Willem Gunning, and Dominique Njinkeu, eds., *The Political Economy of Economic Growth in Africa, 1960–2000*, vol. 2. Cambridge: Cambridge University Press

Mwega, Francis M. and Njuguna S. Ndung'u (2007), "Explaining African Economic Growth Performance: The Case of Kenya," chapter 10 in Benno J. Ndulu, Stephen A. O'Connell, Jean-Paul Azam, Robert H. Bates, Augustin Kwasi Fosu, Jan Willem Gunning, and Dominique Njinkeu, eds., *The Political Economy of Economic Growth in Africa, 1960–2000*, vol. 2. Cambridge: Cambridge University Press

Nath, Shyam and Yeti Nisha Madhoo (2007), "A Shared Growth Story of Economic Success: The Case of Mauritius," chapter 11 in Benno J. Ndulu, Stephen A. O'Connell, Jean-Paul Azam, Robert H. Bates, Augustin Kwasi Fossu, Jan Willem Gunning, and Dominique Njinkeu, eds., *The Political Economy of Economic Growth in Africa, 1960–2000*, vol. 2. Cambridge: Cambridge University Press

Ndiaye, Mansour (2007), "State Control and Poor Economic Growth Performance in Senegal," chapter 12 in Benno J. Ndulu, Stephen A. O'Connell, Jean-Paul Azam, Robert H. Bates, Augustin Kwasi Fossu, Jan Willem Gunning, and Dominique Njinkeu, eds., *The Political Economy of Economic Growth in Africa, 1960–2000*, vol. 2. Cambridge: Cambridge University Press

Nkurunziza Janvier D. and Floribert Ngaruko (2007), "Why Has Burundi Grown So Slowly?: The Political Economy of Redistribution," chapter 2 chapter 12 in Benno J. Ndulu, Stephen A. O'Connell, Jean-Paul Azam, Robert H. Bates, Augustin Kwasi Fosu, Jan Willem Gunning, and Dominique Njinkeu, eds., *The Political Economy of Economic Growth in Africa, 1960–2000*, vol. 2. Cambridge: Cambridge University Press

Roque, Fatima (2005), "Transformation for Post-conflict Angola," in Augustin K. Fosu and Paul Collier, eds., *Post-conflict Economies in Africa*. New York: Palgrave Macmillan: 213–28

Samba Mamadou, Ousmane and Mahaman Sani Yakoubou (2007), "Climate Vulnerability, Political Instability, Investment, and Growth in a Landlocked Sahelian Economy: Niger, 1960–2000," chapter 6 in Benno J. Ndulu, Stephen A. O'Connell, Jean-Paul Azam, Robert H. Bates, Augustin Kwasi Fosu, Jan Willem Gunning, and Dominique Njinkeu, eds., *The Political Economy of Economic Growth in Africa, 1960–2000*, vol. 2. Cambridge: Cambridge University Press

Savadogo, Kimseyinga, Siaka Coulibaly, and Coleen A. McCracken (2007), "Analyzing Growth in Burkina Faso over the Last Four Decades," chapter 20 in Benno J. Ndulu, Stephen A. O'Connell, Jean-Paul Azam, Robert H. Bates, Augustin Kwasi Fosu, Jan Willem Gunning, and Dominique Njinkeu, eds., *The Political Economy of Economic Growth in Africa, 1960–2000*, vol. 2. Cambridge: Cambridge University Press

Tsassa, Célestin and Benjamin Yamb (2007), "Croissance off-shore au Congo et économie rentière," chapter 25 in Benno J. Ndulu, Stephen A. O'Connell, Jean-Paul Azam, Robert H. Bates, Augustin Kwasi Fosu, Jan Willem Gunning, and Dominique Njinkeu, eds., *The Political Economy of Economic Growth in Africa, 1960–2000*, vol. 2. Cambridge: Cambridge University Press

PART 2

Interpretation

4 | Domestic interests and control regimes

Robert H. Bates

The paper was written with financial support from the National Science Foundation (Grant SES 9905568), the Carnegie Corporation, and the Center for International Development and the Weatherhead Center for International Affairs of Harvard University. The chapter was written while the author was a Moore Distinguished Scholar at the California Institute of Technology. The chapter has benefited greatly from comments and criticisms received at seminars held at Harvard University, Guelo Brittany, and at the annual meetings of the AERC 2004 in Nairobi. Special thanks go to Steven Block for his criticisms and corrections. As ever, Karen Ferree and Smita Singh deserve much of the credit for this work. James Habyarimana and Irene Yackolev provided valuable contributions. I wish to thank Bela Prasad, Matthew Hindeman, and Marc Alexander for their technical assistance. The author alone is to be blamed for its shortcomings.

1   Introduction

When imposing a control regime, a government seeks to displace the market as the primary agency for governing the economy. Either by manipulating the structure or operation of markets, or by replacing private markets with public bureaucracies, it seeks to shape the way in which land, labor, and capital are allocated; commodities produced and distributed; services furnished; and incomes determined.

This chapter details the policies that characterize regulatory regimes and documents their economic impact. Stressing the economic costs inflicted by the imposition of control regimes, the chapter asks: given their magnitude, why did governments pursue such policies? And having chosen to regulate their economies, why did governments persist in this decision? The answers it offers not only shed light on why governments may impose control regimes, then, but also on the politics of policy reform.

In analyzing the content of control regimes, this chapter draws on two sets of data. One is the classification of policy syndromes developed by the research teams; the other is an account of the policy choices of twenty-eight African governments published by the World Bank (1994).[1] In its 1994 report, the Bank audited the measures taken by its sample set of governments to regulate financial markets, industries, trade, and services. To illustrate the content of control regimes, the chapter compares the measures taken by governments judged to have implemented control regimes with those judged not to have done so, as documented in the World Bank's report (1994).

2   Prices in the macroeconomy

As shown in the World Bank's report (1994), almost all African governments created banks to promote investment in commerce, industry, and agriculture. Governments that imposed control regimes went further, however: targeting privileged sectors, they actively subsidized the costs of capital for those who invested in them. To encourage investment, they imposed low interest rates, either by constraining the lending practices of private banks or by creating state banks to offer low-cost loans. The result was financial repression. As shown in table 4.1, under governments judged to have imposed control regimes, the mean *ex ante* real deposit interest rate was lower than under governments whose policies were judged to have remained "syndrome-free."

[1] See World Bank (1994).

Table 4.1 *Ex ante real deposit rate.*

	Control regimes	Other syndromes	Syndrome-free
Mean	−66.1	−309.6	−3.9
Median	−6.1	−4.1	−0.3
Count	162	90	165

Table 4.2 *Black market premium.*

	Control regimes	Other syndromes	Syndrome-free
Mean	175.4	133.6	7.4
Median	53.0	27.0	6.3
Count	317	211	314

Governments that operate outside the CFA zone (or RMA) control the means of payment. By setting the price at which local currency exchanges for foreign, and then controlling transactions at this official exchange rate – e.g. via remittance requirements for exporters and foreign-exchange rationing for importers – they can separate local parallel-market prices for traded goods from international prices. One measure of the magnitude of this intervention is the level of the black market premium that then prevails in the market for foreign exchange. As shown in table 4.2, when governments imposed control regimes, the mean level of that premium was more than twice the level of that in economies free of controls.[2]

3 Interventions by sector

Governments that adopted regulatory regimes were not only more likely to distort prices fundamental to the macroeconomy; they were also more likely to champion sectoral policies.

3.1 The industrial sector

Those that adopted control regimes intervened heavily in the industrial sector. Data from the World Bank study (1994: 234) suggest that over one-third secured monopoly rights over mineral production, compared with one-quarter of those judged "syndrome-free." Similarly, the World Bank's data (1994: 234) indicate that governments that adopted control regimes

---

[2] Given the magnitude of the within-group variance, the difference in means implies an F-statistic of 5.44, significant at the 0.02 level.

Table 4.3 *Intervention in food markets.*
(number of countries)

Level of restrictions:	Countries that adopt:	
	Control regimes	Other
Major	12	2
Limited	5	0
None	4	5
Total	21	7

Source: Data from World Bank (1994: 85).

were half-again more likely to form state monopolies in the cement and textile industries.

3.2 The agricultural sector

As seen in table 4.3, in its review of twenty-eight African cases, the World Bank noted that one-half of the governments judged to have imposed control regimes, placed "major" – as opposed to "limited" or "no" – restrictions on the purchase and sale of staple food crops.

All twenty-eight of the governments studied by the World Bank maintained a monopoly over the purchase and export of their country's major cash crops. But by artificially appreciating the value of the domestic currency, governments that adopted control regimes imposed an additional level of taxation. As noted in a variety of studies (most notably, perhaps, in Krueger, Schiff, and Valdes 1992), the manipulation of the exchange rate powerfully and adversely impacted upon the earnings of those producing cash crops for export.

African governments also intervened in the market for food crops: the World Bank (1994) reports that virtually all of the twenty-eight governments in its sample imposed "extensive" price controls (1994: 91). The better to provision consumers with low-priced products, some governments secured monopoly standing in agricultural markets, thus gaining the power to alter prices. Examples would include the creation of the National Milling Corporation by the government in Tanzania, which purchased and processed wheat and maize; the Sugar Board in Kenya, which produced and processed sugar and regulated its distribution; or the National Agricultural Marketing Board in Zambia. Table 4.4 reveals that governments that adopted control regimes more frequently created such marketing agencies than did others. As noted in studies by Killick (1978), Bates and Collier (1991), and others,[3]

---

[3] See, for example, Dodge (1977) and the classic reports of William Jones: World Bank (1975, 1982).

Table 4.4 *Government monopolies in the processing of wheat, maize, sugar, and vegetable oil.*
(number of countries).

Countries that adopt:	Wheat	Maize	Sugar	Vegetable oil	Total
Control regimes	11	6	12	8	21
Other policies	2	2	4	2	7

Source: Data from: World Bank (1994: 234).

Table 4.5 *Government monopoly over the importation of wheat, rice, sugar, other staples, and vegetable oils.*
(number of countries)

Countries that adopt	Wheat	Rice	Sugar	Other staple food crops	Vegetable oils	Total
Control regimes:	10	13	13	8	8	21
Other policies:	4	4	3	2	2	7

Source: Data from World Bank (1994: 235).

when governments created agricultural marketing boards, they employed their market power to provision urban consumers with low-priced food.

In efforts to control domestic markets, governments also created public agencies that purchased food abroad and marketed it domestically. Acquiring foreign exchange at the official rate, the agencies purchased rice, wheat, and other products abroad, which they placed in the domestic market at prices lower than those that would have prevailed had the imports been made by private traders. As seen in table 4.5, the data suggest that such measures were more likely to have been taken by governments that adopted regulatory regimes.

To be noted and stressed is that the financial burden of such interventions was borne by exporters, a portion of whose earnings were appropriated at the official rate. In many African countries, agricultural products – coffee, cocoa, cotton, or other cash crops – numbered among the exports that financed these measures.

4   The economic impact

To address the impact of control regimes, we begin by mapping the incidence of these policies onto the opportunity structure of Africa's economies. As seen in table 4.6, the governments in landlocked and coastal countries more

Table 4.6 *Control regimes and geographic location, 1970–1995.*

	Percent	Number
Landlocked	52.3	193
Coastal	49.6	183
Resource-rich	38.8	143

Note: Because Resource-rich can be either coastal or landlocked, the total is omitted.

Source: Data supplied by Paul Collier and Stephen A. O'Connell, based on the classification developed in chapter 2.

frequently adopted regulatory policies than did those that were resource-rich.

In chapter 2, Collier and O'Connell measure the impact of control regimes on growth rates in Africa. Controlling for the impact of rainfall and fluctuations in the growth rate of major trading partners and introducing country-specific effects – to control for such factors as coastal location or resource endowment – and period effects – to control for the effects of changes in the global economy, such as resulted from the oil price shocks of the 1970s and 1980s – Collier and O'Connell find that economies subject to control regimes achieved a median[4] growth rate that lay nearly 2 percentage points below that achieved by economies governed by policies that were judged "syndrome-free."

As reported in chapter 3, Fosu and O'Connell (2006) disaggregate the average performance of Africa's economies into "growth spells," which they then relate to the policy choices of their governments. Defining a growth collapse as a fall in the three-year centered moving average of growth below the no-growth (0.0 percent) level, they find the frequency of growth collapses under control regimes to be more than twice that under policy regimes that remained syndrome-free. Defining "medium" growth as the achievement of a five-year moving average growth rate of 2.5 percent, Fosu and O'Connell (2006) find that in less than one-quarter of the cases where governments adopted control regimes did economies attain medium rates of growth; by contrast, where policies were syndrome-free, more than half attained such a growth rate. They further find that economies ruled by governments whose policies remained syndrome-free were more than twice as likely to attain high growth rates – a five-year moving average of 3.5 percent or more – than were those ruled by governments that imposed control regimes.

---

[4] Given the dispersion in the data, they employed a least-absolute rather than a least-squares deviation criterion, thus dampening the impact of outliers.

5   A closer look

To illuminate the processes that account for the impact of control regimes, it is useful to move from aggregate, cross-national data to materials gleaned from country studies. In this section we make use of materials gathered at the micro-level, drawing heavily on the work of the country teams as reported in volume 2.

5.1   Manufacturing

Seeking to promote industrial development in Tanzania, the government placed a high priority on securing the local production of consumer products, such as clothing and footwear. The government therefore created the National Textile Corporation (TEXCO), which invested in a series of mills that produced cloth, blankets, and packaging, and the Tanzanian Leather Associated Industries (TLAIA), which invested in the production of shoes. None of the firms created by the two agencies operated at a profit. For want of revenues, their managers skimped on maintenance; they lacked access to the foreign exchange with which to import spare parts. The managers frequently failed to pay suppliers of raw materials, of services, or of the water and electricity necessary to drive looms and lathes. The firms survived by securing loans from the government: funneling money into the shoe plants, one minister declared, "was like pouring water down in a leaking tin" (McHenry 1994). Despite the poor performance of these firms, the government continued to make good their losses. From 1967, the date of Tanzania's official commitment to socialism, to 1982, when that commitment began to erode, public sector firms in Tanzania increased their share of total manufacturing employment from 15.5 percent to 52.7 percent. Fearing to lay off the thousands of workers that these firms employed (McHenry 1994), the government continued to use public revenues to cover their deficits.

As noted in the country studies in volume 2, Tanzania's experience was replicated by that in other nations. Addressing the case of Zambia, for example, Mwanawina and Mulungushi (2007) trace the government's investments in factories for the making of glass, the fabrication of building materials, the extrusion of plastics, and the assembly of automobiles. Quoting Turok (1979: 24) they note that "the parastatal sector, the main arm of government economic muscle, were grossly undercapitalized, over staffed, and faced shortages of raw materials and spare parts due to lack of foreign exchange" (2007: 18). Gogué and Evlo (2007) recount the efforts of the government of Togo: "Public investment represented nearly half of GDP by the end of the 1970s," they note (2005: 16). The government of Togo,

Gogué and Evlo (2007) record, launched its program of industrialization following the influx of foreign revenues inspired by a boom in the price of phosphates. Similar stories are told for Cameroon and Congo (Kobou, Njinkeu, and Powo Fosso 2007; Tsassa and Yamb 2007); Burundi (Nkurunziza and Ngaruko 2007); Zambia (Mwanawina and Mulungushi 2007), and Sierra Leone (Davies 2007). As in the case of Tanzania, these investments often consumed more resources than they generated. Writing of the industries created by the government of Burundi, for example, Nkurunziza and Ngaruko (2007) note:

> By 1995, equity capital of thirty-six such firms with majority state participation represented 20 percent of the country's GDP, but overall, these corporations posted a net loss equivalent to 6 percent of GDP. (Nkurunziza and Ngaruko 2007: 35)

5.2   Public services

Governments that imposed control regimes recruited large numbers of workers. Tsassa and Yamb (2007) report, for example, that the government of the Republic of the Congo increased the size of the public work force by an average of 9 percent per year from 1960 to 1993. Samba Mamadou and Yakoubou (2007) report a 4 percent annual increase in the government work force in Niger over the period 1980–92, while Gogué and Evlo (2007) note a three-fold increase in public sector employment in Togo over the period 1965–79. In Niger, Cameroon, Congo, Guinea, and Benin, the country studies inform us, in the 1960s and 1970s all who secured their diplomas were guaranteed employment by the state.[5]

Tsassa and Yamb (2007) report that by the early 1990s, 97 percent of the receipts of the government of the Congo were targeted for civil servant salaries. One way of relieving the burden was simply to accumulate arrears; the country studies suggest that this tactic was adopted by many of the governments in the franc zone. Where governments could exercise monetary discretion, they often reduced the burden by inflating the currency. According to the International Labour Organization (ILO), in Tanzania, the real salaries of public employees fell by nearly one-half between 1969 and 1980 (cited in McHenry 1994, table 4.1). In her study of workers in Kinshasa, MacGaffey (1991) reports that mid-1980s salaries constituted less than one-half of the incomes of those who worked in the public sector.

One of the major effects of the reduction of salaries was the growth of corruption. Charged with preventing the importation of products that were manufactured locally, a customs official could instead wave such goods through, pocketing a fee for his "service." Or charged with overseeing the

---

[5] Note the relevant country case studies. They are posted at http://www.aercAfrica.org.

Table 4.7 *Distribution of growth performance, by syndrome.*
(% of row)

Panel A: three-year moving average			
Syndrome status	< 0	>=0	Total
Not-free	49.3	50.7	100
Syndrome-free	19.1	80.9	100
Total	39.5	60.5	100
Panel B: five-year moving average			
Syndrome status	<2.5	>=2.5	Total
Not-free	75.9	24.1	100
Syndrome-free	47.5	52.6	100
Total	66.7	33.3	100
Panel C: five-year moving average			
Syndrome status	<3.5	>=3.5	Total
Not-free	80.7	19.3	100
Syndrome-free	55.8	44.2	100
Total	72.6	27.4	100

pricing of products produced at home, an inspector could share with the managers of firms the profits to be made from selling those products on the black market. The result was the erosion of the quality of public services and the rise of corruption.

5.3 Farming

Governments that imposed control regimes formed monopsonies with which to purchase export crops; offering farmers a low domestic price, they re-sold cash crops at prices prevailing in global markets. Dossou and Sinzogan, with Mensah (2007) document the cartelization of the cotton industry in Benin and its subsequent take over by the government. They also document the government's use of its market power to separate the domestic from the international price of cotton and to appropriate a major portion of the differential. Azam and Djimtoïngar (2007) note a similar pattern in Chad, where the government not only imposed a direct tax on farmers but also a profit tax on the reserves of the cotton agency. By dint of the government's ownership of 75 percent of the shares of the parastatal, the majority of the profits also accrued to the government. Nkurunziza and Ngaruko (2007) provide a similar narrative for the coffee industry in Burundi; Samba Mamadou and Yakoubou (2007) for the groundnut industry in Niger; and Davies (2007) for coffee and cocoa in Sierra Leone. As stated by Gogué and Evlo (2005):

The producer price of key export crops fell considerably (40% in the case of cocoa and 20% in the case of coffee) despite the increase in the international prices of these commodities. The power of the agencies created to implement the price control policies (OPAT, Togograin, Togofruit, etc.) grew bigger, as did the anti-rural bias of the government's income distribution policy. At the same time, flattering and deceiving slogans that boasted the merits of the Green Revolution and through which the government conveniently conveyed its demagogical rhetoric lulled farmers. Indeed, Togolese heard so much about something called "the Green Revolution" but they never experienced [it] actually. The beautiful words and great promises of the government were not followed by concrete actions. (2005: 36)

Similar patterns arose in markets for food crops. In Tanzania (Mwase and Ndulu 2007), Mozambique (de Sousa and Sulemane 2007), and Ethiopia (Alemayehu 2007), governments gathered farmers into villages, where they provided land, tools, and credit. With farm production now concentrated in circumscribed locations, the governments sought to control the purchase and distribution of farm products, funneling them through "single-channel" marketing structures, such as marketing boards or cooperative societies. They thereby sought to procure for urban consumers ample supplies of food at affordable prices. The result of this policy was, however, the opposite. As documented for Guinea by Doumbouya and Camara (2007) and for Tanzania by Lofchie (1989), as the bureaucracy charged with procuring grain increased in scope and size, the amount of grain that it marketed declined. One interpretation is that production itself declined; given the forceful relocation of peasant families from private farms to collective villages, this interpretation may be correct. Another is that when confronted with an official market offering low prices for farm products, the producers simply sold their products in unofficial markets, thereby eluding those who monitored the quantities and regulated the prices of agricultural products. The latter possibility is confirmed by Doumbouya and Camara (2007), who report the growth of black markets in Guinea and the movement of producers to regions by the border, where they could sell food crops in private markets and at unofficial rates of exchange. Indeed, in their study of Benin, Dossou and Sinzogan, with Mensah (2007) stress the size of the illicit trade in food products with Nigeria, where "Dutch disease" had led to high food prices.

Writing about Mozambique, Pitcher (2002) notes similar patterns. In the southern portion of Mozambique, the formation of communal villages so disrupted production that shortages of food and high prices for farm products became painfully common in the port cities and national capital, even while the welfare of the peasantry declined (see also Bowen 2000). Indeed, it declined to the point, Pitcher notes, where significant portions of the peasantry shifted their support from the Mozambican Liberation Front (FRELIMO), the governing party, to the Mozambican National Resistance

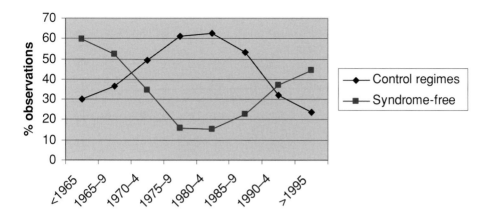

Figure 4.1 Policy regimes over time, 1965–1995

(RENAMO), an armed movement sworn to its forceful overthrow (see also Schutz 1995; Hall and Young 1997).

6 Temporal and political correlates

This section depicts the incidence of control regimes, comparing the frequency with which they were adopted, by time period and by type of political system. The pattern of variation points to forces that may account for the selection of such policies – and thus, too, for their subsequent abandonment.

As seen in figure 4.1, governments in the mid-1970s through to the mid-1980s were more likely to adopt control regimes than were governments in the 1960s or 1990s.

As seen in figures 4.2 and 4.3, control regimes were more likely to be adopted by authoritarian governments: those based on no-party governments or single-party systems (figure 4.2) or military regimes (figure 4.3). Governments in countries with competitive political systems (figure 4.2) and civilian regimes (figure 4.3) were more likely to adopt policies judged "syndrome-free."[6]

Not only has the choice of policy syndromes varied over the post-independence period; so too has the structure of political institutions (figures 4.4 and 4.5). In particular, single-party systems became increasingly scarce and competitive systems more common toward the end of the twentieth century.

---

[6] The relationship between policy choice and political institutions is statistically significant in all cases.

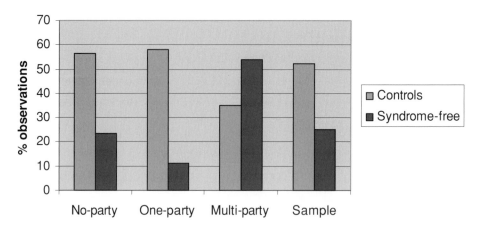

Figure 4.2 Policy choice and political system

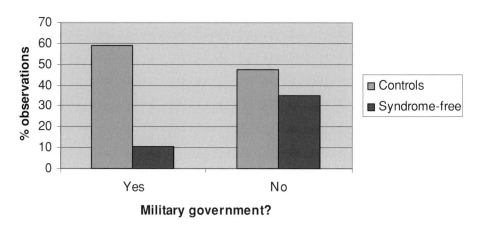

Figure 4.3 Military government and policy regime

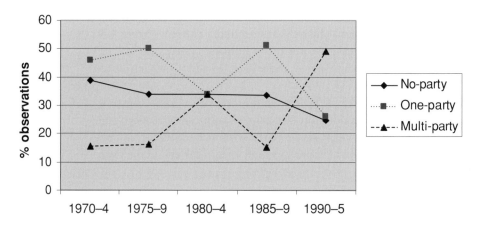

Figure 4.4 Party systems over time, 1970–1995

Table 4.8 *The variables.*

	Number of observations	Mean	Std dev.	Min.	Max.
Control regime	1,196	0.510	0.501	0	1
Syndrome-free	1,163	0.251	0.434	0	1
No-party system	1,196	0.313	0.463	0	1
Single-party system	1,196	0.392	0.483	0	1
Regional polarization	1,118	0.372	0.484	0	1
Privileged region	1,195	0.891	0.311	0	1
President from the non-privileged region	977	0.570	0.495	0	1
Socialism	1,115	0.289	0.450	0	1
Military head of state	1,103	0.441	0.497	0	1
Cold War	1,196	0.692	0.462	0	1

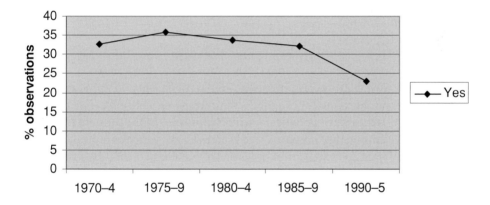

Figure 4.5 Military governments over time, 1970–1995

   Because both policy choices and institutions have co-varied with time, the relationship between them may, of course, be spurious. To address this concern, we therefore turn to multivariate analysis. Table 4.8 describes the variables employed in subsequent models.

   As demonstrated in table 4.9, when period dummies are entered into the equation, the relationship between type of political system and the choice of policy regime remains significant. The coefficients of these dummies capture the temporal pattern of policy choice, with the period before 1975 forming the reference category. The estimates in columns (1) and (3) confirm that governments were more likely to adopt control regimes during the 1970s and 1980s and that they became significantly less likely to adopt such policies in the 1990s. The coefficients in columns (2) and (4) suggest that the trajectory marking the adoption of syndrome-free policy-making traced a mirror image of that traced by the adoption of control regimes.

Table 4.9 *Patterns of policy-making.*
(conditional logistic estimation)

Dependent variable	Control regime (1)	Syndrome-free (2)	Control regime (3)	Syndrome-free (4)
No-party system	0.628	−1.208		
	(3.56)**	(6.62)**		
Single-party system	0.688	−2.021		
	(4.05)**	(10.16)**		
Cold War	0.902	−0.480	1.096	−0.983
	(6.41)**	(2.98)**	(7.76)**	(6.19)**
Military head of state			0.488	−1.676
			(3.80)**	(9.61)**
Constant	−1.046	0.365	−0.920	0.189
	(6.82)**	(2.49)*	(6.88)**	(1.38)
Observations	1092	1071	1059	1038

Absolute value of z-statistics in parentheses.
* Significant at 5%; ** significant at 1%.

Of particular interest, however, are the coefficients on the institutional measures. In columns (1) and (2), the dummy variable indicating the presence of a competitive political system is subsumed by the constant term. The coefficients on the "no-party" and "single-party" variables indicate that the adoption of control regimes is significantly associated with the structure of political competition and that non-competitive systems were far less likely to adopt policies judged to be "syndrome-free." In columns (3) and (4), the coefficient on the variable indicating a military head of state suggests that military governments were significantly more likely to impose control regimes than were civilian. Taken together, the estimates in table 4.9 thus suggest a relationship between authoritarian forms of government and a preference for regulatory regimes.

6.1   A closer look

6.1.1   Early adopters

The first countries to adopt control regimes included the West African states of Ghana, Guinea, and Mali and East African nations such as Tanzania and Uganda. They also included Congo (Brazzaville). The leaders of these governments viewed themselves as socialist and adopted much of the language and some of the institutions of command-and-control economies.

As noted in the country studies in volume 2, socialist governments imposed control regimes. The Convention People's Party (CPP) that ruled

Ghana under Kwame Nkrumah listed among its objectives the creation of "a Socialist State [*sic*] in which all men and women shall have equal opportunity and where there will be no capitalist exploitation" (Aryeetey and Fosu 2005). The ruling parties of Tanzania, Zambia, and Uganda adopted "African socialist" manifestos in the mid-1960s; while the Movement National de la Révolution, the governing party in the Republic of Congo, formerly endorsed Marxism–Leninism in 1968 (Tsassa and Yamb 2007), as did the Parti de la Révolution Populaire in Benin and FRELIMO in Mozambique in the mid-1970s. In each case, the result was the imposition of control regimes. As noted by Dossou and Sinzogan, with Mensah (2007: 3–4) in their study of Benin, when "socialism was proclaimed as the 'route to development' and Marxism–Leninism the 'philosophical guide,' then there began a policy of 'planification' with ambitious objectives." And the state then became "omnipotent . . . with little regard for the interests of the private sector."

The commitment of governments to socialist policies at home was matched by a commitment to non-alignment abroad. As evidenced most vividly, perhaps, by the Congo (Kinshasa) crisis, almost immediately after independence in the early 1960s, the global conflict between capitalism and socialism intruded into the politics of Africa. The independence that its nations had just won now appeared threatened. The states that adopted control regimes numbered among those who most vigorously protested the intrusion of the great powers and advocated a policy of non-alignment in global affairs.

These governments also numbered among the most active opponents of the minority regimes that clung to power in Southern Africa. They channeled funds to liberation movements; maintained schools in which political activists could learn from the histories of the liberation struggles in China, Algeria, and Vietnam; and gave asylum to leaders who faced jail – or worse – at home. Several provided bases where military units could train in preparation for re-deployment to their homelands.

The choice of economic policies by these "early adopters" of control regimes thus fits into a broader profile. The governments that adopted control regimes stood among the charter members of the so-called "Casablanca group." They sought Africa's liberation and championed the cause of African unity. Their adoption of interventionist economic policies appears to reflect their determination to transform the continent.

6.1.2 Embattled reformers

As noted in figure 4.1, the frequency with which governments adopted regulatory regimes increased from roughly 30 percent at the end of the 1960s to over 60 percent by the end of the 1970s. One reason for this increase was the tendency of regimes that were, quite literally, embattled to regulate their economies. Both Ethiopia and Somalia – two nations fighting each

Table 4.10 *Ideology and patterns of policy-making.*
(conditional logistic estimation)

Dependent variable	(1) Control regime	(2) Syndrome-free	(3) Control regime	(4) Syndrome-free
No-party system	0.751	−1.186		
	(1.78)	(2.67)**		
Single-party system	1.105	−0.885		
	(2.48)*	(2.14)*		
Socialist	2.484	−2.455	2.731	−2.533
	(4.70)**	(4.84)**	(5.24)**	(4.79)**
Cold War	2.753	−1.791	3.007	−2.429
	(8.48)**	(5.38)**	(9.06)**	(6.92)**
Military head of state			0.736	−2.414
			(1.84)	(5.23)**
Observations	641	562	631	555
Number of countries	26	23	26	23

Absolute value of *z*-statistics in parentheses.
* Significant at 5%; ** significant at 1%.

other – adopted socialist ideologies and imposed control regimes in order to mobilize for war. To these nations could be added Angola, Mozambique, and Guinea-Bissau, whose military forces in the mid-1970s defeated those of Portugal. The governments of these nations sought to over-ride market forces in order to mobilize for war. Adding further impetus to their decision was the desire of some to signal their good faith to socialist countries abroad and thereby attract military and financial backing.[7]

Table 4.10 captures the relationship between the ideological commitment of the government in power and the pattern of policy-making.

7 The politics of economics

This section has two parts. The first addresses a paradox that has lurked just beneath the surface of the discussion thus far: the seeming willingness of socialist governments, with their commitment to economic equality, to

---

[7] In other instances, it is difficult to detect systematic reasons for the adoption of control regimes. In the case of Kenya, the reasons appear to derive from anxiety concerning food supplies; in that of the Côte d'Ivoire, they appear to be associated with the launching of agricultural projects and industrial schemes following the coffee boom of the mid-1970s. Rwanda, Chad, and Burundi may belong to the class of "embattled" regimes; Senegal, Madagascar, and Mauritius (1960–70) do not. In such instances, the reasons remain as idiosyncratic and therefore difficult to explain.

undermine the well-being of peasants, the poorest of the poor in Africa. Untangling this paradox clarifies the role of political interests in the selection of government policies. The second illustrates the importance of pressures for redistribution, which also appear to promote the adoption of control regimes.

7.1 A fruitful paradox

As seen in table 4.10, socialist governments in Africa tend to impose control regimes. They therefore tend to adopt policies that lower the economic well-being of the peasantry, the poorest of their citizens, and those therefore with the most compelling claim for public assistance.[8] Addressing the disjuncture between the values and the choices of socialist governments brings into sharp focus the political forces that drive policy choices.

The discussion can proceed in several quick steps.

7.1.1 In general

The core of Africa's political regimes was composed of the *government, industry*, and organized *labor*. While accounting for less than 40 percent of the GDP of a typical African state and less than 20 percent of the population, these urban-based interests nonetheless dominated policy-making in the post-independence period:

Governments provide services and, for the most part, public services remain un-priced. Their biggest cost is labor. To defend their budgets, governments therefore adopt policies that lowered the cost of labor.
Industries employ capital and labor to produce commodities. All else being equal, a decrease in the costs of labor results in an increase in profits. Industry therefore joins government in favoring policies that lower the costs of labor.
Labor favors policies that defend the real value of workers' incomes. Given the income of most wage earners in Africa, workers devote a large portion of their expenditures to food.

In seeking to reward the core coalition, governments therefore championed policies that secured low priced food.

7.1.2 In particular

Socialist governments were tightly integrated with the other portions of the core coalition:

---

[8] This tendency has been noted by others. See, for example, Mitrany (1961).

Socialist governments were more likely to nationalize existing firms and to invest in new industries than were others. To a greater degree than other governments, their interests therefore aligned with those of industrial firms.

Socialist governments aspired to the provision of higher levels of health care, education, and other services than did most other governments. As a result, they hired more workers.

As a matter of principle, socialist governments endorsed the interests of workers. And as a matter of practice, socialist parties maintained close ties with organized labor and trade unions based in both private industry and the public services.

Socialist governments therefore possessed a strong interest in adopting policies that lowered the costs of food, even though lowering the incomes of farmers.

The policies that enabled socialist regimes to consolidate their core constituency violated their ideological commitments. That they did so testifies to the power of the political interests that dominated policy-making in the post-independence period. These industries were urban-based, industry-based, and located in the towns, and they possessed close ties to regimes in power.

Having limned the political foundations of control regimes, a second question arises: given the economic costs of these policies, why did governments not abandon them? To comprehend this delay, one need ask only: would any member of the governing coalition have an incentive unilaterally to call upon the government to abandon them? More specifically: would any single player – industry, organized labor, or the government itself – benefit by calling for higher prices for farmers? The answer is of course: "no." No politician would voluntarily defect from the ruling coalition, no firm unilaterally agree to higher costs, no trade unionist call for changes that would lower the incomes of labor. While socially costly, the choice of policies constituted an equilibrium.

7.2   Regional redistribution

Control regimes were employed for purposes of redistribution. Already noted is their use by governments to extract resources from rural dwellers and to transfer them to urban-based industries. Equally important, it would appear, is the use of these policies to transfer resources between regions.

As noted by Tsassa and Yamb (2007), politics in the Republic of the Congo is marked by rivalries between the poorly endowed North and the relatively prosperous South. Following the "Three Glorious Days" of August 1963, a "Conseil National de la Révolution" (CNR) took power and committed the government to building a socialist state. In pursuit of that objective, it created state monopolies to purchase crops at fixed prices; selling them at competitive prices, the center collected taxes from the North. Tsassa and Yamb (2007) note that to defend its monopoly position from new entrants and competitors, the bureaucracies drew on the power of both the army and police. In 1968, the military forcefully seized power. Headed by Marien Ngouabi, a Northerner, the ruling junta then began to install people from the North to key posts throughout the military, the government, and the parastatal sector. Politics was a matter of *regional* redistribution.

Togo provides another example (Gogué and Evlo 2007). Northern Togo is semi-arid, poor, and relatively unpopulated. The South produces the primary cash crops and contains the phosphate deposits that generate the majority of Togo's foreign exchange. It also contains the majority of Togo's population and, for historical reasons, a disproportion of its educated personnel. Most active portions of the independence movement had originated in the South, and it was a Southerner, Sylvanus Olympio, who became Togo's first President. In 1963, however, the military seized office. Gnassingbé Eyadéma was Olympio's rival and after a four-year interval he seized the presidency. Gnassingbé came from Kara, a district in the North. Through a mixture of inducement and intimidation – heavily balanced toward the latter – he rendered the state a means of extracting resources from the South to the benefit of himself and his Northern constituency.

Recalling the Kobou, Njinkeu, and Powo Fosso (2007) analysis of Cameroon, the discussion of Malawi by Chipeta and Mkandawire (2007), and Mwega and Ndung'u's (2007) portrayal of Kenya, we gain a keen appreciation of the extent to which regional competition drives politics in Africa – and the policy choices of its governments.

Table 4.11 illustrates the relationship between policy choice and regional inequality. The variable "Privileged region" takes the value 1 when a nation exhibits a high level of regional inequality and 0 when it does not. The coefficient suggests that when there is a privileged region, governments are more likely to impose control regimes and less likely to adopt policies that are "syndrome-free." Note, too, the coefficient on the variable "Polarized region." A privileged region is coded as polarized when it is ethnically and religiously homogenous and distinctive. The coefficient suggests that cultural uniformity and distinctiveness add to the impact of regional inequality, producing a stronger tendency to introduce control regimes.

Table 4.12 suggests that in countries where the chief executive is from a region that is relatively poor, governments are again more likely to adopt control regimes (column (1)) and less likely to adopt policies that remain syndrome-free (column (2)). The coefficient in column (1) is statistically significant. The coefficient in column (3), moreover, suggests that when the presidency shifts from a privileged to a non-privileged region, then the government is significantly more likely to impose regulatory controls.

Table 4.11 *Regional differentiation and patterns of policy-making.*
(logistic estimation, pooled sample).

Dependent variable	Control regime (1)	Syndrome-free (2)	Control regime (3)	Syndrome-free (4)
No-party system	0.566	−1.339		
	(2.97)**	(5.79)**		
Single-party system	0.485	−1.478		
	(2.50)*	(6.36)**		
Privileged region	1.505	−2.410	1.530	−2.640
	(5.44)**	(8.16)**	(5.78)**	(9.02)**
Polarized region	0.599	−1.215	0.573	−0.814
	(3.81)**	(5.65)**	(3.66)**	(3.81)**
Socialist	1.524	−1.779	1.391	−1.704
	(8.54)**	(6.41)**	(7.75)**	(6.09)**
Cold War	0.994	−0.601	1.118	−1.051
	(6.28)**	(3.16)**	(7.15)**	(5.51)**
Military head of state			0.277	−1.742
			(1.90)	(8.47)**
Constant	−2.771	3.033	−2.592	3.086
	(9.54)**	(9.54)**	(9.36)**	(9.76)**
Observations	1041	1041	1003	1003

Absolute value of *z*-statistics in parentheses.
* Significant at 5%; ** significant at 1%.

Table 4.13 reports marginal effects, thus enabling us to gain a sense of the magnitude of the coefficients contained in table 4.12. The coefficients confirm the importance of party competition; in its absence, the likelihood of adopting a control regime or of abandoning syndrome-free patterns of policy-making rises by about 20 percentage points. Regional inequality increases the likelihood of control regimes by about 15 percentage points; cultural polarization adds an additional 20 percentage points. The impact of these variables is both less and less precisely estimated under military governments than when there are civilian regimes. The results also confirm the arguments of Mwase and Ndulu (2007): both ideology and "the times" appear to have a significant impact upon patterns of policy-making.

7.3 Discussion

The political forces that underpin the choice of control regimes thus appear to arise from three sources. One is ideology. High levels of government intervention occur when governments find principled reasons for over-riding the allocations generated by markets. A second is the power of

Table 4.12 *Presidential origin and patterns of policy-making.*
(logistic estimation, pooled sample).

Dependent variable	Control regime (1)	Syndrome-free (2)	Control regime (3)	Syndrome-free (4)
No-party system	0.532	−1.482		
	(2.29)*	(5.76)**		
Single-party system	0.585	−1.625		
	(2.55)*	(6.40)**		
President from the	0.743	−0.214	0.806	−0.123
non-privileged region	(4.44)**	(1.05)	(4.63)**	(0.60)
Socialist	1.823	−1.506	1.697	−1.558
	(8.85)**	(5.41)**	(8.12)**	(5.52)**
Polarized region	1.001	−1.069	0.987	−0.678
	(5.76)**	(4.93)**	(5.65)**	(3.19)**
Cold War	1.023	−0.568	1.189	−1.026
	(5.76)**	(2.74)**	(6.85)**	(5.20)**
Military head of state			−0.172	−1.374
			(1.01)	(6.22)**
Constant	−1.924	0.831	−1.519	0.376
	(7.98)**	(3.67)**	(7.41)**	(1.83)
Observations	853	853	820	820

Absolute value of z-statistics in parentheses.
* Significant at 5%; ** significant at 1%.

organized interests. In a political world in which governments need not compete for the support of a broad electorate, interest groups constitute the primary means by which political preferences shape policy choices. And in a game best characterized as the interplay of political interests, it is those that are organized that prevail. The third is regional inequality. It generates incentives to adopt policies designed to overcome the economic impact of disparate endowments and to create political institutions with the power to elicit the transfer of resources. Authoritarianism; demands for redistribution between town and country, rich region and poor; and governmental intervention in markets – these tendencies co-vary. They appear to have shaped the political conduct and economic performance of governments in post-independence Africa.

8 Conclusion

This analysis not only furnishes insight into the political logic underlying control regimes but also into the politics of late-twentieth-century reform.

Table 4.13 *Marginal effects on patterns of policy-making.*
(logistic estimation, pooled sample).

Dependent variable	Control regime (1)	Syndrome-free (2)	Control regime (3)	Syndrome-free (4)
No-party system	0.191	−0.180		
	(4.22)*	(7.29)**		
Single-party system	0.221	−0.226		
	(4.76)*	(7.62)**		
President from the	0.151	−0.021	0.176	−0.012
non-privileged region	(4.00)**	(0.82)	(4.53)**	(0.48)
Socialist	0.372	−0.129	0.363	−0.177
	(12.33)**	(5.48)**	(11.85)**	(8.20)**
Polarized region	0.224	−0.163	0.217	−0.087
	(6.43)**	(7.28)**	(6.20)**	(3.64)**
Cold War	0.221	−0.19	0.196	−0.186
	(6.68)**	(5.00)**	(5.56)**	(5.82)**
Military head of state			−0.025	−0.178
			(0.64)	(6.58)**
Constant	−1.924	0.831	−1.519	0.376
	(7.98)**	(3.67)**	(7.41)**	(1.83)
Observations	853	853	820	820

Absolute value of z-statistics in parentheses.
* Significant at 5%; ** significant at 1%.

As noted in chapter 9, with the end of the Cold War global opinion swung in favor of free market policies and competitive political systems. An implication of the arguments in this chapter is that these economic and political reforms of necessity took place together.

When contemplating this proposition, it is useful to cite three cases. The first is policy change in Mozambique; the second, policy reform in Ghana; and the third, policy-making in Botswana.

Mozambique's peasantry faced costs of organizing as high as those faced by the peasantry in other countries. But RENAMO based itself in the rural areas when mounting its armed opposition to the government. RENAMO could successfully operate in the rural areas because it drew logistical support from abroad. What support many peasants could give, however, they did give, and FRELIMO, the governing party, faced the prospect of losing their political allegiance, given its insistence on measures that the peasants opposed (Schultz 1976; Hall and Young 1997; Pitcher 2002). One reason that FRELIMO relaxed and then abandoned its commitment to villagization was that the policies fueled support for RENAMO, its political rival.

Elsewhere peasants lacked such an advocate – organized, armed, and able to resist the governing party – and governments had less reason to alter their policies.

First as a military ruler and then as a head of a single party regime, Rawlings deployed his security services in Ghana to impose price controls, shut down black markets, and evacuate crops from the countryside for sale in urban markets. In face of these policies, the economy still failed to grow and the government began to contemplate abandoning its *dirigiste* policies. For Rawlings, abandoning a control regime was tantamount to abandoning his urban-based, industry-based, class-based constituency and the socialist principles that legitimated his policy commitments.

The solution that Rawlings devised is notable. To defend his political future while altering his public policies, Rawlings had to build a rural base for his governing party. Beginning by organizing village political committees manned by political militants, he then introduced elected local councils. When he later introduced elections for the parliament and presidency, he had therefore already put in place political organizations throughout the townships and villages. Given the structure of Ghana's economy and the composition of its population, rural voters outnumbered urban. For Rawlings, democratization therefore provided a means of shifting from an urban-based constituency, which was hurt by economic reform, to a rural political base, which benefited from them. It provided a means of surviving politically while abandoning a control regime (Leith and Lofchie 1991; Rothchild 1991, 1995; Shillington 1992; Herbst 1993; Oquaye 1995; Gyimah-Boadi 1998; and Aryeetey and Fosu 2007).

If Ghana provides evidence that the abandonment of control regimes creates incentives for political reform, then Botswana provides evidence of how open political competition creates incentives to avoid the extractive policies in the first place. As stated by Maipose and Matsheka (2007):

The leadership in the ruling party had considerable interest in promoting their own version of good government. Because the government knew that it must stand for election every five years, the ruling party pursued policies it believed would gain it the political support necessary to defeat its opponents, seeking "profit" in the form of "political income." The priorities of the key rural development programs, such as the Arable Land Development Programme and the Accelerated Rural Development Programme, initiated during this period, and attention given to the cattle industry, were not biased against rural areas. (2007: 10)

Control regimes can not be sustained when policy results from competition between politicians who had every reason to bid for political majorities. In Africa, farmers constitute that majority, and their interests are violated by these policies.

The introduction of political competition and the abandonment of control regimes thus went together in late-twentieth-century Africa.

References

Alemayehu Geda (2007), "The Political Economy of Growth in Ethiopia," chapter 4 in Benno J. Ndulu, Stephen A. O'Connell, Jean-Paul Azam, Robert H. Bates, Augustin Kwasi Fosu, Jan Willem Gunning, and Dominique Njinkeu, eds., *The Political Economy of Economic Growth in Africa, 1960–2000*, vol. 2. Cambridge: Cambridge University Press

Aryeetey, Ernest and Augustin K. Fosu (2005), "Ghana," African Economic Research Consortium, Nairobi

(2007), "Economic Growth in Ghana," chapter 9 in Benno J. Ndulu, Stephen A. O'Connell, Jean-Paul Azam, Robert H. Bates, Augustin Kwasi Fosu, Jan Willem Gunning, and Dominique Njinkeu, eds., *The Political Economy of Economic Growth in Africa, 1960–2000*, vol. 2. Cambridge: Cambridge University Press

Azam, Jean-Paul and Nadjiounom Djimtoïngar (2007), "Cotton, War, and Growth in Chad, 1960–2000," chapter 3 in Benno J. Ndulu, Stephen A. O'Connell, Jean-Paul Azam, Robert H. Bates, Augustin Kwasi Fosu, Jan Willem Gunning, and Dominique Njinkeu, eds., *The Political Economy of Economic Growth in Africa, 1960–2000*, vol. 2. Cambridge: Cambridge University Press

Bates, Robert H. and Paul Collier (1991), "The Case of Zambia," in Robert H. Bates and Anne O. Krueger, *Political and Economic Interactions in Economic Policy Reform.* Oxford: Blackwell

Bowen, Merle L. (2000), *The State against the Peasantry: Rural Struggles in Colonial and Postcolonial Mozambique.* Charlottesville, VA: University of Virginia Press

Chipeta, Chinyamata and Mjedo Mkandawire (2007), "Man-made opportunities and Growth in Malawi," chapter 5 in Benno J. Ndulu, Stephen A. O'Connell, Jean-Paul Azam, Robert H. Bates, Augustin Kwasi Fosu, Jan Willem Gunning, and Dominique Njinkeu, eds., *The Political Economy of Economic Growth in Africa, 1960–2000*, vol. 2. Cambridge: Cambridge University Press

Davies, Victor (2007), "Sierra Leone's Economic Growth Performance, 1961–2000," chapter 19 in Benno J. Ndulu, Stephen A. O'Connell, Jean-Paul Azam, Robert H. Bates, Augustin Kwasi Fosu, Jan Willem Gunning, and Dominique Njinkeu, eds., *The Political Economy of Economic Growth in Africa, 1960–2000*, vol. 2. Cambridge: Cambridge University Press

de Sousa, Clara and José Sulemane (2005), "Mozambique's Growth Performance, 1960–1996," chapter 24 in Benno J. Ndulu, Stephen A. O'Connell, Jean-Paul Azam, Robert H. Bates, Augustin Kwasi Fosu, Jan Willem Gunning, and Dominique Njinkeu, eds., *The Political Economy of Economic Growth in Africa, 1960–2000*, vol. 2. Cambridge: Cambridge University Press

Dodge, Doris Jansen (1977), *Agricultural Policy and Performance in Zambia.* Berkeley, CA: Institute of International Studies, University of California

Dossou, Antonin S., Jean-Yves Sinzogan, with Sylviane Mensah (2007), "Economic Growth in Benin: Lost Opportunities," chapter 22 in Benno J. Ndulu, Stephen A. O'Connell, Jean-Paul Azam, Robert H. Bates, Augustin Kwasi Fosu, Jan

Willem Gunning, and Dominique Njinkeu, eds., *The Political Economy of Economic Growth in Africa, 1960–2000*, vol. 2. Cambridge: Cambridge University Press

Doumbouya, Sékou F. and Fodé Camara (2007), "Explaining Economic Growth in Africa: The Case of Guinea," chapter 17 in Benno J. Ndulu, Stephen A. O'Connell, Jean-Paul Azam, Robert H. Bates, Augustin Kwasi Fosu, Jan Willem Gunning, and Dominique Njinkeu, eds., *The Political Economy of Economic Growth in Africa, 1960–2000*, vol. 2. Cambridge: Cambridge University Press

Fosu, Augustin and Stephen A. O'Connell (2006), "Explaining African Economic Growth: The Role of Anti-Growth Syndromes," in François Bourguignon and Boris Pleskovic, eds., *Growth and Integration: Annual World Bank Conference on Development Economics 2006*. Washington, DC: The World Bank

Gogué, Tchaboure Aimé and Kodjo Evlo (2005), "Togo." Africa Economic Research Consortium, Nairobi

  (2007), "Togo: Lost Opportunities for Growth," chapter 14 in Benno J. Ndulu, Stephen A. O'Connell, Jean-Paul Azam, Robert H. Bates, Augustin Kwasi Fosu, Jan Willem Gunning, and Dominique Njinkeu, eds., *The Political Economy of Economic Growth in Africa, 1960–2000*, vol. 2. Cambridge: Cambridge University Press

Gyimah-Boadi, Emmanuel (1998), "Managing Electoral Conflicts: Lessons from Ghana," in T. D. Sisk and A. Reynolds, eds., *Elections and Conflict Management in Africa*. Washington, DC: United States Institute of Peace Press

Hall, Margaret and Tom Young (1997), *Confronting Leviathan: Mozambique since Independence*. Athens, OH: Ohio University Press

Herbst, Jeffrey (1993), *The Politics of Reform in Ghana*. Berkeley, CA and Los Angeles, CA: University of California Press

Killick, Tony (1978), *Development Economics in Action*. London: Heinemann

Kobou, Georges, Dominique Njinkeu, and Bruno Powo Fosso (2007), "The Political Economy of Cameroon's Post-independence Growth," chapter 16 in Benno J. Ndulu, Stephen A. O'Connell, Jean-Paul Azam, Robert H. Bates, Augustin Kwasi Fosu, Jan Willem Gunning, and Dominique Njinkeu, eds., *The Political Economy of Economic Growth in Africa, 1960–2000*, vol. 2. Cambridge: Cambridge University Press

Krueger, Anne O., Maurice Schiff, and Alberto Valdes, eds. (1992), *The Political Economy of Agricultural Pricing Policies*, 5 vols. Baltimore, MD: Johns Hopkins University Press for the World Bank

Leith, Clark and Michael Lofchie (1993), "The Case of Ghana," in Robert H. Bates and Anne O. Krueger, *Political and Economic Interactions in Economic Policy Reform*. Oxford: Blackwell

Lofchie, Michael F. (1989), *The Policy Factor: Agricultural Performance in Kenya and Tanzania*. Boulder, CO: Lynne Rienner

MacGaffey, Janet (1991), *The Real Economy of Zaire*. Philadelphia, PA: Unversity of Pennsylvania Press

Maipose, Gervase S. and Thapelo C. Matsheka (2007), "The Indigenous Developmental State and Growth in Botswana," chapter 15 in Benno J. Ndulu, Stephen

A. O'Connell, Jean-Paul Azam, Robert H. Bates, Augustin Kwasi Fosu, Jan Willem Gunning, and Dominique Njinkeu, eds., *The Political Economy of Economic Growth in Africa, 1960–2000*, vol. 2. Cambridge: Cambridge University Press

McHenry, Dean E. (1994), *Limited Choices: The Political Struggle for Socialism in Tanzania*. Boulder, CO: Lynne Reinner

Mitrany, David (1961), *Marx Against the Peasant*. New York: Collier

Mwanawina, Inyambo and James Mulungushi (2007), "Zambia," chapter 27 in Benno J. Ndulu, Stephen A. O'Connell, Jean-Paul Azam, Robert H. Bates, Augustin Kwasi Fosu, Jan Willem Gunning, and Dominique Njinkeu, eds., *The Political Economy of Economic Growth in Africa, 1960–2000*, vol. 2. Cambridge: Cambridge University Press

Mwase, Nkunde and Benno J. Ndulu (2007), "Tanzania: Explaining Four Decades of Episodic Growth," chapter 13 in Benno J. Ndulu, Stephen A. O'Connell, Jean-Paul Azam, Robert H. Bates, Augustin Kwasi Fosu, Jan Willem Gunning, and Dominique Njinkeu, eds., *The Political Economy of Economic Growth in Africa, 1960–2000*, vol. 2. Cambridge: Cambridge University Press

Mwega, Francis M. and Njuguna S. Ndung'u (2007), "Explaining African Economic Growth Performance: The Case of Kenya," chapter 10 in Benno J. Ndulu, Stephen A. O'Connell, Jean-Paul Azam, Robert H. Bates, Augustin Kwasi Fosu, Jan Willem Gunning, and Dominique Njinkeu, eds., *The Political Economy of Economic Growth in Africa, 1960–2000*, vol. 2. Cambridge: Cambridge University Press

Nkurunziza, Janvier and Floribert Ngaruko (2007), "Why Has Burundi Grown So Slowly? The Political Economy of Redistribution," chapter 2 in Benno J. Ndulu, Stephen A. O'Connell, Jean-Paul Azam, Robert H. Bates, Augustin Kwasi Fosu, Jan Willem Gunning, and Dominique Njinkeu, eds., *The Political Economy of Economic Growth in Africa, 1960–2000*, vol. 2. Cambridge: Cambridge University Press

Oquaye, Mike (1995), "The Ghanaian Elections of 1992 – A Dissenting View," *African Affairs* 94: 255–75

Pitcher, M. Anne (2002), *Transforming Mozambique*. New York: Cambridge University Press

Rothchild, Donald (1995), "Rawlings and the Engineering of Legitimacy in Ghana," in I. W. Zartman, *Collapsed States*. Boulder, Co: Lynne Rienner

   ed. (1991), *Ghana: The Political Economy of Recovery*. Boulder, CO: Lynne Rienner

Samba Mamadou, Ousmane and Mahaman Sani Yakoubou (2007), "Climate Vulnerability, Political Instability, Investment, and Growth in a Landlocked, Sahelian Economy: Niger, 1960–2000," chapter 6 in Benno J. Ndulu, Stephen A. O'Connell, Jean-Paul Azam, Robert H. Bates, Augustin Kwasi Fosu, Jan Willem Gunning, and Dominique Njinkeu, eds., *The Political Economy of Economic Growth in Africa, 1960–2000*, vol. 2. Cambridge: Cambridge University Press

Schultz, Theodore W. (1976), *Transforming Traditional Agriculture*. New York: Arno Press

Schutz, Barry (1995), "The Heritage of Revolution and the Struggle for Governmental Legitimacy in Mozambique," in I. W. Zartman, ed., *Collapsed States.* Boulder, Co: Lynne Rienner

Shillington, Kevin (1992), *Ghana and the Rawlings Factor.* London: Macmillan

Tsassa, Célestin and Benjamin Yamb (2007), "Croissance off-shore au Congo et économie rentière," chapter 25 in Benno J. Ndulu, Stephen A. O'Connell, Jean-Paul Azam, Robert H. Bates, Augustin Kwasi Fosu, Jan Willem Gunning, and Dominique Njinkeu, eds., *The Political Economy of Economic Growth in Africa, 1960–2000*, vol. 2. Cambridge: Cambridge University Press

Turok, B. (1979), *Development in Zambia.* London: Zed Press

World Bank (1975), *Republic of Zambia: Agricultural and Rural Sector Survey.* Washington, DC: The World Bank

  (1982), *Tanzania: Agricultural Sector Report.* Washington, DC: The World Bank

  (1994), *Adjustment in Africa: Reform, Results, and the Road Ahead.* Washington, DC: The World Bank

5 Sacrificing the future: intertemporal strategies and their implications for growth

Paul Collier and Jan Willem Gunning

1 Introduction

This chapter focuses on a particular type of policy failure, namely the sacrifice of future income for present gain. All societies and their governments face a trade-off between present and future consumption, but in Africa this has often led to serious policy errors. The core phenomenon we discuss is an unsustainable boom in public spending. However, we also include a less common event, looting. Although fairly rare, when looting occurs its implications for growth have been substantial. Bouts of unsustainable public spending were usually, although not invariably, triggered by booms in revenues from natural-resource rents. These were often amplified by unsustainable debt accumulation. Looting of assets occasionally took the form of dispossession of private assets, but more commonly the target was publicly owned assets.

Both unsustainable public spending booms and asset looting were sometimes simply mistakes, but were more commonly rational strategies. Unsustainable strategies can be rational even though they are socially costly because many of the costs are external to the calculus of decision takers. In section 2, we discuss the episodes of unsustainable public spending, and in section 3 we turn to the looting episodes. As with all our syndromes, it is possible for a single episode to be characterized by multiple syndromes. Thus, the second Nigerian oil boom of 1979–83 features an unsustainable boom in public spending which took the form of looting, so that it is included in both sections.

2   Unsustainable public spending

Many African economies have remarkably undiversified export structures. As a result they are prone to trade shocks to a degree not seen in most Asian and Latin American developing countries. The evidence is not that African economies have done worse in managing such shocks. Rather, African economies, as a result of their relative natural resource abundance, have been more prone to such shocks. Because dependence upon natural-resource rents is much more important for African economies than for those of other developing regions, the problems that are globally associated with natural-resource rents are of disproportionate importance.

Globally, positive shocks in resource rents often lead to short bursts of unsustainable growth. The term 'unsustainable growth' can be used in two different senses: either the *rate of growth* or the *level of output* can potentially be unsustainable. We use the term in the more radical sense that what is unsustainable is the initial increase in output, not merely its rate of increase. Collier and Hoeffler (2005a) measure resource rents country-by-country globally for the period 1970–2002 and estimate their effects on growth rates for each four-year sub-period. Controlling for policies and institutions as measured by the World Bank's Country Policy and Institutional Assessment (CPIA), they find that within a sub-period resource rents significantly increase the growth rate of constant-price GDP. However, there is also a significant and adverse lagged effect of resource rents. Thus, a boom raises the growth rate contemporaneously, but then reduces the growth rate in the subsequent period by half as much as the initial increase. Thus, around half of the contemporaneous increase in output from a natural-resource boom is unsustained.

It is worthwhile noting that in Africa this phenomenon is concentrated in two decades, the 1970s and the 1980s: in our country studies in volume 2 no episodes are classified as intertemporal syndromes before 1970 or after 1990, with a single exception. An obvious explanation is that the 1970s saw some of the biggest trade shocks in recent economic history, including the 1973 and 1979 oil shocks and the beverages (coffee, tea, and cocoa) boom of 1975–9. High real interest rates made deficit spending in the 1980s unsustainable. The colonial institutions still in place in the 1960s made unsustainable spending very difficult. In many former colonies agencies of fiscal restraint were abolished or emasculated in the 1970s. Conversely, the reforms of the 1980s left African economies dramatically less syndrome-prone in the 1990s. Apparently the reforms drastically reduced the incentives for unsustainable spending; in our country studies Cameroon is the only instance of a post-1990 episode of unsustainable spending. Hence the twenty-year period 1970–90 was characterized by a remarkable conjunction of large shocks, weak fiscal discipline, and relatively strong incentives for redistribution at the expense of the future.

Why would a trade shock lead to unsustainable spending? In the static model of "Dutch disease" theory the spending effect of a boom induces expansion of the non-tradable sector at the expense of tradables (other than the booming sector). This optimal adjustment to an improvement in the terms of trade is, of course, welfare-increasing. However, it shows up in the National Accounts as a *fall* in GDP, if GDP is calculated at pre-boom relative prices. In a dynamic version of the model the boom, if correctly recognized as temporary, will induce asset accumulation so that consumption can be permanently maintained at a higher level post-boom.[1] However, in the absence of any distortions this will not involve an increase in *domestic* investment. If the economy was in equilibrium prior to the boom (with the domestic rate of return equal to the world interest rate) then it is obviously optimal to allocate windfall investment entirely to foreign assets: domestic investment would lower the rate of return below the world rate of interest. The National Accounts would again record a fall in GDP. The return on foreign assets would be recorded as an increase in GNP.

This technical point is important since growth regressions typically measure growth in terms of constant-price GDP. Clearly, this biases growth regression evidence on the impact of shocks towards the conclusion that the government and private agents fail to harness a positive shock effectively: the *optimal* response in a distortion-free economy would appear as a reduction in growth. To that extent the observed failures to sustain output increases after a positive trade shock may simply be a statistical artifact.

The "Dutch disease" model and its dynamic (but still distortion-free) extensions serve as a useful theoretical benchmark. However, if a boom is to lead to (temporary) growth in GDP we must introduce other elements. One possibility is that there are price or wage rigidities. Boom-induced spending in sectors with idle resources will then have Keynesian effects: output will increase.

Deaton (1992) found that government expenditure had a much higher persistence than other forms of expenditure. In a sample of thirty-five African countries he found that three years after a one-year export price boom all forms of expenditure had returned to normal with the exception of government consumption. Within government consumption, the wage bill is typically the most persistent component. This is important since a

---

[1] See, e.g., Collier, Gunning, and associates (1999: chapter 1, appendix) for optimal responses to temporary shocks.

particular type of wage rigidity, with public sector wages maintained at levels far exceeding the opportunity cost of labor, was common in Africa until well into the 1980s. In this case an increase in public employment raises GDP (since value added in government is measured at cost) even if new civil servants produce nothing so that aggregate output falls unambiguously. Typically public sector employment is difficult to retrench so that if the increase in public spending proves unsustainable the non-wage-bill components of government consumption are cut. This may then reduce GDP – e.g. if road maintenance is reduced. In this case the increase in wage employment is registered in the National Accounts first, misleadingly, as an increase in output, followed, correctly, by a fall in output.

The second possibility is a capital market imperfection: domestic investment is credit constrained – e.g. because the country cannot borrow abroad. The boom then enables agents to increase investment out of windfall income. In addition, foreign creditors may relax the borrowing constraint in response to the terms of trade improvement and the associated increase in government revenue. For example, in the 1970s the oil economies increased their external debt massively in the wake of the 1973 and 1979 OPEC price increases (Gelb and associates 1988; Collier, Gunning, and associates, 1999). In Africa, Nigeria offers the most striking example of such boom-induced spending sprees.

One of the key messages from the empirical trade shocks literature is that – contrary to what had been the policy consensus until well into the 1990s – private agents respond appropriately to booms, provided they are well informed about the temporary nature of the windfall. If private agents recognize a boom as temporary they will save a large part of their windfall income: assets are accumulated in the boom period so as to smooth consumption over time. One way in which a boom can be wasted is if the government's response to the shock gives noisy signals to private agents so that these are confused about the nature of their windfall income. Not recognizing its temporary nature they would then rationally save very little out of it.

For example, the government might expand public sector employment in response to the increase in its tax revenue during a boom. Since such spending is by its nature difficult to reverse this is clearly an inappropriate public sector response to the shocks: the policy amounts to lock in of an expenditure level that will become unsustainable after the boom. The error can easily spread to the private sector: private agents are unlikely to recognize such government expenditure as temporary. They may therefore well consider part of the increase in their income as permanent and therefore save too little.

This affects the political economy of reform. In the post-boom period the government will find it difficult to adjust its spending to its reduced tax revenue. This may lead to painful adjustment measures with IMF, World Bank, and donor involvement. To the extent that private agents do not recognize that the government response to the boom has made public expenditure unsustainable the adjustment measures may become deeply unpopular: the policy regime in the boom period is nostalgically idealized and reforms are resisted because they are seen as unnecessary. The legacy of the boom then consists of delayed and therefore ultimately very costly adjustment.

Such intertemporal mistakes are very easy to make. For example, the Ugandan government was well aware of the danger of increasing its expenditure in response the coffee boom of 1994. It was careful to identify the increase in government revenue due to the coffee tax. However, it did not realize that as the windfall was spent domestically other forms of government revenue increased substantially. These revenue increases were not attributed to the boom and therefore treated as permanent. The government thereby over-estimated the scope for permanent increases in government spending.

However, the Ugandan case is exceptional. More commonly a government perceives little incentive in asset accumulation to smooth public consumption. The problem is analogous to the political economy of trade policy where the benefits of protection are concentrated on a small number of agents and therefore very visible, while the larger costs are diffuse, involving a very large number of consumers, and therefore much less visible. Similarly, a strategy of public consumption smoothing involves high political costs since claims from spending ministries will have to be resisted at the very time when the government is very liquid so that stringency seems ill advised. Conversely, the benefits of a smoothing strategy are in the future and accrue to a large number of agents who are not clearly identified. Hence, even if the government was *able* to estimate the size of the windfall correctly, it may not be *willing* to treat this income as temporary. A government may therefore rationally decide not to smooth its expenditure. This may have happened in Kenya during the coffee boom period (Bevan, Collier, and Gunning 1989, 1990).[2]

In addition, the government affects, intentionally or not, the scope for consumption smoothing by private agents. This is because in aggregate private agents can accumulate assets only by acquiring claims on the government or by acquiring foreign assets. Many African governments have made the former very unattractive (e.g. by offering negative real interest rates) and the latter illegal.

We have seen that a government may engage in unsustainable spending if the political costs of smoothing are clearly visible while the benefits are not. Unwillingness to smooth can also arise in a very different way. Consider the

---

[2] This episode is not classified as a case of unsustainable spending but would certainly qualify.

model of Adam and O'Connell (1999), where the government's objective is to maximize the welfare of a particular group – e.g. the regime's ethnic base. If this group is sufficiently small, the government has no incentive to promote growth. It will try to grab rents and transfer these to the favoured group. Since this group is small the costs of the distortions the government imposes to generate rents are largely borne by others. A regime that is sufficiently unrepresentative will therefore have no incentive to promote growth. This political-economy model provides a useful framework for analysing government responses to a boom. If the boom accrues to the government (as, for example, in the oil economies or in countries with agricultural exports and controlled producer prices) it changes the costs of transferring rents to the favoured group: this can now be done without imposing taxes on the rest of the economy. The boom may therefore enable the government to transfer rents by lowering the costs thereof. Failing to invest so as to smooth consumption over time is then not a mistake, but a rational government response to the boom. If this interpretation is correct then the unrepresentativeness of African regimes is part of the explanation for the unsustained government spending booms which are often associated with positive trade shocks. Burundi offers a striking example of this mechanism.

In summary, a boom may accrue directly or indirectly to the government. The government may easily mistake some of its windfall income as permanent, as in the Ugandan example. More commonly it may find it politically expedient to engage in consumption smoothing to only a very limited extent, either because the benefits of smoothing are diffuse or because the regime is unrepresentative. In any case the spending boom will (if used to expand employment) be difficult to reverse so that spending becomes unsustainable after the boom, especially if private agents mistakenly come to view the government's fiscal stance during the boom as sustainable.

2.1 Evidence on spending booms

In the country studies in volume 2 we find eight episodes of unsustainable spending (table 5.1).[3] We consider these in turn.

Burundi most closely fits the pattern of a trade shock-induced period of unsustainable spending. A massive increase in public spending became feasible with the revenue from the coffee boom, starting in 1975, and with the improved access to foreign borrowing as a result of that boom. As Nkurunziza and Ngaruko (2003) stress, these resources were used to

---

[3] In the larger set (covering forty-three rather than twenty-seven countries) used by Collier and O'Connell in chapter 2, there is one additional instance of unsustainable growth: Angola 1994–2000. In this period, external debt was contracted on the basis of oil wealth to finance the war against Savimbi.

Table 5.1 *Episodes of unsustainable spending in the country studies.*

Country	Period
Burundi	1972–1988
Cameroon	1978–present
Congo	1978–91
Côte d'Ivoire	1970–90
Guinea	1973–84
Niger	1974–85
Nigeria	1970–87
Togo	1974–79

Source: Classification by the project editors (see chapter 2).

distribute rents to the political elite via public corporations. That this system could survive for a long time is explained by the massive use of rents to reward the army so that predation could continue. Similarly, rigidly enforced capital controls made capital flight very difficult, except for members of the elite. As in the Adam–O'Connell model the government had no incentive to promote growth: since the elite was small it had a strong incentive to grab rents.

In Cameroon, the trade shock was the discovery of oil in 1975; oil exports started in 1978. Initially, this boom was managed remarkably well. The government resisted spending pressures (in part by keeping the size of the windfall a secret, even from the Ministry of Finance), it saved a very large fraction of its windfall income, and it held its savings largely in the form of foreign assets. However, upon repatriation these assets were poorly allocated. Government spending was increasingly used to subsidize state enterprises and (after 1985) to maintain cash crop prices in real terms when world prices had declined substantially.

The case of the Republic of Congo is best seen as the oil boom relaxing a borrowing constraint. The government reacted by borrowing heavily abroad. The proceeds were invested in a heavily regulated non-oil sector, dominated by state enterprises.

Côte d'Ivoire started the 1970s with a conservative policy regime, characterized by fiscal and monetary restraint. This restraint was abandoned in the second half of the 1970s. The five-year plan for 1976–80 was extremely optimistic. Its lack of realism would have made it unsustainable very quickly if the country had not benefited enormously from the beverages boom. (This happened in many African countries. For example, Tanzania's unsustainable economic strategy – including massive investment in heavy industry – was maintained for another five years as a result of the coffee boom.) Côte d'Ivoire was a very substantial exporter of coffee and cocoa. As a result the beverages boom represented a very large terms of trade improvement: the barter terms of trade rose by over 80 percent in 1975–7 and in 1977, at the peak of the boom, the windfall amounted to 26 percent of GDP (Ghanem 1999: 145, and figure 4.1).

Fiscal restraint was abandoned in this period. Current expenditure rose only modestly while government revenue soared. As a result government saving rose massively, reaching an astonishing 18 percent of GDP in 1977. Nevertheless the budget went into deficit: the government embarked on an extraordinary program of public investment, financed in part by external borrowing. Towards the end of the boom, in 1979, public investment amounted to 23 percent of GDP. The fiscal deficit rose from a modest 2 percent of GDP in 1975 to 12 percent by 1980. This public investment had spectacularly low returns. Ghanem (1999: 161) finds a 60 percent increase in the aggregate ICOR between the first and the second half of the 1970s.

The political economy of the public investment program is not entirely clear. Our interpretation is that public investment in office buildings, super-highways, and state enterprises with negative value added at world prices was not a mistake. Such investment was preferred to the accumulation of foreign assets or productive domestic investment because it offered vast opportunities for transferring rents to the elite. Such rent creation through public investment was, of course, already feasible prior to the boom, but it would then have been much more costly. Prior to the boom external borrowing would have been more difficult and raising revenue domestically to finance public investment would have required visible, and therefore politically costly, changes in taxation.

During the boom government revenue rose automatically since price controls delinked producer prices for export crops from world prices. In addition the boom raised the country's creditworthiness. Through these two channels the boom reduced the cost (from the perspective of the elite) of the investment strategy: the need to raise revenues in a politically costly way was reduced. In this view the intertemporal substitution which ended the Ivorian "miracle" economic performance was not a mistake, but a rational response to the boom. Policy-makers knew the strategy was unsustainable, but calculated that it was not in their interest to smooth spending. That the positive shock had such an extraordinary negative long-run effect therefore does not reflect the inability but rather the unwillingness of the regime to harness the boom efficiently.

After the boom this fiscal stance quickly became unsustainable. The strategy of unsustainable spending left the country in economic crisis after one of the largest booms ever recorded. A large part of government debt was held domestically. In a flexible exchange regime adjustment could have relied in part on default on this domestic debt, through evaluation. However, its franc zone membership denied Côte d'Ivoire this instrument. As a result adjustment involved an extended period of painful contraction until the dilemma was resolved by the 1994 devaluation. In the post-devaluation period growth recovered.

In Guinea, the period 1973–84 started with a phase of extraordinary rapid growth (7 percent *per capita*) in 1973–8. This was followed by a period of decline (–1 percent *per capita*) in 1978–84. In the latter period Guinea had a highly interventionist socialist regime, and experienced a negative shock (the oil shock of 1979–80) and a debt servicing crisis. Doumbouya and Camara (2007) describe how in this period the government redistributed resources from peasants (who were heavily taxed) to the urban wage earning elite. This redistribution (not unlike that occurring in Tanzania at the same time) was unsustainable: peasants could shift resources from production of export crops to food crops and Guinea was not in a position to offset the resulting fall in exports through borrowing. This led to economic implosion with private agents retreating from the formal economy into subsistence and informal sector activities. This process ended with a military coup in 1984.

The case of Niger is in some respects similar to that of Côte d'Ivoire. The country enjoyed a uranium boom in 1974–80 (in both price and in quantity terms). The boom enabled the government to embark upon an ambitious program of public investment, partly financed by external borrowing. The return to this investment was very low, leaving the country post-boom indebted and with an unsustainable fiscal stance. Here the similarities end. As Azam (1999) stresses, the government faced a portfolio problem. Mining companies had an incentive to keep uranium in the ground as long as they expected the world price to rise so much that unmined uranium had a higher return (through appreciation) than the opportunity cost of capital. As further price increases became less likely the companies stepped up production. This increased government revenue.

Since uranium is an exhaustible resource this revenue should be seen as an asset to be reinvested rather than as income. Viewed in this light the government was right to increase investment at the end of the uranium price boom. However, this led to a very concentrated investment boom. Very likely this bunching of investment reduced the return on investment through construction boom effects. Ideally, the government would have smoothed investment over time, using external borrowing to bring some of the investment forward. The implication is that the government should have borrowed much more than it did and that investment smoothing would have raised the permanent income.

This is very different from the Ivorian case where unsustainability reflected the unwillingness rather than the inability of the regime to smooth windfall income. For Niger, inability might either have been the result of a capital market imperfection (creditors refusing to lend against future government revenue from uranium exports, as Azam suggests) or of the government's failure to recognize the implications of bunched investment. In the former case, if the government was hampered by a borrowing constraint, the implication is that the government, unable to bring investment forward, should have smoothed by *postponing* investment. Holding the uranium revenue which accrued in the late 1970s initially abroad and repatriating the foreign assets gradually in the 1980s to finance domestic investment could have done this. Under this interpretation Niger's syndrome of unsustainable spending is less unusual than its link to an exhaustible resource suggests: the failure of governments to stretch an investment boom through the use of foreign assets is quite common.

Nigeria experienced two oil booms in the 1970s. Both accrued largely to the government. During the first boom the windfall was, unusually, initially held in the form of foreign assets. This was not a matter of design: reserves accumulated because Nigeria had a fixed exchange rate regime. The technocrats which at that time ran economic policy under the military government were committed to import-substituting industrialization (already discredited at the time, as Harberger 1999 points out). When the foreign assets were repatriated they were accordingly used for investment in large-scale industrial projects, including a massively expensive steel mill which never produced steel. In effect, the oil boom provided the resources to implement the civil servants' industrial vision.

That the technocrats could realize their megalomanic industrial ambitions reflects Nigeria's political economy at that time. The position of civil servants was unusually strong since they were shielded by the military from control by politicians. In addition, the interests of farmers and the urban wage earners were not served by effective interest groups. Hence the bureaucrats enjoyed a period of unconstrained power at the very time when the resources were available to implement their vision. It is worth noting that this is one of the few cases where public spending was driven by a (technocratic) economic vision, rather than by the self-interest of the regime.

During the second oil boom, presided over by a civilian government, public investment continued, now more as a source of rents than as a way of implementing a particular economic vision. Government consumption now also rose massively, financed by external borrowing. In the early 1980s Nigeria's external debt stood at $12 billion. Massive public spending brought the regime victory in the 1983 election. However, it was soon overthrown by a coup. This is another case where intertemporal inefficiency reflects unwillingness rather than inability. The ruling clique was well aware that its spending was unsustainable. The very painful adjustment which occurred in the 1980s was predictable. (In the period 1981–6 gross domestic expenditure fell by an astonishing 35 percent in real terms; Bevan, Collier, and Gunning 1992.) Our interpretation, developed in section 3 on looting, is that the prevailing competitive patronage politics drove those with power into rampant embezzlement.

Devaluation was postponed until 1986. This followed a long period of external pressure (including from the World Bank) for policy reform. The shock of adjustment therefore became associated not with the old policies (including the fixed exchange rate regime) which had led to it, but with the liberalization. Hence unsustainable spending left an unexpected but extremely costly legacy: a widely shared hostility towards economic liberalization.

Togo experienced a series of trade shocks in the 1974–9 period: first the oil shock (negative), then a phosphate boom in 1974–5 (positive), followed by the coffee boom (positive). As in Nigeria, the government had a vision of *grands travaux* and industrial investment which could be realized as a result of the windfalls. Public investment rose massively, to 40 percent of GDP in 1979. A handful of state enterprises accounted for half of industrial investment in the late 1970s. Trade policy was used to make these enterprises viable at domestic prices.[4]

Rents were distributed to favoured ethnic groups through government employment. (The number of civil servants trebled in a decade.) By the end of the 1970s the regime ran large budget deficits and had accumulated a massive external debt. However, it is not obvious that this was unsustainable *ex ante*. As Gogué and Evlo (2007) stress, Togo (like Côte d'Ivoire) enjoyed strong western support in the Cold War period. The regime might rationally have decided that it could continue to run up debt because of its strategic importance in the region (where, for example, neighbouring Benin had adopted Marxist–Leninism). Indeed, the regime was stable until after the fall of the Berlin Wall.

In Guinea, the bauxite boom led to huge civil service employment and subsidization of state enterprises. The government hired all graduates, 70 percent of the budget went on subsidies and civil service salaries, and rice consumption was heavily subsidized.

3 Looting

Our focus in this chapter is on gross failures in social intertemporal optimization. Looting is one such failure: it is a variant of corruption in which the target is assets. Assets are dishonestly acquired and in the process an incentive is created to convert them either into consumption or some socially less productive asset such as flight capital.

---

[4] Gogué and Evlo (2007).

Africa has seen various types of looting. In Uganda during the era of Idi Amin the basic asset transfer was private-to-public, as Asian assets were confiscated and then handed out again in an informal fashion as state patronage. The new "owners" had usage rights but little security – indeed, during the early 1990s their property was returned to its original owners. Hence, their incentive was to deplete it – for example, by neglecting maintenance. A closely analogous process is the public looting of European-owned farms and informal transfer to political clients in Zimbabwe. In Nigeria and Zaire the basic asset transfer was public-to-private, as mineral wealth was siphoned off by politically powerful figures. Again, the new owners had little security and so, to the extent that they wished to retain the wealth as an asset rather than consume it, they had a strong incentive to get it out of the country. A third form of looting occurred in the context of state breakdown. With property rights unenforceable the basic asset transfers are private-to-private. State breakdown is distinctive and is considered as a syndrome in itself. Our concern here is confined to situations in which state power is used either to loot the private sector, as in Uganda and Zimbabwe, or to loot the public sector, as in Nigeria and Zaire.

In addition to the distinction between looting the private sector and looting the public sector, a further important distinction is between looting by an autocratic state and looting by a democratic state. Ideally, political leaders simply lack the opportunity to loot because they are subject to various checks and balances. Such checks and balances do not have to be very effective to stop *outright* looting. The total failure of checks and balances in Africa usually occurred only in the context of military absolutism, such as with Mobutu, Abacha, and Amin, all coup leaders from the army. However, the most important and most troubling case of looting occurred in Nigeria during the democratic period of 1978–83, and indeed probably resumed under the return to democracy in 1998. These were periods of genuinely contested presidential elections. The agendas of the competing political parties were not strongly predetermined by ideological positions, and so in principle it might have been hoped that the electorate would have been able to use its power to secure effective public expenditures on public assets such as roads and private assets such as education. One estimate is that by 1999 Nigerian capital flight had cumulated to $10 billion.[5] Much of this occurred in the democratic period, because this was the period of the peak earnings from oil. The slide of Zimbabwe into looting has coincided with the decline in its democracy. However, to an extent, the looting can be seen as a desperate strategy by an initially democratic government facing the prospect of electoral defeat. A further possible episode of looting in the context of

---

[5] See Collier, Hoeffler, and Pattillo (2005).

Table 5.2 *Episodes of looting in the country studies.*

Country	Looting period	Target	Regime type
Burundi	1972–88	Public	Autocracy
CAR	1965–79	Public	Autocracy
DRC	1973–97	Public	Autocracy
Liberia	1997–2000	Private	Democracy
Mali	1968–91	Public	Autocracy
Mozambique	1974	Public	Autocracy
Nigeria	1973–8	Public	Autocracy
Nigeria	1978–83	Public	Democracy
Nigeria	1983–98	Public	Autocracy
Somalia	1975–91	Public	Autocracy
Togo	1994–2000	Public	Autocracy
Uganda	1971–9	Private	Autocracy
Zimbabwe	1998–2000	Private	Democracy

Source: Classification by the project editors (see chapter 2).

democracy, too recent to be included in our study, is Kenya under President Mwai Kibaki. The highly charged depictions of public 'looting' alleged by the British High Commissioner were endorsed in the resignation statement of the Anti-Corruption Commissioner, John Githongo, in response to which some aid programs were suspended. At present it is unclear whether this is on a scale sufficient to affect macroeconomic performance.

These cases yield a two-by-two disaggregation of African looting: whether the object of looting is the private sector or the public sector, and whether the agency of looting is an autocratic state or a democratic political party. Africa's episodes of looting, so classified, are shown in table 5.2. It was widely hoped that the wave of democracy across Africa in the early 1990s would produce economic discipline. That it has not put an end to looting is both intriguing for analysis and disturbing for policy. We therefore devote most attention to trying to understand the underlying process.

3.1   Looting the private sector in autocracies

Autocracy by its nature destroys checks and balances. However, although such a dismantling is a necessary precondition for looting, it is not sufficient. Most autocrats refrain from looting the assets of the private sector because of the radically unsustainable nature of the strategy: this is the famous distinction between the roving and the stationary bandit. The main example of an autocratic state looting the private sector in Africa is the confiscation of Asian assets in Amin's Uganda.

Amin's strategy is probably best interpreted as a mistake. The unsustainability of the strategy manifested itself both in the rapid withering of the economy and in the collapse of government revenue. Amin was an unsuccessful autocrat in the most basic respect: he was unable to finance his army to an adequate extent to meet a military challenge from a similar-sized, low-income neighboring state. As a result, after a relatively brief rule he was overthrown by external military intervention from Tanzania. A subsequent President of Uganda, Yoweri Museveni, provides an unusually clear confirmation of Amin's error. Museveni adopted precisely the opposite strategy to that of Amin, inviting the Asians to return to Uganda, restoring their property, and avoiding predatory taxation. The resulting rapid growth of the economy dramatically increased government revenue. Museveni prioritized expenditure on the army and was able to achieve a military victory over a much larger neighbor. In January 2006 he celebrated his twentieth year in power.

It is notable that elsewhere in Africa there are many examples of rich ethnic minorities living under autocracies, but there is no other major example of an autocrat looting the private sector. It would not have been surprising had such looting been more common. Some African autocrats should rationally have taken the roving bandit view because they were highly insecure. Africa is by far the most coup-prone region. The risk of a coup is increased by having already had a coup, and so those who achieved the capacity to dismantle checks and balances could rationally see their likely tenure as brief.[6] The rarity of looting of the private sector may reflect a combination of the speed with which the economy collapses in response, and a 'winner's curse' effect of successful coup leaders. The economic consequences of looting the private sector are clear from Uganda and Zimbabwe. In both cases the economy rapidly declined in absolute terms by around 30 percent with tax revenue falling even more rapidly, forcing the government to resort to hyperinflation. Such looting is thus a sensible strategy only for those leaders who expect to lose power within a few years. However, coup winners will be drawn systematically from among those who over-estimate their likely longevity in power. Hence, looting the private sector may seem a sub-optimal strategy even for those who would in fact do well out of it.

3.2 Looting the private sector in democracies

Democracies are normally defended against looting by both electoral competition and by the rule of law. Electoral competition normally ensures that governments will not adopt policies that even over a relatively short

---

[6] On the risk of African coups, see Collier and Hoeffler (2005b).

horizon are ruinous. The rule of law implies that basic property rights must be respected.

If looting the private sector is bad politics for autocrats, it is even more likely to be bad politics for democratic political parties. There are only two examples in Africa, namely Zimbabwe and Liberia. These episodes are best considered as mistakes. The clear evidence for this is that the strategies have not been electorally successful. In order to retain power in Zimbabwe, President Mugabe has needed to resort to increasingly drastic curtailment of electoral competition, including suppression of the media, and violent oppression of the opposition political party. He has also had to dismantle the rule of law so that property rights could be disregarded. In Liberia, Charles Taylor criminalized the state far more dramatically, but rapidly lost power and is now exiled in Nigeria.

Just as Museveni's success from implementing the opposite of Amin's strategy demonstrates that it was simply an error, so the example of the ANC in South Africa and of President Ahmad Tejan Kabbah in Sierra Leone demonstrates the error in the strategies of Mugabe and Taylor. The ANC was faced with a much more lucrative opportunity to loot an ethnic minority private sector than that facing Mugabe in Zimbabwe. For over a decade it has resolutely resisted this option and shows few signs of taking it in the future. Whereas electoral support for Mugabe's party has crumbled, the ANC has actually strengthened its electoral dominance. In Sierra Leone, as in Liberia, the new democratic government inherited a fragile post-conflict situation in the context of substantial natural-resource rents. However, it has been able both to consolidate the democracy through further elections, and at the same time strengthen its own hold on power.

Nevertheless, the existence of the option of democratic looting of an ethnic minority private sector has been significant in some African contexts. We refer to it as "anticipated redistribution." The context in which it is potentially of importance is where ruling ethnic minorities sense that they are likely to lose power to an ethnic majority and that, perhaps because of their own conduct to the majority, they risk confiscation of assets. The cases of Amin's Uganda and Mugabe's Zimbabwe illustrate that minorities face some risk of looting even if the looting strategy is irrational, because leaders have the power to make mistakes. With these expectations, the minority will attempt to shift its assets out of the country *while it is still in power.*

The most high-visibility example of such an exodus was the flight of capital out of Angola in the transitional months between the Portuguese revolution of April 1974 and the Popular Movement for the Liberation of Angola (MPLA) take-over of power in 1975. As well as financial assets, every physical asset that could possibly be dismantled and shipped out was removed to Portugal. This asset stripping would have left Angola with a depleted legacy even had subsequent political developments been more benign. Similar capital flight occurred in all the Portuguese colonies, that of longest duration being Guinea-Bissau which was the origin of the liberation struggle against the Portuguese on the continent.

However, quantitatively the most important examples of capital flight due to anticipated looting were South Africa and Namibia. From the late 1970s it became clear that minority rule was not sustainable, consequent upon the fall of the Portuguese regimes in Angola and Mozambique in 1975 and of the Smith regime in Southern Rhodesia in 1978. The wealthy white elite of South Africa substantially repositioned its asset portfolios. Although the visible signs of this were far less dramatic than in Angola, in South Africa white wealth owners had a far longer period in which to gradually reposition their assets. Although capital flight was illegal in South Africa, the visible sign of a shift in portfolios was a rapid and sustained collapse in the rate of private investment. As a consequence there was also a collapse in the growth rate. There was an analytically similar, but much smaller, flight of capital from the other major settler economy, Kenya, in the early 1960s. Of course, in retrospect this capital flight was unnecessary. Indeed, even at the time that it occurred, the probability of a future episode of looting was probably perceived as relatively low by wealth owners. However, perceived new risks do not have to be high in order to induce substantial shifts in portfolios.

Our case studies in volume 2 also suggest two anticipated redistributions where power has yet to shift: Burundi and Togo. In Burundi, the early loss of power of the parallel Tutsi elite in neighboring Rwanda brought home the vulnerability of elite-owned assets retained within the country, even though to date the Tutsi elite has managed to retain power. In Togo, through the 1990s the world's longest-serving President was becoming increasing likely to die, and so his clients, who had had a long period in which to amass wealth, were increasingly vulnerable. In the event he survived until 2005 and was hastily and unconstitutionally replaced by his son.

3.3   Looting the public sector in autocracies

In Uganda General Amin looted the private sector whereas in Nigeria General Abacha looted the public sector. The difference was obviously in the endowments of natural-resource wealth. In economies with substantial natural-resource rents they are the natural target for looting. The embezzlement of natural-resource rents is also an intertemporal concern because the resource wealth is a depleting asset. However, as a strategy it is sustainable over a far longer horizon than looting the private sector: resources may be depleted for decades. Hence, it can be a rational strategy even for a "stationary bandit."

However, although autocrats have the power to loot, viewed globally, they usually do not do so. Autocratic looting has been much more pronounced in Africa than in other regions. Why might this be the case? Since African autocrats have generally retained power for as long as the global average, the most evident reason for looting – a short time horizon – does not provide an explanation.

Because looting targets assets, it is an extreme case of redistribution at the expense of growth. Two distinctive features of Africa made this a more attractive option for African autocrats than those of other regions.

First, other things equal, there is a stronger incentive to loot public assets *the higher is the ratio of such assets relative to the society's income.* Evidently, the larger are public assets the greater is the gross gain from looting them, but since looting sacrifices the growth of income, the lower is the initial level of income the lower is its opportunity cost. Looking first at the numerator of this ratio, Africa has had far more resource-rich economies than other regions: currently around 30 percent of its population lives in such economies against only 11 percent elsewhere. Thus, there were many more societies in which the looting of public assets was potentially lucrative. Turning to the denominator, even in 1960 the resource-rich developing countries in other regions had *per capita* incomes more than double those of resource-rich Africa, and this gap rapidly widened (see figure 2.2). Thus, since societies rich in public assets but with low private incomes clearly have the strongest incentive for looting, the phenomenon would be more common in Africa than elsewhere.

The other reason why Africa was more prone to the looting of public assets is that the incentive to prioritize redistribution over growth becomes more attractive *the smaller is the group to which the benefits of redistribution can be confined* (Adam and O'Connell 1999). Ethnic differentiation provides the most convenient basis for exclusion: it is easy to identify and people cannot readily change categories. Most societies have some ethnic diversity and in such societies autocrats typically have their own ethnic group as their power base. Through various strategies, autocrats encourage their ethnic group to sustain them: partly by the rewards of redistribution, and partly by the fear of retribution from other groups should there be a change of regime. Hence, we would expect that, globally, autocracy would be more detrimental to growth the greater the extent of ethnic diversity. This is indeed what the econometric evidence finds (Collier 2000; Alesina and La Ferrara 2003). This global relationship is bad news for Africa. As shown in table 2.19 (p. 119), Africa is considerably more ethnically diverse than other regions, and it has been considerably less democratic. The conjunction of these features is most pronounced for those countries with large public assets, namely the resource-rich economies. Measuring the extent of the problem by the ratio of measures of ethnic diversity and democracy, after the 1960s Africa's resource-rich economies on average consistently score more than double those of other regions.

Thus, African autocrats were more likely to be sitting on the opportunity of valuable lootable resources; the opportunity cost of such looting was likely to be lower; and because their identifiable power bases were narrower, the gain from redistribution was magnified relative to its opportunity cost. They thus had a substantially stronger incentive to loot public assets for purposes of redistribution to their clients.

Given that public assets were looted for the benefit of a favored group, the remaining question of importance for growth is why this was not merely an asset transfer: why was there a net reduction in assets? Robinson and Verdier (2002) provide a convincing answer to this question. They argue that once clients are given assets they are no longer dependent upon the patron. To retain loyalty, the patron needs to dispense flows, not stocks. Hence, assets needed to be metaphorically dismantled and transferred as flows. Of course, the clients were free to accumulate these flows as private assets, but in effect the autocrat precluded the option of club assets.

3.4   Looting the public sector in democracies

As with protection against looting of the private sector, a democracy has two mechanisms for protecting against the looting of public assets: electoral competition and the rule of law. At least superficially, it might seem that competitive elections would provide an even stronger defense of public assets than of private assets. Most private assets are necessarily owned by a minority of voters, whereas the looting of public assets implies a diminished provision of public goods that would benefit a majority of voters. Political parties should thus have strong incentives to supply desired public goods in order to survive in power. By contrast, the rule of law is generally better designed to protect private property than public assets. Many of the mechanisms that defend public assets from public officials are either internal civil service procedures or political checks rather than the police and the courts. We therefore refer to these defenses as *due process*, rather than as the rule of law. It is possible for the rule of law to survive in conditions where due process collapses. However, where due process is in place, it ensures that even if politicians want to embezzle public money they are not able to do so without penalty.

It is useful to compare four African democracies to see how electoral competition and due process have worked. Both Botswana and Nigeria have very substantial natural-resource rents. In Nigeria looting has clearly had first-order effects on growth. In Botswana by contrast, despite equally valuable resource rents the government has been disciplined by democracy into delivering public goods. One key procedure for preventing looting has been nothing more than an administrative rule: natural-resource revenue is saved in foreign reserves unless public projects are available that meet a threshold economic rate of return. For various reasons government leaders have chosen to adhere to this aspect of due process, although they would most surely have had the power to dismantle it without jeopardizing the rule of law. Neither Kenya nor Senegal has important natural-resource rents. In Kenya, as discussed above, looting is considerable. By contrast, in Senegal corruption is significantly less severe.

Hence, one puzzle to be explained is why looting is important in Nigeria and Kenya but not Botswana and Senegal. However, although Nigeria and Kenya both have patronage politics, looting is radically more severe in Nigeria. This becomes a second puzzle to be explained. Two defense mechanisms – electoral competition and due process – get undermined.

Natural-resource rents subvert democracy through two routes. Resource-rent democracies are more likely to suffer from patronage politics because the maximum patronage resources available to the government increase. Further, even where societies without natural resources do have patronage politics, the consequences are less dire. Because they have to rely more heavily upon taxation, patronage governments can get away with less, and so have to spend more on public goods provision. Through both these routes, a democracy with large natural-resource rents is liable to have inferior public goods and hence slower growth.

We would characterize Nigeria as the quintessential example of a natural-resource democracy in which during our period both restraints were undermined. Similarly, Kenya is an example of an economy without natural-resource revenues where patronage politics has nevertheless proved to be viable. Consistent with our analysis, looting is manifestly even more of a problem in Nigeria than it is in Kenya.

However, while Nigeria and Kenya suffer from looting, Botswana and Senegal do not. Yet Botswana is a natural-resource economy like Nigeria, and Senegal is structurally similar to Kenya. What might account for such different outcomes? One possible explanation is that in Nigeria and Kenya the episodes of democracy followed prolonged periods of autocracy whereas in Botswana and Senegal democracy has been continuous since independence. When democracy is replaced by autocracy this generally implies more than the end of electoral competition. While the overall rule of law might be retained, thereby defending private assets from looting, there is nothing to prevent the autocrat quietly dismantling due process, and thus the defenses of public assets. Such a dismantling of due process clearly occurred in both Nigeria and Kenya. The restoration of democracy literally means only the restoration of electoral competition. Thus, competitive elections defined the resumption of democracy in Nigeria and Kenya. The restoration of electoral competition reflected the political bankruptcy of the previous regimes – in effect, autocracy collapsed. However, while such a collapse enables the forces of electoral competition to re-emerge, there are no equivalent forces rapidly restoring due process. Unlike electoral competition, due process is a mass of complex rules, procedures, and expectations. Whereas the leaders of a dormant political party have a strong incentive to play their part in restoring electoral competition, no equivalent group stands to benefit from the restoration of due process.

There is thus a major difference between democracies that have persisted continuously from their initial inheritance of due process, such as Botswana and Senegal, and those that have been restored, such as Nigeria and Kenya. As a result of their different histories, Nigeria and Kenya during their looting episodes were characterized by electoral competition in the context of an inherited breakdown in due process whereas Botswana and Senegal have had due process, usually without significant electoral competition. Electoral competition without due process produces patronage politics – looting. Due process with limited electoral competition produces the more conventional politics of public goods. In effect, by preserving their democracies, Botswana and Senegal also preserved the restraints that protected them from patronage politics. It was much less difficult to maintain the restraints than to re-establish them once they had been dismantled under periods of autocracy.

One implication is that Kenya may have a better chance of restoring due process than Nigeria. In Kenya taxation has necessarily to be considerable so that in the long term citizen pressure will be significant. Indeed, in Kenya looting may even be a temporary disequilibrium phenomenon which will cease once citizen pressure resulting from taxation builds to the threshold at which patronage is no longer viable. Nigeria's structurally low taxation suggests that it cannot expect such an easy evolution out of patronage politics. However, even in Nigeria the experience of Botswana carries a somewhat hopeful message. Although in order to *introduce* due process Nigeria may need some idiosyncratic factor such as political leadership rather than just the automatic force of citizen pressure, once introduced due process might be sustainable, as in Botswana.

4 Conclusion and implications

Unsustainable public spending was an important factor in the failure of the growth process in Africa. It need not be related to trade shocks, but it often is. Such spending is often characterized as a symptom of loss of control, or of the government's inability to assess correctly the temporary nature of the boom-related increase in government revenue, or, finally, of the government's failure to understand the case for consumption smoothing. There is probably some truth in all three of these explanations. However, we suggest that in many cases unsustainable spending should not be seen as a sign of incompetence but rather as the result of a rational decision of a narrowly based regime. Such a regime has no incentive to promote growth and may well have an incentive to substitute current for future income. We have suggested that much the same applies to looting. Although some looting episodes can reasonably be seen as mistakes, more commonly they are informed choices.

There is little reason to think that the incidence of intertemporal mistakes was markedly higher in Africa than in other regions. However, some of the mistakes probably had greater potency. In particular, the fear of "democratic looting" – the fear of confiscation of minority assets by newly enfranchised majorities – was much more widespread than the phenomenon itself, which happened only as rare mistakes. This fear induced precautionary capital flight which was destructive of growth.

Intertemporal syndromes as informed choices have rested on one or other of three underlying malfunctions: powerful minorities can gain from socially costly strategies; time horizons of leaders can be dysfunctionally short; and the electorate can reward dysfunctional political behavior. What are the potential defenses against these problems?

In the past the key malfunction has probably been the first. The most straightforward defense is democratization: minorities lose their power. This is rapidly happening across Africa. Indeed, much of the impetus for democracy has come from a recognition of the damage done by power-ful minorities. However, this may only change the cause of the syndrome: switching the malfunction to short time horizons and patronage politics, both intensified rather than resolved by electoral competition. Potentially, given a hardening of the world prices of commodities, Africa will be char-acterized by democracies gearing up resource booms through borrowing to finance patronage politics.

To defend against the intertemporal syndrome in democracies essentially requires that the checks and balances that are common in, but not inherent to, democracy function effectively. Democracy in Botswana has produced an economic success because electoral competition has been modest while the checks and balances from due process have been strong. At the heart of Botswana's success are two simple-looking bureaucratic restraints: pub-lic officials who embezzle face a credible threat of punishment, and public investment projects must pass a rigorous test of their rate of return. These two restraints inhibit looting, provide a sound mix between real and finan-cial assets, and smooth shocks. Thus, while competitive elections solve the perverse incentives that stem from minority power, Africa will need both features of democracy before it transforms resource rents into growth. As Afghanistan and Iraq have demonstrated, competitive elections can rapidly be introduced into the most difficult of conditions. They may well be self-sustaining as political parties develop interests in contesting power. Due process and checks and balances are much more difficult to establish, and there is no equivalent constituency demanding them. It would be unfortunate if democracy in Africa became discredited, inviting a return to the disastrous experience of autocracies, when what is needed is not less democracy, but more.

References

Adam, C. S. and S. A. O'Connell (1999), "Aid, Taxation and Development in Sub-Saharan Africa," *Economics and Politics* 11: 225–54

Alesina, A. and E. La Ferrara (2003), "Ethnic Diversity and Economic Performance," Department of Economics, Harvard University

Azam, J.-P. (1999), "The Uranium Boom in Niger, 1975–82," in P. Collier, J. W. Gunning, and associates, *Trade Shocks in Developing Countries.* Oxford: Oxford University Press, 2 vols.

Bevan, D., P. Collier, and J. W. Gunning (1989), "Fiscal Response to a Temporary Trade Shock: the Aftermath of the Kenyan Coffee Boom," *World Bank Economic Review* 3: 359–78

   (1990), *Controlled Open Economies.* Oxford: Oxford University Press

   (1992), *Nigeria 1970–1990*, ICEG Country Studies 11. San Francisco, CA: ICS Press

Collier, P. (2000), "Ethnicity, Politics and Economic Performance," *Economics and Politics* 12: 225–45

Collier, P., J. W. Gunning, and associates (1999), *Trade Shocks in Developing Countries.* Oxford: Oxford University Press, 2 vols.

Collier, P. and A. Hoeffler (2005a), "Democracy and Natural Resources," CSAE, Department of Economics, Oxford

   (2005b), "Greed and Grievance in Coups d'Etats," CSAE, Department of Economics, Oxford

Collier, P., A. Hoeffler, and C. Pattillo (2005), "Africa's Exodus: Brain Drain and Capital Flight," *Journal of African Economies* 13(O) Supplement 2:15–54

Deaton, A. (1992), "Commodity Prices, Stabilization and Growth in Africa," Discussion Paper 166, Research Program in Development Studies, Princeton, NJ: Princeton University

Doumbouya, Sékou F. and Fodé Camara (2007), "Explaining Economic Growth in Africa: The Case of Guinea," chapter 17 in Benno J. Ndulu, Stephen A. O'Connell, Jean-Paul Azam, Robert H. Bates, Augustin Kwasi Fosu, Jan Willem Gunning, and Dominique Njinkeu, eds., *The Political Economy of Economic Growth in Africa, 1960–2000*, vol. 2. Cambridge: Cambridge University Press

Gelb, A. and associates (1988), *Oil Windfalls: Blessing or Curse?* New York: Oxford University Press

Ghanem, H. (1999), "The Ivorian Cocoa and Coffee Boom of 1976–79: the End of a Miracle?," in P. Collier, J. W. Gunning, and associates, *Trade Shocks in Developing Countries.* Oxford: Oxford University Press, 2 vols.

Gogué, Tchabouré A. and Kodjo Evlo (2007), "Togo: Lost Opportunities for Growth," chapter 14 in Benno J. Ndulu, Stephen A. O'Connell, Jean-Paul Azam,

Robert H. Bates, Augustin Kwasi Fosu, Jan Willem Gunning, and Dominique Njinkeu, eds., *The Political Economy of Economic Growth in Africa, 1960–2000*, vol. 2. Cambridge: Cambridge University Press

Harberger, A. C. (1992), "Introduction," in D. Bevan, P. Collier, and J. W. Gunning, *Nigeria 1970–1990*, ICEG Country Studies 11. San Francisco, CA: ICS Press

   (1999), "Latin America and East Asia: Revisiting the Evidence," in L. Thorbecke and H. Wan, Jr., eds., *Taiwan's Development Experience: Lesson on the Roles of Government and Market*. Boston, Dordrecht, and London: Kluwer Academic: 327–64

Nkurunziza, Janvier D. and Floribent Ngaruko (2007), "Why Has Burundi Grown So Slowly? The Political Economy of Redistribution," chapter 2 in Benno J. Ndulu, Stephen A. O'Connell, Jean-Paul Azam, Robert H. Bates, Augustin Kwasi Fosu, Jan Willem Gunning, and Dominique Njinkeu, eds., *The Political Economy of Economic Growth in Africa, 1960–2000*, vol. 2. Cambridge: Cambridge University Press

Robinson, J. and T. Verdier (2002), "The Political Economy of Clientelism," CEPR Discussion Paper 3205

6 | The political geography of redistribution

Jean-Paul Azam

1 Introduction

Poor countries are not uniformly poor. In many African countries, there is generally a simple mapping between the allocation of wealth across ethnic groups and their geographical distribution. For example, in West African countries, the cultural and religious divisions between ethnic groups are strongly correlated with the difference in wealth between them. There is a sharp contrast between a relatively affluent south and a poorer north in most of the countries of this area. For instance, in Chad, the southerners produce cotton, while the northerners are poor nomadic herdsmen. A similar distribution of activities can be found in Mali and Niger, where southerners are agriculturists, and northerners are nomadic herdsmen. In Côte d'Ivoire, the northerners also produce cotton, but there it is a poorer crop than the coffee and cocoa produced by the southerners. In Nigeria, the giant country of Africa, the northerners rely on a typical Sahelian agriculture, growing cotton and millet, while oil dominates the southern economy.

In these countries, a typical political pattern seems to emerge: a military regime often prevails when the northerners are in power, while civilian

This chapter was presented at the AERC/Harvard University workshop on "Explaining African Economic Growth, 1960–2000" (Weatherhead Center for International Affairs, March, 18–19, 2005). It benefited from comments by Nahomi Ichino, who was the discussant, and by Robert Bates, who also offered editorial remarks, and by Chinyamata Chipeta, Paul Collier, Augustin Fosu, Christine de Mariz, Benno Ndulu, Dominique Njinkeu, Janvier Nkurunziza, Steve O'Connell, and Nicolas van de Walle. These comments are gratefully acknowledged, without implicating their authors.

rule seems to be the dominant mode of government when the southerners are in power. François Tombalbaye in Chad and Félix Houphouët-Boigny in Côte d'Ivoire were from the south of their countries, and ran civilian governments. The Hausa generals from northern Nigeria came to power time and again, while the southerner Olesegun Obasanjo led the return to civilian rule in that country (see Zartman *et al.* 1997). This pattern allows for some exceptions. In Mali, for example, the military rulers Modibo Keïta and Moussa Traoré were also from the south, like the civilian governments that were in power either before or after them. No northerner has ever ruled that country. Nevertheless, the pattern sketched above seems to occur often enough to warrant some further analysis. Azam and Mesnard (2003) and Azam (2006) analyze the theoretical foundations of such a pattern. This analysis is sketched below, spelling out the kind of political determinism that the pattern seems to reveal. The natural endowments of the different ethno-regional groups that are living together in some African countries impose some significant constraints on the sustainable political regimes that can be found there.

Sometimes a more complex pattern emerges, as in Ghana, where the rich cocoa growers have poorer neighbours in both the north and in the south. Nevertheless, a related pattern emerges, as the civilian leader Kofi Busia, for example, came from the richest Akan group, while some of the military rulers, including in particular Jerry Rawlings, came from poorer groups. The pattern is slightly different in East Africa, which has a rough east–west division corresponding mostly to altitude. The rich crops grow mainly on the hills above 3,000 ft, while herdsmen are found mostly below that level. In all these cases, these geographical differences give rise to some form of ethnic rent, as migration from the poorer areas to the richer ones is largely precluded by the rules of land ownership. A fairly tight mapping thus exists between ethnicity and the regional location of the groups. Politics in these countries is thus to a large extent devoted to the redistribution of these rents across groups. Sometimes a civil war breaks out between them. In Chad in the late 1970s and in Nigeria a few years earlier, for example, the civil wars set the rich groups against the poorer ones. In other cases, peace prevails despite this type of inequality across groups.

As proved by the later events starting in September 2002, Côte d'Ivoire was clearly exposed to such a risk. The north–south divide there involves both ethnic and religious aspects. The Djula and the Senufo in the north are Muslim, and grow cotton and millet. In fact, the land of the Djula is so poor that they are mainly found in trade rather than in agriculture. The Akan and the Kru in the south are Christian or Animist and grow cocoa and coffee as well as palm oil and exportable vegetables. However, peace was purchased there for several decades by redistribution. Houphouët-Boigny, the late President of Côte d'Ivoire, tried explicitly to build national unity by taxing his own ethnic group, the Akan cocoa and coffee growers, in order to fund visible public investments in infrastructure in the other regions and some other redistributive public expenditure, like health and education. This strategy was quite successful until Houphouët-Boigny's death in 1993. Since then, his successors have changed the general orientation of this country's public expenditure strategy, keeping the northerners out of the game. There was a *coup d'état* in 1999, which brought General Robert Gueï to power for a year. He was a western Mandé, a group related to the northern ones. Later on, a mutiny split the country into two parts in 2002, the northern one falling under the mutineers' control. Hence, the history of Côte d'Ivoire seems to suggest that this type of country has the choice between orderly redistribution between groups, organized by peaceful means, or violent appropriation. Viewed in this light, the type of redistributive policies that Houphouët-Boigny used consistently from the 1970s to his death played a fundamental part in purchasing the peace in this country. This strategy seems to have a wider domain of application in Africa. For example, Azam, Berthélemy, and Calipel (1996) find a significant negative impact of public expenditures with a strong redistributive content, like education and health, on the probability of the outbreak of political violence using panel data from a series of African countries.

Therefore, the redistribution syndrome which has been identified in many of the case studies of this project is probably a response to some deeper parameters which are somehow rooted in the colonial origins of the national borders. As in medicine, one should never, in political economy, confuse the syndrome with the disease that it reveals. African countries have been delineated either by agreements between competing colonial powers or by a colonial administration for fiscal or economic reasons. For example, modern-day Burkina Faso was twice split between the neighboring countries by the French. The idea was to provide its richer neighbors with a reserve of labor for enhancing their development potentials. No attention was paid at all to the deep cultural unity of the Mossi Empire, rooted in a long and rich common history. The Moro Naba twice got his country back together by providing the French with highly organized military units for fighting its two world wars. Similarly, the northern tip of the then Ubangui-Chari territory was grafted onto Chad in 1936 by the French Popular Front government in order to provide the local colonial administration with some fiscal revenues. The civil war that took place in that country in the second half of the 1970s opposed the original Chadian groups to the people from the grafted south. These examples suggest that some countries have inherited a polarized ethnic division from the past, and so are left with a fairly radical choice of political strategy. They can either buy the peace by the means described below, or go for a civil war instead. Hence, as shown below, redistribution and state breakdown might be the possible syndromes of a common disease related to ethnic division and the polarization of wealth across groups.

The present chapter sheds some light on this type of behavior using developments in the economic theory of conflict. Section 2 presents the relations between ethnicity, the geographic allocation of resources, and the resulting polarization of the distribution of wealth across groups. Section 3 then discusses how redistribution and deterrence can be used for buying the peace in these types of countries. Section 4 goes deeper into the social mechanisms involved in this type of redistribution against the background of the rural–urban migration flows that necessarily come with economic development. Section 5 draws some conclusions.

2   Ethnicity and the polarization of wealth

The mapping between the unequal levels of affluence of the different ethnic groups and the natural resources available in their territory is determined by the history of their migration and settlements. Most African ethnic groups have a long memory of the different places where they came from before they settled in their current location. Most of the people in central and eastern Africa and a large part of southern Africa are descendents of the Bantu migrants. Similarly, in west Africa some of the forest groups, such as the Akan, claim ancestors from the Sahelian region. They sometimes conquered their current territory by force, but they often found an empty land. In some cases, the germs that they brought with them decimated the previous occupants (Diamond 1997). Some ethnic groups have moved in a recent past, and are currently found in recently conquered land. For example, the Djulas from northern Côte d'Ivoire arrived there under the leadership of Samory Touré, at the beginning of the twentieth century. They evicted the Animist Senufo farmers, killing many of them and converting the survivors to Islam. However, these historical roots are now sufficient for founding the perceived legitimacy of the collective ownership of their land by many ethnic groups in Africa. As a result, only farmers from certain well-defined ethnic groups are entitled to get land in some areas. The resulting exclusion of migrants from other groups may create inefficiency and inequality of wealth across groups.

Figure 6.1 describes the type of rent that may result in Africa from the restrictions on labor mobility imposed by ethnicity and collective land ownership. From left to right is measured the quantity of labor used on the land owned collectively by group R. From right to left, the quantity of labor used on group P's land is measured. The vertical line through points R and P represents the natural allocation of labor between the two groups in the absence of migration. Maybe because group R has more fertile land, owns

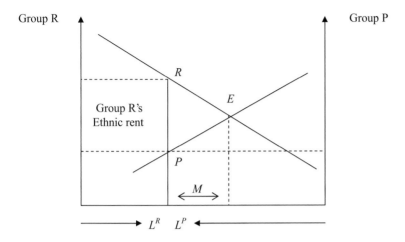

Figure 6.1 Ethnic rent and migration failure

other assets that enhance the productivity of its labor, or has a lower population density on similar land, its marginal productivity is larger than that of group P. Given the supply of labor in each group, the marginal product of labor in group R is at *R*, located above group P's marginal product measured at *P*. Then, the area of the rectangle so labeled measures the ethnic rent that accrues to the members of group R. This is akin to a monopsony rent insofar as the restriction on hiring labor from the other group drives a wedge between the marginal product of labor and its opportunity cost. In the case depicted in figure 6.1, the market equilibrium entails a distortion, as the marginal productivity of labor is not equalized across groups. The social cost of the resulting inefficient allocation of labor is measured by the area of the triangle *REP*, which represents the deadweight loss.

In order to restore productive efficiency, the quantity *M* of labor would have to migrate from the land of group P to that of group R. The marginal product of labor would then be equalized across groups, and output would reach its maximum. Therefore, the large discrepancies that can be observed in some African countries between the marginal productivities of labor across different ethno-regional groups can equivalently be ascribed to either a labor market failure or to a land market failure. However, the latter diagnosis seems more accurate, as it pinpoints the root cause of the problem, namely the collective ownership of land by the whole ethnic group. In fact, the expression "migration failure" encapsulates these two ideas at once. Efficiency could be restored, for example, if *M* units of group P's labor were allowed to migrate to group R's land, and work there for an income equal to the height of point *E*, while the rest of the "Harberger triangle" would be paid to some group R members as rent. Such a move could be

Pareto-improving, depending on the initial distribution of income within group R, and in particular on the functioning of the labor market within that group. It would undoubtedly be socially desirable from a utilitarian point of view.

The distortion described above does not necessarily occur all over Africa. Many ethnic groups have developed a well-functioning market for land where some form of share-cropping contracts have existed for centuries, allowing migrants to make a living on rented land. Hill (1963) has described in detail the *abusa* contract, which solves this problem among the Akan cocoa planters in Ghana. In neighboring Côte d'Ivoire, the same contract exists and is called *abu san*. It gives one-third of the crop to the migrant farmer, and two-thirds to the planter (Gastellu 1989). Some marginal adjustments are made by allocating some land to the migrant's wife (or wives), and by allowing for the gift of some free meals to the planter. Nothing is paid to the collective owner of the land, i.e. the ethnic group. Among the Akan in both countries, the planter traditionally owns the trees but only has usufruct rights on the land for the duration of the life of the trees. This system has been working smoothly for a long time, and largely explains the early success of post-independence Côte d'Ivoire. Azam (1993) shows how smooth immigration allowed that country to engage in a process of endogenous growth. However, the events leading to the civil war starting in 2002 suggest that this migration process could be turned into a time bomb by some simple manipulation of the laws governing land ownership. The 1998 "Reforme foncière" (Land reform), enacted by President Konan Bedié, himself from the Akan group, engineered a massive expropriation of many of the migrants who had bought the orchards from the planters. The distinction between the ownership of the land and that of the trees has been blurred, resulting in massive violence, as alien migrants were then seen as occupying Akan ethnic land. This came with a vengeance, as some Akan migrants had also planted cocoa on Krou land, in the south-west of Côte d'Ivoire, and got expelled as well. President Konan Bedié was ousted by a coup in December 1999, but the smooth functioning of the land market has not been restored.

Land markets seem to be working more efficiently in Muslim countries than in Animist or Christian ones, at least when Islam has been present for a long time. For example, Manchuelle (1997) shows how the flow of migrants from the Soninke group in the Upper Senegal Valley was primed by the possibility of renting some land downstream near the French trading post of Bakel in the nineteenth century. Since then, this ethnic group has been very successful at making up by migration for the secular impoverishment of its land. Inheritance laws force people to define land ownership individually in Muslim societies, although some hybrid systems are still in force in some Muslim African countries.

Several post-independence African rulers did attempt to alleviate such migration failures. For example, Houphouët-Boigny knew very well that his country needed massive imports of manpower from Burkina Faso (then Upper Volta) and Mali for producing the coffee and cocoa that would earn his country the foreign exchange required for development. The colonial French had understood this before, and Upper Volta had been divided between the neighboring countries from 1936 to 1945. Then Côte d'Ivoire got a pool of labor available in its northern part which had been cut off from the Mossi Empire. However, the Mossi emperor Moro Naba recovered his country after the Second World War in return for raising an army that joined the Free French Forces in the Gold Coast during the war. Houphouët-Boigny wanted to make the massive immigration from the north irreversible by granting dual citizenship to the migrants. However, this is one of the few policy decisions that he was unable to get through parliament. Part of the current problems faced by this country since the turn of the twentieth century stems from this failure. However, in some cases, the migration of people from the poorest group follows the military defeat of the rich and does not ensure an optimal use of the land. In Chad since 1990, for example, the northern herdsmen are often trespassing in the cotton fields of the southern cotton growers, which they use as grazing land, and do not hesitate to kill the complaining farmer. This is done with perfect impunity since the northerners won the civil war and are now ruling the country. This example epitomizes how glaring inequalities of wealth across groups are likely to come to a violent end unless some conscious policies are chosen to manage the potential distributional conflict involved in an orderly fashion. Group P may take over, probably by violent means, and then impose some sharing of the rent under some form of threat. The Chadian example just described shows that this is not necessarily done by efficient means. Section 3 describes how this can be prevented if group R is prepared to pay the price of the peace.

Ethnic rent does not only arise from agriculture. The collective ownership of the land extends to the traditional ownership of its mineral wealth. For example, in Côte d'Ivoire and Mali there are quite a lot of gold mines scattered on ethnic land. Modern governments have usually found ways of appropriating these mines, often by compensating some traditional ethnic authority. This is not necessarily easy to enforce, and Sierra Leone provides a sad example where alluvial diamonds have given rise to violent state breakdown. This type of violent expropriation occurs more often with mineral wealth than with agricultural production, although Zimbabwe has provided a recent example to the contrary. The main reason for this fact, which the case of Zimbabwe supports equally, is that farmers are needed for production as much as the land itself. Their know-how is part of the wealth, and cannot be expropriated as easily as mineral wealth. Leonard and Straus

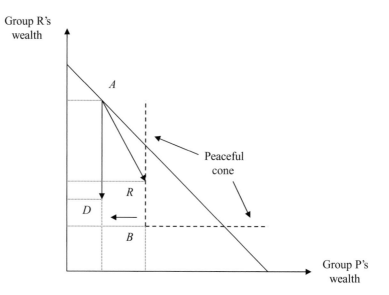

Figure 6.2 Paying for the peace

(2003) use the expression "enclave production" to indicate the latter type of resources, which seems to increase the probability of violent expropriation. These examples illustrate the link between wealth inequality across groups and the incentives they create for violent appropriation.

However, political violence or civil war does not necessarily follow from the polarization of wealth across groups. In most cases, the two sides have an incentive to avoid the outbreak of political violence, as the latter is bound to destroy resources and lives. This is where politics comes in as a way to solve the distributional problem without violence and prevent the outbreak of war. Section 3 describes how the richest group might prevent war by choosing the right combination of redistribution of wealth and accumulation of weapons for the sake of deterrence.

3   How to pay for the peace

When the initial distribution of wealth is too polarized, the richest group has the choice between taking the risk of a war, with all the destruction that this implies, and paying some price for securing the peace. This section sketches how the price of peace is determined within a simple graphical setting. Further analysis can be found in Azam and Mesnard (2003) and Azam (2006).

Figure 6.2 depicts how the richer group can pay for the peace. The setting is similar to that of a standard analysis of the bargaining problem. Point *B* represents the break point, which describes the allocation of wealth that would prevail in case of civil war. Because of the intrinsic uncertainty of the outcome of a war, this point may be interpreted as representing the allocation of *expected* wealth across the two groups in case of war. Then, the efficiency frontier is represented by the downward-sloping line with a slope equal to one. It is the locus of all the possible allocations of a given wealth between the two groups. Peace occurs only if the final allocation of wealth is chosen within the cone located to the north-east of point B, or on its frontier. Otherwise, one group or the other would choose war, which would then promise a higher expected wealth than peace. Call this the "peaceful cone." If the initial allocation of wealth falls within that cone, then the analysis can stop here, as no further policy choice is required for establishing the peace. However, the discussion above has shown that many African countries are in fact characterized by a highly unequal initial distribution of wealth across groups, creating a rent for the lucky ethno-regional groups. As mentioned above, this typical case poses the problem of politics, understood as the collective search for a peaceful equilibrium. Politics then boils down either to the conscious reduction of the polarized distribution of wealth between the two groups or to the modification of their aspirations by some form of military threat. Figure 6.2 illustrates the two pure methods that can be used for buying the peace.

Point A represents the initial allocation of wealth between the two groups, which is assumed to fall outside the peaceful cone. The status quo at A is not an equilibrium outcome, as group P would get a higher expected wealth by choosing to wage a war against group R, thus getting to point B. The first possible strategy for buying the peace is for group R to give away some of its wealth to group P. If no resource cost is involved in such a move, then the allocation of wealth is shifted along the efficiency frontier up to the point where group R's wealth lies on the vertical line above B, may be with a minute addition for breaking the tie between the two points. Peace is then Pareto-improving over B, as both players get a higher payoff in the resulting equilibrium. However, it is realistic to assume that some resource cost might be incurred for making such a transfer of wealth. For example, some taxes might have to be levied on group R's members by its leader, entailing possibly some incentive effects. Some output might be lost if the taxes so levied reduce the marginal reward to labor. However, as discussed above, there are many rents existing in fact in Africa, so that the social cost of taxation might be negligible in some cases. This would require a careful targeting of these rents, as advocated by David Ricardo nearly two centuries ago. For example, the massive implicit taxation of the cocoa crop in Côte d'Ivoire in the 1970s and 1980s, whereby the "Stabilization Fund" was on average taking about 50 percent of the export value of the crop, did not impose much distortion. In fact, the cocoa growers remained by far the best-off group in the country and the quantity exported doubled over about a decade, resulting in a glut that depressed the world market at the end of 1987. Nevertheless, the present framework can easily accommodate such transaction costs. Then, the resulting deadweight loss might entail a move below the efficiency frontier, as depicted in figure 6.2 by the move from A to R. As long as R is located above B, the resulting equilibrium outcome is unanimously preferred to war.

The redistributive policy sketched above raises however a fundamental problem of credibility, described by Azam (2001) and Azam and Mesnard (2003). It is based in fact on the offer by group R of an implicit or explicit contract of the type: "I will give you a transfer T if you do not get armed and engage in a war against me." However, once group P has refrained from arming and engaging in the war, the latter is in a much weaker position, and the incentives for group R to deliver the promised transfer are much weakened. Knowing this, group P might be deterred from accepting the contract, and might go for the war despite the peaceful offer made by group R. This type of commitment problem lies at the heart of the economic analysis of institutions as developed in particular by North (1990), and has wide-ranging applications. In Africa, the historical record suggests that two types of systems have been used by rulers for securing the peace by such a redistribution strategy. The first one is typically based on reputation: the ruler gradually acquires a reputation for keeping his word, and never reneges on his promises. This was the course of action chosen by Houphouët-Boigny, who ruled over Côte d'Ivoire, as a member of the French parliament and as a cabinet minister even before independence, and then as the elected President until his death in 1993. The drawback of this approach is that his reputation died with him, leaving the subsequent governments in an awkward position.

Léopold Sédar Senghor of Senegal used a different approach of a more institutional kind. It is related to the analysis made by Acemoglu and Robinson (2000) of the universal franchise adopted in nineteenth-century Europe. Senghor came from a minority group, the Serer, and was Christian in a predominantly Muslim country (Boone 2003). He very early on relied on democracy with universal franchise, but the secret ballot was not enforced until 1993 (Schaffer 1998). Then, the Sufi brotherhoods, and in particular the Mourides, really controlled the votes, at least in the rural areas. During this whole period, the modernizing government used the traditional brotherhoods as guarantors, making its promises credible by their ability to defeat it in the elections. The brotherhoods thus served as political intermediaries, voicing the demands of the people and mobilizing popular support in return for the kept promises. However, in most other cases the credibility of the promises made will be less than perfect. The promised transfer will then have to be larger the less credible is the promise in order to compensate group P for the risk of default. However, there are limits to this type of compensation, as the ruling group cannot promise more than its available resources. Azam (2001, 2006) and Azam and Mesnard (2003) show how a civil war might break out because of such commitment failure while the ruling group has the resources and is willing to share them. Hence, the commitment technology is a crucial ingredient in a strategy aiming at buying peace by redistributing wealth. This suggests that, when in power, group R has an incentive to build credible political institutions and tie its own hands by creating some system of checks and balances in order to reduce its probability of reneging on its own promises.

When group R does not have a credible enough commitment technology, then it might be profitable to simply hand over the political power to group P. Then, the latter might take over the ability to tax group R and to engineer the required redistribution in an orderly fashion. However, nothing would then prevent the ruling group P from going beyond the necessary redistribution level, described in figure 6.2. When in power, group P would have an incentive to tax group R up to the point where the latter is just indifferent between peace and war – i.e. where group R's wealth falls to the level of *B*, or minutely above it. Because of this prospect, group R might in fact prefer to take a chance and go for a war. If the latter is lost, then political power changes hands, and the analysis just made can be repeated, with group P in power. Here again, building political institutions for reducing the ruling group's ability to tax the other might be the solution for peace to be credible.

The alternative strategy to redistribution is based on deterrence. The latter consists of accumulating weapons in peace time with a view to reducing the potential opponent's payoff in case of war to such an extent that the latter will prefer peace. In figure 6.2, such a move is represented by a shift from point *A* to point *D*. Group R is sacrificing a quantity *AD* of resources, invested irreversibly in weaponry, in order to reduce group P's expected payoff in case of war. In the case of figure 6.2 this is supposed to shift group P's expected payoff in case of war to the vertical of point *A*. Then, *D* will secure peace if it lies above the resulting expected payoff that group R would get in case of war. Deterrence is thus socially costly, as it involves the sacrifice of productive resources in equilibrium in order to prevent the occurrence of a state of nature where the accumulated weaponry could be used for fighting on the off-equilibrium path. Nevertheless, it might be preferable to the outbreak of a war if the resource cost implied is lower than the expected cost of the war – i.e. if point *D* lies above point *B*, as in figure 6.2. In many cases, group R may choose a blend of the two pure strategies described above. For example, in the case of figure 6.2 group R could invest some resources in deterrence in order to shift the break point to the left but not all the way to the vertical of point *A*. Then, the remaining gap would be filled by

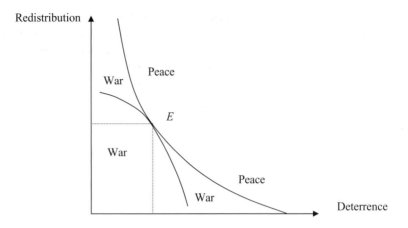

Figure 6.3 The redistribution/deterrence trade-off

redistribution. Such a strategy mix might be optimal – for example, if the marginal cost of deterrence or redistribution is increasing.

In general, then, there exists a locus that describes all the combinations of redistribution and deterrence that provide group P with the same expected payoff in case of peace as the expected payoff from the war. Call this "group P's participation constraint" (Azam and Mesnard 2003; Azam 2006). The position of this curve in this space depends on the relative efficiency at fighting and at producing of the two groups. If group P is very efficient at fighting relative to group R, this participation constraint will be located quite far to the right, as group R would have then to invest more on deterrence for any given level of redistribution. Similarly, if group R is highly productive relative to group P, the latter's participation constraint will be located high up in this space, as the stakes of the potential fighting would be high. Peace is secured if group P is faced with a combination of redistribution and deterrence that yields a higher payoff than this benchmark, even minutely so, while war occurs otherwise. Figure 6.3 represents a plausible shape of this locus as a convex curve. All the points located above that locus are consistent with the peace, as they give more redistribution for any level of deterrence, or vice versa. Then, the peace-seeking government will choose a point on this locus that minimizes the price paid for the peace. The case described in figure 6.3 assumes that the marginal cost of redistribution or deterrence incurred by group R is increasing, so that the iso-cost contours are concave. Then, the equilibrium mix of deterrence and redistribution is found where an iso-cost contour is tangent to group P's participation constraint. This point is labeled E in figure 6.3. The location of E on this locus depends on the efficiency of group R at producing or fighting. If its labor is highly productive, then the opportunity cost of diverting resources for military deterrence is also high, and it will rely more on redistribution. If its soldiers are very efficient at fighting, then any given level of deterrence can be achieved by diverting a small quantity of resources from production, making this solution more attractive. Therefore, the exact location of the equilibrium mix of deterrence and redistribution will be determined by the comparative advantage of the two groups at fighting and at producing. A more precise analysis of this point is presented in Azam (2006), which yields a typology of political regimes as a function of these comparative advantages.

However, group R might choose not to pay for the peace, and to go for the war instead. This would occur if point E turned out to be more expensive than the expected cost of war. Then, group R would be tempted to take a chance at the latter. Hence, the analysis presented above gives group R the choice first between war and peace, and then between redistribution and deterrence. From a utilitarian point of view, the redistributive solution for buying the peace is the best one unless there are huge transaction costs involved. The other two solutions, based on deterrence or civil war, are socially more costly, as they require that some resources be diverted from production into defense expenditures or outright fighting.

One of the crucial issues to be faced when choosing the redistribution strategy is to determine who in group P should be the recipient of the transfer. Should it be broad-based, aiming at giving some benefit of peace to a large number of group P's members, or should it be delegated to some key players from group P, who could then optimize its distribution within their group? The answer to this question depends largely on the pre-existing social structure of the target ethnic group. Redistribution can be at times highly efficient. For example, Houphouët-Boigny used the traditional leader Gbon Coulibaly, and then his family, for exerting social control over the Senufo, in northern Côte d'Ivoire. There was then no need to establish a heavy public administration in the north, as traditional institutions were doing their job. Similarly, as described above, Léopold Sédar Senghor used the traditional authority of the Sufi brotherhoods for managing the redistribution flows. However, this turns out to be very difficult when the target group has a very loose social structure. This problem can arise in particular among the forest people, including for example the Diola from Casamance in Senegal (Boone 2003). There a low-intensity civil war erupted until a credible leader emerged eventually, permitting a political settlement to be found. Similarly, the Bété from south-western Côte d'Ivoire have also been regarded as a politically amorphous group, with no traditional authority with which to negotiate. Section 4 aims to provide a framework for thinking about this issue.

4 Triangular redistribution and political control

The redistribution problem must be analyzed against the background of the rural–urban migration flows that result necessarily from economic and political development (Bates 2000). Village communities send the most promising of their offspring to the urban sector equipped with the required education for hopefully obtaining good positions in the formal sector and preferably in government. They can thus have access to high and regular incomes so that they can in turn remit money to the village community which funded the initial investment in education or fund some investments in local infrastructure. The most talented ones will climb the social ladder and acquire powerful positions that will give them the opportunity to influence the regional allocation of public investments (Ayogu 2000). The migrants to the urban sector thus function as "delegates" of their group of origin, in charge of earning there the means for supporting themselves and returning a share of this income back to the village. Sometimes the resulting transfers come as contingent remittances, triggered by the occurrence of some shock within an implicit insurance contract (Azam and Gubert forthcoming). In a more indirect fashion, they can also direct public spending in social or physical infrastructure to the benefit of their village of origin. However, as mentioned above, some of the resources that are redistributed by this system are levied in a distortionary way, in particular when they are channeled by the public sector. These distortions are liable to impose some cost on the ordinary people, and help maintain them in poverty.

Therefore, part of the African elite can be viewed as collectively redistributing a share of the resources that have been collected through the state apparatus or the public sector in a way that may cause a lot of distortion. This "triangular redistribution" system is illustrated in figure 6.4. As discussed above, the personalized relationships between the elite and the people from their village of origin involve the repayment of some initial investment made by the villagers in the education and the migration of their offspring. However, "bygones are bygones," and some enforcement mechanisms are used by the villagers for securing the inflow of remittances. The precise mechanism involved depends on the ethnic group, and calls for more research. As a first approximation, the exchange between the migrant and the villagers may be understood as an exchange of gifts for prestige and support (Azam 1995b). This is captured in figure 6.4 by the expression "symbolic transaction." The urban elite will eventually be responsible for the development of the state apparatus, which lives to a large extent off the taxes levied on the villagers through the taxation of agricultural exports or the distortions imposed on food markets. However, one should not regard the villagers as the ingenuous victims of this triangular redistribution system. Given that all the other groups in the country have similarly sent some "delegates" to

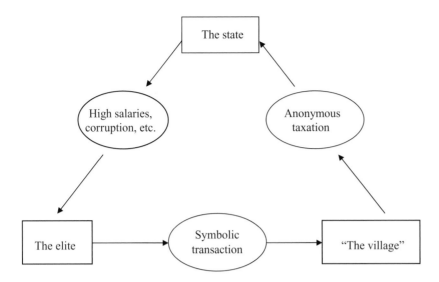

Figure 6.4 The triangular redistribution game

participate in the urban economy and in the political appropriation game, it is optimal for the group to invest in the migration of its best offspring to participate in the scrum and try to get hold of a good share. This can be analyzed as an inefficient Nash equilibrium of the prisoner's dilemma type: given that all the other groups are engaged in the taxation game, it is best for them to have some delegates engaged in this game as well. Otherwise, the burden of the political game that is bearing on them would basically be the same, while the probability of getting some fallout would be zero. The inefficiency results from the fact that none of them takes into account the distortions imposed on the economy by their collective behavior.

The main point of this analysis can be captured by an extremely simple model. Assume that there are two kin groups, each composed of a farmer and an urbanite. The game takes place in two stages and is solved by backward induction. In stage 1, the two urbanites decide collectively through the political process the tax rate t that the government is going to impose on the farmers; this political process also determines the shares of the expected proceeds that each of them will obtain. This determination is modeled here in a fairly general way, somehow related to a bargaining process. The assumed uniform tax rate imposed on the two groups may be regarded as a political or administrative constraint, which is assumed to prevent the tax system from tailoring a different tax rate for each group. This might also reflect a built-in equity consideration characterizing the tax law of this country. For the sake of simplicity, assume that the intra-group redistribution through the "symbolic transaction" mentioned above functions extremely well. Assume that the urbanites remit their entire share as remittances g_i, $i \in \{1, 2\}$ to the farmers. In the real world, the fallout that the groups get from their urban "delegates" does not only take the form of remittances. Ayogu (2000), for example, has shown how the most successful migrants to the city are able to influence the regional allocation of public investment and get political support from their group for that. However, there is no need to go into these details here, as the main point to capture in the model is that the urbanites will return some resources to the benefit of their village of origin. No risk of default is assumed regarding these remittances. This might result from the "gift-for-prestige" redistribution system analyzed by Azam (1995b). For the sake of simplicity, assume that the urbanites do remit voluntarily the whole share that they have gotten from the political process, and derive a utility g_i from doing it. This captures all the symbolic and social rewards that they get from the villagers. It could also be interpreted as an extreme form of altruism, of the kind labeled "warm glow" in the theoretical public economics literature.

In stage 2, the farmer from group $i \in \{1, 2\}$ puts an effort level e_i into production, with a unitary productivity (i.e. output is also e_i). The farmer's utility function is assumed quasi-linear in consumption c_i and effort e_i. The disutility of effort is assumed increasing and convex and, for the sake of simplicity, is specified as $\frac{1}{2}\, e_i^2$. The farmer decides on his (her) effort level knowing the amount of remittances received from the urbanite g_i, as well as the tax rate t that bears on output. Therefore, in stage 2, the farmer from group i will seek to solve the following maximization problem:

$$\max c_i - \frac{1}{2}e_i^2,$$
$$\text{s.t. } c_i = g_i + (1 - t)\, e_i.$$

The following effort and output supply function can be derived easily from the first-order condition of this maximization problem:

$$e_i = 1 - t, \; i \in \{1, 2\}. \tag{1}$$

This supply function shows very clearly the disincentive effect of taxation.

Now, the backward induction solution requires that this function be taken into account when analyzing the political process that takes place at stage 1. For the outcome to be sub-game perfect, we need to assume that the two urbanites correctly anticipate the best-response functions described by (1). The political process is modeled in the simplest and most general way, which encompasses the Nash bargaining solution, generalized or not, as a special case. As suggested above, this political solution should take due account of the two groups' participation constraints – i.e. that no group should get less in the peaceful outcome than its expected gain from a potential war. Now that the ethnic groups are disaggregated by distinguishing the urban elite from the villagers that they represent in the political process, the latter must be defined accordingly.

It is natural in this simple setting to assume that in case of war the urban "delegates" would fight over the power to tax the farmers. Then, the expected payoff from the conflict can simply be modeled for each group's representative as the total value of the tax proceeds at the end of the conflict multiplied by their probability of winning the war. Denote B_1 and B_2 each group's expected payoff from a potential war, so defined. It is natural to assume that the sum $B_1 + B_2$ is smaller than the fiscal revenues collected in the case of peace.

Then the political solution will be a triplet $\{t, g_1, g_2\}$ that maximizes some function $V(g_1, g_2)$, assumed increasing and quasi-concave in its two arguments.[1] For example, the generalized Nash bargaining solution would maximize $(g_1 - B_1)^{\eta}(g_2 - B_2)^{1-\eta}$. If the outcome was determined by some random allocation mechanism after the tax revenues had been chosen, such that group 1 would win the fiscal pot with probability p and group 2 with probability $1 - p$, then $g_1 + g_2$ would be maximized. There is no need to specify so precisely how the political process is solved. However, the following constraints would clearly be taken into account. First, the urbanites cannot deliver back to their kinfolk in the village more than is available in the fiscal revenues. This requires:

$$g_1 + g_2 = t \cdot (e_1 + e_2). \tag{2}$$

This assumes that there are no other sources of finance besides the taxes levied on the farmers, but it would be extremely easy to add some exogenous flow of resources. Then of course, for the equilibrium outcome to be subgame perfect, the urbanites should take (1) into account, for substituting into (2).

In addition, if war is to be avoided, the following two participation constraints should be taken into account:

$$g_1 \geq B_1 \quad \text{and} \quad g_2 \geq B_2. \tag{3}$$

From the first-order conditions of this very general maximization program, one finds that $t = \frac{1}{2}$. This is the main result coming out of this exercise. The intuition for it is simply that the urbanites will select the maximum of the Laffer curve in order to extract collectively the maximum possible resources from the farmers. The Laffer curve here reads: $2t(1 - t)$, as can be seen by substituting (1) in the budget constraint (2). In other words, in maximizing the amount of money that they can remit back to the village, the urbanites have an incentive to impose the tax distortion that maximizes

---

[1] See Anbarci, Skaperdas, and Syropoulos (2002) for a discussion of various bargaining solutions "in the shadow of conflict."

the tax revenue. This is found here in a simple model where the urbanites are assumed to be the most altruistic and devoted to their group's welfare as can possibly be conceived, as they give back their entire income from the urban game. This result goes at the crucial point about the redistribution syndrome: even if the behavior of the elites is driven entirely by altruism and the desire to remit their whole income for the sake of their kinfolks, they will choose a tax rate as high as if they were driven by a pure predatory objective. It follows from (1) that $e_i = \frac{1}{2}$, $i \in \{1, 2\}$, while the optimum would be 1, were the farmers not to reward as they do the remittances that they receive from the urbanites.[2] This captures the distortion entailed by the triangular redistribution game described in this section. Then, from (2), it follows that the fiscal pot to be allocated is equal to $\frac{1}{2}$ also.

Lastly, the sub-game perfect equilibrium of this game is characterized by the allocation of remittances to the two farmers. It is clearly influenced by the expected gains to each group from a potential war. It is also influenced to a large extent by the precise specification of the function $V(g_1, g_2)$ that the political process is supposed to maximize. Here, the simplest effect comes out of the solution of the game. Define $v = V_1/V_2$ as the marginal rate of substitution between the two urbanites' payoffs – i.e. the ratio of the partial derivatives of $V(g_1, g_2)$ with respect to its first and second argument, respectively.[3] There are three possible outcomes where each group gets the following allocation for some $\alpha \in [0, 1]$ depending on the specification of the function $V(g_1, g_2)$:

$$g_1 = B_1 + \alpha[1/2 - (B_1 + B_2)]$$
$$\text{and } g_2 = B_2 + (1 - \alpha)[1/2 - (B_1 + B_2)],$$

where $\alpha = 0$ if $v > 1$, $0 < \alpha < 1$ if $v = 1$, and $\alpha = 1$ if $v < 1$.

This expression brings out nicely both the stakes of the peaceful political process and the constraints bearing on it, namely that the allocation between the two groups of the benefit from the peace cannot fall below the expected payoff that each would get from the war. Each group gets first the equivalent of its expected gain from the war, and then additionally a share of the incremental social gain from the peace: $1/2 - (B_1 + B_2)$. That share may be zero in the two-corner solutions. This completes the formal description of the sub-game perfect equilibrium of this game.

Therefore, this simple game-theoretic model helps us to understand the main features of the "triangular redistribution game" described above: in

[2] In that case, the villagers would have no incentives to invest in their offspring's migration and the political game described here would be stillborn. In a sense, then, the inefficiency identified in this model is simply the price to pay for triggering development, insofar as the latter requires a flow of rural–urban migration.

[3] This formulation can encompass the Rawlsian function $V(g_1, g_2) = \min\{g_1, g_2\}$, provided that v is defined as the ratio of the two *left-hand* derivatives.

order to acquire prestige and support from their kinfolk remaining in the village, the group's "delegates," the urban migrants participating in the political process, have an incentive to extract as much of the resources as possible from the country in an anonymous fashion. Hence, this analysis does not contain any moral overtones that would blame the redistribution game that can be observed on some kind of "evil nature" of the African elite, but traces it instead to the incentives created by the structure of the game. It identifies its root cause in the redistribution system that links the elite to the ordinary people.[4] As discussed elsewhere (Azam 1995a, 2001), this redistribution system is crucial for maintaining civil peace in the ethnically divided African countries. Hence, it will remain in force for the foreseeable future, at least in peaceful societies.

Houphouët-Boigny of Côte d'Ivoire was probably the master of this type of strategy until his death in 1993. Using all the tools made available to him by a relatively well-functioning state, he systematically used the cooptation of rising politicians as a way to remain in power by getting them involved in the government or at the highest levels of the bureaucracy, often in lucrative positions (Azam and Morrisson 1994; Azam 1995a). He knew how to selectively turn a blind eye to some forms of corruption. The aim of this policy was to deprive any potential opposition movement of any effective leader by attracting the latter into the circles of power and even turning their political clout into an asset for the government. On only one occasion, when the Bété Kragbé Gniagbé proved to be insensitive to this type of gift, did he reluctantly let the army suppress the nascent movement in 1970. Moreover, he based his redistribution policy on the implicit taxation of his own unconditional supporters, the Baule cocoa and coffee growers, to fund highly visible public investment in the other regions of the country. Examples of the latter are given by the San Pedro harbor and the related infrastructure in the south-western Bété area or the sugar complexes in the northern Senufo area. In so doing, he was making more difficult, and therefore more costly, the mobilization of the local people along ethnic lines by investing public capital for increasing labor productivity in these areas. Lastly, his education policy, one of the most generous in the world relative to GDP, was explicitly aimed at creating "national unity" by helping elites from all the ethno-regional groups to emerge, ensuring political participation and inclusion for all of them (Azam 1993; Azam and Morrisson 1994). In sum, he was pursuing a strategy aiming at increasing the opportunity cost of opposition or rebellion at the level of both the potential leaders and that of ordinary supporters.

---

[4] The inefficiency brought out here would be mitigated were the migrants rewarded for the welfare level achieved by their kinfolk rather than for the resources that they bring back. Then, however, it is doubtful that the villagers would have an incentive to invest in their offspring's out-migration.

Indeed, when some groups are excluded from the game, they might engage in political violence, trying to acquire by rebellion what is denied to them by the political system (Azam 2001). This can occur either because the government excludes them consciously, preferring to reserve the benefit of participation to its own supporters, or because the social ladder is cut by a shortage of education services, precluding the initial investment in human capital that is the pre-requisite for joining the urban elite. Uganda under Idi Amin or Obote provides an example of the first case, while Mali under Moussa Traoré offers an example of the latter (Mutibwa 1992; Azam *et al.* 1999). Both examples have given rise to a rebellion, leading to the overthrow of the exclusive elite. Azam and Djimtoïngar (2007) show that the Chadian civil war resulted from a similar failure of the Tombalbaye government to leave a fair share to the Northerners.

The triangular redistribution system so described, whereby the state buys some loyalty from the social base via the remittances, and other kinds of redistributive flows, delivered by the urban-based workers to their folks remaining back in the village, is rarely the cause of political violence besides the examples discussed below. It is usually a well-enforced mechanism founded on the initial endowment of ethnic capital, which typically ensures compliance with the rules of the game. It usually forms an almost exhaustive partition of most of the people of the country, with the exception of some migrants of foreign origin. Nevertheless, the study of some recent African conflicts provides some examples of insurrection that were triggered by the discontent of the ethnic base with the fallout from the participation of their elite in the state game.

A first instance is provided by the Tuareg movement in Mali and Niger in the early 1990s. Although this rebellion has been often presented as an ethnic problem between the Tuareg and the other groups of Mali and Niger, closer scrutiny shows that an important reason for this fighting was the discontent of the young jobless Tuareg with their tribal rulers. The *Ishumar* (derived apparently from the French word *chômeur*, meaning unemployed), were former soldiers from the Libyan army that Colonel Khadafi had to fire when the oil money started to dry up. Upon returning to their homeland, these young Tuareg realized that there was no opportunity for them, in particular because of the poor education that they had received and the very poor infrastructure invested in their region by the Mali or Niger governments. General Moussa Traoré of Mali had purchased the quiescence of the Tuareg by distributing some advantages to the members of the Tuareg traditional chieftaincy, with very little fallout for the rest of the people. Then, the north witnessed an insurrection, which was initially directed as much against the feudal leaders as against the Mali and Nigeri states (Gaudio 1992; Azam *et al.* 1999). Another example of the breakdown of the redistribution system within the ethnic framework is provided by the insurgency in Sierra Leone in the early 1990s, described by Abdullah and Muana (1998) as a revolt of the lumpen proletariat. Without any ethnic support or any national program, the Revolutionary United Front, formed from the underclass of Freetown and the illegal diamond miners, turned into a sort of bandit movement, committing atrocities against the people from all groups. Another example is provided by Bates (1989), who presents an analysis of the *Mau-mau* insurgency in Kenya in the 1950s. He suggests that it was also triggered by a breakdown of the relationship between the *Kikuyu* elite and its ethnic base. These examples illustrate the fact that the ethnic group can fail to provide the required link between its members and the higher levels of the state, and, in this case, a type of political violence that is particularly difficult to control erupts.

Most of the time, however, a violent insurgency arises when the elite from one or several ethnic groups are excluded from the sharing of the state bounty rather than when the remittance flow between the elite and the villagers is cut. It is fairly significant to notice that the insurgent groups are very much a reflection of the structure of the ethnic groups described above: the analysis of guerrillas presented in Clapham (1998) shows that most insurgent groups are led by their most educated members, and that the loyalty that they get from their followers depends to a large extent on their ability to secure and redistribute resources within the group. Among others, Pool (1998) for the case of the Eritrean People's Liberation Front (EPLF), and Young (1998) for the Tigray People's Liberation Front (TPLF), illustrate precisely how the educated elite members have organized the distribution of resources among their supporters, and how this has helped attract more of them. Then, the cross-border relationships with each other, as well as with southern Sudan, played a crucial role. However, in the days of the Cold War it was relatively easy to get funding from one of the superpowers, so looting was not necessary. Nowadays, absent foreign support, which is more and more difficult to mobilize in the post-Cold War period, the looting of alien groups is often the only solution left. In some cases, looting allows some warlords to sustain long-duration insurgencies, which do not really seem aimed at toppling the government, but at creating an enclave under the control of the insurgents in a sort of partial secession. This is just an extension of the framework presented here, where the redistribution of wealth is done by conquest.

5 Conclusion

This chapter has shown how peaceful African societies are organized around an elaborate "triangular" redistribution system. The state and the rest of the urban formal sector collect or produce a lot of resources that "delegates" from the different ethno-regional groups attempt to control for the benefit of their group of origin. This analysis does not assume any kind of evil nature on the part of the individuals involved, and assumes instead that they are mainly motivated by altruism. However, because the resources of the government, as well as other formal sector resources, are collected anonymously, no individual would do any good to his own ethnic group if he refrained from participating in the scramble. In fact the opposite, he would simply by so doing leave a larger share of the resources to the others. Then, the collective behavior of all the participants in the political process results rationally, from the individual viewpoint, in the maximization of the resources collected by the state, at the maximum of the Laffer curve. Hence, even altruistic "delegates" will eventually inflict a lot of distortions on the economy in order to extract collectively as much of the resources as possible. The villagers would in fact be better off if none of them sent any "delegates" to the capital city, at least in the short run. However, once the scramble is on, as it is in the transitional phase of political and economic development analyzed here, each group has an incentive to send its own "delegates" to the scrum.

Then, the sharing rule among the different groups has been shown to depend crucially on the expected gains from a potential war that each group could secure. This is why the "shadow of conflict" lies at the heart of this complex redistribution system that is dissected here. If the government is credible enough, then redistribution will prevent war from erupting, and each group will get a share that depends somehow on its efficiency at fighting. If credibility is not sufficient, then the civil war will break out and the sharing of resources will be performed by wasteful means.

This line of analysis suggests that economic reform and structural adjustment should be designed in such a way that the most efficient ways of redistributing income between groups should be selected, while the most distortionary ones should be avoided (Coate 2000). The aid community should avoid slashing the most conspicuous methods of redistribution between groups, as this would at best divert the collection of resources to more discrete, but probably more distortionary, methods. At worst, succeeding in repressing redistribution would in many cases eventually trigger civil war. Priority should be given to the fight against self-serving diversion, whereby the ruling group grabs resources to its own benefit only, while efficient redistribution policies that benefit the excluded groups should be favored. Broad-based education policy, which favors the future political participation of all groups while increasing the opportunity cost of soldiering, should thus be the mainstay of the strategy of political and economic development.

References

Abdullah, Ibrahim and Patrick Muana (1998), "The Revolutionary United Front of Sierra Leone," in Christopher Clapham, ed., *African Guerrillas*. Oxford: James Currey: 172–193

Acemoglu, Daron and James Robinson (2000), "Why Did the West Extend the Franchise? Democracy, Inequality, and Growth in Historical Perspective," *Quarterly Journal of Economics* 115(4): 1167–99

Anbarci, Nejat, Stergios Skaperdas, and Constantinos Syropoulos (2002), "Comparing Bargaining Solutions in the Shadow of Conflict: How Norms against Threats Can Have Real Effects," *Journal of Economic Theory* 106: 1–16

Ayogu, Melvin D. (2000), "The Structure of Power and the Pattern of Public Spending in a Fiscal Federalism," Paper presented at the ABCDE–Europe Conference, Paris, June (forthcoming in *Journal of Policy Modeling*)

Azam, Jean-Paul (1993), "The 'Côte d'Ivoire' Model of Endogenous Growth," *European Economic Review* 37(2/3): 566–76

(1995a), "How to Pay for the Peace? A Theoretical Framework with References to African Countries," *Public Choice* 83(1/2): 173–84

(1995b), "L'Etat auto-géré en Afrique," *Revue d'économie du développement* 4: 1–19

(2001), "The Redistributive State and Conflicts in Africa," *Journal of Peace Research* 38(4): 429–44

(2006), "The Paradox of Power Reconsidered: A Theory of Political Regimes in Africa," *Journal of African Economies* 15(1), March: 26–58

Azam, Jean-Paul, Jean-Claude Berthélemy, and Stéphane Calipel (1996), "Risque politique et croissance en Afrique," *Revue économique* 47(3): 819–29

Azam, Jean-Paul and Nadjiounoum Djimtoïngar (2007), "Cotton, War, and Growth in Chad, 1960–2000," chapter 3 in Benno J. Ndulu, Stephen A. O'Connell, Jean-Paul Azam, Robert H. Bates, Augustin Kwasi Fosu, Jan Willem Gunning, and Dominique Njinkeu, eds., *The Political Economy of Economic Growth in Africa, 1960–2000*, vol. 2. Cambridge: Cambridge University Press

Azam, Jean-Paul and Flore Gubert (forthcoming), "Migrants' Remittances and the Household in Africa: A Review of Evidence," *Journal of African Economies* (forthcoming)

Azam, Jean-Paul and Alice Mesnard (2003), "Civil War and the Social Contract," *Public Choice* 115(3): 455–75

Azam, Jean-Paul and Christian Morrisson (1994), *The Political Feasibility of Adjustment in Côte d'Ivoire and Morocco*. Paris: OECD, Development Centre Studies with Sophie Chauvin and Sandrine Rospabé (1999), *Conflict and Growth in Africa, Vol. 1: The Sahel*. Paris: OECD, Development Centre Studies

Bates, Robert H. (1989), *Beyond the Miracle of the Market: The Political Economy of Agrarian Development in Kenya*. Cambridge: Cambridge University Press

(2000), "Ethnicity and Development in Africa: A Reappraisal," *American Economic Review* 90(2): 131–4

Boone, Catherine (2003), *Political Topographies of the African State: Territorial Authority and Institutional Choice*. Cambridge: Cambridge University Press

Clapham, Christopher, ed. (1998), *African Guerrillas*. Oxford: James Currey

Coate, Steven (2000), "An Efficiency Approach to the Evaluation of Policy Changes," *Economic Journal* 110, April: 437–55

Diamond, Jared (1997), *Guns, Germs, and Steel: The Fates of Human Societies*. New York: Norton

Gastellu, Jean-Marc (1989), *Riches paysans de Côte-D'Ivoire.* Paris: L'Harmattan

Gaudio, Attilio (1992), *Le Mali*, 2nd edn. Paris: Khartala

Hill, Polly (1963), *The Migrant Cocoa Farmers of Southern Ghana: A Study in Rural Capitalism.* Cambridge: Cambridge University Press

Leonard, David K. and Scott Straus (2003), *Africa's Stalled Development: International Causes and Cures.* Boulder, CO and London: Lynne Rienner

Manchuelle, François (1997), *Willing Migrants: Soninke Labor Diasporas, 1948–1960.* Athens, OH: Ohio University Press

Mutibwa, Phares (1992), *Uganda since Independence: A Story of Unfulfilled Hopes.* London: Hurst

North, Douglass C. (1990), *Institutions, Institutional Change and Economic Performance.* Cambridge: Cambridge University Press

Pool, David (1998), "The Eritrean People's Liberation Front," in Christopher Clapham, ed., *African Guerrillas.* Oxford: James Currey: 19–35

Schaffer, Frederic C. (1998), *Democracy in Translation: Understanding Politics in an Unfamiliar Culture.* Ithaca, NY and London: Cornell University Press

Young, John (1998), "The Tigray People's Liberation Front," in Christopher Clapham, ed., *African Guerrillas.* Oxford: James Currey: 36–52

Zartman, I. William, with Tessy D. Bakary, A. Adu Boahen, Alex Gboyega, and Donald Rothchild (1997), *Governance as Conflict Management.* Washington, DC: Brookings Institution Press

7 | Political conflict and state failure

Robert H. Bates

1 Introduction

In his chapter on Ethiopia in volume 2, Alemayehu Geda contends that
in addition to the "vagaries of nature," growth performance in Ethiopia

The chapter was written with financial support from the National Science Foundation
(Grant SES 9905568), the Carnegie Corporation, and the Center for International
Development and the Weatherhead Center for International Affairs of Harvard University. I
wrote it while a Moore Distinguished Scholar at the California Institute of Technology. The
chapter has benefited greatly from comments and criticisms received at seminars held at
Harvard University, Guelo Brittany, and at the annual meetings of the AERC 2004 in
Nairobi. Special thanks go to Steven Block for his criticisms and corrections. As ever, Karen

"is largely determined by [the] strength and efficiency of institutions, [the] efficacy of public policies, and risk related to war" (Alemayehu 2007: 2). Of these factors, Alemayehu emphasizes the last, placing special emphasis on *internal* war. Internal conflict also emerges as a major determinant of economic performance in the chapters in volume 2 on Chad (Azam and Djimtoingar 2007), Sudan (Ali and Elbadawi 2007), Sierra Leone (Davies 2007), Burundi (Nkurunziza and Ngaruko 2007), Mozambique (de Sousa and Sulemane 2007), Kenya (Mwega and Ndung'u 2007), and Uganda (Kasekende and Atingi-Ego 2007), or in nearly one-third of the country studies.

In Chad and Sudan, provinces in the North have sought to dominate those in the South, and in both countries' natural resources – specifically oil – represent a major prize. In Sierra Leone, diamonds rather than petroleum constitute the spoils of war, and rival political machines – each as adept at campaigning in the field of battle as in the electoral arena – seek to capture power and thus control over diamond revenues. In Burundi, a fraction of the ruling elite used their position in the military to slaughter their opponents, capture the state, and employ public power to secure private privilege. In Kenya, incumbents mobilized private militias to clear key districts of opposition voters as they reacted to the threat posed by the re-introduction of electoral competition. The stories that underlie the cases thus differ; but in each, political conflict imposed major costs upon the economy.

These cases illustrate the patterns of politics that characterize the state failure syndrome: societies militarize, governments turn predatory, and life and property become insecure. This chapter offers a theory of state failure, captures its incidence, and explores its costs in post-independence Africa.

2   Patterns of state breakdown

To portray and analyze patterns of state failure in Africa, this chapter makes use of two samples of African countries. The first, which I shall call the forty-six-nation sample, covers the period 1970–95 (see table 7.1) and was assembled by the Africa project at Harvard University.[1] The second, the which I shall call the twenty-six-country sample, comprises the country cases of the AERC Growth Project and covers the period 1960–2000 (table 7.2).

Those who analyze state failure and civil war tend to make use of one of three datasets: those compiled by James Fearon of Stanford University,

---

Ferree and Smita Singh deserve much of the credit for this work. I also wish to thank Matthew Hindeman and Marcus Alexander for their technical assistance. The author alone is to be blamed for its shortcomings.
[1] www.people.iq.harvard.edu/~rbates

Table 7.1 *Countries in the forty-six-nation sample, 1970–1995.*

1. Angola	17. Gabon	33. Nigeria
2. Benin	18. The Gambia	34. Rwanda
3. Botswana	19. Ghana	35. São Tomé & Principe
4. Burkina Faso	20. Guinea	36. Senegal
5. Burundi	21. Guinea-Bissau	37. Seychelles
6. Cameroon	22. Kenya	38. Sierra Leone
7. Cape Verde	23. Lesotho	39. Somalia
8. CAR	24. Liberia	40. Sudan
9. Chad	25. Madagascar	41. Swaziland
10. Comoros	26. Malawi	42. Tanzania
11. Congo, Republic	27. Mali	43. Togo
12. Côte d'Ivoire	28. Mauritania	44. Uganda
13. Djibouti	29. Mauritius	45. Zambia
14. DRC	30. Mozambique	46. Zimbabwe
15. Equatorial Guinea	31. Namibia	
16. Ethiopia	32. Niger	

Table 7.2 *Countries in the twenty-six-nation sample, 1970–1995.*

1. Benin	10. Guinea	19. Senegal
2. Botswana	11. Kenya	20. Sierra Leone
3. Burkina Faso	12. Malawi	21. South Africa
4. Burundi	13. Mali	22. Sudan
5. Cameroon	14. Mauritius	23. Tanzania
6. Chad	15. Mozambique	24. Togo
7. Congo, Republic	16. Namibia	25. Uganda
8. Ethiopia	17. Niger	26. Zambia
9. Ghana	18. Nigeria	

the World Bank, or the researchers at the Peace Research Institute, Oslo (PRIO).[2] Focusing on the first, Fearon classifies 15.1 percent of its 1,196 observations as experiencing civil war, the World Bank 17.7 percent, and PRIO only 10.8 percent.[3] Inspection reveals that PRIO excludes from its list conflicts in Angola and Chad; the violence that engulfed Burundi beginning in 1972 and Rwanda in 1990–5; and the collapse of Sierra Leone (1972–96). These omissions make it difficult to justify the use of PRIO's data in this study.

---

[2] Fearon (2003), Sambanis (2001), Gleditsch *et al.* (2002).

[3] I here refer to Prio1000, a variable that takes the value 1 when the conflict results in an average of at least 1,000 battle deaths per year.

Table 7.3 *Observations positive for civil wars, forty-six African countries, 1970–1995.*

		World Bank data		
		Yes	No	Row totals
Fearon data	Yes	912	51	963
	No	29	152	181
Column totals		941	203	1144

Note: Pearson chi2(1) = 646.24, p = 0.000.

Fearon includes in his list civil wars in Mozambique, Senegal, Uganda, and Zimbabwe that the World Bank omits; in my judgment, Fearon misclassifies years of resistance to colonial rule (as in the case of Mozambique) and of sheer repression (as in the case of Zimbabwe) as periods of civil war. The World Bank includes conflicts in Burundi (1973, 1991–3), Zaire (1992–5) and Kenya (1991–3) that Fearon excludes; and in these instances, I would concur with the judgment of the Bank. Fearon's data set includes countries with minuscule populations (e.g. Comoros, Equatorial Guinea) which the Bank's does not. I will therefore employ the World Bank's list in this chapter, while stressing the degree to which the two sources concur in their classification of the country-year observations (see table 7.3).

Figure 7.1 depicts the incidence of civil war, by year and country. As exemplified by Angola, Chad, and Ethiopia, some countries experienced perpetual violence over the sample period. As exemplified by Burundi, Nigeria, Sudan, and others, if a country experienced a war early on, it was likely to experience one later on as well. Note, too, that civil wars in Africa became more common with time. Later sections of this chapter will seek to account for these patterns in the data.

The modal number of years for which the countries remained at war was 0: over the period 1970–95 most African countries remained at peace. The median (0) lay below the mean (7.19 years), reflecting the impact of the persistently violent states. With the variance (10.7) half again as large as the mean, there was a broad distribution of durations of violence – one that, save for states that remained at peace, is nearly flat (see figure 7.3).

Figure 7.4 is based on the twenty-six-nation sample and depicts the distribution of wars across the landlocked and coastal states and those abundantly endowed with natural resources (I use the time-varying classification developed in chapter 2). Civil wars were present in fewer than 2 percent of the observations gathered from the coastal states; by contrast, they appear in over 20 percent of those gathered from resource-rich nations and in nearly 40 percent of the observations taken from landlocked countries.

3   The costs of civil war

The costs of war are both immediate and longer term. The immediate costs are the destruction of life and property and the loss of income. The longer-term costs result from the loss of capital and the reluctance, because of insecurity, to invest.

3.1   Immediate costs

The most obvious way in which conflict impacts upon economic growth is through the destruction of output and the means of producing it. Viewers of the news will recall with horror the devastation visited upon Freetown, Monrovia, and Mogadishu. Most Africans live in the rural areas rather than in cities, however; the largest single sector in most of Africa's economies remains agriculture. But when fighting takes place in the countryside, the destruction of life and property can be fully as devastating as that in town. A World Bank study of Mozambique found that in the war zones the agricultural sector lost 40 percent of its immobile capital, such as buildings, and 80 percent of its mobile capital, such as cattle (Collier *et al.* 2003). A similar study in Uganda found that in regions of active fighting, two-thirds of the households lost not only their homes and livestock but virtually *all* of their possessions (Collier *et al.* 2003: 16).

Economic decline occurs not only because of the destruction of goods and property. It also occurs because conflict raises the costs of engaging in economic activity. Alex de Waal's study (1991) of the wars between the Mengistu regime and the TPLF in Ethiopia provides a vivid illustration. The fighting destroyed crops and livestock; additional goods were lost as the army forcibly appropriated farm products in order to feed its soldiers. More significant than the loss of property, Waal reports, was the inability to employ the market. Food deficits had long characterized important regions in Ethiopia, such as those along the coast; and within the grain-producing areas there were seasonal shortfalls, particularly just prior to the time of harvest. In peaceful times, merchants from the coast would therefore import manufactured goods into the food-producing areas and sell them in the towns; using the proceeds to purchase grain, they would then return to the coastal lowlands. And within the grain-producing zones, those whose crops had yet to ripen would enter the labor market, earn wages by harvesting the crops of others, and use their earnings to purchase food for their families. During the war, however, the government leveled the towns in Tigray; it destroyed the capacity of buyers and sellers to meet and transact. By impressing private transport, seizing shipments of goods, and restricting the movement

Africa — periods of instability/conflict, by country, 1970–1995

Country	1970	71	72	73	74	75	76	77	78	79	80	81	82	83	84	85	86	87	88	89	90	91	92	93	94	95
Angola																	■	■	■	■	■	■	■	■	■	■
Benin																										
Botswana																										
Burkina Faso																			■							
Burundi			■	■																		■				■
Cameroon																										
Cape Verde																										
CAR																										
Chad	■	■	■	■	■	■	■	■	■	■	■	■	■	■	■	■	■	■	■	■	■	■	■	■	■	■
Comoros																										
Congo, Rep.																							■			■
Côte d'Ivoire																						■				■
Djibouti																						■				■
Eq. Guinea																										
Ethiopia					■	■	■	■	■	■	■	■	■	■	■	■	■	■	■	■	■	■				
Gabon																										
Gambia																										
Ghana																										
Guinea																										
Guinea-Bissau																										
Kenya																						■	■	■		
Lesotho																										
Liberia																					■					■
Madagascar																										
Malawi																										
Mali																					■	■	■	■	■	

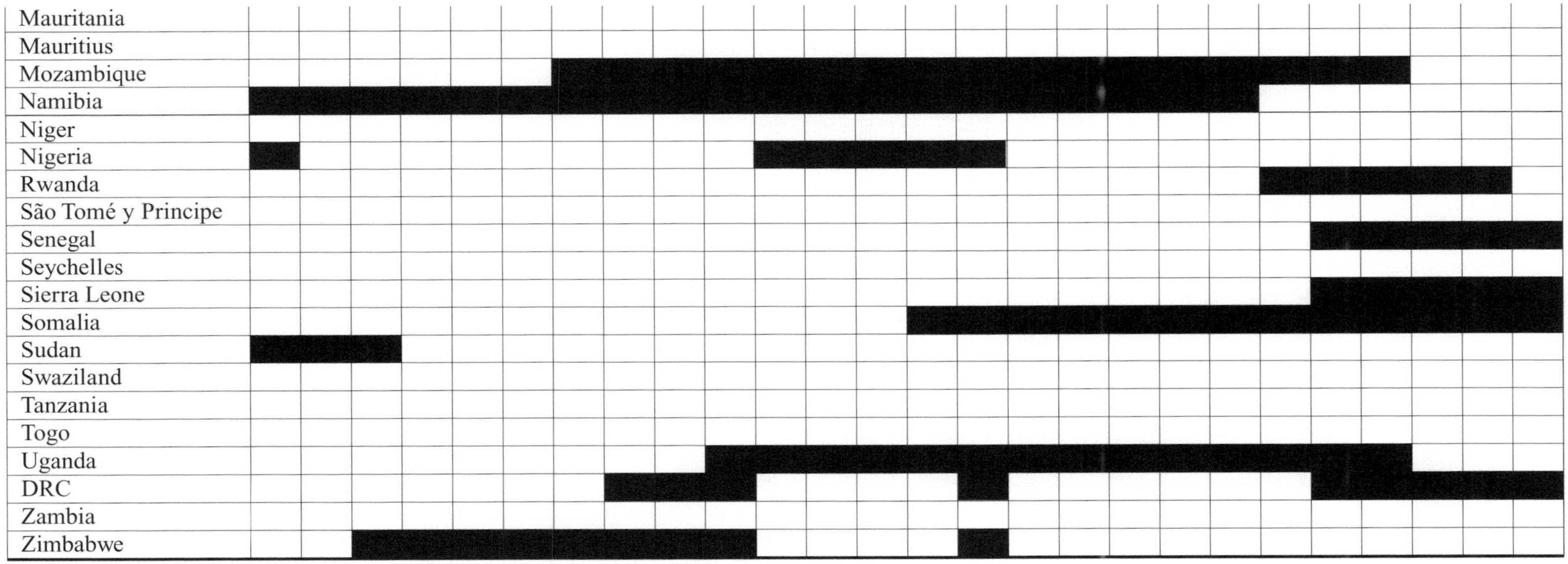

Figure 7.1 Civil war, by country and by year, World Bank data, 1970–1995

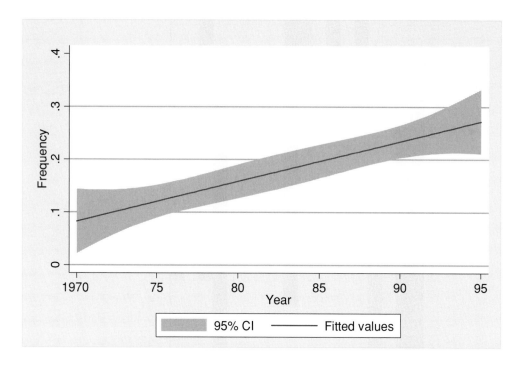

Figure 7.2 Civil wars, by year, World Bank Classification, 1970–1995

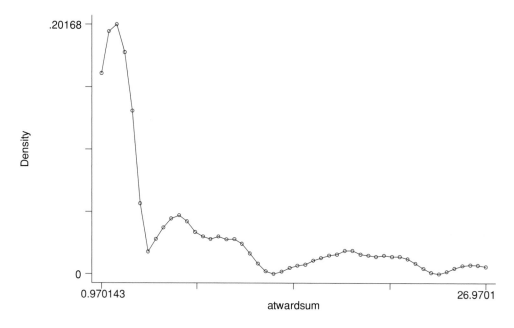

Figure 7.3 Total number of years of civil war

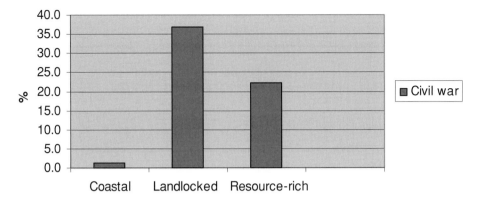

Figure 7.4 Civil war, by opportunity group

of merchants and laborers, it also forestalled the movement of grain to food deficit areas.

The result, as stated by de Waal, was that

> there was almost no local trade . . . In Meqele, the price of grain in December 1982 was 181 Birr per quintal . . . In Shire it was 60 Birr and in North Wollo 40–90 Birr. If . . . trade had been possible, the surpluses . . . would have been taken to Meqele, at a transport cost of about 47 Birr and 23 Birr per quintal respectively. (de Waal 1991: 152)

Those with surpluses experienced a loss of income; those with deficits starved. Had markets functioned and exchange been possible, the one would have been better off; the latter would have survived.

As families sought the means to purchase food, de Waal notes, they sold off livestock; but with many families responding in this manner, the price of cattle plummeted. Failing to gain incomes from livestock sales, rural families then turned to off-farm employment. But with the price of necessities, such as food, rising, people stopped spending on other things. Because of the impact of the war on the urban centers of Tigray, the demand for labor declined just when the supply was increasing. Wages therefore plummeted and, with them, the capacity to purchase food. War led to famine in Tigray, de Waal writes. And the famine that resulted came not so much from physical shortages but rater from the collapse of incomes.[4]

3.2   Lagged effects

Civic conflict thus destroys physical assets and sparks sharp recessions. Adding to its impact on growth is its impact on capital formation. The

---

[4] Note the obvious parallels with Sen's analysis of the impact of famine (Sen 1984).

Table 7.4 *Ratio of value of debt to value of annual exports.*
(Study sample of African countries)

State breakdown?	Mean	Std dev.	Number of observations	F	P > F
No	311.37	517.13	824		
Yes	615.79	660.73	59	15.50	0.0001
Total	331.70	578.16	883		

Source: World Bank, *World Development Indicators* data.

evidence suggests that civil war lowers the rate of capital formation in both the public and private sector.

It may appear incongruous to talk of government policy in the midst of political collapse. But even in periods of maximal disorder, governments continue to command public bureaucracies; they enlist them in their campaigns for military victory. In such crises, governments are impatient, however; and this impatience shapes the nature of their policies. Being insecure, governments discount long-term economic costs in favor of short-term benefits. In poor countries,[5] the World Bank reports, military spending rises from an average of 2.8 percent of GDP to an average of 5 percent (Collier *et al.* 2003), while spending on education, infrastructure, or health care declines. In the words of the World Bank, expenditures on the military "crowd out" public investments.

Consider the findings reported in chapter 10 on political reform: in both the African and the global samples, the governments of countries listed in the problem sets of the State Failure Task Force tended to be more likely to be rated as opportunistic by investors. In the judgment of private businessmen, these governments were significantly more likely to repudiate contracts or to seize property. These actions, too, represent evidence of a strong preference for short-term gains, even at the cost of future losses from a tarnished reputation.

Turning to the twenty-six country cases studied in the AERC Growth Project, the evidence suggests that insecure governments are more likely to incur debt. As noted in table 7.4, in the years in which states were judged to have collapsed, the ratio of debt to exports doubled. And as noted in table 7.5, there was a 25 percent increase in level of government consumption – something that had to be financed either through the short-term loss of purchasing power (as a result of inflation) or by sacrificing growth (as a result of higher interest rates).

---

[5] I.e. countries with a *per capita* income of less than $3,000.

Table 7.5 *Government consumption as a percent of GDP.*
(Study sample of African countries)

State breakdown?	Mean	Std dev.	No. of observations	F	P > F
No	16.28	7.04	548		
Yes	18.46	9.18	64	5.13	0.024
Total	15.51	7.32	612		

Source: World Bank, *World Development Indicators* data.

Research by Collier, Hoeffler, and Pattillo (2002) offers insight into the impact of violence on private capital. Conflict affects both the composition and the quantity of capital, they stress. In the face of possible violence, people prefer to hold portfolios weighted toward more mobile forms of capital; they prefer liquid to fixed investments. And in an environment in which fighting destroys the fruits of productive effort, the productivity of capital declines; when fighting begins, people therefore adjust downward the amount of capital they wish to employ. The reduction in the demand for capital and the shift from fixed to liquid capital promote capital flight. As reported by Collier, Hoeffler, and Pattillo (2002), the data suggest that in 1980 40 percent of private wealth had been moved offshore (2002: 1). "That Africa has such a high proportion of its wealth abroad despite being capital-scarce is an indication of how much . . . other variables matter" (2002: 22). Among the most important of these variables, they imply, is the threat of conflict.

It was Fosu (1992) who first reported systematic evidence of the decline of growth in the presence of political instability and of the importance of the impact of political instability on capital formation. Rather than civil wars, Fosu focused on "elite instability," as measured by a weighted sum of reported, attempted, and successful coups. Using a sample of thirty-one African countries over 1969–86, he interacted this measure with the variables in an augmented growth equation. He found that in the presence of instability the coefficients linking capital to output declined. Countries with levels of political instability above the sample mean, Fosu reports, tended to grow an average of 1.14 percentage points more slowly than did their more stable counterparts.

Like Fosu, Gyimah-Brempong and Traynor (1999) estimate the impact of political instability on growth; they, too, explore both its direct effect on growth as well as its effect through its impact on capital. Rather than restricting attention to coups, however, Gyimah-Brempong and Traynor instead build a composite measure of political instability, using data from thirty-nine

African countries over 1975–88 and weights derived from a principal components analysis of data on guerrilla warfare, political purges, riots, anti-government demonstrations, politically motivated strikes, and assassinations.[6] A 1 standard deviation increase in political instability leads to a reduction of 0.15 percentage points in the mean rate of growth, the authors report; by influencing capital formation, violence subtracts an additional 0.25 percentage points with a one-year lag.

In 2005, Gyimah-Brempong, working with Marva Corley, returned to the study of civil war (Gyimah-Brempong and Corley 2005). Using data for 1960–96 from forty-three African countries, Gyimah-Brempong and Corley find a "very large [effect] relative to the average growth rates" in SSA (2005: 296) – something in excess of 4 percentage points. They confirm that the more intense the war – i.e. the longer it lasts and the higher the death rate – the greater its impact. And they once again underscore the significance of the link between violence and the growth rate that runs through the formation of capital.

By affecting the quantity as well as the productivity of capital, political conflict thus has both a short- and long-term impact on growth. Adding to the latter is the fear that countries that have been violent may become violent once again, the impact of conflict on growth can be long lasting. By Collier and Hoeffler's calculations (Collier, Hoeffler, and Pattillo 1999), the longer-term effect – or the "overhang" as Collier, Hoeffler, and Pattillo (1999) phrase it – amounts to a reduction of 2.10 percentage points over the five years following a civil war.

At the end of the Cold War, Africa contained roughly 30 percent of the world's nations, 10 percent of the world's population, and 5 percent of the world's economic product.[7] If marked by the toppling of the Berlin Wall in 1989, the end of the Cold War found 46 percent of the world's civil wars taking place in Africa; if by the fall of the Soviet Union in 1991, a full

---

[6] These are the "standard" Banks measures of conflict (Banks 1999). Gyimah-Brempong and Traynor (1999) use Arellano and Bond's (1991) two-step procedure to control for the impact of reciprocal causation in the relationship between conflict and both income and growth.

[7] We can select as our denominator the number of members of the United Nations (call that number UN) or the number of nations with a population of 1 million or more (call that number POP). We can select as our numerator the number of countries in SSA (call that number SSA); the total number of countries on the African continent (AF); or the number of countries in Africa (SSA-POP) or on the continent (AF-POP) with a population of 1 million or more. Africa's percentage of the world's nations (WT for world total; WT-POP for the total number of nations in the world with 1 million or more people) can then be calculated alternatively as: SSA/UN = 25 percent; AF/UN = 28 percent; SSA/WT = 22 percent; AF/WT = 27 percent; (SSA-POP)/(WT-POP) = 23 percent; (AF-POP)/(WT-POP) = 29 percent.

53 percent.[8] In recent years, then, Africa has over-supplied political conflict. It is perhaps for this reason that political risk services rate Africa as the riskiest continent for investors (Collier, Hoeffler, and Patillo 1999).

4 State failure

Two major literatures address the sources of political disorder in contemporary Africa. One is political and points to the low quality of "governance" (World Bank 1991; Fukuyama 2004) and the other to the weakness of political institutions (Jackson and Rosberg 1982; Bratton and van de Walle 1997). Both, it is claimed, result in personalistic forms of rule based on clientelism, corruption, and repression. As stated by Christopher Clapham, the emergence of insurgency movements in West Africa in the 1990s "can be ascribed to the experience of post-independence government so bad as to lead . . . to resistance . . . and to the consequences of . . . immiseration, exploitation, and state decay" (quoted in Adibe 2001: 28). Such accounts remain unpersuasive, however. How can one recognize which institutions are weak, which states fragile, or which governments "bad" other than by the rise of political disorder? Insofar as these "causal" factors are characterized by their consequences, then they add little by way of explanation. They may highlight what has been observed, but they do little to explain it.

A second approach is economic and is best exemplified by the World Bank study, *Breaking the Conflict Trap* (Collier *et al.* 2003). As stated by its authors, "the key root cause of conflict is the failure of economic development" (Collier *et al.* 2003: 53). Stated more fully, the approach contends that

countries with low, stagnant, and unequally distributed per capita incomes that have remained dependent on primary commodities for exports face dangerously high risks of prolonged conflict. In the absence of economic development, neither good political institutions, nor ethnic and religious homogeneity, nor high military spending provide significant defenses against large scale violence. (Collier *et al.* 2003: 53)

The primary weakness of the political approach is that it borders on tautology. That of the economic approach is that it fails to point to the mechanisms that link economic conditions to political outcomes. While pointing to a set of relationships between macroeconomic aggregates and political behaviors, it fails to specify the micro-level mechanisms that generate those relationships or the incentives that animate them.

A fresh look is thus in order.

---

[8] The figures are calculated from data gathered by the Peace Research Institute in Oslo on conflicts between insurgent groups and governments that generate 1,000 or more battle deaths per annum (Strand, Wilhelmsen, and Gleditsch 2002).

5   Framing the problem

In choosing a vantage point from which to cut into this problem, the chapter takes counsel from both the "theory" of the state and the realities that prevail in contemporary Africa.

5.1   Theory of the state

According to Max Weber, the state is "a human community that successfully claims the monopoly of the legitimate use of physical force within a given territory" (Weber 1921: 1). Two features of this definition command attention: the importance of coercion and the state's claim to a monopoly of it.

In political science, many who study the politics of advanced industrial nations find Weber's emphasis on physical force largely irrelevant to the study of politics. Rather than emphasizing coercion, they instead concentrate on civic participation; and rather than putting the military at the center of the state, they instead focus on the civilian branches of government. In the context of contemporary Africa, however, Weber's characterization rings true.

Consider, for example, the prominence of the military in African politics. As documented in chapter 10 on political reform, the armed forces provided the head of state in over a third of the 1,196 country-year observations gathered from a sample of forty-six African countries over a twenty-six-year period (1970–95). In recent years civilians have increasingly replaced military officers as chief executives; but one need only reflect upon the Eastern portion of contemporary Africa to appreciate the central role of the military. The presidents of Eritrea, Ethiopia, Uganda, Rwanda – members of the so-called "new generation" of African leaders – seized power by fighting for it. Consider, too, the presidents of Burundi, Mozambique, and Namibia. At the head of each country stood the leader of the movement that had prevailed in armed struggle.[9]

Given the ease with which Weber's characterization of the state maps on to the realities of Africa, when we focus on the state in this analysis, we shall focus on coercion. And we shall refer to those who head the state as "specialists in violence."

Weber emphasizes not only the importance of force; he also suggests that a political community becomes a state when it can successfully command

---

[9] While some might dismiss this pattern as distinctive of Africa, idiosyncratic and therefore of no general significance, a glance at the history that informed Weber's vision should provoke reappraisal. In Medieval Europe, the Angevins and Lancasters placed generations of warriors on the throne of England and the Merovingians and Capetians on the throne of France. As Tilly famously states, throughout the Medieval and Early Modern period, "war made the state and the state made war" (Tilly 1975: 42).

a *monopoly* over its use. He thus points to an observable symptom of state failure: the inability of governments to secure a monopoly of violence. Taking guidance from the theory of the state and the realities of contemporary Africa, this chapter will therefore explore the conditions under which governments – or specialists in violence – succeed or fail to acquire a monopoly over the use of force. And it will take as evidence of state failure the militarization of civic society.

5.2   The logic of political order

Three questions thus form the agenda for this analysis. One is: under what conditions will citizens choose to disarm, leaving the government to protect their life and property? Closely related is a second: under what conditions will specialists in violence choose to employ force to defend their citizens rather than to prey upon them? And because neither political order nor the "Weberian state" are givens, there arises a third: when will these choices prevail as an equilibrium? Addressing these questions offers a deeper understanding of the nature of political order and of the conditions under which it fails.

   In search of answers, I turn from the theory of the state to the theory of games.[10] The players are two citizens and a specialist in violence. The equilibria of this game suggest the conditions under which order can prevail; by the same token, they suggest the conditions under which political disorder will arise. The remainder of the section presents the logic of the argument; by applying the model to African data, section 6 assesses its validity.

5.3   The model

Consider the behavior of three players: G, a specialist in violence, and two citizens, $i \in \{1, 2\}$. Although G is a specialist in violence, she is not endowed with a monopoly over it; the citizens, too, have access to arms and G can achieve a monopoly of physical force only when the citizens set theirs aside.

   By assumption, each citizen possesses a given amount of resources, denoted by T_i (as in time), that she can allocate between work (w_i), military preparedness (m_i), and leisure (l_i). That is,

   Citizen $i \in \{1, 2\}$ chooses $w_i, m_i, l_i \geq 0$ subject to $w_i + m_i + l_i \leq T_i$.

The resources devoted to work, w_i, are productive; they result in an output of $F(w_i)$ for player i.[11] Those devoted to military activity are unproductive. Rather than creating wealth, they merely redistribute it – or provide a defense against its redistribution.

---

[10] More accurately, Avner Greif, Smita Singh, and I (Bates, Greif, and Singh 2002).
[11] The function F is assumed to be twice continuously differentiable and concave.

After allocating their resources, each citizen observes the decision of the other; they then (sequentially) decide whether or not to attempt to raid the other's possessions, with player 1 choosing first. The amount that one can gain from raiding depends not only on the quantity of the other's assets but also on the relative strength of the players.[12]

As is conventional, the citizens derive their utility from income and from leisure. They can increase their incomes by working or by employing their military capabilities to raid.

G, too, seeks to maximize her utility, which, like that of the citizens, derives from income and leisure. As a specialist in violence, however, G does not need earn her income from laboring in a farm or factory; rather, she gains it through the use of force. She can increase her income by engaging in predation or by collecting fees for the provision of a valued service: the provision of security for those who seek to relax or to create wealth.

Three assumptions characterize the military balance between G and private citizens. Given that private agents are themselves capable of violence, (i) when G preys upon the economic output of a citizen i, G succeeds in capturing her wealth only with some probability. (ii) G engages in predatory activity only if the expected revenue from its use of violence exceeds its cost of military activity. (iii) And G can dispossess only one agent per period.

Should G engage in predation, then the revenue she seizes from i equals the probability of successful predation, multiplied by player i's income from work and raiding, net the amount i has paid in taxes. Should G choose to

---

[12] More generally, throughout the chapter we ignore the possibility that one agent eradicates the other. Similarly, we do not consider a situation in which one group gains military resources by raiding the other. When this is the case, one group is likely to come to dominate the other. This is the situation we do not consider here. Alternatively, one can consider our analysis as related to a situation in which property rights are determined endogenously through interactions among the economic agents. The degree to which one can secure property rights depends upon relative coercive capabilities. See, for example, Skaperdas (1992), Grossman (1995), and Muthoo (2000). The model also puts to one side evolutionary forces and specialization in the use of violence (as in Moselle and Polak 2001); asymmetries among the agents (as in, for example, Grossman and Kim 1995 and Muthoo 2000); the impact of past conflicts on one's current military capabilities (Fearon 1998); uncertainty and loss of potential exchange (discussed in Skarpedas 1996) and moral hazard issues.

By the same token, this framework enables us to extend the analysis beyond that possible in other works. Specifically, it allows us to examine the endogenous determination of prosperity and violence. See the papers cited above, as well as Usher (1989) and Skaperdas (1992). The model in Muthoo (2000) is closest to ours. While it explores the impact of asymmetries (which we do not), it does not enable agents to invest in military capabilities (as we do), explore such issues as deterring raids by consuming leisure, or examine the welfare implications of the state.

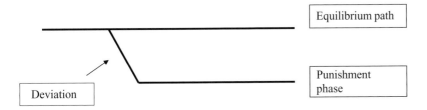

Figure 7.5 The path of play

secure her income from taxes, then her income is simply the amount of taxes paid by each private agent who has chosen to do so.

The tableau is thus peopled by a specialist in violence and two citizens, each seeking to maximize her utility and each endowed with the capacity to consume leisure or to secure income, if necessary, by the use of force. The foundations of political order are captured by the conditions for an equilibrium in which the specialist chooses to refrain from predation and to provide security instead and in which the citizens refrain from taking up arms and engage in leisure and productive activity instead.

To locate such an equilibrium, we cast the interaction between G and the citizens as a repeated game; in such a setting, prospective losses help to define the equilibrium path of play (figure 7.5). The principal threats of interest in this game are the losses that arise from state failure. When states fail, specialists in violence turn to predation; they become warlords. Rather than earning her income from safeguarding the possessions of others, G instead seizes them. The citizens, for their part, stop paying taxes and re-arm, either so as to raid or to defend themselves against raids by G or other citizens. Because the citizens re-allocate resources from leisure and production to military endeavors, both income and security decline.

The equilibrium of this sub-game can be called the state failure equilibrium. In it, there is neither security nor prosperity. It is the possibility of a reversion to the payoffs under state failure that constitutes the threat that promotes – or fails to promote – the decision to adhere to the choices that yield political order (figure 7.5).

5.4   *Political order as an equilibrium*

To be more precise, then, the conditions for political order are:

- Each private agent chooses w_i, m_i, l_i optimally (given the strategies of other players); refuses to raid; and pays taxes to G, if the other agent has not raided or if G has refrained from seizing the wealth of a private agent.

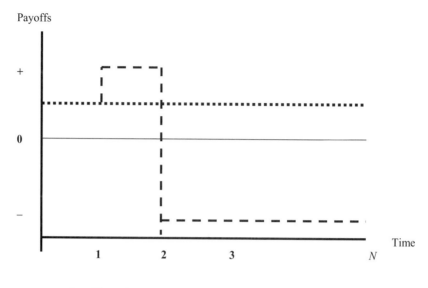

Payoffs on the equilibrium path

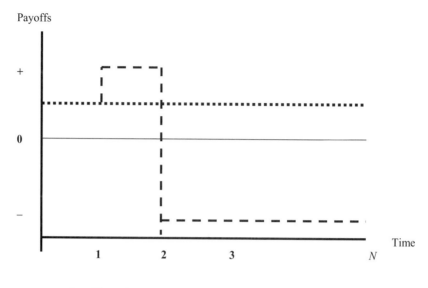

.... Payoffs on the equilibrium path

— — — Payoffs from defection and subsequent punishment

Figure 7.6 Payoffs from strategy choices

Otherwise, the private agents "revolt," refuse to pay taxes, and revert to self-defense.
- *G* refrains from predating as long as neither private agent raids or fails to pay taxes. If either agent raids or fails to pay taxes, *G* then becomes predatory and seizes the wealth of the private agents.[13]

Under what conditions will these strategies be sustained as an equilibrium? For a strategy to be an equilibrium strategy, no player should be able to gain from deviating after any history, when deviation results in a reversion to the state failure equilibrium. That is:

- No private agent should be able to gain by raiding or refusing to pay taxes
- Nor should an agent be able to gain by altering the allocation of her resources between work, leisure, and military preparation
- *G*'s threat to predate must be credible
- And *G* must find it optimal not to predate if the economic agents adhere to their strategies.

In pondering these conditions, focus upon *G*, noting both the incentives that prevail in equilibrium and those that arise should a deviation occur

---

[13] Considering a similar equilibrium in which *G* punishes an agent who raided or failed to pay tax without reverting to the state failure equilibrium does not change the analysis.

(consult once again figures 7.5 and 7.6). Because the citizens and G are locked in a game, their fates are interdependent. The citizens' expectations of G and their response to changes in her incentives also affect their willingness to adhere to the equilibrium path of play.

G's incentives to adhere to the equilibrium choice of strategies derive from the revenues she can secure from taxation (figure 7.6). To induce G to refrain from predation, the tax level, τ, needs to be high enough that G finds it optimal, given the private agents' strategies, to refrain from confiscating the agents' wealth if they have paid their taxes. But taxes must also be sufficiently low that private agents prefer to purchase the services of G rather than to incur the costs of providing their own security. That is, the level of revenues needs to satisfy both G's and the citizens' participation constraints.

Should taxes not be fully paid, G must choose between punishing and thereby triggering a reversion to the state failure equilibrium or continuing to play the strategies that define political order. Should public revenues exceed the payoffs under state failure, then G would prefer to continue to receive them rather than to punish, thus triggering state failure. The tax level must therefore not be so high that G's threat to predate if taxes are not fully paid remains credible. Both the need to fulfill the citizens' participation constraint and the need to fill G's credibility constraint thus imply an upper bound on the level of public revenues.

As suggested by figure 7.6, however, conditions off the equilibrium path also shape the incentives for G. In particular, for G to forswear the short-term benefits of opportunism, she needs to fear the shadow cast by state failure.

The low levels of payoffs under state failure help to deter predation. Should G be assured of high levels of income even in the midst of political disorder, however, she may not fear the loss of tax payments that would result were she to behave opportunistically. And should G discount the future at too high a rate, then immediate prospects may outweigh future losses, weakening G's incentives to behave in a prudential manner. Should G consider her future insecure, then the long-term but moderate gains to be reaped by acting with restraint would decline in value; so, too, would the long-term losses that G would endure by way of punishment. The temptation to veer from the equilibrium path would thus strengthen, raising the likelihood of actions that would provoke state failure.

The discussion thus far has focused on the incentives of G. But note, too, the behavior of the private citizens. If public revenues decline, then, understanding G's incentives, the citizens might fear their government's behavior. They might expect the specialist in violence to begin to behave as a predator, using her power to extract resources from the private economy. So, too, if G's hold on power becomes less secure: the citizens might then fear that their government – now facing greater prospects of the loss of power – would now begin to despoil rather than to protect. And should a major new source of wealth arise – a resource boom, say; or discoveries of oil or mineral deposits – comprehending the incentives that shape the choices of the specialist in violence, the citizens might anticipate a change in the conduct of their government. They might anticipate that the government would forswear costly efforts on their behalf and turn instead to consuming the bounty created by the bonanza. In anticipation of the transformation of the specialist's role – her change from protector to predator – the citizenry would itself then alter its behavior: it would revert to the private provision of security and pick up arms.

The model thus suggests three testable propositions:

1. That the likelihood of state failure should be related to the level of public revenues.
2. That insofar as governments become more myopic when they face higher levels of risk, the likelihood of state failure should rise when their political fortunes become insecure.
3. And that governments in economies that contain valuable resources should experience higher levels of disorder than governments in other economies.

5.5   Qualitative support

Note that these propositions map closely onto key features of Africa's development experience. Because the propositions limn African realities, the logic that generates them gains credibility.

5.5.1   Revenue

Consider public revenues. Taxes on trade provide the bulk of public revenues in Africa. When oil prices rose in the 1970s, they triggered a recession in the global economy, resulting in a fall in the demand for Africa's exports. Government incomes atrophied as a result.

The late-century rise of the informal economy added to the damage inflicted by the decline of exports. Where governments had imposed price controls, production and exchange exited the formal economy and shifted to the "shadow" economy, where prices remained uncontrolled and incomes exempt from taxation.[14] Where governments had over-valued the national currency, exports flowed through "illicit" channels; when smuggled, goods

---

[14] See the remarkable trilogy: MacGaffey (1987, 1991) and MacGaffey and Bazenguissa-Ganga (2000).

remained untaxed (see World Bank 1994; Dossou and Sinzogan, with Mensah 2007; Doumbouya and Camara 2007). And where crop prices were controlled by marketing boards, the rise in prices for goods bought off the farm posed a threat to farm incomes. In response, peasants either sold their crops in "parallel" markets, where they could command higher prices, or withdrew from the market economy (Bates 1981; Hyden 1981; de Sousa and Sulemane 2007). In both town and country, then, the response of the private sector to the policy choices of governments led to the contraction of the tax base.

5.5.2 Uncertainty

Until the mid-1990s, the majority of the African governments were authoritarian: on average, one-third of the heads of state came from the military and three-quarters presided over no-party or single-party systems (see chapter 10 on political reform). The late 1970s marked the peak period of military rule; the late 1980s that of single-party systems (see chapter 10). Then came the period of political reform. As the number of competitive party systems rose so, too, did the percentage of states in which incumbents were openly subject to organized political opposition. In the last decade of the sample period 1970–95, multi-party political systems became the modal form of government in Africa. Governments that had faced no challengers now had to compete for office. They became less secure.

As noted by Bratton and van de Walle (1997), in 1980–5, nine of the seventeen countries in their sample held competitive elections; in the period 1990–4, the number rose to thirty-eight. And while before the 1990s only one African head of state had been voted out of office, between 1990 and 1994 the number rose to eleven, with three others choosing not to run (Block 2002: 206).

5.5.3 Natural resources

Consider, too, the impact of natural resources. Cilliers (2000), Hirsch (2001), Collier and Hoeffler (2002), and others (Human Rights Watch 1999) stress the link between diamond deposits and the war in Angola. Reno (Reno 1998, 2000) emphasizes the link between natural resources and civil wars in Sierra Leone and Liberia. Johnson (2003) stresses the role of oil in the civil war in Sudan, and Zinn and others (Kirk-Greene 1971; Suberu 2001; Zinn 2005) the impact of oil on political conflict in Nigeria. So pervasive is the link between resource wealth and political conflict that it has given rise to a literature on the "resource curse" – a force disrupting politics, it is claimed, in Indonesia, Russia, and the Middle East as well (Chaudry 1997; Ross 2003).

Table 7.6 *Variables employed in the analysis.*

Variable	Units	Mean	Std dev.	Source
Dependent variable				
Formation of domestic military groups?	0 = No, 1 = Yes	0.247	0.431	*Keesings Contemporary Archives, Africa Confidential, Economist Intelligence Unit*
Independent variables				
Core model				
REVENUES	Central government revenues as percent of GDP	19.486	10.165	*Penn World Tables Mark 5.6*
NO-PARTY system	0 = No, 1 = Yes	0.313	0.463	*Keesings Contemporary Archives, Africa Confidential, Economist Intelligence Unit*
ONE-PARTY system	0 = No, 1 = Yes	0.392	0.483	ditto
DURATION;				
No-party system	Length of time in years of duration of political system	2.405	4.685	ditto
One-Party system	ditto	3.415	5.551	ditto
Multi-Party system	ditto	1.271	3.934	ditto
PETROLEUM	Value of exports *per capita* in constant US dollars	86.071	473.730	Data collected by research team from commercial sources
Control variables				
Modernization variables:				
LITERACY	Percent of adult population that is literate	58.917	19.921	*World Development Indicators*
URBAN POPULATION	Percent of population living	25.849	13.476	ditto
INCOME	Log of GDP *per capita* (PPP)	6.851	0.605	*Penn World Tables Mark 5.6*
MODERNIZATION	Factor score derived from principal components analysis of INCOME, LITERACY, and URBAN POPULATION	1.60 E_02	0.024	

Variable	Description			Source
GROWTH	Annual rate of change of INCOME in cities	0.152	8.290	Penn World Tables Mark 5.6
DROUGHT	Arable hectares of land *per capita*	0.304	0.347	World Development Indicators
ELECTIONS	1 if year before national election 0 otherwise	0.191	0.392	Keesings Contemporary Archives, Africa Confidential, Economist Intelligence Unit
NEIGHBOR	Total level of conflict in neighboring states (number of coups, domestic military groups, and civil wars)	1.514	1.953	ditto
CROSS-BORDER	Percent of population *not* belonging to an ethnic group that spills over national boundary	0.427	0.318	Englebert (2000)
POPULATION	Total Population	0.707	0.455	World Development Indicators
TIME SINCE LAST REPORT	Number of years since a domestic military group was last reported	5.994	6.235	Keesings Contemporary Archives, Africa Confidential, Economist Intelligence Unit
Other variables				
Exchange rate	Local currency units per US dollar	1150.831	20261.547	Penn World Tables Mark 6.0
Government consumption	Government consumption as percent of GDP	16.757	7.737	World Development Indicators
Debt	Foreign debt as multiple of annual exports	331.718	578.461	World Development Indicators
State breakdown	1 = Yes, 0 = No	0.108	0.310	Keesings Contemporary Archives, Africa Confidential, Economist Intelligence Unit

The logic that underlies our analysis of political disorder thus resonates with accounts of politics in Africa. The argument is thus plausible. It is time to assess its validity.

6   Testing the argument

6.1   Variables

According to the model, when people anticipate that incentives now favor predation by the specialists in violence, they revert to the private provision of security. That is, they arm themselves. We therefore take as our indicator of state failure the formation of private militias.[15] In gathering data to test the argument, coders answered the following question: "For a given country in a given year: were there reports of a private military organization?"[16] If the answer was "yes," then the dependent variable takes the value 1; if "no," the value 0.

Dividing the magnitude of central government's revenue for a given year by the magnitude of its GDP generated a measure of PUBLIC REVENUES. Price data and production figures collected from commercial sources yielded the value of each country's annual, *per capita* PETROLEUM production. Data on Africa's political systems indicated for each year whether the head of state presided over a NO-PARTY, ONE-PARTY, or MULTI-PARTY political system, thus capturing the level of political competition and suggesting the rate of discount. Table 7.6 provides a list and description of the variables and notes the sources from which they were taken.

The dependent variable is qualitative. Because it is bounded from above by 1 and from below by 0, the errors from regression will not be identically distributed. I therefore employ the probit rather than the normal distribution; when introducing fixed effects, I employ the conditional logistic model.

Missing values in the data pose a major problem for the analysis. Not only is there a great deal of it, but also there is every reason to presume that it correlates with the likelihood of violence.[17] Resorting to case-wise deletion – that is, to dropping observations that lack data for key variables – would decrease the efficiency and increase the potential for bias in the estimates. It would also reduce the number of cases relative to the depth of the panel, thereby introducing an additional source of bias (Judson and Owen 1999).

---

[15] It is the militarization and not the violence that the model explains. For a thoughtful treatment of the implication of rationality for conflict, see Fearon (1995).

[16] Recall the sources in n.2.

[17] This will come as no surprise to anyone who studies Africa. See Honaker (2000).

A second major problem arises from the impact of variables omitted from the models; should they affect both the dependent and independent variables, any relationship between the two would be spurious. Endogeneity poses yet another problem. Changes in the dependent variable (the level of insecurity) could yield changes in the independent variable (such as public revenues); the estimated relationship between the two would thus include a component of reciprocal causality.

Methods developed by Rubin and others (Rubin 1996; Schafer 1997) provide an alternative to case-wise deletion, generating imputed estimates of the missing values and their distributions. Given the magnitude and nature of the problems posed by missing data, I employed no method that could not be implemented on multiple, imputed data sets. The introduction of fixed effects provided a response to the second difficulty. I addressed the third by introducing instrumental variables.

6.2 Core model

Table 7.7 presents the core model. The model contains measures of the variables whose values affect the possibility of political order. The dependent variable is the likelihood that civil society will take up arms.[18] Column (1) contains estimates drawn from the pooled set of data using a probit model; column (2) includes fixed effects and employs a conditional fixed-effects logit model; column (3) also applies a probit model, but one that employs instrumental variables to correct for the endogeneity of public revenues.[19]

Estimates from the pooled sample suggest that states whose governments collect a large percentage of their GDP as government revenues are less likely to exhibit symptoms of state failure. When corrected for endogeneity bias (column (3)), the quadratic term is positive and significant, suggesting an upper bound to the range in which additional revenues dampen the tendency of armed groups to form. When fixed effects are included in the estimations,

---

[18] More precisely, the likelihood that there will be a report of the formation of domestic military groups.

[19] The instruments included first- and second-period lagged values of public revenues; first- and second-period values of primary product exports; lagged measures of the portion of government taxes derived from trade; and the weighted annual average growth rate of the G7 economies. The instruments are strongly correlated with the present level of public revenues; there is no reason to regard them as possessing a strong relationship with the likelihood of the formation of armed groups in the present period. Nor are past levels of public revenues likely to be correlated with the shock on the probability of the formation of private militias. Standard tests suggest that the instruments are "strong." For reasons given above, the level of public revenues enters the equation in quadratic form. The value of petroleum production enters in quadratic form as well, not for theoretical reasons but because that specification yields more precise and robust estimates.

Table 7.7 *The core model.*

Variable	Pooled sample (probit estimates) (1)	Conditional logits (fixed effects) (2)	Instrumental variables (probit estimates) (3)
REVENUES	−0.055	−0.055	−0.151
	(0.025)**	(0.063)	(0.069)***
REVENUES SQUARED	0.001	0.001	0.002
	(0.00)	(0.001)	(0.00)***
NO-PARTY	−0.407	−1.110	−0.539
	(0.214)*	(0.430)***	(0.12)***
ONE-PARTY	−0.691	−2.240	−0.610
	(0.258)***	(0.470)***	(0.09)***
DURATION			
...No-Party	0.07	0.024	0.074
	(0.021)***	(0.037)	(0.00)***
...One-Party	0.045	0.171	0.038
	(0.016)***	(0.037)***	(0.00)***
...Multi-Party	0.001	0.077	0.006
	(0.025)	(0.065)	(0.00)***
PETROLEUM	0.190	0.293	0.295
	(0.269)	(0.441)	(0.02)***
PETROLEUM SQUARED	−0.031	−0.047	−0.041
	(0.037)	(0.059)	(0.00)***
TIME SINCE LAST REPORT	−0.087	−0.019	−0.082
	(0.017)***	(0.024)	(0.00)***
Constant	0.429	–	1.529
	(0.340)	–	(6.550)
No. observations	1084	847	1084

Robust standard errors in parentheses; Significance levels: ***0.01; **0.05; *0.1.

the coefficients become insignificant, however. One reason may be that the variables are "slow-moving" and thus may not generate much variation in differenced form.

Each of the three statistical models indicates that states governed by no-party and one-party systems are significantly less likely to yield reports of the formation of armed groups. In this instance, it is the fixed effects estimates that yield the most relevant insights. Because of differencing, the coefficients can be interpreted as indicating the impact on political order of a change from a no- or single-party to a multi-party system. Note that the coefficients of the party system variables are larger than those derived from the pooled sample. The results suggest that a change to competitive politics is significantly associated with an increase in the likelihood of political disorder.[20]

Basing estimates upon the coefficients of the instrumental variable model (results not shown here) indicates that the largest (marginal) effects arise from petroleum production and the party system. When, on average, the *per capita* value of petroleum production reaches $100, then the likelihood of the formation of private militias rises by nearly 3 percentage points. A change from a no-party to a competitive party system increases the likelihood by 5 percentage points; a change from a one-party to a competitive party system increases it by 6.

Table 7.8 adds a collection of control variables to the model. These include measures of modernization: INCOME, LITERACY, and URBAN POPULA-TION, plus a composite MODERNIZATION score (see table 7.6 for details). The controls also include measures of shocks. Two are economic: short-term changes in GROWTH and DROUGHT.[21] A third is political and records the incidence of a national ELECTION. Others (e.g. Sambanis 2001; Fearon and Laitin 2003; see also Herbst 2000) stress the importance of state size, noting that large states are more costly to police. To control for size, I include a measure of POPULATION.

Political disorder in one country affects the likelihood of disorder in its neighbors (Murdoch and Sandler 2002); and the presence of military groups in one year can increase the likelihood of their presence in the next. The variable NEIGHBOR provides a measure of the number of domestic military groups, civil wars, and international conflicts in neighboring countries and another, CROSS-BORDER, records the percentage of the state's population that belong to groups whose membership spills across national boundaries. As data for the last have been gathered for only one period (see Morrison *et al.* 1989; Englebert 2000; Englebert, Tarango, and Carter 2002), the measure is time-invariant; it is therefore interacted with NEIGHBOR when entered in the fixed-effect equations. A measure of the TIME SINCE LAST REPORT helps to correct for the interdependence between the annual observations.

---

[20] The introduction of period effects does not alter this finding.

[21] Unlike Miguel, Shanker, and Sergenti (2004), I include both DROUGHT and GROWTH in all equations. During periods of drought, pastoralists seeking grazing land alter their migration routes and therefore pose a threat to the land rights of others. Because drought thus affects the likelihood of disorder through its impact on land rights as well as on growth, it is not a valid instrument for growth. I therefore include it among the control variables.

Table 7.8 *The core model plus controls.*

Variable	Pooled sample (probit estimates)		Conditional logits (fixed effects)		Instrumental variables (probit estimates)	
	(1)	(2)	(3)	(4)	(5)	(6)
REVENUES	-0.047	-0.049	-0.085	-0.062	-0.245	-0.248
	(0.029)*	(0.028)*	(0.061)	(0.065)	(0.051)***	(0.052)***
REVENUES SQUARED	0.001	0.001	0.001	0.001	0.004	0.004
	(0.00)	(0.00)	(0.001)	(0.001)	(0.000)***	(0.000)***
NO-PARTY	-0.542	-0.536	-0.958	-0.969	-0.602	-0.592
	(0.258)**	(0.262)**	(0.523)*	(0.486)**	(0.140)***	(0.240)**
ONE-PARTY	-0.676	-0.659	-2.227	-2.208	-0.683	0.265
	(0.254)***	(0.259)**	(0.547)***	(0.533)***	(0.137)***	(0.265)
DURATION						
. . . No-Party	0.063	0.065	0.03	0.032	0.067	0.066
	(0.024)***	(0.024)***	(0.044)***	(0.04)	(0.002)***	(0.004)***
. . . One-Party	0.037	0.037	0.168	0.179	0.036	0.036
	(0.018)**	(0.019)**	(0.042)***	(0.041)***	(0.001)***	(0.002)***
. . . Multi-Party	0.004	0.004	0.052	0.058	0.002	-0.004
	(0.024)	(0.024)	(0.066)	(0.066)	(0.002)	(0.028)
PETROLEUM	0.301	0.314	0.286	0.226	0.357	0.370
	(0.341)	(0.341)	(0.528)	(0.498)	(0.029)***	(0.028)***
PETROLEUM SQUARED	-0.039	-0.041	-0.043	-0.036	-0.045	-0.028
	(0.045)	(0.045)	(0.080)	(0.071)	(0.001)***	(0.001)***
TIME SINCE LAST REPORT	-0.08	-0.08	-0.009	-0.015	-0.075	-0.077
	(0.017)***	(0.017)***	(0.024)	(0.024)	(0.001)***	(0.001)***
INCOME	-0.28	–	0.155	–	-0.305	–
	(0.267)	–	(0.504)	–	(0.225)	–

LITERACY	−0.004	—	0.052	—	0.005	—
	(0.005)	—	(0.021)**	—	(0.001)***	—
URBAN POPULATION	0.006	—	−0.054	—	0.017	—
	(0.008)	—	(0.032)*	—	(0.000)***	—
MODERNIZATION	—	−0.134	—	0.45	—	0.000
	—	(0.188)	—	(0.479)	—	(0.060)
GROWTH	−0.017	−0.012	−0.024	−0.025	0.048	0.069
	(0.006)***	(0.006)***	(0.017)	(0.016)	(0.016)***	(0.145)
ELECTION	−0.292	−0.3	−0.698	−0.682	−0.305	−0.298
	(0.156)*	(0.155)**	(0.316)**	(0.314)**	(0.066)***	(0.113)***
DROUGHT	−0.449	−0.445	−0.979	−0.918	−0.402	−0.458
	(0.199)**	(0.193)**	(1.048)	(1.101)	(0.014)***	(0.452)
POPULATION	0.121	0.116	—	—	0.037	0.039
	(0.094)	(0.094)	—	—	(0.013)***	(0.062)
NEIGHBOR	0.157	0.123	0.227	0.3	0.263	0.194
	(0.08)**	(0.080)	(0.136)*	(0.132)	(0.013)***	(0.047)***
CROSS-BORDER	−0.229	−0.154	—	—	−0.38	−0.226
	(0.135)*	(0.127)	—	—	(0.033)***	(0.232)
NEIGHBOR*CROSS-BORDER	—	—	−0.063	−0.073	—	—
	—	—	(0.029)**	(0.03)	—	—
Constant	0.432	−1.4	—	—	3.747	1.96
	(2.504)	(1.553)	—	—	(9.087)	(31.20)
No. observations	1084	1084	847	847	1084	1084

Robust standard errors in parentheses; Significance levels: ***0.01; **0.05; *0.1.

Endogenous variables: crev, crev2, lgw.

Instrumental variables: ltxtrd l2crev l3crev lsxp lsxp2 bizcycsh.

In this instance, the instrumental variables seek to correct for the endogeneity of GROWTH as well as REVENUES.

With one significant exception, the coefficients of the theoretical variables behave in the equations that include the control variables in the same manner, by and large, as they do in the equations of the core model. The exception is REVENUES, where the coefficient becomes much larger in the equations that incorporate instruments when the additional variables are entered into the equation.[22]

The coefficients linking the modernization variables to political disorder are insignificant in estimates drawn from the pooled sample. Those drawn from the fixed-effects equations suggest that increases in LITERACY and URBAN POPULATION can lead to increases in the likelihood of political disorder.

The estimates from the pooled equation suggest that GROWTH shocks and DROUGHT also affect the likelihood of disorder. Higher levels of GROWTH reduce the likelihood of domestic militarization; DROUGHT increases it.[23] The estimates for GROWTH are not robust, however. When fixed effects or instrumental variables are introduced, the coefficient for GROWTH reverses in sign and it become insignificant in the fixed-effects models. Those for DROUGHT retain a positive sign, although they, too, lose significance when fixed effects are incorporated into the models.

More robust is the coefficient on the measure of political shocks, ELECTIONS. It is has been argued that elections are politically destabilizing.[24] Our estimates offer little support for that argument: in each specification, the evidence indicates that there were fewer reports of militarized groups in the year before elections. One possibility is that political organizations alter the means by which they compete for power, changing from the use of violence to the search for votes. Another is that governments simply may not hold elections during periods of great insecurity and that the estimate is therefore biased.

As suggested by Herbst (2000) and Fearon and Laitin (2003), the coefficients on POPULATION suggest that larger countries may be more difficult to pacify. But differences in size do not bear a significant relationship to the likelihood of disorder in most specifications.

The coefficients on NEIGHBOR and CROSS-BORDER are of the expected sign and are significant in most equations.

---

[22] Again, tests indicate that the instruments are not "weak."

[23] The measure is the number of hectares of land *per capita*. Decreases in the measure therefore indicate increases in drought, and a negative sign on the coefficient suggests a positive relationship between drought and disorder.

[24] Thus the title of Snyder's justly famous work (Snyder 2000).

Turning to the estimates of the marginal effects of the variables, employing the coefficients generated when using instrumental variables, the results (not shown here) again confirm the importance of petroleum and the party system among the theoretical variables. The magnitude of their effect remains virtually unaltered when control variables are entered into the equations. Among the latter set of variables, it is income that emerges as the strongest correlate of disorder. The estimates suggest that moving 1 standard deviation above the mean in *per capita* income would reduce the likelihood of the formation of militias by 7 percentage points.

6.3   *Discussion*

The literature on political conflict in Africa stresses its economic origins. The results above suggest the need for greater nuance. While societies with lower incomes are more prone to political disorder, the evidence underscores the importance of political factors. While the literature emphasizes the role of GDP, this analysis emphasizes the role of public revenues: poorer *states*, it argues, are more likely to experience state failure. And while these accounts stress the role of economic factors, this points to the central importance of the party system.

Other literatures do emphasize political rather than economic sources of conflict. One variant focuses on the destabilizing role of democratization, stressing in particular the role of competitive elections (Zakaria 1997; Snyder 2000). The findings reported here call once again for a more nuanced interpretation. While competitive political systems are more likely to generate reports of private military groups than are no- or single-party systems, there is no evidence that elections themselves provoke the formation of private militias. The link between political reform and political disorder runs, the evidence suggests, not through electoral competition but rather through the fear of, and reaction to, the prospects of losing office.

The findings suggest that when states are starved or sated with revenues; when the incumbents in regimes hitherto immune to open political opposition must face organized political challengers; and when those in power have access to resource rents, then elites and citizens behave in ways that lead to state failure.

7   In search of causal paths

In closing, we return to the qualitative literature in search of the links between resource rents, political competition, and government revenues on the one hand, and state failure, on the other.

7.1   Petroleum production

Regional conflict provides one link, be it between center and periphery or between those regions that lack and those that are blessed with an abundance of natural resources.

Among the issues that motivated the people of eastern Nigeria to take up arms against the central government in 1967 was their demand for control over petroleum deposits in the region. In key meetings between the leaders of the Eastern Region and the Central Government, Colonel Chukwuemeka Ojukukwi indicated that the Eastern Region would remain within Nigeria were the nation structured as a confederation – one in which the East would secure control over petroleum resources. The Central Government refused to accede to this proposal, however, largely (in the words of Khan 1994: 10) because of "the issue of oil revenue distribution."

With the breakdown of negotiations came the outbreak of the war. The Central Government's primary military objective (Dudley 1982: 113) was to seize the oil fields. The commander of the forces that secured that objective, Olesegun Obasanjo, still fights for control over Nigeria's petroleum deposits: now President of Nigeria, he has again moved troops to the oil-producing regions, seeking to repress rebels who, for their part, seek to check his attempts to seize the resources of their region on behalf of the central government (*New York Times* September 30, 2004: A11).

A similar narrative characterizes the Sudan. The central government and Southern Region had long struggled over issues as commonplace as political preferment and as volatile as race and religion. Shortly after independence, a mutiny of southern units of the armed forces led to the outbreak of war; years of fighting and subsequent compromises led to its termination. In 1978 came reports of the discovery of oil deposits in the northern reaches of the southern region. The national assembly then altered the regional boundaries, separating the oil fields from the south and locating them in the north, thereby placing them under *de facto* control of the central government. In combination with the political marginalization of Southern leaders and the imposition of Sharia law in the north, where many southerners lived, the loss of oil revenues led to the resumption of civil war (Mitchell 1993; Woodward 1995; de Waal 1997; Ali and Matthews 1999; Johnson 2003).

These narratives suggest that forces at the center mobilize their political and military might to capture the streams of income that emanate from Africa's natural resources, while those who dwell in the richly endowed region seek to capture that income for themselves. Both back up their claims with military force, thereby establishing a link between resource endowments and political conflict.

Qualitative accounts suggest an additional tie between resource wealth and state failure. They suggest that when the center succeeds in appropriating the wealth generated by natural endowments, the government no longer strives to provide services for its citizens. Recoded in terms of our analysis, the political contract between G and the citizens appears then to break down: the specialist in violence no longer needs to exchange services, such as the protection of property rights, for the receipt of public revenues.

To illustrate, Amos Sawyer – once an opponent of the government of William Tolbert and later himself Liberia's President – points to the growth of government revenues from natural resources and its impact on the government's behavior: "iron ore royalties and other forms of business, especially multinational corporations, relieved the government from reliance on hut taxes," he writes, and "the government thus gained sources of income independent of the performance of its . . . administrative apparatus" (Sawyer 1992: 10). The result, in Sawyer's words, was the "emergence of autocracy": a presidency that ruled the country as a "personal domain" (1992: 10). Cilliers (2000) notes a similar pattern in Angola, where the revenue-sated political elites have retired to the presidential mansion, leaving it to the people themselves to provide their own health care, sanitation, housing, and security.

Returning to Nigeria, we can also turn to the comments of Billy Dudley (Dudley 1982): "the oil boom," he writes, "was a disaster" – one made worse by military rule. As Dudley states:

Under military rule, with no constituents to conciliate and no electorate to be accountable to – in however weak a sense one interprets the notion of accountability – the effect of the oil boom was to convert the military political decision makers into a new property-owning, rentier class working in close and direct collaboration with foreign business interests with the sole aim of expropriating the surpluses derived from oil for their own private benefit. (Dudley 1982: 116)

Qualitative materials thus suggest possible links between petroleum production and political order. One runs through the politics of income distribution, not between rich individuals and poor but rather between the center and the periphery or between regions endowed with natural resources and those that are not.[25] A second runs through the incentives that shape the behavior of elites. Sated with resource wealth, those who govern no longer have an incentive to safeguard the welfare of their people in exchange for public revenues. Instead they abandon the strategies that, in equilibrium, support political order.

---

[25] While a new theme in this chapter, the impact of regional tensions is addressed in greater depth in chapter 6 by Azam and it is one to which we shall shortly return (see below).

7.2   Revenues

Specialists in violence can transmute force into security; but they need to be paid to do so. If the flow of earnings from the provision of this service is worth less than the immediate benefits from predation (less the subsequent losses from state failure), then they will instead use force to engage in predation, rendering the citizenry less secure and more likely to pick up arms. This is one strand of the logic advanced in this chapter, and the estimates lend support to the argument.

The evidence from the literature suggests that the relationship runs along several different paths. One is through the non-payment of the military. Rather than paying their salaries, some governments instead accumulate arrears. This form of non-payment characterizes the francophone states, which are unable to monetize their debts. Decalo discusses the example of Benin (Decalo 1997: 11); O'Toole (1997) the case of the CAR; Yates (1996) the case of Gabon; and Mundt (1997), Huband (1998), and Hills (2000), the example of Côte d'Ivoire. In each instance, non-payment resulted in riots and looting by soldiers. Outside of the franc zone, non-payment takes a different form: the erosion of the real value of the soldiers' pay. Where central banks are able to lend to governments so that they can pay their debts, then governments can renege on those debts by increasing the supply – and thus lowering the value – of their currencies. Perhaps the best example comes from Zaire.[26] When in 1993 Mobutu tried – once again – to pay his debts by issuing bank notes, his soldiers at last refused to accept them. They rebelled, refused payment, and turned to looting.

When left unpaid by their governments, specialists in violence seek to pay themselves. One way is through extortion. As stated by Kasozi (1994), in Uganda in the 1980s,

> Any soldier who needed money . . . would just pick an isolated . . . part of the road, put logs or chains across it, and wait for unfortunate travelers. These twentieth century highwaymen would rob anyone of anything they fancied: cash, watches, cassette radios, clothes, and the like. (1994: 164)

General Kpama Baramoto, commander of the Civil Guard in Zaire, levied a toll on mineral and diamond production in Eastern Zaire, issued trading licenses, and, for turning a blind eye, took payments from smugglers (MacGaffey 1987: 60–2; Pech 2000). Or, as in Liberia, soldiers can turn into "sobels" – soldiers by day, rebels by night – thus enjoying the non-monetary perquisites of public employment, such as housing, and the financial rewards of rebellion: ransoms, loot, and plunder (Howe 2000: 57; see also Ellis 1999).

---

[26] Among the numerous accounts, see Nzongola-Ntanlaja (2002).

Soldiers possess another option, of course, and that is themselves to seize power. Illustrative are the memoirs of one James Waore Dianga, a junior officer who in August 1982 attempted to overthrow the government of Daniel Arap Moi, president of Kenya. Dianga and his colleagues witnessed a decline in the ability or inclination of the government to provide equipment that worked, uniforms that fitted, housing that was adequate, food that was palatable, or pay that would enable the soldiers to live in reasonable comfort. As stated by Dianga: "A soldier . . . signs a contract with the State . . . The soldier, on his/her part, is under oath to defend the State . . . The government enters into an agreement . . . to supply the soldier" (Dianga 2002: 48–9). The declining fortunes of the soldiers broke the letter of the contract, and the rising fortune of the President's cronies violated its spirit; in response, Dianga writes, the soldiers rebelled.

The attempted coup led by Flight Lieutenant Jerry Rawlings in Ghana in 1979 offers another example. Under-paid and without decent clothing or adequate shelter, the rank and file seethed in resentment as their officers – themselves now in charge of the state – enriched themselves while abandoning to their fate those whom they commanded. Rawlings' denunciation of Ghana's elite and of their violation of the contract between the soldier and the state occupies a prominent place in Ghana's – indeed, in Africa's – political heritage.[27]

Regionalism provides a second link. In Africa, as elsewhere, the desire for redistribution motivates politics. Regions that are relatively poor seek to extract revenues from those that are rich. Such efforts need not lead to conflict, however: with sufficient public revenues, elites from richer regions can retain the loyalty of those from the less prosperous regions by channeling benefits to them, thus forestalling armed challenges (Azam 1994).

Evidence comes from Côte d'Ivoire, where political order rested on a series of pacts negotiated between regional elites and the center (see Boone 2003 and Azam 1994). Southerners, and in particular the Akan, controlled the center. Prominent in the periphery were the Senoufo, who possessed a well-organized polity in the north. "The complaint of the north," Boone writes, was that "their region was impoverished and relegated to backward political status" (2003: 263). To counter mounting discontent, President Houphouët-Boigny launched "a massive infusion of resources" (2003: 263), starting projects that led to the opening of parastatal agencies, the construction of roads, and the founding of cotton and livestock industries in the region. Channeling an intensive flow of benefits in the area dominated by

[27] Ironically, the statement emanates from the prosecution's depiction of the motives for the coup, rather then from the mouth of Rawlings himself. See the account in Shillington (1992) and Appiah (1996).

the Senoufo, the government recruited members of the ruling clans into the agencies that managed these projects (Boone 2003: 267ff.).

This tactic is, of course, risky: should revenues fall, then the government may be unable to fulfill the key periphery's participation constraint. With the end of the coffee boom of the late 1970s, those in the center could no longer credibly pledge to target the north with projects (Rapley 1993). The north therefore began to organize against the central government. After the death of Houphouët-Boigny, the forces of the north gathered about Allasane Outtara: once Prime Minister, he now sought to become President. Led by Laurent Gbagbo, southern politicians rallied to check the rise of Outtara, portraying him as a non-national and therefore ineligible for high office. The courts agreed. Following a coup by soldiers whom the government had failed to pay, the rival politicians transformed their political organizations from political parties into armed militias and plunged Côte d'Ivoire into war.[28]

A second source of risk arises from the inconsistency of preferences and resultant inability to commit. In order to secure the demobilization of the periphery, the government may pledge to transfer resources. Once the periphery surrenders, however, the government may prefer to renege on its pledges. Knowing that, the periphery may therefore ignore the government's promises and refuse to demobilize. As stressed by Fearon (1998), Acemoglu and Robinson (2001), Azam and Mesnard (2003), and others, for co-optation to work, promises must be credible.[29]

In compiling data for the sample of forty-six African countries over 1970–95, I noted whether countries were marked by regional inequalities and whether the Chief Executive came from an economically privileged or a poorly endowed region. As seen in table 7.9, when the Chief Executive came from a less prosperous region, the likelihood of mass militarization declined. The marginal effects (not shown here) are large, suggesting that having a President from a non-prosperous region reduces the likelihood of militarization by 19 percentage points. The evidence thus suggests that insofar as regional differences matter, pledges of transfers tend to be incredible. Defusing the political tensions that arise between rich regions and poor appears to require that the elite from the poorer region secure the power to allocate the state's resources.

---

[28] The split between the north and south was not the sole line of cleavage, it should be stressed. Particularly within the south, major animosities set the western regions against those of the east.

[29] This arguments draws on the logic of the "security dilemma" that pervades multi-ethnic societies. See Posen (1993) and Fearon (1998). It also echoes the arguments advanced by Acemoglu and Robinson (2001) and Acemoglu and Robinson (2006), as they strive to identify when political order will give way to conflict or persist because of reform. It parallels most closely, however, the analysis of Azam and Mesnard (2003), who strive to explain the disintegration of Côte d'Ivoire.

Table 7.9 *President from non-prosperous region.*

Variable	Pooled sample (probit estimates) (1)	Conditional logits (fixed effects) (2)	Instrumental variables (probit estimates) (3)
REVENUES	−0.053	−0.051	−0.159
	(0.03)*	(0.07)	(0.04)***
REVENUES SQUARED	0.001	0.001	0.002
	(0.00)	(0.00)	(0.00)***
PRESIDENT FROM NON-	−0.362	−0.727	−0.476
PROSPEROUS REGION	(0.17)**	(0.35)*	(0.08)***
NO-PARTY	−0.588	−0.669	−0.545
	(0.26)**	(0.51)	(0.29)*
ONE-PARTY	−0.728	−1.812	−0.822
	(0.28)***	(0.58)***	(0.33)**
DURATION			
...No-Party	0.073	0.008	0.069
	(0.02)***	(0.04)	(0.00)***
...One-Party	0.046	0.141	0.056
	(0.02)**	(0.05)***	(0.00)***
...Multi-Party	0.001	0.012	−0.007
	(0.02)	(0.07)	(0.00)
PETROLEUM	0.227	1.404	0.244
	(0.33)	(1.18)	(0.03)***
PETROLEUM SQUARED	−0.029	−0.161	−0.031
	(0.04)	(0.14)	(0.00)***
MODERNIZATION	−0.128	1.122	−0.044
	(0.18)	(0.80)	(0.06)
GROWTH	−0.019	−0.025	0.127
	(0.01)***	(0.02)	(0.16)
DROUGHT	−0.430	−0.855	−0.540
	(0.19)**	(0.95)	(0.48)
ELECTIONS	−0.305	−0.607	−0.283
	(0.16)*	(0.31)*	(0.10)***
POPULATION	0.105	1.384	0.071
	(0.09)	(1.35)	(0.05)
NEIGHBORS	0.160	−	0.189
	(0.079)**	−	(0.041)***
CROSS-BORDER	−0.216	−	−0.202
	(0.121)*	−	(0.190)
NEIGHBOR*CROSS-	−	−0.026	−
BORDER	−	(0.019)	−
TIME SINCE LAST	−0.080	−0.005	−0.047
REPORT	(0.02)***	(0.03)	(1.190)
Constant	−0.971	−	0.851
	(1.552)	−	(20.701)
No. observations	1048	813	1048

Robust standard errors in parentheses; Significance levels: ***0.01; **0.05; *0.1.

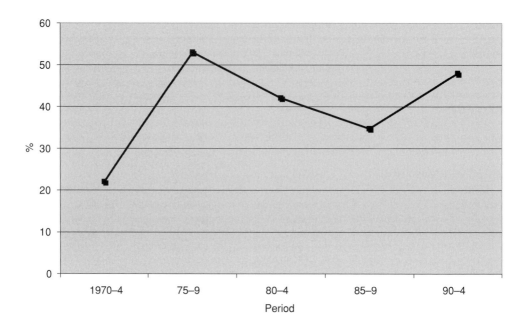

Figure 7.7 Rate of loss of office, by period, 1970–1994

7.3 Political reform

To probe the link between political reform and state failure, consider the level of risk faced by incumbent regimes. We have information concerning the departure from office of eighty-eight leaders over the period 1970–95. The number of incumbents rose from thirty-six at the beginning of the period to forty-six at the end. Figure 7.7 portrays the rate at which they lost office in each period; figure 7.8 the manner of their exit.

Viewed one way, the data suggest that African leaders faced less risk after the period of reform than they did in earlier periods. As seen in figure 7.7, in the period 1975–9, 53.5 percent of the leaders lost office as opposed to 48.8 percent in 1990–4. And as seen in figure 7.8, following the onset of political reform in 1989, the relative frequency of peaceful exits – resulting from resignations, electoral losses, or natural deaths – for the first time exceeded that of violent departures – resulting from coups, assassinations, or forceful expulsion from office. Data not presented here indicate that over 80 percent of the violent departures took place in no-party states – i.e. in states often ruled by the military. Over 60 percent of the peaceful exits took place in competitive party systems. These data give reason, then, to argue that political reform led to a less risky political environment.

Viewed another way, however, the data support an alternative vision. The risks to incumbents of coming to a violent end may have declined in the

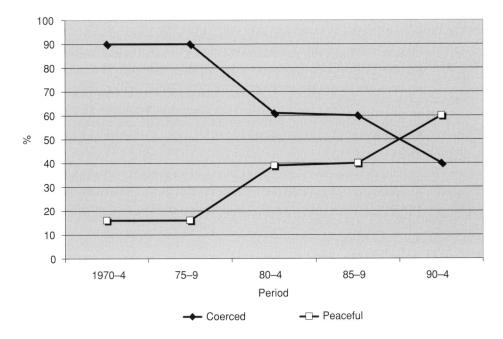

Figure 7.8 Forms of exit from office, by period, 1970–1994

sample period (figure 7.8). But the risk of loss of office rose (figure 7.7), returning to the level it had been in the late 1970s – the least stable period in post-independence Africa. Consider, moreover, the period just prior to reform: over the previous decade, the prospects of losing office had been declining and political leaders appeared to have gained an increasingly secure hold on power. As seen in figure 7.7, however, with 1989 came a rise in the level of political insecurity: the risk of loss of office rose sharply. Indicative of the leaders' own assessment, perhaps, is that 70 percent of the total voluntary exits from the post of Chief Executive took place in the period 1985–94 – 40 percent in 1985–9 and 30 percent in 1990–4 – suggesting a downward revision in the leaders' assessment of their political prospects.

Some of Africa's leaders may have stepped down in the face of the threat posed by political reform; others fought back. Consider, for example, the case of Kenya in the 1990s. Daniel Arap Moi, the incumbent, came from the Rift Valley. The Valley contained forty-four of the 188 parliamentary constituencies. As the President could fill twelve other seats with nominees of his own, if he could consolidate his political base he would then be assured close to 30 percent of the parliamentary seats even before the outset of the campaign. But ethnic groups from other regions had migrated into the Rift Valley in search of land; and they tended to vote for the political parties that they had supported in their place of origin, which in key instances stood in opposition to the ruling party. The President and his backers, Kimenyi and Ndung'u (2005) claim, therefore launched a program of political intimidation.[30] Organizing private militias, they invaded settler communities, beat and killed their residents, drove off their livestock, and burnt down shops, schools, and homes. Fearing the loss of power, the incumbent turned predatory and used force to violate rather than to safeguard the security of citizens. As Kimenyi and Ndung'u (2005) conclude, "the main motivation behind the violence was to influence voting in favor of the [ruling party]" (2005: 326).

Consider, too, the case of Sierra Leone. Most accounts of political conflict in Sierra Leone begin with the 1991 invasion of the RUF. But other accounts, especially those written by scholars from Sierra Leone, start earlier, focusing on the conduct of the APC, the ruling party.

In the 1970s, the APC faced challenges from its traditional rival, the SLPP, and from dissidents disillusioned by the decline in Sierra Leone's economy under the APC.[31] The APC responded violently to these threats to its power. In a manner that foreshadowed later events in Rwanda and Zimbabwe, the governing party mobilized the party's youth league and the government's police to break up the rallies of the opposition parties; to beat up its sympathizers; and to intimidate those in the media that might sympathize with their cause. Fearing the loss of power, the ruling party turned violent. As stated by a prominent member of the opposition, the APC

had no support in the East. So how were they going to win? They knew they would win in the North and Western areas, but not in the East. Parliament would then be balanced between the two parties. They wanted to win, so there was violence.[32] (Quoted in Hayward and Kandeh 1987: 50)

When civil war later broke out in Sierra Leone, a major goal of the combatants was to rid themselves of a political elite that was willing to attack its own people in order to retain political office.

It was when the political elite faced the prospect of losing office that governments turned predatory. Table 7.10 notes the dates when "national conferences" were convened. At these conferences, citizens joined politicians in debating the performance and structure of their governments. Several conferences assumed sovereign powers; virtually all reintroduced multiparty systems. In the face of such challenges, governments began to attack their citizens. Consider figure 7.9, for example, which presents the mean Freedom House Ratings for all countries which were independent by 1988. On the surface, it portrays Africa's widely celebrated move to democracy.

---

[30] For confirmation of this account, see also Kenya (1992); Human Rights Watch/Africa (1993); Hempstone (1997).

[31] Which started in 1968.

[32] See also Barrows (1976); Abdullah (2004); Kandeh (2004).

Table 7.10 *National conferences.*

Country	Date	Duration	Election		Outcome: Incumbent	
			Month	F&F?	Ousted	Retained
Benin	Feb. 1990	1 week	Feb. 1991	yes	✓	
			Mar. 1996	yes	✓	
Congo	Feb. 1991	3 months	Aug. 1992	yes	✓	
Gabon	Mar. 1990	3 weeks	Dec. 1993	no		✓
Mali	Jul. 1991	2 weeks	Apr. 1992	yes	✓	
Niger	Jul. 1991	6 weeks	Feb. 1993	yes	✓	
Burkina Faso	Aug. 1991	2 months	Dec. 1991	no		✓
Ghana	Aug. 1991	7 months	Dec. 1992	yes		✓
Togo	Aug. 1991	1 month	Aug. 1993	no		✓
Zaire	Aug. 1991	1 year	–	–		
CAR	Oct. 1991	2 months	Aug. 1992	yes	✓	
Chad	Jan. 1993	3 months	Jun. 1996	no		✓

Note: F&F refers to whether international observers ruled the election "free and fair."
Source: Zartman (1997): 41.

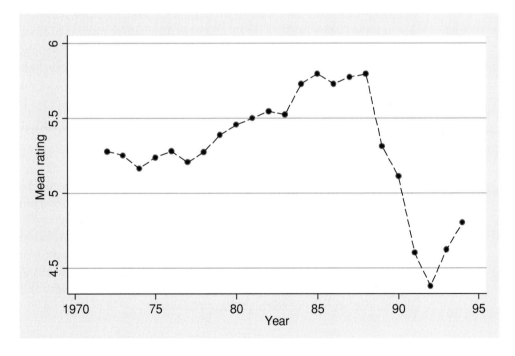

Figure 7.9 Civil liberties, by year, Freedom House Ratings, 1970–1995

But then take a deeper look and remove from the sample "sharp improvers," countries whose scores improved by more than 2 points between 1988 and 1994. These were São Tomé and Principe (−5), Benin, Cape Verde, and Malawi (−4), and Guinea-Bissau and South Africa (−3). Setting these aside, we can see higher (and therefore worse) average scores for the remaining forty countries, suggesting their relative failure to reform and, more relevantly, an upward spike in their scores in the early 1990s. Lying below such figures are such incidents as the Saba Saba killings in Kenya, when government forces shot down twenty-eight people at a rally called by an opposition party; the drowning of protestors in the Bé Lagoon of Lomé in 1991 and the slaughter of protestors by soldiers in 1993, which resulted in the fleeing of Togo by thousands of refugees (Heilbrunn 1993); the 1993 massacres of the ruling armed forces in Burundi; and genocides in Kasai, orchestrated by Mobutu to disrupt the political opposition (Huband 2001; see also Monga 1996 and Hempstone 1997). Just as political reform became more likely, so, too, did many governments become more willing to violate the rights of their citizens.

Recall the findings above: most elections do not result in the taking up of arms; they appear to induce demobilization. What appears to trigger the militarization of political life is the prospect of the loss of power. When incumbents sense that they will lose in open competition for office, they then mobilize the power of the state to vanquish their opponents. As phrased by Keen, there is an "elite backlash" (Keen 2000: 24). And civic society, feeling insecure, becomes more likely to organize in defense of their lives and property.

8 Conclusion

This chapter has probed the roots of political disorder and state collapse. Analyzing the conditions under which governments would use force to protect rather than to predate and people would delegate the use of coercion to those who govern, this chapter has addressed the causes of state breakdown in contemporary Africa. Africa shows that the Weberian state is not a given. It results when these choices form an equilibrium. The poverty of the state, the prospects of wealth from predation, and the prospect of losing office form the conditions under which this equilibrium will collapse and governments trigger the rise of political disorder.

References

Abdullah, Ibrahim, ed. (2004), *Between Democracy and Terror*. Dakar: CODESRIA
Acemoglu, Daron and James A. Robinson (2001), "A Theory of Political Transitions,"
    American Economic Review 91: 938–63

(2006), *Economic Origins of Dictatorship and Democracy*. Cambridge: Cambridge University Press

Adibe, Clement A. (2001), "Foreign Policy Decisionmaking in Anglophone West Africa," in G. M. Khadiagala and T. Lyons, eds., *African Foreign Policies*. Boulder, CO: Lynne Rienner

Alemayehu Geda (2007), "The Political Economy of Growth in Ethiopia," chapter 4 in Benno J. Ndulu, Stephen A. O'Connell, Jean-Paul Azam, Robert H. Bates, Augustin Kwasi Fosu, Jan Willem Gunning, and Dominique Njinkeu, eds., *The Political Economy of Economic Growth in Africa, 1960–2000*, vol. 2. Cambridge: Cambridge University Press

Ali, Ali Abdel Gadir and Ibrahim A. Elbadawi (2007), "Explaining Sudan's Economic Growth Performance," chapter 7 in Benno J. Ndulu, Stephen A. O'Connell, Jean-Paul Azam, Robert H. Bates, Augustin Kwasi Fosu, Jan Willem Gunning, and Dominique Njinkeu, eds., *The Political Economy of Economic Growth in Africa, 1960–2000*, vol. 2. Cambridge: Cambridge University Press

Ali, Taisier M. and Robert O. Matthews (1999), "Civil Wars and Failed Peace Efforts in Sudan," in T. M. Ali and R. O. Matthews, eds., *Civil Wars in Africa*. Montreal: McGill–Queen's University Press

Appiah, Joe (1996), *The Autobiography of an African Patriot*. Accra: Asempa Publishers

Arellano, M. and S. Bond (1991), "Some Tests of Specification for Panel Data," *Review of Economic Studies* 58: 277–97

Azam, Jean-Paul (1994), "How to Pay for Peace? A Theoretical Framework with Reference to African Countries," *Public Choice* 83: 173–84

Azam, Jean-Paul and Nadjiounoum Djimtoïngar (2007), "Cotton, War, and Growth in Chad, 1960–2000," chapter 3 in Benno J. Ndulu, Stephen A. O'Connell, Jean-Paul Azam, Robert H. Bates, Augustin Kwasi Fosu, Jan Willem Gunning, and Dominique Njinkeu, eds., *The Political Economy of Economic Growth in Africa, 1960–2000*, vol. 2. Cambridge: Cambridge University Press

Azam, Jean-Paul and Alice Mesnard (2003), "Civil War and the Social Contract," *Public Choice* 115: 455–75

Banks, Arthur (1999), "Cross-national Times Series Data Archive," Center for Social Analysis, Binghamton, NY. State University of New York at Binghamton

Barrows, Walter (1976), *Grassroots Politics in an African State*. New York: Africana Publishing

Bates, Robert H. (1981), *Markets and States in Tropical Africa*. Berkeley, CA and Los Angeles, CA: University of California Press

Bates, Robert H., Avner Greif, and Smita Singh (2002), "Organizing Violence," *Journal of Conflict Resolution* 46: 599–628

Block, Steven A. (2002), "Political Business Cycles, Democratization, and Economic Reform: The Case of Africa," *Journal of Development Economics* 67: 205–28

Boone, Catherine (2003), *Political Topographies of the African State: Territorial Authorities and Institutional Choice*. Cambridge and New York: Cambridge University Press

Bratton, Michael and Nicolas van de Walle (1997), *Democratic Experiments in Africa*. Cambridge: Cambridge University Press

Chaudry, Kiren Aziz (1997), *The Price of Wealth*. Ithaca, NY: Cornell University Press

Cilliers, Jakkie (2000), "Resource Wars – A New Type of Insurgency," in Christian Dietrich and Jakkie Cilliers, eds., *Angola's War Economy: The Role of Oil and Diamonds*. Pretoria: Institute for Security Studies

Collier, Paul, V. L. Elliott, Havard Hegre, Anke Hoeffler, Marta Reynal-Querol, and Nicolas Sambanis (2003), *Breaking the Conflict Trap*. Washington DC: Oxford University Press for the World Bank

Collier, Paul and Anke Hoeffler (2002), "Greed and Grievance in Civil Wars," CSAE, Oxford

Collier, Paul, Anke Hoeffler, and Catherine Pattillo (1999), "Flight Capital as a Portfolio Choice," Washington DC: International Monetary Fund

  (2002), "Africa's Exodus: Capital Flight and the Brain Drain as Portfolio Decisions," Washington, DC: The World Bank

Davies, Victor (2007), "Sierra Leone's Economic Growth Performance, 1961–2000," chapter 19 in Benno J. Ndulu, Stephen A. O'Connell, Jean-Paul Azam, Robert H. Bates, Augustin Kwasi Fosu, Jan Willem Gunning, and Dominique Njinkeu, eds., *The Political Economy of Economic Growth in Africa, 1960–2000*, vol. 2. Cambridge: Cambridge University Press

de Sousa, Clara Ana and Jose Sulemane (2007), "Mozambique's Growth Performance, 1960–1996," chapter 24 in Benno J. Ndulu, Stephen A. O'Connell, Jean-Paul Azam, Robert H. Bates, Augustin Kwasi Fosu, Jan Willem Gunning, and Dominique Njinkeu, eds., *The Political Economy of Economic Growth in Africa, 1960–2000*, vol. 2. Cambridge: Cambridge University Press

de Waal, Alex (1991), *Evil Days*. New York: Human Rights Watch

  (1997), *Famine Crimes: Politics and the Disaster Relief Industry in Africa*. Oxford: James Currey with African Rights and the International African Institute

Decalo, Samuel (1997), "Benin: The First of the New Democracies," in J. F. Clark and D. E. Gardinier, eds., *Political Reform in Francophone Africa*. Boulder, CO: Westview Press

Dianga, James Waore (2002), *Kenya, 1982: The Attempted Coup*. London: Penn Press

Dossou, Antonin S., Jean-Yves Sinzogan, with Sylviane Mensah (2007), "Economic Growth Benin: Lost Opportunties," chapter 22 in Benno J. Ndulu, Stephen A. O'Connell, Jean-Paul Azam, Robert H. Bates, Augustin Kwasi Fosu, Jan Willem Gunning, and Dominique Njinkeu, eds., *The Political Economy of Economic Growth in Africa, 1960–2000*, vol. 2. Cambridge: Cambridge University Press

Doumbouya, Sékou F. and Fodé Camara (2007), "Explaining Economic Growth in Africa: The Case of Guinea," chapter 17 in Benno J. Ndulu, Stephen A. O'Connell, Jean-Paul Azam, Robert H. Bates, Augustin Kwasi Fosu, Jan Willem Gunning, and Dominique Njinkeu, eds., *The Political Economy of Economic Growth in Africa, 1960–2000*, vol. 2. Cambridge: Cambridge University Press

Dudley, Billy (1982), *An Introduction to Nigerian Government and Politics*. Bloomington, IN: Indiana University Press

Ellis, Stephen (1999), *The Making of Anarchy*. New York: New York University Press

Englebert, Pierre (2000), *State Legitimacy and Development in Africa*. Boulder, CO: Lynne Rienner

Englebert, Pierre, Stacy Tarango, and Matthew Carter (2002), "Dismemberment and Suffocation: A Contribution to the Debate on African Boundaries," *Comparative Political Studies* 35: 1093–1118

Fearon, James D. (1995), "Rationalist Explanations for War," *International Organizations* 49: 379–414

(1998), "Commitment Problems and the Spread of Ethnic Conflict," in D. A. Lake and D. Rothchild, *The International Spread of Ethnic Conflict*. Princeton, NJ: Princeton University Press

(2003), "Ethnic Structure and Cultural Diversity by Country," *Journal of Economic Growth* 8: 195–222

Fearon, James and Laitin, David (2003), "Ethnicity, Insurgency and Civil War," *American Political Science Review* 97: 75–90

Fosu, Augustin (1992), "Political Instability and Economic Growth: Evidence from Sub-Saharan Africa," *Economic Development and Cultural Change* 40: 823–41

Fukuyama, Francis (2004), *State-building: Governance and World Order in the 21st Century*. Ithaca, NY: Cornell University Press

Gleditsch, Nils Petter, Peter Wallensteen, Mikael Eriksson, Margareta Sollenberg, and Havard Strand (2002), "Armed Conflict 1946–2001: A New Data Set," *Journal of Peace Research* 39: 615–37

Grossman, Herschel I. and D. Kim (1995), "The Economics of Revolutions," Department of Economics, Brown University, Providence, RI

Gyimah-Brempong, Kwabena and Marva E. Corley (2005), "Civil Wars and Economic Growth in South Africa," *Journal of African Economies* 14: 270–311

Gyimah-Brempong, Kwabena and Thomas L. Traynor (1999), "Political Instability, Investment, and Economic Growth in Sub-Saharan Africa," *Journal of African Economies* 8: 52–86

Hayward, Fred M. and Jimmy D. Kandeh (1987), "Perspectives on Twenty-five Years of Elections in Sierra Leone," in F. M. Hayward, ed., *Elections in Independent Africa*. Boulder, CO: Westview Press

Heilbrunn, John (1993), "Social Origins of National Conferences in Benin and Togo," *Journal of Modern African Studies* 31: 277–99

Hempstone, Smith (1997), *Rogue Ambassador: An African Memoir*. Sewanee, TN: University of the South Press

Herbst, Jeffrey (2000), *States and Power in Africa*. Princeton, NJ: Princeton University Press

Hills, Alice (2000), *Policing Africa*. Boulder, CO: Lynne Rienner

Hirsch, John (2001), *Sierra Leone: Diamonds and the Struggle for Democracy*. Boulder, CO: Lynne Rienner

Honaker, James (2000), "Issues in Multiple Imputation of Data of the African Research Program," Department of Government, Harvard University, Cambridge, MA

Howe, Herbert M. (2000), *Ambiguous Order: Military Forces in African States*. Boulder, CO: Lynne Rienner

Huband, Mark (1998), *The Liberian Civil War*. London: Frank Cass

(2001), *The Skull beneath the Skin: Africa After the Cold War*. Boulder, CO: Westview Press

Human Rights Watch (1999), *Angola Unravels.* New York: Human Rights Watch

Human Rights Watch/Africa (1993), *Divide and Rule: State Sponsored Ethnic Violence in Kenya.* New York: Human Rights Watch

Hyden, Goran (1981), *No Shortcuts to Progress.* Berkeley, CA and Los Angeles, CA: University of California Press

Jackson, Robert H. and Carl G. Rosberg (1982), *Personal Rule in Black Africa.* Berkeley, CA and Los Angeles, CA: University of California Press

Johnson, Douglas H. (2003), *The Root Causes of Sudan's Civil War.* Bloomington, IN: Indiana University Press

Judson, R. and A. Owen (1999), "Estimating Dynamic Panel Data Models: A Guide for Macroeconomists," *Economics Letters* 65: 9–15

Kandeh, Jimmy D. (2004), "In Search of Legitimacy: The 1966 Elections," in I. Abdullah, ed., *Between Democracy and Terror.* Dakar: CODESRIA

Kasekende, Louis A. and Michael Atingi-Ego (2007), "Restarting and Sustaining Growth in a Post-conflict Economy: The Case of Uganda," chapter 8 in Benno J. Ndulu, Stephen A. O'Connell, Jean-Paul Azam, Robert H. Bates, Augustin Kwasi Fosu, Jan Willem Gunning, and Dominique Njinkeu, eds., *The Political Economy of Economic Growth in Africa, 1960–2000,* vol. 2. Cambridge: Cambridge University Press

Kasozi, A. B. K. (1994), *The Social Origins of Violence in Uganda, 1964–1985.* Montreal: McGill–Queen's University Press

Keen, David (2000), "Incentives and Disincentives for Violence," in M. Berdal and D. Malone, eds., *Greed and Grievance: Economic Agendas in Civil Wars.* Boulder, CO: Lynne Rienner

Kenya, Republic of (1992), "Report of the Parliamentary Select Committee to Investigate Ethnic Clashes in Western and Other Parts of Kenya," Nairobi: Government Printer

Khan, Sarah Ahmed (1994), *Nigeria: The Political Economy of Oil.* Oxford: Oxford University Press for the Oxford Institute for Energy Studies

Kimenyi, Mwangi S. and Njuguna Ndung'u (2005), "Sporadic Ethnic Violence: Why Has Kenya not Experienced a Full Blown Civil War?," in Paul Collier and Nicholas Sambanis, eds., *Understanding Civil War: Evidence and Analysis (Volume 1: Africa).* Washington, DC: The World Bank

Kirk-Greene, A. H. M. (1971), *Crisis and Conflict in Nigeria.* London: Oxford University Press

MacGaffey, Janet (1987), *Entrepreneurs and Parasites: The Struggle for Indigenous Capitalism in Zaïre.* Cambridge: Cambridge University Press

   (1991), *The Real Economy of Zaire.* Philadelphia, PA: University of Pennsylvania Press

MacGaffey, Janet and Rémy Bazenguissa-Ganga (2000), *Congo–Paris: Transnational Traders on the Margins of the Law.* Oxford: James Currey

Miguel, Edward, Shanker Satyanath, and Ernest Sergenti (2004), "Economic Shocks and Civil Conflict," *Journal of Political Economy* 112(4): 725–53

Mitchell, Christopher (1993), "The Process and Stages of Mediation: Two Sudanese Cases," in D. Smock, ed., *Making War and Waging Peace: Foreign Intervention in Africa.* Washington, DC: United States Institute of Peace Press

Monga, Celestin (1996), *The Anthropology of Anger.* Boulder, CO: Lynne Rienner

Morrison, Donald, Robert Mitchell, John Paden, and Hugh Stevenson (1989), *Black Africa: A Comparative Handbook*. New York: Paragon House

Moselle, Boaz and Ben Polak (2001), "A Model of a Predatory State," *Journal of Law Economics and Organization* 17(1): 1–33

Mundt, Robert J. (1997), "Côte d'Ivoire: Continuity and Change in a Semi-democracy," in J. F. Clark and D. E. Gardinier, eds., *Political Reform in Francophone West Africa*. Boulder, CO: Westview Press

Murdoch, J. and Todd Sandler (2002), "Economic Growth, Civil Wars, and Spatial Spillovers," *Journal of Conflict Resolution* 46: 91–110

Muthoo, Abhinay (2000), "On the Foundations of Property Rights, Part 1: A Model of the State-of-nature with Two Players," TJJ

Mwega, Francis M. and Njuguna S. Ndung'u (2007), "Explaining African Growth Performance: The Case of Kenya," chapter 10 in Benno J. Ndulu, Stephen A. O'Connell, Jean-Paul Azam, Robert H. Bates, Augustin Kwasi Fosu, Jan Willem Gunning, and Dominique Njinkeu, eds., *The Political Economy of Economic Growth in Africa, 1960–2000*, vol. 2. Cambridge: Cambridge University Press

Nkurunziza, Janvier and Floribert Ngaruko (2007), "Why Has Burundi Grown so Slowly? The Political Economy of Redistribution," chapter 2 in Benno J. Ndulu, Stephen A. O'Connell, Jean-Paul Azam, Robert H. Bates, Augustin Kwasi Fosu, Jan Willem Gunning, and Dominique Njinkeu, eds., *The Political Economy of Economic Growth in Africa, 1960–2000*, vol. 2. Cambridge: Cambridge University Press

Nzongola-Ntanlaja, Georges (2002), *The Congo from Leopold to Kabila*. London: Zed Books

O'Toole, Thomas (1997), "The Central African Republic: Political Reform and Social Malaise," in J. F. Clark and D. E. Gardinier, eds., *Political Reform in Francophone Africa*. Boulder, CO: Westview Press

Pech, Khareen (2000), "The Hand of War: Mercenaries in the Former Zaire 1996–97," in A.-F. Musah and J. K. Fayemi, eds., *Mercenaries: An African Security Dilemma*. London: Pluto Press

Posen, Barry (1993), "The Security Dilemma and Ethnic Conflict," *Survival* 35: 27–47

Rapley, John (1993), *Ivoirien Capitalism: African Entrepreneurs in Côte d'Ivoire*. Boulder, CO: Lynne Rienner

Reno, William (1998), *Warlord Politics and African States*. Boulder, CO: Lynne Rienner
  (2000), "The Real (War) Economy of Angola," in Christian Dietrich and Jakkie Cilliers, eds., *Angola's War Economy*. Pretoria: Institute for Security Studies

Ross, Michael (2003), "The Natural Resource Curse: How Wealth Can Make You Poor," in I. Bannon and Paul Collier, eds., *Natural Resources and Violent Conflict*. Washington, DC: The World Bank

Rubin, D. B. (1996), "Multiple Imputation after 18+ years (with Discussion)," *Journal of the American Statistical Association* 91: 473–89

Sambanis, Nicholas (2001), "A Review of Recent Advances and Future Directions in the Quantitative Literature on Civil War." New Haven, CT: Yale University

Sawyer, Amos (1992), *The Emergence of Autocracy in Liberia.* San Francisco, CA: ICS Press

Schafer, Joseph L. (1997), "Imputation of Missing Covariates in the Multivariate Linear Mixed Model." Department of Statistics, University Park, PA: The Pennsylvania State University

Sen, Amartya (1984), *Poverty and Famines.* Oxford: Clarendon Press

Shillington, Kevin (1992), *Ghana and the Rawlings Factor.* London: Macmillan

Skaperdas, Stergios (1992), "Cooperation, Conflict, and Power in the Absence of Property Rights," *American Economic Review* 82: 720–38

(1996), "Gangs and the State of Nature," in P. Newman, *The New Palgrave Dictionary of Economics and the Law.* London: Palgrave

Snyder, Jack (2000), *From Voting to Violence.* New York: W.W. Norton

Strand, Havard, Lars Wilhelmsen, and Nils Petter Gleditsch (2002), "Armed Conflict Data Codebook," Peace Research Institute, Oslo

Suberu, Rotimi T. (2001), *Federalism and Ethnic Conflict in Nigeria.* Washington, DC: United States Institute of Peace Press

Tilly, Charles (1975), "Reflections on the History of State Making," in Charles Tilly, ed., *The Formation of National States in Western Europe.* Princeton, NJ: Princeton University Press

Usher, Dan (1989), "The Dynastic Cycle and the Stationary State," *American Economic Review* 79: 1031–44

Weber, Max (1921), "Politik als Beruf," *Gesammelte Politische Schriften.* Munich: Duncker & Humblot

Woodward, Peter (1995), "Sudan," in O. Furley, *Conflict in Africa.* London: I.B. Tauris

World Bank (1991), *Governance and Development.* Washington, DC: The World Bank

(1994), *Adjustment in Africa: Reform, Results, and the Road Ahead.* Washington, DC: The World Bank

Yates, Douglas (1996), *The Rentier State in Africa: Oil Rent Dependency and Neocolonialism in the Republic of Gabon.* Trenton, NJ: Africa World Press

Zakaria, Fareed (1997), "The Rise of Illiberal Democracy," *Foreign Affairs* 76: 22–43

Zartman, I. W. (1997), *Governance as Conflict Management.* Washington, DC: Brookings Institution Press

Zinn, Annalisa (2005), "Theory versus Reality: Civil War Onset and Avoidance in Nigeria Since 1960," in Paul Collier and Nicholas Sambanis, eds., *Understanding Civil War: Evidence and Analysis (Volume 1: Africa).* Washington, DC: The World Bank: 89–122

8 | Shocks, risk, and African growth

Jan Willem Gunning

1 Introduction: Hamlet without the prince?

Perhaps the most striking fact about the empirical growth literature is that risk, clearly a key determinant of investment behavior, plays only a peripheral role in it. Easterly *et al.* (1993) had already noted that the growth-regressions literature stresses country characteristics which are relatively stable over time whereas growth rates are very volatile. They concluded that shocks are apparently important relative to country characteristics in determining economic growth.

In the literature on the reasons for poor African growth, risk has long been a key suspect. Collier and Gunning (1999b), in a thematic paper for the AERC project, stressed that there are inherent reasons for Africa to be more risk-exposed (e.g. many African countries face a combination of semi-arid conditions and a very short growing season). In addition, policy regimes in Africa have often left a legacy of poor infrastructure, poor contract enforcement, weak financial sectors, policy uncertainty, and risk of conflict. Governments have thereby both increased the risk to which private agents are exposed and have undermined risk-coping mechanisms.

While there is consensus that risk is an important reason for Africa's poor growth performance, there still is remarkably little evidence. Simply put, the literature provides no firm basis for statements on the quantitative importance of risk for growth.

In section 2 we discuss some basic concepts. The standard growth regression implies, even if it does not include any measures of risk among the regressors, an effect of risk on growth. Remarkably, this implication seems to be universally ignored. We show that it might well be quantitatively important. Section 3 discusses the channels through which growth can be affected by risk. In section 4 we consider the scant empirical evidence. Here we focus on recent work using micro data sets for rural households. Section 5 draws some conclusions.

2   Growth and risk: the basics

We have noted that risk plays only a peripheral role in the empirical growth literature. To illustrate, consider the stochastic loglinear growth equation

$$y_{t+1} = \exp(A^*)s_t y_t^\alpha, \tag{1}$$

where y denotes income, s a multiplicative shock and A^* a constant (which could pick up the effect of a set of time-invariant regressors measuring, for example, initial educational endowments or the quality of institutions). The shocks s are i.i.d. and their distribution is lognormal: $\ln s \sim N(-\sigma/2, \sigma^2)$ so that $E s = \exp(-\frac{1}{2}\sigma^2 + \frac{1}{2}\sigma^2) = \exp(0) = 1$.[1] The parameter α satisfies $0 < \alpha < 1$.

Taking logs:

$$\ln y_{t+1} = A^* + \alpha \ln y_t + \ln s_t, \tag{2}$$

hence

$$\ln y_{t+1} - \ln y_t = (A^* + E \ln s) + (\alpha - 1)\ln y_t + (\ln s_t - E \ln s). \tag{3}$$

Substituting $A = A^* + E \ln s$ and $\varepsilon = (\ln s - E \ln s)$ gives

$$\ln y_{t+1} - \ln y_t = A + (\alpha - 1)\ln y_t + \varepsilon_t, \tag{4}$$

where the errors are i.i.d. and $\varepsilon \sim N(0, \sigma^2)$.

The loglinear specification (4) has become the workhorse of the growth regressions literature and it also plays a central role in the *Explaining African Growth Performance* project.

The deterministic growth model embedded in (2) is obtained by eliminating the error term $\ln s_t$:

$$\ln y_{t+1} - \ln y_t = A + (\alpha - 1)\ln y_t.$$

---

[1] Recall that if x is distributed lognormally: $\ln x \sim N(\mu, \sigma^2)$ then its mean is given by $Ex = \exp(\mu + \sigma^2/2)$. An important corollary is that if the variance σ^2 changes then the mean Ex is affected.

Clearly, this model exhibits (conditional) convergence[2] with a steady state

$$y = \exp[A^*/(1-\alpha)].$$

Note that the long-run income level y^* is independent of the initial income level y_0: there is, of course, hysteresis in this growth model, but the economy's starting position does not matter in the long run.

Returning to the stochastic model, from (4) $\ln y_{t+1}$ can be written as a constant plus an infinite series of normally distributed terms

$$\ln y_{t+1} = A[1 + \alpha + \alpha^2 + \ldots] + [\varepsilon_t + \alpha\varepsilon_{t-1} + \alpha^2\varepsilon_{t-2} + \ldots].$$
$$(5)$$

Note that the effect of any shock ε_τ wears off exponentially: while a shock obviously can dramatically affect growth (either positively or negatively) in the short run, there is no effect in the limit

$$\lim_{\tau \to \infty} \frac{\partial \ln y_{t+\tau}}{\partial \varepsilon_t} = \lim_{\tau \to \infty} \alpha^{\tau-1} = 0. \qquad (6)$$

The second term in square brackets in (5) involves only zero-mean shocks. It might therefore appear that risk has no long-run effect. After all $E \ln y_{t+1} = A[1 + \alpha + \alpha^2 + \ldots]$ and therefore $E\lim_{\tau \to \infty} = A/(1-a)$. This would seem to imply that the mean of the ergodic distribution of y, $E y_\infty$, is independent of the distribution of shocks.

If this were true then two economies which differed only in terms of the risk they faced would have the same expected value $E y_\infty$. Starting from the same y_0 they would therefore have (on average) the same growth rate: there would be no effect of risk on growth. The ride would, of course, be bumpier for the economy with more risk, but the two economies would (in expectation) reach the same destination.

However, while intuitively appealing, this inference is wrong. To see why, note from (5) that the ergodic distribution of $\ln y$ is normal

$$\ln y_\infty \sim N\left(\frac{A}{1-\alpha}, \frac{\sigma^2}{1-\alpha^2}\right).$$

Hence $E \ln y_\infty = A/(1-a)$. It follows that the mean of the ergodic distribution of y is given by:

$$E y_\infty = \exp\left[\frac{A}{1-\alpha} + \frac{\sigma^2}{2(1-\alpha^2)}\right]$$
$$= \exp\left[\frac{A^*}{1-\alpha} - \frac{\sigma^2}{2(1-\alpha)} + \frac{\sigma^2}{2(1-\alpha^2)}\right] \qquad (7)$$

---

[2] Convergence is conditional because A^* will differ between countries so that the income level in the steady state is country-specific.

since $A = A^* + E \ln s$ and $E \ln s = -\sigma^2/2$.   Substituting $y^* = \exp[A^*/(1-a)]$ it follows that

$$E y_\infty = y^* \exp\left[\frac{-\alpha}{1-\alpha^2}\frac{\sigma^2}{2}\right]. \tag{8}$$

This is an important result. It shows that a change in risk (i.e. a mean-preserving change in the distribution of ε through a change in the variance σ^2) does affect long-run growth. This effect is unambiguously negative: the expected value $E y_\infty$ is decreasing in the variance σ^2. (Note that if the variance goes to 0 then the mean $E y_\infty$ approaches the steady-state value of the deterministic model, y^*.)

Does this matter? Yes, it does: this effect of risk on the mean $E y_\infty$ can be substantial. For example, for Africa a fairly typical value for $\alpha - 1$, the coefficient of lagged income in the growth regression (4), would be -0.01. Also, African growth is highly volatile so that two-thirds of annual shocks might fall in, say, the range of $\pm 6\%$ of GDP. This would imply $\alpha = 0.99$ and $\sigma = 0.06$. For these parameter values we find from (9) (p. 301) that $E y_\infty = 0.91 y^*$: the effect of risk is to reduce the expected value of income 9 percent below the steady-state value. This is equivalent to the destruction of some 13 percent of the capital stock in the steady state of the deterministic model.[3] Alternatively, we can measure the effect in terms of the increase in income from some starting position to the steady state (or to the mean of the ergodic distribution). If the economy started at, say, 60 percent of the steady-state income level: $y_0 = 0.6 y^*$ then growth (in the sense of the long-run increase in income) would be $y^* - y_0 = 0.4 y^*$ in the deterministic case. Under risk growth would be (in expectation)

$$E y_\infty - y_0 = 0.91 y^* - 0.6 y^* = 0.31 y^*,$$

almost a quarter less than in the deterministic case. Again, the effect is large.

Clearly, the error term in (4) need not reflect risk: it could also capture measurement or specification error. Also, note that if ε does stand for risk then the specification is quite restrictive: all countries are assumed to face the same risk. In applications with micro datasets this may be realistic (e.g. if farm households face the same climatic risks) but for country growth regressions it is obviously implausible. This can be overcome by introducing country-specific measures of risk exposure as regressors. We return to this in section 4.

To summarize, it is often taken for granted that a standard growth regression such as (4) implies that risk has no effect on growth in the long run. The intuition for this is based on the correct observation that the effect of shocks wears off, as shown by (6). However, the intuition is wrong, for two reasons. First, an increase in risk (σ^2) does *not* amount to a mean-preserving spread

---

[3] Assuming a Cobb–Douglas technology with a capital exponent of $2/3$: $0.91 = (0.87)^{2/3}$.

of the ergodic distribution of ln y. That distribution has mean $A/(1 - \alpha)$ and, as we have seen, a change in risk affects A. Secondly, even if the change were to be mean-preserving for ln y, that would not preserve the mean of y since the logfunction is, of course, non-linear. For both these reasons the mean of the ergodic distribution of income, $E y_\infty$, *is* affected. In this particular case we can derive the distribution analytically. As shown in (8), the mean is decreasing in risk. Hence risk reduces growth.

This might be no more than a theoretical detail if it were not for our numerical example, which suggests that this effect of risk on growth might well be strong. However, this is only part of the story and very likely not the most important part. This is because we have until now implicitly assumed, rather implausibly, that risk does not affect economic behavior.

To see this note that (2) can be written as a policy function

$$\ln y_{t+1} = f(\ln y_t, s_t) \tag{9}$$

which summarizes agents' accumulation decisions. The policy function can be seen as a behavioral "rule" (which might well involve optimization), mapping current income and shocks (y_t, s_t) into next year's income level y_{t+1}. So far we have assumed that risk does not affect behavior: risk affects growth only because s is an argument of the policy function. This gives the *ex post* effect of risk: the ergodic distribution is affected for a *given* policy function, i.e. for unchanged behavior. Hence for the *ex post* effect the agent's perception that he faces risk is of no importance: growth is affected only if and when shocks actually occur. As illustrated by our numerical example, this *ex post* effect can be substantial.

The theoretical literature on growth under uncertainty is concerned with the effect of risk on the policy rule itself. In that literature, the question is whether agents change their behavior, i.e. the policy function f, in response to a perceived change in their exposure to risk. In this case the effect of risk will be to change next year's income level, controlling for the current level of income *and also for the current shock*. Risk then affects growth through a change in investment behavior rather than through the realized shocks. This is the *ex ante* effect of risk.[4] Analytical work suggests that this effect, too, can be substantial. Unfortunately, there is very little empirical material.

3   How does risk affect growth? Plausible channels

"Everyone knows that political instability is inimical to economic growth" (Bates 2004: 494). Bates' explanation for this folk wisdom is that political instability leads to uncertainty, notably concerning property rights. "If economic activity takes place amidst political turmoil, then changes in the law,

---

[4] See e.g. Dehn (2000); Elbers, Gunning, and Kinsey (2006).

regulations, or policies might alter the *expected value* of an investment program . . . leading to less capital formation and less growth" (Bates 2004: 496, my italics). Note that political instability is here interpreted as an increased probability of a bad outcome (such as expropriation). Hence the investor's expected return is affected: risk is not interpreted as a mean-preserving spread. I should emphasize that I use risk in this latter, technical sense, i.e. keeping the mean constant. If this is the way we understand instability (risk, volatility, . . .) then it is, of course, *not* self-evident that it reduces economic growth.

This technical point is of some importance: an increase in risk may well lead to *higher* growth. Consider a risk-neutral, profit-maximizing entrepreneur. How is he affected by risk in terms of the volatility of the price of his output? As long as there is any substitutability between fixed and variable inputs (so that he can vary output in response to price changes) he will benefit from volatility. This is a straightforward implication of Jensen's inequality: since the profit function is strictly convex in the output price, greater risk (a mean-preserving spread in the price distribution) raises the expected value of profits.

The condition that there is some scope for varying output *ex post* is not restrictive. For example, farmers can and do vary their effort in coffee harvesting in response to price changes, they can increase their non-agricultural labor supply in case of a drought, and they can delay planting until at least some of the rainfall risk has been resolved. Such *ex post* responses are well documented and they are sufficient for the profit function to be strictly convex.

However, under capital market imperfections the agent is unlikely to be risk-neutral. Whether a risk-averse agent who maximizes expected utility benefits from volatility is ambiguous: the flexibility effect (the increase in expected profits) and the effect of risk-aversion work in opposite directions. If risk aversion is sufficiently strong the agent's expected utility will be reduced by an increase in risk even though expected profits increase.[5] In models with a single asset this may lead to a negative effect of risk on investment; in models with multiple activities (e.g. rural household models with crop diversification) it affects not only the level of investment but also its composition: the agent may respond to an increase in risk by shifting savings to a safe asset.[6]

---

[5] Mash (1995) quantifies the welfare effect of commodity price volatility for producing countries. He shows that in many cases a substantial part of the welfare loss associated with risk aversion is offset by the increase in producers' mean income.

[6] Adam and O'Connell (1997, appendix 1; this does not appear in the published version of their paper) analyze the effect of risk on growth in such a context with a peasant household allocating its labor between a risky and a safe crop *ex ante*. There is no

The argument in section 2 was extremely general: risk is likely to affect growth, both *ex ante* and *ex post*. Theory does not tell us whether the effect is positive or negative, let alone whether it is quantitatively important. An obvious question is whether there are reasons to expect that the impact of risk on growth is negative and particularly severe in Africa. This could arise because African countries are more exposed to risk or because there is less scope for risk-coping strategies than in non-African developing countries. We consider both types of explanations.

Farmers face greater risks than elsewhere because in many African countries the growing season is very short so that minor climatic variations can have devastating consequences for agricultural production. For example, in Ethiopia, Zimbabwe, and Tanzania farmers face a probability of total crop failure of about 10 percent. Also, the prevalence of illnesses is high in rural areas. In addition there are policy-related risks. Price volatility is high as a result of poor market integration, often reflecting poor public provision of infrastructure. In addition, there is often considerable uncertainty regarding policy itself, e.g. taxation levels.

Africa's soil characteristics have led to very low population densities on much of the continent, in marked contrast to the Indian sub-continent. This makes risk-coping vastly more difficult. Credit markets, informal insurance, and other institutions which help agents to pool idiosyncratic risks typically require physical proximity to overcome moral hazard and informational asymmetry problems. Basing credit on collateral rather than reputation is seldom feasible. Of the key rural assets cattle is vulnerable to sickness and theft and land is, in many areas, abundant. Where risks are co-variant (most climatic risks and some of the disease risks) low population density precludes insurance. Risk pooling would work only if done over large geographical areas and with low population densities that option is likely to be undermined by informational asymmetries.[7]

In addition, there is a long history of government interventions undermining financial intermediation, particularly in rural areas. For example, the "soft-controls" regimes typically intervened to channel investment resources to urban activities.

---

flexibility *ex post*. This makes the profit function linear so that an increase in risk leaves expected profits unchanged. Any risk aversion is then sufficient for an increase in risk to reduce the optimal allocation of labor to the risky crop. Unfortunately, this neat result hinges on the extreme assumption ruling out *ex post* flexibility. Their key conclusion, that risk reduces the growth rate in this economy, is not true under flexibility without further restrictions – e.g. on the degree of relative risk aversion.

[7] At least under the usual institutional arrangements. A combination of local, informal insurance (which could overcome informational asymmetries) and formal reinsurance (to overcome co-variance by pooling risk over large geographical areas) might well be feasible but has not yet been attempted.

In these circumstances there is no scope for risk pooling (through insurance or credit) for co-variant risks. Rather, farm households adopt individual risk-coping strategies, notably diversification and consumption smoothing. One striking characteristic of African farm households is that they are highly diversified. Non-agricultural activities often account for a very large part of household income while farming operations themselves are highly diversified between various crops and livestock and also in space (multiple plots). Such diversification is a response to risk: there is, for example, evidence that in areas where rainfall is more reliable households are less diversified.[8]

Diversification is, of course, costly: the household forgoes the gains from specialization. In itself, this is a level effect which does not necessarily affect growth. However, level effects easily translate into growth rate effects, e.g. when there are indivisibilities in investment and imperfections in credit markets. This conjunction is typical for many rural areas in Africa.

The second risk-coping strategy which is common in the rural economy is consumption smoothing, typically using food stores, livestock, or both. These assets are themselves subject to substantial risks (livestock illnesses, theft, vermin, spoilage). As Dercon (2005) has stressed this makes consumption smoothing much less effective than suggested by consumption smoothing models with a riskless asset, notably Deaton (1991). (Note that the effectiveness of consumption smoothing is essentially the ability of the household to reduce the welfare loss induced by risk. This is conceptually distinct from the effect of risk on growth.)

Risk can affect growth both by changing the level of saving and its composition in terms of assets. Obviously, in models with a single asset (e.g. Deaton 1991; Elbers, Gunning, and Kinsey 2007) only the level of savings can be affected. That effect can go either way. If shocks affect only non-asset income but not the asset and the return on it then (as is well known) the sign of the effect of risk on savings depends on the sign of the third derivative of the utility function. In particular, if marginal utility is strictly convex in consumption than an increase in risk leads to more (precautionary) saving. However, if risk affects the asset itself (or, equivalently, the return on the asset) then the effect may well be negative (for the same utility function). Hence the precautionary motive and the fact that the agent has access only to an unsafe asset work in opposite directions.

There is nothing in theory to suggest the sign of the balance of these effects. Hence we do not know whether risk will reduce or increase savings and thereby growth. This depends on the specifics of the utility function, the production technology, and the nature of capital market imperfections. In Deaton's simulations (with a safe asset) the effect is positive: agents save

---

[8] See the discussion in Collier and Gunning (1999a) and the sources there cited.

when facing risk whereas otherwise they would not have saved. In the Elbers, Gunning, and Kinsey (2007) simulations (where the asset is risky) discussed in section 4 the effect is, however, negative.

We can say more when investment is difficult to reverse. Dixit and Pindyck (1994) have shown how irreversibility undermines the incentive to invest. This may well be particularly relevant for Africa. Monopolistic market structures make it difficult to reverse investment. For example, the market for second-hand machinery is very thin. (See Pattillo (1999), who documents this for Ghana.)

Now consider how the composition of savings would be affected. Consumption smoothing requires savings to be held in liquid form and this may not be compatible with an expansion of the household's production capacity. For example, the household may invest in food stores or cash holdings at the expense of investment in tree crops or land improvement. This composition effect of risk on growth might well be more pertinent for Africa than elsewhere. For example, Fafchamps, Gunning, and Oostendorp (2000) show that manufacturing firms in Zimbabwe hold large inventories (of inputs and outputs) in response to risk, notably the risk of late deliveries of inputs. These risks are unusually large in Africa, partly as a result of the neglect of transport infrastructure. The opportunity cost of this risk-induced stock holding may well be lower fixed investment. Similarly, in Nigeria manufacturing firms have invested heavily in diesel generators in response to the unreliability of the public sector provision of electricity. Again, this has presumably been at the expense of equipment investment (Collier and Gunning 1999a).

4   Does it matter? Empirical estimates

In Elbers, Gunning, and Kinsey (2007) we have estimated the effect of risk on growth using a micro-panel dataset. Hence in this study the unit of observation is the household rather than a country, as in the growth-regressions literature. The data are for a sample of 400 rural households in Zimbabwe who were resettled in the early 1980s under a (remarkably successful) land reform program. The sample households were first interviewed in 1983–4 (with some retrospective questions on asset holdings in 1980), again in 1987, and annually since 1992. There has been very little sample attrition, making this a unique African panel dataset.

All households received the same area of arable land. Since land cannot be sold (and there is virtually no land rental) households are basically identical in terms of land holding. However, after twenty years of heterogeneity in terms of demographic growth they differ markedly in land/man ratios. They also differ in terms of TFP: there are very large yield differences, controlling for farm inputs. Some are simply much better farmers than others. There are also very large differences in livestock ownership, livestock being the most important asset in this rural economy.

The key risk in these village economies is rainfall. This risk is, of course, highly co-variant, limiting the scope for local risk pooling. While there is some informal insurance in the survey villages there is no formal credit or insurance and the dominant risk-coping strategy is consumption smoothing through the use of livestock. Herds are built up after a good harvest while in bad times cattle are used for own consumption, either directly or by selling cattle to finance the purchase of maize, the staple crop.

Elbers, Gunning, and Kinsey (2007) model each household as a Ramsey-economy.[9] There is a single asset, livestock, which is an input into production and which can also be used for smoothing. The household maximizes expected utility over an infinite horizon, choosing optimal levels of consumption and investment (i.e. livestock accumulation). It takes into account that it faces risks and that today's investment affects its ability to cope with tomorrow's shocks. There are two types of shock, one affecting income (a good or a bad harvest), the other assets (e.g. a livestock birth or death). The households have rational expectations: they know the distribution of shocks. The outcome of the household's optimization can be written as a policy function which gives the optimal level of next year's capital stock (and hence also the optimal levels of this year's consumption and investment) as a function of the current asset position (livestock ownership) and current shocks.

In principle, given a utility function, a production function, and the distribution of shocks one could solve the model and derive the household's (recursive) policy function. However, analytical solutions can be obtained for only a few (uninteresting) cases. In the macro-growth literature exactly the same problem arises. The standard solution in that literature is to abandon the attempt to estimate the structural model: typically some linearization is adopted instead. For example, most textbooks show that the canonical growth regression can be obtained either from the Solow model (i.e. with a fixed savings rate) or from the Ramsey model (with forward-looking investment behavior) by loglinearization around the steady state. This is expedient but for our present purposes very problematic: once we abandon the structural form of the model little can be said on how risk affects investment behavior and hence growth.

Elbers, Gunning, and Kinsey (2007) use econometric simulation techniques to estimate their micro-model in its structural form. The survey did

---

[9] This is clearly extreme: each household is, like Robinson Crusoe, entirely on its own: it cannot share inputs or outputs with other households. Elbers, Gunning, and Kinsey (2007) relax this assumption and perform a test of risk pooling, but they conclude that in this sample there is indeed little risk pooling.

not collect consumption data but it did collect data on agricultural production, inputs, and the capital stock (herd size).[10] In addition rainfall data were available. This was sufficient to identify the model. The estimated model was then used, again by employing simulation techniques, to generate growth paths (time series of income or of the capital stock) for each household in the sample. For each path shocks are generated in every year as random draws from a given joint distribution.

Figure 8.1 shows simulation results for a particular household, showing the real value of the capital stock (scaled by the household's labor force) over a fifty-year period, starting at $t = 0$ from the household's actual starting position in 1980. (This household has values for TFP and initial livestock ownership very close to the sample average. The results are therefore very similar to those for the whole sample.) The figure shows four paths.

The "sample path under risk" is one possible growth path, defined by a particular series of fifty randomly drawn shocks, one for each year. The point to note is how very volatile this path is: the herd size frequently changes by as much as 50 percent up or down in the course of one or two years. Clearly, the econometrician who had time-series data for part of this growth path would find it very difficult to say something about the underlying growth process.

For each household a large number (100,000) of such growth paths were generated. In each year the expected value of the household's capital stock was then calculated as the mean over these paths. The time path of this mean ($E k_t$) is shown in figure 8.1 as "average under risk." The averaging procedure, of course, removes the volatility. The path shows what herd size the household would expect to attain at future dates, from the standpoint of $t = 0$.

Note that the path shows very rapid growth in the first twenty years: in this period, k trebles. This reflects the very low initial asset holding of this particular household. After the first twenty years the path levels off: $E k_{20}$ is apparently already close to the mean of the ergodic distribution, $E k_\infty$.[11] What this "average under risk" path illustrates is the power of convergence. Since the household starts out very poor it grows initially very rapidly, at some 9 percent per year in the first ten years.

Now consider the effect of risk on growth. We remove risk in two steps so as to be able to decompose the effect of risk on growth into the *ex ante* and the *ex post* effect. In the first step the policy function

$$k_{t+1} = f(k_t, \varepsilon_t) \tag{10}$$

[10] Using capital stock rather than consumption data probably reduces measurement error.
[11] There still is growth in the long run: TFP grows exogenously at about 1 percent per annum. However, since in figure 8.1 the capital stock is scaled by the household's labor supply measured in efficiency units its long-run level is (in expectation) constant.

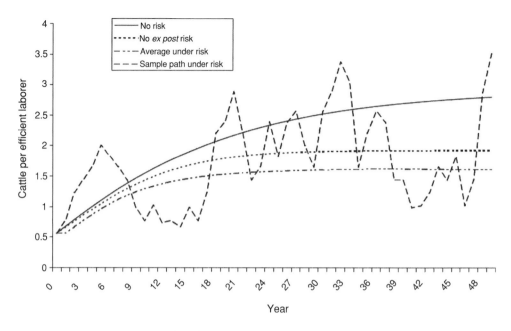

Figure 8.1 Growth and risk, selected households
Source: Elbers, Gunning, and Kinsey (2007).

is kept unchanged but instead of drawing shocks ε_τ randomly $\varepsilon_\tau = 0$ is imposed for all years: the agent expects to be hit by shocks but these never occur. This eliminates the *ex post* effect but leaves the *ex ante* effect intact: by construction the agent continues to behave as if shocks are generated from the original distribution. This procedure generates a single path, designated "No *ex post* risk" in figure 8.1.

The final step is to eliminate the *ex ante* effect as well by removing variance from the distribution of shocks. In the limit ε_τ is not only actually equal to zero for all t, but is known to be zero in advance. In other words, the agent experiences no shocks and is fully aware that he faces no risk. This changes the policy function f: the agent behaves differently when he perceives that there is no risk. The result is the path denoted "no risk."

The effect of risk on the level of the capital stock can now be measured in figure 8.1 as the vertical distance between the "no risk" and "average under risk" paths. Clearly, the effect is massive: the household would have accumulated much more capital in the absence of risk. The effect can be decomposed into the *ex ante* and the *ex post* effect by measuring the distance from the "No risk" to the "No *ex post* risk" path and from there to the "Average under risk" path. Note that for this household the total effect of risk is dominated by the *ex ante* effect.

These results also apply to the sample households as a group. In the sample risk reduces the expected long-run value of the capital stock, $E K_\infty$ 46 percent below the steady-state value in the deterministic case, $y^*: E k_\infty = 0.54 k^*$. This is a striking result. Risk does not only make growth very volatile (illustrated vividly by the "Sample path under risk") but it very much lowers growth *on average*. Of this reduction two-thirds is accounted for by the *ex ante* effect, the rest by the *ex post* effect. This also is a remarkable result. In much of the empirical literature (e.g. on vulnerability) it is implicitly assumed that the actual shocks are an adequate measure of the effect of risk. But they are not: most of the impact is internalized in the form of different investment decisions. Hence growth is very much affected *even when no shocks occur.*

The Zimbabwe study appears to be the first micro-based study finding a strong effect of risk on growth. The famous study of Rosenzweig and Wolpin (1993) used the Indian International Crops Research Institute for the Semi-Arid Tropics (ICRISAT) data and concluded that introducing formal insurance would have *no* effect on growth. Their explanation was that households engaged in efficient informal insurance (risk pooling within the village) so that if actuarially fair insurance were to be offered there would be no takers. There are technical problems with the way they modeled risk. However, if we accept their finding it can, obviously, be true only if risk is largely idiosyncratic. For otherwise there would be only limited scope for informal insurance.

Whatever may be the case in the ICRISAT villages, the literature on African economies stresses the importance of co-variant risks (related to climate, warfare, and government policies). In Africa, co-variant risks are dominant and typically there are no formal financial markets to enable risk pooling at a higher level or borrowing at a given interest rate. Under these circumstances the situation will be more like that in the Zimbabwean villages with self-insurance through consumption smoothing as the key risk-coping strategy. That makes the Zimbabwe results interesting for the study of African growth. However, they are only suggestive. Whether the key result – that risk in those circumstances massively reduces growth – generalizes to other contexts, we do not know.

Note that we get an effect of risk on growth without appealing to endogenous growth mechanisms such as productivity spillovers. These might well be important. For example, there are likely to be learning-by-doing externalities in manufacturing which are not captured if risk induces portfolio adjustment at the expense of investment in manufacturing. Adam and O'Connell (1997) emphasize such compositional effects.

What about the macro-evidence? Easterly *et al.* (1993) included trade shocks variables in country growth regressions and concluded that trade shocks were a major part of the story. They did not attempt to distinguish between the *ex ante* and *ex post* effects of risk or between positive and negative shocks. Dehn (2000) made both these distinctions. He found that trade shocks have no significant *ex ante* effect: contrary to popular belief the fact that African countries are exposed to large trade shocks does not in itself explain their poor growth performance. Dehn did find a strong *ex post* effect, but only for negative shocks. Booms are apparently by and large handled in such a way that they do not contribute to sustained growth while busts have a significant negative growth effect.[12]

Measures of internal shocks (e.g. political assassinations) are often included in growth regressions. There are obvious endogeneity problems here. In addition, inevitably risk is measured as the actual number of shocks in a short period (e.g. a decade). This introduces a bias towards identifying risk only with the *ex post* effect and thereby understating its importance.

5   Conclusion

In cross-country growth regressions the effect of risk is inadequately accounted for. First, the standard loglinear specification implies an effect of risk on growth which may well be substantial but which is invariably ignored in the analysis. Secondly, while often some attempt is made to capture the effect of risk directly by introducing regressors which capture a country's exposure to risk (e.g. the volatility of its terms of trade or the number of political assassinations), deriving good measures from short time series is difficult and in practice the measures may capture the *ex post* effect but only a small part of the *ex ante* effect of risk. The effect of risk on growth may thereby be seriously under-estimated.

We noted that African economies may well face more risk than other countries (e.g. because of their reliance on rainfed agriculture in a situation where growing seasons are extremely short). In addition, the scope for risk-coping is often lower than elsewhere: low population density makes it difficult to rely on insurance or credit. Governments have increased the risk exposure of private agents while at the same time undermining institutions which support risk-coping.

There is unfortunately very little empirical evidence on the effect of risk on growth. The macro-literature usually fails to distinguish between the *ex post* and *ex ante* effects and may well miss much of the latter.[13] For example, the *ex ante* effect may reduce growth for a long period in, say, Cameroon, because agents take into account the possibility of war, even when

---

[12] This supports the case study evidence on trade shocks, e.g. Collier and Gunning (1999c).
[13] A notable exception is Ramey and Ramey (1995).

peace is preserved throughout the period considered.[14] More generally, we would want to know to what extent growth is reduced by governance-based risk or by governance-related restrictions on risk-coping by private agents. However, on these questions there is as yet no evidence. The micro-evidence for Zimbabwe showed a very strong impact of risk, mostly through the *ex ante* effect. This type of work is currently being extended to other African countries. This will enable us to assess whether the Zimbabwe results are very special or whether they generalize.

References

Adam, C. S. and S. A. O'Connell (1997), "Aid, Taxation and Development in Sub-Saharan Africa," CSAE Working Paper 97/5, CSAE, University of Oxford and World Bank Working Paper 1885

Bates, R. (2004), "On *The Politics of Property Rights* by Haber, Razo, and Maurer," *Journal of Economic Literature* 42: 494–500

Collier, P. and J. W. Gunning (1999a), "Explaining African Economic Performance," *Journal of Economic Literature* 37: 64–111

  (1999b), "The Microeconomics of African Growth, 1950–2000," Thematic Paper for the AERC Collaborative Research Project on "Explaining African Economic Growth, 1950–2000," World Bank and CSAE, University of Oxford, mimeo

  (1999c), *Trade Shocks in Developing Countries*. Oxford: Oxford University Press

Deaton, A. (1991), "Saving and Liquidity Constraints," *Econometrica* 59: 1221–48

Dehn, J. (2000), "Commodity Price Uncertainty and Shocks: Implications for Investment and Growth," D. Phil. thesis, University of Oxford

Dercon, S. (2005), "Risk, Insurance and Poverty: A Review," in S. Dercon, ed., *Insurance against Poverty*. A Study Prepared by the World Institute for Development Economics Research of the United Nations University (UNU-WIDER). Oxford and New York: Oxford University Press

Dixit, A. and R. Pindyck (1994), *Investment under Uncertainty*. Princeton, NJ: Princeton University Press

Easterly, W., M. Kremer, L. Pritchett, and L. H. Summers (1993), "Good Policy or Good Luck? Country Growth Performance and Temporary Shocks," *Journal of Monetary Economics* 32: 459–83

Elbers, C., J. W. Gunning, and B. Kinsey (2007), "Growth and Risk: Methodology and Micro Evidence," *World Bank Economic Review* 21: 1–20 forthcoming

Fafchamps, M., J. W. Gunning, and R. Oostendorp (2000), "Inventories and Risk in African Manufacturing," *Economic Journal* 110: 861–93

Mash, R. (1995), "The Consequences of International Trade Price Volatility for National Income and Welfare: Theory and Evidence," D. Phil. thesis, University of Oxford

Pattillo, C. (1999), "Risk, Financial Constraints and Equipment Investment in Ghana: A Firm-Level Analysis," in P. Collier and C. Pattillo, eds., *Investment*

---

[14] I am indebted to Steve O'Connell for this suggestion.

and Risk in Africa. Basingstoke and London: Macmillan and New York: St. Martin's Press: 120–1

Ramey, G. and V. A. Ramey (1995), "Cross-Country Evidence on the Link Between Volatility and Growth," *American Economic Review* 85: 1138–51

Rosenzweig, M. and K. I. Wolpin (1993), "Credit Market Constraints, Consumption Smoothing and the Accumulation of Durable Production Assets in Low-Income Countries," *Journal of Political Economy* 101: 233–44

PART 3

Explanation

9 | The evolution of global development paradigms and their influence on African economic growth

Benno J. Ndulu

1 Introduction: growth syndromes and ideas

A key feature of the African growth experience is that it is predominantly episodic and that these episodes are largely driven by policy choices. A key question of interest for this chapter is what explains these policy choices. Many of the case studies in the AERC Growth Project adopt an interest-based neoclassical political-economy framework to explain the policy choices that

I would like to thank Lopamudra Chakraborti for very able assistance in the compilation and analysis of World Values Survey and African leadership data.

have impacted the episodic growth performance. This chapter complements such analyses by exploring how global ideas influenced policy choices and hence growth syndromes.[1] The argument is that global ideas have had a powerful role in shaping the growth environment in African countries. They have influenced the ideological and technical content of chosen development strategies; standards of peer review, peer pressure, and performance assessment; and the levels and character of official development assistance (ODA). The development paradigms have been shaped, in turn, by the dominant ideologies of the time; the evolving frontier of development economics in response to actual experience; and the changing attitudes towards the roles of the market, state, private sector, institutions, and political regimes.

A key theme of this chapter is how the influence of global ideas and development paradigms is mediated through human agency, particularly leaders, but also through interaction between governments and aid agencies in shaping these attitudes, and through interaction between world and local societal values. It is also worth exploring the extent to which domestic values and paradigms of leading nations like the USA (and the UK) can indirectly influence policy in the developing world through their leadership in international aid agencies, such as the World Bank and the IMF, and through multinational corporations. The role of aid agencies in transmitting global ideas and standards, particularly through aid conditionality, is likely to be uncommonly strong in Africa, given the significantly higher dependence on ODA within the region than elsewhere in the world.

The evolution of national policy paradigms evident in the African case studies entailed simultaneous changes in political regimes and policy choices. In chapters 2 and 3 of this volume, the most dramatic change in the growth syndromes over time is the displacement of syndrome-free cases by control regimes between the late 1960s and the mid-1980s, and their subsequent restoration post-1990, during the period of intense democratization in Africa (Bratton and van de Walle 1997). The periodization of dominant growth syndromes and associated political regimes, as discussed later, closely corresponds to the shifts in the global development paradigms.

Following the discussion of the evolution of global development paradigms in section 2, I explore the workings of three key channels of transmission of global ideas to the process of shaping the growth syndromes (environment) of African economies. In section 3.1, I explore how global development paradigms shaped the visions and the attitudinal disposition of leaders towards the market, trade, and business. The particular focus

---

[1] In chapter 2, Collier and O'Connell identify beliefs to be one of the motivators for such choices, the other two being institutions and interest groups, as discussed earlier.

here will be on the first generation of African leaders, who embraced vision-ary roles in shaping the development paths of their countries and operated under relatively weak institutional and donor conditionality constraints. The second channel of influence, elaborated in section 3.2, is the influence of global opinion leaders on shaping local societal views on acceptable pol-icy choices and governance standards. This is complemented by patterns of private resource flows often reflecting global norms of acceptable economic and political behavior. The third channel, discussed in section 3.3, is exter-nal advice given by aid agencies and application of external conditionality to discipline policy choices. More specifically, in section 3.3, I undertake an analysis of the systematic link between development paradigms, country performance assessment and aid allocation using the World Bank's Coun-try Policy and Institutional Assessment (CPIA) rankings. Section 4 of the chapter draws some conclusions.

2   The evolution of global development paradigms

During the 1960s and 1970s the primary concern among the international development community was market failure, and hence a perceived need for state intervention to engender development. The mid-1980s saw a major shift towards emphasis on government failure; hence, constraining the state was seen as a prerequisite for growth. The 1990s saw a moderation of this position to that of making the state work with the market through improved governance structures and more inclusive political processes. The role of the state, in this regard, is primarily to address coordination failure, where opportunities are substantial but need purposive government action to real-ize them. Papers by Adelman (2000) and Collier, Dollar, and Stern (2000) presented at ABCDE Europe are among the more recent ones to discuss this evolution.

   This global evolution of the size and role of the state is partly mirrored by trends in government consumption expenditure as a proportion of GDP. Figure 9.1 shows unambiguously that the African governments' claims on GDP grew virtually in tandem with the rest of the developing world during the 1970–85 period, consistent with the sharp rise in *dirigisme* as the global paradigm of the day. This happened in Africa despite the fact that actual resources commanded and expended on consumption by African govern-ments *per capita* never grew as fast as in the rest of the world. The sharp drop in this ratio after 1985 in the rest of the developing world and after 1990 in Africa reflected the swing of the pendulum to the paradigm of a minimalist state and greater concern with government failures.

   The schematic table below (table 9.1) illustrates how the global devel-opment paradigms have shifted over time. It is noteworthy that what is

Table 9.1 *Evolution of the global development paradigms.*

Dominant paradigms	Role of state	Role of market	Institutions	Political paradigms
1960–70 Market-friendly	Supportive of market	Dominant	Not focal	Not focal
1970–85 Emphasis on market failure CONTROLS (Regulatory, populist)	Dominant and leads market	Residual	Not focal	Not focal
1985–90 Market-oriented	Minimalist	Dominant	Increasingly important to support markets	Not major expressed concern
1990–to date	Supportive of (follows) the market	Dominant	Governance and social cohesion/ capital	Inclusive political regimes

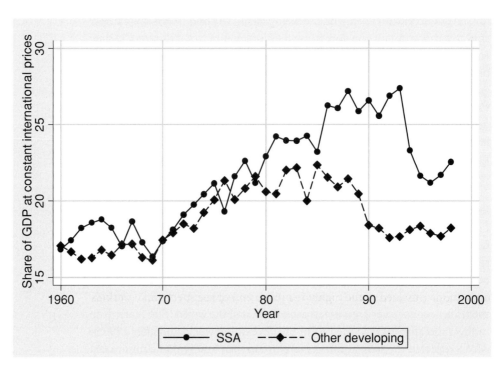

Figure 9.1 Median government consumption, thirty-nine SSA versus forty-five Other developing, 1960–2000.

characterized as "syndrome-free" in the 1960s and in the post-1990 period entails very different types of desired involvement of the state and very different societal values, as we shall later show in section 3.

The schematic partially adopts Robert Wade's (1993) distinction between two types of government intervention: "leading the market" and "following the market." "Leading the market" means that government initiates projects that private business people would not undertake at current prices (*ex ante* unviable at current prices, but viable at shadow prices) or that are unviable at both current and shadow prices. "Following the market" means that the government wants to assist in projects that private business wants to undertake at current prices (*market-oriented dirigisme*). In East Asia, for example, successful states either followed the market or, where they led the market did so via projects that were in most cases *ex ante* viable at shadow prices. Botswana would fall in the latter group. Success depended on the institutional capacity of a state to define (and redefine) and pursue realistic long-term development policies in a given socio-economic setting.

Below, I elaborate on the three main phases in the evolution of the global development paradigm and its influence on the dominant growth syndromes adopted in African case study countries.

2.1   Phase 1: 1960s–mid-1980s – the dominance of control regimes

Migdal (1988) describes the development paradigm in this phase as follows: the notion of "development" rested on the concept of state as the "primum mobile" of socio-economic progress. The idea of "developmentalism" and the idea of state intervention were seen as inseparable, and policies and planning were seen as offering boundless possibilities. Leaders of third world countries as well as the entire international community saw development as a matter of "social engineering." A country without a five-year plan was not worth its salt. The UN and its agencies defined norms and targets to be reached within a certain decade or sector. It was taken for granted by multilateral and bilateral development agencies that the state had a pivotal role to play in transforming societies from backwardness to modernity (Ljunggren 1993: 7–8). The role of the state was pervasive as the "great majority of the developing nations clustered at the highly regulated end of the spectrum" (Perkins 1988: 5).

The painful experience from the great depression and the effects of the First World War, which amplified the concerns with poverty, particularly in "backward" agrarian economies, combined to strongly underpin the emergence of this paradigm. Development economics provided the rationale and instruments for its implementation.

Three features were deemed fundamental to economic development of the poor countries. First, latecomers could learn from the development experience of pioneers. Gerschenkron (1962) emphasized the advantages of "backwardness," citing free access to a "book of blue print for development." The state would play an active role, he envisioned, in utilizing the stock of technological knowledge garnered by the pioneering group. Many of Africa's early leaders, as we discuss later, espoused the possibility of accelerated development and the imperative of catching up with the prosperity of the industrial countries ("We must run while they walk": Julius Nyerere).

Secondly, it was clear that affluence was strongly associated with industrialization, an empirical regularity that was later confirmed by Kuznet's work (1966) and amplified by Chenery and Syrquin (1975). Therefore, an important part of the development agenda (which was widely believed by the first generation of African leaders) was to achieve structural change towards a larger share of national income being sourced from industry. Two major bottlenecks lay in the way of the big push towards industrialization. The first constraint was the lack of an abundant labor supply whose absorption into industry would not bid up wages and thereby undermine the profitability of industrialization. Lewis' (1954) seminal paper on the dual economy provided the rationale for perfectly elastic supply of labor released from agriculture where its marginal product was zero or released at a constant, institutionally set wage below the industrial wage (Ranis and Fei 1961). Much of this was later questioned by an equally important work by Schultz (1964), which provided the intellectual underpinning to explain the rapid industrialization that took place in the developing world until 1974. The second constraint was that of foreign exchange, since industrialization depended significantly on foreign inputs. Inelasticity of export demand, particularly of primary commodities, was believed to constrain the generation of requisite import capacity. As a result, import substitution was sought out as the only secure means to indirectly earn foreign exchange for industrialization.

Thirdly, the workings of the market were deemed inadequate for the "great development project" on account of several failures necessitating the use of planning to address coordination failures. Theorists of growth and development had been preoccupied with market failures since the 1920s, but these concerns only intensified after the Second World War. Thus Keynesian macroeconomics, the economics of imperfect competition, and the principles of economic planning embodied in the new "market socialism" were first developed in the 1930s (Bell 1994). But these ideas found broad application within development circles only after 1945, in response to three conceptual developments: (1) a systematic reconsideration of Marshall's microeconomic grounds for government intervention;

(2) Rosenstein-Rodan's Investment Board (Rosenstein-Rodan 1943) for the big push, later elaborated by Nurkse (1953), who advocated a full-bodied Ministry of Planning to address coordination failures; and (3) a subsequent shift of focus to a decentralized approach to planning under a Central Office of Project Evaluation using shadow prices derived from the analyses by Balassa (1971), Diamond and Mirrlees (1971a, 1971b), and Little, Scitovsky, and Scott (1970) (the former on optimal taxation).

2.2   Phase 2: 1980s – a sharp turn away from the strong role of the state

The next phase in the evolution of the global development paradigm was based on the questioning of the notion of "government failure" as well as the validity of the dual development paradigm. The state had been previously viewed as having a substantial role in repairing *market failures*. This approach, which had been predominant since the 1950s, began to lose its credibility in the 1980s as it became clear that *government failure* was an equally pervasive and serious problem (Wade 1990: 8–9).

Two sets of factors were important for the change: (1) conceptual developments that questioned much of the earlier work on market failure and therefore a minimal role for the state; and (2) significant changes in the leadership of several countries that were accompanied by changes in attitudes towards the old paradigm. The changes in the 1980s were largely in reaction to the failure of the state to engender growth and much less to changing concepts of what was needed for growth, which became a major preoccupation of empirical and conceptual growth research in the 1990s.

One pillar of the old paradigm rested on assumptions about the rural economy. The first of them, which supported the claim that agriculture is a source of abundant cheap labor supply for industrialization, was shaken by the work of Schultz (1964). Stiglitz (1988) contended that the imperfections in the rural credit market were necessarily welfare-reducing and argued that state intervention was not justified because planners did not have the information to eliminate this market failure.

The second pillar was skepticism regarding the ability of developing countries to access capital and international markets. The "Four Dragons consensus" challenged this skepticism (Little, Scitovsky, and Scott 1970; Balassa 1971). The strategy of planning and import substitution was abandoned for outward-oriented growth by policy-makers of the governments of South Korea and Taiwan, who showed that people from developing countries could produce goods that satisfied consumers in the North and could function in an industrialized world (Wade 1990).

Partly questioning Rostow's (1965) and Denison's (1967) "big push" theory of development, Stiglitz (1988) argued that a country's growth involved more than the accumulation of factors of production. Invoking

Schumpeter's (1954) theory, he underlined the importance of efficient financial intermediation in steering existing resources to their most efficient uses. Stiglitz's critique also challenged the effectiveness of government intervention in setting up development banks. Emphasis was laid instead on the development of capital markets to exploit the positive relationship between economic development and financial intermediation (Goldsmith 1969).

2.3   Phase 3: 1990s onwards – the paradigm of balance and one-world consensus

The "one-world consensus" that emerged during the decade and a half that followed the 1982 debt shock represented an important shift from the 1980s focus on a minimalist state. The consensus was prompted by the preponderant government failures of the 1970s. It originated from the recognition that structural and market-oriented reforms tended to be astonishingly slow in producing positive effects. This new consensus advocated a balance between market and political institutions.

This position was clearly articulated in the World Bank's 1991 *World Development Report* (WDR) (World Bank 1991), which concluded that the challenge to policy-makers in developing countries was to exploit the complementarities between state and the market. Some of the WDR's policy prescriptions are outlined below:

- Investing in people requires an efficient public role since the supply of basic social services (e.g. education, healthcare, and nutrition) would remain sub-optimal if left to the private sector.
- An enabling climate – including emphasis on competition (to foster innovation and cost efficiency), infrastructure, and institutions – is essential for private enterprise to flourish.
- In a globally integrated world, high rates of growth will be achieved only if openness to trade and flow of productive resources is not excessively constrained.
- Macroeconomic stability is an essential part of a stable development environment.

As I shall argue in section 4, the consensus also reflected changes in societal values both globally and within Africa. These changes have been reflected in the standards applied by development institutions for assessing the policy environment for growth and poverty reduction, a leading example of which is the World Bank's Country Policy and Institutional Assessment (CPIA), discussed further below.

3 From global ideas to African syndromes: channels of transmission

3.1 Development paradigms, leaders, and growth syndromes: Fabianism and African control regimes

Recent research demonstrates the importance of leadership in achieving and sustaining growth. Glaeser *et al.* (2004) find that in an initially poor economy, economic growth since the 1960s has been to a significant extent a consequence of having the right leader. The authors establish that in the post-1960 growth record, leader fixed effects have been huge and widely dispersed, implying that some leaders have been associated with rapid growth while others have not. They show that good leaders accumulate capital, avoid wars, and are rewarded with longer tenure in countries with higher educational achievements. Jones and Olken (2004), citing Easterly *et al.* (1993), argue that the weak correlation of growth in different time periods and within countries is symptomatic of the existence of different growth regimes. They find robust empirical evidence that national leaders, particularly in autocratic settings, matter in explaining these shifts in growth. They do so either directly through influencing the policy environment or indirectly through shaping institutions.

Rodrik and Subramaniam (2004) demonstrate the importance of attitudinal disposition of leadership towards markets and business for growth in a country context, using the example of India's growth revival since 1980, well before the market liberalization phase of the 1990s. They make an important distinction between a "pro-market" and "pro-business" orientation. The former is concerned with removing impediments to the market, favoring entrants and consumers. The latter, on the other hand, is focused on raising the profitability of established enterprises – favoring incumbents and producers. The sequence adopted by countries has varied, with differential impacts.

Evolution of global development paradigms and ideas has been influential in shaping the kind of policy choices leaders make, with consequences for the growth environment and ultimately growth outcomes. This channel of influence was particularly potent among the first generation of African leaders. At independence, these leaders typically promised growth and poverty reduction in exchange for development autocracy anchored on their ideals. Although there were variations across countries, the promise typically combined a sense of urgency in achieving catch-up with developed countries, economic nationalism through indigenization, and the pursuit of development through redistribution. Governments were to use their fiscal powers, the external resources channeled through them, and indirect controls on private sector resource allocation to these ends. The most influential among

Table 9.2 *Episodes of growth syndromes and leadership, African countries.*

a   Episodes of occurrence of different types of leadership

Period	Autocracy	Military	Democracy
1970–90	44	27	24
1991–2000	19	6	30

b   Frequencies of growth syndromes with their corresponding episodes of type of leadership

Syndrome	Autocracy	Military	Democracy
Hard	12	7	3
Soft	24	16	11
Free	11	5	31

Source: Calculation based on data in appendix 1.

these leaders were not merely heads of their governments, but also idealists and visionaries. The majority of them operated under autocratic settings that provided a wide scope for the implementation of their ideas.

Although control regimes accounted for around 32 percent of African economic history during 1960–2000 (chapter 2), their occurrence is particularly concentrated from the late 1960s to the mid-1980s, a period also of preponderant autocratic leadership regimes. Using data on the type of African leadership, autocratic leadership regimes (civilian and military) during 1970–90 accounted for 75 percent of leadership episodes (see table 9.2). What is more striking is that, based on the combination of syndrome and type of leadership, 80 percent of autocratic leadership regimes over the entire period of African economic history have predominantly coexisted with control regimes (hard and soft), while nearly 70 percent of democratic regimes have coexisted with syndrome-free growth episodes (table 9.2 and figure 9.2).

We also analyzed the odds of having a syndrome-free growth environment under autocratic or democratic leadership. The ANOVA test (see appendix 2) shows that if the type of leadership prevailing in a country is democracy then there is a significantly greater chance that there is no regulatory (control) regime in the country; in other words, the country is more likely to be "syndrome-free."

The coefficient estimates of an ordered logit model lead to the same conclusion. As discussed in appendix 3, a likelihood-ratio test fails to reject the proportionality of odds assumption that is critical to identifying the impact of leadership regime in this model. Given this result, the logit estimates imply that the risk (odds) of exhibiting a "syndrome-free" regime as opposed to

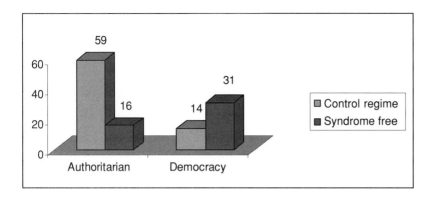

Figure 9.2 Syndromes and their corresponding episodes of types of leadership in SSA, 1970–2000

a "hard-" or "soft-"control regime is fully seven times higher for countries that have "democracy" as the prevailing type of leadership than for those with "authoritarian" leaders. These patterns are further explained in chapter 10 by Bates.

The most prominent among the first-generation African leaders (for example, Nkrumah, Nyerere, Kaunda, Kenyatta, Senghor, Ramgoolam) espoused the Fabian socialist intellectual tradition as well as ideology. These leaders had come into direct contact with Fabian socialists during their education in Britain or with social democrats in continental Europe. Samir Amin (Egyptian-born and Paris-trained) is one of the better known neo-Marxian thinkers who locally wielded particularly strong influence among francophone African intellectuals and development practitioners. He promoted conscious self-reliance of developing countries through the development of internal mass markets. The Non-aligned Movement (NAM) became a potent international avenue for keeping this idealistic tradition alive, as it kept African leaders in touch with some of the strongest believers/proponents of this ideology outside the region (e.g. Nehru, Nasser, Tito, and Sukarno). Within the region, OAU – which was closely associated with African communalism – became the Pan African venue for affirmation of this model.[2]

---

[2] Some African academics viewed the close tie to external ideas as being diversionary and at the expense of engagement with local intelligentsia. For example Mkandawire (2000) laments: "African governments relied heavily on foreign mentors, admirers or sycophants for intellectual inspiration or affirmation." Thus according to him Nyerere had a band of foreign "Fabian socialists" who had easy access to him, in sharp contrast to Tanzanians who had difficulties seeing Nyerere. Kaunda had John Hatch as a close intellectual associate, who was invited to be the first director of the Institute for Humanism; Nkrumah

The influence of Fabian socialism in Africa began during the colonial period, and the exposure to these ideas went beyond leaders to include their local advisers. Reviewing Bauer (1984), for example, Chamberlain (1985) writes rather cynically that:

It was the triumph of Fabian ideas in Europe in the late Thirties that changed everything in West Africa and Malaysia for the worse. Government marketing boards were set up with monopoly powers. The free trader was practically abolished. Little proprietors had to sell to the marketing boards at specified prices. The boards, with surpluses to use as the politicians saw fit, were, in a way, functioning as tax collectors. A younger generation of native intellectuals journeyed to London to study economics under Fabian professors such as Harold Laski. They returned home to become the advisers to government. When, in the last years of British colonial rule, the situation was described to colonial secretary Oliver Lyttleton and to Andrew Cohen, the head of the African Development Department of the colonial office, they remarked cynically that the African peasant had no future anyway.[3]

The Fabian approach to economics and the flourishing growth of development economics in the post-war period reviewed earlier provided a solid basis for adoption of control regimes. The Fabian approach to economics held that (1) the state has responsibility for collecting and redistributing rents from capital, land, and labor to achieve egalitarian goals; and (2) the state has a responsibility to manage resource allocation because, left to its own devices, the market and the private sector (businesses) will not reach a socially optimal allocation due to a variety of market failures. A major task of Fabian socialist thinkers was to find a practical (workable) construct for implementing a planning system that redressed the failures or achieved "market socialism." Fabian thinkers such as Hugh Gaitskell, Henry Douglas Dickinson, and Evan Durbin recognized that the market system could neither price collective goods nor reflect the true social value of externalities, and hence could not guarantee allocative efficiency. Not keen on Soviet-style planning systems, they sought to develop a system that would address coordination failures arising from indivisibilities in investment, scale economies in production, and the failure of market prices to convey all relevant information to private investors.

Although the "state interventionist" stance describes economic management of a substantial proportion of the African continent during the 1960s and through the mid-1980s, important differences did exist across three groups of countries. The differences were largely characterized by relative

---

had surrounded himself with pan-Africanists, such as George Padmore and W. E. B. Dubois. In later years there were European and America "radicals" who were to appear as peripatetic advisers to a whole range of "progressive" regimes in Africa.

[3] Chamberlain (1985) is available at
www.fee.org/publications/the-freeman/article.asp?aid=2001.

emphases on (1) the pursuit of nationalism and the related pressures for indigenization of the economy; and (2) the balance between redistribution and growth strategies:

- The first category grouped such countries as Côte d'Ivoire in the 1960s and 1970s, and Mauritius since the 1970s, which pursued a relatively open and liberal system with the view to encouraging foreign and domestic investment. State intervention was in the earlier phase aimed at achieving this goal through an incentive structure to offer attractive returns to investors and reduce infrastructural transactions costs. The state was largely supportive of private capital. Subsequent pressure for economic nationalism and regional redistribution in the case of Côte'd Ivoire led to increased state participation in enterprise partnership with the private sector. In the case of Mauritius shared growth was a principle pursued throughout.
- The second category grouped countries which although predominantly market-oriented espoused an early nationalist and indigenization strategy – e.g. Kenya and Zambia. Unlike the first category, however, the basic strategy was growth-oriented with a trickle down for redistribution of benefits from growth. Towards the 1980s these countries adopted an intensification of the indigenization strategy and redistribution through increased state participation in enterprise and pursuit of a (globally sanctioned) basic needs strategy involving enhanced participation of government in the provision of basic social services and ambitious targets.
- The third group of countries – such as Tanzania, Mozambique, and Ethiopia – pursued a popular state interventionist strategy, overhauling ownership patterns, emphasizing redistribution over growth, and adopting state ownership and control of markets as the main instruments for redistribution.

The ability of Mauritius to break away from the stranglehold of the control syndrome despite adopting that approach in the early post-independence period, and the significant presence of the market economy and private sector in Kenya and Zambia, deserve some explanation.

The story for Mauritius revolves very much around the first Prime Minister, Seewoosagur Ramgoolam. While studying in England, the young Ramgoolam was fascinated by the heat of political discussion which he nurtured through membership with the Fabian Society, which further initiated him into the secrets of British politics, parliamentary democracy, and socialism. He was a keen student of the great Fabian intellectuals including Sidney and Beatrice Webb, George Bernard Shaw, G. D. H. Cole, and Harold Laski, who were preaching a kind of reformist socialism and the virtues of the welfare state while avoiding the pitfalls of radical socialism or communism. But as a Fabian socialist with his feet firmly on the ground, Ramgoolam came to believe in the virtues of "enlightened capitalism" and a mixed economy, mobilizing the enterprise and intelligence of the capitalists as the engine of economic growth and of higher productivity and the sharing of profits with the people at large. As a deep thinker, genuinely committed to the modernization of his country, Ramgoolam held as his central belief that a mixed-economy democracy would ensure economic growth with social justice. This is consistent with his resisting the temptation to redistribute the large rents from sugar price subsidies in the 1970s, despite strong pressures from the radical groups, and instead leaving a sizeable portion of the windfall to the sugar growers who used it partly to diversify their investment into the initial phase of the export processing zones.

While studying in England, Ramgoolam struck up life-long friendship with many leading African students in London including Jomo Kenyatta and Kenneth Kaunda. The latter two appear to have adopted a similar approach of a mixed economy in their own presidencies, as reflected in the case studies in volume 2.

3.2   An emerging African consensus on societal values?

The second channel is the influence of global opinion leaders in shaping local societal views on acceptable policy choices and governance standards. Spurred on by the rapid globalization process, the world has been shifting away from the nation-state ideal that was taken for granted after 1945 towards the rising pressure and willingness of countries to submit to quasi-legal obligations and pay greater heed to international public opinion. It influences the pattern of global resource flows and local opinions regarding the desirable features of an economic and political system. In the context of the growing adoption of democracy in Africa since the 1990s, the importance of local opinion has strengthened since undesirable regimes and leadership can actually be voted out.

In this section, I show what the African social values are (based on perception survey data) and compare these with those in other regions. This confirms, based on information from two data sets, the World Values and Afrobarometer surveys, that there is a fairly strong correspondence between societal values and perceptions about political and economic systems in Africa and those in other regions of the world.

3.2.1   The World Values Survey

The first wave of the World Values Survey was conducted in 1981–2 with developed nations comprising the majority of the countries surveyed. The second round, in 1990–1, increased the scope of this investigation by sampling more developing nations. By the third round, in 1995–7, sixty-four independent nations had been surveyed at least once. The last round

Table 9.3 *World, LDC, and African values, 1999–2002.*

Opinion (1999–2002 wave)	World (% of global population)	Africa (% of African population)	Other LDCs (% of population in other LDCs)	ROW (% of population in developed nations)
Against strong autocratic leader	65	69	60	77
In favor of experts	58	55	65	45
Against army rule	83	80	77	95
In favor of democracy	91	92	90	93
Democracy is good for the economy	68	64	65	75
Overall good opinion on democracy	88	77	87	93
In favor of equity (1–4 on a 1–10 scale)	33	34	32	37
Against the country being run by a few big interests	69	66	71	59
In favor of mixed economy	61	66	55	78
Government more responsibility against poverty (1–4 on a 1–10 scale)	34	26	29	47

Source: Authors' calculations based on the World Values Survey data: 2000–2 wave.

was conducted over the period 1999–2002 and involved five African countries – Nigeria, Zimbabwe, Uganda, Tanzania, and South Africa – among forty-three developing countries. For the purpose of this study the relevant questions selected focused mainly on the aspects of market orientation as opposed to state control, awareness of poverty and equity issues, opinions on democracy, and reforms being implemented in their economies. The pattern of views on which opinions were elicited evolved from a focus on macroeconomic and structural reforms to equity considerations and democracy.

The analysis broadly confirms the convergence of values across the world on what a desirable society and economy is – consistent with the "one-world consensus." Based on the last wave of the World Values Survey (1999–2002), on average the world and African societies prefer democracy and a mixed economy with the state playing a supportive role to the market, and value technocracy and equitable treatment (table 9.3). It is also instructive that about a third of respondents consider poverty reduction to be a government responsibility. Responses to the individual questions are discussed below, showing a trend of opinion in the direction described above. ANOVA tests were conducted to check whether there were any statistically significant differences in responses between those from African countries and the rest of the developing regions.

The percentage of people who believed that "having a strong leader who does not have to bother with parliament and elections" was either "very bad" or "fairly bad" was 65 percent in the fourth wave. There were no statistically significant differences in the opinions held world-wide and in SSA in 1995–7. The average score for an African country against having this type of a strong leader was significantly higher in the SSA region in 1999–2002 when compared to the average response in all other developing countries.

Over and above supporting democracy, "practicing authoritarianism" or exercising any kind of control was also unanimously condemned, with some 74 percent of people surveyed (in the 1995–7 wave) believing that "a party leader should be prepared to cooperate with other groups, even if it means compromising some of his or her important beliefs as opposed to a party leader who stands firm for what he or she believes, even if others disagree." This percentage remained high at 72 percent in the fourth wave.

On average, more people in the 1999–2002 wave (58 percent) believed that "having experts, not government, make decisions according to what they think is best for the country" was either a "very good" or "fairly good" means of governing their country, in contrast to the average response in the third wave.

The majority of respondents have opinions against military rule in both the waves (54 percent). The ANOVA test showed less tolerance in SSA of "having the army rule" as a means of governing their country in comparison to the rest of the developing world (1999–2002).

Conforming to the one-world consensus, the world population unanimously supported the democratic system (88 percent in the third wave and 91 percent in the fourth wave). The ANOVA results show significantly that more Africans were in favor of a democratic political system, in comparison to the average responses from the rest of the developing countries.

More people believed that democracy was also conducive to the economic system functioning well – about 65 percent in the 1995–7 wave and 68 percent in the 1999–2002 wave. The mean responses from the Africa region were significantly higher than those from the other LDCs in the mid-1990s and about even in 1999–2002.

Answers to "democracy may have problems but it's better than any other form of government" met with unanimous "strongly agree" and "agree" responses of 87 percent in the 1995–7 wave and 88 percent in the 1999–2002 wave. Again, Africa region responses were significantly higher than the other less-developed countries (LDCs) in 1999–2002.

Responses to concerns based on equity issues went in favor of incomes being made more equal, as opposed to a preference for having larger income differences as incentives for individual effort. On average, more people towards the late 1990s thought that equitable income distribution was more important than market forces of competition. Based on ANOVA tests, the average responses from Africa and the rest of the LDCs did not significantly differ.

About 76 percent agreed that the government was doing too little for people trapped in poverty in the fourth wave, which rose from 72 percent expressing similar dissatisfaction in the third wave. The ANOVA results confirm the upward trend in the proportion of those with this view across the third and fourth waves. The percentage of people who thought that the poverty situation worsened in their country went up by 11 percent from 69 percent in the 1995–7 wave to 80 percent in the 1999–2002 wave, with no statistically significant differences in the average response rates from the Africa region when compared to those elicited from the other LDCs.

57 percent of respondents in 1990–3, 72 percent in 1995–7, and 69 percent in 1999–2002 thought that a few big interests were looking out for themselves. ANOVA tests of the third-wave data reveal that responses from the Africa region were not significantly different from those elicited from the other LDCs.

When asked if "private ownership of business and industry should be increased as opposed to government ownership of business and industry," more people at the global level wanted to see government ownership increase since the early 1990s, rising over time. However, a greater proportion of the African population in the third wave believed that there should be greater private participation in contrast to the other developing-world responses.

Opinions on whether "the government should take more responsibility to ensure that everyone is provided for" in contrast to "the people should take more responsibility to provide for themselves" again portrayed the changing beliefs over the different snapshots in time. On average, more people wanted government "intervention" to address equity concerns in the mid-1990s.

Another place where one can draw proof for this assessment of people's beliefs is that more people in the 1999–2002 wave believed that "most poor people in their country have a chance of escaping from poverty in contrast to very little chance of escaping from poverty." Six percent more people (46 percent in 1999–2002 compared to 40 percent in 1995–7) thought that the poverty problem was not irreparable when compared to the fraction of people who thought similarly in the third round.

3.2.2   The Afrobarometer survey

Two rounds of Afrobarometer surveys, involving twelve African countries in 2000–1 and fifteen countries in 2002–3, largely confirm the above values and attitudes in African countries. Although the country-sample selection targeted those undergoing political or economic reforms, there are significant differences of views by respondents in each of the surveyed countries. The

Table 9.4 *Comparison of African opinions, World Values Survey and Afrobarometer.*

Opinion	World Values Survey (1999–2002 wave) (%) Africa	Afrobarometer (2000–1 wave) (%) 12 African countries
Against strong leader (one-man rule)	69	80
Against one-party rule	–	69
Against army rule	80	82
In favor of democracy	92	69
Democracy is good for the economy	64	75
In favor of equity	34	89
(1–4 on a 1–10 scale)	(44% chose 1–5)	
Country is run by a few big interests	66	52
In favor of mixed economy	66	59
In favor of equity	34	89
Avoid large gaps between the rich and the poor		56
Women should be treated the same as men		66
How much government is doing against poverty	26 (% think that it's the right amount)	29

Source: World Value Survey and Afrobarometer Working Papers 1, 34.

2000–1 wave has been analyzed fully and is used here to make comparison with the 1999–2002 results from the World Values Survey. Comparatively, the scores in the Afrobarometer survey in favor of democracy and eschewing authoritarian rule are even stronger than in the World Value Surveys (see table 9.4 for partial comparisons).

Based on the first round of the survey, Africans unanimously prefer multi-party democracy to authoritarian alternative forms of government such as one-party rule, one-man rule, or even military rule. However, they rarely associate democracy with voting and elections. To most of them, democracy means civil liberties like freedom of speech and government by the people. They also expect democracy to ensure a baseline welfare level, where citizens have access to the basic necessities of life such as food, water, shelter, and basic education. Almost half of the population prefers a free market economy to a planned economy, which implies that the other half prefers the opposite.

Based on the analysis by Bratton *et al.* of the second round of the survey (Bratton *et al.* 2006), politically Africans (1) prefer democracy and reject authoritarian rule; (2) intend to stick with democracy while only moderately satisfied with the way it works now; and (3) think they are better off politically since the arrival of competitive politics.

On the market economy, the second round suggests that Africans prefer a mixed economy with active but not overbearing state regulation and with a tilt of preference towards a "free market" (44 percent) rather than a "government-run economy" (37 percent). Eighty-two percent insist that government should protect property rights; and almost 70 percent are in favor of collective, as opposed to individual, responsibility for the well being of people.

On equity, Africans affirm discomfort with wide wealth differentials, have very strong commitment to political equality (voting not a privilege of the better educated), and have a clear popular preference for gender equality.

From these public opinions, one can clearly observe that it reflects the global values prevalent in the one-world consensus of the 1990s. A sense of balance between market-oriented and state control, both in the formulation of the structure of development strategy as well as the means to achieve it (through reforms), and an increased awareness of poverty and distributional issues are the two focal aspects that characterize the one-world consensus.

3.3   Influence of global development ideas through aid conditionality and selectivity

The third transmission channel of global ideas to growth syndromes in African economies is via the international development agencies that offer advice, aid, and technical assistance to developing countries with its associated conditionality.

It is noteworthy that aid conditionality has emerged since the late 1970s to counter deteriorating policy choices associated with increasingly non-representative political structures and weak autocracies in Africa. This channel of influence became particularly significant in the case of African countries in light of the high level of aid in their resource envelopes. Even though the ability of aid conditionality to shape commitment to reforms has been put into question, it continues to be actively used. More recently donor-disciplined "process conditionality" has been added to the tool kit – e.g. making aid conditional on adopting inclusive processes in the preparation of Poverty Reduction Strategies or adopting democratic institutions (Ndulu 2004).

In the first two decades of independence, apart from the technical assistance from multilateral agencies, development plans were also prepared with technical support from outside the multilateral agencies (e.g. Harvard Group, Sussex University, etc.). The influence of development economics was particularly strong in this regard, given that it was the channel through which the frontier of the discipline was brought to application.[4]

---

[4] Mkandawire (2000) saw the use of foreign expertise as part of the domination of policy-making by the aid establishment. The "experts" are part of the paraphernalia of

Below we focus on the extent to which selectivity in aid allocation, conditionality, and technical advice is shaped by changing international public opinion. We focus on the influence of global opinion on policy choices for growth using the allocation of World Bank IDA credit as an example. A country receives more aid (IDA plus bilateral aid leveraged by IDA) based on, among other things, willingness to conform to policy thrusts consistent with addressing weaknesses identified through the assessment of Country Policy and Institutional Assessment (CPIA). We argue that what is assessed as good performance measures through CPIA changes with the global opinions on what constitutes acceptable norms and values.

3.3.1   CPIA and African growth syndromes

The World Bank annually assesses the quality of International Bank for Reconstruction and Development (IBRD) and IDA borrowers' policy and institutional performance in areas relevant to economic growth and poverty reduction. These assessments began in the late 1970s to help guide the allocation of lending resources. The criterion of good performance has evolved over time, reflecting lessons learned and mirroring the evolution of the development paradigm. While in earlier years assessments focused mainly on macroeconomic policies, they now include other factors that reflect changing notions of what produces economic development. It is important to note that CPIA scores for individual countries have been found to be closely correlated with private sector country ratings, such as those by the *Institutional Investor, International Country Risk Guide (ICRG)*, and *Euromoney* (Easterly *et al.* 1993).

For low-income countries, this rating is a significant factor determining their access to IDA credit and hence a key incentive for compliance to world norms represented in the decision-making bodies of the World Bank. For the typical African country case studied in this project, borrowing from the IDA represented a large proportion of their development financing. The IDA credit allocation formula enforces "selectivity." The CPIA typically accounts for 80 percent of the criteria for allocation of IDA credit and, as Collier and Dollar (2002) show, the World Bank has actually followed this criterion of allocation in practicing selectivity in contrast to bilateral aid.

There is some empirical evidence that this approach to selectivity in IDA credit allocation is associated with enhanced growth outcomes. Collier and Hoeffler (2004) show that there is a strong correlation between high CPIA scores and actual growth outcomes, with 30–40 percent return to aid

conditionalities. He argues that, ideally, the recipient state should coordinate development activities under its jurisdiction. In reality, most recipient states relate to foreign donors in a supine position, leaving the thinking, planning, experimenting – and, therefore, learning – to foreign institutions.

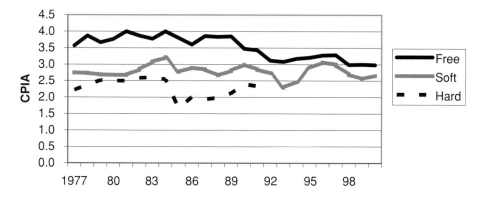

Figure 9.3 Annual average CPIA scores for three policy syndromes, 1977–2000.

provided to a country with a CPIA score at the overall mean. Indeed, although aid is subject to diminishing returns, Collier and Hoeffler (2004) conclude from their analysis that a country's absorptive capacity is dependent upon the quality (level) of policy and institutions as measured by the CPIA. Easterly (1998) reached similar conclusions when CPIA measures of policy were introduced into a regression equation involving several other conditioning variables. The CPIA in 1977, the CPIA in 1990, the average of CPIAs in 1990–8, and the CPIA in 1998 were all generally statistically significant in explaining *per capita* growth outcomes. A point of caution here also made by Easterly (1998) concerns the potential endogeneity in these relationships, since growth outcomes are partly considered in the assessment.

Our classification of policy syndromes provides interesting insights into the evolution of the World Bank's conception of "good" economic policy. To characterize the evolution of the global development paradigms, we limit our analysis to the Bank's assessment of control regimes (hard and soft), as compared to the syndrome-free environment. The following are the main findings.

CPIA scores broadly reflect the desire to rid countries of anti-growth syndromes. From a core group of twenty-two African countries, the scores for "syndrome-free" regimes are generally higher than those of "controlled" regimes throughout the period – i.e. 1977–2000 (figure 9.3) for which data on CPIA exist. This appears to reflect the continuity of the core assessment of macroeconomic stability even when the balances between the roles of state and markets, and between poverty reduction and growth change over time with development paradigms.

Looking at the trends, the average CPIA scores of "free" regimes marginally decline during the 1977–2000 period. On the other hand, average

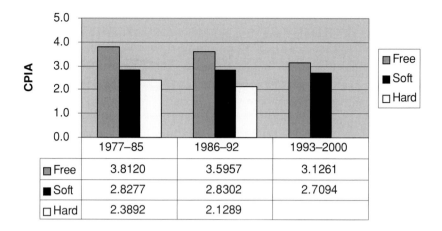

	1977–85	1986–92	1993–2000
▣ Free	3.8120	3.5957	3.1261
■ Soft	2.8277	2.8302	2.7094
☐ Hard	2.3892	2.1289	

Figure 9.4 Performance CPIA scores in paradigmatic periods, 1977–2000.

CPIA scores for "controlled" regimes slightly drop from the first to second periods, but rise again in the last period (figure 9.4). One interpretation is that although reality does not change, the normative evaluation of that reality appears to have changed with changes in the development paradigm. An alternative but complementary interpretation is that these changes correspond to evolving societal views on the "quality" of growth and the willingness to trade off growth for collective responsibility for the poor.

It is also worth explaining the changes in the scores of the control regimes over time. Until 1980, the global development paradigm emphasized "market failures" that led to interventions by local or foreign governments to correct them. Under this paradigm, there was a higher tolerance of controlled regimes, particularly those that were in pursuit of poverty reduction. Taking Tanzania as an example, the highest CPIA score (3.8) between 1977 and 2000 was achieved in 1977, while the country was in a hard-control regime but widely lauded for its social development and poverty programs (figure 9.5). The 1980s saw much less tolerance for *dirigisme* reflected in the very sharp decline in the scores for control regimes and among those African countries as there was a sharp shift from concerns with "market failures" to those with "government failures," and "advocated minimalist states." During this period, Tanzania's scores dropped. Since the 1990s, the focus has shifted towards embracing a "mixed economy" – an approach in which there are supportive roles of the state to market operation, greater attention to governance, and increased awareness of poverty concerns. The weight of these additional criteria counterbalance traditional considerations leading to decline in the scores of syndrome-free regimes as we knew them in the 1980s. And Tanzania's scores rise again.

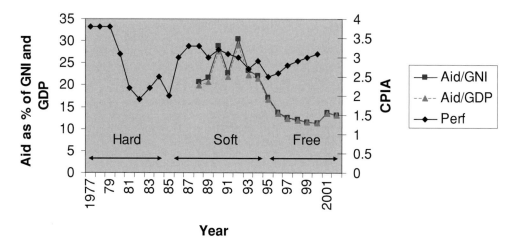

Figure 9.5 Tanzania, CPIA scores and growth syndromes, 1977–2001.

Finally, there is a clear tendency towards the convergence of CPIA scores between "free" and "controlled" regimes. The convergence of the two trends may well be mainly due to the global societal attention to poverty and equity. Equity, institutions, and politics become focal points for poverty reduction and economic development and, as we saw in section 3, there is also a growing view that governments have responsibility for the poor.

4   Conclusion

We began our chapter by noting that, based on case studies and the synthesis by Collier and O'Connell in chapter 2, policy syndromes do matter for growth outcomes, with a syndrome-free growth environment associated with a clear 1 percentage point growth performance advantage and certainly avoidance of growth collapse, which is so prevalent in SSA (figure 9.6). Our interest was to explore the reasons behind the policy choices characterizing the growth syndromes, and in particular by exploring how global ideas influenced policy choices and hence growth syndromes. While acknowledging the importance of an interest-based explanation for the preponderance of anti-growth syndromes in the region, we were interested in understanding the link between what appeared as dominant phases of global policy paradigms and what has been recognized as the most dramatic change in the growth syndromes over time – the displacement of syndrome-free cases by control regimes between the late 1960s and the mid-1980s and their subsequent restoration during the 1990s.

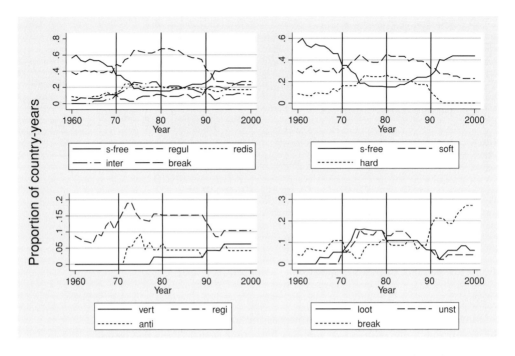

Figure 9.6 Policy syndromes in forty-six SSA countries, 1960–2000
Source: Judgmental classification by the editorial committee based on country studies
and broader literature.

From the analysis, three conclusions seem to be borne out. First, all the
three channels of transmitting ideas from the global development paradigms
to the African policy choices appear to have done so potently. The first generation of African leaders, partly influenced by the post-war development
perspectives, and particularly Fabian socialism, embarked on an autocratic
development strategy that was heavily suspicious of the private sector and
overly concerned with market failures and hence adopted a stance of the state
as the modernizing agent. The preponderance of control regimes between
the late 1960s and early 1980s is partly a result of this approach to development. Correspondingly, as we have seen, this was also a phase of preponderance of autocratic leadership in SSA. Subsequent changes away from this
approach first swung towards a minimalist state and later to a mixed economy with democracy taking a strong root. Given the result in the analysis
that the odds of having a syndrome-free growth environment are six times
higher when an African country has an episode of democratic leadership,
the recent rapid democratization process may hold good promise for better
growth outcomes, given other constraints.

Secondly, from the analysis it is clear that African values of consequence to growth syndromes are in tandem with the world values. Recent world values which favor a state supportive of the private sector and markets are also in favor of democratic practice and caring for the unfortunate. In addition, the global preference tends toward governments which are increasingly egalitarian, which have been obtained in Africa. And, indeed, it is through the practice of democratic rights that the opinion of the public will come to bear on policy choices.

Finally, given Africa's high dependence on aid, international multilateral agencies have played a disproportionately larger role in shaping African policy syndromes – through technical advice, conditionality, and now increasingly through selectivity in aid allocation to engender adoption of globally desirable policies.

Appendix 1: Growth syndromes and types of leadership in Africa, 1970–2000

Table 9.A1 *Syndromes and types of leadership*

Country (1)	Period (2)	Syndrome (3)	Leaders (4)	Type of leadership (5)
Angola	1975–9	hard	Antonia Neto (1975–9)	autocracy
	1979–90	hard	José dos Santos (1979–90)	autocracy
	1991–2000	soft	José dos Santos (1991–2000)	autocracy
Benin	1970–2	soft	Coutoucou Hubert (1970–2)	military
	1972–4	soft	Maga Mathieu Kérékou (1972–91)	autocracy
	1975–89	hard	Mathieu Kérékou (1972–91)	autocracy
	1990–2000	free	Nicéphore Dieudonné Soglo (1991–6) Mathieu Kérékou (1996–)	democracy
Botswana	1970–80	free	Seretse Khama (1966–80)	democracy
	1980–98	free	Quett Ketumile Joni Masire (1980–98)	democracy
Burkina Faso	1970–80	soft	Abubakar Sangoulé Lamizana (1966–80)	democracy
	1980–2	soft	Saye Zerbo (1980–2)	military
	1983–90	hard	Jean-Baptiste Ouedraogo (1982–3) Thomas Sankara (1983–7) Blaise Compaoré (1987–)	military
	1991–2000	free	Blaise Compaoré (1987–)	democracy
Burundi	1972–88	soft	Michel Micombero (1966–76) Jean-Baptiste Bagaza (1976–87)	military
	1988–93	state breakdown	Pierre Buyoya (1987–93)	military

(cont.)

Table 9.A1 *(cont.)*

Country (1)	Period (2)	Syndrome (3)	Leaders (4)	Type of leadership (5)
	1993–2000	state breakdown	Sylvie Kinigi (1993–4) Sylvestre Ntibantunganya (1994–6) Pierre Buyoya (1996–)	democracy
Cameroon	1970–82	soft	Ahmadou Babatoura Ahidjo (1960–82)	autocracy
	1982–93	soft	Paul Biya (1982–)	autocracy
	1994–2000	free	Paul Biya (1982–)	autocracy
Cape Verde	1975–91	soft	Aristides Maria Pereira (1975–91)	autocracy
	1992–2000	free	Antonio Manuel Mascarenhas Gomes Monteiro (1991–)	democracy
CAR	1970–81	soft	Jean-Bédel Bokassa (1966–79) David Dacko (1979–81)	autocracy
	1981–5	soft	André Kolingba (1981–5)	military
	1985–93	soft	André Kolingba (1985–93)	autocracy
	1993–2000	soft	Ange-Félix Patassé (1993–)	democracy
Chad	1970–5	soft	François Ngarta Tombalbaye (1962–75)	military
	1975–90	soft	Félix Malloum N'Gakoutou (1975–9) Goukouni Oueddei (1979–82) Hissène Habré (1982–90)	autocracy
	1990–2000	soft	Idriss Déby (1990–)	democracy
Comoros	1975	free	Said Mohamed Jaffar (1975–6)	autocracy
	1976–8	hard	Ali Soilih Mtsashiwa (1976–8)	autocracy
	1979–89	soft	Ahmed Abdallah Abderemane (1978–89)	autocracy
	1990–5*	state breakdown	Said Mohamed Djohar (1989–95)	democracy
Congo, Rep.	1970–7	hard	Marien Ngouabi (1969–77)	autocracy
	1977–92	hard	Jacques-Joachim Yhombi-Opango (1977–9) Denis Sassou-Nguesso (1979–92)	military
	1992–7*	free	Pascal Lissouba (1992–7)	democracy
Côte d'Ivoire	1970–90	soft	Félix Houphouët-Boigny (1960–)	democracy
	1991–9	free	Félix Houphouët-Boigny (1960–93) Henri Konan Bédié (1993–9)	democracy
Djibouti	1977–90	free	Hassan Gouled Aptidon (1977–)	autocracy
	1991–9	state breakdown	Hassan Gouled Aptidon (1977–99)	autocracy
DRC	1979–97	soft	Joseph-Désiré Mobutu/Mobutu Sese Seko (1965–97)	autocracy
Equatorial	1970–9	state breakdown	Francisco Macías (Masie) Nguema (1968–79)	autocracy

Table 9.A1 *(cont.)*

Country (1)	Period (2)	Syndrome (3)	Leaders (4)	Type of leadership (5)
Guinea	1980–2000	soft	Teodoro Obiang Nguema Mbasogo (1979–)	autocracy
Ethiopia	1970–3	free	Haile Selassie I (1930–74)	autocracy
	1974–87	hard	Tafari Benti (1974–7)	military
			Mengistu Haile Mariam (1977–)	
	1987–91	hard	Mengistu Haile Mariam (1977–91)	democracy
	1992–2000	free	Meles Zenawi (1991–5)	democracy
			Negaso Gidada (1995–)	
Gabon	1970–97	soft	Omar Bongo (1967–)	autocracy
	1998–2000	free	Omar Bongo (1967–)	democracy
Gambia	1970–94	free	Dawda Kairaba Jawara (1970–94)	democracy
	1994–6	free	Yahya A. J. J. Jammeh (1994–6)	military
	1996–2000	free	Yahya A. J. J. Jammeh (1996–)	democracy
Ghana	1970–1	free	Kofi Busia (1969–72)	democracy
	1972–8	soft	Ignatius Kutu Acheampong (1972–8)	military
	1979–83	hard	Frederick Kwasi Akuffo (1978–9)	military
			Hilla Limann (1979–81)	
			Jerry John Rawlings (1981–)	
	1984	soft	Jerry John Rawlings (1981–)	military
	1985–92	free	Jerry John Rawlings (1981–)	military
	1992–2000	free	Jerry John Rawlings (1981–2000)	democracy
Guinea	1970–7	hard	Ahmed Sékou Touré (1961–)	autocracy
	1978–84	soft	Ahmed Sékou Touré (1961–84)	autocracy
	1985–93	free	Lansana Conte (1984–)	military
	1993–2000	free	Lansana Conte (1984–)	democracy
Guinea-Bissau	1974–84	soft	Luís Cabral (1974–80)	military
			João Bernardo Vieira (1980–4)	
	1984–99	soft	João Bernardo Vieira (1984–99)	autocracy
Kenya	1970–1	free	Jomo Kenyatta (1964–74)	autocracy
	1972–91	soft	Daniel Arap Moi (1978–)	autocracy
	1992–2000	free	Daniel Arap Moi (1978–)	democracy
Lesotho	1970–86	free	Joseph Leabua Jonathan (1965–86)	autocracy
	1986–93	free	Justin Metsing Lekhanya (1986–91)	military
			Elias Phisoana Ramaema (1991–3)	
	1993–8	free	Ntsu Mokhehle (1993–8)	democracy
Liberia	1970–80	free	William Tubman (1944–71)	democracy
			William Tolbert (1971–80)	
	1980–90	free	Samuel Doe (1980–90)	military
	1990–5	free	No leaders	–

(cont.)

Table 9.A1 *(cont.)*

Country (1)	Period (2)	Syndrome (3)	Leaders (4)	Type of leadership (5)
Madagascar	1970–1	free	Philibert Tsiranana (1960–72)	democracy
	1972–5	soft	Gabriel Ramanantsoa (1972–5)	democracy
	1976–85	hard	Didier Ratsiraka (1975–)	autocracy
	1986–92	soft	Didier Ratsiraka (1975–93)	autocracy
	1993–6	soft	Albert Zafy (1993–6)	democracy
Malawi	1970–94	free	Hastings Kamuzu Banda (1966–94)	autocracy
	1994–2000	free	Elson Bakili Muluzi (1994–)	democracy
Mali	1970–9	hard	Moussa Traoré (1968–91)	military
	1979–91	hard	Moussa Traoré (1968–91)	autocracy
	1992–2000	free	Amadou Toumani Touré (1991–2)	democracy
			Alpha Oumar Konaré (1992–)	
Mauritania	1970–3	free	Moktar Ould Daddah (1961–78)	autocracy
	1974–85	soft	Moustafa Ould Mohamed Salek (1978–9)	military
			Mohamed Mahmoud Ould Ahmed Louly (1979–80)	
			Mohamed Khouna Ould Haidalla (1980–4)	
			Maaouya Ould Sid'Ahmed Taya (1984–)	
	1986–2000	free	Maaouya Ould Sid'Ahmed Taya (1984–)	democracy
Mauritius	1970	soft	Seewoosagur Ramgoolam (1968–82)	democracy
	1971–2000	free	Anerood Jugnauth (1982–95)	democracy
			Navin (Chandra) Ramgoolam (1995–2000)	
Mozambique	1975–6	soft	Samora Machel (1975–)	autocracy
	1977–86	hard	Samora Machel (1975–86)	autocracy
	1987–92	state breakdown	Joaquim Chissano (1986–)	autocracy
	1992–2000	free	Joaquim Chissano (1986–)	democracy
Namibia	1990–2000	soft	Sam Shafishuna Nujoma (1990–)	democracy
Niger	1970–4	soft	Hamani Diori (1960–74)	autocracy
	1974–87	soft	Seyni Kountché (1974–87)	military
	1987–9	soft	Ali Saïbou (1987–)	military
	1990–6	state breakdown	Ali Saïbou (1987–91)	democracy
			Andre Salifou (1991–3)	
			Mahamane Ousmane (1993–6)	
Nigeria	1970–9	soft	Yakubu Gowon (1966–75)	military
			Murtala Ramat Mohammed (1975–6)	
			Olusegun Obasanjo (1976–9)	
	1979–82	soft	Shehu Shagari (1979–83)	democracy

Table 9.A1 *(cont.)*

Country (1)	Period (2)	Syndrome (3)	Leaders (4)	Type of leadership (5)
	1983–6	hard	Muhammadu Buhari (1983–5)	military
			Ibrahim Babangida (1985–)	
	1987–98	soft	Ibrahim Babangida (1985–93)	military
			Sani Abacha (1993–8)	
Rwanda	1970–2	free	Grégoire Kayibanda (1961–73)	democracy
	1973–8	soft	Juvénal Habyarimana (1973–4)	military
	1978–94	soft	Juvénal Habyarimana (1973–94)	autocracy
	1995–2000	free	Pasteur Bizimungu (1994–2000)	democracy
São Tomé & Principe	1975–91	not classified	Manuel Pinto da Costa (1975–91)	democracy
Senegal	1970–93	soft	Leopold Sédar Sénghor (1960–80)	democracy
			Abdou Diouf (1981–)	
	1994–2000	free	Abdou Diouf (1981–2000)	democracy
Seychelles	1976–7*	free	James Richard Mancha (1976–7)	democracy
	1977–2000*	free	France-Albert René (1977–)	autocracy
Sierra Leone	1970–85	hard	Siaka Stevens (1968–85)	democracy
	1985–9	hard	Joseph Saidu Momoh (1985–)	democracy
	1990–6	state breakdown	Joseph Saidu Momoh (1985–92)	military
			Valentine Strasser (1992–6)	
Somalia	1970–6	hard	Muhammad Siyad Barre (1969–91)	military
	1976–91	hard, followed by state breakdown after 1991	Muhammad Siyad Barre (1969–91)	autocracy
South Africa	1994–2000	free	Nelson Mandela (1994–9)	democracy
			Thabo Mbeki (1999–)	
Sudan	1970–85	soft	Ja'far Muhammad Numayri (1969–85)	military
	1985–9	state breakdown	Abd Siwar ad-Dhahab (1985–6)	autocracy
			Ahmed Ali al-Mirghani (1986–9)	
	1989–2000	state breakdown	Umar al-Hasan Ahmad al-Bashir (1989–)	military
Swaziland	1970–2000	free	King Sobhuza II (1968–82)	autocracy
			Queen Dzeliwe Shongwe (1982–3)	
			Queen Ntombi Thwala (1983–6)	
			King Mswati (1986–)	

(cont.)

Table 9.A1 *(cont.)*

Country (1)	Period (2)	Syndrome (3)	Leaders (4)	Type of leadership (5)
Tanzania	1970–85	hard	Julius Nyerere (1964–85)	autocracy
	1986–94	soft	Ali Hassan Mwinyi (1985–95)	autocracy
	1995–2000	free	Benjamin Mkapa (1995–)	democracy
Togo	1970–3	free	General Gnassingbé Eyadema (1967–)	democracy
	1974–2000	soft	General Gnassingbé Eyadema (1967–)	autocracy
Uganda	1970	hard	Apolo Milton Obote (1966–71)	autocracy
	1971–9	soft	Idi Amin Dada (1971–9)	military
	1979–86	state breakdown	Godfrey Lukongwa Binaisa (1979–80) Apolo Milton Obote (1980–5) Tito Okello (1985–6)	autocracy
	1987–91	soft	Yoweri Kaguta Museveni (1986–)	autocracy
	1992–2000	free	Yoweri Kaguta Museveni (1986–)	autocracy
Zambia	1970–91	soft	Kenneth Kaunda (1964–91)	autocracy
	1992–2000	free	Frederick Chiluba (1991–)	democracy
Zimbabwe	1970–80	soft	Ian Smith (1965–79) Abel Muzorewa (1979–80)	autocracy
	1980–2000	soft	Robert Mugabe (1980–)	democracy

Note: In column (3), "soft" and "hard" controls are sub-headings of the "excessive regulatory controls" syndrome defined by Collier and O'Connell in chapter 2, and "state breakdown" refers to the state breakdown syndrome. The "free" category here refers to the absence of soft or hard controls or state breakdown; this category therefore amalgamates the "syndrome-free" category of Collier and O'Connell with episodes in which the redistributive or intertemporal syndrome was present but the regulatory control syndrome and state breakdown were not. In a very few cases, marked by asterisks, there are differences with respect to the classification in chapter 2, based on our own judgment. Under the Leaders column, the notation (1990–) indicates that the leader came into power in 1990 and was still in place in 2000, which is the end-year of this data table.
Source: CIA *World Fact Book* and the online encyclopedia at www.encyclopedia.com.

Appendix 2: Syndromes and political regimes

The dependent variable "syndromes" was generated using the following scale:
    0 denoted a "hard-"control regime, 1 a "soft-"control regime, and 2 the absence of syndromes ("syndrome-free").
    0/1 dummy variables were created denoting different types of leadership (table 9.A2).

Table 9.A2 *The ANOVA test*

anova syndrome democracy autocracy

| | Number of obs = 120 | | | $R^2 = 0.1940$ | |
| | Root MSE = 0.6629 | | | Adj $R^2 = 0.1803$ | |
Source	Partial SS	df	MS	F	Prob > F
Model	12.3780	2	6.1890	14.08	0.0000
democracy	8.3048	1	8.3048	18.90	0.0000
autocracy	0.4413	1	0.0441	0.10	0.7519
Residual	51.4136	117	0.4394		
Total	63.7192	119	0.5361		

Appendix 3: Ordered logit model

The coefficient estimates from the ordered logit model (table 9.A3) are consistent with our ANOVA result (table 9.A2). Note first that a likelihood-ratio test suggests that the proportional odds approach is reasonable – i.e. that the impact of the leadership regime on the odds of a country's exhibiting a "syndrome-free" regime as opposed to "hard-" or "soft-"controls is approximately equivalent to the impact of leadership regime on the odds of syndrome-free status or soft controls versus hard controls to the odds of a country exhibiting "soft" and "syndrome-free" regimes as opposed to a "hard-"control regime.

Table 9.A3 *Logit results*

	Ordered logit (*t*-statistic)	Odds ratio	ANOVA coefficients (*F*-value)
Democracy	2.01	7.45	1.62
	(4.89)**		(28.28)**
Authoritarian		0.14	0.96
			(28.28)**
Observations	120	120	120
Pseudo-R²	0.1086		
Prob > chi²(1)	0.0000		

Given this, we infer from table 9.A3 that the risk (odds) of exhibiting a "syndrome-free" regime as opposed to "hard-" or "soft-"controls is *7 times* higher for countries that have "democracy" as the prevailing type of leadership than for those with "authoritarian" leaders.

References

Adelman, I. (2000), "Fifty Years of Economic Development: What Have we Learned?," Keynote address at the Annual Bank Conference on Development Economics, June 26–28, Paris

Balassa, B. (1971), *The Structure of Protection in Developing Countries*. Baltimore, MD: Johns Hopkins University Press

Bauer, P. T. (1984), *Reality and Rhetoric: Studies in the Economics of Development*. Cambridge, MA and London: Harvard University Press and Weidenfeld & Nicolson

Bell, D. (1994), "Socialism and Planning: Beyond the Soviet Economic Crisis," in F. Roosevelt and D. Belkin, eds., *Why Market Socialism? Voices from Dissent*, Armonk, NY: M. E. Sharpe: 165–73

Bratton, M. and N. van de Walle (1997), *Democratic Experiments in Africa: Regime Transitions in Comparative Perspective*. Cambridge: Cambridge University Press

Bratton, M. *et al.* (2004), "Afrobarometer Round 2: Compendium of Comparative Results from a 15-Country Survey," Afrobarometer Working Paper 34

Chamberlain, J. (1985), "A Reviewer's Notebook: Reality and Rhetoric," *The Freeman: Ideas on Liberty* 35 (12)

Chenery, H. and M. Syrquin (1975), *Patterns of Development 1950–1970*. New York: Oxford University Press for the World Bank

Collier, P. and D. Dollar (2002), "Aid Allocation and Poverty Reduction," *European Economic Review* 46(8): 1475–1500

Collier, P., D. Dollar, and N. Stern (2000), "Fifty Years of Economic Development: What Have We Learned?," World Bank, mimeo

Collier, P. and A. Hoeffler (2004), "Aid, Policy and Growth in Post-conflict Societies," Policy Research Working Paper Series 2902, Washington, DC: World Bank

Denison, E. (1967), *Why Growth Rates Differ: Post-war Experience in Nine Western Countries*. Washington, DC: Brookings Institution

Diamond, P. A. and J. A. Mirlees (1971a), "Optimal Taxation and Public Production I: Production Efficiency," *American Economic Review* 61: 8–27

(1971b), "Optimal Taxation and Public Production II: Tax Rules," *American Economic Review* 61, 261–76

Easterly, W. (1998), "Are All Countries Growth Projections Above Average?," World Bank Policy Research Working Paper. Washington, DC: World Bank

Easterly, W., M. Kremer, L. Pritchett, and L. Summers (1993), "Good Policy or Good Luck? Country Growth Performance and Temporary Shocks," *Journal of Monetary Economics* 32: 525–57

Gershenkron, A. (1962), *Economic Backwardness in Historical Perspective*. London: Praeger

Glaeser, E., R. La Porta, F. Lopez-de-Silanes, and A. Shleifer (2004), "Explaining Growth: Institutions, Human Capital, and Leaders," Paper Presented at the Brookings Panel on Economic Activity, March 25. The Brookings Institution, Washington, DC

Goldsmith, R. W. (1969), *Financial Structure and Economic Development*. New Haven, CT: Yale University Press

Jones, B. F. and B. A. Olken (2004), "Do Leaders Matter? National Leadership and Growth since World War II," Working Paper, Harvard University, March

Kuznets, S. (1966), *Modern Economic Growth: Rate, Structure, and Spread*. New Haven, CT: Yale University Press

Lewis, W. A. (1954), "Economic Development with Unlimited Supplies of Labor," *The Manchester School* 22: 139–91

Little, I., T. Scitovsky, and M. Scott (1970), *Industry and Trade in Some Developing Countries*. London: Oxford University Press

Ljunggren, B., ed. (1993), *The Challenge of Reform in Indochina*. Cambridge, MA: Harvard University Press

Migdal, J. (1988), *Strong Societies and Weak States: State–Society Relations and State Capabilities in the Third World*. Princeton, NJ: Princeton University Press

Mkandawire, T. (2000), "Non-Organic Intellectuals and 'Learning'," in Policy-Making Africa EGDI Seminar "What do Aid Agencies and their Co-operating Partners Learn from their Experiences?," August 24

Ndulu, B. J. (2004), "Inclusiveness, Accountability, and Effectiveness of Development Assistance in Sub-Saharan Africa," in F. Bourguignon and B. Pleskovic, eds., *Annual World Bank Conference on Development Economics 2004: Accelerating Development*. Washington, DC: World Bank

Nurkse, R. (1953), *Problems of Capital Formation in Underdeveloped Countries*. Oxford: Basil Blackwell

Perkins, D. (1988), "Reforming China's Economic System," *Journal of Economic Literature* 26: 601–45

Ranis, G. and J. Fei (1961), "A Theory of Economic Development," *American Economic Review* 51(4): 533–65

Rodrik, D. and A. Subramaniam (2004), "From 'Hindu Growth' to Productivity Surge: The Mystery of the Indian Growth Transition," NBER Working Papers 10376, National Bureau of Economic Research

Rosenstein-Rodan, P. (1943), "Problems of Industrialization of Eastern and South-Eastern Europe," *Economic Journal* 53: 202–11

Rostow, W. (1965), "The Take-Off Into Self-Sustaining Growth," *Economic Journal* 66: 25–48

Schultz, T. W. (1964), *Transforming Traditional Agriculture*. New Haven, CT: Yale University Press

Schumpeter, J. (1954), *The History of Economic Analysis*. Oxford: Oxford University Press

Stiglitz, J. E. (1988), "Economic Organization, Information, and Development," in H. Chenery and T. N. Srinivasan, eds., *Handbook of Development Economics*, volume 1. Amsterdam: North-Holland: 93–160

Wade, R. (1990), *Governing the Market: Economic Theory and the Role of Government in East Asian Industrialization*. Princeton, NJ: Princeton University Press

(1993), "Managing Trade: Taiwan and South Korea as Challenges to Economics and Political Science," *Comparative Politics* 25(2): 147–67

World Bank (1991), *World Development Report 1991: The Challenge of Development*. Oxford and New York: Oxford University Press

10 | Political reform

Robert H. Bates

This chapter describes the process of political reform in late twentieth-century Africa and explores its impact on the economic behavior of governments. When I speak of "political reform," I refer to the movement from no-party or one-party to multi-party political systems or from military to civilian regimes. Largely ignoring political liberties – freedom of association

This chapter draws extensively from Humphreys and Bates (2005). The chapter was written with financial support from the National Science Foundation (Grant SES 9905568), the Carnegie Corporation, and the Center for International Development and the Weatherhead Center for International Affairs of Harvard University. I wrote it while a Moore Distinguished Scholar at the California Institute of Technology. The chapter has benefited greatly from comments and criticisms received at seminars held at Harvard University, Guelo Brittany, and at the annual meetings of the AERC 2004 in Nairobi. Special thanks go to Steven Block for his criticisms and corrections. As ever, Karen Ferree and Smita Singh deserve much of the credit for this work. I also wish to thank Matthew Hindeman and Marcus Alexander for their technical assistance. The author alone is to be blamed for its shortcomings.

and expression, for example – and political rights – such as the right to vote and campaign for office – I join with Ottaway (1997), Ihonovbere (1998), and others (e.g. Hutchful 1997)) in distinguishing between *democratization* and *reform*, and focus solely on the latter.[1]

To trace the trajectory of political reform, I turn to the standard chronicles[2] and for forty-six countries over a twenty-six year period (1970–95) I ask: did the head of state in place on December 31 of that year preside over:

- A no-party system – i.e. a political system in which parties were legally banned and effectively suppressed?
- A single-party system?
- Or a multi-party political system?[3]

I also ask whether the head of state was – or was not –a military official. Political reform involves the transition from a no- or single-party to a multi-party political system, or from a military to a civilian regime.

1   Background

In the course of their strategic retreat from the continent, imperial governments first granted power to local legislatures, then shared power with cabinets that included local politicians, and finally surrendered power to local executives. These executives then briefly governed their nations before the devolution of full sovereignty. The culmination of each step was the introduction of elections in which rival parties put forward competing candidates for office. In the last few years before independence, rather than being selected by a bureaucrat, the legislator or executive was instead chosen by a local electorate.

In a careful study of political change in twenty-six francophone and anglophone polities in Africa, Ruth Berns Collier (1982) reports that in this period of self-government, nine of these countries formed a single-party system. "In most," she writes, "the overwhelming electoral victory of a single party or the [voluntary] merger of two parties into one made it possible for that party effectively to eliminate all competition" (Collier 1982: 95). In these

---

[1] This distinction also implies that the measure of political reform overlooks the quality of multi-party competition; that is, whether elections were free and fair.

[2] *Keesing's Contemporary Archives*, *Country Profiles* of the *Economist Intelligence Unit*, *Africa Research Bulletin*, *Africa Contemporary Record*, *Africa Confidential*, and *Africa South of the Sahara*.

[3] The category "competitive political system" includes both multi-party systems and systems where party competition was legal but did not take place. The latter category contained too few observations (twenty-one) to support meaningful analysis.

Table 10.1 *The sample set of forty-six countries.*

1. Angola	17. Gabon	33. Nigeria
2. Benin	18. The Gambia	34. Rwanda
3. Botswana	19. Ghana	35. São Tomé & Principe
4. Burkina Faso	20. Guinea	36. Senegal
5. Burundi	21. Guinea-Bissau	37. Seychelles
6. Cameroon	22. Kenya	38. Sierra Leone
7. Cape Verde	23. Lesotho	39. Somalia
8. CAR	24. Liberia	40. Sudan
9. Chad	25. Madagascar	41. Swaziland
10. Comoros	26. Malawi	42. Tanzania
11. Congo, Republic	27. Mali	43. Togo
12. Côte d'Ivoire	28. Mauritania	44. Uganda
13. Djibouti	29. Mauritius	45. Zambia
14. DRC	30. Mozambique	46. Zimbabwe
15. Equatorial Guinea	31. Namibia	
16. Ethiopia	32. Niger	

nine countries, then, multi-party competition came to an end even before independence.

In the post-independence period, seven more of Collier's sample of twenty-six states adopted single-party systems: "In most of these," she writes, "the one-party states did not result from electoral victory or merger but from the banning of all opposition parties or the outright rigging of elections" (Collier 1982: 95).[4]

Within three years after independence, a new form of authoritarianism emerged. In the early 1960s, the armies of Benin, Madagascar, Sudan, Togo, and Congo (Brazzaville) overthrew their civilian leaders. In the forty-six-country sample employed for the present study (see table 10.1), by 1970, only nine – or 25 percent of those that had achieved political independence – retained competitive systems.

Table 10.2 presents the distribution of the types of party systems that prevailed over the sample period (1970–95). Table 10.3 portrays the incidence of military rule. To be noted is that the two are correlated (see table 10.4), with the great majority of military rulers presiding over no-party systems.

The late 1970s marked the peak period of military rule (table 10.3); the late 1980s that of single-party systems (table 10.2). Overall, until the mid-1990s the majority of the African governments were authoritarian: on average, a

---

[4] For an overview of the formation of single-party regimes, see Coleman and Rosberg (1964).

Table 10.2 *Nature of party system, 1970–1995.*

Time period	Distribution of country-years			
	No-party	One-party	Multi-party	Total
1970–4				
Number	70	83	28	181
%	38.67	45.86	15.47	100.00
1975–9				
Number	93	97	25	215
%	43.26	45.12	11.63	100.00
1980–4				
Number	75	111	36	222
%	33.78	50.00	16.22	100.00
1985–9				
Number	72	110	33	215
%	33.49	51.16	15.35	100.00
1990–5				
Number	64	68	127	259
%	24.71	26.25	49.03	100.00
All years				
Number	374	469	249	1,092
%	34.25	42.95	22.80	100.00

third of the heads of state came from the military and three-quarters presided over no-party or single-party systems.

The period of most rapid change came in the period of political reform: the late 1980s and early 1990s. In that era, the percent of heads of state who came from the military fell from 33 percent to 23 percent and the portion of the chief executives that presided over single-party regimes fell from one-half to one-quarter. For the first time in the sample period (1970–95), multi-party political systems became the modal form of government in SSA.

Throughout this book, we partition the cases into three "growth opportunity" categories: landlocked and resource-scarce, coastal and resource-scarce, and resource-rich (see table 10.5 and chapter 2). Doing so here, we find that throughout most of the sample period, no-party government provided the modal form of rule in the landlocked and resource-scarce regions of Africa; single-party systems held sway in the countries on the coast. Resource-rich nations proved more variable. When political reform took place, it struck with particular force in the latter two groups, where 60 percent or more of the sample set of countries adopted multi-party political regimes.

Table 10.3 *Military head of state, 1970–1995.*

	Distribution of country-years		
	Military head of state?		
Time period	No	Yes	Total
1970–4			
Number	129	63	192
%	67.19	32.81	
1975–9			
Number	141	79	220
%	64.09	35.91	
1980–4			
Number	146	74	220
%	66.36	33.64	
1985–9			
Number	149	71	220
%	67.73	32.27	
1990–5			
Number	164	49	213
%	77.00	23.00	
Total			
Number	729	336	1,065
%	68.45	31.55	

Table 10.4 *Military rule and the party system.*

			Type of party system			
Distribution of country-years			No-party	One-party	Multi-party	All
Chief executive in military?	No	Number	107	372	239	718
		% of systems	14.90	51.81	33.29	100.00
		% of execs	29.32	82.48	98.35	
	Yes	Number	258	79	4	341
		% of systems	75.66	23.17	1.17	100.00
		% of execs	70.68	17.52	1.65	
	Total	Number	365	451	243	1,059
		% of systems	34.47	42.59	22.95	100.00
		% of execs	100.00	100.00	100.00	

Table 10.5 *Party system, by opportunity group, 1970–1994*
A 1970–4 and 1975–9

Distribution of country-years	Time period							
	1970–4				1975–9			
	No-party	Single-party	Multi-party	Total	No-party	Single-party	Multi-party	Total
Landlocked								
Number	36	23	1	60	45	14	2	51
%	60.0	38.33	1.67		73.8	23.0	3.28	
Coastal								
Number	27	45	19	91	32	68	17	117
%	29.7	49.5	20.9		27.35	58.1	14.5	
Resource-rich								
Number	7	15	8	30	16	15	6	37
%	23.3	50.0	26.67		43.2	40.5	16.2	
Total								
Number	70	83	28	181	93	97	25	215
%	38.7	45.9	15.47		43.3	45.1	11.6	

Notes: The classification by opportunity group applies to country-years and is time-varying. Here "landlocked" and "coastal" refer to country-years that are not only geographically either landlocked or coastal, but also resource-scarce by the criteria developed in chapter 2. Resource-rich country-years refer to geographically landlocked or coastal countries in which natural-resource exports pass various thresholds (see chapter 2).

B 1980–4 and 1985–9

Distribution of country-years	Time period							
	1980–4				1985–9			
	No-party	Single-party	Multi-party	Total	No-party	Single-party	Multi-party	Total
Landlocked								
Number	34	21	10	65	33	27	5	65
%	52.3	32.1	15.4		50.8	41.5	7.69	
Coastal								
Number	25	70	17	112	15	67	23	105
%	22.3	62.5	15.2		14.3	63.8	21.9	
Resource-rich								
Number	16	20	9	45	24	16	5	45
%	35.6	44.4	20.0		53.3	35.6	11.1	
Total								
Number	75	111	36	272	72	110	33	215
%	33.8	50	16.2		33.5	51.2	15.4	

Notes: See table 10.5, panel A.

C 1990–4

Distribution of country-years	Time period			
	1990–4			
	No-party	Single-party	Multi-party	Total
Landlocked				
Number	30	24	24	78
%	38.5	36.8	30.8	
Coastal				
Number	19	38	61	118
%	16.1	32.2	51.7	
Resource-rich				
Number	15	6	42	63
%	23.8	9.52	66.67	
Total				
Number	64	68	127	259
%	24.7	26.3	49	

Notes: See table 10.5, panel A.

2 Explaining political reform

In their attempts to account for the change from authoritarian forms of government, scholars have advanced two major explanations. One emphasizes the role of global forces and in particular the role of donors and financial institutions. The second stresses the importance of political forces that operate within Africa.

2.1 The international path

As noted in Ndulu's chapter 9, by the end of the 1970s, the international community was fully aware of the failure of African development. Emboldened by the reformist mandate bestowed by its President, Robert McNamara, the World Bank had financed a dazzling array of small-farmer and community-level projects. As recounted in its official history, the World Bank's own evaluations revealed a distressingly low rate of return for its Africa projects: "More than any other task the Bank had undertaken, its engagement with Sub-Saharan Africa sapped the institution's ... confidence," it reports (Kapur 1997: 720). When seeking reasons for the failure of its projects, the Bank found them in "the policy environment." As documented in its famed "Berg Report,"[5] Africa's economies were subject to a mix of policies that distorted market prices and undermined economic incentives and so crippled growth and development.

In addition to being a financer of projects, the World Bank then became an advisor to governments. In pursuit of policy change, it drew upon two sources of strength. The first was expertise. Through publications, seminars, and the training of public servants, the Bank sought to expose the economic costs of prevailing policies and to offer alternatives. The second was capital. In any given country at any given time, the Bank would normally finance a multitude of projects, the cancellation of any one of which would go largely unnoticed by the national government. To gain the attention of policy-makers, Please (1984) writes, the Bank therefore began to bundle its projects into sectoral programs; more would then be at risk were the Bank to suspend its lending. Sectoral programs soon gave way to country programs and to conditionality, as the Bank sought to strengthen further its leverage over policy-makers in debtor nations and to sharpen the incentives for policy reform.

The World Bank was but one of several sources of finance, however; private banks, bilateral donors and increasingly the IMF also provided credit to African governments. In pursuit of power, the Bank therefore sought to build coalitions among creditors. Given international realities, however, a united front proved difficult to achieve. In the midst of the Cold War, the USA, for example, simply refused to join any coalition threatening to suspend aid to Mobutu, who was providing arms and bases to those fighting Marxists in Angola. And when the USA might pursue collective efforts to elicit changes in socialist countries, other nations – those in Scandinavia, for example – would then breach the creditors' alliance out of ideological sympathy or humanitarian concerns.

As donors focused on the behavior of African governments, they necessarily struggled with the question: why would these governments adopt policies that undermined economic prosperity? Over time, a consensus emerged: that the behavior of these governments reflected their lack of political accountability. Not being accountable, governments in Africa could adopt policies that conferred concentrated benefits on the elites while imposing widely distributed costs on those who generated the wealth of the nation. In its pursuit of ways to alter the economic environment faced by private agents in Africa's economies, the World Bank therefore began to focus not only on policy choices but also on institutional reform.[6]

In the late 1980s and early 1990s, changes at the global level strengthened the hand of Africa's creditors. Under the presidency of Ronald Reagan, the USA vigorously backstopped the efforts of international financial

---

[5] World Bank (1981).   [6] See, for example, World Bank (1989, 1991).

institutions to reduce the role of governments and to strengthen that of markets in the developing countries. The collapse of the Labour Party and the eleven-year rule of Margaret Thatcher aligned Britain's agenda with that of the USA. And after the fall of the Labor government in Norway in 1981 and the Social Democratic government a decade later, African governments seeking to resist reforms could no longer count on support from the Scandinavian countries.

The fundamental change came, however, with the collapse of communism. The new democracies in middle-income Europe now had a stronger claim on international assistance than did the impoverished authoritarian regimes of Africa. The ability of the international financial community to elicit institutional reform rose accordingly.

The "international" explanation of political reform thus focuses on the place of Africa within the global system and stresses the role of foreign creditors and international capital. There exists a second account, however, which I label the "domestic" narrative. By way of introduction, consider the words of Adu Boahen, a long-term challenger of Ghana's military regimes: "Adu Boahen [*sic*] was detained . . . for [my] role in . . . campaigns for the reintroduction of multiparty democracy in Ghana . . . long before anybody heard of Mikhail Gorbachev or of World Bank and IMF conditionalities" (Boahen 1997: 146). Boahen's indignation imparts weight to his claim that the source of political change lay in the townships of Africa rather than in the offices of the international financial community.

2.2   The domestic path

With the decline of Africa's economies in the 1970s came the erosion of government revenues and the quality of the services that they could provide. When Sahr Kpundeh examined the pay slip of Freetown's Commissioner of Taxes, for example, he noted a monthly salary of Le 13,941.00.[7] "If [the Commissioner] buys a bag of rice at Le 8,200 . . . every month to feed his family," Kpundeh wrote, "and pays Le 300 for transportation to and from work every day, . . . his expenses exceed his earnings" (Kpundeh 2004: 67). The Commissioner's response, Kpundeh reports, was to devote less time to collecting the public's revenues and to devote more to generating an income for himself and his family (2004: 67).

MacGaffey (1991: 14) finds similar patterns in the DRC. Drawing on a survey of household finances in Kinshasa, she notes that over two-thirds of the expenditures made by public employees went to the purchase of food and that the portion had increased in recent years while that spent on meat

---

[7] US $28 (!) at the time of writing.

and fish had declined. The first, she stresses, is the mark of poverty; the second, of immiseration.

In response to the erosion in their salaries, government workers exited the public domain and turned to private economic activity.[8] They also joined the ranks of those who opposed the governments that employed them.

Côte d'Ivoire offers an apt example. During the recession of the 1970s, its economy was fortuitously buoyed by favorable prices for coffee and cocoa, its principal exports. In 1978, however, these prices, too, declined – just as petroleum prices doubled. During the export boom, the government had launched massive development programs in the North, a region long disgruntled by its marginal position in the forest-based economy. The bills for this expansion came due just as the capacity to finance them declined and the government sought to retrench. As stated by Rapley (1993: 58–9), the

austerity program hit with particular force on the civil servants, who found their budgets frozen; their programs cut; and their salaries left unpaid. In response, public servants turned on the government that employed them: transport workers closed down bus lines, workers disrupted the supply of electricity to Abidjan, the national capital, and airport employees closed down the national airport (see also Faure 1989).

For public servants, the economic collapse of the state represented a threat to private incomes; for private citizens, it resulted in a loss of public services. Clinics were left without medicines, as governments could not afford to import them – or as the staff would sell them to supplement their meager wages. Schools were left without textbooks, and teachers often spent as much time in commerce as they did in instruction. Private traders faced increased costs from the decay of the roads, the inefficiency of the harbors, and the extraction of bribes. Telephone facilities decayed and postal workers trimmed their hours to fit their pay. Many in the private sector therefore turned from activities that made extensive use of public services to those that did not, shifting from production for exchange into self-sufficiency. Many also joined in demands for political reform (Bratton and van de Walle 1997).

Two accounts thus lead to the same end: protests against authoritarian rule. In several countries, the opposition organized national conferences that transformed military governments into civilian regimes and uncompetitive into competitive party systems. In 1990, Benin became the first to convene such a conference. Seeking to emulate Benin's achievements, reformers in

---

[8] By the mid-1980s, MacGaffey (1991) notes, salaries constituted less than one-half of the incomes of those who worked in the public sector.

neighboring states then organized conferences of their own. A wave of political reform spread first through West Africa and then inland and to the south, encompassing both French- and English-speaking states.[9]

3 Empirics

To deepen our understanding of political reform, we turn from qualitative accounts to quantitative data drawn from forty-six countries over the period 1970–95 (see table 10.1).

The most straightforward way of exploring the patterns described in section 2 would be to estimate the entries in a transition matrix that would represent the probability of a political system enduring from one period to the next or of altering in form. The paucity of information confounds this approach, however. Given the high degree of persistence in the political systems of Africa, the number of informative observations is small. Even when applying techniques designed for the investigation of rare events (King and Zeng 2001), I have been unable to secure precise estimates of the impact of key variables upon the likelihood of such transitions.

Rather than employing Markov models to explore transitions, I therefore rely upon probit and logit estimation. Both treat the dependent variable as a binary variable. A country then is either reformed and thus 1, or authoritarian and thus 0.

I have offered two interpretations of the process of reform, one based on international forces and the other on those within Africa. To capture the first, I include a measure of AID, or more precisely, aid dependence; the variable represents the value of international grants measured as a percent of the central government's budget. Designating with a dummy variable all observations recorded after 1988, I distinguish the period after the Cold War; I call this variable POST-1988. The dependent variable is the likelihood of abandoning authoritarian forms of government. Insofar as international factors shaped the process of reform, the coefficients on these variables should be positive in sign and statistically significant.

It was by all accounts the literate, urban-based, middle class that provided the impetus for political reform. Insofar as reform stemmed from sources internal to Africa, then the likelihood of reform should be significantly and positively related to (the log of) *per capita* INCOME, to the percent of the adult population that could read or write (LITERACY), and to the percentage living in urban areas (URBAN POPULATION). The influence of local sources of reform should also become evident in the relationship between UNREST and reform. UNREST registers whether there were reports

---

[9] It will be noticed that South Africa is excluded from this part of the analysis.

of mass demonstrations in any given year (1) and whether, if so, they became violent (2). It should also become evident in the relationship between the likelihood of reform in one country and the level of reform in its neighbors, with the latter being captured in a variable called NEIGHBORHOOD.

Both the "international" and "domestic" accounts of reform emphasize the role of economic decline, be it of the private economy or of public services; I therefore include GROWTH and public REVENUES in the equations. To control for the strong inertial property of political arrangements, I also include a measure of the "stock" of political institutions. The variable DURATION indicates the number of years in which the incumbent political system – be it no-party, one-party or multi-party – has been in place.

A major difficulty confronting these attempts at estimation is the prevalence of missing values in the data.[10] Resorting to case-wise deletion – that is, to dropping observations which lack data for key variables – decreases the efficiency and increases the potential for bias in the estimates. I therefore employ the methods developed by Rubin (1996) and Schafer (1997) to impute multiple estimates of the missing values and to calculate their distributions, and the techniques developed by the Harvard Data Center to estimate and to interpret the estimates derived from the resultant data.[11] Another difficulty is the possible significance of omitted variables, which could either cause spurious relationships or endogeneity. To counter those possibilities I introduce fixed effects and instrumental variables.

Table 10.6 provides a description of the variables, their distribution, and the sources from which they were taken. Table 10.7 contains the probit estimates drawn from pooled samples and table 10.8 conditional logit estimates that allow for country-specific effects. In each table, (2) and (4) employ the composite score, MODERNITY rather than INCOME, LITERACY AND URBAN POPULATION. The variable NEIGHBORHOOD registers the average level of political reform in the neighboring states.

In both tables 10.7 and 10.8, the coefficients relate the value of the independent variables to the likelihood of reform. In column (1) and (2), the dependent variable takes the value of 1 if the country possesses a multi-party political system and 0 otherwise. In column (3) and (4), the dependent variable takes the value 1 if the government is headed by a military official and 0 otherwise. In all equations, the standard errors are robust and clustered by country. The values of all right-hand-side variables are lagged by one year.

The estimates document the inertial property of political institutions and the tendency of institutions to persist; in so doing, they also highlight the magnitude of the challenge that faced the reformers. In column (1) and (2) in table 10.7, the coefficients on the duration indicators

---

[10] This will come as no surprise to anyone who studies Africa. See Honaker (2000).
[11] King, Tomz, and Wittenberg (2000).

Table 10.6 *Description of variables used in tables 10.7 and 10.9.*

Variable name	Definition/Units	Mean	Standard error of mean
Dependent variables:			
MULTI-PARTY	1 if multi-party system, *de facto* or *de jure*; 0 otherwise	0.208	0.406
MILITARY	1 if chief executive a military official; 0 otherwise	0.441	0.479
Explanatory variables:			
INCOME	log of GDP *per capita* (PPP)	6.851	0.605
LITERACY	Percent of adult population literate	58.917	19.921
URBAN POPULATION	Percent of population living in cities	25.849	13.476
MODERNITY	Factor score derived from principal components factor analysis of INCOME, URBAN POPULATION, AND LITERACY	−1.6 E-02	0.024
GROWTH	Annual rate of growth of GDP	0.152	8.290
REVENUES	Central government revenues as percent of GDP	19.486	10.165
AID	International grants as percent of central government budget	53.643	68.934
OIL	Dollar value of oil exports *per capita*	86.071	473.730
DURATION:			
No-party	Length of time NO-PARTY system in place (see below)	2.405	4.685
Single-party	Length of time SINGLE-PARTY system in place (see below)	3.415	5.551
Multi-party	Length of time MULTI-PARTY system in place (see above)	1.271	3.934
NO-PARTY	1 if chief executive achieves power without an election; 0 otherwise	0.313	0.463
SINGLE PARTY	1 if chief executive elected to office but faced no opposition party	0.392	0.483
NEIGHBORHOOD	Average level of reform in neighboring states	2.741	1.112
POST-1988	1 if year 1988–95; 0 otherwise	0.269	0.444

Table 10.7 *Probit estimation of covariates of reform.*

	MULTI-PARTY political system		MILITARY rule	
Variable	(1)	(2)	(3)	(4)
INCOME	0.287	–	−1.317	–
	(1.600)	–	(−7.176)***	–
LITERACY	0.011	–	−0.007	–
	(2.302)**	–	(−2.315)**	–
URBAN POPULATION	0.008	–	0.018	–
	(1.440)	–	(3.892)***	–
MODERNITY	–	0.440	–	−0.518
	–	(3.315)***	–	(−5.264)***
GROWTH	0.008	1.361	−0.002	−0.009
	(1.191)	(0.174)	(−0.257)	(−1.400)
REVENUES	−0.009	−0.007	−0.033	−0.042
	(−0.649)	(−0.532)	(−3.718)***	(−4.667)***
AID	−0.004	−0.005	−0.007	−0.005
	(−1.726)*	(−2.049)**	(−3.090)***	(−2.026)*
OIL	−0.001	0.001	0.001	0.001
	(−1.286)	(−1.682)*	(1.771)*	(0.180)
UNREST	−0.007	−0.001	0.007	0.028
	(−0.105)	(−0.022)	(0.139)	(0.556)
DURATION:				
No-party	−0.010	−0.099	0.103	0.101
	(−4.383)***	(−4.323)***	(6.571)***	(6.961)***
Single-party	−0.105	−0.103	−0.029	−0.014
	(−4.8)***	(−4.689)***	(−2.207)**	(−1.173)
Multi-party	0.243	0.245	−0.022	−0.060
	(2.006)**	(2.023)**	(−0.443)	(−1.172)
NEIGHBORHOOD	0.174	0.161	−0.216	−0.108
	(2.927)***	(2.728)***	(−3.768)***	(−2.079)**
POST-1988	1.132	1.185	−0.125	−0.016
	(7.452)***	(8.249)***	(−0.851)	(−0.120)
No. obs.	1,088	1,088	1,088	1,088

Note: *t*-statistic in parentheses. *= 0.10 confidence level; ** = 0.05 confidence level; *** = 0.01 confidence level.

Table 10.8 *Conditional fixed-effects estimation of covariates of reform.*

Variable	Dependent variable			
	MULTI-PARTY political system		MILITARY rule	
	(1)	(2)	(3)	(4)
INCOME	1.139	–	−2.552	–
	(1.461)	–	(−3.815)***	–
LITERACY	0.024	–	0.013	–
	(0.963)	–	(0.599)	–
URBAN POPULATION	0.091	–	0.009	–
	(1.655)	–	(0.254)	–
MODERNITY	–	2.288	–	−1.266
	–	(3.117)***	–	(−1.958)*
GROWTH	0.017	0.013	−0.008	−0.022
	(0.982)	(0.777)	(−0.502)	(−1.556)
REVENUES	−0.009	−0.010	−0.004	−0.010
	(−0.279)	(−0.304)	(−0.158)	(−0.420)
AID	−0.008	−0.007	−0.004	−0.001
	(−1.216)	(−1.104)	(−0.803)	(−0.229)
OIL	0.001	0.001	0.001	0.001
	(0.326)	(0.293)	(0.306)	(0.213)
UNREST	−0.034	−0.029	0.140	0.165
	(−0.209)	(−0.178)	(0..967)	(1.225)
DURATION:				
No-party	−0.152	−0.151	0.298	0.317
	(−2.905)***	(−2.945)***	(6.011)***	(6.535)***
Single-party	−0.147	−0.146	−0.107	−0.082
	(−3.793)***	(−3.838)***	(−2.390)**	(−1.931)*
Multi-party	0.529	0.515	−0.031	−0.097
	(4.001)**	(3.925)***	(−0.246)	(−0.723)
NEIGHBORHOOD	0.366	0.384	−0.597	−0.454
	(2.017)**	(2.255)**	(−3.791)***	(−3.046)***
POST-1988	1.683	1.826	−0.977	−0.437
	(3.551)***	(4.146)***	(−2.255)**	(−1.210)
No. obs.	710	710	710	710

Note: *t*-statistic in parentheses. *= 0.10 confidence level; ** = 0.05 confidence level; ***= 0.01 confidence level.

for no- and single-party systems are highly significant;[12] as seen in table 10.8, they remain significant even after the introduction of fixed effects. Returning to table 10.7, notice, too, the coefficients on government REVENUES: all are negative and, for military governments, they are highly significant. Governments with higher revenues were more likely to be civilian than were those that lacked financial resources. As seen in table 10.8, the signs but not the significance levels persist in the fixed-effects, conditional logistic estimations.

The estimates in tables 10.7 and 10.8 provide support for the "domestic" path toward political reform. In both, the greater the percent of the adult population who were literate (LITERACY) and the higher the average (log of) INCOME, the more likely were authoritarian regimes to fall. In the estimates that incorporate fixed effects (table 10.8), the coefficients on the individual components of modernity become insignificant; evidence for the broader argument nonetheless remains the coefficient on the aggregate measure, MODERNITY, which is statistically significant and of the expected sign.[13] The data also confirm the importance of political contagion within Africa. As seen in the coefficient on NEIGHBORHOOD, the higher the average level of political reform in surrounding countries, the greater the likelihood of reform in a given nation. Unexpectedly, the level of domestic UNREST bears little relationship to the outcome of the struggle for reform. Inspection of the data indicates that the level of unrest was high in countries where reform triumphed (e.g. Benin) as well as in countries where it failed (e.g. Togo). Authoritarian governments appear to have fallen not because they faced more unrest but because they were unable to respond to it

Turning to the indicators of international forces, interesting differences emerge between the two kinds of reform: the movement to MULTI-PARTY political systems and from MILITARY to civilian government. In tables 10.7 and 10.8, the coefficient on POST-1988, the dummy variable marking the post-Cold War period, shifts positively and significantly for the movement to a competitive political system (table 10.7). In the case of military regimes, the coefficient on POST-1988 is insignificant in three of the four equations: the toppling of military governments failed to accelerate after the Cold War. The late-century increase in the number of competitive regimes resulted more from the fall of single-party systems than it did from the fall of no-party (and therefore largely military) systems.[14]

---

[12] That the coefficients on no-party systems are positive in (3) and (4) merely re-confirms that military governments tend to form no-party regimes.

[13] Recall that the variable MODERNITY is derived from a principle components analysis of INCOME, LITERACY, and URBAN POPULATION.

[14] Interacting the period dummy with the "stock" of different kinds of governments confirms that it was the no-party systems that tended to become competitive in the post-war period; the no-party systems – the regimes of choice for military governments – behaved no differently in this respect in the periods before and after 1988.

The data suggest that AID dependence played a different role in the two kinds of transitions. The probit estimates computed from the pooled sample (column (1) and (2) in table 10.7) suggest that higher levels of aid dependence rendered no- and single-party governments *less* likely to transition to multi-party political regimes. The signs but not the significance levels persist in the conditional logit (fixed effects) estimates (column (1) and (2) in table 10.8). By contrast, in *all* models, higher levels of aid dependence rendered the transition from military rule *more* likely (column (3) and (4) in tables 10.7 and 10.8). Aid dependence thus appears to have played a greater role in the transition from military government to civilian rule than it did in the transition from no- or single- to multi-party systems.

Note the coefficients on OIL in column (2) and (3) in table 10.7. In keeping with the literature on the "resource curse" (Ross 1999; Sachs and Warner 1999), the coefficient suggests that governments blessed with an abundance of natural resources may be more likely to be authoritarian. But note also the coefficient in column (3) and (4): the greater the access to oil revenues, the less likely the government is military.

A problem confronting the estimates reported in tables 10.7 and 10.8 is the possible impact of reciprocal causation: GROWTH or REVENUES could be affected by changes in political regime, for example, and the estimates therefore need to be corrected for the impact of endogeneity. Particularly when estimating equations that include qualitative dependent variables and multiple data sets, it proves difficult to correct for this source of bias. Suitable techniques[15] exist only for probit estimation. When addressing the problem of endogeneity, I used for instruments lagged values of the endogenous variables, the rate of growth of the OECD economies, the percent of exports comprising primary products, and the percent of tax revenues derived from international trade. The coefficients on most variables remained virtually unchanged. Not surprisingly, given the volatility of short-run growth rates, the coefficients for the instrumented values of GROWTH were poorly estimated. Those for REVENUES were more precise and suggest that the uncorrected estimates understate the impact of government revenues on political stability by roughly 50 percent.

It is useful to shift our focus from the sign and significance of the coefficients to an assessment of their magnitude. The data in table 10.9 provide estimates of the magnitude of the change in the likelihood of reform that is associated with a change in the magnitude of a given independent variable, while the other such variables are held at their median values. Recall that "reform" refers to the movement *to* a competitive party system and *away*

---

[15] "Suitable" implies, among other things, that the technique can be applied to multiple imputed data sets.

Table 10.9 *Political reform (first differences).*

	Dependent variable			
Variable	Multi-party rule (1)	Multi-party rule (2)	Military rule (3)	Military rule (4)
INCOME	0.045	–	−0.275	–
Lowest → highest	(−0.008 0.110)	–	(−0.348 −0.202)	–
LITERACY	0.080	–	−0.073	–
Lowest → highest	(0.017 0.171)	–	(−0.131 −0.002)	–
URBAN POPULATION	0.033	–	0.101	–
Lowest → highest	(−0.01 0.086)	–	(0.051 0.152)	–
MODERNIZATION	–	0.105	–	−0.162
Lowest → highest	–	(0.04 0.187)	–	(−0.223 −0.106)
GROWTH	0.016	0.017	−0.005	−0.024
Lowest → highest	(−0.01 0.043)	(−0.007 0.044)	(−0.038 0.032)	(−0.507 0.10)
REVENUES	−0.024	0.018	−0.121	−0.147
Lowest → highest	(−0.008 0.044)	(−0.007 0.048)	(−0.179 −0.061)	(−0.202 −0.091)
AID	−0.045	−0.051	−0.105	−0.071
Lowest → highest	(−0.103 0.003)	(−0.106 −0.044)	(−0.181 −0.046)	(−0.148 −0.015)
OIL	0.0	0	0	0
Lowest → highest	(0.0 0.0)	(0.0 0.0)	(0.0 0.0)	(0.0 0.0)
UNREST	−0.002	0.001	0.006	0.019
0 → 1	(−0.060 0.065)	(−0.054 0.069)	(−0.060 0.076)	(−0.044 0.085)
DURATION:				
NO-PARTY	−0.023	−0.022	0.035	0.033
0 → 1	(−0.042 −0.009)	(−0.04 −0.09)	(0.026 0.043)	(0.025 0.040)
SINGLE-PARTY	−0.024	−0.023	−0.009	−0.005
0 → 1	(−0.044 −0.010)	(−0.042 −0.009)	(−0.019 −0.001)	(−0.012 0.002)
COMPETITIVE	0.062	0.061	−0.008	−0.019
0 → 1	(0.001 0.111)	(0.003 0.109)	(−0.041 0.024)	(−0.052 0.012)
NEIGHBORHOOD	0.050	0.045	−0.083	−0.041
Lowest → highest	(0.018 0.086)	(0.015 0.078)	(−0.127 −0.041)	(−0.08 −0.002)
POST-1988	0.386	0.402	−0.037	−0.004
0 → 1	(0.278 0.492)	(0.294 0.503)	(−0.117 0.053)	(−0.082 0.089)

Note: "Lowest → highest" indicates a movement from the lowest to the highest quartile, i.e. over the interquartile range. In the case of POST-1998, 0 → 1 indicates a movement from before to after. In the case of the DURATION variables, 0 → 1 represents an increase of an additional year. The values in parentheses define the 95% confidence interval of the estimate.

from a military regime. For the DURATION variables, the estimates indicate the impact of an additional year of a no- or single-party system or a multi-party political regime. For the POST-1988 dummy, the change ranges from 0 to 1 – i.e. from before to after the Cold War. For the other variables, the value is changed from the 25th to the 75th percentile of the sample values.

The results in column (1) suggest that if a country like Liberia (which is in the lowest quartile) could increase its literacy rate to that of Zimbabwe (which is in the highest), then the likelihood of adopting a competitive political system would increase by 8 percentage points (with the 5 percent confidence interval of 0.017 to 0.171 percent). Those in column (3) suggest that had the central government of Chad (which in 1974 occupied the 75th percentile) derived as small a percent of its revenues from international grants as did Mauritius (which occupied the 25th), then the likelihood of Chad adopting a civilian regime would have increased by 11 percentage points (with the 5 percent confidence interval of 4.6 to 18.1 percent). Interestingly, it is the end of the Cold War that appears to have had the greatest effect upon the change to a competitive political system. For the change from military to civilian regimes, the major force appears to have been internal rather than global in origin, with the so-called "modernization" variables having the greatest effect. In both cases, AID dependency appears, however, to have accelerated the reform of military regimes.

4   The impact of political reform

While champions of political reform viewed it as good in itself, they also viewed it as a means for securing economic reform. Being unconstrained by the need to compete for popular support, it was argued, authoritarian governments were more likely to engage in economic predation. They were less likely to govern with economic restraint and therefore prone to distort key prices in the macroeconomy: the exchange rate, the interest rate, the aggregate price level. Such arguments were championed both by African intellectuals who posited a link between poor governance and poverty (Ake 1990) and by international donors who increasingly viewed political accountability as a necessary precondition for economic reform (World Bank 1994).

In this section, I explore and evaluate the logic of this argument.[16] In doing so, I find that while political accountability appears to relate to reduced opportunism by governments, it fails to relate to our (less than perfect!) measure of macroeconomic restraint. In subsequent sections, I therefore explore the possibility that political accountability fails because political competition creates incentives for governments to manipulate the macroeconomy for short-term political advantage.

---

[16] More accurately, Macartan Humphreys and I: see Humphreys and Bates (2005).

4.1   Political accountability

Using a principal–agent framework, Barro (1973), Ferejohn (1986), Persson and Tabellini (2000), and others (see Besley 2006) have crafted models of political accountability and derived from them the equilibrium behavior of governments. In this section, I employ such a model in order to explore the link between political reform in Africa and the policy choices of its governments.

In models of political accountability, the citizens move first, choosing a minimum level of acceptable performance by their government. Knowing how the citizens have chosen, the government then chooses public policies, seeking to offer sufficient benefits to win renewal in power and to secure private benefits from office that are consistent with its retention of office. After its term has been completed, the citizens evaluate the government's performance. If some decisive group of citizens approves – a group that we call the selectorate – the citizenry may choose to renew the government's contract. If the selectorate fails to do so, the government departs from office and another is installed in its place. The game between the citizens and their government is played over an infinite number of periods of fixed length; each player's valuation of utility is given by the sum of welfare in each period, discounted for risk and time.

One way of securing greater accountability is to compel those who seek office to compete for the votes of the electorate. One step toward reform, then, is the change from a military to a civilian regime. Another is introducing multi-party systems where single- and no-party (i.e. nakedly authoritarian) systems had hitherto held sway. As we shall see, there exists an equilibrium for this game in which the strategy followed by citizens compels the government to produce more public goods and fewer private benefits than it might otherwise desire, and in which a wider selectorate (a larger M) increases the quality of policy on the margin. The model thus demonstrates that institutions of accountability – arrangements that allow the popular replacement of executives based on performance, or that widen the selectorate – *can* generate incentives that influence economic policy in the ways claimed by political reformers. I explore later why they fail in important respects to do so.

4.2   The economy

In this model, we think of an economy containing N individuals, indexed by $i \in \{1, 2, \ldots, N\}$ in which production is governed by an agent – the government – that manages the transformation between public goods – denoted by π – and private goods – denoted by ϕ – subject to the constraints that $f(\pi, \phi) \leq 1$ and $\pi, \phi \geq 0$. The function $f(\pi, \phi)$ captures the ease with which the agent can transform public into private goods. The income of each player – the government and all others – is written as $y_i = \pi + \phi_i$, where ϕ_i denotes individual i's allocation of the private good and where $\Sigma_i \phi_i = \phi$. The total income of the economy is $\Sigma_i y_i = N \cdot \pi(\phi) + \phi$.

Along the frontier defined by $f(\pi, \phi) = 1$, the supply of private goods is implicitly a function of the supply of private goods: $\phi = \phi(\pi)$. We assume that production sets are convex, so that $\phi_\pi \leq 0$ and $\phi_{\pi\pi}, \pi_{\phi\phi} < 0$. We also assume that $\phi_\pi(0) = 0$ and that $\pi_\phi < -1/N$, so that even the smallest transformation of public into private goods reduces total income. Under these conditions, the economy's income is maximized when the government refrains completely from transforming public into private goods. Put another way, rent-seeking is inefficient.

4.3   The polity

The government, acting as an agent, implements a set of policies that apportions resources between public and private goods. It can retain some of the private goods for its own consumption (i.e. generate and consume political rents). Alternatively, it can distribute such goods to influential followers.

The government is forward-looking and confronts two streams of future benefits. One is the reward of holding office, which it discounts for political risk and time at rate $\delta \in [0, 1]$. The other is the most rewarding alternative offered in the private sector, the per-period value of which is given by v, also discounted for time.[17] So long as the rewards from holding office exceed those from alternative employment, the government seeks to retain office.

Call the set of principals whose support is sufficient to return the government to office the selectorate; the selectorate is a strict sub-set of the principals and is of fixed size M. I assume that the government is incapable of credibly committing to honor its promises. It is the power of the selectorate to reward (or to punish) the government for meeting (or failing to meet) its expectations that generates incentives for it to adopt particular policies. If a sufficient number, M, of principals chooses not to re-select the government – alternatively, if the government fails to satisfy the demands of M principals – then the government is dismissed with some positive probability.

4.4   The game

In each period, there are three phases of play. In the first, each citizen has the option unilaterally to select a minimum satisfaction level, $y_i = \pi + \phi_i$,

---

[17] We treat v as exogenous and time-invariant and we assume that it is of less value to the government than the most attractive gains that can be made from the unconstrained use of office.

that represents the lowest level of performance that she will tolerate before seeking to dismiss the government. In the second, the government chooses a mixture of public and private goods and an allocation of the latter between itself and selected principals. In the third, the principals choose non-cooperatively whether to take some costless action to return the government to office.

Because the government cannot commit, the citizens "vote" retrospectively. Observing the government's performance in office and applying their performance standards, they express or withhold their approval of the government. If the members of the selectorate choose to return the government to office, they succeed in doing so. Should the government fail to satisfy the selectorate, it remains in power with probability $q \in (0, 1)$; otherwise, with probability $1 - q$, the government is dismissed and a new one is installed. In either case, play returns to the first phase in which principals can again choose performance criteria for the new term of office.

Within this framework, I look for an equilibrium in which principals employ a retrospective voting rule with cutoff points $\{y_i\}$ and the government undertakes actions that are feasible; that meet the demands of some set of M principals; and that leave no reason for any principal to alter her threshold in an effort to increase her well-being.

4.5 The impact of accountability

In what follows I denote possible allocations of public and private goods by $(\pi, \{\phi_{gov}, \phi_{pri}\})$ where $\{\phi_{gov}, \phi_{pri}\}$ describes the distribution of private goods between the government and private citizens. Note three benchmark values for public goods provision π.

4.5.1 The government's ideal

Like all actors in the model, the government seeks to maximize its income defined over private and public goods. If unconstrained, the government would appropriate all of the private goods and produce a level π_{min} of the public good satisfying $\phi_\pi = -1$.[18] The government's ideal allocation is therefore

$$(\pi_{min}, \{\phi(\pi_{min}), 0\}).$$

4.5.2 Participation constraint

A second benchmark value for π, which I label π_{max}, is the maximum value of π (and thus the minimum value of ϕ) that yields benefits to the

---

[18] Note that π_{min} will always exceed zero because of the properties of the transformation function, which render it increasingly costly to transform public into private goods.

government that are at least as valuable as those it could gain were it to choose opportunistically and suffer dismissal. $\pi_{\max}$ sets an upper bound on the level of collective goods that a government is willing to produce while seeking to remain in office. Assuming that the government consumes all private goods, this upper bound is given by the largest feasible value of π that satisfies:

$$\pi + \phi(\pi) \geq \left[\pi_{\min} + \phi(\pi_{\min}) + v\frac{\delta - \delta_q}{1 - \delta}\right]\frac{1 - \delta}{1 - \delta_q},$$

where δ_q is the component of the government's overall discount rate δ that is attributable to the probability of losing office.

The proof for this claim is given as Lemma 1 in the published article, where it is also demonstrated that $\pi_{\max} < \pi_{\min}$ and that $\pi_{\max}$ always exist.[19]

4.5.3 Feasibility constraint

The government manages the transformation of private into public goods. Should the government seek to secure office by generating private benefits for the selectorate, it would then have to produce less π and so would impose losses upon the economy. A third benchmark, then, is the value of π below which the costs that result from the distortion that arises from the transformation of public benefits into private goods become too great to allow the government to compensate the politically decisive set of M players through private transfers. It is given by the value of π for which the slope of $\phi(\pi)$ is $-(M + 1)$ – or, if no such point exists, by the maximal feasible supply of public goods, which satisfies $f(\pi, 0) = 1$. We call this value π_*, the corresponding value of private goods production is $\phi_* = \phi(\pi_*)$. Note that since $\pi_{\phi\phi} < 0$, $\pi_* > \pi_{\min}$.

When π is greater than π_*, then, the government can find M players that will be willing to accept a reduction in π in exchange for some increase in ϕ – an increase which the government can feasibly supply.

4.6 Equilibrium

These benchmark values of π help us to portray the equilibrium of this game.

Claim: It is a sub-game perfect stationary equilibrium for each principal, i, to demand $y_i^* = \pi^*$ in each period; for the government to produce $(\pi^*, \{\phi(\pi^*, 0\})$ in each period, where $\pi^* = \min(\pi_*, \pi_{\max})$; and for the selectorate to re-select the government.

---

[19] Humphreys and Bates (2005).

In equilibrium therefore, an accountable government satisfies its selectorate by supplying *public* goods. In addition, it shirks, producing positive amounts of private goods and consuming them itself.[20] But it consumes fewer private goods and produces more public goods than it would do were it left unaccountable. Moreover, the quality of policy is an increasing function of the size of the selectorate. A larger M means more public goods and less diversion of the economy's resources into the hands of political incumbents.

The logic of the model thus confirms the intuition of those who advocate greater levels of accountability for governments in Africa.

4.7   Testing the model[21]

The question remains: does accountability work in practice? Has *political* reform led to *economic* reform in Africa? Two measures can be employed to address this question. Both reflect the assessments of informed observers and both offer insight into the policy choices of governments. The first comes from the *International Country Risk Guide (ICRG)* and is produced by Political Risk Services (PRS).[22] Each year, the PRS convenes a panel of international investors to rate governments on a series of dimensions, each relevant to the political, economic, and financial risks faced by investors. For each country, our measure, OPPORTUNISM, combines ratings of the government's propensity to repudiate its financial obligations and its likelihood of expropriating private investments. To produce the measure, the two ratings are weighted by the loadings derived from principal components estimation. The resulting score provides a measure of the tendency to make opportunistic use of public power.

The World Bank's Country Policy and Institutional Assessment (CPIA) provides a second measure. The CPIA provides an annual evaluation of the conduct of governments that have loans outstanding with the Bank. The Bank's rating covers the policy performance of the government in twenty specific areas, grouped into four major categories (see table 10.10). Scoring the country's performance in each area from 1, for low, to 5, for high, the Bank calculates an aggregate score, or CPIA, which is the un-weighted average of the rating in each of the twenty areas.

---

[20] The proof is reported in Humphreys and Bates (2002). The logic derives from Adam and O'Connell (1999). Note that while formally this equilibrium is not unique, most of the other stationary sub-game perfect equilibria that we have identified are similar to that stated.

[21] For additional evidence, see Kanz (2005) and Stasavage (2005).

[22] http://www.countrydata.com/wizard/.

Table 10.10 *Country Policy and Institutional Assessments (CPIA).*

Disaggregated Elements of CPIA Index

  I. Macroeconomic management
1. General macroeconomic performance
2. Fiscal policy
3. Management of external debt
4. Macroeconomic management capacity
5. Sustainability of structural reforms

 II. Public sector management
1. Quality of budget and public investment process
2. Efficiency and equity of resource mobilization
3. Efficiency and equity of public expenditures
4. Accountability of the public service

III. Policies for sustainable and equitable growth
1. Trade policy
2. Foreign exchange regime
3. Financial stability and depth
4. Banking sector efficiency and resource mobilization
5. Property rights and rule-based governance
6. Competitive environment for the private sector
7. Factor and product markets
8. Environmental policies and regulations

IV. Policies for reducing inequalities
1. Poverty monitoring and analysis
2. Pro-poor targeting of programs
3. Safety nets

Rating scale: 1 = low; 5 = high

Source: Country Policy and Institutional Assessments, *Report on 1998 Ratings.* Washington, DC: The World Bank.

In essence, the CPIA provides a measure of the government's adherence to the so-called "Washington Consensus" (Williamson 1990, 1994). While the measure contains several flaws,[23] it provides an informed assessment of the

---

[23] Regressing the aggregate score against measures of macroeconomic balances – levels of government consumption, fiscal deficits, inflation, and so on – shows the measure to yield highly significant relationships with objective measures of policy choices and enhances our confidence in it. There are however some significant limitations. The measure mixes assessments of policies with outcomes; it assigns equal weights to each policy; and the policies in Category IV are largely irrelevant to the arguments of this chapter. Furthermore, there is evidence that the criteria for determining the score have varied over time. Note that while the CPIA index is based in part on assessments of institutions, (a) these assessments constitute only a minor portion of the total rating and

government's efforts to generate a sustainable macroeconomic environment, free of major policy distortions.

4.7.1   Independent variables

Table 10.11 reports the definitions and distributions of the independent variables and the sources from which they were drawn.

4.7.2   Institutions

According to the logic of accountability, the incentives that drive government responses bite because the government wants to return to office but faces the prospects of the loss of power. A measure of COMPETITION captures these incentives. By the rules governing the creation of this measure, a polity receives a score of 1 if there is no executive in place; 2 if there is a non-elected executive; 3 if there is an elected executive but no electoral competition; 4 if there is an elected executive, and competition between candidates but not between parties (because opposition parties are banned); 5 if there is an elected executive and competition between candidates but not between parties (even though opposition parties are legal); and 6 if there is an elected executive, with competition between candidates backed by opposing parties taking place during the electoral campaign. A score of 7 is assigned if the executive's vote share is less than 75 percent (Beck *et al.* 2001).[24]

4.7.3   Discount rate

In the model, the government is forward-looking: it compares the short-term benefits from adopting self-interested policies with the longer-term costs of the loss of office. The power of the incentives to which institutions of accountability give rise thus depends upon the government's rate of discount. Affecting the value the government places upon future benefits from office is its assessment of political risk.

The State Failure Task Force (Goldstone *et al.* 2003) offers a suitable measure. This measure – labeled PROBLEM – indicates whether each country was a part of the State Failure Task Force's "problem set" in the previous year

---

(b) were the Bank raters inclined to give higher ratings to countries that exhibited higher levels of political accountability, then this would bias us towards finding such a positive correlation in the data, contrary to what we in fact find (see below).

[24] The variable MULTI-PARTY, employed earlier, is a proper sub-set of this scale. It possesses fewer categories than COMPETITION simply because Africa contains no countries that exhibit the requisite characteristics for some of them. Here we employ global samples and therefore use the fully articulated scale.

Table 10.11 *Definitions, sources, and descriptions for tables 10.12 and 10.13.*

Variable	Definition	Source	Units	Range	Mean
QUALITY	See text	PRS, ICRG data	Index	−2.3–1.73	0
CPIA	See text	World Bank	Index	1–5	2.86
COMPETITION (Executive scales)	See text	Beck *et al.* (2001); Ferree and Singh (2002)	Categorical	1–7	4.56
RISK	Is there a finite term of office? If so are multiple terms in office allowed?	Constructed from data in Beck *et al.* (2001)	Dummy	0–1	0.63
PROSPECTS	Expectation of regime collapse: see text	Calculated using Przeworski *et al.* (1990), ACLP regime data	Probability	0–0.86	0.024
REGIONAL (EXECREG)	Does the executive draw its support from a regional base?	Beck *et al.* (2001); (EXECREG)	Dummy	0–1	0.025
CHECKS	Number of veto players + 1 for each veto player whose orientation is closer to the opposition than to the government	Beck *et al.* (1997); (CHECKS2)	Count	1–14	2.55

PROBLEM	See text	Goldstone et al. (2003)	Dummy	0.1	0.18
AGRIPOP	See text	World Bank: WDI 2000	Percent	0.1	0.47
OIL	See text	World Bank: WDI 2000	Percent	0.1	0.05
Per capita GDP	Real GDP per worker at 1995 prices	Penn World Tables	Constant 1985 dollars	480–37,089	8,822
Growth of GDP	Percent change in GDP	Penn World Tables	Percent	–50–85	3.69

by virtue of being embroiled in a civil conflict, undergoing extreme levels of violence, or experiencing an adverse regime change.[25]

4.7.4 Properties of the selectorate

According to the logic of the model, the degree to which a government will employ political power to produce collective benefits depends upon the size of the selectorate. The larger the number of veto points within the institutions of government, the more inclusive must be the government's core coalition. The logic of the model therefore suggests that the larger the number of veto points in the institutions of government, the more likely will policy-makers be to promote the creation of collective goods. The variable, CHECKS, is based upon the number of independent parts of the political process. It uses information regarding the number of different parties in a governing coalition and the extent to which there is a competitive legislature independent of the President or Prime Minister's party.[26]

4.7.5 Economic structures

Policy-makers are constrained by the types of economies in which they function. In particular, if economic agents are able to protect themselves from predation by reducing production or by moving their assets, then extractive policies will yield fewer benefits to government and governments will possess stronger incentives to refrain from them. Two variables capture the ease with which rents can be extracted. The first, AGRICPOP, measures the share of the population that is dependent upon agricultural production. The second, OIL, measures the value of oil production as a share of GDP. In each case, we expect negative relations between these measures of economic structure and the government's policy choices.

4.7.6 Control variables

A small set of variables provides information on the wealth of the country, GDP growth rates, and time. The Africa dummy in the pooled regressions that employ the global dataset provides an important check on our argument. For if the reasoning provides an adequate theory of the policy preferences of Africa's governments, then the coefficient on the African dummy should fail to attain statistical significance, when included in models that contain the variables that capture the logic of accountability.[27]

---

[25] More information on this measure can be found on the homepage of the State Failure Task Force, http://www.cidcm.umd.edu/inscr/stfail/sfcodebk.htm.

[26] Each of the DPI variables, CHECKS1 and CHECKS2 were used in the analysis.

[27] We stress that the results presented here do not take account of the possible impact of policy on the supposedly independent variables. Our results are robust to the replacement of independent variables with their lags. We have yet to model these endogenous

4.8   Estimation

I first estimate our statistical models using a pooled sample of observations. I then re-estimate each model introducing country-specific effects and the lag of the dependent variable. Since a fixed-effects model that includes a lagged dependent variable may introduce bias in finite samples (Wooldridge 2002), I report one version of each model that employs the Arrelano and Bond Generalized Method of Moments (GMM) estimator and a second that employs systems GMM.[28]

Table 10.12 presents results for OPPORTUNISM for both an African and a world sample. Table 10.13 presents similar results for CPIA. In the case of OPPORTUNISM, the analysis is based upon data from 103–104 nations, of which 28–29 are from Africa, depending on-data availability; the samples cover the period 1985–95. In the case of CPIA, the global sample includes 95–96 nations and the African sample 36–37 and covers the period 1975–90.

Positive coefficients for the variables relating to OPPORTUNISM indicate that higher levels of the variable yield a lower tendency for the government to employ public powers to extract private benefits from the economy. In the case of CPIA, positive coefficients suggest that higher levels of the independent variable yield a stronger tendency on the part of governments to use public policy to generate a stable macroeconomic environment.

4.8.1   Control variables

Turning first to the control variables, note the pronounced tendency for hysteresis in public policy: the magnitude and significance of the coefficients on the lagged dependent variables indicate that policies, once chosen, tend to persist. As expected, wealth and GDP growth are associated with more favorable policy ratings.

4.8.2   The Nature of the economy

When corrected for bias arising from the incidence of a lagged dependent variable, there is scattered evidence in the Africa sample that increases in the importance of primary products in the private economy lead to the adoption of self-interested policies. When OIL is employed as a measure of resource appropriability, the results for the pooled regressions support the

---

relationships directly, but we note that insofar as public goods provision, as recorded by the World Bank, may increase the competitiveness of institutions, this should lead to an *upward* bias in the estimated correlation, and hence, a bias *against* our result.

[28] Arellano and Bond (1991). The results reported do not take account of the categorical and censored nature of the dependent variable. While formally categorical, the dependent variables in fact contain as many as thirty values. And although formally bounded, there is little clustering of data on the boundaries. We therefore find that employing Tobit models made little impact on our estimates.

Table 10.12 *OPPORTUNISM as dependent variable.*

Sample	Africa			World		
method	Pooled[a]	FE	AB[a]	Pooled[a]	FE	AB[a]
Model	(I)	(II)	(III)	(IV)	(V)	(VI)
Theoretic variables						
COMPETITION	0.01	0.032	0.027	0.049	0.019	0.023
	0.67	3.62***	2.14**	5.05***	2.71***	2.07**
CHECKS	0.079	−0.021	−0.029	0.045	−0.003	0.016
	3.08***	1.23	1.05	3.95***	0.28	1.25
PROBLEM (lag)	−0.225	−0.09	−0.013	−0.243	−0.079	−0.012
	4.16***	2.33**	0.30	5.75***	2.60***	0.16
AGRIPOP (Lag)	−0.524	−1.136	−1.768	−0.521	−1.184	−1.294
	2.90***	1.60	1.27	3.87***	2.58**	1.47
OIL (lag)	−0.372	0.287	0.141	−0.785	0.346	1.016
	2.62***	1.34	0.54	6.27***	1.76*	2.71***
Control variables						
GDP (lag)	0.134	0.037	0.025	0.076	−0.015	−0.025
	7.40***	0.87	0.23	12.75***	1.71*	1.27
GROWTH (lag)	0.002	0	−0.001	0.023	0.003	−0.002
	0.53	0.12	0.40	6.09***	2.33**	0.93
YEAR	0.027	0.01	0.014	0.075	0.028	0.023
	4.03***	1.96*	1.33	18.02***	7.53***	2.66***
Lag of the dependent	–	0.789	0.521	–	0.772	0.812
variable	–	19.02***	4.52***	–	40.62***	16.58***
Dummy variable for SSA	–	–	–	0.024	–	–
	–	–	–	0.43	–	–
Constant	−53.39	−19.2	–	−150.238	−54.971	–
	4.07***	1.83*	–	18.10***	7.36***	–
N	338	314	285	1,273	1,180	1,074
R^2	0.37	0.74		0.65	0.82	
No. cross-sectional units			29	28	104	103
Arellano–Bond test that average autocovariance in residuals of order 2 is 0: (z-statistic)			1.06			−1.49

Notes: Absolute value of *t*-statistics listed below coefficients.
[a] Robust *t*-statistics reported, * significant at 10%; ** significant at 5%; *** significant at 1%.

Table 10.13 CPIA *as dependent variable.*

Sample	Africa			World		
method	Pooled[a]	FE	AB[a]	Pooled[a]	FE	AB[a]
Model	(VII)	(VIII)	(IX)	(X)	(XI)	(XII)
Theoretic variables						
COMPETITION	0.011	0.001	−0.004	−0.015	0.012	0.004
	0.71	0.05	0.15	1.32	1.24	0.17
CHECKS	0.11	−0.001	−0.026	0.056	−0.005	−0.01
	3.55***	0.02	0.55	3.31***	0.32	0.41
PROBLEM (lag)	−0.091	0.034	−0.015	−0.093	−0.065	−0.147
	1.25	0.48	0.16	1.96*	1.55	1.90*
AGRIPOP (Lag)	−0.33	−1.72	−3.344	−0.155	−1.033	−1.89
	1.72*	1.71*	1.41	1.13	1.63	1.56
OIL (lag)	−1.505	−0.068	−0.439	−1.346	−0.303	−0.127
	7.74***	0.13	0.72	9.31***	0.90	0.34
Control variables						
Per capita GDP (lag)	0.127	0.022	−0.179	0.107	−0.038	−0.16
	4.90***	0.39	1.38	7.17***	1.50	3.17***
Growth of GDP (lag)	0.023	0.008	0.005	0.031	0.009	0.004
	6.02***	2.75***	1.32	8.23***	3.88***	1.45
Year	0.01	−0.005	−0.009	0.019	0	−0.001
	1.75*	0.71	0.81	4.84***	0.05	0.08
Lag of the dependent	–	0.635	0.641	–	0.664	0.687
variable	–	17.15***	10.42***	–	29.14***	16.11***
Dummy variable for SSA	–	–	–	−0.032	–	–
	–	–	–	0.63	–	–
Constant	−16.896	12.093	–	−35.919	2.038	–
	1.51	0.83	–	4.50***	0.21	–
N	507	501	463	1227	1198	1099
R^2	0.27	0.46		0.24	0.49	
No. cross-sectional units		37	36		96	95
Arellano–Bond test that average autocovariance in residuals of order 2 is 0: (z-statistic)			−0.97			0.10

Notes: Absolute value of *t*-statistics listed below coefficients.
[a] Robust *t*-statistics reported, * significant at 10%; ** significant at 5%; *** significant at 1%.

hypothesized relationship between the costs of private goods extraction for the choices of governments. Higher values of oil production correlate with higher levels of OPPORTUNISM. The results for the equations that employ differenced data do not behave in a similar manner, however; in addition, three of the coefficients derived from the global sample yield evidence *against* this argument.

More consistent is the evidence of the impact of agriculturally dependent economies. In the case of both dependent variables – OPPORTUNISM and CPIA – and both samples, the pooled regressions drawn from African data suggest that the greater the weight of the agricultural sector, the more opportunistic a government's policy choices. Fixed-effects estimates from the global sample yield further support for the argument, when ratings from private investors are employed. The sign on this measure of the importance of agriculture is negative for both samples. It fails to attain significance, however.

4.8.3   The selectorate

The model underscores the importance of a third set of variables: those relating to the size of the selectorate. The larger the size of the selectorate, the logic suggests, the stronger the incentives for the government to reward its supporters by producing public goods.

One indicator of the size of the selectorate is the number of veto points in the institutions of government, and thus the number of points of entry for political interests; the greater the number of veto points, the larger the effective selectorate. The pooled regressions suggest that governments that are constrained by checks and balances, and so face multiple veto points, adopt policies that elicit higher investor ratings. This is true for both dependent variables and for both samples in the pooled regressions. These institutional features are "slow moving," however. Possibly for this reason, measures of their impact fail to emerge in the equations that use differenced values of the variables.

4.8.4   Discount rate

The data provide evidence of the impact of discounting. If a government is sufficiently unstable to fall into the State Failure Task Force's problem set (i.e. PROBLEM $= 1$), the policy environment deteriorates for private investors, as measured by OPPORTUNISM. The same relationship holds for the World Bank ratings of government policies in the pooled global sample. The magnitudes in regressions (I), (II), (IV), and (V) associate a change in PROBLEM from 1 to 0 with a fall in OPPORTUNISM of between one-tenth and one-fifth of a standard deviation.

4.8.5 Institutions

Of greatest interest, however, are our results regarding political institutions. Both the African and global samples offer evidence of a relationship between electoral competition and OPPORTUNISM. The results are strongly significant in all but one specification. The magnitudes of the coefficients suggest that an increase in COMPETITION from its lowest to its highest value is associated with an increase in the OPPORTUNISM score of approximately one-fifth of a standard deviation; as noted above, this increase in turn associates with an increase in growth rates of approximately one-quarter of a percentage point.

Note, however, that when CPIA is used as a measure of policy choice, then there is *no* evidence for a relation between institutions and public policy, once other determinants of policy choice are taken into account. Indeed in some models there is evidence that when governments face risks from electoral competition, they then choose policies that distort the macroeconomy ((IX) and (X)) and so receive lower ratings from the World Bank.

Note the African dummy in the global sample in tables 10.2 and 10.3. In both cases, the coefficients are insignificant. Within the context of the model, African governments behave in ways that are indistinguishable from governments elsewhere.

4.9 *Political business cycle*

The evidence thus suggests that introducing political competition stays the hand of predatory governments but fails to inspire them to manage better the macroeconomy. Indeed, the evidence suggests the opposite may be true: that governments subject to electoral risk are less willing to adhere to the Washington consensus.

To aid in interpreting these findings, I turn to the work of Block (2002) and of Block, Ferree, and Singh (2003). Employing data from forty-seven African states over the period of political reform, 1980–94, Block (2002) sought to determine whether the introduction of elections affected the policy choices of governments; Block, Ferree, and Singh (2003) narrowed the focus to elections in which opposition parties could challenge incumbent regimes.

In exploring the link between elections and policy choice, Block (2002) draws on the so-called "naïve" and "rational" models of politically induced business cycles.[29] In both, politicians seek office and are fully informed; the citizens prefer better economic conditions to worse and lack full information. In the "naïve" models, citizens can observe aggregate features of the macroeconomy: inflation and unemployment. Being unsophisticated, they

---

[29] See Nordhaus (1975), Rogoff (1990), and also Lindbeck (1976).

react only to present information: if the present level of inflation is low and employment high, then they are more likely to vote for the incumbent, even if neither level is sustainable. Their naïveté leaves them open to manipulation. Given the citizens' decision rule, the government retains office by producing unsustainable economic booms in election years followed by contractions in the post-election period. The failure to smooth intertemporal consumption imposes welfare losses on the economy, even while the politicians reap the political benefits.

In the second version of the model, the voters prefer politicians who can competently manage the economy. To signal their competence, the politicians generate public services, and the more competent they are the greater the amounts of such services they can generate for any given level of revenues. Because citizens are sophisticated, political competition offers competent incumbents the opportunity to reveal their type: they signal their type by financing public services even in bad times. Divisible goods can be consumed immediately while the benefits of capital goods accrue with a lag: not only greater expenditure but also the displacement of capital formation by public consumption thus result in equilibrium. Political competition thus leads not only to the failure to smooth intertemporal consumption but also to the failure to achieve high levels of growth.[30]

In testing the first of these models, Block finds significant evidence of pre-election increases in the growth of money supply and decreases in the nominal rate of interest and the exchange rate in non-CFA countries. The pro-cyclical impact of these changes emerges in the post-election period, when the rate of money growth turns negative and the interest and exchange rates rise. While the rates of inflation in pre-election periods remain higher than expected, given the logic of the model, they rise significantly in the post-election period, thus lending additional support to the theory. Block also finds evidence in support of the political competence model, with public expenditures and government consumption rising significantly in the pre-election periods, along with the level of government debt.

Block, Ferree, and Singh (2003) restrict their attention to presidential elections in which there was competition for office. In years in which there are competitive elections, they find, the share of government consumption in GDP increases on the order of 1.5 percentage points, which is significantly greater than that for non-competitive elections (Block, Ferree, and Singh

---

[30] As noted in Block (2001) and Block, Ferree, and Singh (2003). See also Drazan (2000). The absence of strong and independent monetary institutions in Africa removes a basic objection to the application of models of the political business cycle. In addition, African governments tend to be presidential and with fixed-term limits, thus limiting the possibility of endogeneity. To be noted is that struggles between capital and labor rarely follow the lines of partisan cleavage in Africa, thus diminishing the value of the standard partisan models of the political business cycle (e.g. Hibbs 1977).

2003: 460). Competitive elections are "associated with a nearly 13 percentage point increase in the rate of real money growth over that observed in non-competitive election years" (2003: 461). And "competitive elections are typically followed by devaluations on the order of 20 percentage points greater than [for] non-competitive elections" (2003: 462) – an adjustment made necessary by the imbalances introduced by the changes in fiscal and monetary policy and by the postponements of adjustments in the pre-election periods. In no case do they find non-competitive elections yielding evidence of politically induced business cycles; evidence of political shocks is confined to elections in which there is political competition.

In absorbing these findings, it is important to stress the second major finding reported by Brock, Ferree, and Singh (2003): that the relationship between electoral competition and macroeconomic distortions peaks with the so-called "founding election" – the election that occurred at the time of the transition from authoritarian rule. Thereafter, the relationship attenuates. This finding may suggest a growing sophistication on the part of the electorate and an increased conviction on the part of those in power that the electorate may punish rather than reward incumbents who manipulate the macroeconomy in search of political advantage.

4.10   Discussion

Why does accountability fail to induce monetary restraint? Addressing once again the logic of political accountability, I search for answers to this question by focusing on several key assumptions of the model.

4.10.1   Candidates

According to the model, if the incumbent fails to meet the performance criterion set by the selectorate, then she is replaced by another randomly selected from a pool of identical candidates. But what if the candidates are heterogenous? Might not the selectorate then be tempted to reinstate an incumbent who possessed qualities that it admired, even were she to fail to deliver decent economic performance? And, anticipating that behavior, might the incumbent not then find the performance criteria incredible and therefore ignore them?

Addressing this possibility compels us to realize that party competition and competitive elections are not themselves sufficient to ensure accountability. Phrased differently, buried in the accountability model lies an assumption of political convergence: it is convergence that renders the selectorate willing to accept a random draw in place of an incumbent who has failed to meet their performance standards. Convergence results when parties and candidates cater to the tastes of the median voter in order to win elections. Such behavior is most likely when there are two parties and plurality voting. But, in Africa, virtually all of the French-speaking, states and several of the anglophone ones employ proportional representation.[31] And even where plurality voting is employed, regional, religious, and ethnic differences make it difficult to reduce the number of parties such that the centripetal incentives created by plurality voting override the centrifugal forces arising from substantive differences (Cox 1997).

To illustrate, consider the case of Kenya. When in 1991 the Kenya African National Union (KANU) government of Daniel Arap Moi legalized the formation of other parties, leading dissidents formed the Forum for the Restoration of Democracy (FORD). But in 1992, FORD split, with leaders from the Central Province forming FORD-Asili (or "original") while Western Province, especially Luo-speaking leaders, formed FORD-Kenya. Further clouding the picture was the formation of the Democratic Party by Mwai Kibaki, former Vice President, and yet a third unit of FORD by Simeon Nyachae, a prominent advisor to previous presidents. Given that a plurality of votes was sufficient to win, the number of opposition parties made it possible for Moi to remain in office, even when opposed by 60 percent of the electorate in the 1992 election (Throup and Hornsby 1998). Behaving in a sophisticated fashion, party leaders responded as theory would predict (Cox 1997; Magaloni 2004): they sought alliances and mergers. This strategy offered the benefits of defeating their least preferred candidate (the incumbent, President Moi) but at the cost of the possible loss of their most preferred (themselves). It was not until the twenty-first century that the opposition parties agree to merge. When they did, KANU was swept from power. That it had remained in power for over a decade while facing competitive elections and exhibiting extraordinary incompetence in its management of the Kenyan economy underscores the power of the assumption of convergence underlying the accountability model, and how this assumption may limit its applicability in contemporary Africa.

4.10.2   Voter sophistication

The accountability model demands that the voters be able to optimize. When they set performance benchmarks, should they place them too high the incumbent may despair of meeting the standard for re-selection; knowing she is likely to be "fired," she will indulge herself while in office. If the criteria are set too low, then the incumbent need not deliver good policy in order to stay in power.

There is scattered evidence that Africa's electorates may be too demanding. Reports from the Afrobarometer surveys comment that "the general public may have an overly rosy view of the diminished capabilities of the

---

[31] See the important contributions: Mozaffar (1998) and Mozaffar *et al.* (2003).

African state" (Afrobarometer, 2004b: 38): over 52 percent of those surveyed in fifteen countries thought that "the government can solve . . . all or most of the country's problems" (2004b: 38). When entertaining such lofty expectations, electorates can be unforgiving. Bratton and van de Walle (1997) note between 1990 and 1994, eleven heads of state were voted out of office, with three others choosing not to run (Block 2002: 206). If such behavior is evidence of excessively high expectations, rulers may behave as unconstrained even in competitive political environments.

Recall the ICPR ratings by private investors, however, that suggest that governments in competitive political environments *do* behave with greater restraint: COMPETITION is associated with less OPPORTUNISM. Recall, too, the evidence marshaled by Block, Ferree, and Singh (2003): even if incumbents are defeated in competitive elections, it is not for want of striving to stay in office. Rather than resigning themselves to defeat in the face of excessively high performance standards, as this argument suggests, they instead manipulated fiscal and monetary policy in an attempt to remain in office.

What if voters evaluated politicians in terms of who they were rather than what they achieved? That is, what if rather than setting performance standards too high, voters instead set them too low, allowing politicians to shirk. Beliefs that voters behave this way are commonly held both by citizens and by students of Africa: the African electorate is held to engage in identity rather than performance voting. But if this were in fact the case, then once again we would not expect to find increased accountability leading to increased restraint, as noted by investors' ratings. When there is political competition, these data suggest, elites find it necessary to abjure the use of power for self-aggrandizement, which they surely could do if receiving the unreserved support of co-ethnics.

While still focusing on the preferences of voters, we can focus on yet another assumption of the argument: that voters would prefer policies that conform to the Washington Consensus. Return once again to the portrait of Africa's electorates presented in the Afrobarometer studies (Bratton, Mattes, and Gyimah-Boadi 2004). "By a large margin" (Afrobarometer 2004a: 14), these surveys report, African citizens support an active economic role for governments and prefer a mixed to a market-based economy. They support trade protection. "There is widespread popular resistance to public sector reform" (2004a: 14). And "most people want the government to remain involved in agricultural marketing" (2004a: 14). In the words of the authors of the Afrobarometer survey "their vision favors state intervention above market forces" (2004a: 14).

Even though Africa's citizens may prefer state intervention, however, the data from the surveys indicate that also they loathe inflation and desire employment (Bratton, Mattes, and Gyimah-Boadi 2004). Preferring an

activist government is not the same as preferring a government that main-
tains an unsustainable monetary policy. Given these considerations, national
politicians might then be reluctant to generate macroeconomic booms for
short-term political advantages.

The failure of political accountability to induce macroeconomic restraint
may therefore not derive from the preferences of citizens. If Africa's voters
can not optimize, then why does political competition lead to lower levels
of OPPORTUNISM? If Africa's voters were lulled by the forces of identity
politics, then why does accountability appear to curb elite predation? And if
Africa's voters were insensitive to the costs of macroeconomic mismanagement, why would they so strongly condemn inflation and unemployment?
Perhaps political accountability fails to induce macroeconomic discipline
not because of the voters' unwillingness to impose the evaluative standards
required to make accountability work, but rather because of their inability
to do so.

4.10.3   Information

To apply the standards required to induce macroeconomic constraint, voters
presumably have to monitor the levels of inflation and unemployment.
Employment figures are difficult to come by in Africa, however; indeed, given
the size of the subsistence sector and the informal economy, employment
is difficult to define. Nor are average price levels common knowledge; even
when calculated with precision, their release is too long delayed to assist in the
making of voting decisions. It is therefore difficult for citizens to monitor the
management of the national economy, to judge the economic performance
of incumbents, and thus to be able to implement punishment strategies.
Knowing that, politicians would have less reason to practice macroeconomic
restraint.

Note that while the assumption of complete information works against the
accountability model, it works in favor of models of the politically induced
business cycle. Such models stress politicians' ability to exploit informational
asymmetries and thus their ability to manipulate the economy in ways that
while economically harmful are politically advantageous. This characteristic
of Africa's political economies – the lack of information – thus stands as the
best candidate for exploring why political reform failed to produce a more
stable macroeconomic environment.

5   Conclusion

Many in Africa championed political reform for its own right. They desired
liberty, freedom, and a government that placed the public interest above their
own. Many also championed reform as a means of securing better economic

policies. By introducing competition into political life, they sought to render governments accountable to private citizens, thereby aligning the political interests of incumbents with the collective interest in policies that would strengthen the economy.

The evidence suggests that political reforms have rendered Africa's governments less opportunistic: private investors rated them as less likely to repudiate debts or to expropriate investments. But reform appears to have had less impact upon the management of the macroeconomy. In the face of prospective political defeat, the evidence suggests, governments in competitive systems tend to spend more, to borrow more, to print money, and to postpone needed revaluations of their currencies than do those not facing political competition. The relationship between political competition and macroeconomic mismanagement appears to have weakened over time, suggesting that voters have learned, or that politicians believe them to have become more sophisticated. The empirical results nonetheless pose a challenge to those who seek in political reform the remedy for Africa's economic malaise.

References

Adam, Christopher S. and Stephen A. O'Connell (1999), "Aid, Taxation, and Development in Sub-Saharan Africa," *Economics and Politics* 11: 225–54
Afrobarometer (2004a), "Afrobarometer Round 2: Compendium of Comparative Results from a 15-country Survey," East Lansing, MI: Michigan State University
    (2004b), "Afrobarometer Round 2: Compendium of Comparative Results from a 15-country Survey," Ann Arbor: Michigan State University
Ake, Claude (1990), *The Case for Democracy*. Atlanta, GA: The Carter Center
Arellano, M. and S. Bond (1991), "Some Tests of Specification for Panel Data," *Review of Economic Studies* 58: 277–97
Barro, Robert (1973), "The Control of Politicians," *Public Choice* 14: 19–42
Beck, Nathaniel, Jonathan Katz, and Richard Tucker (1997), "Beyond Ordinary Logit: Taking Time Seriously in Binary Time-series-cross-section Models," California Institute of Technology, Division of the Humanities and Social Sciences, Working Paper 1017
Beck, Thorsten, George Clarke, Alberto Groff, Philip Keefer, and Patrick Walsh (2001), "New Tools and New Tests in Comparative Political Economy: The Database of Political Institutions," *World Bank Economic Review* 15(1): 165–76
Besley, Timothy (2006), *Principled Agents? The Political Economy of Good Government*. Oxford: Oxford University Press
Block, Steven A. (2001), "Does Africa Grow Differently?," *Journal of Development Economics* 65: 443–67
    (2002), "Political Business Cycles, Democratization, and Economic Reform: The Case of Africa," *Journal of Development Economics* 67: 205–28

Block, Steven A., Karen Ferree, and Smita Singh (2003), "Multiparty Competition, Founding Elections and Political Business Cycles in Africa," *Journal of African Economies* 12: 444–68

Boahen, A. Adu (1997), "Ghana: Conflict Reoriented," in I. W. Zartman, *Governance as Conflict Management.* Washington, DC: Brookings Institution Press

Bratton, Michael, Robert Mattes, and E. Gyimah-Boadi (2004), *Public Opinion, Democracy, and Market Reform in Africa.* New York: Cambridge University Press

Bratton, Michael and Nicolas van de Walle (1997), *Democratic Experiments in Africa.* Cambridge: Cambridge University Press

Coleman, James S. and Carl G. Rosberg (1964), *Political Parties and National Integration.* Berkeley, CA and Los Angeles, CA: University of California Press

Collier, Ruth Berns (1982), *Regimes in Tropical Africa.* Berkeley, CA and Los Angeles, CA: University of California Press

Cox, Gary (1997), *Making Votes Count.* New York: Cambridge University Press

Drazan, Allan (2000), *The Political Business Cycle at 25 Years.* Cambridge, MA: MIT Press

Faure, Yves A. (1989), "Côte d'Ivoire," in D. B. C. O'Brien, J. Dunn, and R. Rathbone, *Contemporary West African States.* Cambridge: Cambridge University Press

Ferejohn, John (1986), "Incumbent Performance and Electoral Control," *Public Choice* 50: 5–26

Ferree, Karen and Smita Singh (2002), "Political Institutions and Economic Growth in Africa: 1970–1995," in Steve Chan and James Scarritt, eds., *Coping with Globalization: Cross-national Patterns in Domestic Governance and Policy.* Boulder, CO: Frank Cass

Goldstone, Jack, Monty Marshall, Robert Bates, and David Epstein (2003), "State Failure Task Force Project, Phase iii Report." McLean, VA: SAIC

Hibbs, Douglas (1977), "Political Parties and Macro-economic Policy," *American Political Science Review* 71: 467–87

Honaker, James (2000), "Issues in Multiple Imputation of Data of the African Research Program." Department of Government, Cambridge, MA: Harvard University

Humphreys, Macartan and Robert H. Bates (2002), "Political Institutions and Economic Policy Making: Lessons from Africa," *CID Working Paper* 94, September (2005), "Political Institutions and Economic Policies: Lessons from Africa," *British Journal of Political Science* 35: 403–28

Hutchful, Eboe (1997), "Militarism and Problems of Democratic Transitions," in M. Ottaway, ed., *Democracy in Africa.* Boulder, CO: Lynne Rienner

Ihonovbere, Julius (1998), "Where is the Third Wave? A Critical Evaluation of Africa's Non-transition to Democracy," in J. M. Mbaku and J. Ihonvbere, eds., *Multiparty Democracy and Political Change.* Aldershot: Ashgate

Kanz, Martin (2005), "The Price of Democracy? Political Pressures and Fiscal Policy in Sub-Saharan Africa." University of Oxford, Department of Economics

Kapur, Devesh (1997), "The Weakness of Strength: The Challenge of Sub-Saharan Africa," in D. Kapur, J. P. Lewis, and R. Webb, eds., *The World Bank: Its First Half Century.* Washington, DC: The Brookings Institution Press

King, Gary and Langche Zeng (2001), "Explaining Rare Events in International Relations," *International Organization* 55: 693–715

King, Gary, Michael Tomz, and Jason Wittenberg (2000), "Making the Most of Statistical Analyses," *American Journal of Political Science* 44: 347–61

Kpundeh, Sahr J. (2004), "Corruption and Political Insurgency in Sierra Leone," in I. Abdullah, *Between Democracy and Terror*. Dakar: CODESRIA

Lindbeck, A. (1976), "Stabilization Policies in Open Economies with Endogenous Politicians," *American Economic Review Papers and Proceedings:* 1–19

MacGaffey, Janet (1991), *The Real Economy of Zaire*. Philadelphia, PA: University of Pennsylvania Press

Magaloni, Beatriz (2004), "Voting for Autocracy: The Politics of Hegemony and its Demise." Stanford University

Mozaffar, Shaheen (1998), "Electoral Systems and Conflict Management in Africa," in T. D. Sisk and A. Reynolds, eds., *Elections and Conflict Management in Africa*. Washington, DC: United States Institute of Peace

Mozaffar, Shaheen, James R. Scarritt, and Glen Galaich (2003), "Electoral Institutions, Ethnopolitical Cleavages, and Party Systems in Africa's Emerging Democracies," *American Political Science Review* 97: 379–90

Nordhaus, William (1975), "The Political Business Cycle," *Review of Economic Studies* 42: 169–90

Ottaway, Mariana, ed. (1997), *Democracy in Africa*. Boulder, CO: Lynne Rienner

Persson, Tosten and Guido Tabellini (2000), *Political Economics*. Cambridge, MA: MIT Press

Please, Stanley (1984), "The World Bank: Lending for Structural Adjustment," in Richard E. Feinberg and Valeriana Kelb, eds., *Adjustment Crisis in the Third World*. Overseas Development Council, US, Third World Policy Perspective Series 1. New Brunswick, NJ and London: Transaction Books: 83–98

Przeworski, Adam, Michael E. Alvarez, José Antonio Cheibub, and Fernando Limongi (1990), *Democracy and Development: Political Institutions and Well-being in the World, 1950–1990*. Cambridge and New York: Cambridge University Press

Rapley, John (1993), *Ivoirien Capitalism: African Entrepreneurs in Côte d'Ivoire*. Boulder, CO: Lynne Rienner

Rogoff, K. (1990), "Equilibrium Political Budget Cycles," *American Economic Review* 80: 21–36

(1999), "The Political Economy of the Resource Curse," *World Politics* 51: 325–61

Rubin, D. B. (1996), "Multiple Imputation after 18+ Years (with Discussion)," *Journal of the American Statistical Association* 91: 473–89

Sachs, Jeffrey D. and Andrew M. Warner (1999), "The Big Push, Natural Resource Booms, and Growth," *Journal of Development Economics* 59: 43–76

Schafer, Joseph L. (1997), "Imputation of Missing Covariates in the Multivariate Linear Mixed Model." Department of Statistics, University Park, PA: The Pennsylvania State University

Small, Melvin and J. David Singer, with the collaboration of Robert Bennett, Kari Gluski, and Susan Jones (1982), *Resort to Arms: International and Civil Wars, 1816–1980*. Beverly Hills, CA: Sage

Stasavage, David (2005), "Democracy and Education Spending in Africa," *American Journal of Political Science* 49: 343–58

Throup, David and Charles Hornsby, eds. (1998), *Multiparty Politics in Kenya.* Athens, OH: Ohio University Press

Williamson, John (1990), "What Washington Means by Policy Reform," in J. Williamson, ed., *Latin American Adjustment: How Much has Happened?* Washington, DC: Institute for International Economics

   ed. (1994), *The Role of Technocrats in Economic Policy Reform.* Washington, DC: Institute for International Economics

Wooldridge, Jeffrey M. (2002), *Econometric Analysis of Cross Section and Panel Data.* Cambridge, MA: MIT Press

World Bank (1981), *Accelerated Development in Sub-Saharan Africa: An Agenda for Action.* Washington, DC: The World Bank

   (1989), *Sub-Saharan Africa: From Crisis to Sustainable Growth.* Washington, DC: The World Bank

   (1991), *Governance and Development* ("Berg Report"). Washington, DC: The World Bank

   (1994), "Adjustment in Africa: Reforms, Results, and the Road Ahead," *World Bank Policy Research Bulletin* 5

11 | Endogenizing syndromes

Paul Collier and Robert H. Bates,
with Anke Hoeffler and Stephen A. O'Connell

1 Introduction

We have seen that Africa's geography has distinctively shaped its opportunities. Two-thirds of Africa's population live in countries that are either dominated by natural resource wealth, or are landlocked and resource-scarce. Both of these conditions are difficult to cope with, and both are far more common in Africa than in other parts of the developing world. In this chapter we suggest that not only have Africa's opportunities been shaped by its geography, but that to a significant extent so have its choices.

Policy choices do not lend themselves to quantitative analysis: they are highly multifaceted with no obvious procedure for aggregation, and they are often continuous but ordinal, lying on the qualitative spectrum better–worse. In addition, individual variables often measure policy outcomes rather than policy settings: they become endogenous to growth. We have reduced this complexity to a manageable set of "syndromes" – patterns of policy choice that are plausibly causally prior to growth outcomes and that an economist would expect to be seriously dysfunctional for growth. This simplification has naturally come at the price of a substantial loss of information. However, as we saw in chapter 2, the syndromes are associated with a substantial part of Africa's growth shortfall. If this association is causal, which we shall investigate, then the loss of information is not overly severe, at least in terms of the impact of policies on growth. Attention then properly shifts to *explaining* policy choices, and here the syndrome structure provides a powerful focal point for analysis. Under what circumstances did particular syndromes arise in post-independence Africa, and under what circumstances were they abandoned? Earlier chapters – including the whole of part 2 – have already begun the task of explanation. We continue it here by exploring the conditions under which the syndromes occurred, both individually and as a group.

In addressing the origins of policy choice we concentrate on the manner in which those who operate in the real economy – private citizens – can affect the behavior of their governments. We focus on the role of interest groups and political parties, and particularly on the role of the party system, emphasizing not only the role of political parties in representing private interests but also the impact of the party system on the incentives of politicians. In addition, we emphasize the size and composition of what, following Roeder (1993) and Bueno de Mesquita *et al.* (2003), we call the selectorate: the group that mediates the political life chances of politicians. As stressed by Zolberg (1966) and Kasfir (1976), in post-independence Africa there was a "shrinking" of the political arena: the selectorate narrowed. Following the logic of Adam and O'Connell (1999) and Bueno de Mesquita *et al.* (2003), we argue that as a selectorate diminishes in size, the incentives to engage in redistribution rise; the benefits become more concentrated and the costs more dispersed, thus leading to a greater demand for redistributive transfers to the powerful few. Moreover, by the logic of Humphreys and Bates (2005), as a selectorate increases in size, the incentives to form public goods increase as well; as the number of people that a government must reward rises, it becomes less expensive to reward them through the provision of a public good rather than through the distribution of private payoffs. Focusing on the instruments of representation – political parties and interest groups – and the changing scope of the selectorate yields, we argue, provides insight into the origins of the anti-growth patterns of policy-making that characterize late-twentieth-century Africa.

2   Building blocks of political geography

Policy choices reflect who holds power, what growth opportunities they face, and what they understand about those opportunities. We consider these three building blocks of political choices in turn.

2.1   Power structures

The impact of political power structures on policy choices is mediated, we shall argue, by the concentration, composition, and durability of executive power. The more concentrated is power, the greater are the returns to redistribution to the group in power, relative to the public good of inclusive growth. For a given concentration, in turn, the distortions imposed to achieve redistribution depend on the match between political and economic power, so that policy will depend on precisely which group is incumbent. The expected durability of rule, finally, affects the incentives of those in power to sacrifice the future for the present.

Anti-growth syndromes, by this logic, are more likely to emerge where power is highly concentrated, is held by economically less productive groups, and is viewed by those in power as precarious.

In much of Africa, power gradually shifted from being highly diffuse to being radically concentrated. Its composition, meanwhile, shifted from groups that broadly reflected the interests of citizens to groups that acquired influence wholly disproportional to their numbers. Finally, the durability of African executive power has been distinctively bimodal: many leaders have ruled only briefly, but many have ruled for decades. In this section, we explore the motive forces and implications of this evolution by tracking a "representative" political system over the decades following the end of colonial rule. We focus on the manner in which changes in the structure of representation and the size of the selectorate altered incentives for policy-making. Our purpose in following this fictive polity through its four canonical stages – starting and ending with constitutional democracy – is to advance a line of argument. At the end of the chapter, we move from conjecture to evidence, making use of data from our sample of countries in the post-independence period to test hypotheses advanced in this and subsequent sections.

2.1.1   Stage 1: constitutional democracy in conditions of ethnic identity

Our representative polity embarks upon independence with a constitution that, formally at least, is democratic. Power is diffused across the electorate as parties compete for votes. The selectorate is large: to win a party needs to attract the support of at least 50 percent of the electorate. Politicians therefore have strong incentives to champion the delivery of national public goods.

Some countries – Botswana, Mauritius, and Senegal, for example – remained at this stage throughout.

If voters identify with ethnic groups, a cost-effective way of forming a political party may be to base it on ethnic allegiance rather than upon a program that is nationally appealing. Thus the chapter on Uganda that appears in volume 2 (Kasekende and Atingi-Ego 2007): the governing party (the United People's Congress, UPC, headed by Milton Obote) drew solid electoral support from the Acholi and Langi in the North while the Kabaka Yekka and the Democratic Parties drew their support from kingdoms in the south. Thus, too, the case of Nigeria (Iyoha and Oriakhi 2007), where immediately after independence three major parties competed for power, each based on a major ethno-regional group: the Hausa–Fulani in the North, the Yoruba in the West, and the Ibo in the East.

In a competitive political setting, political parties face a choice between offering programs that feature national public goods and programs that offer ethno-regional goods. Should some parties offer regional public goods, then the nationally oriented parties face the prospect of free-riding. It is rational for each ethnic group to vote for its "own" party, even though all groups would gain were they to vote for parties that championed the provision of national rather than regional public goods. In competitive political settings, regional public goods may therefore crowd out national public goods in the political marketplace.

Implicitly, at least, much of the literature on post-independence politics stops at this point: electoral competition, it argues, leads to ethnic capture as office-seeking politicians trim their policy platforms to the preferences of their constituencies.[1] But consideration of the size and partitioning of the selectorate suggests a more nuanced account, including the circumstances under which the championing of redistributive, sub-national political agendas will be most likely.[2]

The incentive to adopt ethno-regional politics rather than national public goods depends in part upon the ethnic composition of the population. If the majority of the population is from a common ethnic group, as in Botswana (Werbner 1993), then there is little incentive for ethno-regionalism: even were the ethnic majority to use its power for redistribution, it would be too large to secure big gains. Conversely, if the society is ethnically highly fragmented, as in Tanzania (Norris and Mattes 2003), in a majoritarian political system, no ethnic party could credibly gain from political redistribution. The incentive for ethno-regional politics may therefore peak when there are a few large groups, each able to become a substantial political force. The impetus may intensify insofar as the groups are polarized – that is to say, internally compact but with large differences between them, so that differences between groups become salient relative to differences within.

---

[1] See the contributions in Rothchild and Olorunsula (1983).
[2] The contributions of Posner are highly relevant to this line of analysis; see, for example, Posner (2005).

There are additional reasons for locating the "danger zone" at the intermediate level of ethic concentration. As stressed by Fearon and Laitin (1996),
Collier (2000), and Bates and Yacolev (2002), in a majoritarian electoral
environment high levels of ethnic fragmentation may in fact strengthen
rather than weaken incentives to provide national public goods.[3] Although
each party would like to deliver only regional public goods to its own group,
unless it is a majority it will not be able to do so. The ethnic parties would
need to form coalitions. Further, an ethnic group that is initially excluded
from the coalition can bid its way into it by offering its votes at a lower price
in terms of ethno-regional public goods than some group in the coalition.
Hence, in an ethnic democracy, while parties would like to deliver regional
public goods to their own group, they may be driven to supplying national
public goods as the only thing that they can agree upon.

Further, we have already seen that if the winning ethnic party does not
need to form a coalition because it is a *large* majority, it will not have much
incentive to favor regional public goods over national public goods. Hence,
the danger zone for democratic politics would be where the largest ethnic
group forms a small majority of the population, – large enough to control
the polity but small enough for it to be worthwhile sacrificing the national
for the ethnic interest. This phenomenon is termed "ethnic dominance."
We would thus predict that under conditions of ethnic dominance even
democratic politics would not deliver national public goods.[4]

2.1.2 Stage 2: single-party systems

As documented in chapters 9 and 10, within a decade after independence, most states in Africa abandoned multi-party systems of government.
Roughly 50 percent adopted single-party systems; over 30 percent no-party
systems;[5] while fewer than 20 percent gave legal sanction to the formation
of opposition parties. In one-third of the cases, the military seized power;
when they did so, they tended to suspend the holding of elections and to
outlaw the formation of parties.

In terms of the framework advanced in this chapter, the end of party
competition led to a change in both the system of representation and the
size and composition of the selectorate. Interest groups, rather than political
parties, dominated the process of representation; the selectorate narrowed;
and the result of both was an intensification of the incentives to employ
public policy to seize wealth rather than to foster its creation.

---

[3] Note the contrast with Easterly and Levine (1997) and Alesina, Baqir, and Easterly (1999).
[4] For a formal model of the conditions under which parties will appeal to "ethnic" as
opposed to "national" interests, see Penn (2006).
[5] That is, systems of personal rule.

Returning to our representative state, we can follow the impact upon the policy-making elite of the termination of party competition. Our illustration assumes a change from a competitive to a single-party system. But the arguments linking changes in the party system to changes in policy preferences would apply as well to a shift to a no-party system – i.e. one ruled by a big man and his cronies.

With the abandonment of multi-party democracy, the incentive for the ruling party to appeal to a mass base diminishes. Rather, depending upon the arrangements for internal party democracy, the maximum requirement is that the leader retain the support of the majority of the original party. Whereas to win the first election the leader needed to secure the support of at least 50 percent of the electorate, he now needs as little as 25 percent.

Two groups lose from the banning of opposition parties. One is the voters who supported these opposition parties, potentially 50 percent of the electorate. In multi-party, coalition politics these groups are not powerless: they retain the power to bid themselves into the ruling coalition by demanding a lower price than some group already in the coalition. The banning of rival parties essentially removes this right to bid into the ruling group.

The other groups that lose power reside *within* the ruling party. The President needs to retain the support of the party, but not its universal support. Even if internal party structures are democratic, he is compelled to retain the support of only half of the voters who originally supported the party. Thus, supposing the party to have gained 50 percent of the votes, the President now has to retain the support of only 25 percent of the national electorate.

One result of the change in the party system, then, is that the selectorate shrinks in size. Another is that the incentives that shape policies change. The President and his remaining supporters are now in a position to set policies so as to benefit the 25 percent support they need to retain in order to rule. To the extent that internal party structures are less than fully democratic, the ruling group may be able to retain power while being supported by even less than half of the original party.

If the ruling faction of the single party is ethno-regional, regional public goods now become a more efficient way of targeting benefits to the 25 percent than national public goods, which wastefully also benefit the remaining 75 percent who are now disempowered. The more ethno-regionally fragmented is the society, the narrower the support base of a single party is likely to be. As in the case of Burundi (Nkurunziza and Ngaruko 2007) or in Mobutu's Zaïre (Nzongola-Ntanlaja 2002), the support base of the President may narrow to his district, his co-ethnics, or his family. The narrower the support base, the stronger the incentive for regional as opposed to national public goods.

Hence, the more ethnically fragmented the society, the more damaging would we expect to be the move from competitive party politics.[6]

When representation is achieved through electoral competition, numbers count. Because politicians have an incentive to recruit supporters, large groups become influential even if widely scattered. And because political parties bear the costs of organizing, these groups can be powerful even though they are poor. When interest groups, rather than political parties, represent the interests of citizens, however, then the political advantage shifts.[7] In particular, it shifts in favor of minorities and especially wealthy minorities. Geographically, the costs of organizing are lower the more concentrated the group; large groups that lie widely scattered are less likely to form organized interests. Economically, industries in which production is concentrated are more likely to exert political pressure; when a firm's decisions can alter market prices, it can perceive the benefits that can be derived from collusive agreements.

It is the politicians who provide the regulations that lead to the restructuring of markets. The more wealthy the interests, the better they can afford to pay for the services of politicians. In exchange for financial contributions from businesses, members of the ruling group forge licensing agreements, impose restrictions on trade, and regulate prices in markets. Escaping the pressures of market competition, businesses gain the power to restrict output and set prices and thereby secure greater profits than would be possible in a competitive market. The mass of the consumers pay the costs. Because of the change in the system of representation, the power of numbers is reduced; in the absence of electoral competition, the majority cannot secure a change in the policies that benefit the concentrated minority. One result is the adoption – or retention – of the kinds of policies that we have characterized as "control" or "redistributive" regimes (see chapters 3, 4, and 6). Another is the creation of a narrow elite, in which wealth melds with power.

Note a basic problem with this account: as 75 percent of the population loses out from this transition, the change should be blocked, especially as it takes place while under majority rule. How, then, could so many states abandon competitive party systems?

One reason is that people may have misread the implications of the move to single-party rule. The political opposition may recognize that they may lose the power to bid themselves into the ruling coalition. But the half of the winning coalition that is due to lose its power may be deceived into thinking that it is actually gaining power at the expense of the 50 percent

---

[6] Subject to a qualification discussed below concerning resource rents.

[7] See Olson (1977), Becker (1983), and Adam and O'Connell (1999); for an application to Africa, see Bates (1981).

who will undoubtedly lose it. As noted in the chapter by Mwanawina and Mulungushi (2007), such appears to have been the case in Zambia. The Bemba-speaking politicians from the Northern Province had been among the most militant supporters of the United National Independence Party (UNIP), the governing party. They had vigorously campaigned on behalf of the formation of a single-party state. But, when UNIP became the sole legal party, then found themselves marginalized by a coalition based in the Eastern Province and were later excluded from power.

Secondly, few of the parties that ended up with power in Africa had campaigned on a program of national public goods. Elections had been contested by parties based on ethnic–regional coalitions. Hence, the switch from the championing of national programs to the sponsorship of ethno-regional "club" goods was not a difficult one. For many in the governing party, even those who were eventually marginalized, it represented a return to a familiar – and appealing – political formula.

Third, the leaders that presided over the transition to one-party or no-party states invariably argued that multi-party competition would validate and deepen existing ethno-regional cleavages, and thereby undermine polit-ical and economic progress. Our own argument – along with those of Azam in chapter 6 and Bates in chapter 7 – gives more credence to this under conditions of polarization than when fractionalization is high. Experience suggests, however, that the political valence of an appeal for "national unity" may be robust to these distinctions of degree.

Lastly, resistance to political restructuring was costly. For some, it meant forgoing rewards for compliance: a job as the head of a parastatal or a junior ministry, for example. For others, it meant running the risk of financial losses or physical harm. Presidents are powerful; they control the means of rewarding or punishing others; and they could selectively target sanctions so as to disorganize those who opposed the suppression of party competition. They could and did make it privately advantageous for individual opponents to endorse policy changes that would be harmful to the opposition as a group.

2.1.3   Stage 3: rule by fear

By the late 1980s, the vast majority – 80 percent or more – of Africa's political systems were authoritarian: they were based on no- or one-party political systems. The nature of the party system narrowed the scope of the selectorate, allowing elites to adopt policies that redistributed income from the mass of the population to finance narrowly targeted benefits: profits for protected industries or regional or ethnic public goods.

In a no- or single-party system, power need not be highly concentrated in the President. It could be dispersed around a range of interest groups, with the President having to appease powerful groups or to play them off against each other. Such appears to have been the case in the early days of

Moi's presidency in Kenya, as he played one of the Central Province barons off against another, or in the early days of single-party rule in Zambia, when President Kaunda sometimes appeared a captive of the powerful politicians in the Central Committee.

By the figures employed in our example, 75 percent of the population were excluded from power. And in particular, in some instances, the figures were even greater. In Equatorial Guinea, the Nguema family controls the government and pockets the earnings of the oil industry. In Rwanda, the families of Juvénal Habyarimana and his wife formed the *akasu* – the little house – that dominated the government, until overthrown by the Rwandan Patriotic Front (RPF). And as argued by Nkurunziza and Ngaruko (2007), following the coup of Micombero in Burundi, the denizens of Bururi seized power, retaining it for more than three decades. Power, and the benefits it could supply, became narrowly concentrated.

A major reason that narrowly based regimes could remain in power is that their leaders ruled by fear. A review of the conduct of African presidents suggests that in roughly 40 percent of the country-years in our sample, they based their rule to a significant degree on the use of force. Examples would include Marien Ngouabi in Congo; Hissène Habré in Chad; Siaka Stevens in Sierra Leone; and Jose Eduardo dos Santos in Angola.

Those who ruled by fear mobilized the coercive apparatus of the state to jail, kill, or exile political opponents and to intimidate those who might otherwise be drawn into the ranks of their political opponents. Note, for example, the commentary of Nguza Karl-i-Bond, the chimerical politician from Shaba Province in Zaire (now DRC), whose memoirs document political practices in Mobutu's Zaire. As he recounts, when Mobutu convened a new Council of Ministers – and he convened many new ones – he gave a set speech. "The responsibility of the . . . men of state," Mobutu would pronounce, "was to know how to guard secrets." "If we decide to kill someone for reasons of state," he would declare, "it must remain between us" (Huband 2001: 227). As did other heads of state, Mobutu controlled a variety of organizations capable of killing "for reasons of state"; these included the Civil Guard, commanded by his brother-in-law, Kpama Buramoto; the Special Research and Surveillance Brigade, commanded by General Blaise Bolozi, also related to the President by marriage; the Special Action Forces, a paramilitary unit, commanded by Honore Ngabanda Nzambo-ku-Atumba, a close aide of Mobutu and his chief of intelligence; and the Special Presidential Division, by all accounts the most effective unit of them all, commanded by General Nzimbi Ngabale, a "close relative" (Nzongola-Ntanlaja 2002: 154).

Others, such as Mathieu Kérékou in Benin, presided over a less baroque security apparatus: a People's Militia, a Presidential Guard, an army, and a Ministry of Interior (Allen 1989: 52, 71). While modest in scope by

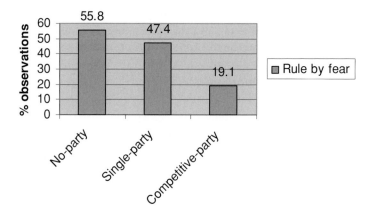

Figure 11.1 Rule by fear and party system

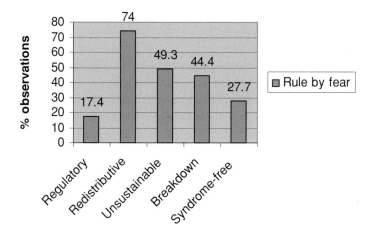

Figure 11.2 Rule by fear

comparison with those of Mobutu, the forces at Kérékou's disposal suf-
ficed to detain political rivals, jail students, and to drive into exile those who
actively opposed his regime. The units were so organized that, in the words
of Allen (1989: 52) they "concentrate[d] the entire repressive apparatus in
the hands of the President."

Observing the distribution of regimes based on fear, we note that they
tended to prevail in one or no-party systems (figure 11.1).

The narrow scope of the selectorate in such regimes, in turn, creates incentives to employ public policies to secure the redistribution of
economic resources. As seen in figure 11.2, in states ruled by fear, economic
redistribution constitutes the modal choice of public policy.

How did some African societies get to rule by fear? One route is a *gradual exclusion* from power starting from a stage-2 single-party system. The leader dismantles whatever checks and balances are in place and replaces party supporters in positions of power with family members. Newly excluded supporters have an incentive, as a group, to arrest the process, but face a free-rider problem: to arrest the process essentially involves challenging the President, and this exposes those making the challenge to risk. As the support base shrinks below the 25 percent of stage 2, even ethnically specific public goods become wasteful relative to private patronage. The redistribution ceases to be ethno-regional and becomes family-based looting.

Gradual exclusion, in which a single-party system erodes into personal rule, is not the only means by which rule by fear has evolved, however. There are two other routes: coups and rebellions. Both place the head of a hierarchical military organization at the head of the government, and the President therefore enters office with the tools in place to rule by fear.

The only effective threat to this concentration of power comes from a blocking coalition within the military: that is, a further coup or rebellion. The risk of a coup is roughly 6 percent in states ruled by fear; among others, it is roughly 4 percent, and the difference is significant at the 0.01 level. Rule by fear thus associates with political instability. And the combination of political risk and economic redistribution is costly, lowering the prospects for growth.

2.1.4   Stage 4: restored democracy

A final step, which may come after stages 2 or 3, is the restoration of democracy. Democracy has two distinct dimensions; electoral competition (Schumpeter 1950), which is relatively easy to introduce, and checks and balances (Dahl 1971), which are not. By the mid-1990s, one-half of the states of Africa were governed by regimes chosen in competitive elections. More elusive has been the creation of checks and balances. Whether judged in terms of electoral competition or checks and blances, the nations of Africa continue to lodge at the lower end of the global distribution of the democracy ratings. The form of democracy that they exhibit more closely resembles the illiberal democracies of Farheed Zakaria (Zakaria 1997) than the polyarchies of Robert Dahl (Dahl 1971).

2.1.5   Concentration, composition, and duration: a summary of their implications for growth

The greater is the concentration of power the greater the incentive for the group in power to choose the private rewards of redistribution over the public good of growth. As interest groups come to dominate the process of representation, their differential abilities to overcome the collective action problem shape who is going to benefit from redistribution. In Africa, the biggest single industry is agriculture; but because it was dominated by small-holders, once contested elections were banned, the costs of collective action lowered the power of farmers. Instead, power shifted to well-organized inter-ests such as public sector employees and large firms.

When leaders see their position as precarious, their discount rates rise. The higher the discount rate the lower the payoff to the gains from a growth strategy, and so the more attractive is redistribution at the expense of growth. Superficially, African leaders should in retrospect usually not have seen their positions as precarious: they include many of the longest-serving rulers in the world and the single-party systems and rule-by-fear systems over which they presided eliminated constitutional means for their replacement. However, unconstitutional means of replacement were common through coups and rebellions. Unlike democratic challenges, these could occur at any moment: leaders were never safe. Again unlike democratic challenges, the consequences could be violent: *vide* President Doe of Liberia, tortured to death by his political opponents. While facing an objectively low probability of being replaced, and so ending up holding office for long periods, leaders felt endangered.

2.2   Opportunities

Opportunities affect the magnitude and distribution of costs and benefits of the syndromes.

2.2.1   Landlocked, resource-scarce countries

One of the key choices is between short-term gains to the group in power and long-term growth for the country as a whole. As argued by Sachs and Warner (1995), landlocked countries that are resource-scarce simply lack good growth opportunities. The returns to the choice of a strategy of long-term national growth are therefore going to be more modest than in other settings. Realizing this, the group in power has a stronger relative incentive to opt for redistribution. In keeping with this reasoning, we find (figure 11.3) that landlocked countries are more likely to have either single-party or no-party systems than are coastal regions or regions that are resource-rich; they are more likely than coastal regions to be ruled by fear (figure 11.4); and they are more likely to exhibit redistributive and less likely to adopt syndrome-free policy regimes than are coastal or resource-rich nations (figure 11.5). They are also more likely to experience state breakdown and civil war (figures 11.5 and 11.6), themselves the result of attempts to use the power of the state to engage in, or to protect against, redistribution.

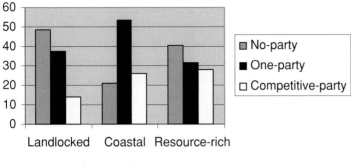

% observations

Figure 11.3 Opportunities and party system

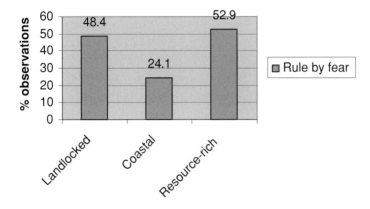

Figure 11.4 Opportunities and rule by fear

2.2.2 Resource-rich countries

Resource-rich countries have the potential for national growth and so do not have the same political economy problems of landlocked, resource-scarce societies. However, because they have low levels of taxation they are likely to under-supply the public good of scrutiny, as discussed in chapter 7. With low scrutiny, rulers are in a position to divert public funds to improper uses. In the context of democratic competitive electoral politics, this diversion can make patronage politics financially feasible: the massive patronage needed to win elections despite failing to deliver public goods can be financed by the resource rents. In this situation, the more competitive is party competition, the more will parties be driven to spend on patronage. The political equilibrium is when the party maximizes the amount of public funds that can be diverted into patronage, and this patronage in turn is sufficient to maintain it in power. Indeed, with sufficiently intense competition the government will need to raid the commons of the future by borrowing in an unsustainable

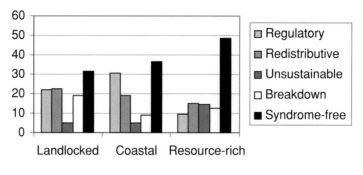

Figure 11.5 Opportunities and syndromes

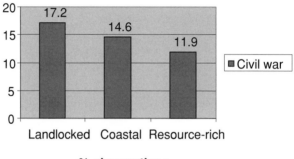

Figure 11.6 Civil war

way. Hence, we would expect that in the context of large resource rents electoral competition would lead to the syndrome of unsustainable spending. Large resource rents make the syndrome of unsustainable spending much more likely because they provide the government with the collateral against which it can borrow.

2.2.3   Coastal, resource-scarce countries

During a part of our period coastal, resource-scarce countries had remarkable opportunities for growth, namely through breaking into international markets for manufactures. Even without this, they had superior opportunities to the landlocked, resource-scarce countries due to their lower costs of international trade. Lacking large natural resource rents, they do not face the problems of low scrutiny common to the resource-rich. Hence, this group should have good returns to a strategy for national growth, while having sufficient scrutiny to impose constraints on patronage. We would therefore expect democratic politics in this group of countries to work better than elsewhere in Africa.

2.3 Influences on knowledge

Power structures determine who gets to choose, and opportunities combine with these choices to determine economic payoffs. However, people take decisions in the context of limited information. Influences on knowledge therefore potentially shape choices. We distinguish between three levels of influence: in-country, regional, and global.

2.3.1 In-country knowledge

In-country knowledge can usefully be divided into the knowledge base of the leader and the knowledge base of the population. As argued in chapters 4 and 9, many of Africa's first generation of leaders were influenced by socialism, whether in its Fabian or Marxist varieties. Socialist beliefs directly suggested that control regimes were a necessary strategy for economic development.

The knowledge base of the population, which can be proxied by its education, might affect political choices in two main ways. First, conditional upon democracy, a higher level of knowledge might increase the pressure to choose national public goods over regional public goods and private patronage. Second, even in the absence of democracy, the more educated is the population the more rapidly is the society likely to learn from errors. Hence, we might expect the syndromes to be less persistent the more educated is the population.

2.3.2 Learning from the region

Potentially, countries can learn from the successes of their neighbors. For example, in Latin America the Chile model was influential, while in East Asia the "gang of four" provided a role model that was widely emulated. In Africa there is some limited evidence for this: during the 1990s Madagascar started to copy Mauritius, and Namibia may have copied Botswana. Countries can also learn from the failure of neighbors: the fact that the ANC was based in Zambia during a phase of manifest economic failure is sometimes used to account for the careful economic management that the ANC has adopted since coming to power in South Africa. We would thus expect the adoption and escape from the syndromes to be serially correlated across the region.

2.3.3 Learning from the world

All societies learn from others. The global fashion for privatization that started in the 1980s was clearly sparked by the example of the Thatcher government in the UK. In Africa, two major world phenomena are of sufficient importance to warrant explicit investigation: the rise of Asia and the fall of the USSR. The rise of East Asia as a global exporter beginning in the 1980s provided a new role model for coastal, resource-scarce low-income countries. Potentially, the success of such countries in Asia revealed to those in Africa that the cost of the syndromes was higher than they had previously realized. The fall of the USSR was an important learning event for those societies with control regimes. Examples of its influence are that the governments of Eritrea and ANC South Africa which formed shortly afterwards did not adopt the socialist model, even though while liberation movements they had espoused it.

3 Predicting the syndromes

Our analysis relates the occurrence of syndromes to the nature of power structures, opportunities, and influences on knowledge. To test these hypotheses empirically we begin by pooling the syndromes and considering only what determines whether a society is free of them. We then conduct a similar analysis for the individual syndromes.

3.1 Determinants of syndrome-free status

Table 11.1 presents our analysis of the characteristics that are significant in determining whether a country is free of the syndromes. The statistical method is logit analysis, with each country-year experience in Africa since 1970 forming an observation. A positive sign indicates a variable which increases the likelihood that a country will be free of all syndromes. The estimates have been derived after employing multiple imputation methods to derive estimates of the values for missing observations.[8]

We begin with variables that describe power structures, whether via the political system or the structure of ethnic allegiances. Consider first the variable indicating the mode of representation: "multi-party." When this variable takes the value 1, the head of state was picked in an election contested by competing political parties. When 0, there was a single party or personal rule, and representation is undertaken by organized interests. The "multi-party" variable itself is highly significant and its coefficient is large and positive: multi-party competition makes an African country much more likely to be syndrome-free.

---

[8] We use methods developed by Rubin (1996) and Schafer (1997) to impute multiple estimates of the missing values and to calculate their distributions, and techniques developed by the Harvard Data Center to estimate and to interpret the estimates derived from the resultant data. See Honaker (2000) and King, Tomz, and Wittenberg (2000).

Recall our discussion of the role of the size of the selectorate. A measure would be the degree of ethnic concentration, for which we have two measures. The first is "ethnic dominance," which takes a value of 1 if the largest group constitutes 45 percent or more of the population and 0 otherwise. Given such preponderance, our reasoning would suggest, the group would tend to use the state to promote prosperity through the creation of collectively rather than privately beneficial policies and through growth-oriented rather than redistributive measures. As we would expect, the coefficient for this variable is positive, although the level of significance is low (see table 11.1).

A second measure is ethic diversity, as measured by the probability that any two people, selected from a country's population at random, would belong to different ethno-cultural groups. In this instance, we enter the variable in interaction with an indicator of "rule by fear." We do so because we believe that when minorities, which in Africa are often ethnically defined, seize power, they then use the coercive apparatus of the state to implement policies of redistribution. The combination of rule by fear and high levels of fractionalization should therefore produce a significantly negative relationship with syndrome-free policy-making.

To interpret the relevant results in table 11.1, note that "rule by fear" takes on the values of 1 for present and 0 for absent. Note, too, that the average level of ethnic fractionalization in the sample set of counties is 0.725, and let the variable take on the values of 0, indicating complete homogeneity; 0.725, indicating average diversity; and 1, indicating total fractionalization. Employing the coefficients from the model in column (1), we note that were the population ethnically homogenous (i.e. when ethnic diversity = 0), even a government that ruled by fear would adopt syndrome-free policy-making: the coefficient would be positive and significant. Given the size and significance of the coefficient on the interaction term, however, at the average level of ethnic fractionalization (0.725), rule by fear exercises a significantly negative effect on the dependent variable. So too when the measure of fractionalization equals 1. As the level of ethnic diversity rises, then rule by fear impacts more negatively upon the likelihood of syndrome-free policy-making. The results thus suggest that regimes that possess a narrow ethic base – i.e. that have a small selectorate – are willing to employ force to distort markets using the power of the state to create and enforce pubic policies that secure redistribution rather than growth (see also table 11.2, column (1)).

We next investigate the variables that capture economic opportunities. The coefficients for landlocked and coastal resource-scarce variables are each significant and negative. Note that the coastal states chose policy regimes that tended to impose regulatory regimes and to engage in redistribution. That they did so just as coastal states in Asia embraced the international economy

Table 11.1 *Explaining the syndromes: what keeps countries syndrome-free?*

	Syndrome-free (1)	Syndrome-free (2)	Syndrome-free (3)	Syndrome-free (4)
Multi-party	1.176	1.376	1.220	1.093
	(0.239)***	(0.244)***	(0.246)***	(0.238)***
Ethnic dominance	0.417	0.290	0.409	0.487
	(0.231)*	(0.244)	(0.231)*	(0.242)**
Rule by fear	1.902	2.05	1.916	1.977
	(0.513)***	(0.505)***	(513)***	(0.487)***
Ethnic diversity	−0.483	−0.723	−0.482	−0.379
	(0.754)	(0.767)	(0.753)	(0.760)
Rule by fear × Ethnic diversity	−3.889	−4.158	−3.907	−3.915
	(0.718)***	(0.723)***	(0.719)***	(0.687)***
Accumulated knowledge	6.018	10.562	5.851	6.672
	(1.429)***	(1.741)***	(1.443)***	(1.460)***
Landlocked, resource-scarce	−1.024	−1.029	−1.019	−0.869
	(0.216)***	(0.218)***	(0.216)***	(0.228)***
Coastal, resource-scarce	−1.021	−0.912	−1.018	−1.013
	(0.205)***	(0.205)***	(0.206)***	(0.208)***
Proportion of nat. res. rents in GDP	−1.650	−1.702	−1.469	−1.581
	(0.458)***	(0.459)***	(0.471)***	(0.470)***
Trend	−0.008	0.029	−0.010	−0.018
	(0.015)	(0.017)*	(0.015)	(0.016)
Secondary enrollment in 1970	0.059	0.076	0.059	0.048
	(0.015)***	(0.017)***	(0.015)***	(0.017)***
Post-1989	1.215	1.552	1.208	1.266
	(0.280)***	(0.249)***	(0.281)***	(0.289)***
Average syndrome-free for neighbors		−1.839		
		(0.393)***		
Nat.-res. rents × Multi-party			−0.571	
			(0.979)	
Risk of coup d'état				−8.609
				(3.748)**
Obs.	1,645	1,645	1,645	1,645
McFadden R^2	0.26	0.27	0.26	0.26
Adjusted R^2	0.24	0.26	0.24	0.25

Notes: Logit estimation, *p*-values in parentheses.
* Significant at 10 percent; ** significant at 5 percent; *** significant at 1 percent; all regressions include an intercept.

Table 11.2 *Explaining the syndromes individually.*

	Regulatory (1)	Redistribution (2)	Unsustainable spending (3)	State breakdown (4)
Multi-party	−0.207	−1.130	−0.637	−0.021
	(0.174)	(0.264)***	(0.349)*	(0.297)
Ethnic dominance	−0.316	−1.30	0.428	−1.169
	(0.222)	(0.264)***	(0.352)	(0.347)***
Rule by fear	0.444	−0.569	0.968	−1.808
	(0.451)	(0.531)	(0.691)	(0.872)*
Ethnic diversity	1.028	−1.917	0.276	−3.506
	(0.746)	(0.836)***	(1.096)	(1.087)***
Rule by fear ×	−0.815	3.624	−0.690	2.911
Ethnic diversity	(0.602)	(0.709)***	(−0.758)	(1.120)**
Accumulated	−5.323	−1.333	−4.679	−1.731
knowledge	(1.438)***	(1.674)	(3.494)	(1.835)
Landlocked,	−0.223	1.293	−1.084	0.085
resource-scarce	(0.192)	(0.218)***	(0.326)***	(0.243)
Coastal,	0.418	0.580	−0.611	−0.116
resource-scarce	(0.175)**	(0.193)***	(0.272)***	(0.226)
Proportion of nat.-	−0.273	2.547	2.312	−2.997
res. rents in GDP	(0.357)	(0.383)***	(0.410)***	(1.097)***
Trend	−0.025	0.007	−0.012	0.006
	(0.015)*	(0.017)	(0.037)	(0.018)
Secondary	−0.146	0.075	−0.076	−0.068
enrollment in 1970	(0.016)***	(0.017)***	(0.025)***	(0.021)***
Post-1989	−1.264	−0.301	−1.701	1.058
	(0.237)***	(0.264)	(0.500)***	(0.305)***
Obs.	1,645	1,645	1,645	1,645
McFadden R^2	0.18	0.23	0.21	0.15
Adjusted R^2	0.17	0.22	0.19	0.11

Notes: Logit estimation, *p*-values in parentheses.
* Significant at 10 percent; ** significant at 5 percent; *** significant at 1 percent; all regressions include an intercept.

and adopted growth-promoting polices helped to lay the foundation for Africa's long-run growth shortfall, as argued in chapter 2. As an indicator for resource wealth, we introduce a continuous variable: the value of the resource rents as a share of GDP. The coefficient on this variable is significantly negative: resource rents systematically make syndromes more likely.

Finally, we investigate a range of knowledge variables. The proportion of the population aged over twenty-five that had been educated significantly increases the predicted frequency of syndrome-free status in subsequent years. We measure cumulative experience by the population-weighted cumulative proportion of country-years that are syndrome-free. We measure the impact of neighbours by noting the portion of neighboring states that are symptom-free at any given time. The first is highly significant and the coefficient is positive; the second (see table 11.1, column (2)) is significant and negative. The first represents learning; the second, efforts to avoid mistakes made by others.[9]

The data suggest that the fall of the USSR influenced policy choices. Given the impact of this and other temporally-specific variables, the time trend is insignificant, though negative.

As shown in table 11.1, column (3), party competition has less effect in resource-rich countries. While consistent with the hypothesis of the "resource curse" (Ross 2003), the finding is not statistically significant. Equation (4) introduces a measure of coup risk: countries at high levels of risk from coups are significantly less likely to choose a mix of policies that is "syndrome-free."

The central conclusion from this analysis is thus that the syndromes move in concert with the three sets of influences discussed in the previous sections: the nature of the party system, the size and composition of the selectorate, and the level of knowledge.

3.2   Syndrome by syndrome

We now consider how each of the syndromes may be induced by particular power structures, opportunities, and influences on knowledge.

3.2.1   Redistribution

The redistribution syndrome takes three forms: excessive ethno-regional redistribution, looting, and inadequate ethno-regional redistribution.

We have suggested that excessive ethno-regional redistribution is more likely with single-party rule, where power becomes concentrated in a single minority group, and if there are substantial resource rents, since these are likely to be regionally concentrated.

The looting form of redistribution is predicted to be generated by rule by fear, which in turn can develop from single-party rule, coups or rebellions.

Inadequate ethno-regional redistribution occurs where a rich and productive group with power fails to buy off a poorer and potentially aggressive group, and as a result suffers violent expropriation. At the heart of such a

---

[9] We also investigated whether the rise of East Asian manufactured exports influenced the coastal countries. We found no significant effect: countries did not change behavior despite the mounting evidence that they were missing an unprecedented opportunity for rapid growth.

missed opportunity is an ability to make binding agreements (Acemoglu and Robinson 2001; Azam and Mesnard 2003). Promises by the rich to transfer resources to the poor lack credibility, given time-inconsistent preferences.[10]

3.2.2 Unsustainable spending and anticipated redistribution

The degree to which countries adopt unsustainable policies is likely to depend upon the scope for debt accumulation. In turn, this will depend upon the initial level of indebtedness and the level of exports. Countries with natural-resource booms are therefore most vulnerable to this syndrome. Unsustainable spending – typically generating a period of rapid but unsustainable growth – results when there is no institutional capacity to protect the "commons" of the future against claims made in the present. When, as is often the case in Africa, states are weak, the governing group may find it difficult to control the level and rate of current public consumption.

Anticipated redistribution occurs where a ruling group, whether ethno-regional or looting, has good reason to believe that it will lose power in the near future. It then has an incentive to asset strip, even if this is costly. The scope for anticipated redistribution depends in part upon the clarity of the threat of loss of power, and the extent to which assets can be run down. Potentially, the group can run down its net assets position without stripping assets by borrowing. However, the same information that tells the group that it risks loss of power may make it non-creditworthy to lenders. An example is South Africa in the later days of minority rule.

An apparently milder form of anticipated redistribution which may enable borrowing, and thus potentially be more damaging, is where the ruling group has an unspecific fear of loss of power, rather than having clear information about a specific threat. Thus, an autocrat may feel insecure due to the possibility of a coup. This is very different from the urgent end-game that likely characterized the behavior of the Afrikaners in the late 1980s.

3.2.3 State breakdown

State breakdown occurs as a result of the capturing of political power by a small, authoritarian minority. One result is the disempowerment and political alienation of a large percent of the population; a second is the adoption of redistributive policies. Such outcomes are more likely when there is a mixture of rule by fear and ethnic fractionalization. There is some evidence that resource rents make rebellions more likely, though not coups – perhaps because, unlike rebellions, coups do not need to be financed.

---

[10] Recall the discussion in chapter 7 where it was shown that, in keeping with the argument above, where power has shifted into the hands of more resource-scarce regions, there are lower levels of militarization. This finding, too, is consistent with an argument that stresses the importance of credibility; it may find its cause in the inability of the richer regions to make credible promises of redistribution.

3.2.4 Control regimes

As discussed in chapter 6, single party rule and rule by fear both make control regimes more likely. There are also likely to be role-model effects, with the collapse of the USSR making control regimes much less attractive.

3.2.5 The statistical evidence

We now look at how each particular syndrome deviates from the core regression, the results being reported in table 11.2. Because the dependent variable is now a syndrome rather than the absence of syndromes, we should expect the signs to be the opposite of those observed in table 11.1.

Consider, first, the regulatory syndrome. Consistent with the arguments of chapter 6, the ending of the Cold War, a large proportion of adults with secondary education, and party competition made the adoption of control regimes less likely; the last is not statistically significant, however. Ethnic dominance is now insignificant: the urge to excessive regulation was not affected by a society having a dominant ethnic group. Coastal economies were more likely to adopt such policies than were those that were landlocked.

Now consider the redistribution syndrome. When there is a dominant ethnic group, the incentives to adopt redistributive policies appear to decline. Rather, the important drivers of the syndrome are ethnic diversity joined with rule by fear and the existence of rich resources. When opposition parties can openly contest elections, governments are less likely to engage in redistribution. Somewhat surprisingly, increases in education actually raise the likelihood of the syndrome.

The major driver of the unsustainable spending syndrome is, unsurprisingly, the magnitude of resource wealth. Ethnic diversity and rule by fear appear to have little bearing on the likelihood of exhibiting this syndrome. A more educated population and multi-party democracy make this syndrome less likely.

Finally, turning to state breakdown, it is here that the interaction of rule by fear and ethnic diversity appears to be most potent. In the light of recent scholarship, it is surprising to find that high levels of resource wealth appear to reduce, rather than increase, the likelihood of this syndrome.

4 Conclusions

We close by reiterating our core findings. The form of representation counts: it affects the degree to which policy will be used to promote the formation of national public goods, such as growth, as opposed to targetable "club" goods, such as ethno-regional transfers or private benefits for the elite. So, too, does the selectorate: the narrower the selectorate, the greater the incentives to secure wealth through redistribution rather than growth. And the states of Africa have learned: from their own experiences, from the fall of communism, and from the mistakes of their neighbors.

Appendix: Data used in analysis of syndromes

Table 11.A1 *Descriptive statistics.*

Variable	Mean	Std dev.	Min	Max	Obs.
Syndrome-free	0.341	0.012	0	1	1645
Regulatory	0.421	0.012	0	1	1645
Redistribution	0.315	0.012	0	1	1645
Unsustainable spending	0.098	0.007	0	1	1645
State breakdown	0.146	0.009	0	1	1645
Rule by fear	0.410	0.014	0	1	1645
Ethnic dominance	0.277	0.011	0	1	1645
Ethnic diversity	0.725	0.014	0.255	0.953	1645
Accumulated knowledge	0.238	0.001	0.172	0.372	1645
Neighbors' syndromes	0.323	0.009	0	1	1645
Landlocked, resource-scarce	0.283	0.011	0	1	1645
Coastal, resource-scarce	0.454	0.012	0	1	1645
Proportion of natural-resource					1645
rents in GDP	0.061	0.005	0	1	1645
Trend	28	10.10	11	45	1645
Secondary enrollment in 1970	8.258	0.151	1	30	1645
Multi-party	0.151	0.359	0	1	1645
Coup risk	0.046	0.001	0	0.16	1645
Resource-rich*					
Competitive parties	0.034	0.013	0	11.5	1645
Rule by fear*					
Ethnic diversity	0.311	0.010	0	1	1645
Post-1989	0.429	0.249	0	1	1645

Sample: Angola, Benin, Botswana, Burkina Faso, Burundi, Cameroon, CAR, Chad, Côte d'Ivoire, DRC, Ethiopia, Gabon, The Gambia, Ghana, Guinea, Guinea-Bissau, Kenya, Lesotho, Liberia, Mali, Mauritius, Mozambique, Niger, Nigeria, Senegal, Sierra Leone, Somalia, South Africa, Sudan, Tanzania, Togo, Uganda, Zambia, Zimbabwe

Variables:

Syndrome-free

Takes a value of 1 if the country is free of any syndrome in the year in question.

Regulatory

Takes a value of 1 if the country is either in a hard or a soft regulatory regime.

Redistribution

Takes a value of 1 if the country is in any of the three variants of the redistribution syndrome.

Unsustainable spending

Takes a value of 1 if the country is in a phase of the unsustainable spending syndrome.

State breakdown

Takes a value of 1 if the country is experiencing state breakdown.

Rule by fear

Dummy variable taking a value of 1 if authority is highly concentrated in a political leader who indeed "rules by fear." *Source:* classification by authors.

Ethnic dominance

Takes a value of 1 if the largest ethnic group in society makes up between 45 and 90 percent of the total population. *Source:* based on Fearon and Laitin's (2003) "plural" variable.

Ethnic diversity

This cultural fractionalization measure takes a value of 0 for homogenous societies, higher values describe more heterogenous societies. The number is obtained by drawing two people at random from a country and measuring the probability that they belong to the same culture. *Source:* Fearon (2003).

Accumulated knowledge

Population-weighed average (using 1980 populations) of the syndrome-free status for all countries in SSA. This variable is time-varying but the same for all countries. *Source:* authors' calculations.

Neighbors' syndromes

Average of the syndrome-free status of the country's neighbors. *Source:* authors' calculations.

Landlocked, resource-scarce

Dummy variable taking a value of 1 for landlocked, resource-scarce countries. *Source:* classification by authors.

Coastal, resource-scarce

Dummy variable taking a value of 1 for coastal, resource-scarce countries. *Source*: classification by authors.

Proportion of natural-resource rents in GDP

Using data from the World Bank's adjusted savings project we calculated the rents for each commodity by subtracting the cost from the commodity price. We then multiplied the rents per unit by the amount extracted and summed across the different commodities. We then calculated the share of rents in GDP. Since the rents are provided in current US dollars we used the WDI 2003 GDP in current dollars to calculate this share. Natural resources for which rent data were available are: oil, gas, coal, lignite, bauxite, copper, gold, iron, lead, nickel, phosphate, silver, tin, and zinc. The data are available from http://lnweb18.worldbank.org/ESSD/envext.nsf/44ByDocName/GreenAccountingAdjustedNetSavings.

Trend

A linear trend term, incremented one unit per year.

Secondary enrollment in 1970

Ratio of number of persons enrolled in secondary school to number of persons of secondary school age.

Multi-party

Dummy variable taking a value of 1 if the country has a multi-party system. *Source*: http://africa.govt.harvard.edu.

Coup, risk of

This variable was calculated using the model of *coup d'état* presented in Collier and Hoeffler (2005).

Resource rich × Competitive parties

Interaction between two dummy variables, one taking the value of 1 if the country is resource-rich (and 0 otherwise) and the other taking on the value 1 if the country has a multi-party system (and 0 otherwise).

Rule by fear × ethnic diversity

Interaction between a dummy variable taking a value of 1 if authority is highly concentrated in a political leader who "rules by fear" (and 0 otherwise) and the Fearon index of ethnic diversity.

Post-1989

Dummy variable taking a value of 1 for 1990 and later years.

References

Acemoglu, Daron and James A. Robinson (2001), "Inefficient Redistribution," *American Political Science Review* 95: 649–61

Adam, Christopher S. and Stephen A. O'Connell (1999), "Aid, Taxation, and Development in sub-Saharan Africa," *Economics and Politics* 11: 225–54

Alesina, Alberto, Reza Baqir, and William Easterley (1999), "Public Goods and Ethnic Divisions," *Quarterly Journal of Economics* 114: 1243–84

Allen, Chris (1989), "Benin," in C. Allen, M. S. Radu, K. Somerville, and J. Baxter, *Benin, the Congo, Burkina Fasu: Economics, Politics, and Society.* London and New York: Pinter

Azam, Jean-Paul and Alice Mesnard (2003), "Civil War and the Social Contract," *Public Choice* 115: 455–75

Bates, Robert H. (1981), *Markets and States in Tropical Africa.* Berkeley, CA and Los Angeles, CA: University of California Press

Bates, Robert H. and Irene Yackolev (2002), "Ethnicity in Africa," in C. Grootaert and T. van Bastelaer, eds., *The Role of Social Capital in Development.* New York: Cambridge University Press

Becker, Gary S. (1983), "A Theory of Competition among Pressure Groups for Political Influence," *Quarterly Journal of Economics* 98: 371–400

Bueno de Mesquita, Bruce, Alastair Smith, Randolph Siverson, and James Morrow (2003), *The Logic of Political Survival.* Cambridge, MA: MIT Press

Collier, Paul (2000), "Ethnicity, Politics, and Economic Performance," *Economics and Politics* 12: 225–45

Collier, Paul and Anke Hoeffler (2005), "Grand Extortion Coup Risk and the Military as a Protection Racket," University of Oxford, mimeo

Dahl, Robert (1971), *Polyarchy.* New Haven, CT: Yale University Press

Easterly, William and Ross Levine (1997), "Africa's Growth Tragedy: Policies and Ethnic Divisions," *Quarterly Journal of Economics* 112: 1203–50

Fearon, James (2003), "Ethnic and Cultural Diversity by Country," *Journal of Economic Growth* 8(2): 195–222

Fearon, James D. and David D. Laitin (1996), "Explaining Interethnic Cooperation," *American Political Science Review* 90: 715–35

  (2003), "Ethnicity, Insurgency and Civil War," *American Political Science Review* 97: 75–90

Honaker, James (2000), "Issues in Multiple Imputation of Data of the African Research Program," Department of Government, Cambridge, MA: Harvard University

Huband, Mark (2001), *The Skull beneath the Skin: Africa after the Cold War.* Boulder, CO: Westview Press

Humphreys, Macartan and Robert H. Bates (2005), "Political Institutions and Economic Policies: Lessons from Africa," *British Journal of Political Science* 35: 403–28

Iyoha, Milton A. and Dickson E. Oriakhi (2007), "Explaining African Economic Growth Performance: The Case of Nigeria," chapter 18 in Benno J. Ndulu, Stephen A. O'Connell, Jean-Paul Azam, Robert H. Bates, Augustin Kwasi Fosu, Jan Willem Gunning, and Dominique Njinkeu, eds., *The Political Economy of*

Economic Growth in Africa, 1960–2000, vol. 2. Cambridge: Cambridge University Press

Kasekende, Louis A. and Michael Atingi-Ego (2007), "Restarting and Sustaining Growth in a Post-conflict Economy: The Case of Uganda," chapter 8 in Benno J. Ndulu, Stephen A. O'Connell, Jean-Paul Azam, Robert H. Bates, Augustin Kwasi Fosu, Jan Willem Gunning, and Dominique Njinkeu, eds., *The Political Economy of Economic Growth in Africa, 1960–2000*, vol. 2. Cambridge: Cambridge University Press

Kasfir, Nelson (1976), *The Shrinking Political Arena*. Berkeley, CA and Los Angeles, CA: University of California Press

King, Gary, Michael Tomz, and Jason Wittenberg (2000), "Making the Most of Statistical Analyses," *American Journal of Political Science* 44: 347–61

Mwanawina, Inyambo and James Mulungushi (2007), "Zambia," chapter 27 in Benno J. Ndulu, Stephen A. O'Connell, Jean-Paul Azam, Robert H. Bates, Augustin Kwasi Fosu, Jan Willem Gunning, and Dominique Njinkeu, eds., *The Political Economy of Economic Growth in Africa, 1960–2000*, vol. 2. Cambridge: Cambridge University Press

Nkurunziza, Janvier and Floribert Ngaruki (2007), "Why Has Burundi Grown so Slowly? The Political Economy of Redistribution," chapter 2 in Benno J. Ndulu, Stephen A. O'Connell, Jean-Paul Azam, Robert H. Bates, Augustin Kwasi Fosu, Jan Willem Gunning, and Dominique Njinkeu, eds., *The Political Economy of Economic Growth in Africa, 1960–2000*, vol. 2. Cambridge: Cambridge University Press

Norris, Pippa and Robert Mattes (2003), "Does Ethnicity Determine Support for the Governing Party?," The John F. Kennedy School of Government, Harvard University, Cambridge, MA

Nzongola-Ntanlaja, Georges (2002), *The Congo from Leopold to Kabila*. London: Zed Books

Olson, Mancur (1977), *The Logic of Collective Action*. Cambridge, MA: Harvard University Press

Penn, Elizabeth Maggie (2006), "Citizenship versus Ethnicity: The Role of Institutions in Shaping Identity Choice," Institute for Quantitative Social Science, Department of Government, Harvard University, Cambridge, MA

Posner, Daniel (2005), *Institutions and Ethnic Politics in Africa*. New York and London: Cambridge University Press

Roeder, Philip (1993), *Red Sunset*. Princeton, NJ: Princeton University Press

Ross, Mark (2003), "The Natural Resource Curse," in I. Bannon and P. Collier, eds., *Natural Resources and Violent Conflict*. Washington, DC: The World Bank

Rothchild, Donald and Victor Olorunsula, eds. (1983), *State vs Ethnic Claims*. Boulder, CO: Westview Press

Rubin, D. B. (1996), "Multiple Imputation after 18+ Years (with Discussion)," *Journal of the American Statistical Association* 91: 473–89

Sachs, Jeffrey D. and Andrew M. Warner (1995), "Natural Resource Abundance and Economic Growth," National Bureau of Economic Research, Inc., NEBR Working Papers 5398

Schafer, Joseph L. (1997), "Imputation of Missing Covariates in the Multivariate Linear Mixed Model," Department of Statistics, University Park, PA: The Pennsylvania State University

Schumpeter, Joseph A. (1950), *Capitalism, Socialism and Democracy*. New York: Harper & Row

Werbner, Richard (1993), "From Heartland to Hinterland: Elites and the Geopolitics of Land in Botswana," in T. J. Bassett and D. E. Crummey, eds., *Land in African Agrarian Systems*. Madison, WI: University of Wisconsin Press

Zakaria, Fareed (1997), "The Rise of Illiberal Democracy," *Foreign Affairs* 76: 22–43

Zolberg, Aristide (1966), *Creating Political Order: The Party States of West Africa*. Chicago: Rand McNally

PART 4

Looking ahead

12 | Harnessing growth opportunities: how Africa can advance

Paul Collier, Jan Willem Gunning, Stephen A. O'Connell, and Benno J. Ndulu

1 Introduction

Our analysis has been retrospective: Africa's economic growth over the period 1960–2000. The primary purpose in understanding Africa's past is to help guide its future. Our main conclusion from our review of Africa's past has been that while its opportunities were atypically difficult, its politics evolved in such a way that it largely failed to harness them. The politics was transmitted into the economy through syndromes: growth-constraining packages of policies, institutions, and behavior.

In this chapter we look forward. Opportunities, as we define them, are geographical characteristics and hence, for better or for worse, there is little one can do to change them. Africa can, however, make much better use of its opportunities and, where opportunities are adverse, mitigate their economic impact. We consider in turn the three big opportunity groups that we have used throughout the study – landlocked and resource-scarce, resource-rich, and coastal and resource-scarce countries. For each we ask two types of question. First, what proximately is needed in order for opportunities to be harnessed? For example, landlocked Africa needs better transport infrastructure. Second, what are the political underpinnings that would enable such proximate changes to be made and sustained? For example, what political structures would provide the incentive for neighboring countries to maintain the transport corridors that landlocked countries need?

As background, we stress four major lessons from our analysis of Africa's experience. First avoiding policy mistakes continues to be the single most important choice in the hands of African governments intent on closing the growth gap with fast-growing regions of the world. Remaining syndrome-free alone accounts for between a quarter and a half of the growth gap, and is virtually a necessary condition for surpassing global averages on a sustained basis. The political and institutional requirements for remaining syndrome-free may vary systematically across opportunity groups – resource-rich countries, for example, are unusually exposed to intertemporal errors.

Second, the geographical disadvantages faced by a large proportion of African countries can be offset with appropriate choices and investments. Taking appropriate action to address locational and demographic challenges, and to manage natural-resource wealth effectively, would enable the region to close another third of the growth gap.

Third, Africa's societies are distinctively diverse: citizens have strong ethno-regional identities. Where these create a platform for conflict, the costs of violence invite a concentration of state power sufficient to provide internal security. But autocracy can be ruinous under conditions of ethnic diversity, with a dictator basing power on his own ethnic group and maintaining allegiance through redistribution to the group at the expense of the public good of growth. This tension cannot be resolved in the abstract: autocratic regimes flourished in much of Asia, for example, over the period of study. But under the very different social conditions of many African countries, the downside risks of autocracy are multiplied relative to the appeal of participatory institutions that disperse power. In short, Africa needs democracy. There are no guarantees of success, and young and weak democracies may require security support from regional and global partners, particularly in the short run. Moreover, much of Africa is resource-rich and in these geographic conditions democracy itself needs to be distinctive. The rents from natural resources can easily corrupt democratic competition into the politics of patronage. Ethnically diverse societies with resource wealth need not only democracy but unusually strong checks and balances on how governments can use public money.

The final lesson concerns the detailed design of growth strategy. We have defined growth opportunities geographically and categorically: coastal, landlocked, resource-rich. In reality, the economic constraints on growth – even geographical ones – are multi-dimensional and vary in intensity across countries. Some of this complexity can be accommodated by combining analytical categories: resource-scarce economies with substantial primary export sectors, for example, may share key features of resource-rich economies. But the multi-dimensionality of constraints raises deeper issues, and growth strategists have taken two broad approaches. One approach stresses the interdependence of economic constraints and argues that the success of any individual reform may require the simultaneous implementation of many other reforms (Banerjee and Newman 1993; Acemoglu and Zilibotti 2001; Sachs *et al.* 2004). The second looks for binding constraints and argues that reforms can and should be sharply prioritized on a country-by-country basis (Hausmann, Rodrik, and Velasco 2005; Easterly 2006). We view these approaches as complementary rather than competing. Our synthesis taxonomy operates at the intermediate level, stressing aspects of opportunity and choice that are themselves multi-dimensional and that may involve strategic complementarities, but that vary systematically enough across countries to provide a powerful platform for country-specific analysis.

2 Harnessing opportunities in landlocked Africa

Recall that Africa is highly distinctive in having around 33 percent of its population living in countries that are both landlocked and resource-scarce and therefore have very limited opportunities. In other developing regions the proportion is a mere 1 percent. Thus, outside Africa, areas with such unpromising endowments have seldom become countries.

We first consider a range of growth strategies that might be feasible for a typical landlocked, resource-scarce African country, and then turn to the political underpinnings that might be needed for these strategies.

2.1 Strategies for growth in landlocked Africa

Landlocked, resource-scarce countries have no single obvious winning growth strategy that will take them to middle-income status. Instead, like Switzerland, they need to be ingenious. We consider nine different possible strategies. These are not alternatives and could in principle be adopted in parallel, although it would probably spread effort too widely for all nine to be implemented together.

2.1.1 Strategy 1: increase neighborhood growth spillovers

Growth spills over across borders. All countries, whether landlocked or not, can benefit from the growth of their neighbors. Because landlocked countries have worse access to global markets, a good strategy is to integrate as strongly as possible into neighboring economies to maximize these spillovers.

Outside Africa this is precisely what the landlocked countries do. Recall from chapter 2 what happens if the neighbors grow by an extra 1 percent. The typical non-African coastal country gains from this extra growth of neighbors by 0.4 percent on its own growth rate. The typical non-African landlocked country gains much more: 0.6 percent. How much extra growth does the typical African landlocked country get if its neighbors grow by an extra 1 percent? The answer is zero. This tells us something important, namely that these countries are not adequately integrated into their sub-region and that this substantially reduces their potential for growth.

What can be done? Cross-border trade is primarily a matter of trade policy, infrastructure policy, and practical on-the-ground implementation. Within this list the key obstacles will differ country-by-country. However, while the landlocked countries have a strong interest in regional integration, including the elimination of intra-regional trade barriers, they also have a strong interest in reducing the external trade barriers of the region. Regional trade barriers generate an invisible transfer from the poor landlocked countries to their more industrialized and richer neighbors (Venables 2003). Within a regional trade bloc the landlocked countries should therefore lobby for the lowest possible external trade barriers. African governments have typically pursued regional integration for political rather than economic reasons. To the extent that economic objectives were important, the idea was that regional integration would enable small African economies to realize economies of scale (Oyejide, Elbadawi, and Collier 1997; Gunning 2001). In practice, regional integration often led to divergence within a trade bloc with the benefits concentrated in richer, coastal countries (such as Kenya in the East African Community in the 1970s) and the poorer, landlocked members left behind in relative terms. While this experience has made policy-makers wary, it reflects high external barriers rather than an intrinsic effect of integration. That integration with low external barriers offers hope for the disadvantaged group of landlocked and resource-scarce countries is not yet well appreciated by African policy-makers or donors.

2.1.2   Strategy 2: improve neighbors' economic policies

A second implication is that once economies are better integrated, the economic performance of neighbors matters. The faster neighbors grow, the faster the landlocked country will grow. Not only can the landlocked not afford to make policy mistakes, they cannot afford their more fortunate neighbors to make mistakes. Good policy choices of the more fortunately endowed African countries are regional public goods and hence tend to be under-supplied through individual national decisions. This is not a recipro-cal relationship: it matters to Niger enormously that Nigeria should adopt good policies, but whether Niger adopts good policies is of little consequence for Nigeria.

2.1.3   Strategy 3: improve coastal access

Access to the sea is a vital interest for landlocked countries that they do not control. Studies confirm the evident fact that your costs of access depend upon the transport infrastructure and policy decisions of your coastal neighbors (Limão and Venables 2002). The transport costs of landlocked countries vary enormously depending upon these decisions of neighbors. However, since they are providing a regional public good, they usually have insufficient incentive to provide as much of it as is needed.

2.1.4   Strategy 4: become a haven for the region

Many business services are traded regionally rather than globally – for example, some financial services. Often these services depend upon a good policy environment. If one country in a region manages to set policies clearly superior to those of its neighbors it will attract these services and export them around the region. The classic example of such a role was Lebanon, which became a financial center for the entire Middle East (as Switzerland did for Europe). As Lebanon demonstrates, a country does not need to be landlocked in order to become a regional haven. The landlocked have no absolute advantage. However, they do have a comparative advantage: with fewer alternative strategies than more fortunately endowed countries, they can be seen to have a stronger incentive to sustain necessary reforms. The possibility of becoming the center for those regional goods that are highly policy-sensitive, such as finance, gives landlocked countries a differential incentive to adopt good policies, qualitatively countering the weaker incentive argument of Gallup and Sachs with Mellinger (1999) discussed in chapter 2.

2.1.5   Strategy 5: don't be air-locked or E-locked

The technology of trade has to some extent shifted in favor of landlocked countries.

Air transport is much more important than it used to be. Landlocked Africa is the closest low-income developing area by air to Europe, and so it has a potential niche market in airport-intensive activities. Distance itself is becoming a less important component of transport costs than loading and unloading, but these costs can be lowered by policy. There are significant economies of scale in air transport and in this respect the landlocked countries are at a disadvantage because they are small markets for air services. However, low costs are possible even on a modest scale: the key is deregulation. Nigeria provides a good model of how an open-skies policy can radically reduce the cost of air services and increase their frequency. Possibly these very companies might provide the foundation for a region-wide low-cost air service for landlocked Africa. Once air-freight is cheap, landlocked Africa has a comparative advantage in horticultural exports to Europe, as demonstrated by Zambia's success with air-transported flowers.

E-services now have the potential to deliver rapid economic growth. This is the story of recent economic development in India. Because India is a coastal economy it has many options for global integration. Landlocked Africa does not have such a range of options. E-services are attractive because distance is irrelevant. Indeed, the fact that Africa's location is in the same time zone as Europe gives it a major advantage over Asia. The twin pillars of E-services are telecommunications and post-primary education. Good telecommunications depends upon getting regulatory and competition policies right. It is a relatively simple matter to tell when they are wrong: prices are too high relative to global benchmarks and coverage is inadequate. Post-primary education represents a clear opportunity, not least in the sense that it has tended to be poorly targeted and supported in the past. Secondary-school training served as a near-automatic conduit for public sector employment until the late 1980s in many countries, and well before that time aid donors shifted their priorities to the primary level where social returns were less sensitive to the policy environment. To the degree that the economic reforms of the 1990s brought the private and social returns to post-secondary education into better alignment, these same reforms now place a premium on policies to increase the private return – on the supply side, through public investments in school quality and on the demand side, through policies favorable to direct foreign investment (FDI) in both services and manufacturing.

2.1.6   Strategy 6: encourage remittances

Because landlocked economies have fewer options for growth they are likely to experience substantial emigration. However, emigration can be turned to advantage through remittances. Maximizing remittances depends upon several steps. One is to educate people so that they are employable in higher-income economies rather than simply as unskilled workers in neighboring countries that are almost as poor. The second is to facilitate the finding of jobs in such economies. A model for such practices is the Philippines, where training is targeted to the needs of high-income economies and the government provides information and embassy services to make hiring of its citizens easy. The third is to encourage emigrant workers to remit part of their incomes. This depends upon banking systems and exchange rates. An over-valued exchange rate taxes remittances and therefore discourages them. The fourth is to encourage the diaspora to invest in the country – for example, building homes for family and retirement. The fifth is to encourage second-generation emigrants to retain their ties with the country. Finally, banking system reform is crucial, not just for inducing remittances, but for improving the allocation of remittances within the economy. Ghana (in spite of its coastal position) now receives huge remittance flows, including about

$1 billion annually through official channels. However, total remittances from Ghanians abroad are very much larger. The bulk of their remittances are carried, transferred to friends and relations or to NGOs, with inevitable costs in terms of poor intermediation. Financial sector reform is therefore a priority for landlocked countries wishing to harness migration as a source of growth.

2.1.7   Strategy 7: design the budget so as to encourage big aid inflows on a long-term basis

Even if landlocked Africa adopts shrewd growth strategies it is likely to be poor relative to most other countries for the foreseeable future. The coming expansion in aid to Africa can potentially provide the governments of land-locked countries with a large revenue source on a long-term basis. It is highly desirable that this should support the budget rather than become a prolifer-ation of donor projects or humanitarian interventions. This depends upon governments building transparent and reliable systems of public expendi-ture which satisfy the dual hurdle of integrity and efficiency. This is an enormous undertaking but the payoff would also be enormous. With effec-tive public services many other activities would become feasible. Equally, a large aid inflow as budget support would enable taxes to be lowered. Coun-tries at the level of development of landlocked Africa should concentrate upon spending money effectively rather than raising it effectively. The gov-ernments that spend money effectively should and will get substantial aid.

2.1.8   Strategy 8: create a transparent and investor-friendly environment for resource prospecting

The area of landlocked Africa currently classified as "resource-scarce" is enormous. It seems likely that there are valuable resources in the ground that have not yet been discovered. Creating a political and commercial envi-ronment in which these resources are located and extracted for the bene-fit of citizens will be difficult. However, there are examples, most notably Botswana.

The main impediments to prospecting are likely to be the risks as perceived by resource-extraction companies. Some of these are political, but the more important ones are probably the risk to the reputation of the company should the governance of the resource revenues become manifestly problematic. Not all companies are concerned about the risk to their reputation because not all companies have good reputations to protect. However, this gives rise to an adverse selection problem: the companies attracted in to the risky environments of landlocked Africa are those that are not concerned about poor governance and so have no interest in helping to avoid the problems that have been common in resource-rich Africa.

2.1.9   Strategy 9: rural development

Because landlocked countries do not have the option of rapid industrialization, the bulk of their populations will continue to be rural for a long
time. In turn, this implies that policies for rural development should receive
higher priority than in other economies. Whereas the policies needed for
industrial exports are pretty standard around the world, policies for rural
development must be adapted to local circumstances and so require a much
larger investment in local knowledge. A further constraint upon rural development is the limited market access in Europe and the USA for products
such as cotton in which landlocked Africa has a comparative advantage.

2.2   The political foundations for growth in landlocked Africa

The nine growth strategies considered above each have political requirements for sustained implementation. We now consider these requirements
and how they might be met.

2.2.1   Political requirement 1: internalize neighborhood externalities

All countries depend on others to some extent, but the landlocked countries
of Africa are unusual in their degree of dependence. They are dependent
upon their more fortunate neighbors in three respects: regional integration;
the spillovers that come if their neighbors adopt good policies; and access
to the sea.

The benefits of regional integration are at least to some extent reciprocal.
The road network that facilitates regional trade is a regional public good from
which all benefit. The appropriate political response is therefore cooperation
at the neighborhood level. The incentives for such regional cooperation can
be enhanced by providing aid for regional public goods rather than just for
national public goods, as has been common in the past. The debate on global
public goods has made donors acutely aware of the importance of trans-
border externalities. This awareness can be harnessed to ensure funding for
the sort of infrastructure which otherwise would be under-supplied.

Similarly, the benefits of good policies are also at least to some extent
reciprocal, although as our example of Niger and Nigeria shows, there are
large asymmetries of power. Nevertheless, there is the possibility of internal-
izing the externalities through peer pressure. For such pressure there needs
to be a forum in which peers can compare each other's performance. A
neighborhood-level Annual Peer Review Mechanism along the lines of the
Organization for Economic Co-operation and Development (OECD) and
NEPAD would be one approach.

The benefits of access to the sea are not reciprocated: the landlocked country depends upon its coastal neighbor but not vice versa. Hence, the coastal

country needs to be given an incentive to provide better access to the sea than it would otherwise choose. In principle, the landlocked country could provide financial assistance to its more fortunate neighbor to cover these costs. However, given the disparity in incomes, a more natural way of providing the necessary incentive is for some of the aid to the coastal country to be made conditional upon the coastal country providing a specified level of access for the landlocked country. Evidently, this would need to be supported by a verification system in which the assessment of the landlocked country was critical. Alternatively, such conditional aid could be provided to a regional bloc which would then be responsible for the verification system.

2.2.2   Political requirement 2: internalize international externalities

In addition to neighbors, landlocked countries are dependent upon the international community, partly for market access, partly for aid, and partly for the institutions that would protect the reputation of reputable investors in extractive industries.

The international community expresses concern for the acute problems of landlocked Africa – for example, in periodic massive emergency relief programs. However, there is a failure to connect between the parts of OECD governments and societies that deliver emergency relief and the parts responsible for market access and for long-term aid.

Negotiations over market access for agricultural products have been dominated by the interests of European and American farmers rather than by concerns for producers in landlocked Africa. This culminated in the remarkable proposal from the trade negotiators of the EU and USA that landlocked Africa should be compensated for diversifying out of cotton, a proposal that was withdrawn following opposition. Given the enormous differential in opportunities available to those cotton farmers in landlocked Africa and those in the OECD, once externalities are properly internalized it is the latter who should be induced to diversify into other activities.

Landlocked Africa needs to be recognized as a distinctive recipient of aid. Because it is already poorer than other regions and has inferior prospects of growth, it is likely to be a long-term recipient of aid, not merely to raise growth, that is aid-for-development, but to raise current consumption. At present this is not reflected in aid allocation criteria, for there is no intermediate category between development assistance and emergency relief.

The institution designed by the World Bank in 1998 to manage the revenues from the Chad–Cameroon pipeline is the prototype for providing protection of reputation for firms in the extractive industries. The government of Chad created a system of scrutiny by civil society of the oil revenues, a system that was underwritten by World Bank conditionality. In turn, this provided the oil companies with the degree of comfort needed to invest to extract oil reserves which had been discovered in the 1950s but left unexploited. While the detailed design of the institution may prove to have some weaknesses, the core idea has considerable potential to encourage reputable firms into other difficult environments.

2.2.3   Political requirement 3: rebalancing interest groups

The governments of landlocked countries are evidently central to most of the growth strategies discussed above. In turn, changed behavior of government implies changed power structures: the public goods needed by those interest groups that have been politically weak have been under-supplied.

For better rural development policies to be sustained the rural population needs to be able to overcome the impediments that it faces for collective action that are so much greater than for urban groups. The essential step in such a rebalancing of power is multi-party competitive democracy. Once farmers have votes that matter, politicians have some incentive to deliver the public goods that matter for agriculture.

Another under-supplied public good is scrutiny of public expenditure. Recall that if effective scrutiny can be put in place, aid is likely to be greatly increased. Scrutiny is thus a national public good, so no single individual or group has an incentive to provide it. Worse, scrutiny curtails the actions of the powerful and so they have an active interest against its supply. Scrutiny of public expenditure can be done in three complementary ways: top-down systems such as audit; bottom-up systems such as providing communities with information about their entitlements, as demonstrated by a celebrated initiative in Uganda (Reinikka and Svensson 2004); and sideways pressure from peer groups, as when district governments compete with each other to look the most effective.

The provision of good air services and E-services would enable new economic activities to develop. Until these activities emerge their interest remains latent and so is unexpressed. This may enhance the potential for a "big-push" strategy to improve air and E-services. A temporary aid-for-infrastructure effort may have a lasting impact if it enables industries to develop which are then in a position to defend their interest in the mainte-nance of good air and E-services.

Just as industries dependent upon air and E-services lack influence because they do not exist, emigrants lack influence because they are absent. This weakens the support base for remittance-friendly policies. One strategy for increasing the influence of the diaspora is to give them some formal rep-resentation in government, something adopted by Eritrea during the 1990s. Alternatively, the diaspora can be given a favorable legal status, as done by the government of India through the category of Non-Resident Indians.

3   Harnessing opportunities in resource-rich Africa

Recall that Africa is distinctive in having around a third of its popula-tion living in countries that are resource-rich. In other developing regions the proportion is only 11 percent. Moreover, resource abundance (unlike landlockedness) is subject to change, and here again Africa's trajectory is distinctive: the past decade alone has seen the emergence of major new oil exports in Angola, Chad, Equatorial Guinea, and Sudan. Globally, the management of resource riches has proved to be problematic.

We first consider a range of growth strategies that might be feasible for a typical resource-rich African country, and then turn to the political under-pinnings that might be needed for these strategies.

3.1   Strategies for growth in resource-rich Africa

Unlike landlocked, resource-scarce countries, resource-rich countries have a single dominant growth strategy that can take them to middle-income status.

3.1.1   Strategy 1: governments should transform the resource rents efficiently into public goods and private capital formation

In Africa, resource rents usually accrue largely to the public sector. In many cases, notably in the oil economies, resource rents have been squandered. (This response is not specific to Africa, e.g. Gelb 1988, but Africa has rela-tively more resource wealth.) The policy debate has focused on the extent to which foreign assets can be used to make an orderly and effective transla-tion of resource wealth into public goods possible. This involves four distinct policies. First, because revenues are generally volatile, the government needs to smooth expenditures over the medium term. Note that this is very dif-ferent from accumulating financial assets for future generations, a strategy which will be inappropriate for a poor country unless its opportunities for domestic investment are exceptionally limited. Accumulating assets for a shorter period in order to smooth consumption over the medium term raises difficult technical issues of economic management, concerning the choice of assets, the appropriate savings rate out of resource rents, and the coordination of fiscal and monetary policies in a situation when money demand is unstable. However, there is ground for optimism: as noted in chapter 5, the gross mismanagement of resource booms (common in the 1970s), which we classified as the "intertemporal syndrome," has not hap-pened on a significant scale in the past decade. Second, it needs to scrutinize public expenditures on the criterion of economic efficiency, with projects selected on a technical assessment of their likely return rather than on the basis of political lobbying. Third, it needs to protect public revenues from embezzlement. Fourth, it needs to create incentives for cost-effective delivery of public services by public employees: that is, expenditures need to be well implemented.

An additional challenge for the government of a resource-rich economy is to transfer some of the wealth to the private sector. Botswana has managed this transfer partly by using diamond wealth to finance relief in drought years and, more importantly, by transfering public savings through the banking system thereby allowing the private sector to run a deficit. Without some transfer to the private sector the private capital stock would become inefficiently small relative to the stock of public capital. One way to redress the balance is for the government to use resource rents to retire domestic debt (Collier and Gunning 2006). In resource-rich countries with coastal locations – a category that includes most of Africa's oil exporters – another option is to use resource rents to support a robust program of export diversification. In combination with policies that avoid macroeconomic distortions from booms and busts, such rents could be directed to competitiveness-enhancing investments in infrastructure, higher education and the upgrading of skills, and information and communication technology.

3.2   The political foundations for growth in resource-rich Africa

The desirable growth strategy for resource-rich countries is obvious. The key issue is how this strategy can be politically adopted and sustained. The required political conditions are different from those needed for the land-locked countries.

3.2.1   Political requirement 1: protecting the commons of the future

The future is an under-represented interest group. As a result, the discount rate of the government is likely to be too high. One approach is to build formal institutions with rules that specify the relationship between current revenue and warranted spending. For example, Russia now has a four-year averaging rule for the price of oil that it uses to estimate the warranted expenditures from oil revenues. No such rule can have an immaculate justification in terms of optimally smoothing expenditure, but an advantage is that it is clear when it is being breached and this may protect against the unsustainable growth syndrome. However, formal institutions tend to be fragile unless they have some support in terms of interests. One factor which has tended to increase discount rates is the threat of coups. The incidence of coups d'état in Africa has continued to be high – for example, in the period 2000–5 there were successful coups in the CAR, Mauritania, and Togo. The African Union (AU) has begun to condemn coups, and was successful in putting down one in São Tomé and Principe. However, at present it lacks the logistics to make its condemnation effective. Since states have little effective internal defense against coups the provision of international assistance to put them down, under the authority of the AU, might make leaders feel more secure and thereby lower the discount rates of leaders. A different approach to strengthening the interest of the future is to increase the voice of youth, which in Africa is surely assisted by competitive elections.

3.2.2 Political requirement 2: checks and balances

One of our themes has been that in resource-rich countries electoral competition is not in itself sufficient to ensure accountability. The resource rents enable the government to have low taxation, and because taxes are low the public good of scrutiny is not provoked by the burden of taxation. The global evidence is that electoral competition actually lowers growth rates in resource-rich societies unless it is combined with checks and balances.

Hence, a critical aspect of governance in a resource-rich society is the provision of effective checks and balances. These can range from the constitutional, such as multiple veto players, to the informal, such as unrestricted and privately owned media. Evidence from Peru on how checks and balances can be undermined suggests that the media are more important than constitutional checks and balances such as parliament and the judiciary (McMillan and Zoido 2004). In Peru, the key part of the media was the television channels; however in Africa, because of its lower level of income, the most effective part of the media is probably radio. Multiple privately owned radio stations may be the best restraint.

3.2.3 Political requirement 3: an informed electorate

Citizens and the media cannot scrutinize government behavior without information on its performance. In particular, citizens need information on how public resources are being used. The Extractive Industries Transparency Initiative (EITI) establishes a clear code of practice for the reporting of resource revenues. This is an important input into scrutiny, since without knowledge of revenues there can be no scrutiny of expenditure. However, the larger task is to improve information on the scale, composition, and effectiveness of expenditures, using the top-down, bottom-up, and peer pressure approaches discussed above.

3.2.4 Political requirement 4: protecting the technocrats

While public scrutiny can protect against dishonesty it cannot protect against folly. The defense against wasteful, populist projects is essentially technocratic. An excellent example of such a defense system in a resource-rich African country is Botswana where each public project is subject to a technocratic rate-of-return analysis and not undertaken unless it meets a required minimum return. The key step in such a system is to protect the decisions of technocrats from political interference. One approach is to make such a unit quasi-independent, analogous to an independent central bank.

4   Harnessing opportunities in coastal, resource-scarce Africa

Recall that Africa is distinctive in having a much smaller share of its population in coastal, resource-scarce countries than the proportion elsewhere. However, even so the proportion, at 35 percent, is substantial. The other distinctive feature is that it is this group that during our period most diverged from the growth performance of this group elsewhere. From the 1980s onwards, many coastal, resource-scarce countries outside Africa achieved remarkably rapid growth that put them on track to reach middle-income status within a generation.

Again, we first consider the appropriate growth strategy and then turn to the political underpinnings that might be needed for it.

4.1   Strategies for growth in coastal, resource-scarce Africa

4.1.1   Strategy 1: emulate the Asian model

The obvious growth strategy for a coastal, resource-scarce African economy is to emulate the Asian model of diversified export growth, whether for manufactured goods, services, or agro-processing.

In turn, this requires that the costs of some such exports be brought down to world levels. This is not an easy matter. The relevant infrastructure for exporting needs to be brought up to standards comparable with competitors, and this is likely to be expensive. Often the returns on the required infrastructure investments will not be high unless diversified exporting becomes viable, which requires crossing some threshold of cost reduction. Yet individual components of infrastructure in isolation are unlikely to be the only constraint upon reaching such a threshold, and even in aggregate infrastructure is not the only obstacle to African exporting, so that investing in it will not automatically trigger the emergence of the activities needed to validate the investment in infrastructure. A cost-benefit analysis of infrastructure investment except in the context of a broader strategy of promoting export growth is likely to conclude that other uses of public money are more warranted. One reason why infrastructure alone is likely to be insufficient is that Asian exporters of competing goods still benefit from cheap labor, but also benefit from economies of agglomeration which cannot be available to Africa until after similar agglomerations have been built up. Finally, new export activities which became profitable would need to be protected from predatory activity by politicians and public officials. The fear of likely predation in itself may be sufficient to discourage investors who have a wide choice of alternative locations.

4.2   The political foundations for growth in coastal, resource-scarce Africa

The desirable growth strategy for coastal, resource-scarce countries is obvious since Asia has already established the model. The key issue is how politically this strategy can be adopted and sustained. Again, the political requirements are quite distinctive. Whereas the resource-rich countries fundamentally need systems that enable public money to be spent well, the coastal countries need a far more focused change in governance that permits export platforms to function competitively.

4.2.1   Political requirement 1: protecting exporters from predation

The lack of a diversified export sector creates a threshold problem in which until exports have been successfully diversified there is no effective lobby for pro-export policies. In turn, the absence of such a lobby creates risks that deter the entry of exporting firms.

To solve this problem requires a temporary institutional guarantee that substitutes for an export lobby. The donors are in a position to provide such a guarantee. For example, they could put aid into an escrow account that would automatically provide compensation for exporting firms if the government failed to deliver specified conditions. While it is admittedly not possible to specify a contract that provides complete protection, such a system could go some way to reducing the risks for export investors. The established practices of investor guarantee organizations such as the Multinational Investment Guarantee Agency (MIGA) are a basis for such an approach, although ideally a new system would, for example, guarantee all firms in an Export-Processing Zone (EPZ), regardless of whether they were foreign or domestic.

Temporary external guarantees would provide the government with a financial incentive to honor commitments made to exporters, since default would result in its aid being used for compensation. However, the government would also need to take practical steps to ensure that public employees did not engage in predatory behavior. One advantage of an EPZ is that it enables easy coordination among exporting firms, so that lobbying and complaints to government can be made more easily. A variant adopted in Cambodia was for the EPZ to employ staff seconded to the Minister of Trade whose job was simply to patrol the corridors of the ministry, detecting impediments to exports as they occurred and reporting weekly to the minister. Such arrangements do not need to be permanent, but they are probably necessary to break existing behavioral patterns on the part of public officials.

4.2.2   Political requirement 2: an infrastructure big push

Protecting exporters from predation is unlikely to be sufficient. The existence of complementarities and thresholds in different types of infrastructure implies that a "big-push" approach is necessary, with the investment being evaluated as a package in the context of a wider strategy rather than item-by-item. Financing such a big push would be both expensive and risky, and would need to come from aid rather than normal government revenue. In turn, the aid would need to be exceptional. An implication of a big-push strategy is that aid should be concentrated in one or a few countries at a time, even if all countries were equally "deserving" of aid, or equally promising. By spreading aid thinly over all equally deserving countries no country might get sufficient aid to push it over the threshold into international competitiveness. However, such an allocation would require explicit acknowledgment of a catalytic role for aid.

4.2.3   Political requirement 3: temporary protection from Asia

Even with a big push of infrastructure and a temporary governance structure that protected exporters, Africa's coastal economies might not be able to compete with Asia because of the problem of Asia's economies of agglomeration. To overcome this problem may require that African producers be given temporary privileged access to OECD markets. While this may seem politically fanciful, the principle has in fact already been conceded for both the EU and the American market. The schemes which provide this protection are the Everything but Arms initiative in Europe and the Africa Growth and Opportunity Act (AGOA) in the USA. A third preferential scheme was proposed as part of the Hong Kong negotiations of the Doha Round in December 2005. Unfortunately, while these schemes have some merit, and clearly accept the principle of protection, they fail at the level of detail. Everything but Arms and the Hong Kong offer apply only to the least developed countries, whereas the most likely African countries to break into global markets are the more developed: Senegal rather than Liberia. The Everything but Arms scheme has complex and highly restrictive rules of origin which make it expensive to benefit from the scheme and limited in its scope. AGOA also has highly restrictive rules of origin and additionally is time-limited to a mere three years. With such a short horizon firms are reluctant to make new investments, so that they can be profitable and yet not expand. If any preferential scheme is likely to be effective, it should be pan-OECD, with more generous rules of origin and a time horizon of around a decade: sufficient to pump prime a more diversified African export sector but still time-bound so as to encourage speedy action. The rationale for such a scheme would be to get Africa across the threshold of competitiveness artificially in the first instance. Once over it, Africa might then start to build export agglomerations and the resulting economies might then drive down costs approximately to Asian levels. While the approach might seem theoretical, in fact Africa's one major success in manufacturing exports, Mauritius, broke into markets in entirely this way. It received temporary protection for twelve years from its allocation under the Multi-Fiber Agreement (MFA), a trade restriction that has now been eliminated. We should stress that this strategy can only be speculative. While the benefits of getting some African countries decisively into diversified export markets would surely be considerable, it is unlikely that trade preferences in themselves are either necessary or sufficient. Nevertheless, they might be useful, both increasing commercial feasibility and making complementary changes in policies and infrastructure politically more likely.

5   Conclusions

Growth strategy took a back seat to economic and political reforms in Africa throughout much of the period from the late 1970s to the mid-1990s. Indeed, to the degree that the reforms of the 1980s and 1990s sought to scale back and refocus the economic role of the state, they repudiated the one grand economic strategy that has ever commanded broad appeal within independent Africa, that of state-led and inward-looking industrialization. Throughout this book and in the accompanying volume 2 of country studies, we have sought to understand the drivers of growth in contemporary Africa, and in doing so to lay the groundwork for a renewed debate on growth strategy.

Our analysis of anti-growth syndromes has cross-cutting relevance for all of Africa. While there is some evidence of differential exposure to the syndromes by opportunity group, each group provides multiple episodes displaying each of the syndromes. Taken together, these episodes provide a powerful and reasonably complete account of growth failure. Remaining syndrome-free is a *sine qua non* of sustained rapid growth in Africa, and must be at the center of any viable growth strategy.

If remaining syndrome-free is necessary for sustained rapid growth, however, it is not sufficient. We have stressed that opportunities vary: the growth frontier for a landlocked and resource-poor country is less favorable than that for a coastal or resource-rich country. But opportunity is not destiny, and the variation in growth outcomes within opportunity groups, even among syndrome-free countries, is wide. Opportunity-specific analysis is required to identify strategies with high potential growth payoffs. We have made a start in this chapter, drawing on the global evidence and on our own synthesis of the country studies of the Africa Growth Project. A central lesson of these studies is that the political foundations of growth strategy must be constructed alongside the economic ones.

References

Acemoglu, D. and F. Zilibotti (2001), "Productivity Differences," *Quarterly Journal of Economics* 116(2), May: 563–606

Banerjee, A. and P. Newman (1993), "Occupational Choice and the Process of Development," *Journal of Political Economy* 101(2), April: 274–98

Collier, P. and J. W. Gunning (2006), "Asset Policies During an Oil Windfall: Some Simple Analytics," *The World Economy* 28(5): 1401–15

Easterly, W. (2006), "The Big Push Déjà Vu: A Review of Jeffrey Sachs's *The End of Poverty: Economic Possibilities for Our Time*," *Journal of Economic Literature* 44(1), March: 96

Gallup, J. L. and J. D. Sachs with A. D. Mellinger (1999), "Geography and Economic Development," in B. Pleskovic and J. E. Sachs, eds., *Annual Bank Conference on Development Economics 1998*. Washington, DC: The World Bank: 127–70

Gelb, A. (1988), *Oil Windfalls: Blessing or Curse?* Oxford: Oxford University Press

Gunning, J. W. (2001), "Trade Blocs: Relevant for Africa?," *Journal of African Economies* 10: 311–35

Hausman, R., D. Rodrik, and A. Velasco (2005), "Growth Diagnostics," The John F. Kennedy School of Government, Harvard University, Cambridge, MA

Limão, N. and A. J. Venables (2002), "Transport Costs, Infrastructure and Growth," *World Bank Economic Review* 15(3): 451–79

McMillan, J. and P. Zoido (2004), "How to Subvert Democracy: Montesinos in Peru," *Journal of Economic Perspectives* 18(4), Fall: 69–92

Oyejide, A., I. Elbadawi, and P. Collier, eds. (1997), *Regional Integration and Trade Liberalization in SubSaharan Africa. Vol. 1: Framework, Issues and Methodological Perspectives*. Basingstoke and London: Macmillan

Reinikka, R. and J. Svensson (2004), "Local Capture: Evidence from a Central Government Transfer Program in Uganda," *Quarterly Journal of Economics* 119(2), May: 679–705

Sachs, Jeffrey D., John W. McArthur, Guido Schmidt-Traub, Margaret Kruk, Chandrika Bahadur, Michael Faye, and Gordon McCord (2004), "Ending Africa's Poverty Trap," *Brookings Papers on Economic Activity* 1: 117–216

Venables, A. (2003), "Winners and Losers from Regional Integration Agreements," *Economic Journal* 113: 747–61

Index